DATE			

HANDBOOK OF LABOR ECONOMICS
VOLUME II

HANDBOOKS
IN
ECONOMICS

5

Series Editors

KENNETH J. ARROW
MICHAEL D. INTRILIGATOR

NORTH-HOLLAND
AMSTERDAM · NEW YORK · OXFORD · TOKYO

HANDBOOK OF LABOR ECONOMICS

VOLUME II

Edited by

ORLEY ASHENFELTER
Princeton University

and

RICHARD LAYARD
London School of Economics

1986

NORTH-HOLLAND
AMSTERDAM · NEW YORK · OXFORD · TOKYO

ISBN North-Holland for this set 0 444 87858 0
ISBN North-Holland for this volume 0 444 87857 2

Publishers
ELSEVIER SCIENCE PUBLISHERS B.V.
P.O. Box 1991
1000 BZ Amsterdam
The Netherlands

Sole distributors for the U.S.A. and Canada
ELSEVIER SCIENCE PUBLISHING COMPANY, INC.
52 Vanderbilt Avenue
New York, N.Y. 10017
U.S.A.

Library of Congress Cataloging-in-Publication Data

Handbook of labor economics.

  (Handbooks in economics ; 5)
  Includes bibliographies.
  1. Labor economics.   I. Ashenfelter, Orley,
1942-   . II. Layard, R.   III. Series.
HD4802.H36   1986   331   86-16730
ISBN 0-444-87858-0 (set)
ISBN 0-444-87856-4 (v. 1)
ISBN 0-444-87857-2 (v. 2)

PRINTED IN THE NETHERLANDS

INTRODUCTION TO THE SERIES

The aim of the *Handbooks in Economics* series is to produce Handbooks for various branches of economics, each of which is a definitive source, reference, and teaching supplement for use by professional researchers and advanced graduate students. Each Handbook provides self-contained surveys of the current state of a branch of economics in the form of chapters prepared by leading specialists on various aspects of this branch of economics. These surveys summarize not only received results but also newer developments, from recent journal articles and discussion papers. Some original material is also included, but the main goal is to provide comprehensive and accessible surveys. The Handbooks are intended to provide not only useful reference volumes for professional collections but also possible supplementary readings for advanced courses for graduate students in economics.

CONTENTS OF THE HANDBOOK

PREFACE TO THE HANDBOOK

The modern development of labor economics is a bold effort to use systematic theory to explain important empirical facts about the labor market. The results of this effort are topical, lively, and sometimes controversial, because the findings are relevant to both public and private decision-making. This Handbook brings together for the first time a systematic review of the research topics, empirical findings, and methods that comprise modern labor economics.

The chapters, which have all been written by leading contributors to the original research on each topic, are designed both to evaluate what has been learned *and* where further research may be profitable. We believe they will therefore be valuable to a wide range of readers, both those who wish an introduction to what has been done *and* those who wonder where things are heading.

The reader will find three common themes running through these chapters. In every case a guiding principle is the search for a parsimonious and systematic theoretical framework that both is consistent with the known facts about the labor market and that has further implications for empirical analyses. Also common to these chapters is a familiarity with some common empirical methods and empirical results and the clear perception that further empirical testing is necessary. Finally, a common theme that runs through the chapters is the presumption that an understanding of the way labor markets work will lead all of us to better decisions in both our public and private lives. In our view it is these common features of the chapters in this Handbook that represent the high standards set for the finest work in applied economics.

Volume I is concerned with the classic topics of labor supply and demand and their impact on the wage structure. These topics have been of interest to social scientists for many centuries, since they bear on two fundamental questions. First, what are the sources of income inequality, and second, what are the disincentive effects of attempts to produce a more equal income distribution? Labor supply is concerned with the incentives which individuals have to provide labor services, and labor demand is concerned with the incentives which firms have to use them. The more elastic the demand and supply, the greater the efficiency costs of interventionist policies. Thus, a key theme running through many of these chapters is just how big these elasticities are.

Until recently the data available to answer these questions were very limited, as were the computational facilities to handle them. But on the labor supply side this has changed drastically with the advent of large data sets on individuals, and

Frank Stafford (Chapter 7) shows the tremendous impact which this has had on the output of good empirical work in labor economics.

Labor supply has many dimensions. Even the apparently simple question of hours worked breaks down into hours per week, weeks per year, and years per lifetime. For most prime-age men the issue is less whether to work at all than how much to work. As John Pencavel (Chapter 1) shows, the evidence suggests that men's choice between hours of work and leisure is only weakly influenced by the available wages. For married women, there are more alternative uses of time than for men, since in the majority of households they do more of the household work. This has led many researchers to conclude that wages affect women's work more than men's. James Heckman and Mark Killingsworth (Chapter 2) examine the evidence using a host of different approaches to explain the division of women's time between paid work and other activities. Of course, much of the variation in female labor supply is not explained by wages and income, but by changes in family status. Montgomery and Trussell (Chapter 3) survey the connection between demography and labor economics this implies. Finally, Reuben Gronau (Chapter 4) surveys the whole range of different possible activities, including paid work and others, and attempts to explain it. Needless to say all the four chapters we have mentioned embed their analyses, where relevant, in a model of family decision-making.

A person's lifetime labor supply is much affected by when he stops (retires) and when he starts (quits education). The decision to retire is profoundly affected by the availability of social security and private pensions, which in turn raises the question of how private pensions are determined. The research on these issues is fully explored by Edward Lazear (Chapter 5). Turning to education, this is important not only for its effect on the duration of work-life but upon the skills of those people who are at work. Richard Freeman (Chapter 6) surveys the research on the productive role of education and its effect on earnings, and evaluates the effect of financial rewards in affecting the number of people wishing to stay in school.

We know less about labor demand than about labor supply, because we have less cross-section data on firms than on households. Thus, most work on labor demand is based on time-series analysis. Work has tended to fall into two rather distinct groups: that which mainly aims to estimate the effects of wages, and that which mainly aims to track the detailed quarter-by-quarter adjustment of employment to external shocks. Daniel Hamermesh (Chapter 8) surveys the theory and evidence about wage effects, where there are two rather separate issues: first the effects of relative wages on the skill- or age-mix of employment at given output, and second the effect of real wages on the aggregate level of output and employment. Stephen Nickell (Chapter 9) is concerned, in contrast, with the detailed path through which employment adjusts to a shock, given that full immediate adjustment is too costly.

The wage structure is determined as a first approximation by demand and supply, though Volume II also treats the impact of other institutional structures. There is a supply of workers with given characteristics to jobs of given quality, and there is a corresponding demand. Each depends on the wages paid for given worker and job characteristics. This wage structure adjusts until supply and demand are equal. The wage structure can thus be described by a functional relationship between the wage on the one hand and, on the other, the characteristics of the worker and of the job he is in.

Robert Willis (Chapter 10) surveys this relationship beginning with the famous human capital model. His review establishes the wide empirical applicability of this framework in a variety of circumstances. Yoram Weiss (Chapter 11) concentrates on one particular dimension of the wage structure: its variation over the life-cycle. He models this, allowing individuals to choose their rate of human capital investment at all points of time. Variation of wages over time to compensate for earlier human capital investment is but one example of the more general role of compensating differentials in the wage structure. Sherwin Rosen (Chapter 12) examines a whole range of other differences between jobs for which compensating differentials are paid – differences in risk to life and health, climatic conditions, convenience of hours, uncertainty of prospects and so on.

One glaring feature of the wage structure is the lower wages paid to women and blacks. This may be so even when they are compared with otherwise identical white males. If so, this raises the question of how such discrimination can persist in a competitive economic environment, and a host of possible explanations are surveyed by Glen Cain (Chapter 13).

The papers in Volume II generally proceed from the common observation that heterogeneity in worker skills and employer demands often tempers the outcomes that would be expected in frictionless labor markets. Donald Parsons (Chapter 14) surveys the burgeoning and very recent work that documents and attempts to explain the nature of long-term employment relationships. Much of this work has started from empirical observations on the length of employment relationships and attempted to present alternative theoretical set-ups that may justify alternative employment arrangements. The primary motives singled out for the nature of long-term employment relationships in this literature are employer and employee attitudes toward risk and the incomplete information they bring to employment bargains.

Much the same motivation underlies the models of search in the labor market that Dale Mortensen (Chapter 15) reviews, but the emphasis is different. Here the goal is to explore the determinants of the allocation of worker resources to searching across job opportunities.

Two chapters deal with the modern analysis of unemployment. George Johnson and Richard Layard (Chapter 16) explore the determination of the structure of unemployment. Here the goal is to describe the longer-term level and persistent unemployment structures that exist and to assess the various explanations for them. Another feature of unemployment in modern economies is the business cycle. David Lilien and Robert Hall (Chapter 17) review the broad evidence on the nature of the cyclical movements in unemployment and the theoretical explanations for why this puzzling phenomenon exists.

The last section of the Handbook deals explicitly with the institutional structures that are a part of modern labor markets. Henry Farber (Chapter 18) reviews the considerable work on trade union decision-making that has emerged in the last two decades. One particularly important aspect of trade union behavior is the strike activity that seems to insert inexplicable costs into the bargaining relationship. John Kennan (Chapter 19) reviews the empirical and theoretical work in this field with a view to establishing the extent to which the former is consistent with the latter.

In the following chapter, Gregg Lewis (Chapter 20) turns his hand to an updated survey of the impact of trade union bargaining on relative wages. Since the publication of his classic *Unionism and Relative Wages in the U.S.* over twenty years ago, both new data and new methods have been brought to the discussions of this topic. Lewis reviews this modern research with the same meticulous care and fine judgment he brought to this topic two decades ago.

Paul Taubman and Michael Wachter (Chapter 21) explicitly take up the discussion of earnings mobility and the extent to which social and familial class structures result in labor market outcomes nearer the Marxist than the classical explanations. The empirical work in this area concentrates on the extent of income mobility across families and over time, which is of considerable importance in the minds of many in establishing the operating characteristics of any society.

Ronald Ehrenberg and Joshua Schwarz (Chapter 22) survey the special characteristics of labor markets in the public sector. Recognizing that the motivations of public-sector employers may be more complex than in the private sector, the survey provides a wealth of information on the special structures in public-sector labor markets and the analyses of how they operate.

Like most good research, the material reviewed in this Handbook raises as many questions as it answers. Future research will no doubt continue to emphasize the interaction between systematic explanation and careful data analysis, which seems to us the key to continued success in economics.

CONTENTS OF VOLUME II

Chapter 16
The Natural Rate of Unemployment: Explanation and Policy

2.1. The SE estimates 1144
2.2. The panel estimates 1144
2.3. Macro estimates 1146
3. Variation in the wage gap across the U.S. work force 1148
4. Micro, OLS, and CS estimates: Data problems 1155
4.1. Errors resulting from the omission of fringe benefits 1156
4.2. Weekly or annual wage and the hours gap 1156
4.3. Errors from union status misclassification 1157
4.4. Nonrandomness in the NLS, SEO, and PSID data sets 1157
5. Adjusting the Micro, OLS, and CS wage gap estimates 1159
5.1. Adjusting for nonrandomness in the SEO, NLS, and PSID data files 1159
5.2. Adjusting for differences in the dependent wage variables 1160
5.3. Adjusting for incomplete worker coverage 1161
5.4. Adjusting for differences in the set of right-hand variables 1162
6. The adjusted Micro, OLS, and CS gap estimates 1163
6.1. Adjusted estimates from CPS data 1163
6.2. Adjusted estimates from 1967 SEO data 1168
6.3. Adjusted estimates from the PSID data 1168
6.4. Adjusted estimates from other Michigan Survey Research Center (SRC) data 1171
6.5. Adjusted estimates from the National Longitudinal Surveys 1173
6.6. Adjusted estimates from other sources 1174
6.7. Upper bounds for the overall mean wage gap 1174
Appendix 1176
References 1176

Chapter 21
Segmented Labor Markets
PAUL TAUBMAN and MICHAEL L. WACHTER 1183
1. Introduction and summary 1183
2. The internal labor market 1186
2.1. Historical antecedents 1187
2.2. Internal labor markets 1188
2.3. The question of allocative efficiency 1190
2.4. The role of labor unions 1192
3. The secondary sector 1195
3.1. Finding the demarcation line that distinguishes sectors 1196
3.2. The impact of human capital 1199
3.3. Negative feedback effects 1202
4. Models of earnings mobility over the life cycle 1203
4.1. The permanent income model 1203
4.2. The Markov model 1204
4.3. The human capital model 1206

PART 4

LABOR MARKET EQUILIBRIUM
AND FRICTION

Chapter 14

THE EMPLOYMENT RELATIONSHIP: JOB ATTACHMENT, WORK EFFORT, AND THE NATURE OF CONTRACTS

DONALD O. PARSONS*

The Ohio State University

1. Introduction

In the U.S. economy approximately 100 million workers are matched with market work activities on any given day. Millions more are matched with nonmarket activities of various kinds, including child rearing, home production of a variety of goods and services, and schooling. Economic efficiency requires that (1) specific individuals and activities be appropriately matched and that (2) the individuals, once matched, undertake the activity with an appropriate level of effort or intensity. In this chapter I focus on the economic forces that influence and define important aspects of these elements of the employment relationship in a market economy.

Historically the employment relationship in the United States has been a simple one. In the last century most individuals worked for themselves or in small firms, employees of the railways being the most notable exception. The individual undertook his chosen activity at an effort level that he judged appropriate and received income according to the market evaluation of the resulting good or service. Although simple, the outcome could also be harsh since family income was heavily dependent on earnings and earnings insurance was unavailable, except through public and private charity and of course the family.

The institutional structure of the employment relationship has, however, been transformed in this century. The nature of the workplace has changed radically.[1] The share of the workforce that was self-employed or unpaid family workers declined from almost 50 percent (47.08 percent) in 1900 to less than 10 percent (9.22 percent) in 1978. See Table 14.1.

*Support for this chapter was provided in part by the National Institute on Aging. The comments of John Garen, Thomas Kniesner, Howard Marvel, Randy Olsen, and Timothy Perri are gratefully acknowledged.
[1] One of the major transformations, the growth in trade unionism, is considered at length in Chapter 18 by Henry Farber in this Handbook.

Handbook of Labor Economics, Volume II, Edited by O. Ashenfelter and R. Layard
©Elsevier Science Publishers BV, 1986

Table 14.1
Self-employed and unpaid family workers as
a share of total employees, 1900–1978.

Year	Self-employment share (%)
1978	9.22
1970	10.21
1960	16.25
1950	20.50
1940	26.83
1930	29.44
1920	32.35
1910	38.57
1900	47.08

Source: 1900–1960, S. Lebergott, *Manpower in Economic Growth*. New York: McGraw-Hill, 1964, p. 513; 1970, 1978, *Statistical Abstract of the United States, 1979*, p. 403.

The average size of workplace in the non-self-employed sectors of the economy moreover has increased rapidly over this period. In the manufacturing sector, for example, the proportion of employment in small workplaces with less than twenty workers declined from 14.4 percent in 1909 to 6.5 percent in 1977 (Table 14.2). Over the same time period, the proportion employed in establishments of 1000 or more workers doubled from 15.3 percent to 27.5 percent.

Table 14.2
Share of manufacturing employment by establishment size in the United States, 1909–1977.

	Establishment size (employment)					
	1–19 (%)	20–49 (%)	50–249 (%)	250–499 (%)	500–999 (%)	1000+ (%)
1977	6.5	8.8	28.1	15.6	13.5	27.5
1972	6.2	8.7	27.8	15.4	13.1	28.7
1967	5.6	8.3	26.0	14.5	12.8	32.8
1963	7.2	9.1	26.6	14.2	12.4	30.5
1958	7.8	9.4	26.0	14.0	12.3	30.5
1954	7.6	8.7	25.0	13.5	12.6	32.6
1947	7.2	8.7	24.7	13.5	13.1	32.8
1939	9.5	9.7	29.4	16.1	13.0	22.3
1929	9.9	9.2	28.1	15.1	13.3	24.4
1919	10.4	9.1	27.2	13.8	13.2	26.4
1914	13.1	10.6	30.0	15.3	13.2	17.8
1909	14.4	11.6	30.8	15.2	12.7	15.3

Source: Various Censuses of Manufacturing. The employment size intervals for 1939 and before include next highest integer, e.g. 1–20. The 1939 data are reported in the 1940 census.

As the size of the workplace grew, the need for explicit and implicit employment contracts to define and regulate the employment relationship grew correspondingly. At the same time, however, the information necessary for efficient employment contracts became for the most part more expensive. Information on employer and employee circumstances and activities that might in a small workplace be free or quite inexpensive, a byproduct of other productive activities, may be observable in a large firm only at prohibitive cost to all parties to the contract. Much of the recent literature on the employment relationship has stressed the interplay of efficiency objectives and the limitations imposed on the form of employment contracts by information costs.

The developments in each of the three areas reviewed below (work effort, specific human capital, and earnings insurance) have in many respects been independent but, as we shall see, the underlying approach in each is remarkably similar. Each focuses on the potentially distorting effect of contract enforceability and asymmetric information on efficient employment relationships. In each area, moreover, two broad questions have formed the bases for the analyses:

(1) among homogeneous workers, what is the optimal employment "contract" (service agreement and compensation package)? and

(2) among heterogeneous workers with identical observable traits, how can the provisions of the optimal contract be altered to secure a more appropriate match of worker and firm?

In the specific human capital literature, for example, the obvious returns to reduced job mobility suggest that backloaded compensation packages such as nonvested pensions are likely to be optimal among homogeneous workers. As it happens, if apparently identical workers differ in their mobility propensities, this same compensation scheme may have important self-selection effects as well. With a backloaded compensation package, the expected value of the package will be highest for the workers with the lowest self-perceived mobility propensity. Since contract considerations will play an important part in much of the discussion that follows, Section 2 is devoted to a brief review of several major themes in contract theory.

Contracts, whether implicit or explicit, can do no more than make feasible what would otherwise be mutually agreeable joint activities. The employment relationship is primarily formed by more basic considerations. In this chapter three aspects of the employment relationship will be reviewed in detail: (1) the supply of work effort by the employee, (2) the investment in employer–employee match specific skills, and (3) the provision of earnings insurance by the employer. The supply and demand for work effort of individual workers is an obvious and crucial factor in the employment relationship. Employers have preferences about the intensity with which employees undertake their tasks, preferences which may be quite at variance with those of the employees. It is essential that the employee be motivated to undertake the assigned task at the mutually agreed intensity. This may require no more than a handshake, although the large array of employment incentive devices suggests otherwise. More typically some combination of incentives and employer monitoring may be required. The forces that determine the form of the optimal compensation package under various economic circumstances are developed in Section 3. Worker reliability is not likely to be homogeneously distributed over the workforce so that the job matching of earnest workers and vulnerable firms, as well as appropriate effort incentives once matched, may be important in the optimal employment relationship. The impact of worker heterogeneity on employment contracts is therefore also considered in this section.

More than optimal work effort is required of an efficient economy. Efficient job mobility is important as well if the economy is to respond to the rapid changes in product demand that characterize market economies. In the U.S. manufacturing sector between 1972 and 1977, for example, employment increased by 50 percent or more in several industries, including X-ray appliances and tubes (155 percent), fluid meters (80 percent), and oil field equipment (63 percent), while declining by 50 percent or more in others such as ammunition (-63 percent) and wool yard (-51 percent).[2] The rate of turnover in the economy, in part required to accommodate these changes, is large. In the manufacturing sector, for example, the average *monthly* employee separation rate fluctuated between 3.8 percent and 4.9 percent during the 1970s, suggesting that a 50 percent turnover rate over the course of a year is not unusual.[3]

Perfect fluidity among jobs is not likely to be optimal, however. Indeed, a large part of the workforce in the United States secures long time employment with a single firm. Two recent studies [Akerlof and Main (1981) and Hall (1982)] have attempted to estimate job duration in the British and U.S. economies. Hall (1982, p. 720) estimates that eventual completed tenure for all U.S. workers with a job in 1978 has a median of 7.7 years and that 28 percent are currently with a job that will last 20 years or more.

Fruitful models of the employment relationship must explain the individual incidence of job attachment and job turnover (and unemployment) as well as aggregate levels since job turnover probabilities are not uniform across individuals and groups. In particular, turnover and unemployment are concentrated among the inexperienced and among the poorly educated. Mincer and Jovanovic (1979) report two-year job separation probabilities that vary from more than 70 percent for males who have been working for less than a decade and who have less than one year on their current job to 5 to 6 percent for individuals who have

---

[2] One important dimension of job mobility, job search, will not be reviewed systematically in this chapter since the topic is reviewed in Mortensen (Chapter 15 in this Handbook). For an earlier theoretical and empirical survey of job search, see Parsons (1977); see also the still excellent theoretical survey by Lippman and McCall (1976).

[3] U.S. Bureau of the Census (1977).

Table 14.3
The ten-year retention rate within the firm
among older males, by race and education,
1966–1976.

Schooling attainment (in years)	Race	
	White (%)	Black (%)
0–8	35	32
9–11	44	47
12	49	51
13–15	44	61
16+	55	71
Total	44	39

Source: National Longitudinal Surveys. The sample was limited to males 45 to 51 years of age in 1966 (55–61 in 1976). Sample size is 2006: 1454 whites and 552 blacks.

been working 40 to 44 years and have been with their current firm for more than 10 years.

Ten-year longitudinal data from the National Longitudinal Surveys similarly indicates that prevalence of job stability and illustrates as well systematic differences by skill. In Table 14.3 I report the ten-year retention rate among male respondents who were 45 to 51 years of age in 1966. For the group as a whole 44 percent of the surviving whites and 39 percent of the surviving blacks were with the same firm ten years later. The retention rate rises from 35 percent to 55 percent among whites as education increases from 0–8 years of schooling to 16 or more years of schooling and from 32 percent to 71 percent among blacks for the same schooling increase.

One factor that alters the economic value of job attachment is on-the-job learning, particularly learning specific to the firm, e.g. attributes of its suppliers, capital, personnel, and customers. Obviously a job match that has value specific to the firm and the individual will reduce mobility in any sensible economic regime, although, with fluctuating market conditions, not necessarily to zero.

The measurement of these direct and indirect job specific investments in the work force is imprecise since most costs are indirect. Nonetheless the few management studies reported in the economics literature suggest that the invest-ment costs are substantial. Mincer (1962, p. 62) cites an American Management Association study of California firms which reported hiring, training, and sep-aration costs per worker of $1535 in 1982 dollars. Oi (1962, p. 546) reports fixed employment costs at International Harvester of $1418 per worker in 1982 dollars. The investment expenditures apparently rise rapidly with skill level. Oi, for

Table 14.4
Firm investment per employee, 1969 (in 1982 dollars).

Skill level	Firm investment ($)
Least skilled (e.g. materials handler)	911
Semi-skilled (e.g. maintenance mechanic)	5 715
First-line supervisor	13 353
Middle manager	53 413
Top level manager	113 503

Source: Parsons (1972). All dollar figures are readjusted to 1982 $ levels.

example, reports estimates of $470 for a common laborer, $44 765 for a two-year progressive student and $69 778 for a four-year apprentice, again all in 1982 dollars. Parsons (1972) discusses a study undertaken in 1969 by a manufacturing firm, R. G. Barry, that indicates that the firm's investment in employees ranged from $911 for the lowest skill category to $113 503 for a top level manager (1982 dollars). The full results are reported in Table 14.4.

The observed patterns of turnover are consistent with the importance of preserving match specific skills and with the positive correlation of general and specific skills illustrated in Table 14.4. Whether these separation rates are fully efficient, however, depends very much on the nature of feasible contracts. Efficiency is not assured by the usual competitive assumptions since the unique value of the specific job match implies that this income generating asset lacks the labor market guarantees carried by more widely demanded skills. Contracting problems may induce inappropriate initial job matching as well as subsequent job attachment if workers are heterogeneous in their mobility propensities. Unobservable heterogeneity among workers may induce firms to introduce a variety of ancillary employment practices such as screening and self-selection devices when specific human capital investments are heavy.[4] The nature of contracting and its implications for job separation in the presence of specific human capital are developed in Section 4.

In Section 5 a second factor that may alter the stability of the employment match is considered, namely worker and owner preferences for stable incomes. The income of the self-employed is, of course, vulnerable to business cycle fluctuations and more idiosyncratic, firm-specific reversals.[5] Among employees the important role of job loss in the cyclical behavior of experienced worker

[4] U.S. Department of Labor (1980).
[5] Aggregation phenomena that may be important in cyclical unemployment, e.g. the labor market congestion problems that arise with a greater number of simultaneous layoffs [Parsons (1980)], will be ignored below.

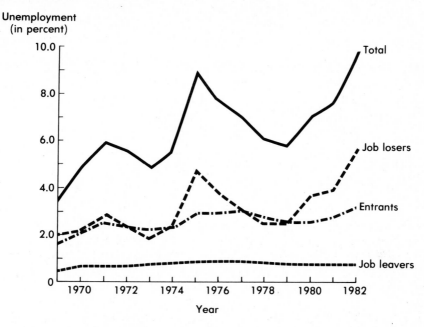

Figure 14.1. Unemployment rate by reason. *Source: Handbook of Labor Statistics*, 1980, p. 82.

unemployment and consequent earnings losses is apparent in Figure 14.1 in which the unemployment rate is separated into components by "cause" over the period 1969–1979. Clearly unemployment due to job loss is a powerful factor in the determination of total unemployment over the business cycle.

Section 5 will focus primarily on the attempts by individual workers to secure from the firm some form of earnings insurance. Although the individual may have alternative income sources, both public and private, standard insurance policies against the possibility of reduced earnings are not widely marketed. Presumably potential insurers perceive substantial moral hazard and adverse selection problems, induced by the insurer's inability to distinguish exogenous, random earnings losses from those due to choice or foreknowledge. The employing firm knows the nature of its own business conditions and the prospects of its employees better than a third party insurer and, if sufficiently large, may serve the function of insurer, either by offering direct cash payments to those laid off or by retaining them on payroll. The most direct application of this reasoning suggests that job attachments will be more secure (less likely to be broken) during periods of declining demand in large firms. Recently more complex models have been developed, combining aggregate nondiversifiable risk and severe information problems of a particular sort, which yield contrary implications. Again these insurance models of the employment relationship are the focus of Section 5.

The review below will concentrate on theoretical models, in part because the review is already overlong and in part because empirical work has lagged substantially behind theoretical developments in this area. Unfortunately, given the scarcity and general primitiveness of existing employer data sets and the relative subtlety of many of the theoretical implications, this imbalance is likely to remain for some time.

2. The employment contract

A mutually advantageous exchange of services and payments for services between two parties may not be instantaneously and verifiably executed; either the service or payment exchange may be incompletely monitored or deferred in time. The reliability of performance by the contracting parties may therefore be a crucial characteristic of the economic environment. Indeed a theme that reoccurs throughout the following sections is the potentially important effect that contract enforceability may have on the employment relationship. In this section important elements of the current theory of contracts of particular relevance to the employment relationship will be reviewed.

The main function of any contract is to constrain behavior, behavior that in a broader context is nonoptimal but which at the moment the decision is made is attractive to some economic agent.[6] Life cycle reallocation of consumption by borrowing when young and repaying the loan when older, for example, may be optimal for a given individual; repayment of the loan as an isolated activity is surely unattractive to this same individual. In a sense, what follows can be viewed as an analysis of the limitations of contract relationships, most frequently as a consequence of information and enforcement difficulties.

The most prominent restrictions on employment contracts are legal, a reflection of the fact that human capital is embodied in individuals with certain "inalienable rights". Slavery and indentured servant contracts, for example, are not enforceable and long-term contracts that restrict individual mobility and behavior generally are viewed skeptically by the courts. While themselves not burdensome, these restrictions are only the most dramatic of a wide range of restrictions derived from the same philosophic base. Bankruptcy laws are a reflection of the same concerns, leading to the peculiar difficulty individuals have when young (and without collateral) of borrowing for schooling, apprenticeship

---

[6] Occasionally the term contract is used to mean repeated exchange *voluntarily* entered into in *each* period, e.g. Bull (1983). The standard notion of a contract as a "binding agreement" is lost with such a usage.

costs, and other employment expenditures. Sensitivity to this borrowing constraint is important since a frequently proposed solution to reliability problems is some form of bonding which may in fact not be feasible.

A second contracting problem is that of information difficulties, particularly the asymmetric access to information that economic agents may have at a given time.[7] Certainly since much information (knowledge) relevant to the employment contract is generated (learned) as a byproduct of other activities the individuals and firms may undertake, information costs may differ across agents. Of particular consequence, the joint-product nature of information acquisition implies that unrelated third parties are likely to find information on employer and employee behavior relatively more costly to obtain than do the employer and employee themselves.

Insurance models make clear the importance of the information available to the contracting parties in determining equilibrium behavior and contract form. Theoretical models of the insurance industry, for example, have long recognized two information problems that, if sufficiently severe, make insurance contracting infeasible, namely moral hazard and adverse selection.[8] A contract may affect an insurer's loss experience adversely if losses are determined in part by the activities of the insured and if it is costly or impossible for the insurer to monitor these activities (moral hazard). Moreover, if the population is heterogeneous in the likelihood of loss and if this is known to the insured but not the insurer, the insurer may find his losses greater than would be anticipated by preinsurance loss rates because those with the greatest likelihood of loss will be the most eager to secure coverage (adverse selection). A third information problem, the inability to determine accurately and costlessly which state of nature has in fact occurred (imperfect state verification), has also recently received attention in the literature.[9] Parallels to the effort-monitoring issue in employment contracts should be self-evident. In one form or another, these same problems limit the range of feasible employment contracts and thereby alter the employment relationship.

Depending on the circumstances, the time dimension may be important in the information process. Information on a specific event may be relatively less

---

[7]Access to information is of course a loose but customary way of asserting that information acquisition may be costly. See Wachter, Williamson, and Harris (1975) for a detailed discussion of transactions costs underlying information collection. The term efficiency will often be used in the customary if misleading sense of optimal performance under the assumption that information acquisition is free.

[8]Important formal models of these problems include Spence and Zeckhauser (1971) and Pauly (1974); for a discussion of market equilibrium in the presence of adverse selection, see Rothschild and Stiglitz (1976). See also Akerlof (1970) for an early but still valuable discussion of the general problem of market problems that arise because of adverse selection.

[9]Townshend (1979) discusses an interesting model of state verification in which the agent who does not have access to critical information may purchase it. The agent will tend to do so optimally only if he suspects the informed agent's claim is quite wide of the mark; suspected minor violations will be ignored. Parsons (1984) develops a model with imperfect state verification.

expensive to collect at one point in time than at another. Generally one would expect information to be less costly if one were willing to wait longer for it, although even that process has obvious limits. This aspect of the process is not considered carefully in the literature; typically the time dependence of costs is simply characterized by its presence or absence at a particular time a decision must by assumption be made.

2.1. Explicit contracts

Contracts may be formal, explicit documents or less well-defined implicit agreements. Formal, explicit contracts have one major advantage, enforcement costs of contract performance are in part subsidized by the state. A wide range of penalties or damages can be imposed on a nonperforming party by the courts. In an uncertain world in which no individual is absolutely reliable, such a subsidized enforcement mechanism has a transparent appeal.

Explicit contracts, however, are quite demanding of information and may not be feasible. As a practical matter explicit contract contingencies must be limited to readily observable outcomes, a rather powerful restriction. Frequently only one of the two immediate parties to the relationship may know an important piece of information with any precision. The other contracting party, much less an uninvolved third party, may not have access to the information at any reasonable cost. Subtle questions such as whether a worker voluntarily quit because he felt he had prospects of a better job elsewhere or whether he was coerced to leave through an employer's manipulation of nonpecuniary job conditions are crucial to the efficient contracts considered below yet are not easily answered by a third party uninvolved in the case. This information verification problem surely limits the role that third parties can play in the enforcement of agreements and ultimately limits the exchanges that can be undertaken.

It is important to recall that performance bonding and the use of collateral make damage collection easier but do not eliminate the need for the courts or other contract enforcement mechanisms.[10] Someone, the courts or otherwise, must determine whether a bond or other form of collateral is to be forfeited.[11] Presumably this judgment requires observation of the agent's behavior and any appropriate contractual contingencies. The importance of institutional constraints, specifically the bankruptcy constraint on borrowing without collateral,

---

[10] See Benjamin (1978) for a discussion of the role of collateral in contract performance.

[11] Landes and Posner (1979) provide an insightful discussion of private "courts"; ultimately an agreement to abide by binding private arbitration if a dispute arises in the execution of a contract requires an enforcement mechanism to ensure that the binding arbitration agreement is itself honored by the parties.

must also be considered in assessing the effectiveness of explicit performance "bonding".[12]

Other informational requirements for explicit contracting may be important. Courts enforce contracts primarily through the imposition of damages. Many theories exist of how damages ought to be assessed in a situation of contract breach due to unforeseen contingencies but little empirical research exists on how damages are in fact imposed in such situations.[13] There is little reason to suppose court behavior is consistent. It is important that all contingencies which could lead to contract breach be foreseen and that the damages be prespecified if uncertainty about the outcome of the contract is to be eliminated. All possible states of the world can rarely be foreseen and precontracted, so that even a carefully considered, explicit contract will involve some degree of undesirable uncertainty.

2.2. Implicit contracts

Information costs may make third party enforcement of explicit contracts infeasible. The two parties to a contract may know whether or not satisfactory performance on a contract has been undertaken, yet find it prohibitively expensive to demonstrate that to another, unrelated individual. Almost surely, certain mutually beneficial exchanges will be hindered by this infeasibility. Private agreements or implicit contracts that are not enforceable in the courts may, in such circumstances, be attractive and, depending on circumstances, more or less efficient. The efficiency of the arrangement depends critically on the extent to which the agreement can be enforced by less formal mechanisms. The literature has focused on two possible economic enforcement mechanisms: subsequent, profitable relationships between the two contracting parties (repeated exchange) and reputational effects of contract performance that might alter subsequent contracting by other individuals and firms with the parties involved.

Concern about future, potentially profitable exchange between the two parties may provide some assurance of contract performance. Information requirements are limited since only the parties to the contract need have access to the information, so such contracts may be feasible when explicit contracts are not. Simple game theory examples, for example the prisoner's dilemma, illustrate that the enforcement power of such relationships may be more apparent than real [Luce and Raiffa (1957)]. Specifically if the relationship has a finite, known end

---

[12] See Kennan (1979) and MacDonald (1982) for discussions of borrowing constraints on bonding of specific human capital investments and Eaton and White (1982) for a similar discussion on effort bonding.

[13] Useful discussions of economic models of contract damages can be found in Barton (1972) and Shavell (1980).

point, it may be equivalent in a behavioral sense to a single period model. Since the last period is equivalent to a single period, the party coerced to perform would default in the last period since the contract is no longer multi-period, which in turn suggests that the next-to-last period is the "final" contract period from an economic viewpoint. This process leads to the conclusion that such a contract is not viable in any period. Infinite relationships avoid this problem, most plausibly those with random end points [Telser (1980)]. The use of approximate solution algorithms suggests that repeated exchanges may be self-enforcing if the number of exchange periods, although finite, is sufficiently large [Radner (1981)]. The introduction of some uncertainty in the expected behavior of the other party may also lead to more cooperative solutions [Kreps and Wilson (1982)].

The termination of any subsequent profitable relationships between the two contracting parties is only a special case, though perhaps an important one, of indirect, economic damages imposed on an individual who breaches an implicit contract. Other parties, somehow made aware of the contract breach, may alter their behavior in a manner which is adverse to the defaulter. These third party effects will be labelled reputational effects.

Reputational models were to my knowledge first developed extensively in the advertising and product quality literature. Nerlove and Arrow (1962) explored the dynamics of reputation development through advertising. Gould (1970) developed models of information dissemination more explicitly within the Nerlove–Arrow framework. Obviously the extent and speed with which information spreads to interested economic agents is crucial to the contract enforcement function of reputation. Nelson (1974) first linked the reputational process with product quality, essentially arguing that the building of brand identity (reputation) through advertising creates a performance bond of sorts such that heavy advertising and product quality will be positively linked. See Klein and Leffler (1981) for a general, informal discussion of this idea. The heart of the process is the notion that reputation is a bond that an individual posts for good performance, a bond not in the traditional sense of forfeiture of a tradeable asset but rather in the sense that poor performance will reduce the individual's wealth or asset holdings. Kotowitz and Mathewson (1979) and Schmalensee (1978) attempt to model this process formally (using the Nerlove–Arrow framework and a Markov process, respectively) and find not surprisingly that such reputational enforcement mechanism need not function desirably in all circumstances. If, for example, consumers rely heavily on the notion that advertised brands are high quality products, they may be profitably fooled by a cunning advertiser [Schmalensee (1978)]. Kihlstrom and Riordan (1984) note that such notions would not persist in the long run among rational consumers and consider the demand and cost structures that would lead to reputational equilibria. See also Shapiro (1982).

Presumably employment contracts enforced by reputational capital may be similarly secure under some circumstances yet vulnerable to breach under others, although the circumstances have yet to be well specified.[14] One might conjecture that, for given market size, reputation effects will be more important for large firms than small. A dissatisfied employee of a large firm is more likely to communicate directly or indirectly with a potential employee of that firm than is a dissatisfied employee of a smaller firm. Memory of an incident at a better known firm is also more likely to be persistent among uninvolved third parties. Empirical evidence for such size effects can be found in the noncontracted inflation adjustments that firms have made in retiree benefits in recent years. Allen, Clark and Summer (1984) report that such adjustments are positively and systematically related to firm (pension plan) size.[15]

A similar line of reasoning would suggest that individual employees will be less bound by reputational effects than will firms.[16] Inexpensive information on a specific individual is unlikely to be readily available to the firm and reputationally enforced reliability correspondingly less powerful. If sufficiently important, of course, information on any individual's past performance can be secured, so reputational effects may be important for sensitive jobs such as top management positions for which firms will be willing to invest substantial resources in search and information collection [Fama (1980), Perri (1983)]. Contract default may be expensive to such individuals and therefore implicit contracts relatively secure.

Although not directed explicitly at the reputational issue, empirical evidence does exist that past labor market behavior has effects on current labor market opportunities for both firms and workers. Abowd and Ashenfelter (1981), for example, estimate substantial compensating wage differentials for industries with histories of high past layoffs. Whether such informational effects hold at the individual firm level was not considered. Mincer and Jovanovic (1981) and Bartel and Borjas (1981) both present evidence that persistent job turnover by older workers has negative effects on the subsequent wages such individuals can secure. Much remains to be done of a theoretical and empirical nature on this issue.

I should stress that an "enforceable" implicit agreement does not require that both parties be reliable. Even if only one of the parties to an agreement, say the firm, is reliable, information costs and contract monitoring costs are much reduced and a variety of otherwise infeasible agreements may be undertaken. It only becomes necessary that appropriate information be known to the reliable

---

[14] Holmstrom (1981) and Charmichael (1984) provide brief discussions of reputational issues in the labor market.

[15] See also Hatch (1982).

[16] Firms may be more reliable because the end pointed problem that limits the repeated-exchange enforcement technique should be less severe than it would be for an individual. John Garen made this point to me.

party at the time of contract execution, not the unreliable party nor any uninvolved third party. The performance of the less reliable party in such circumstances may be more explicitly bonded, with the bond held by the reliable party. If the appropriate information is not costlessly available to the reliable party, some form of more costly performance monitoring may be necessary.

Some individuals not only appear to be more reliable, they are in fact more reliable, whether because of some innate differences in ethical standards or because of ancillary social pressures that make breaching a contract costly. To the extent such traits are observable, such individuals will be differentially attractive for situations in which monitoring and enforcement possibilities are weak. It is surely not inadvertent that many of the world's more repressive dictators have assigned brothers to head the army or police. Most firms have long since passed the stage in which family members can staff all responsible positions, but other selection devices may achieve something of the same goal. Firms may screen workers for reliability (in work effort or job attachment) both through initial statistical discrimination according to observable correlates of reliability and through trial periods of employment. The compensation schedule may also be structured to induce self-selection if the worker but not the firm is aware of the worker's reliability. Such mechanisms may make possible some attractive but otherwise infeasible exchanges.

3. Work effort and compensation

The employer and employee must negotiate a variety of terms for the provision of labor services. At least two dimensions of work commitment are fundamental: the number of hours the individual will spend at the work place and the intensity with which he undertakes the assigned tasks during that period. Traditionally factor demand theory, indeed demand theory in general, has assumed that the quantity and quality of services purchased can be perfectly and costlessly observed by the buyer. In the labor market, the time commitment is observable at relatively low cost in most circumstances. Even here exceptions come to mind, including the work hours of individuals who perform work away from any central work place, for example many types of salesmen. The quality of the input, in the present context work intensity or effort, typically involves greater measurement difficulty.[17] Compensation structures designed to minimize these difficulties are the focus of this section.

---

[17]Effort supply functions will be ignored below. See Pencavel (1977) for a discussion of such models analogous to traditional work hours supply models.

3.1. The compensation of homogeneous workers

The employee of course knows the level of intensity he is undertaking without incurring any substantial monitoring costs. Were he a reliable agent, his compensation could be based on his reported effort level. The models discussed in this section assume that the employer cannot systematically rely on these reports but instead must undertake some direct metering of worker activities and base the worker's compensation upon that metering.

The firm faces the choice of metering and rewarding input quantity and quality or output quantity and quality. Consider, for example, a value production function of the form:

$$V(q,Q) = f(h, H; \theta),\qquad(3.1)$$

where V is the value of output, a function of the quantity (q) and quality (Q) of output, and $f(\cdot)$ is the production function with the quantity (h) and quality (H) of work effort and a random element (θ) as arguments.

If no randomness exists in the production technology, an incentive system based on output measures would be equivalent to one based on input measures. The system chosen would depend solely on observability considerations. Output quantity and quality need not be any easier to measure than input attributes. The output of white-collar tasks is often difficult to measure as is the output of many low-skilled tasks such as general maintenance. In large-scale production processes, individual output is often not even well defined conceptually. If one set of quantity/quality pairs, either for input or output, is observable at little cost, however, it will presumably form the basis for an incentive contract in this circumstance.

If workers and employers are both risk neutral, the introduction of randomness in the production process would not alter the certainty conclusion in any significant way. If, however, the standard assumption is maintained that workers are risk averse and firms risk neutral, the two methods are no longer equivalent. The worker presumably knows with certainty the hours and effort he provides to the firm and would, other things equal, prefer to be paid a certain wage based on that effort. If output alone is observable, the wage payment must in part be based on output, however random, if the worker is to be given an incentive to expend effort. Such a piece rate system will unfortunately introduce unwanted variability into the worker's earnings. The optimal compensation scheme must balance these considerations.

In the analysis that follows, I consider in turn the case in which there is no production function randomness and the case in which there is significant randomness in "production". I will label these cases the production worker model and the managerial model since productivity risk is not likely to be a significant concern for most forms of production work.

I should note before beginning that the role of firm size on the optimal compensation scheme is not transparent. In small firms with nonstochastic production processes, the owner or manager is likely to observe both input intensity and output quality and the particular payment scheme may be a matter of indifference. If substantial risk does exist in the production process, the small firm owner may be less willing to absorb the risk entirely so that risk sharing may be more prevalent than in large firms with diversified owners.

3.1.1. The compensation of production workers

Large differences exist in the compensation structure of production workers. In a sample of 58 manufacturing industries subject to BLS nationwide occupational surveys between 1963 and 1968, six industries, primarily in apparel and footwear, reported 70 percent or more of their production workers were paid on an incentive basis. Two, Work Clothing and Men's and Boys' Shirts, reported that more than 80 percent of their production workers were paid on an incentive basis. Conversely seven industries reported that 2 percent or less of their workforce were paid on an incentive basis. In cigarette manufacturing and petroleum refining the percentage was less than one half a percent. See Table 14.5.

Table 14.5
Percent of production workers paid under incentive
wage plans in selected manufacturing
industries, 1963–68.[a]

Work Clothing	82%
Men's and Boys' Shirts	81
Men's and Boys' Suits and Coats	74
Footwear, except Rubber	70
Women's Hosiery	70
Children's Hosiery	70
Flour and Other Grain Products	2
Motor Vehicles	2
Paints and Varnishes	1
Fertilizer	1
Synthetic Fibers, Noncellulose	1
Cigarettes	0
Petroleum Refining	0

Source: Stelluto (1969).
[a]For precise industry definition and dates, see source.

What could account for these large differences in compensation systems? The industries at the two extremes suggest the possibility that firm size may be important although it is not altogether clear why smaller firms (as would typically be found in the apparel industry) would be more likely to use incentive pay than would larger firms (such as those that characterize petroleum refining). Indeed, one might expect that the greater information decentralization of large firms would lead to greater reliance on incentive pay.

Alchian and Demsetz (1962) propose two factors that may affect the relative efficiency of (1) output oriented reward systems such as incentive pay and (2) input oriented systems with direct supervision of effort. The principal of these is the difficulty of designing incentive pay when workers are organized in teams. If a large number of workers are needed to operate a single blast furnace, for example, aggregate output is a poor measure of performance by one single individual of the team; individual shirking remains a problem and direct monitoring of effort is likely to be necessary. A second argument with many of the same empirical implications is that employer monitoring of the worker's treatment of the firm's capital may be important in any case, the more so the greater the amount of capital and its complexity. If output is the sole reward criterion, the worker has an obvious incentive to use the cooperating capital in a nonoptimal way much as a renter of a house may treat it differently than would the home owner. If indeed the employer is already directly monitoring the worker's treatment of the capital equipment, the marginal cost of direct supervision of worker effort is surely reduced as well.

Both arguments by Alchian and Demsetz suggest that the prevalence of incentive pay should decrease with the capital intensity of the industry; conversely direct supervision of effort should increase. A multivariate analysis of the

Table 14.6
Determinants of the percentage of production workers
paid on an incentive basis in selected
manufacturing industries, 1963–68.[a]

	Coefficient	Standard error	t-statistic
Constant	56.107	8.318	6.74
Emp 500[b]	0.217	0.100	2.18
$\log(K/L)$[c]	−17.317	2.632	−6.58
$\bar{R}^2$	0.43		

[a] The dependent variable is the percentage of production workers paid on an incentive basis. The sample size is 55 manufacturing industries, primarily at the 4-digit SIC level.

[b] The percentage of workers in establishments with 250 or more workers.

[c] The log of the capital-to-labor ratio.

complete set of incentive pay data collected by Stelluto (1969) strongly confirms these conjectures. An ordinary least squares regression of the percentage of production workers paid on an incentive basis on establishment size (the percentage of workers in establishments with 250 or more workers) and the log of the capital to labor ratio was undertaken and the results reported in Table 14.6. The coefficient of the log of the capital-to-labor ratio is negative and strongly statistically significant with a t-statistic of -6.58. The coefficient implies that a 10 percent increase in capital intensity will induce a 1.7 percentage point decline in production workers on incentive pay. Controlling for capital intensity, firm size has a positive coefficient significant at the 5 percent level. Apparently incentive pay probabilities do increase with firm size once the dominating effect of capital intensity is removed from the data. The effect is not large, however. A one percentage point increase in the prevalence of large establishments induces a 0.2 percentage point increase in the prevalence of incentive pay for production workers.

3.1.2. Models of effort monitoring and compensation

Much of the supervision process has not been carefully modelled. Several aspects of job supervision and compensation policies have been developed, however, and warrant discussion. In particular, economists have developed models that clarify the nature of the optimal employment relationship when input monitoring is incomplete, presumably because effort monitoring is costly. These models take two forms, occasional but precise monitoring and continuous but imperfect monitoring. The behavioral distinction is primarily in the introduction of risk to the reliable worker that imperfect monitoring introduces into the process.

The question of the optimal amount of sampling of behavior and of the corresponding penalty to impose for detected malfeasance has arisen naturally in the law and economics literature [Becker and Stigler (1974)].[18] Although the discussions focus on optimal compensation schemes for law enforcers subject to bribes, the extension to shrinking or malfeasance by a firm's employee is self-evident.

Becker and Stigler, for example, consider the question of the optimal employment contract of law enforcement officials who are subject to the temptation of bribes (b). Becker and Stigler conclude that a bond/severance pay compensation scheme will generally be efficient. If monitoring is costless and complete, the performance bond (B) must equal or exceed the magnitude of the bribe and performance is assured. If, however, monitoring is costly and perhaps incomplete, so that the probability of the detection of malfeasance and the forfeiture of the bond (p) is less than one, then performance is assured for all but risk-preferring

---

[18] See also Becker (1968).

individuals if

$$pB \geq b,$$

where p = detection probability, B = magnitude of bond, and b = magnitude of bribe. The expected return from accepting the bribe must be negative for bribery to be forestalled.

Any combination of detection magnitude and bond size that satisfies this inequality will secure complete compliance in this model [Harris and Raviv (1979) label complete compliance contracts "forcing contracts"]. Since performance monitoring normally requires the expenditure of real resources and posting of the bond does not, efficiency would seem to require an infinitesimally small level of monitoring activity and an infinitely large bond. Reasons why bonds and monitoring are finite are many. Capital difficulties facing workers may limit the size of the bond a worker is willing to post. The reliability of the firm in detecting (claiming) malfeasance will be strained with a sufficiently large bond. Risk aversion becomes a potentially important constraint on the equilibrium size of the bond when the possibility of misclassification arises since not even those workers making the contractually required effort are totally secure from bond forfeiture.

The Becker–Stigler model need involve no question of risk preferences since the monitoring is 100 percent accurate when undertaken; the reliably performing agent will never be disciplined. Harris and Raviv (1979) propose an alternative monitoring model in which the monitor is imperfect. They present an example of a market structure in which the optimal employment structure is quite similar to the Becker–Stigler bonding model, estimated effort above a critical level is paid a fixed wage, below the critical level a different, possibly zero wage (the worker is discharged). The worker's risk preference becomes central to the optimal level of the critical effort requirement and fixed wage in this situation.

Consider the example more specifically. Assume in particular that the value of production (V) is equal to the effort expended (H) so that

$$V = H,$$

and that the worker's utility function has the explicit form:

$$U = W^{\gamma} - H^{(1+\gamma)}/(1+\gamma),$$

where γ is a risk preference parameter in the interval $0 < \gamma < 1$. The individual therefore is risk averse with respect to wealth in this model and experiences increased disutility at an increasing rate with effort. Effort is unobservable but a "monitoring technology" exists that provides an unbiased estimate of effort, say $\hat{H}$, $E(H) = \hat{H}$, that is subject to a uniformly distributed random error over the interval

$$[\hat{H} - \varepsilon, \hat{H} + \varepsilon].$$

Harris and Raviv assert that the optimal compensation contract in this case has the form:

$$W = \begin{cases} W^*, & \text{if } \hat{H} > H_c, \\ 0, & \text{otherwise,} \end{cases}$$

where $W^* = (1 + \gamma)\varepsilon$ and $H_c = \varepsilon + \delta\gamma$ with $\delta = (2\varepsilon^{1-\gamma})^{-1/\gamma}$. The firm will pay a wage W^* if the monitoring index equals or exceeds a predetermined minimum enforcement level H_c and will discharge the worker without payment if the performance index falls short of that level. If the monitoring device is sufficiently accurate ($\varepsilon < 2^{-(1+\gamma)}$), the individual will choose an effort level at which dismissal probabilities will be zero, specifically the equilibrium level of effort will be $H^* = H_c + \varepsilon$.

If the monitoring index is subject to sufficiently large error ($\varepsilon \geq 2^{-(1+\gamma)}$), the dismissal probability will be positive. Specifically, with such monitoring error, equilibrium effort will be

$$H^* = (1 + \gamma)\delta,$$

and the equilibrium dismissal rate (p^*)

$$p^* = 1 - (2^{1+\gamma}\varepsilon)^{-1/\gamma}.$$

In this simple model, the impact of an increase in the imperfection of effort monitoring (an increase in ε) takes the following forms:
   (1) the equilibrium wage if retained increases,
   (2) the equilibrium level of effort declines, and
   (3) the equilibrium dismissal rate (with no wage payment) increases.
The model is somewhat peculiar in that the firm knows (from its knowledge of the environment assumed here) that all the workers, including those discharged, are performing faithfully, but it must nonetheless discharge workers according to its announced policy, presumably to maintain future credibility.

3.1.3. *Performance monitoring and life cycle compensation*

In the Becker–Stigler bonding model, variations in reliability with age may induce corresponding variations in the optimal bond and therefore variations in wage profiles over the life cycle. Difficulties in instantaneous monitoring of work

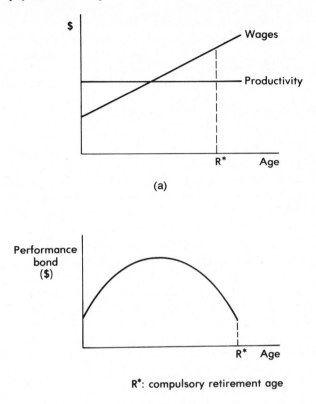

Figure 14.2. (a) Life cycle wages and productivity. (b) Life cycle (implicit) bonding.

effort suggest that a multiperiod compensation contract, perhaps even a lifetime compensation contract may be desirable. If the observation lag on effort is long, a deferred, contingent compensation contract may be optimal.

Lazear (1979, 1981) claims that job monitoring may induce a life cycle wage profile similar to the traditional human capital investment profile with wages below marginal productivity early in the life cycle and above marginal productivity later in the life cycle [see Figure 14.2(a)]. The back loaded wage payments provide a performance bond of sorts and Lazear claims that such a profile might therefore be induced by job monitoring considerations.

The Lazear model is an extension of the bonding model developed by Becker and Stigler (1974) discussed above in which the individual posts a bond of sufficient size to guarantee faithful performance of his duties and then receives severance pay at the end of the period equal to the bond plus accrued interest if he is faithful. Becker and Stigler discuss a model of bonding and life cycle wage profiles but the specific model they develop has no interesting intertemporal linkage and reduces to a series of single period bonds. Lazear develops a more elaborate structure, indeed one sufficiently complex that he is unable to derive a solution or any properties of the solution.[19] In the absence of such results, he argues that the model may yield a wage profile as in Figure 14.2(a).

Consideration of the implied Becker–Stigler bond of such a wage profile makes the Lazear conjecture unlikely. What is the life cycle bond profile implied by a wage/productivity profile of the form illustrated in Figure 14.2(a)? In any period in which productivity exceeds wages, the individual is increasing the size of his performance bond. Conversely, if one ignores interest rate effects (assume $r = 0$), the individual is drawing down his bond in any period in which wages exceed productivity. The linear models of wages and productivity imply a life cycle pattern of bonding quite unlike what one might intuitively expect. In particular the performance bond behaves quadratically, increasing to a peak at midlife and declining after that point [see Figure 14.2(b)]. In such a regime it is the relatively stable age-intervals of midlife that bear the heaviest performance bond. Intuitively one might have expected just the opposite pattern of life cycle bonding with the heaviest bond for (1) young, immature workers with a disproportionately high predilection for shirking and malfeasance and perhaps for (2) older workers with their vulnerability to adverse health shocks. None of the additional considerations introduced by Lazear would seem to lead to the bonding scheme he discusses. A bonding profile of this sort, however, may be appropriate for the bonding of unilateral separations in the presence of specific human capital investments. See Section 4 below and particularly Kennan (1979).

3.1.4. Managerial compensation

The interest of economists in the behavioral consequences of (1) independent agent preferences and (2) incomplete information by the principal on the agent's activities has been a long-standing one, in large part because of its importance in the modelling of managerial behavior and its relationship to the theory of the firm. In the debate over owner versus managerial control, a variety of behavioral models of the firm have been constructed based on the notion that owners, for

---

[19]A two-period model of the Lazear structure is derived in Lazear and Moore (1984). The model is essentially a generalization of the Becker–Stigler bonding model with the possibility of contract breach by the firm and like the original model fails to provide a monitoring argument for life cycle compensation schemes. These remarks should not detract from the fundamental insight of the original Lazear (1979) paper that in a market economy quantity restrictions on purchase (in this case mandatory retirement) usually imply some pricing difficulty. See Parsons (1984a) for an adverse selection model of the demand for retirement aged workers.

Table 14.7
Incentive share of top management compensation in selected
manufacturing and retail firms, 1960–63.[a]

	Total sample (%)	Extreme values deleted[b] (%)
Large manufacturing firms:		
Top executive	86.7	73.4
Top five executives	88.1	73.6
Small manufacturing firms:		
Top executive	91.1	46.0
Top five executives	81.5	50.4
Retail firms:		
Top executives	67.2	61.3
Top five executives	70.6	54.1

Source: Lewellan (1971).
[a] Incentive income was defined as the sum of after-tax stock-based remuneration, after-tax dividend income and absolute after-tax capital gains.
[b] Those with total compensation which deviated from the mean by more than two standard deviations were deleted.

whom profit maximization seems a thoroughly sensible assumption, are unable to monitor perfectly their agents, the managers. As a consequence, a variety of managerial objective functions have been proposed for the firm, e.g. sales maximization [Baumol (1967)] and perquisite maximization [Williamson (1963)]. Each assumes a considerable inability of the firm's owners to control managerial behavior.

The widespread practice of performance-related bonuses for top executives has been held to be a response to this control problem. In an important, early study, Lewellan (1971) reported that performance based rewards were the greater part of the compensation of top executives. In the 1960–63 period, for example, 70–90 percent of a top executive's wealth increments came from stock options and dividends and capital gains from company stock (see Table 14.7). Even when the sample is clipped at ± 2 standard deviations of average compensation to eliminate the handful of extremely large (and possibly unanticipated) capital gain winners and losers, the incentive share of income is in the range of 50–75 percent across the three groups (large manufacturers, small manufacturers, and retailers). In the clipped sample, at least, the incentive share is higher in large firms.

Randomness in the productivity process cannot be neglected in the managerial model. Shocks to firm performance are generated by a variety of factors outside the manager's control, e.g. business cycle fluctuations and more industry and firm-idiosyncratic fluctuations in consumer demand. This randomness adds a new dimension to the optimal compensation calculus. The manager's decisions will be completely efficient only if the manager bears all the risk of the enterprise (collects all rents) and pays the owner of physical capital a fixed fee. Such a compensation policy, however, raises important questions of preferences for risk and optimal risk bearing if, as is frequently assumed, capital owners are risk neutral and employees risk averse since it implies that the employees bear all the risk of the enterprise. A tradeoff between productivity and efficient risk bearing arises, a tradeoff likely to be more severe the poorer the owner's ability to monitor the manager.

A number of fundamental considerations of optimal incentive systems can be illustrated in an example that did much to mold the early literature in this area, namely share cropping contracts between farmer and land owner, Cheung (1969) and Stiglitz (1974). The land owner is presumed (implicitly) to be able to measure *output* quantity and quality costlessly. Direct monitoring of work effort of the farmer by the land owner is assumed to be prohibitively expensive. The land owner must therefore design an output-based contract that will induce the farmer to work the land efficiently. An obvious incentive efficient contract would be a simple fee rental contract in which the farmer paid the land owner a fixed fee in return for the right to all crops grown on the land for a specified period of time.

Uncertainty of crop production due for example to variations in weather may, however, make the tenant farmer an inefficient residual claimant if he is risk averse. If the presumably wealthier landlord is risk neutral for gambles of this size, he would seem a logical insurance provider to the tenant, paying the tenant a fixed wage and "owning" the crop production himself. This insurance contract is of course the opposite of that proposed for pure incentive purposes. With these conflicting forces at work, the optimal linear contract can be shown to be one in which the farmer will be paid a fixed fee less than his alternative wages and will receive as well a share of the crop production. The fixed wage component of the compensation package will increase with the worker's risk aversion and will decrease with a greater need for effort incentives.

Consider this process more formally. A simple example in the spirit of Berhold (1971) and Stiglitz (1975) is useful in illustrating the interrelationship of the equilibrium employment contract and the economic behavior of the employer and employee. Assume a linear production function with an additive shock,

$$V = \mu H + \theta, \quad \mu > 0, \tag{3.1'}$$

where $V \equiv$ the value of the worker's output, $H \equiv$ the worker's effort level or intensity, and $\theta \equiv$ a random element with $E(\theta) = 0$. Assume further that:
  (i) the employer is in a competitive industry and is risk neutral, and
  (ii) the worker is risk averse.
More specifically assume that the worker has a utility function of the form

$$U = U(W - RH^2), \quad U' > 0, \quad U'' < 0, \tag{3.2}$$

where $R \equiv$ a fixed disutility of work parameter and the disutility of work effort increases quadratically with effort and W of course is the wage payment. In this model income will not affect the worker's optimal intensity level.

The compensation and work effort agreement that will result from this market situation will depend on the information available to the two parties. If all desired information is available to both parties and freedom to contract is complete, the risk neutral firm would absorb all production risk and would pay the worker a wage based on the worker's expected production, $W = \mu H$. Confronting this wage gradient, the worker would choose to expend effort H^*, where

$$H^* = \mu/2R, \tag{3.3}$$

that is effort will rise proportionately with productivity and decrease inversely with the disutility of effort parameter R. The worker's earnings will be W^*, where

$$W^* = \mu H^* = \mu^2/2R. \tag{3.4}$$

This efficient earnings–effort pair would be the one chosen for example by the risk neutral self-employed worker.

Consider now a more restricted information environment in which the employer cannot observe work effort directly but can costlessly measure the value of output V. Since eq. (3.1') can be rewritten as

$$H = \frac{1}{\mu}V - \frac{1}{\mu}\theta, \tag{3.5}$$

it is clear that a perfect effort monitor could be constructed if θ as well as V were known, assuming of course that the employer knew his production function parameter μ. In particular, if the production process is subject to no random element, $\theta \equiv 0$, the monitoring of effort by output would be perfect. Indeed, a compensation scheme of payment according to product would be fully efficient,

$$W = \mu H = \mu \left(\frac{1}{\mu}\right)V = V. \tag{3.6}$$

Payment strictly according to product would yield the efficient level of effort in this model even with an unobservable θ with positive variance since the optimal effort is independent of θ. Such a contract would, however, not generally induce a risk averse worker to accept employment if competitive firms with equivalent technology exist. Such firms could offer different contracts that have equivalent (expected) profit potential yet offer the risk averse worker greater expected utility.

The nonoptimality of strict payment by value of product can be demonstrated by deriving the optimal compensation for a class of compensation rules that include strict payment by product as a special case, namely the class of linear wage functions,

$$W = \alpha_0 + \alpha_1 V. \tag{3.7}$$

Clearly strict payment by value is the special case $\alpha_0 = 0$ and $\alpha_1 = 1$.

As a first step in the derivation of the optimal linear compensation function, consider the worker's optimal choice of effort when faced with an arbitrary linear compensation schedule as in eq. (3.7). The precise nature of the worker's decision will in general depend on whether he knows the realized value of the random element θ before he decides on the appropriate effort level or not. If he does, the worker is assumed to maximize his utility as in the standard labor supply problem:

$$\max_{H} U = \max_{H} U(W - RH^2) = \max_{H} U(\alpha_0 + \alpha_1 \mu H + \alpha_1 \theta - RH^2). \tag{3.8}$$

If θ is not known to the worker prior to the effort decision, it will be assumed that he maximizes his expected utility:

$$\max_{H} EU = \max_{H} \int U(\alpha_0 + \alpha_1 \mu H + \alpha_1 \theta - RH^2) \cdot f(\theta) \, \mathrm{d}\theta. \tag{3.9}$$

In this simple model with an additive production error term, the effort level is independent of the realization of θ so the distinction between the known and unknown error term is unimportant. In particular the solutions to (3.8) and (3.9) are the same:

$$H^* = \alpha_1 \frac{\mu}{2R}. \tag{3.10}$$

Only if $\alpha_1 = 1$ in the optimal contract will the equilibrium effort level be equal to the full information effort level [eq. (3.3) above].

Direct substitution of the optimal effort level (3.10) into the worker's expected utility function (3.9) provides a measure of the worker's preferences for compensation rules. Expected utility is appropriate here since the compensation regime is assumed to be determined prior to the employment match and any subsequent realization of productivity. Of course the worker cannot choose among all possible combinations of compensation rules. The employer must be able to break even (achieve zero pure profit) on the employment contract for it to be offered to the worker so expected productivity must equal expected wages for a contract (α_0, α_1) to be offered or

$$E(V - W) = E\left(\mu \frac{\alpha_1 \mu}{2R} + \theta - \left(\alpha_0 + \frac{(\alpha_1 \mu)^2}{2R} + \alpha_1 \theta \right) \right) = 0. \tag{3.11}$$

Since $E\theta = 0$, the zero profit constraint implies that the fixed payment (α_0) and piece rate (α_1) must bear the following relationship:

$$\alpha_0 = \alpha_1(1-\alpha_1)\frac{\mu^2}{2R}. \tag{3.12}$$

The direct substitution of (3.10) and (3.12) into (3.9) yields a single variable problem, say α_1, with a necessary condition for a maximum of

$$\frac{\mathrm{d}\,EU}{\mathrm{d}\alpha_1} = (1-\alpha_1)\left(\frac{\mu^2}{2R}\right)\int_a^b U'(\cdot)f(\theta)\,\mathrm{d}\theta + \int_a^b U'(\cdot)\theta f(\theta)\,\mathrm{d}\theta = 0. \tag{3.13}$$

Since $U' > 0$, the expected value of U' (the first integral) must be positive while the concavity of the utility function insures that the second integral is negative, marginal utility is higher at lower productivity realizations. Thus eq. (3.13) suggests that

$$\alpha_1 \leq 1$$

with strict inequality, unless
   (1) the worker is risk neutral, in which case U' is a constant, or
   (2) the distribution of θ is degenerate, that is there is no randomness.
In all other cases the optimal contract will involve risk sharing between employer and employee with the contract specifying a fixed payment and partial piece rate compensation schedule. Effort will be less than the complete information contract [compare (3.3) and (3.10) with $\alpha_1 < 1$].

This compensation schedule, it should be stressed, is only the optimal *linear* compensation schedule. Nonlinear compensation schemes may and generally will dominate these linear structures [e.g. Shavell (1979), Holmstrom (1979), and Harris and Raviv (1979)]. The analysis of nonlinear structures, however, requires a substantial increase in the sophistication of mathematical technique, specifically calculus of variation and optimal control, with few substantive implications to date.

Nonetheless examples exist of highly nonlinear optimal compensation schemes. The Harris and Raviv (1979) example, for instance, changes in no significant way if production risk is introduced as a linear additive term in the value of production function. Risk is already present in this structure through the imperfect monitor. Again an absolute standard is asserted to be optimal, estimated effort above a critical level is paid one wage, below that level a different, possibly zero wage (the worker is discharged). Obviously the compensation scheme is nonlinear.

Lazear and Rosen (1981) propose a similar discrete, output-oriented compensation scheme based on an ordinal measure, productivity ranking in a multiagent situation. Consider, for example, a situation of such complexity that an employer can judge which of two workers has performed more productively, but is unable to assign a cardinal value to the output of each.[20] To provide effort incentives, the employer must offer compensation based on the observable rank order, prizes in the terminology of contests. Lazear and Rosen explore the optimal prize structure in the two agent case. An important new feature is required in the analysis. Since compensation of a given worker's effort is dependent on the effort of his coworker, an assumption must be made of the game aspect of the model, that is how each expects the other to react. In particular, Lazear and Rosen assume a Nash noncooperative game solution in the two agent problem, a rather unattractive assumption when collusion among workers would be terribly valuable to them, but useful for illustrative purposes.

Lazear and Rosen then compare the efficiency of the rank order compensation system with the linear piece rate model and find that circumstances exist under which the rank order contest would be preferred to the linear piece rate system. This result may seem striking since the rank order compensation scheme ignores information used in the piece rate system, namely the actual value of output; the superiority of the rank order contest, when it occurs, must be due to the linearity constraint on piece rates. One could imagine, for example, that the rank order system would approximate the optimal absolute standard model in the Harris and Raviv example better than would the optimal *linear* piece rate model, although the comparison is between two inefficient structures and not in itself terribly interesting.

Lazear and Rosen consider another information structure that would make a rank order contest potentially attractive even if absolute measures of output were available, namely a random shock that is common to all agents. Indeed, Green and Stokey (1983), Holmstrom (1982), and Nalebuff and Stiglitz (1983) demonstrate under varying conditions that a component of the random element common to all agents is necessary if a rank order contest is ever to be optimal when cardinal output measures are available. The reason is intuitively appealing, namely that the rank of the worker's effort, unlike its absolute measure, is independent of the common random shock. Green and Stokey demonstrate in a model similar to that developed above that, with a sufficiently large number of agents (and prizes), the rank order model can approximate arbitrarily closely a nonlinear compensation scheme *with the common element observable*, i.e. the first best solution. Nalebuff and Stiglitz (1983) argue that this conclusion is dependent on the particular form of the production process, the additive error term, and is not in general true. Generally, some cardinal measure of the performance of

---

[20] Medoff and Abraham (1980, 1981) report several instances of relative performance monitoring among managers.

other agents, for example average output, will be usefully included in the employment contract if a component of the random shock is common to all agents and, as always, if collusion among workers is ruled out.

Indirect measures of environmental shocks may be available that are independent of the actions of the agents themselves and are therefore not vulnerable to collusion. The sales performance of an individual firm's sales staff in a region, for example, is likely to be correlated with aggregate demand measures such as income growth in the area; the crop yield of one's tenants is likely to be correlated with (observable) periods of moisture and temperature, independent of work effort. These measures may not capture industry-specific random effects, but other publicly available statistics may and would be sensibly included in an optimal contract in which individual productivity within the firm is subject to a common random element.

3.2. The compensation of heterogeneous workers

The importance of collecting high-quality information on individual workers, their productivity, reliability, etc. may itself justify long-term employment relationships if worker attributes are in part permanent and not simply a function of current incentives. If observationally equivalent workers systematically differ in the effort they will expend on an activity in a given incentive structure, the firm may adjust its compensation scheme over time as additional information on the reliability of each worker becomes known. In an excellent paper, Freeman (1977) develops a model of life cycle job mobility and compensation in an environment in which productivity assessments accumulate slowly over time. Although the model is based on a research firm example, the model applies equally well to productivity in general.

Freeman imagines a situation in which first period workers are observationally equivalent but in fact differ in the likelihood of making significant discoveries. Freeman assumes that the labor market is composed of two types of workers, high productivity researchers and low, and that the life cycle has two contract periods. After the initial period, workers are distinguished by their observable discoveries. As long as the discovery probability is not zero for the low-productivity individuals, the observed pool of successful discoverers will include a mix of individuals with high probability of success in the second period and low probability. The average probability of success in the second period will be higher among first period successes than among first period failures and the firm will optimally adjust its employment policy to reflect this additional information.

In an auction model of the second period, the firm would simply set wages equal to the expected productivity of each of the two observable groups: the discoverers and the nondiscoverers. If the expected productivity of the nondiscoverers is less than the value of their time in alternative activities (work or leisure) they would separate from the firm in the second period.

In a long-term contract market, the first period worker may purchase insurance against being revealed as a low productivity worker (through the lack of significant first period discoveries). The second period wages of nondiscoverers may therefore be above auction market levels. The extent of this insurance is limited by the constraint that workers cannot be held to long-term contracts; successful discoverers must be paid the expected value of their second period productivity (or more) if they are to remain with the firm.

The compensation of unsuccessful discoverers need not be in the form of higher wages. Indeed, if an efficient separation policy is to be maintained, the compensation may instead take the form of severance pay or early pension rights. Freeman makes the interesting point that early pension rights to *all* employees is not generally efficient since the best workers may choose to accept the pension and seek work elsewhere unless their wages are raised above competitive levels by the amount of the severance payments, which itself would be inconsistent with the productivity insurance function.

Freeman considers the interesting question of how the research firm's employment policies would be altered if workers know *at the beginning of their careers* whether they are high productivity researchers or not, but that the firm does not. This asymmetric productivity foreknowledge alters dramatically the firm's optimal second period compensation structure in a manner quite similar to that for mobility [Salop and Salop (1976) and Nickell (1976)]. The difference in wage payments between discoverers and nondiscoverers in the second period becomes a self-selection mechanism. Low (or negative) wages among all workers in the first period and among nondiscoverers in the second period and correspondingly high wages among discoverers in the second would make employment in the firm attractive only to high productivity researchers. The asymmetry of information shifts the compensation package toward greater production rewards for the agent with the relevant information.[21]

4. Firm specific human capital

The incidence of job separation and consequently of unemployment is not uniform across the major demographic groups in the work force, but is systematically larger among the low skilled and the young. The strong, negative relationship between job separation and education was noted earlier (Table 14.2). Mincer

---

[21] Screening devices used to identify high productivity workers may themselves induce a variety of activities that would not be undertaken were information free. See Spence (1973) on the general question and Akerlof (1976), Miyazaki (1977), and Guasch (1983).

and Jovanovic (1981) report data from the National Longitudinal Surveys of Young Men that indicates that the annual separation rate drops by 90 percent from the first year to the sixth year with the firm (see Table 14.8 below).

The firm specific human capital hypothesis has been proposed as an explanation of these and other turnover patterns. As noted earlier (Table 14.3) firms (and worker) may have relatively heavy investments in their employees. The business firm, after all, is more than a physical plant and pieces of equipment. Imagine a new firm which is about to commence operation. A variety of human capital expenses must be incurred. Hiring costs (advertising, interviewing, etc.) will be generated if new workers are to be attracted to the firm. Screening costs will arise if worker quality is not immediately observable. Optimal job assignments are rarely obvious a priori. Allocating workers to jobs typically requires substantial trial and error with a corresponding loss of productivity. Over time a new worker will learn about his job, about the characteristics of other workers in the firm, and about the nature of the firm's markets or individual customers, as well as the reliability of suppliers of various factors. These investments are specific to the unique match between a firm and worker and will be lost if the match is broken.

Even among established firms employee separations (and the need to invest in replacements) are inevitable, whether through death or through economic turnover such as retirement, discharges, quits and layoffs. A successful, long-lived firm must establish employee compensation policies that economize on the rate of depreciation of this organizational capital. The employment policies undertaken by individual firms may have important implications for the performance of the economy through the balance struck between (1) the need for a fluid, mobile labor force to accommodate inevitable fluctuations in product demand and (2) the need for work force stability to protect heavy investments in firm specific capital.

4.1. Job attachment in a homogeneous work force

4.1.1. Specific human capital, job turnover, and feasible contracts

Large investments in a unique relationship between an individual and a single firm will almost surely reduce the efficient rate of separation between the two agents and is therefore likely to reduce actual separation rates in any but the most unfavorable contracting environments. Contracts, explicit and implicit, are important in the efficient resolution of this process since match-specific capital lacks the usual competitive labor market guarantees that more widely demanded skills carry. In this section, the interrelationship of firm specific investments, job attachment, and feasible contracts is specified and their implications for life cycle mobility are discussed. Finally, the impact of (mobility) heterogeneous workers and imperfect information on the form of the firm's compensation package is developed for a market in which specific human capital investments are heavy.

The original theoretical literature in this area [Becker (1975), Oi (1962), Parsons (1972), Pencavel (1972), and Salop (1973)] focused on the effect of firm specific human capital on firm compensation policies and their consequences for firm layoff and quit experiences. More recently the literature has focused on a simple but expositionally powerful model of individual decision-making and randomness in job matching and separation [Mortensen (1978), Hashimoto and Yu (1980), and Hashimoto (1981)]. Contract effects on behavior are well illustrated at the individual level so this case forms an excellent introduction to the specific human capital investment process.

Single period efficiency requires that the individual be matched with the activity that is the highest valued use of his time. An employment contract that specifies complete worker immobility subsequent to specific human capital investment will typically not be efficient since worker productivities both inside the firm and out are likely to fluctuate randomly over time. The firm may experience product demand reversals, the worker sudden increases in the value of his general human capital in alternative firms. In both cases efficiency may require a reassignment of the individual to a different job.

Consider, for example, a simple model in which the worker and firm must undertake an organizational capital investment if the worker is to be an efficient employee.[22] Assume that the worker's productivity in the firm and his productivity in the labor market are subject to random shocks but that the investment must be undertaken prior to the discovery of these random effects. In particular assume that

$$V_i = \mu_i + \theta_i, \quad i = 0, 1, \tag{4.1}$$

where V_i denotes productivity; μ_i a fixed parameter; and θ_i the random productivity element with $i = 0$ the specific firm in question and $i = 1$ all other firms. Assume that $E(\theta_i) = 0$ so that the μ_i reflect "permanent" productivity differences. Presumably $\mu_0 > \mu_1$ by an amount sufficient to make the investment in the employee profitable on average.

The efficient separation policy is transparent. The firm and the worker should agree to separate if and only if the worker's actual productivity in the firm is less than his productivity outside the firm,

$$V_0 < V_1$$

or

$$\mu_0 + \theta_0 < \mu_1 + \theta_1. \tag{4.2}$$

[22]Again this model is in the spirit of those developed by Mortensen (1978), Hashimoto and Yu (1979), and Hashimoto (1981).

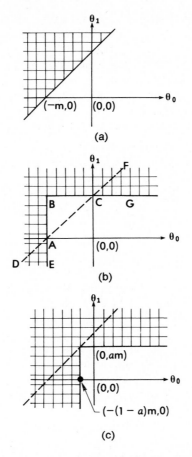

Figure 14.3. (a) The efficient job separation region. (b) The job separation region with bonding. (c) The job separation region with investment sharing.

Defining m as the difference between the expected productivities in the two activities ($m \equiv \mu_0 - \mu_1$), efficient separation will occur whenever

$$m < \theta_1 - \theta_0. \tag{4.3}$$

Unusually high productivity in the outside sector ($\theta_1 \gg 0$) and unusually depressed conditions within the firm ($-\theta_0 \gg 0$) will induce efficient separation.

Graphically the combination of inside and outside productivity shocks that will optimally induce job separations is represented by the cross-hatched area in Figure 14.3, part (a). The critical boundary of the separation–attachment region, of course, is determined by inequality (3.3). The optimal separation rate in this environment will be determined by the frequency distribution of outcomes of θ_0 and θ_1. In a bivariate normal distribution with θ_0 and θ_1 independent and with $E\theta_0 = E\theta_1 = 0$, an increase in the variance of either variable will induce greater efficient separation rates. If, as seems plausible, θ_0 and θ_1 are positively correlated so that productivity in the economy and in the firm fluctuate together (as might occur in a business cycle) then efficient separations will be less. If they are perfectly (positively) correlated no efficient separations may occur.

The efficient rate of job separation depends completely on the difference in expected productivity between the two activities, m, and of course on the size of random shocks, θ_0 and θ_1. The expected margin in productivities is of course not exogenous to the system but is determined by the size of the investment cost, say c. In the case of permanent occupational choice (no separations) in a market with risk neutral economic agents, the investment must provide an expected return (productivity margin) such that

$$\mu_0 - \mu_1 \geq c. \tag{4.4}$$

In a competitive product market with free entry, the relationship will hold as an equality. It is easily demonstrated in this model that larger specific human capital investments will generate lower equilibrium separation rates.

An important implication of this analysis is that no meaningful causal distinction exists between layoffs and quits. The separation rate is a function of the joint distribution of productivity shocks to the firm and to the economy. Job separation conditions are mutually agreed upon, based on complete information on the nature of these shocks. Turnover will occur only when job mobility is efficient because it is in the interest of both parties to agree to such a contract and information and contracting conditions are such that all desirable contracts are attainable.

The informational requirements of an efficient separation contract are large. Hashimoto (1981) proposes a "profit" sharing contract in which factor payments are determined as a share of the difference between current firm and alternative firm productivity. Defining the factor payments to the worker as w (wages) and to the firm as π (profits) the distribution rule would be

$$w = V_1 + \alpha(V_0 - V_1) = V_1 + \alpha m + \alpha(\theta_0 - \theta_1) \tag{4.5}$$

and

$$\pi = V_0 - w = (1 - \alpha)(V_0 - V_1) = (1 - \alpha)m + (1 - \alpha)(\theta_0 - \theta_1), \tag{4.6}$$

where α is a predetermined sharing rule, $0 < \alpha < 1$. Clearly, under this rule each would choose to separate if and only if $m + (\theta_0 - \theta_1) < 0$ or, as in (3.3), $m < \theta_0 - \theta_1$, for then $w < V_1$ and $\pi < 0$.

For such an agreement to be explicitly contracted, an unrelated third party must be able to observe the random elements θ_0 and θ_1 as well as the permanent factors μ_0 and μ_1 and as a consequence m. Such observability is unlikely, even for the two parties actively engaged in the contract. If, as is plausible, only the firm has good information on θ_0, the random shock in current firm productivity, and only the worker on θ_1, the random element in the worker's outside alternatives, then the contract as stated is not feasible. Other mechanisms also yield the efficient separation rate but have the same information requirements. Mortensen (1978), for example, considers an "offer matching" option to the contract that would achieve efficiency in this model, the other party would be willing to bid up the return to the party that wishes to leave to the point that only efficient separations would occur. Clearly the bidding party needs information on the offer the other party receives if strategic games are to be avoided. Indeed in the more general model discussed by Mortensen that incorporates endogenous search activity, search intensity must be observable as well or offer matching will promote excessive search and separation.

An alternative compensation mechanism that requires less information is one that specifies fixed wages and a separation bond equal to the other's capital investment in the match.[23] In this compensation scheme each party's investment is protected. The worker, for example, will quit only if he receives an alternative wage bid greater than his contract wage by the amount of the firm's investment in him and the firm receives the forfeited bond as compensation. Assuming the worker's own investment is reflected in his wage (as must be the case in a competitive labor market), the worker will leave only if his alternative bid exceeds the total investment costs.

Formally the worker will quit when

$$V_1 > w + B_w, \tag{4.7}$$

where B_w denotes the bond the worker must forfeit upon departure and the firm will lay off the worker whenever

$$V_0 < w - B_F, \tag{4.8}$$

where B_F denotes the firm's bond it forfeits upon laying off the worker. Assuming the expected return margin m is equal to investment cost c [see eq. (4.4)] so that $m = c$, then

$$B_w = (1 - \alpha)m \tag{4.9}$$

---

[23] Mortensen (1978) formally considers such a structure.

and

$$B_F = \alpha m, \tag{4.10}$$

each bonds the other's share of the original investment. Recall α is the worker's share of the investment. If the worker is risk neutral and in a competitive labor market, he must be offered a fixed wage equal to the expected alternative wage plus the return on the worker's investment, or

$$w = EV_1 + \alpha m = \mu_1 + \alpha m. \tag{4.11}$$

This fixed compensation–bonding contract is not fully efficient because the returns to the investment are random.[24] The separation decision rules (4.7) and (4.8), following the substitution of the relationships in (4.9)–(4.11) reduce to the rules that the worker should quit if

$$\theta_1 > m, \tag{4.12}$$

that is, if he experiences an outside demand shock greater than the full investment cost, and that the firm should lay off the worker if

$$\theta_0 < -m, \tag{4.13}$$

that is, if his productivity in the firm drops by more than the full investment cost. The separation region of the (θ_0, θ_1) plane under this set of decision rules is illustrated in part (b) of Figure 14.3. The boundary of the efficient separation rules is marked by the dashed line for comparison purposes.

In some circumstances [realizations of (θ_0, θ_1)], bonded individuals will separate from the firm when they should have remained matched (triangle ABC). In others they will remain with the firm even though they should optimally have separated (the regions ADE and CFG). The reason the fixed bond model is not fully efficient is that the total value of the match is a random variable and the fixed bond model gives the other party no opportunity to express actual as opposed to prospective match value.

The information requirements of the bonding scheme are, moreover, not zero, particularly if the scheme must be administered by a third party. The bonding administrator must be able to identify which party wishes to end the match if the appropriate bond is to be forfeited. As a practical issue this decision is more

---

[24] The bonding model is fully efficient in the discussion by Mortensen (1978). He assumes a Poisson arrival process for random shocks to current productivity and alternative activity and considers an instant in time during which no more than one shock in total can occur. He further assumes a fixed and known cost to the party *not* receiving the shock of breaking the job match. A fixed value bond is efficient in this situation.

difficult than one might expect (unless one were familiar with the problems that confront unemployment insurance administrators in systems that distinguish by eligibility or benefit level between layoffs and quits). Both parties can alter other, less observable aspects of contract performance to induce the other to break the match. A firm can make a worker's life quite intolerable by varying the non-pecuniary returns of the job. The worker on the other hand can induce the firm to break the match by an appropriate display of sloth or ineptitude.

The information problem required for bonding is eliminated if one of the two parties is reliable, for both parties presumably know whether or not they are themselves responsible for inducing the separation. The reliable party could therefore hold the bond of the less reliable party, keeping the bond if that is appropriate or returning it, with or without its own forfeited bond as the agreement stipulates.

Becker (1975) proposes that nonvested pensions serve as such a bonding scheme, an idea worked out more formally by Kennan (1979). If the bond is substantial, of course, the worker may confront borrowing constraints that force the bond to be "posted" or accumulated over time with the relatively full efficiency of the bond secured only after some period with the firm. McDonald (1982) models the interrelationship of specific human capital and capital difficulties.

Earlier papers on specific human capital finance and turnover [Becker (1975), Oi (1962), and Parsons (1972)] explored a weak form of employment agreement, a fixed wage contract with no separation damages. No information problems arise in this structure since the payments are not contingent on the realizations of possibly unobservable market processes. In this compensation environment, the worker will quit whenever

$$V_1 - w > 0, \tag{4.14}$$

and the firm will lay off the worker whenever

$$w - V_0 > 0. \tag{4.15}$$

In a competitive labor market, the wage would be set as earlier, as the expected value of the alternative wage plus the worker's share of the investment costs ($w = \mu_1 + \alpha m$). The separation region for a given investment sharing parameter (α) is illustrated in Figure 14.3, part (c). Again the efficient separation boundary in the complete information case is indicated for comparison purposes by the dashed line. The fixed wage separation region is unambiguously larger than the efficient separation region.

Becker (1975) first proposed that there may be some optimal investment sharing (α) that will minimize this inefficient separation. The financing of and returns to the investment will be shared between firm and worker since some investment by each in the relationship reduces the incentives for unilateral withdrawal from the relationship by either; the sharing is a form of mobility bond. The worker's investment in the activity provides the firm with a greater likelihood that the worker will not quit the firm after the investment period and thereby depreciate its investment in the worker's organizational capital. Similarly, the worker has greater security that he will not be subject to permanent layoff (and the depreciation of his organizational human capital) if the firm invested in him as well.

In the framework of the individual's quit decision [part (c)], the sharing should be undertaken such that the separation region *outside* the efficient separation region should include as little probability density of (θ_0, θ_1) as possible.[25] It is easily demonstrated that, if the variances of θ_0 and θ_1 are equal (the size of the random shocks to the individual's productivity inside the firm and outside are equal), then equal sharing of the investment will minimize the separation in-efficiencies due to the nonobservability of θ_0 and θ_1 by both parties. As the variance of θ_0 increases relative to that of θ_1, the firm should optimally undertake an increasing share of the investment if inefficient separations are to be mini-mized.

The sharing hypothesis requires for its execution no information on realized values of (θ_0, θ_1) since a fixed wage contract underlies it. For the same reason, it will not be fully efficient. Hashimoto and Yu (1980) argue that, even though the realizations of θ_0 and θ_1 may not be observable, flexible wage contracts contin-gent on observables correlated with θ_0 and θ_1 will generally be desirable, that is will be more efficient than the fixed wage contract. As the correlation between the proxies for θ_0 and θ_1 and their corresponding true values increase, the contingent contract will approach the fully efficient separation behavior. Certainly it is easy to imagine aggregate observables such as vacancy rates, want ad lineage, etc. that proxy more or less well fluctuations in the worker's wage prospects. Similar data may also provide good indicators of firm demand conditions. Other potentially useful data include industry sales and, if the firm is a large, publicly held corporation, actual firm sales and profits.

Parsons (1972) develops formally Becker's sharing hypothesis in a two period framework in which the first period is devoted to specific training and the second to production. He reports a number of comparative static results. The employer's share of the investment will be higher (1) the less responsive worker quit rates to wage changes, (2) the more responsive trainee supply to wage variations, and (3) the higher the worker's rate of discount. The firm's layoff propensity will be greater the lower unemployment insurance costs and required severance pay-

---

[25]More precisely the expected loss should be minimized which involves the size of a specific misallocation as well as its probability.

ments, the greater the likelihood of eventual rehire, and the more insensitive quits are to wage variations. Independently Pencavel (1972) and Salop (1973) developed elegant optimal wage policies for the zero layoff environment and derived many of the same quit rate implications.

The best evidence to date on the specific human capital sharing hypothesis suggests that the Becker limited information model is valid. Quits (worker initiated job separations) are affected by the worker's share of such investments [Pencavel (1972), Parsons (1972)] and layoffs by the employer's share [Parsons (1972)]. Nonetheless, the measurement of specific human capital is uncertain and the measurement of worker/firm shares of the capital verges on the speculative. The worker's investment in specific human capital (and therefore his incentive to quit) is typically indexed by the difference between actual wages and predicted wages (or proxies for the latter such as schooling) and the firm's investment (and therefore its incentive to lay off the worker) by the difference between total human capital and wages. Clearly this aspect of the firm's organizational capital formation remains very much an open research question.[26]

4.1.2. Life cycle separation behavior

If job matching costs are incurred only at the time of hire, say as job search and mobility costs, then one would expect that separation rates would remain constant over the life of the job match. The wage–separation models discussed above [Pencavel (1972), Salop (1973)] have such a property. If, however, firm specific human capital investment occurs, then one would expect an individual's separation rate to fall over time. Mincer and Jovanovic (1981) provide persuasive evidence that separation rates decline sharply with length of current job tenure and that what appears to be age effects on separation behavior are primarily a reflection of the tenure dependence of separations. In Table 14.8 two-year separation probabilities of young males from the National Longitudinal Surveys, reported in Mincer and Jovanovic, illustrate the tenure dependence of separation probabilities. Whether the individual has zero-to-four years of total work experience or five-to-nine, the separation rates drop from more than 70 percent in the first year on the job to less than 10 percent in the fifth year and beyond. Similar, if lower, separation patterns hold for older males.

The precipitous decline in mobility in the first few years could well be due to factors other than specific human capital, at least in its simplest form. Intuitively one might suppose that the individuals are in part "job shopping", learning about attributes of the firm that are not readily observable prior to working with

---

[26] Elizabeth Peters (1983) presents an interesting study of efficient separation in a small firm, in this case the family. Peters found that the wide differences across states and in divorce laws affected the distribution of assets after the marriage dissolved but had no significant effect on the incidence of divorce.

Table 14.8
Job mobility among young males by experience and tenure,
pooled 1967–73 (percent moving in a two-year period).

Total work experience (years)	Tenure (years with current job)					
	0–1	1–3	3–5	5–7	7–9	9–11
			Total separations			
0–4	0.73	0.58	0.28	0.07	0.12	0.04
5–9	0.77	0.60	0.38	0.08	0.07	0.06
			Quits			
0–4	0.48	0.41	0.20	0.06	0.08	0.04
5–9	0.48	0.42	0.26	0.06	0.05	0.07
			Layoffs			
0–4	0.26	0.17	0.08	0.01	0.05	–
5–9	0.28	0.18	0.11	0.03	0.02	–

Source: Mincer and Jovanovic (1981, p. 25). The basic data set is the younger male cohort of the National Longitudinal Surveys. The total sample size is 3443.

the firm, experience goods in Nelson's terminology [Nelson (1970)]. The experience attribute could be the nonpecuniary nature of the job, e.g. coworkers, bosses, and job stress [Johnson (1978), Viscusi (1980)] or the worker's productivity in the firm [Jovanovic (1979)]. Burdett (1978) proposes a pure search model in which equivalent workers search their way to better and better jobs over time. If jobs are guaranteed at a fixed wage for a lifetime, then workers will face an upward drift in wages and a decline in the quit rate over the life cycle; adversity is assumed away. Mortensen (Chapter 15 in this Handbook) reviews this model at some length.

The tenure patterns, however, hold for layoffs as well as quits (Table 14.3), suggesting that the phenomenon is more than simply a reflection of job shopping and that the job match does grow in value with time with the firm. Indeed, the one empirical, if crude attempt to unravel these various factors (Mincer and Jovanovic) indicates that perhaps a third of the tenure dependence phenomenon is due to worker heterogeneity (individuals with intrinsically lower separation probabilities have disproportionately longer job tenure, ceteris paribus). Further, they decomposed life cycle wage growth by source: one half is general on-the-job training, one-quarter the worker's share of specific human capital investments, and one-quarter job search related, primarily real productivity effects, i.e. the individual finds a more productive match (pure wage search factors do not appear to be a major factor in life cycle wage profiles).

Jovanovic (1979) develops an interesting model that combines alternative wage search (wage growth by job change) and specific human capital investment (wage growth within the firm). The model is sufficiently complex that it has not been systematically exploited but suggests a number of important interactions. On the one hand, search and consequently mobility decline with greater amounts of accumulated specific human capital (Jovanovich assumes complete and efficient contracting here). On the other hand, the attractiveness of specific human capital investments may change with the optimal level of productive search. If the intrinsic value of a match is not immediately evident to a worker, specific investments may not be undertaken at once (if production technology offers a choice) but may instead be undertaken only after active job shopping is past.

4.2. Employment contracts with mobility – heterogeneous workers

If workers differ intrinsically in their job mobility propensities, efficiency would surely require, ceteris paribus, that low mobility workers be matched with jobs in which large, firm-specific investments are profitable. If low-mobility individuals are easily identifiable, by themselves and by firms, this mobility consideration could be easily handled within a competitive labor market, job mobility propensity would simply be another attribute of the individual worker. If, as seems plausible, the worker but not the firm is aware of the individual's mobility propensity, however, the question arises of whether the firm can design a compensation scheme that will cause the worker to reveal his perceived characteristics. In the insurance literature, for example, Rothschild and Stiglitz (1976) consider the question of whether high-risk individuals can be induced to reveal to the insurance firm their riskiness by manipulation of price and extent-of-coverage tie-ins, high-risk individuals being induced to purchase more complete coverage and to pay disproportionately heavier premiums.

Salop and Salop (1976) and Nickell (1976) independently proposed alteration of the tenure structure of wages as a self-screening device which would induce highly mobile individuals to identify themselves. In particular, if firms with heavy specific investments offer low wages in the first period and high wages in the second, the expected compensation stream should be relatively attractive to those with low mobility. One could presume that an appropriately steep wage gradient could separate the workers, if no other factors intervened. Indeed, Salop and Salop argue that the optimal wage pattern would be one in which the individual worker's first period wage would be entirely reduced by the amount of the specific investment and raised correspondingly in the second period (or future periods in a multiperiod model). The logic of the argument is transparent. In a world in which only the worker can observe his innate mobility trait, the worker must bear all the costs of the specific human capital investment for the incentives to be perfect. Obviously this solution ignores the firm/worker contracting problems discussed above. Moreover, as Nickell points out, such a solution ignores other plausible sources of heterogeneity. Specifically workers may systematically differ in access to borrowed funds. This source of heterogeneity is particularly significant since the optimal mobility-revealing strategy is to force the worker to make all specific investments. Random differences in access to capital would make the wage gradient an imperfect selection device, the more so the larger the randomness in discount rates and the less positively correlated these rates are with immobility traits. Nonetheless, these self-selection arguments provide an important, additional reason why workers may share in specific human capital financing.

5. Employment insurance contracts

Empirically wages appear to fluctuate little in response to relatively large fluctuations in product demand. Employment levels also fluctuate proportionately less than do sales and the employment adjustments that do occur are quite slow.[27] Nadiri and Rosen (1974), for example, report that in the manufacturing sector only about 40 percent of the adjustment in production worker levels to a decline in sales occurs in the first quarter, with the full adjustment requiring five to six quarters. The estimated adjustment among nonproduction workers is minimal even in the long run. The large procyclical fluctuations in average productivity are apparently a reflection of the "labor hoarding" that occurs during economic downturns.

As discussed above, the specific human capital hypothesis has predictions for both the existence and incidence of the observed labor hoarding consistent with these observations. A number of papers in the macroeconomic literature, especially Baily (1974), Gordon (1974), and Azariadis (1975), have proposed an alternative explanation, that employment stability is directly purchased from the firm as a part of the employee's compensation package. Among experienced workers, job layoffs seem to be the primary force driving cyclical unemployment rates (see above Figure 14.1). Given the potentially large earnings losses generated by any significant period of unemployment, it is natural to imagine that layoff probabilities under various demand conditions are an important aspect of a worker's compensation.

Since the early literature had a strong macroeconomic orientation, it focused primarily on the implication of the worker's earnings security demands for wage "stickiness"; only recently have the full implications of the models for labor hoarding become fully appreciated [e.g. Akerlof and Myazaki (1980)]. In the same tradition, papers by Calvo and Phelps (1977), Hall and Lilien (1979), Grossman and Hart (1983), Azariadis (1983), Chari (1983), and Green and Kahn

---

[27] Beyond the Nadiri and Rosen work discussed below, see the earlier work by Brechling (1965) and Ball and St. Cyr (1966) and also Clark (1973).

(1983) consider employment contracts under more complex informational assumptions. In this section I explore the motivations and consequences of risk reallocation in employment contracts within the contract framework developed above.[28]

The literature discussed in this section focuses on unemployment as the alternative activity to working for the current firm. All studies assume that unemployment has some value, at the very least respite from work effort and related stress. Nonetheless, the unemployment activity is likely to have a value considerably less than customary wages if not less than current productivity. In the absence of earnings insurance, the loss of any substantial amount of labor income is likely to have severe, negative consequences on family well-being, since for the majority of families in the United States, earnings are the sole source of income of any consequence. Assets, particularly relatively liquid assets which can be cheaply converted into consumption, are few. The ability to borrow against future earnings to finance current consumption is severely restricted as well.

The traditional private insurance market for earnings security is primarily limited to life insurance; private disability insurance is not widespread and unemployment insurance essentially nonexistent. Reasons for the absence of a vigorous, private market for unemployment insurance are not difficult to enumerate:

(1) the difficulty of state verification,
(2) moral hazard, and
(3) adverse selection.

Each of these is a serious problem in the provision of unemployment insurance.

Consider the question of state verification; that is, did the insured event in fact occur? Particularly at the lower skill levels at which unemployment is a considerable risk, an unrelated, private third party may have considerable difficulty determining whether or not an individual is currently employed. Even the government tax collectors with their unique access to information and their tremendous array of coercive powers have significant problems monitoring the earning activity of this group. The difficulties for private insurers are surely more substantial.

Moral hazard and adverse selection problems compound an insurer's problems. Moral hazard problems of two kinds may arise: layoffs (entry into unemployment) may be excessive as firms and workers treat unemployment insurance as subsidized leisure [Feldstein (1975)]. The duration of unemployment may be increased as well if the laid off workers reduce the intensity of their search for alternate jobs. Adverse selection is also likely to be a problem since individuals

---

[28] Excellent reviews of this literature are available. See Azariadis (1981) for a fine discussion of the original rigid wage literature and Hart (1983) and Azariadis and Stiglitz (1983) for critical discussions of the more recent literature on employment contingent wage contracts.

are likely to have better prior information on their prospects for layoff and unemployment than are private insurers of those individuals.

The public provision of unemployment insurance eliminates some but not all of these insurance difficulties. Adverse selection problems are eliminated in a universal system. Access to information unavailable to private insurers reduces but does not eliminate the state verification problem. Still the moral hazard problems remain. With incomplete experience rating, firms and workers have an incentive to treat unemployment insurance as subsidized leisure; workers have a reduced incentive to seek alternative employment, the firm an increased incentive to put them on layoff status. No doubt as a consequence of these insurance difficulties, public unemployment insurance is incomplete. Many unemployed workers are not covered by the system. Of those that are, few receive payments that come close to replacing lost earnings, although they receive some compensation through additional leisure.[29]

The limited private and public availability of earnings insurance suggests that the employer himself may find it profitable to provide some level of protection to the worker against unemployment earnings losses. Certainly the employer has access to higher quality information, both on his own intentions and that of his employees, than do private insurance firms or even the government. One aspect of state verification, whether the individual has been laid off, is obviously known to the employer. Adverse selection is not likely to be a serious problem since again the firm is aware of future layoff probabilities. Some aspects of the problem do remain outside its control; the firm is unlikely to know for example whether the laid off worker is seeking alternative employment diligently or indeed whether he has already found alternative employment.

The ability of the firm to provide employment insurance is dependent on the information available to the agents. Under what conditions will insurance be a feasible part of the employment contract? How much will the worker's earnings fluctuations be moderated? Perhaps most importantly, how will employment behavior be affected in the optimal contract? The models discussed below are the first important steps in answering these questions.

Whatever its specific content, the earnings insurance "contract" will presumably be an implicit one. If the various contingencies were observable at reasonable cost to third parties as is necessary for explicit, legally enforceable contracts, the insurance function would be undertaken by specialized insurance firms. Employers, for example, typically provide life insurance with its rather fewer ambiguities through insurance firms and are not themselves the primary insurer. As with any implicit contract, the reliability of the agents as well as their differential access to information is an important factor in forming the agreement and in determining subsequent behavior.

---

[29]See Topel and Welch (1980) for a review of the literature on public unemployment programs.

The attitudes of the agents toward risk, only briefly considered in the specific human capital discussion, becomes crucial in the analysis of employment of earnings insurance contracts. Since the purpose of insurance is to reallocate risk bearing, the attitudes of the parties toward risk and the cost to each of diversifying this particular risk are crucial to the bargain. The most common assumption is that the worker is risk averse, that the employer behaves as though he is risk neutral, and that as a consequence the employer sells insurance to the worker within the constraints of the information set available to each. The risk neutrality of employers is based on either of two arguments, that capital owners as a group are wealthier and less concerned by a given wealth fluctuation or, more compellingly, that physical capital owners can diversity their portfolios more cheaply than can human capital owners.

However plausible, the assumed risk preferences of the two groups are based on empirical conjecture and indeed models have been developed and are discussed below which assume the converse. One should note that the diversification argument has implications that the simple difference-in-risk-preference argument does not. One would expect that diversification among owners and therefore the willingness to insure workers is more complete in large, publicly held firms. Secondly, aggregate risk due to business cycle fluctuations is not diversifiable and is therefore less likely to be insured by the firm than are random shocks to the firm or industry if the two agents' attitudes toward risk are similar.[30]

In the section that follows I consider first the random firm specific shocks to worker productivity that are most amenable to internal insurance. The nature of the employment contract under various assumptions of information availability and contract reliability is explored. The difficulties and behavioral changes that arise with aggregate, nondiversifiable risk are then considered.

5.1. Individual productivity risk

In this section I assume that the productivity of the individual in the current firm and elsewhere in the economy are subject to individual-specific random shocks that are unrelated to aggregate or business cycle fluctuations. In such an environment it is natural to assume that employers act as if they are risk neutral and therefore that they act as insurers of risk averse workers if information problems are not too severe. This assumption captures the intuitive notion that owners can more easily diversify their physical capital holdings than can workers diversify their human capital position in the firm.

---

[30] See Reagan and Stulz (1982) for a more extended discussion of labor contracts with aggregate and disaggregate risk.

5.1.1. Job attachment with complete information

Consider again the simple two activity model of the previous section:

$$V_i = \mu_i + \theta_i, \quad i = 0,1, \tag{5.1}$$

where V_i denotes productivity, μ_i a fixed productivity parameter, and θ_i the random shock to productivity with $i = 0$ the current firm and $i = 1$ the alternative activity. The alternative activity could be another job or unemployment (leisure, home productivity, job search, etc.). Assume that $E(\theta_0) = E(\theta_1) = 0$, so that $m = \mu_0 - \mu_1$ reflects the permanent difference in productivity between the two activities; in this case m need not be positive although it presumably would be whenever specific investments or mobility costs had been incurred.

The efficient separation policy in the risk neutral (expected productivity maximization) case is, as discussed above, to separate if productivity in the firm is less than productivity outside the firm. Symbolically:

$$V_0 < V_1$$

or

$$\theta_1 - \theta_0 > \mu_0 - \mu_1 \equiv m.$$

In a world of risk neutral competitive firms and complete information, earnings insurance will be provided at zero cost and the efficient separation rule is unaffected by worker risk aversion.

Not all the efficient separation contracts discussed in the previous section will be optimal, however, when workers are risk averse since different contract forms have different implications for earnings stability. In the profit sharing contract, for example, in which wage (W) is set according to the rule:

$$W = V_1 + \alpha(V_0 - V_1).$$

Wage payments to the worker have a nonzero variance, namely

$$V(W) = \alpha^2 \sigma_0^2 + (1 - \alpha^2)\sigma_1^2,$$

where $\sigma_0^2 = V(\theta_0)$ and $\sigma_1^2 = V(\theta_1)$ and by assumption $\text{cov}(\theta_0, \theta_1) \equiv 0$.

In the complete information case, risk neutral employers can (profitably) guarantee workers a fixed wage payment, independent of outcome. In the competitive case with equal expected value for either outcome ($\mu_0 = \mu_1 = \mu$) the payment would be μ. The worker would remain with the firm or separate as efficiency required ($V_0 \gtrless V_1$); he would receive a fixed wage $W = \mu$ if he remained with the firm. If separation is efficient, appropriate side payments would be made from firm to worker if $V_1 < \mu$ and from worker to firm if $V_1 > \mu$.

The courts, of course, might refuse to enforce a requirement of severance payments from worker to firm, although the same transaction could perhaps be designed less transparently. For example, an implicit bond could be posted that would be forfeited to the firm upon a job separation at the worker's initiative. In a multi-period framework this could be executed through low entry wages and high subsequent compensation (seniority-based wage increases, noninvested pensions, etc.).

Conversely, the firm may have some limitation on its ability to pay severance benefits to workers it chooses to lay off, perhaps because of moral hazard problems due to reduced work effort by workers desiring to induce layoff and consequently receive severance benefits payments. Such an economic environment underlies the now famous set of papers on wage rigidity and employment contracts of Baily (1974), Gordon (1974), and Azariadis (1975).[31] The mechanism underlying these models can be illustrated in a special case of the two activity choice models. Label the second activity unemployment. Presumably the value of this activity (V_1) is a function of the value of leisure or job search time, government unemployment compensation payments, etc. Assume that the value of unemployment is fixed, $\sigma_1^2 = 0$ or $V_1 = \mu_1$, and, though plausible but not essential, that the value of unemployment is less than the mean value of productivity in the firm, $\mu_1 < \mu_0$. Assume further that V_0 is distributed over the interval $-\infty$ to ∞ according to the density function $f(V_0)$.

It is easy to demonstrate formally that, with complete information and no contract constraints, the risk neutral firm will offer the risk averse worker an employment contract with the following features:

(1) the firm will lay off the worker if and only if $V_0 < \mu_1$, that is the critical current productivity threshold for separation, say V_c, is $V_c = V_1 \equiv \mu_1$;

(2) the worker will be offered a wage (if retained) that is independent of the productivity realization V_0; and

(3) the severance payment, say K, will be such that the "worker" is equally well off whether employed or unemployed: he is fully insured.

The precise level of the wage–severance-pay package will depend on the value of compensation available elsewhere, that is, the compensation necessary to attract workers to this firm's contract prior to realization of actual productivity.

What now if the firm is unable to offer severance pay or (loosely) unemployment compensation? The effect on the firm's separation policy is unambiguous; the firm will enter into an employment contract with the worker which specifies that the separation rate will be less than efficiency considerations alone would dictate. The layoff threshold V_c will be strictly less than the alternative value of

---

[31]Again see the review of these and subsequent papers in Azariadis (1981).

the individual's time ($V_c < \mu_1$). The reason is transparent; because of the severance pay restrictions, the firm can insure the worker against adverse demand fluctuations only by retaining him on the payroll. As long as the real cost of doing so is not too great, that is V_0 is not too much less than V_1, such a contract is attractive. The result is a quite plausible motivation for "labor hoarding" independent of specific human capital considerations.

Ironically, the pioneering literature in this area, again Baily (1974), Gordon (1974), and Azariadis (1975), stressed the wage rigidity aspect of this structure; the "overemployment" implication was not stressed [Akerlof and Myazaki (1980)]. Although the overemployment implication is quite consistent with what we know of employment behavior, it has a rather obvious deficiency in explaining unemployment, an objective of the early studies.

5.1.2. Asymmetric information

The discussion to this point has assumed complete information, most critically on the realization of V_0 or alternatively θ_0, so that the firm and worker can write explicit contracts guaranteeing performance if they wish. What if the employer alone observes the true productivity realization? If the firm is reliable, perhaps motivated by reputational effects, the previous analysis is unchanged. If private unemployment insurance payments are not feasible, labor hoarding will result.

If the firm is not reliable, the labor hoarding contract is no longer viable. The worker would undertake *only* rigid wage contracts with an unreliable firm in this simple model since wages but not the realized V_0 are observable and therefore amenable to explicit contracts. Not only would the firm find it profitable to lay off workers whenever V_0 fell below $V_1 = \mu_1$, if it contracted for a rigid wage $W > \mu_1$, it would lay off workers profitably whenever $V_0 < W$. Rigid wage contracts with unreliable firms, if they existed at all, would be characterized by high wages and high layoff rates. The existence of such contracts in equilibrium is dependent on the shape of the distribution of realized productivities, V_0 or alternative θ_0.

The worker negotiating with the "unreliable" firm has somewhat less stark alternatives available than is suggested by this simple model. Even though the actual realization of θ_0 is not available for inclusion in the employment contract, presumably quantities correlated with θ_0 are observable to the worker and to third parties. Most obviously wage and employment prospects could be tied to the firm's profitability if it is a large, publicly held firm or perhaps to government statistics on industry sales if profitability or other firm specific data is not available. If these measures are relatively highly correlated with the firm's demand, then contracts may be feasible that approximate efficient separation and complete insurance. Similarly, if severance pay payments are restricted, the second-best contract of labor hoarding may at least be obtainable. The degree to which firm demand can be predicted by public statistics is an important empirical issue which has not to my knowledge been pursued.

Recently researchers have proposed the firm's employment level itself as an indicator of product demand conditions, albeit an endogenous one, e.g. Calvo and Phelps (1977) and Hall and Lilien (1979).[32] At the individual level the discrete (zero–one) nature of employment and layoff in the models considered makes the employment variable useless as a contract performance monitor. However, if a work sharing arrangement is contracted, that is each individual's work hours are reduced proportionately and no one is laid off, more subtle contract relations can be designed. Alternatively, if a firm's work force can be viewed collectively, as might be appropriate for a trade union, the percentage of the work force laid off could be a sensible employment stipulation equivalent to hours reduction for an individual.

The basic intuition behind employment-contingent wage policies is that wage and employment options may be designed in such a way that the employer is induced to reveal accurately the realized state of product demand that he alone can observe. In particular, focusing on the wage attribute alone, if stipulated wages differ across states (and are presumably lowest in the worst states), the firm would always have an incentive to declare that the worst state has occurred. Clearly this makes contracts with wage adjustments across states infeasible. A wage–hours contract, however, that penalizes the firm for declaring a low state of demand by requiring it to employ the worker for less hours in that state may be feasible. The usefulness of such contracts requires that the hours reduction penalize the firm more than the worker, which suggests that the effect of hours variations on (1) worker productivity in the various states and (2) on the worker's utility (the marginal value of leisure) will be crucial to the desirability of such a contract.

The introduction of variable work hours adds an element to the choice set that requires additional discussion even in the complete information case. The unemployment activity and the work activity are no longer simple either/or alternatives but rather may be chosen in any linear combination that add to total time available; the classical labor supply analysis is appropriate. Consider an example in which only two states of the world are possible and that product in each of these two states is a linear function of work hours so

$$V = \mu^j h, \quad j = 1, 2, \tag{5.2}$$

where μ^j is a positive productivity parameter and $h \equiv$ hours worked. Assume

---

[32] More complete reviews of this literature can be found in Hart (1983) and Azariadis and Stiglitz (1983).

$\mu^1 > \mu^2$, i.e. state 1 is the high demand state. Firm profits can be represented by

$$\pi = V - W, \tag{5.3}$$

and worker utility by

$$U = U(W, h), \quad \text{with } U_1 > 0 \text{ and } U_2 < 0. \tag{5.4}$$

In a competitive labor market (zero firm profits) without insurance, the individual would in equilibrium be at the points (W^j, h^j) if the wage rate is $W^j = \mu^j h^j$ in each state; see the somewhat unconventional representation of the labor–leisure graph in Figure 14.4(a).[33] The usual labor–leisure analysis suggests that the substitution effect of greater productivity will induce greater work hours but that the income effect, if leisure is a normal good (as it seems to be empirically), induces fewer work hours, so that the gross or total effect on equilibrium work hours is ambiguous. In the case illustrated, work hours are higher in the high productivity case ($h^1 > h^2$).

Consider now the insurance attribute of the decision process. The worker is quite clearly better off in the high productivity state in Figure 14.4(a) and the question arises whether the firm could not (at least in the full information case) profitably supply security to the worker. Clearly the risk neutral firm could provide such a contract. Assume for simplicity that each of the two states is equally probable and that the prior expected value of the two auction market contracts is sufficient to attract workers into this firm's employment. Assume further that the worker's preference function is such that the income effect on leisure is zero.[34] The employer could improve the worker's expected well-being without reducing his own by offering to transfer equal increments of income (ΔW) from the good state to the bad state until worker utility is equalized across the two states. The resulting full insurance contract is illustrated in Figure 14.4(b). This is the optimal contract in the full information case (the contract that would maximize expected profits, given an expected utility constraint, or conversely maximize expected utility, given an expected profit constraint).

Is this contract feasible if only the employer knows which state is realized? In this special case the answer is clearly yes. Consider again Figure 14.1(b). For a given state of demand parameterized by μ, isoprofit lines can be constructed of the form

$$d\pi = \mu\, dh - dW = 0,$$

---

[33]At least as a labor economist if not a macroeconomist would view it. This representation appears for example in Azariadis and Stiglitz (1983).

[34]Formally this restricts the worker's utility function to those of the form $U = V(W - g(h))$, where presumably $g' > 0$ and $g'' > 0$.

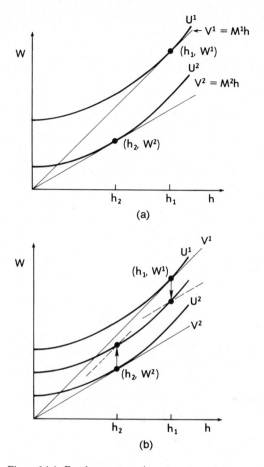

Figure 14.4. Employment-contingent wage contracts.

with the property that all combinations of h and W above and to the left of the line will be less profitable to the firm than those on the line for a given state of demand μ. The isoprofit line through $(h^1, W^1 - \Delta W)$ when $\mu = \mu^1$, denoted by the dashed line through that point, indicates that the employer has a profit incentive to reveal the true state in this case. He can reach no larger isoprofit line by claiming $(h^2, W^2 + \Delta W)$. Similarly, it is more profitable to report state 2 when state 2 in fact occurs; the isoprofit line through the state 2 contract point when $\mu = \mu^2$ indicates profits are greater than if state 1 is falsely announced.

The feasibility of the full insurance contract for the no-income effect utility function rests on the fact that insurance contracting brings the worker to the same indifference curve and that the indifference curve is convex to the hours axis. In the more general case in which income effects are not zero, insurance motives will not lead to the same level of utility in both states and the analysis is more complex. Chari (1983) demonstrates in a model similar to the one discussed here that the "truth-telling" constraints, the requirement that the wage–employment induce the firm to reveal product demand accurately, will distort the wage–employment package if leisure is a normal good and that, moreover, employment will be too large in the low demand state in this framework. Again labor hoarding will occur. Green and Kahn (1983) consider an otherwise similar model with a continuously distributed random productivity shock and prove that in that case overemployment will occur if leisure is a normal good and conversely underemployment will occur if leisure is an inferior good. Since the empirical literature strongly supports the claim that leisure is a normal good, these models would seem to be quite consistent with the earlier work of Baily (1974), Gordon (1974), and Azariadis (1975).

5.2. Aggregate productivity risk

The simple characterization of the employer as risk neutral must be questioned in the case of aggregate business cycle risk since the firm owners can no longer diversity away any risk they bear in this job match; total wealth is reduced, not simply reallocated. The standard risk neutrality argument must instead be based on the empirical conjecture that risk aversion decreases with wealth and that owners are wealthier than workers. One would expect that workers would never be fully insured in this case but would enter into a coinsurance agreement with firm owners, with the sharing of the risk dependent on the relative risk aversion of each party. Indeed optimizing models of this sort are straightforward to construct [Reagan and Stulz (1983)].

Grossman and Hart (1983) and Azariadis (1983) in a framework similar to that discussed above demonstrate that in the situation in which (1) demand information is held solely by a risk averse, unreliable firm and (2) the worker's utility function is characterized by zero income effect on leisure, a wage–hours contract may lead to underemployment, not overemployment of workers. Indeed, if workers are risk neutral, a model similar to that discussed above not only may but will lead to underemployment.

It is perhaps not surprising that a model as counterintuitively constructed as this one will lead to counterintuitive implications. The contracting problems in the asymmetric information case are unusually severe. The firm's incentive to deceive, and therefore the need to impose employment penalties if a low demand state is reported, is a function of the difference in wage payments between the two states. If the risk neutral worker is to insure the firm's owners, however, the wage differential between the high productivity state and the low productivity state must be *larger* than the auction market outcomes. The worker must accept less than his productivity in the bad state and more in the good state. The greater fluctuations of wages than productivity implied by this model will induce unusually severe employment penalties on the firm if it is to report the state of demand truthfully.

Empirically one might imagine that this structure is uninteresting; theoretically however it is important. It is a reminder that what appears to be a theoretical result is in fact based on implicit empirical propositions (in this case of observability of key variables, desire for risk bearing of economic agents, etc.). More importantly the recognition that employers may be risk averse to some extent explains why insurance within the firm may not be complete even in a situation of complete information and complete freedom of contracting. Additional empirical work on risk sharing in employment contracts is clearly needed.[35]

6. Conclusion

An efficient economy requires that individuals be appropriately matched with a job or other productive activity and that, once matched, the individual undertake the assigned activity with an appropriate level of intensity or effort. Extensive, if nonrigorous, empirics suggest that free markets perform these functions well in economies largely composed of self-employed individuals and small firms, although earnings insurance and other distributional issues may remain problems. The rapid increase in firm size in the United States and other industrialized countries in this century and the related decline in self-employment raises anew these critical efficiency questions. Does the introduction of an arms length relationship between employer and employee change the nature and quality of the economic outcomes?[36] How well do employment contracts, implicit and explicit, facilitate the efficient outcome?

---

[35] Much empirical evidence exists to support the notion that wages and employment do not respond in the short run as the simplest auction market model would suggest. Focused analyses of the earnings insurance function of the firm, however, are few. Hashimoto (1975) and Raisian provide evidence that suggests that wages are less rigid than commonly supposed. Brown (1982) explores the time limitation of wage rigidity in the U.S. manufacturing sector and finds that this sector approximates the auction market in the long run, although the long run is indeed long, approximately six years. Kniesner and Goldsmith (1984) provide a comprehensive review of this literature.

[36] Certainly compensation schedules appear to differ in large firms. Economists, for example, have known for some time that large firms pay an average higher wages for the same skills than do small firms [Mellow (1982)]. Garen (1982) has presented convincing, if not conclusive evidence that the large firm wage differential is the result of differential information on employees and as a consequence adverse selection among new hires in large firms. Parsons (1983) documents the large firm size effects on mandatory retirement and the provision of actuarially unfair pensions in large firms. He develops an adverse selection model that explains the relative lack of demand for retirement aged workers in such firms.

In the previous sections I have examined what I believe are three important aspects of the employment relationship. The limitations on contracts are central to the resolution of these questions. The limitations derive primarily from two sources. The fact that human capital is embodied in individuals whose liberty is independently valued has led to restrictions on the individual's freedom to contract about future earnings, both directly and indirectly through bankruptcy clauses. The availability of information (or at a deeper level the magnitude of information costs) is a second source of contract limitations. Obviously, for formal contracts to be enforced, all important information must be observable to a third party at some reasonable cost. Implicit contracts between the parties are less demanding of information availability since third party observability is not necessary. Other questions of contract reliability and enforcement arise when contract performance is no longer overseen by the courts. Agent reliability must be induced by other mechanisms, perhaps by the value of repeated exchange or by reputational considerations.

This chapter focuses on three important areas of the employment relationship: (1) the effort intensity of employees, (2) the acquisition and retention of firm specific human capital, and (3) employment and earnings stability as insurance. In each case the fundamental economic issues are outlined and then the likelihood and consequences of contracting limitations are explored. A common pattern has evolved, to some extent independently, in these three literatures. In the case of homogeneous workers, the crucial questions become: (1) Which agents, if any, have relatively inexpensive access to high quality performance information? (2) What is the contract reliability of the agent with this information access? (3) What form of contract (compensation package) will lead to accurate revelation of the information or appropriate agent behavior without explicit information revelation? The important supplementary question of the optimal *costly* information collection process has been less systematically pursued, although such considerations will surely reduce the most aberrant consequences of employment contracting difficulties.

The various literatures also explore optimal compensation schemes when workers are heterogeneous in one or another performance–reliability dimension. The effect on compensation practices may be great if the employee knows this characteristic of himself but the employer does not. The question then becomes: How can the compensation package be altered to induce the worker to reveal through his actions this private information?

A more detailed review of the various findings is not warranted at this point. I should mention, however, that these three substantive areas are only a subset of the interesting theoretical work on the employment relationship that has recently been undertaken. The reader is particularly referred to the theoretical literature on seniority [Gordon (1974), Grossman (1977, 1978), and Reagan (1984)] and on the independent effect of effort monitoring on hierarchies and firm size [e.g.

Williamson (1967), Alchian and Demsetz (1972), Calvo and Wellicz (1978), and Rosen (1983) and from a different perspective, Lucas (1978) and Oi (1983)].[37]

The empirical analysis of employment contracting has only begun. I suspect that much more empirical work is now necessary if progress in this area is not to degenerate into the relatively uninsightful enumeration of the theoretical possibilities. I suspect moreover that the collection of new data specifically focused on employment practices and policies will be essential if the empirical work is to illuminate employment contracting in any serious way.[38] Unfortunately, as empirical researchers in industrial organization have found, firms tend to be much more wary of providing information than individuals and families tend to be, so that large scale survey research may not be as rewarding as it has been in other areas of labor economics.

References

Abowd, John M. and Orley Ashenfelter (1981) "Anticipated unemployment, temporary layoffs, and compensating wage differentials", in: Sherwin Rosen, ed., *Studies in labor markets*. Chicago: University of Chicago Press, 141–170.

Abraham, Katharine G. and James L. Medoff (1983) "Length of service and the operation of internal labor markets", NBER Working Paper No. 1085.

Abraham, Katharine G. and James L. Medoff (1983) "Length of service, terminations, and the nature of the employment relationship", NBER Working Paper No. 1086.

Akerlof, George (1970) "The market for lemons: qualitative uncertainty and the market mechanism", *Quarterly Journal of Economics*, 84:488–500.

Akerlof, George (1976) "The economics of caste and of the rat race and other woeful tales", *Quarterly Journal of Economics*, 80:599–617.

Akerlof, George A. and Brian G. M. Main (1981) "An experience-weighted measure of employment and unemployment duration", *American Economic Review*, 71:1003–1011.

[37] The empirical analysis of economic behavior within and between firm job hierarchies shows considerable promise. Medoff and Abraham (1980, 1981) have found that within managerial and professional job grades job performance ratings and relative wage are inversely related across experience levels; relative performance is lower, relative wages higher for individuals within a job category the longest. Medoff and Abraham argue that if performance ratings are meant to be narrowly defined measures of actual productivity, this relationship is inconsistent with a simple auction model and suggests other forces are at work, plausibly productivity insurance. This interpretation is not valid if worker performance ratings are based on all tasks assigned, including training. If training is important, as it will be for newer workers, performance could be outstanding yet actual product and auction wages minimal. Indeed, Brown (1983) presents evidence that positive experience effects on wages end with the end of the (self-reported) training period. Exploring the interaction of the internal and external market Cho (1983) has found that the job search activities and the quit propensities of young workers are powerfully affected by their promotion prospects as well as more customary variables such as wages, education, etc.

[38] For recent promising analyses of employment behavior based on employer samples, see Abraham and Medoff (1983a, 1983b) and Bishop (1982). Wolpin (1977) and Lazear and Moore (1984) attempt to use behavioral comparisons of the self-employed and wage and salary earners to explore firm size effects. This is certainly a promising approach, although rather little is known of the decision to become a self-employed individual so that such comparisons must be approached with caution.

Akerlof, George A. and Hajime Miyazaki (1980) "The implicit contract theory of unemployment meets the wage bill argument", *Review of Economic Studies*, 47:321–338.

Alchian, A. A. and H. Demsetz (1972) "Production, information costs, and economic organization", *American Economic Review*, 62:777–795.

Allen, Steven G., Robert L. Clark and Daniel A. Sumner (1984) "Post retirement adjustments of pension benefits", working paper, North Carolina State University.

Azariadis, Costas (1975) "Implicit contracts and underemployment equilibria", *Journal of Political Economy*, 83:1183–1202.

Azariadis, Costas (1981) "Implicit contracts and related topics: a survey", in: Zmira Horstein, Joseph Grice and Alfred Webb, eds., *Economics of the labor market*. Her Majesty's Stationery Office, 221–248.

Azariadis, Costas (1983) "Employment with asymmetric information", *Quarterly Journal of Economics*, 98(Supplement):157–172.

Azariadis, Costas and Joseph E. Stiglitz (1983) "Implicit contracts and fixed-price equilibria", *Quarterly Journal of Economics*, 98(Supplement):1–22.

Baily, M. N. (1974) "Wages and employment under uncertain demand", *Review of Economic Studies*, 41:37–50.

Ball, R. J. and E. B. A. St. Cyr (1966) "Short-run employment functions in British manufacturing", *Review of Economic Studies*, 33:179–207.

Bartel, Ann P. and George J. Borjas (1981) "Wage growth and job turnover: an empirical analysis", in: Sherwin Rosen, ed., *Studies in labor markets*. Chicago: University of Chicago Press, 65–84.

Barton, John H. (1972) "The economic basis of damages for breach of contract", *Journal of Legal Studies*, 1:277–304.

Baumol, William J. (1967) *Business behavior, value, and growth*. New York: Harcourt, Brace and World.

Becker, Gary (1975) *Human capital*. New York: Columbia University Press.

Becker, Gary (1968) "Crime and punishment: an economic analysis", *Journal of Political Economy*, 76:169–217.

Becker, G. and G. Stigler (1974) "Law enforcement and compensation of enforcers", *Journal of Legal Studies*, 3:1–18.

Benjamin, Daniel K. (1978) "The use of collateral to enforce debt contract", *Economic Inquiry*, 16:333–359.

Berhold, Marvin (1971) "A theory of linear profit-sharing incentives", *Quarterly Journal of Economics*, 85:460–482.

Bishop, John H. (1982) "The social payoff for occupationally specific training: the employers' point of view", National Center for Research in Vocational Education.

Brechling, F. (1965) "The relationship between output and employment in British manufacturing industries", *Review of Economic Studies*, 32:187–216.

Brown, James N. (1982) "How close to an auction is the labor market?", in: Ronald Ehrenberg, ed., *Research in labor economics*. Volume 5, 189–235.

Brown, James (1983) "Are those paid more really no more productive? Measuring the relative importance of tenure versus on-the-job training in explaining wage growth", Working Paper No. 169, Industrial Relations Section, Princeton University.

Bull, Clive (1983) "Implicit contracts in the absence of enforcement and risk aversion", *American Economic Review*, 73:658–671.

Burdett, K. (1978) "Theory of employee search: quit rates", *American Economic Review*, 68:212–220.

Calvo, Guillermo A. and Edmund S. Phelps (1977) "Employment contingent wage contracts", in: Karl Brunner and Allan H. Meltzer, eds., "Stabilization of the Domestic and International Economy", *Journal of Monetary Economics*, *Supplement*:160–168.

Calvo, Guillermo A. and S. Wellisz (1978) "Supervision, loss of control, and the optimum size of the firm", *Journal of Political Economy*, 86:943–952.

Chari, V. V. (1983) "Involuntary unemployment and implicit contracts", *Quarterly Journal of Economics*, 98(Supplement):107–122.

Charmichael, H. Lorne (1984) "Reputations in the labor market", *American Economic Review*, 74:713–725.

Cheung, S. (1969) "Transaction costs, risk aversion, and the choice of contractual arrangements", *Journal of Law and Economics*, 12:23–42.

Clark, C. Scott (1973) "Labor hoarding in durable goods industries", *American Economic Review*, 63:811–824.

Cho, Woo (1983) "Promotion prospects, job search and the quit behavior of employed youth", mimeo, The Ohio State University.

Eaton, B. Curtis and William D. White (1982) "Agent compensation and the limits of bonding", *Economic Inquiry*, 20:330–343.

Fama, Eugene F. (1980) "Agency problems and the theory of the firm", *Journal of Political Economy*, 88:288–307.

Feldstein, M. (1976) "Temporary layoffs in the theory of unemployment", *Journal of Political Economy*, 84:937–957.

Freeman, S. (1977) "Wage trends as performance displays productivity potential: a model and application to academic early retirement", *Bell Journal of Economics*, 8:419–443.

Garen, John (1982) "Worker heterogeneity, costly monitoring, wage rates, and firm size", mimeo, Wayne State University.

Gould, John P. (1970) "Diffusion processes and optimal advertising policy", in: Edmund S. Phelps et al., eds., *Microeconomic foundations of employment and inflation theory*. New York: W. W. Norton & Co.

Green, Jerry and Charles M. Kahn (1983) "Wage-employment contracts", *Quarterly Journal of Economics*, 98(Supplement):173–188.

Green, J. R. and N. L. Stokey (1983) "A comparison of tournaments and contracts", *Journal of Political Economy*, 91:349–364.

Gordon, D. F. (1974) "A neo-classical theory of Keynesian unemployment", *Economic Inquiry*, 12:431–459.

Grossman, H. I. (1977) "Risk shifting and reliability in labor markets", *Scandinavian Journal of Economics*, 79(2):187–209.

Grossman, H. I. (1978) "Risk shifting, layoffs, and seniority", *Journal of Monetary Economics*, 4:661–686.

Grossman, Sanford J. and Oliver D. Hart (1983) "Implicit contracts under asymmetric information", *Quarterly Journal of Economics*, 98(Supplement):123–156.

Guasch, J. Luis (1983) "Disturbing effects of contracts based on effort supervision", *Economic Letters*, 11:305–310.

Hall, R. E. (1982) "The importance of lifetime jobs in the U.S. economy", *American Economic Review*, 72:716–724.

Hall, R. E. and D. M. Lilien (1979) "Efficient wage bargains under uncertain supply and demand", *American Economic Review*, 69:868–879.

Harris, Milton and Bengt Holstrom (1982) "A theory of wage dynamics", *Review of Economic Studies*, 49:315–333.

Harris, M. and A. Raviv (1979) "Optimal incentive contracts with imperfect information", *Journal of Economic Theory*, 20:231–259.

Hart, Oliver D. (1983) "Optimal labour contracts under asymmetric information: an introduction", *Review of Economic Studies*, 50:3–35.

Hashimoto, M. (1975) "Wage reduction, job separation and specific human capital", *Economic Inquiry*, 13:485–504.

Hashimoto, M. (1981) "Firm-specific human capital as a shared investment", *American Economic Review*, 71:475–482.

Hashimoto, M. and B. T. Yu (1980) "Specific capital, employment contracts and wage rigidity", *Bell Journal of Economics*, 11:536–549.

Hatch, Sara P. (1982) "Pension plan provisions that directly affect retirement age choice", Urban Institute Project Report.

Holstrom, B. (1979) "Moral hazard and observability", *Bell Journal of Economics*, 10:74–91.

Holstrom, B. (1981) "Contractual models of the labor market", *American Economic Review Proceedings*, 71:308–313.

Holstrom, B. (1982) "Moral hazard in teams", *Bell Journal of Economics*, 13:324–340.

Jensen, M. C. and W. H. Mechling (1976) "Theory of the firm: managerial behavior, agency costs, and ownership structure", *Journal of Financial Economics*, 3:304–360.

Johnson, W. R. (1978) "A theory of job shopping", *Quarterly Journal of Economics*, 92:261–278.

Jovanovic, B. (1979) "Firm specific capital and turnover", *Journal of Political Economy*, 87:1246–1260.

Kennan, John (1979) "Bonding and the enforcement of labor contracts", *Economic Letters*, 3:61–66.

Kihlstrom, Richard E. and Michael H. Riordan (1984) "Advertising as a signal", *Journal of Political Economy*, 92:427–450.

Klein, Benjamin and Keith B. Leffler (1981) "The role of market forces in assuring contractual performance" *Journal of Political Economy*, 89:615–641.

Kniesner, Thomas J. and Arthur H. Goldsmith (1984) "Is the labor market an auction market, a contract market or something in between? A survey of the evidence for the United States", mimeo, University of North Carolina.

Kotowitz, Y. and F. Mathewson (1979) "Advertising, consumer information, and product quality", *Bell Journal*, 10:566–588.

Kreps, David M. and Robert Wilson (1982) "Reputation and imperfect information", *Journal of Economic Theory*, 27:253–279.

Landes, W. M. and R. A. Posner (1979) "Adjudication as a public good", *Journal of Legal Studies*, March:235–283.

Lazear, E. (1979) "Why is there mandatory retirement?", *Journal of Political Economy*, 87:1261–1284.

Lazear, E. (1981) "Agency, earnings profiles, productivity, and hours restrictions", *American Economic Review*, 71:606–620.

Lazear, Edward P. and Robert L. Moore (1984) "Incentives, productivity, and labor contracts", *Quarterly Journal of Economics*, 99:275–296.

Lazear, E. P. and S. Rosen (1981) "Rank-order tournaments as optimum labor contracts", *Journal of Political Economy*, 89:841–864.

Lebergott, Stanley (1964) *Manpower in economic growth: the American record since 1800*. New York: McGraw-Hill.

Lewellen, Wilbur G. (1971) *The ownership income of management*. New York: National Bureau of Economic Research.

Lippman, S. A. and J. J. McCall (1976a) "The economics of job search: a survey", *Economic Inquiry*, 14:155–189.

Lippman, S. A. and J. J. McCall (1976b) "The economics of job search: a survey", *Economic Inquiry*, 14:347–368.

Lucas, Robert E., Jr. (1978) "Adjustment costs and the theory of supply", *Bell Journal of Economics*, 9:508–523.

Medoff, James L. and Katharine G. Abraham (1980) "Experience, performance, and earnings", *The Quarterly Journal of Economics*, 94:703–735.

Medoff, James L. and Katharine G. Abraham (1981) "Are those paid more really more productive? The case of experience", *Journal of Human Resources*, 16:186–216.

Luce, R. D. and H. Raiffa (1957) *Games and decisions*. New York: Wiley.

MacDonald, Glenn M. (1982) "Specific investments and nonlabor income", *Bell Journal of Economics*, 13:225–233.

Mellow, Wesley (1982) "Employer size and wages", *Review of Economics and Statistics*, 64:495–501.

Mincer, Jacob (1962) "On-the-job training: costs, returns and some implications", *Journal of Political Economy*, 70(Supplement):50–79.

Mincer, J. and B. Jovanovic (1981) "Labor mobility and wages", in: S. Rosen, ed., *Studies in labor markets*. Chicago: University of Chicago Press, 21–64.

Miyazaki, Hajime (1977) "The rat race and internal labor markets", *Bell Journal of Economics*, 8:394–418.

Mortensen, D. (1978) "Specific capital and labor turnover", *Bell Journal of Economics*, 9:572–586.

Nadiri, M. Ishaq and Sherwin Rosen (1973) *A disequilibrium model of demand for factors of production*. New York: National Bureau of Economic Research.

Nalebuff, B. and J. E. Stiglitz (1983) "Prizes and incentives: towards a general theory of compensation and competition", *Bell Journal of Economics*, 14:21–43.

Nelson, Phillip (1974) "Advertising as information", *Journal of Political Economy*, 82:729–754.

Nerlove, Marc and K. J. Arrow (1962) "Optimal advertising policy under dynamic conditions", *Economica*, May:124–142.

Nickell, S. J. (1976) "Wage structures and quit rates", *International Economic Review*, 17:191–203.

Oi, W. Y. (1962) "Labor as a quasi-fixed factor", *Journal of Political Economy*, 70:538–555.

Oi, W. Y. (1983) "Heterogeneous firms and the organization of production", *Economic Inquiry*, 21:147–171.

Parsons, Donald O. (1972) "Specific human capital: an application to quit rates and layoff rates", *Journal of Political Economy*, 80:1120–1143.

Parsons, David O. (1977) "Models of labor market turnover: a theoretical and empirical survey", in: R. Ehrenberg, ed., *Research in labor economics*. Greenwich, Conn.: JAI, vol. 1.

Parsons, David O. (1980) "Unemployment, the allocation of labor, and optimal government intervention", *American Economic Review*, 70:626–635.

Parsons, David O. (1983) "The industrial demand for older workers", mimeo.

Parsons, David O. (1984) "Social insurance with imperfect state verification: income insurance for the disabled", Working paper #84-27, Economics Department, Ohio State University.

Pauly, M. V. (1974) "Overinsurance and public provision of insurance: the role of moral hazard and adverse selection", *Quarterly Journal of Economics*, 88:44–54.

Pencavel, John H. (1972) "Wages, specific training, and labor turnover in U.S. manufacturing industries", *International Economic Review*, 13:53–64.

Pencavel, John H. (1977) "Work effort, on-the-job screening, and alternative methods of remuneration", in: R. G. Ehrenberg, ed., *Research in labor economics*. Greenwich, Conn.: JAI, vol. 1.

Perri, Timothy J. (1983) "Explicit labor contracts, shirking, and turnover costs", *Atlantic Economic Review*, December:59–65.

Peters, Elizabeth (1984) "Marriage and divorce in a private contracting framework", mimeo, Center for Human Resource Research, Ohio State University.

Radner, Roy (1981) "Monitoring cooperative agreements in a repeated principal-agent relationship", *Econometrica*, 49:1127–1148.

Raisian, John (1983) "Contracts, job experience, and cyclical labor market adjustments", *Journal of Labor Economics*, 1:152–170.

Reagan, Patricia (1984) "Seniority in hierarchical labor markets", mimeo, Ohio State University.

Reagan, Patricia B. and René M. Stulz (1982) "Risk bearing, labor contracts, and capital markets", mimeo.

Rosen, Sherwin (1972) "Learning and experience in the labor market", *Journal of Human Resources*, 7:326–342.

Rosen, Sherwin (1982) "Authority, control, and the distribution of earnings", *Bell Journal*, 13:311–323.

Rothschild, M. and J. Stiglitz (1976) "Equilibrium in competitive insurance markets: an essay on the economics of imperfect information", in: Diamond and Rothschild, eds., *Uncertainty in economics*.

Salop, S. (1973) "Wage differentials in a dynamic theory of the firm", *Journal of Economic Theory*, 6:321–344.

Salop, J. and S. Salop (1976) "Self-selection and turnover in the labor market", *Quarterly Journal of Economics*, 90:619–628.

Schmalensee, Richard (1978) "Advertising and product quality", *Journal of Political Economy*, 86:485–503.

Shapiro, Carl (1982) "Consumer information, product quality, and seller reputation", *Bell Journal of Economics*, 10:55–73.

Shapiro, Carl (1980) "Damage measures for breach of contract", *Bell Journal of Economics*, 11:466–490.

Shavell, Steven (1979) "Risk sharing and incentives in the principal and agent relationship", *Bell Journal*, 10:55–73.

Spence, Michael (1973) "Job market signaling", *Quarterly Journal of Economics*, 87:355–374.

Spence, Michael and Richard Zeckhauser (1971) "Insurance, information, and individual action", *American Economic Review*, 61:380–387.

Stelluto, George L. (1969) "Report on incentive pay in manufacturing industries", *Monthly Labor Review*, 92:49–53.

Stiglitz, J. E. (1974) "Incentives and risk sharing in sharecropping", *Review of Economic Studies*, April:219–255.

Stiglitz, J. E. (1975) "Incentives, risk, and information: notes toward a theory of hierarchy", *Bell Journal of Economics*, 6:552–579.

Telser, Lester G. (1980) "A theory of self-enforcing agreements", *Journal of Business*, 53:27–44.

Topel, Robert and Finis Welch (1980) "Unemployment insurance: survey and extensions", *Economica*, 47:351–379.

Townsend, Robert M. (1979) "Optimal contracts and competitive markets with costly state verification", *Journal of Economic Theory*, 21:265–293.

U.S. Bureau of the Census (1977) *1977 Census of Manufacturers*. Washington: U.S. Government Printing Office.

U.S. Bureau of the Census (1979) *Statistical Abstract of the United States: 1979*. Washington: U.S. Government Printing Office.

U.S. Department of Labor (1980) *Handbook of Labor Statistics*. Washington: U.S. Government Printing Office.

Viscusi, W. K. (1980) "Self-selection, learning-induced quits, and the optimal wage structure", *International Economic Review*, 21:529–546.

Williamson, O. E. (1967) "Hierarchical control and optimal firm size", *Journal of Political Economy*, 75:123–138.

Williamson, O. E. (1963) "Managerial discretion and business behavior", *American Economic Review*, 53:1032–1057.

Williamson, Oliver E., Michael L. Wachter and Jeffrey E. Harris (1975) "Understanding the employment relation: the analysis of idiosyncratic exchange", *Bell Journal*, Spring:250–278.

Wolpin, Kenneth I. (1977) "Education and screening", *American Economic Review*, 67:949–958.

Chapter 15

JOB SEARCH AND LABOR MARKET ANALYSIS

DALE T. MORTENSEN*

Northwestern University

1. Introduction

The theory of search is an important young actor on the stage of economic analysis. It plays a major part in a dramatic new field, the economics of information and uncertainty. By exploiting its sequential statistical decision theoretic origins, search theory has found success by specializing in the portrayal of a decision-maker who must acquire and use information to take rational action in an ever changing and uncertain environment. Although its specific characterizations can now be found in many arenas of applied economic analysis, most of the theory's original roles are found in the labor economics literature. The purpose of this chapter is to review its performances to date in labor market analysis.

That the theory's services have found useful employment is not particularly surprising. Actors that portray only self seeking workers in certain and static environments cannot represent many of life's real work experiences. The time workers spend unemployed, movements from job to job during the work life, and the allocation of the working life between market work and alternative activities in a dynamic environment are all left inadequately characterized in dramas that feature such actors. Although it is too soon for either an "Oscar" or knighthood, the talents of job search theory for the consistent portrayal of the dynamic dimensions of worker experience can be demonstrated. Furthermore, methods for empirically testing the theory's adequacy as a principal in future plays with these plots are becoming discernible as a consequence of this consistency. These serve as the two principal themes of this review.

The classic income–leisure choice model continues to enjoy a very successful run as a tool for formulating the decision to seek employment. Its extensions to the analysis of investment in education and training, retirement, the labor force

*The work has benefited from comments made by a host of colleagues too numerous to mention by name. I would particularly like to acknowledge the significant contributions of my students – both past and present. All errors of fact and judgment remain mine.

participation of married women, taxes on labor income, and the decision to have and invest in children have greatly enriched the collection of hypotheses concerning household behavior. The theory of job search has developed as a complement to the older theoretical framework. Many writers found that the classic labor supply model with its emphasis on unilateral and fully informed choice could not explain important features of the typical individual's experience in the labor market. The experience of unemployment is an important example. Within the income–leisure choice framework, unemployment simply has no interpretation as a consequence of the assumptions that jobs are instantaneously available at market clearing wage rates known to the worker.

The profession's view of both the employment and non-employment experiences of individual workers changed dramatically in the late 1960s and early 1970s as a consequence of studies of flows in and out of employment at the firm level, of propensities of workers to leave unemployment in cross-section data, and of the labor market experience of individual workers over time found in various panel data sources. In a given population of labor force participants, the steady state fraction who are unemployed is equal to the product of the average frequency and duration of unemployment spells. These data sources revealed that unemployment spells are typically frequent but short in all phases of the business cycle although counter-cyclic increases in both frequency and duration contribute to the well-known time series behavior of unemployment rates. Furthermore, differences in unemployment and participation rates across different demographic groups reflect differences in durations and frequencies of unemployment and participation spells. These empirical contributions suggested the idea of viewing a worker's labor market history as the realization of a stochastic process. This view contributed significantly to the development of the search theoretic approaches to the analysis of unemployment durations, job turnover, and individual labor market experience reviewed in Section 2 of this chapter.

The search theoretic approach to the analysis of unemployment spell durations was the original contribution of search theory to labor market analysis. The presentation of the original formal wage search model and its empirical implications are the topics of Section 2 of this chapter. This model, which is derivative of developments in the theory of sequential statistical decision theory, is designed to focus on the typical worker's problem of finding employment in a decentralized labor market. Information regarding the location of vacant jobs and the compensation that they offer is recognized as imperfect. This information must be acquired and evaluated before a worker can or is willing to become employed. Viewing this process as costly and sequential provides a framework for the analysis of observed variation in the unemployment spells that individual workers experience and in the wages received once employed. Formally, the length of time a worker spends unemployed and the subsequent wage received once employed are both random variables with distributions that depend on the worker's characteristics and those of the environment both directly and indirectly through the worker's determination of conditions for acceptable employment. Because the framework has implications for the distribution of observables, econometric methods for estimation and testing are suggested by the theory.

Section 3 of the chapter reviews more recent theoretical extensions of the search theoretic approach designed for the analysis of job turnover behavior, wage growth, and other dynamic features of an individual's labor market experience.

As a consequence of search costs and time discounting, no rational worker waits indefinitely for an opportunity to be employed in the best of all jobs that might be available. Hence, even employed workers have incentives to continue the search for a better employment opportunity. The first topic considered in Section 3 is an extension of the standard wage search model to search on the job at effort levels that are endogenously determined. This form of the model provides an explanation for the observed negative association between the propensity to separate from a job and the wage earned on a job, holding earnings ability constant. Furthermore, the theory suggests that productivity growth attributable to the acquisition of human capital need not be required as an explanation for positively sloped wage–experience profiles. Although this explanation is now generally acknowledged in the literature on turnover and wage dynamics, its relative importance as an explanation for individual wage growth is still an open question.

Many relevant characteristics of a job–worker match cannot be observed without error but must be experienced. These experiences as they occur provide information about the expected future quality of a specific job–worker match relative to the set of alternatives. This information is useful in the decision to continue the match. This process of learning about jobs and occupations as a means of finding a satisfactory place in the work world has long been thought an important explanation for high turnover rates among young workers. The second topic of Section 3 is a review of the first formal models of learning on the job about the quality of the match. The model considered in detail is another version of the general sequential search model. It implies the wages earned by those who stay on a job increases with tenure even when productivity and tenure are unrelated. Although these implications are broadly consistent with empirical observations, particularly in the most relevant case of young workers, only recently has the stochastic structure of the model been applied in econometric work in a manner that permits the testing of the quantitative importance of the theory.

Longitudinal observations on the labor force histories of individual workers reveal that varied patterns of sequences of spells of employment in different jobs, spells of unemployment, and spells of non-participation characterize worker labor market experience. Empirical attempts to isolate the differences in the frequencies, durations, and patterns of such spell sequences experienced by workers with different demographic characteristics have been based, either explicitly or implicitly, on the assumption that an individual's spell history can be modelled as a Markov chain. Recently, theoretical models based on Markov decision theory have been developed that permit a more "structural" interpretation of these histories. In these models, movements among jobs and labor force states are viewed as the consequence of actions taken by the worker in response to stochastic changes in a worker's opportunity to work, the wage given such an opportunity, and the alternative value of time spent in non-work activities. A brief introduction to this type of modelling is the final topic considered in Section 3. Although the development of this approach is in its infancy, the method promises new insights into how the dynamic processes influencing an individual's opportunities at any point in time and the individual's responses to the realizations of these processes determine the observed distribution of earnings and the distribution of workers over participation categories.

Answers to two purely theoretical questions raised by the sequential search approach to the problem of finding acceptable employment, more generally the problem of "shopping", are reviewed in Section 4 of the chapter. First, is a distribution of price offers for an identical good sustainable when agents on one side of the market act as price setters while agents on the other side are searching price takers? Second, is the level of unemployment that necessarily arises as a consequence of the time required to find employment, more generally the level of the stock that acts as a buffer between the decision to transact and the actualization of the exchange, socially efficient? Although affirmative answers to both questions have been constructed, "no" seems to be the more reasonable theoretical answer to both.

A brief word on the approach taken in this review is in order. Although the references include a reasonably comprehensive list of works on the theory of search and its applications in labor economics, the chapter is not intended to be an exhaustive survey of individual contributions. Instead, the presentation is constructed with two goals in mind. First, the theoretical formulations that have been or are most likely to be applied in empirical studies are emphasized. Second, these models are presented in a manner that illustrates their common formal structure. The hope is that this form of presentation will communicate the unity of the theoretical ideas, on the one hand, and the potential usefulness of that unity for the purpose of empirical estimation and testing, on the other.

2. The wage search model

That the typical worker has a variety of earnings opportunities available but has to shop to find the "best" one is the principal observation that motivated the original formulation of search models and continues to motivate the development of search theory. The worker's decision problem under these conditions involves a choice of a strategy for "shopping" and the selection of a criterion that determines when an offered wage is "acceptable". Stigler's (1961, 1962) original formulation of the worker's decision was as an optimal sample size problem. He views the worker as selecting a random wage sample of size n at a cost of c per wage sampled. The worker accepts employment at the firm offering the highest wage in the sample. The worker's problem is to choose the size of the sample. This formulation has a certain appeal in that one can imagine n to be the number of applications filed with prospective employers. Furthermore, the perfect information case corresponds to a sampling cost of zero. In this case, each worker would sample the entire wage population and go to work for the employer offering the highest wage rate.

Subsequent theoretical analyses of the job search problem are, based on the sequential "stopping" approach borrowed from statistical decision theory.[1] In these formulations, the worker is viewed as sampling wage offers one at a time and deciding on the basis of the sample obtained to date whether or not to stop the search or to continue. This procedure generally dominates the fixed sample size strategy in the sense that its maximal expected present value of future income is higher. In addition, the approach has the advantage of allowing for numerous realistic complications, e.g. that "shopping" takes place in real time, that offers must be accepted shortly after they are made, and that learning about the nature of the true distribution of offers may be an important part of the shopping process, etc. Of course, when a sequential strategy is used, the realized sample size is a random variable whose distribution is determined in part by the nature of the "stopping rule". Hence, in real time, the random sample size may be interpreted as a distribution of lengths of the random search spell. The implications of this interpretation of the theory for the distribution of search spell lengths have proven to be important in attempts to empirically estimate search models and to apply them to policy related issues. Early examples of applications of the sequential sampling approach that exploit these features include Gronau (1971), McCall (1970), and Mortensen (1970).

This section of the chapter has three subsections. In the first, the so-called "standard" or "original" model of sequential wage search is presented. The second is devoted to an exposition of its implications, particularly for the probability distribution over completed spells of unemployment. The third and final section introduces applications of the model and the problems encountered in recent attempts to empirically estimate its parameters and test its implications.

2.1. Wage search in "real" time

If economics can be defined as the study of the allocation of scarce resources, then the central focus of labor economics is the investigation of the way that time

---

[1]See DeGroot (1970) and Chow et al. (1971) for extensive treatment of optimal stopping as a statistical decision theory problem.

endowments of individual human beings are spent. Shopping is one of the numerous activities that tend to absorb time. Little quantitative information is available about the costs and the technology of shopping other than impressions based on personal experience. However, given the fact that the labor market itself accounts for more than two-thirds of household income, one would not be surprised that the time spent shopping in that market is of significant importance and value what ever may be its quantitative magnitude and economic efficiency.

The purpose of this section is to illustrate how contributors to the literature on shopping in the labor market have adapted the statistical theory of optimal stopping to the problem of finding a job paying the "best" wage taking the costs of finding that wage into account. The focus here is not only on the microeconomics of job search. The intention is to develop a theoretical foundation which is strong enough to support an understanding of subsequent applications of the theory to a variety of substantive issues of interest to labor economists and subsequent contributions to the theory of equilibrium wage dispersion and unemployment. The foundation stones underlying this structure are the dual suppositions that search for any job, let alone a better one, requires time and resources and that the returns to this investment in search are uncertain and in the future.

Lags in the process by which information is transferred from prospective employer to willing employee are everywhere. Of course, there are many channels of information transfer. One often thinks of workers trudging from personnel office to union hiring hall looking for an employment opportunity when the term "job search" is used. Yet, a casual conversation with a friend or relative over a beer is a surprisingly common method of finding a job. Obviously, other methods include reading the want ads, which we are told are always there even in the midst of even the worst recession, registering at the public employment office, and hiring the services of a private employment agency. Still, whatever the method used, the interested worker must devote time and money to the search activity which could otherwise be allocated elsewhere and the investment has an uncertain and variable future payoff.[2]

In order to take appropriate account of the fact that search requires time and that the consequences of that search are uncertain, the classic optimal stopping problem must be adapted and generalized in several respects. First, the cost of search should be interpreted as a flow per unit search time, a net deduction from the value of the time which could otherwise be spent in some other activity, plus out-of-pocket financial costs. Second, one must recognize that job availability is

---

[2] See Felder (1975) for an empirical analysis of the method of search used by individual workers based on data from the Denver/Seattle Income Maintenance Experiment.

as important as search effort in determining the time required to locate a job.[3] Finally, the costs and returns attributable to future search activities need to be discounted. Although these additions have little mathematical significance, they do enrich the stopping model considerably.

When search takes place in real time, it is time spent rather than the number of wage rates sampled that is the focus of the analysis. Initially, let time be represented by a sequence of discrete periods of variable length h. Let b denote the value of the time that could be spent in some other activity per unit time. Finally, let $\beta(h)$ represent the discount factor applied to future costs and benefits incurred per period of length h. To account for both job availability and the uncertainties inherent in the job search process, we introduce $q(n, h)$ as a probability distribution over the number of offers received per period of length h spent searching. Let the c.d.f. $F(w)$ represent the distribution of the wage offers. Any offer received is viewed as a random sample from this distribution. It is important to point out that both the distribution of the number of offers received per period and the wage offer distribution are assumed to be unchanging over time and known to the worker.[4] In addition, the analysis is restricted to the case of no recall of offers received in previous periods, mainly for the purpose of simplifying the exposition, although the worker is able to choose among the offers received within the period. Of course, the results reviewed can usually be generalized to the case of recall, when they in fact differ, by simply regarding the "wage" currently considered as the highest of those previously seen and still available.[5]

$$w = \max[w_1, \ldots, w_n], \tag{2.1}$$

where the distribution of w_i is $F(\cdot)$ for all $i = 1, 2, \ldots, n$. An important point to note here is that the receipt of no wage offer, $n = 0$, during the period is a possibility.

Let $G(w, n)$ represent the probability that the best of n offer is less than or equal to w given that $n \geq 1$. It is the distribution that is induced by (2.1) and the assumption that each of the n wage offers received during a period of length h is

[3]Authors of original formulations of the wage search model implicitly assume that offers arrive at an average rate equal to one per unit time period. The empirical importance of the rate at which offers arrive as a determinant of unemployment durations was clearly demonstrated by Barron (1975). Lippman and McCall (1976a) treat the case of random offer arrivals of no more than one per unit time period. The formulation of the offer arrival process adopted in this paper follows that of Wilde (1977).

[4]See DeGroot (1970) for an analysis of the optimal stopping problem in the case of an unknown distribution and Rothschild (1974) for an application of the optimal stopping approach to the problem of price search when the distribution is not known. Lippman and McCall (1976b) study the case of a known but time varying distribution of wage offers.

[5]For a discussion of differences that arise when recall is allowed, see Lippman and McCall (1976a).

an independent random draw from $F(\cdot)$. Let $q(n, h)$, $n = 0, 1, \ldots$, represent the probability that the worker will receive n offers during a period of length h. The purpose of introducing this concept is to allow for job availability. Because it imposes the restriction that time is required to find a job and that job opportunities are found sequentially, a natural specification for this distribution is the Poisson,

$$q(n, h) = e^{-\lambda h}(\lambda h)^{n}/n!, \tag{2.2}$$

where λ denotes the offer arrival rate and its inverse is the expected length of time between offer arrivals. The crucial assumption underlying (2.2) is that the instantaneous probability of the next arrival is independent of the length of time since the last. This assumption would seem to be as appropriate in the job search context as it has been proven to be in so many other applications.

The mathematical decision framework within which both the optimal stopping and the wage search problem are set is the theory of dynamic programming. Essentially the "trick" of the theory is Bellman's (1957) principle of dynamic optimality. Stated in words, the principle asserts that the present decision in a sequence of decisions maximizes current net return plus the expected future stream of returns, appropriately discounted, under the presumption that decisions in the future are made optimally where the expectation taken is conditional on current information. In short, a multi-stage decision problem is converted by the principle into a sequence of single-stage decision problems. Appropriate conditions for application of the principal require that the decision-makers preferences over the future can be regarded as the discounted sum of returns accruing over the future. Bellman's principle is applied liberally throughout this essay.

Although the stream of future returns can be interpreted as von Neumann and Morgenstern "utilities", in most of the wage search literature they are taken to be net incomes and the discount rate is called the interest rate.[6] Hence, the worker is regarded, at least implicitly, as risk neutral and not constrained in the capital market. Typically the worker is also assumed to live forever, i.e. the decision horizon is infinite. Obviously, all three of these assumptions are absolutely ridiculous in the context of an unemployed worker seeking an employment opportunity. Nevertheless, they have been maintained in the literature because doing so permits a relatively simple means of gaining insight into the essentials of the problem. We follow the literature's dictates here.

Let $W(w)$ represent the given present value of stopping, accepting the best offer received, w, during any period and working forever after at that wage. The

---

[6] Notable exceptions to the general rule include Danforth (1979), Hall et al. (1979), and Burdett and Mortensen (1978).

function is continuous, and strictly increasing, and such that $W(0) = 0$ by assumption. Let $V(\ )$ denote the value of searching during the next period given the worker's information. It is the expected present value of future net income given that the optimal strategy will be pursued in the future conditional on the worker's current information. In order to maximize wealth, the worker continues to search while unemployed given an available best wage offer w if and only if $V(\Omega) > W(w)$. Since the analogous acceptance rule applies to the next period,

$$V(\Omega) = (b - c)h + \beta(h)E\{\max[V(\Omega(t + h)), W(x)]|\Omega(t) = \Omega\}, \quad (2.3)$$

where x is the random best offer realized during the next period of length h and $\Omega(t + h)$ is the information, possibly a random variable, that the worker will have in the next period. The first term on the right-hand side of (2.3) is the difference between the value of time spent as "leisure" less the value of time and out of pocket costs spent searching a period of length h. The second term is the expected present value of tomorrow's optimal stopping decision made once the next period's best offer and information is known conditional on the information available today.

Given the assumption that the future sequence of best offers is i.i.d. and the assumption that the distribution for each period is known, the worker learns nothing over time, i.e. $\Omega(t) = \Omega(t + h)$. Consequently, the value of continued search is a constant through time, denoted as V. By virtue of eqs. (2.1)–(2.3), V solves

$$V = (b - c)h + \beta(h)\left[\sum_1^\infty q(n, h)\int_0^\infty \max[V, W(x)]\, dG(x, n) + q(0, h)V\right],$$

or equivalently,

$$(1 - \beta(h))V = (b - c)h$$
$$+ \beta(h)\left[\sum_1^\infty q(n, h)\int_0^\infty \max[0, W(x) - V]\, dG(x, n)\right]. \quad (2.4)$$

Since (2.4) has a unique solution for the value of search, V, provided that the mean of the wage offer distribution is finite, the worker's optimal search strategy satisfies the reservation property and the reservation wage, w^*, is the unique solution to

$$W(w^*) = V. \quad (2.5)$$

By the *reservation property*, we mean that the worker's expected wealth maximizing stopping strategy has the property that it is optimal to accept employment (stop searching) when the highest offered wage in any period is equal to or in excess of a critical number called the reservation wage, which in this case is w^*. The fact that $W(w) \geq V$ for all such wage rates and Bellman's principal imply that the optimal strategy has the property in this particular case.

Given the definition of best offer in (2.1) and the Poisson offer arrival specification in (2.2), eq. (2.4) simplifies considerably in the continuous time version of the analysis which corresponds to the limiting case of an infinitesimal period length. Specifically, (2.2) implies that the probability of a single offer arrival per period of length h is approximately equal to λh, while the probability of more than one arrival is approximately zero when the length of the period is small. Formally,

$$\lim_{h \to 0} q(1, h)/h = \lambda \quad \text{and} \quad \lim_{h \to 0} q(n, h)/h = 0, \quad \text{for } n > 1.$$

In addition, the discount factor is

$$\beta(h) = e^{-rh}, \text{ so that } \lim_{h \to 0} [1 - \beta(h)]/h = r,$$

where r represents the interest rate. Hence, by dividing both sides of (2.4) by h and taking the limit of the results as $h \to 0$, one obtains the following continuous time analogue:

$$rV = b - c + \lambda \int_0^\infty \max[0, W(x) - V] \, dF(x). \tag{2.6}$$

Since V represents the worker's "wealth" when searching, rV is the imputed "income" derived from that wealth per unit time period. Equation (2.6) asserts that it is equal to the difference between the value of time spent not working and the cost of search plus the expected rate of capital gain attributable to search, the product of the instantaneous offer arrival rate and the expected difference, when positive, between the wealth associated with employment and that imputed to search. Since the present value of a future earning stream given a wage equal to x is $W(x) = x/r$, the reservation wage is equal to imputed search income,

$$rV = rW(w^*) = w^*, \tag{2.7}$$

by virtue of eq. (2.5).

To recover the fundamental reservation wage equation for this model, simply use (2.7) to eliminate V is (2.6) and let $W(x) = x/r$. The result is

$$(\lambda/r) \int_{w^*}^\infty [x - w^*] \, dF(x) = c + w^* - b. \tag{2.8}$$

The left-hand side is interpretable as the marginal return to continued search given an offer equal to the reservation wage, the present value of the expected capital gain attributable to finding an acceptable offer next period with due account taken of the frequency with which offers arrive. The right-hand side, which is the cost of search this period when the reservation wage is offered, is composed of two parts. The first is the out-of-pocket cost while the second is an opportunity cost term equal to the difference between the value of working at the reservation wage and the value of "leisure".

Notice that (2.8) suggests the possibility $w^* < b$, that the job an unemployed worker is willing to accept pays less than the value of "leisure". This possibility seems and is inconsistent with a rational participation decision on the worker's part. Indeed, were the worker not to participate, his "wealth" would be b/r, the present value of an infinitely long life spent in leisure. In order to induce him to participate as an unemployed searching worker the value of search V must be at least as large. Taking this participation condition into account, we find that eqs. (2.5)–(2.8) imply

$$rV = w^* > b, \quad \text{if and only if } (\lambda/r)\int_b^\infty [x - b]\, \mathrm{d}F(x) > c. \tag{2.9}$$

In other words, a worker is a willing participant in the labor market, equivalently the reservation wage is at least as large as the value of leisure, if and only if the return to search, given a reservation wage equal to the value of leisure, is at least as large as the out of pocket cost of search.

The idea that the reservation wage might be different from the value of leisure in the face of time and money costs of job search was well established in the literature before formal derivations of the type just presented appeared. However, it was thought that the reservation wage of unemployed workers should fall over time. In a classic and influential article, Kasper (1967) reported empirical evidence in support of this hypothesis. Among the original formalizations of the reservation wage theory, Gronau (1971) demonstrated that the stopping model has such an implication when a finite work life is assumed simply because the return to search, like the return to any other investment in human capital, falls as a worker's retirement date is approached. However, this is an aging effect, not a search tenure effect. Given the relatively short duration of unemployment spells and any reasonable interest rate, one can easily show that the aging effect fails to explain the relatively large rates of decline in the reservation wage that Kasper and others since have reported for relatively young workers. In sum, except for those very near retirement age, the infinite working life abstraction is not a problem.

Still the constant reservation wage result is inconsistent with reported empirical fact. An alternative and I feel more convincing explanation for a declining reservation wage is the likely possibility that most unemployed workers are liquidity constrained. The well-known inability of unemployed workers to borrow money in the official credit market supports this contention. The simplest way to formally incorporate a liquidity constraint into the simple model is to assume that the worker can self-finance the out-of-pocket cost of search only for a finite time period of length T. Specifically, the funds available for the purpose of seeking a job equal cT. In this case, the value of search will depend on time left until the liquidity barrier is binding which will be denoted as $\tau = T - t$, where t is the length of the unemployment spell to date. Since the index τ reverses the order of time, the value of searching one more period given that there are τ periods left is given by the following recursive analogue of eq. (2.3):

$$V(\tau) - V(\tau - h) + (1 - \beta(h))V(\tau - h)$$
$$= (b - c)h + \beta(h)\left[\sum_1^\infty q(n, h)\int_0^\infty \max[0, W(x) - V(\tau - h)]\, dG(x, n)\right].$$

By dividing both sides by h and taking limits as $h \to 0$, one obtains the differential equation:

$$dV(\tau)/d\tau = \lambda \int_0^\infty \max[0, W(x) - V(\tau)]\, dF(x) + b - c - rV(\tau). \qquad (2.10)$$

Since the worker's only alternative when the liquidity constraint is binding is to drop out of the labor force,

$$V(0) = W(b) = b/r. \qquad (2.11)$$

The reservation wage given τ period remaining $w(\tau)$, solves

$$V(\tau) = W(w(\tau)) = w(\tau)/r. \qquad (2.12)$$

Consequently, eqs. (2.10), (2.11), and (2.12) imply

$$dw(\tau)/d\tau = r[w^* - w(\tau)] + \lambda \int_{w(\tau)}^\infty [x - w(\tau)]\, dF(x)$$
$$- \lambda \int_{w^*}^\infty [x - w^*]\, dF(x) \qquad (2.13a)$$

and

$$w(0) = b. \qquad (2.13b)$$

Because $w^* \geq b$ is required for participation and the right-hand side of (2.13a) is non-negative for all $w(\tau) \leq w^*$,

$$w^* \geq w(\tau) \geq b \quad \text{and} \quad \mathrm{d}w(\tau)/\mathrm{d}\tau \geq 0, \tag{2.14}$$

for any willing participant with the inequalities holding strictly when the participation condition of (2.9) holds strictly. In other words, the reservation wage falls toward the value of leisure with search tenure as the limit T of the search period is approached.

The explanation of a reservation wage that declines with search tenure given by this version of the model is that the likelihood of finding a better wage in the future diminishes as time passes. The chance that the worker takes of running out of the means of financing further search increases as time passes. In the end, the worker must accept any wage that will compensate for the value of leisure. However, one would not expect a worker facing an imperfect capital market to be risk neutral, i.e. act as if he were simply an expected wealth maximizer operating subject to a liquidity constraint, as we have assumed. Fortunately, Danforth (1979) has established the essence of the conclusion, namely that the reservation wage and financial wealth are positively related, in the more general context of a risk averse worker.

2.2. The duration of search spells

Obviously, wage search theory views the time spent searching for an acceptable job as a "productive" activity, at least from the point of view of the searching worker. Hence, to the extent that non-employed workers who are classified as unemployed are searching, the theory suggests that "unemployment" is a productive state of labor force participation. This inference caused a lot of controversy in the early 1970s, particularly among the then still dominant school of Keynesian macroeconomics.

However, for labor economists trained in the neo-classical tradition of Marshallian microeconomics, this idea was not so objectionable. Even the institutionalist school had a certain sympathy for a theory that dealt with some of the dynamic questions which they had long insisted were important but outside the supply and demand model. A number of labor economists soon found in the theory an optimizing framework that would permit the formation of empirically meaningful hypotheses about phenomena that quite simply could not be explained by either Marshall's or Keynes' theoretical structures. The obvious set of hypotheses that the original model wage search generates concern the distribution of search-unemployment spell lengths.

Given a stationary reservation wage, w^*, the probabilistic rate at which a worker escapes unemployment is simply

$$\phi = \lambda [1 - F(w^*)], \qquad (2.15)$$

the rate at which offers arrive times the probability that a random offer is acceptable. Since the escape or "hazard" rate is the instantaneous probability of leaving unemployment given unemployment at any date, the constant reservation wage model predicts that the length of a completed search-unemployment spell is distributed exponential with mean equal to the inverse of the escape rate. In the more general case of a reservation wage that varies with the duration of search to date, $w(t)$, because say the worker is liquidity constrained in the manner modeled in the previous section, the distribution of completed spells is given by

$$P(t) = 1 - \exp\left(- \int_0^t \phi(\tau)\,d\tau\right), \quad \text{where } \phi(t) = \lambda [1 - F(w(t))]. \qquad (2.16)$$

In this case $\phi'(t) > 0$, the hazard rate is said to exhibit positive duration dependence. Hence, the wage search model not only makes suggestions about what to include in a duration of search regression but has implications for the distribution of the observed random variable.

In the remainder of this section, we focus on the implications of the model for the determinants of the reservation wage and the rate of escape from unemployment in the constant reservation wage case. In the analysis to follow, it is important to note that there is both a direct and an indirect effect of changes in the "demand" factors in the model – the offer arrival rate and the wage offer distribution – on the escape rate. The direct effect is that obtained holding the reservation wage constant and the indirect effect is the change in the escape rate induced by a change in the reservation wage. Of course, other parameters affect only the reservation wage and these – the value of leisure, the cost of search and the interest rate – might be regarded as the "supply" factors is the model. For these there is no direct effect on the escape rate, only an indirect effect. Specifically, the fundamental equation of the decision model, eq. (2.8), implies that the reservation wage increases with the value of leisure and decreases with both the cost of search and the interest rate. (Simply completely differentiate the equation.) Hence, these facts and (2.15) imply that the rate of escape from unemployment decreases with the value of leisure but increases with the cost of search and the rate at which future returns to search are discounted. All of these implications are easily understood given the fact that the time spent searching is an investment made now in return for higher income in the future.

The distribution of wage offers, $F(w)$, summarizes a worker's employment opportunities given job availability and job availability is indicated by the offer arrival rate λ. These two elements represent two different aspects of the "demand" for the worker's services. We begin our analyses of these by considering the effects of changes in the "mean" and "variance" of the wage offer distribution holding constant the offer arrival rate. Because we do not wish to specify a specific functional form for this distribution, the results below make use of well-known generalized notions of mean and variance.

A cumulative distribution function G is said to be a "translation" of another, F, if there exists a constant μ such that

$$G(w + \mu) = F(w), \quad \text{for all } w. \tag{2.17}$$

For $\mu > 0$, the translation is to the right and G is said to first-order stochastically dominate F in the statistics literature. Of course, G can be formed from F by shifting the latter uniformly to the right a distance μ. Clearly, then, the mean of G is exactly μ units larger than the mean of F but all higher moments around the mean are the same for both distributions. Hence,

$$\lim_{\mu \to 0} \left\{ [G(w) - F(w)]/\mu \right\} = \lim_{\mu \to 0} [G(w) - G(w + \mu)]/\mu = -F'(w),$$

which tells us that a marginal increase in the mean of F, holding other moments constant, decreases the probability of obtaining an offer less than or equal to the given value w by an amount equal to the density of F at w, at least when F is differentiable which we assume for the purposes of this analysis.

The now standard generalized notion of the "variance" is that introduced into the economics literature under the name "mean preserving spread" by Rothschild and Stiglitz (1970). The distribution H is a mean preserving spread of F given that both are defined on the positive reals and have the same mean if and only if

$$\int_0^w H(x)\,dx \ge \int_0^w F(x)\,dx, \quad \text{for all } w > 0.$$

Hence, if one regards $H(w, \sigma)$ as a family of mean preserving spreads of F where σ is a parameter of relative dispersion so that $\sigma = 0$ defines the member F, then

$$\lim_{\sigma \to 0} \int_0^w \left\{ [H(x, \sigma) - F(x)]/\sigma \right\} dx = \int_0^w H_\sigma(x, 0)\,dx \ge 0, \quad \text{for all } w, \tag{2.18}$$

where $H_\sigma(x, \sigma)$ is the partial derivative of $H(\cdot)$ with respect to σ.

These two concepts are useful for our purpose because of the following transformation:

$$\int_w^\infty [x - w]\,dF(x) = E_F\{x\} - w + \int_0^w F(x)\,dx, \quad \infty > w \ge 0. \tag{2.19}$$

This fact can be verified by noting that the two sides are indeed equal when $w = 0$ and that the two expressions have the same derivative. As a consequence, eq. (2.8) can be rewritten as

$$(\lambda + r)w^* = \lambda E_F\{x\} + \lambda \int_0^{w^*} F(x)\,dx + r(b - c). \tag{2.20}$$

Defining $w^*(\mu)$ as the reservation wage associated with the translation G of F defined in eq. (2.17), we have

$$(\lambda + r)w^*(\mu) = \lambda E_G\{x\} + \lambda \int_0^{w^*(\mu)} G(x)\,dx + r(b - c)$$

$$= \lambda\mu + \lambda E_F\{x\} + \lambda \int_0^{w^*(\mu)} F(x - \mu)\,dx + r(b - c).$$

Therefore,

$$\frac{\partial w^*}{\partial \mu} = \frac{\lambda[1 - F(w^*)]}{r + \lambda[1 - F(w^*)]} = \frac{\phi}{r + \phi} > 0 \text{ and less than 1.} \tag{2.21}$$

In words, an increase in the mean of the wage offer distribution increases the reservation wage but by an amount which is less than the increase in the mean. Note that the response is very close to unity when the rate of escape from unemployment is large relative to the interest rate. Indeed, the response is exactly the discount factor one would apply to a dollar expected to be received $1/\phi$ periods hence, which is the expected time until employment at every date during the search process.

In the case of an increase in mean preserving spread, let $w^*(\sigma)$ denote the reservation wage associated with the more spread distribution $H(w, \sigma)$. Since this distribution and F have the same mean by definition:

$$(1 + r)w^*(\sigma) = E_F\{x\} + \lambda \int_0^{w^*(\sigma)} H(x, \sigma)\,dx + r(b - c).$$

Consequently, a marginal increase in spread also increases the reservation wage by virtue of (2.18), i.e.

$$\frac{\partial w^*}{\partial \sigma} = \left[\lambda \int_0^{w^*(\sigma)} H_\sigma(x, 0)\,dx\right] \Big/ (r + \phi) \geq 0. \tag{2.22}$$

This famous result from the stopping literature has its own economic translation. Shoppers love bargains, and bargains are only possible when prices are disperse.

More seriously, it is the consequence of the fact that the worker has the option of waiting for an offer in the upper tail of the wage distribution.

We have already warned the reader that a knowledge of the comparative static results regarding the relationship between the wage is not sufficient for valid inferences about the relationship between the probability of escape from search unemployment and those same parameters. In the case of the mean,

$$\phi(\mu) = \lambda [1 - G(w^*(\mu))] = \lambda [1 - F(w^*(\mu) - \mu)],$$

by virtue of (2.15) and (2.17). Consequently, a marginal increase in the mean increases the escape probability because the reservation wage increases by less, i.e.

$$\partial \phi / \partial \mu = F'/(w^*)[1 - \phi/(\phi + r)] > 0, \tag{2.23}$$

but the effect will be very small if the escape rate is large relative to the interest rate. In the case of spread,

$$\phi(\sigma) = \lambda [1 - H(w^*(\sigma), \sigma)].$$

Therefore, the marginal effect,

$$\frac{\partial \phi}{\partial \sigma} = -\lambda F'(w^*) \frac{\partial w^*}{\partial \sigma} - \lambda H_\sigma(w^*, 0), \tag{2.24}$$

has an ambiguous sign in general.

An increase in job availability as measured by the instantaneous rate at which a worker receives offers, λ, increases the reservation wage by virtue of (2.20), as one would expect. However, given the reservation wage, the same increase also increases the escape rate by virtue of (2.15). The net effect is the sum of the positive direct effect and negative indirect effect. Formally,

$$\frac{\partial \phi}{\partial \lambda} = [1 - F(w^*)] - \lambda F'(w^*) \frac{\partial w^*}{\partial \lambda}, \tag{2.25}$$

where

$$\frac{\partial w^*}{\partial \lambda} = \int_{w^*}^{\infty} [x - w^*] \, dF(x) / [r + \phi] > 0. \tag{2.26}$$

Burdett (1981) shows that the net effect can be negative although a sufficient condition for the intuitively plausible implication that an increase in job availability reduces the expected duration of a search unemployment spell is a "log-concave" wage offer probability density function.

2.3.   Problems in and methods of estimation

One of the first empirical applications of the wage search model concerns the analysis of the effects of unemployment insurance benefits on the duration of unemployment. Numerous authors realized that the value of leisure b can be interpreted to include the insurance benefit paid to covered employed workers. Hence, the model's prediction that the reservation wage increases with the value of leisure also implies that those who receive benefits relative to like workers who do not and those receiving relatively higher benefits under the program should be observed to experience longer unemployment spells. Furthermore, their post unemployment spell wage should be higher. An extensive empirical literature was born that continues to live today devoted to testing and estimating these and related effects of UI.[7]

The standard econometric methodology applied in the early work is the OLS estimation of "reduced form" relationships between both observed unemployment spell lengths and post unemployment earnings and various measures of the liberality of UI benefits, typically replacement ratios and maximum benefit period lengths. Generally speaking, the evidence obtained from many data sources supports the hypothesis that unemployment durations are affected as expected although the evidence on the effects on post unemployment wage is less clear. There are numerous criticisms that can and have been made of the methodological approach taken [see Welch (1977)]. Since actual observations on worker reservation wages are not typically available, the method does not permit a test of the mechanism of causality suggested by the wage search model. Duration observations drawn from any finite period of observation will include many incomplete spells. Observations on the eventual wage are not available for workers who do not complete their spells within the observation period. OLS estimates are biased when these spells are excluded, which was typically done. Finally, the expected length of the spell and the expected post spell wage are jointly determined endogenous variables for each individual.

Unlike most theories of individual economic decisions that are set in the context of a deterministic environment, search theory explicitly deals with the uncertain world that the worker faces when attempting to find a job. As a consequence, the theory has implications for the stochastic relationship one

---

[7]Examples of the original literature on the topic are included in Katz (1977). Also see Ehrenberg and Daxaca (1976) and Klassen (1979). More recent related contributions include Topel (1983) and Clark and Summers (1982).

might expect between "endogenous" and "exogenous" variables as well as the qualitative relationships between them. Specifically, if the reservation wage is stationary, then the distribution of the length of a worker's completed search unemployment spell is exponential with a hazard rate proportional to the probability of sampling an acceptable wage offer and the distribution of the worker's post spell wage is the conditional distribution of wage offers given that it exceeds the reservation wage. Recent empirical work by Kiefer and Neumann (1979a, 1979b, 1981), Nickell (1979), Lancaster and Nickell (1980), and Flinn and Heckman (1982b) exploit these properties. Although it is not my role in this chapter to deal with either the econometrics of estimation or to report on actual estimates obtained, it is useful to illustrate the relationship that does exist between stochastic sequential search models and empirical specification.

Suppose that one has access to observations that include for each of n individuals a post unemployment spell wage and the completed length of the spell, denoted as

$$(w_i, t_i), \quad i = 1, 2, \ldots, n. \tag{2.27}$$

Imagine that the value of leisure net of search cost and the mean wage offer are also observed which are denoted as

$$(b_i - c_i, \mu_i), \quad i - 1, 2, \ldots, n. \tag{2.28}$$

Assume that the wage offer distribution is from a two parameter family with common known form for all workers, an individual mean, and a common but unknown variance σ^2. Further suppose that the offer arrival rate λ, to be estimated, is the same for all workers. Then, conditional on the worker's reservation wage, the model implies the following distributions of the two endogenous variables as we have already noted:

$$\Pr\{w_i \leq w\} = F(w; \mu_i, \sigma^2)/[1 - F(w_i^*; \mu_i, \sigma^2)], \tag{2.29}$$

$$\Pr\{t_i \leq t\} = 1 - \exp(-\lambda[1 - F(w_i^*; \mu_i, \sigma^2)]t). \tag{2.30}$$

It follows immediately that the contribution of the individual to the sample likelihood is

$$L_i = \frac{F'(w_i; \mu_i, \sigma^2)}{1 - F(w_i^*; \mu_i, \sigma^2)} \sigma \times [1 - F(w_i^*; \mu_i, \sigma^2)]$$

$$\times \exp(-\lambda[1 - F(w_i^*; \mu_i, \sigma^2)]t_i),$$

the product to the probability densities associated with the wage and spell length observations. Hence, the sample log-likelihood function given the data and the individual reservation wages is

$$\ln L = \sum_{1}^{n} \left\{ \ln F'\left(w_i; \mu_i, \sigma^2 \right) + \ln \lambda - \lambda \left[1 - F\left(w_i^*; \mu_i, \sigma^2 \right) \right] t_i \right\}. \qquad (2.31)$$

Were one able to observe each worker's reservation wage, maximum likelihood estimates of the unknown parameters, the common offer arrival rate and variance, could be obtained in the obvious manner. Although the reservation wage is not observed by assumption, it is a function of the data implicitly specified by eq. (2.8). A reasonable approximation is the linear form

$$w_i^* = \alpha + \beta \left(b_i - c_i \right) + \gamma \mu_i. \qquad (2.32)$$

Furthermore, for a common positive interest rate, the decision model implies the restrictions

$$\beta > 0, \quad \gamma > 0, \quad \text{and} \quad \beta + \gamma = 1. \qquad (2.33)$$

Hence, by substituting for the individual's reservation wage rates in (2.31) from (2.32), one observes that the parameters of the reservation wage equation can be estimated and the restrictions tested as well, at least in principle. In practice, some spells observed in a finite time interval will not be complete. Such spells are said to be censored. Statistical methods for appropriately estimating duration distributions with a mix of complete and censored duration observations is the subject matter of "survival" or "failure time" analysis. Kalbfleish and Prentice (1980) provide an extensive recent treatment of the subject.

Although natural extensions of the method can be used to test for the positive duration dependence in the hazard rate implied by a falling reservation wage in principle, unobserved heterogeneity complicates the issue. Contrary to the hypothetical example outlined above, the econometrician does not observe either the mean wage offer, μ, or the opportunity cost of accepting employment, $b - c$, for each worker in the sample. Instead, worker characteristics are observed which only proxy for these determinants of the reservation wage. One might expect that the observed characteristics do not capture all relevant differences in the determinants of reservation wage differences across the individuals in a given sample. It is now well known that unobserved heterogeneity of this form induces spurious negative duration dependence. Specifically, for any observationally equivalent subsample, the fact that those with higher individual hazards will leave unemployment sooner implies that fraction of those still unemployed who leave unemployment per period will fall with the observed duration of unemployment even if the hazard for each individual exhibits no duration dependence. [See Salant (1977) and Heckman and Borjas (1980) for discussions of this point.]

In their test of the constant reservation wage hypothesis Kiefer and Neumann (1981) apply the so-called "random effect" model to correct for unobserved heterogeneity. For a discussion of the econometrics of the problem, see Flinn and Heckman (1982b). Heckman and Singer (1982) study the problem of identifying duration dependence when unobserved heterogeneity is present and develop a non-parametric approach for estimating duration dependence in search and related models.

3. Job turnover, earnings paths, and participation histories

The purpose of this section is to describe several important extensions of the original wage search model that have been developed to help understand job turnover, the dynamic behavior of earnings, and the labor market experiences of individual workers more generally over time. As the title of the section suggests, the substantive topic coverage of the literature discussed in the section is quite varied. What ties this literature together is the common approach taken by many different authors to a variety of worker labor supply decisions that arise in a dynamic context. The principal starting point for all the research reviewed is that the worker lives in a changing environment that requires a continual reevaluation of the decision of whether to work now and/or to seek some employment opportunity in the future under conditions of uncertainty. Each of the models reviewed considers a particular version of this problem using a theoretical framework which is derivative of the original model of unemployed search.

It is important to point out that the literature on subsequent developments not included for discussion in this section is far vaster than that which is presented. For example, a review of recent contributions to the literature on the effects of the unemployment compensation system on individual search decisions and on unemployment behavior could now fill a volume. Furthermore, not all contributors to the innovations that are discussed in this section get equal treatment. Instead, my method of presentation has biased my choices in favor of those authors with models that can be conveniently presented within the decision theoretic framework developed in the first section.

3.1. Search on the job

The assumption that workers search only while unemployed is obviously not realistic and subject to criticism. Tobin (1972) makes the point that one observes hardly any search unemployment among many professions, his own for example. The available quantitative information about the process by which workers make transitions to employment and from one job to another is very limited. However, in his review of the available evidence, Mattila (1974) concludes that indeed most workers who quit move to another job without an intervening period of non-employment. More recently, Topel (1983) reports that the vast majority of workers classified as unemployed in the CPS were laid off. These facts suggest the need for allowing search to take place while employed as a means of understanding the behavior of unemployed workers and understanding of the job turnover process.

The model of worker search while employed presented here is constructed in the image of the original developed by Burdett (1978). Although there are reasons to believe that the cost of search is higher for many when employed than it is when unemployed, only the results for the case of no differential will be presented here.[8] An important implication of the model in this case is that the reservation wage of an unemployed worker is simply the value of "leisure" as in the classical participation model. Specifically, when the cost of search is the same when employed or not, the worker accepts the first job that compensates for the value of foregone leisure and then generally continues to search for a higher paying one while employed.

Although this result establishes that speculative waiting to find a higher paying job need not contribute to unemployment, it does not imply that the worker search behavior while unemployed is unimportant as a determinant of the unemployment rate. Specifically, if the intensity with which the worker searches as well as when to accept employment is a part of the search decision, then as before the distribution search unemployment durations is endogenous as Burdett and Mortensen (1980) have shown. The search on the job model presented here includes a search intensity decision for the purpose of analyzing this dependence.

The assumption that workers can only search or not obviously abstracts from the reality that a worker can and does decide to devote more or less effort to search activities. From the worker's point of view, the purpose of searching more intensely is to shorten the expected time period required to find an acceptable or better job. However, one expects that the returns to more intensive search diminish, at least beyond some point. The simplest way to build these features into the model is to assume that the offer arrival rate is proportional to the worker's "search effort" and that the cost of search is an increasing convex function of "effort". In other words, let $s\lambda$ denote the offer arrival rate and $c(s)$ the cost of search function where s represents search effort. In this generalization, λ is a market determined search efficiency parameter or "potential" offer arrival rate. An increasing marginal cost of search requires that the cost function has the properties $c(0) = 0$, $c'(s) > 0$ and $c''(s) > 0$. Notice that the original model can

---

[8] Burdett (1978) analyzes the general case.

be regarded as the boundary case of a constant marginal cost on the unit interval and an infinite cost beyond.[9]

Let b represent the value of leisure, r the discount rate and $F(w)$ the distribution of wage offers as before. A worker's search strategy is now a choice of the lowest acceptable employment wage and an intensity of search effort both when not employed and employed at a particular wage. Let V denote the worker's discounted future net income, with appropriate account taken of the value of leisure, when unemployed given that an optimal search strategy is pursued in the future and let $W(w)$ represent the value of being employed at wage w given the optimal search strategy.

Since the current search effort affects only the cost of search incurred now and the probability of generating an offer in the next instant, its optimal value maximizes the sum of today's income net of search costs and the expected capital gain attributable to search. Hence, when the worker is unemployed,

$$rV = \max_{s \geq 0} \left[b - c(s) + \lambda s \int_0^\infty \{ \max[V, W(x)] - V \} \, dF(x) \right], \qquad (3.1)$$

while when employed at a wage w

$$rW(w) = \max_{s \geq 0} \left[w - c(s) + \lambda s \int_0^\infty \{ \max[V, W(x), W(w)] - W(w) \} \, dF(x) \right]. \qquad (3.2)$$

These equations are natural extensions of (2.6).

Equation (3.2) implies that the value of employment increases with the wage received.[10] Therefore, a comparison of (3.1) and (3.2) implies that the value of leisure is the lowest wage at which the worker will accept employment, i.e.

$$V = W(b) \leq W(w), \quad \text{for all } w \geq b. \qquad (3.3)$$

Given this fact, the first order conditions for the search intensity choice problems on the right-hand sides of (3.1) and (3.2) can be written as

$$\lambda \int_w^\infty [W(x) - W(w)] \, dF(x) = (\leq) c'(s^*(w)), \quad \text{as } s^*(w) > (=) 0, \qquad (3.4)$$

---

[9] Generalizations and applications of the job search model with an endogenously determined search intensity are contained in Mortensen (1977), Burdett and Mortensen (1978), and Burdett (1979).

[10] This assertion can easily be proved by contradiction. The supposition that $W(w)$ in non-increasing implies that the right-hand side of (3.2) is strictly increasing in w.

where $s^*(w)$ is the optimal search intensity choice when the worker is employed at wage $w \geq b$ and $s^*(b)$ is the choice when the worker is unemployed. In other words, optimal search effort equates its marginal return and cost. Because $W(w)$ is strictly increasing, eq. (3.4) and the assumption of increasing marginal cost of effort imply that the optimal search effort declines with the wage earned while employed. Finally, at some sufficiently high wage, w^*, and beyond, the return will not justify the cost of positive search effort at the margin. Since eq. (3.2) implies that $W(w) = w/r$ when $s = 0$, the critical wage, properly called the search reservation wage, solves

$$(\lambda/r)\int_{w^*}^{\infty}[x - w^*]\,dF(x) = c'(0). \tag{3.5}$$

Finally, the unemployed worker is willing to search if and only if the marginal return to search effort at wage b exceeds the marginal cost of no search effort, i.e. $w^* > b$.

In sum, we have established that

$$s^*(b) > 0, \quad \text{if and only if } w^* > b, \tag{3.6a}$$

$$ds^*(w)/dw < 0, \quad \text{for all } b \leq w < w^*, \tag{3.6b}$$

and

$$s^*(w) = 0, \quad \text{for all } w \geq w^*. \tag{3.6c}$$

These results have the following interpretations. The worker is a participant in the sense that he or she looks for employment when unemployed when the marginal return to search effort evaluated at the value of leisure exceeds the marginal cost of effort evaluated at no effort. If a participant, the worker accepts the first job that compensates for the value of leisure and then generally continues to search with an intensity that equates the marginal cost and return to effort. Because the return to search effort declines with the wage earned, so does the optimal search effort choice. Finally, once a sufficiently well paid job is found, the worker stops searching altogether.

The search on the job extension of the basic model contains a theory for both the completed lengths of unemployed search and job spells. Specifically, both are exponential distributions with constant "hazard" rate

$$\phi(w) = \lambda s^*(w)[1 - F(w)], \quad w \geq b, \tag{3.7}$$

where the hazard is the instantaneous rate of escape from unemployment when $w = b$ and is the worker's instantaneous quit rate when employed at wage $b \le w$. Hence, in this model, the expected duration of search–unemployment declines with the value of leisure both because optimal search effort and the probability of finding an acceptable wage decline with the value of leisure. The quit rate when employed declines with the wage earned for analogous reasons. The latter implication of the model is consistent with virtually every empirical study of quit behavior, e.g. see Pencavel (1970), Parsons (1977), and Mincer and Jovanovic (1981).

As Burdett (1978) points out, the model also provides an alternative explanation for why wages generally increase with years of work experience. The standard argument is that workers become more productive with experience as a consequence of learning and training. Here earnings rise because workers with longer experience are more likely to have found a higher paying job. Formally, the model implies that the wage process for an individual over time $\{w(t)\}$ is Markov with state space X, the support of the wage offer distribution F. The instantaneous rate of transition from the current wage w to any other $x \ne w$ in the support of F is zero if $x < w$ and is the product of the rate at which new offers arrive, $\lambda s^*(w)$, and the probability density of receiving the offer x, $F'(x)$, when $x > w$. By virtue of (3.6c), the set $\{x \ge w^*\}$ are the absorbing states of the process and the stationary distribution of the process, which represents the distribution of earnings that any worker can expect in the "long run", is given by $F(x)/[1 - F(w^*)]$ defined on set of absorbing states. Hence, the implied time path of an individual's wage is a stochastically increasing function of length of work experience which is eventually absorbed into the set where the worker is no longer motivated to search.

It is important both conceptually and from an econometric point of view that one not confuse the hypothesis that the quit rate for a given individual declines with the wage earned across jobs with the cross individual effect of different earnings opportunities on their respective quit rates. In this model, the latter is the effect of a change in the mean wage offer on the individual's quit rate holding current earnings constant. This effect can be derived by first using the fact that eqs. (3.2) and (3.4) imply

$$rW(w) - w = s^*(w)c'(s^*(w)) - c(s^*(w)). \tag{3.8}$$

By the convexity of the cost of search effort function, the right-hand side of (8) is positive and increasing in $s^*(w)$. Therefore, the optimal search effort given the wage currently paid and the interest rate, increases with $W(w)$, the worker's future discounted net income stream given that his or her current wage is w. Not surprising, the latter can be shown to increase with a right translation of F, i.e. a ceteris paribus increase in the mean of the wage offer distribution. Since $F(w)$ decreases at every value of w given such a change, the theory predicts that workers facing wage offer distributions with higher means, holding other moments constant and holding the wage currently earned constant, quit more frequently and have more steeply sloped wage experience profiles. Finally, the same argument implies that the rate of escape from unemployment is higher for workers facing a wage offer distribution that is more favorable in this sense. Since the effects of a ceteris paribus increase in the wage currently earned and in the mean wage offer expected are opposite in sign and workers who do face a more favorable wage offer distribution are more likely to be paid more in any sample, the estimated wage "coefficient" in any quit equation is upward biased unless care is taken to include human capital and ability variables that adequately condition for this form of worker heterogeneity.

In the preceding discussion it was asserted that a worker's wealth given the wage currently earned increases with the mean of the wage offer distribution, which we denote as μ. One might also expect that wealth increases with the offer arrival rate parameter λ. However, a formal demonstration of these conjectures requires a more powerful method than that applied in the case of the original stopping version of the model. Because we will have need of the method in the subsequent exposition and because it can also be used here to obtain results concerning the qualitative relationship between maximal wealth and other parameters characterizing the worker's environment, the remainder of this sub-section is devoted to a brief outline of the method.

Let $F(w, \mu)$ denote a family of offer distribution that differ only with respect to their means parameterized by μ. Specifically, one member of the family is a right translation of the other if and only if its μ is greater than the other's. Let $W(w, \mu, \lambda)$ denote the maximal discounted expected future worker net income stream when employed at a wage w given that the worker's mean wage offer in the future is μ and offer arrival rate parameter is λ. Let $s^*(w, \mu, \lambda)$ represent the optimal search effort given w, a wage offer distribution with mean μ and offer arrival parameter λ. Now, observe that eq. (3.2), given condition (3.3), can be rewritten as

$$
W(w, \mu, \lambda) = \max_{s \geq 0} \left\{ \left[w - c(s) + \lambda s \int_w^\infty W(x, \mu, \lambda) \, dF(x, \mu) \right] \Big/ \right.
$$

$$
\left[r + \lambda s [1 - F(w, \mu)]] \right\}
$$

$$
= \max_{s \geq 0} \left\{ \frac{w - c(s)}{r} + \beta(s, w, \mu, \lambda) \right.
$$

$$
\times \left[\int_w^\infty W(x, \mu, \lambda) \frac{dF(x, \mu)}{1 - F(w, \mu)} - \frac{w - c(s)}{r} \right] \right\}, \tag{3.9}
$$

where

$$\beta(s, w, \mu, \lambda) = \lambda s [1 - F(w, \mu)] / [r + \lambda s [1 - F(w, \mu)]]. \tag{3.10}$$

The right-hand side of (3.9) is a map that transforms an arbitrary bounded, continuous function defined on $[0, \infty) \times [0, \infty) \times [0, \infty)$ into another with the same range and $W(w, \mu, \lambda)$ is a fixed point of the map. Furthermore, $r > 0$, $s^*(b, \mu, \lambda)$ bounded, which is guaranteed by the assumption that $c'(s)$ tends to infinity with s for all finite μ, $F(0) = 0$ and (3.6b) imply

$$0 \leq \beta(s^*(w, \mu, \lambda), w, \mu) \leq \beta(s^*(b, \mu, \lambda), b, \mu, \lambda) \equiv \beta < 1, \quad \text{for all } w \geq b. \tag{3.11}$$

Blackwell (1965) has shown that any such transformation $T(W)$ is a contraction map if (i) $|T(W + \delta)| \geq |T(W)|$ for every positive constant δ and (ii) a non-negative constant $\beta < 1$ exists such that $|T(W + \delta)| \leq |T(W)| + \beta \delta$, where $|\cdot|$ denotes the sup norm. A contraction map has the property that any sequence of functions generated by repeated application of the transformation converges to its unique fixed point. Since (3.9)–(3.11) imply that the conditions are satisfied, the value function $W(w, \mu, \lambda)$ is uniquely defined. This argument is a standard method for demonstrating the existence and uniqueness of a solution to stochastic dynamic infinite horizon programming problem.

However, notice that if the value function $W(w, \mu, \lambda)$ is differentiable with respect to the mean wage offer, then the partial differential function, $W_\mu(\cdot)$, must satisfy the following equation by virtue of a complete differentiation of eq. (3.9) with respect to μ:

$$W_\mu(w, \mu, \lambda)$$

$$= \beta_\mu(s^*(w, \mu, \lambda), w, \mu) \left[\int_w^\infty W(x, \mu, \lambda) \frac{dF(x, \mu)}{1 - F(w, \mu)} - \frac{w - c(s)}{r} \right]$$

$$+ \beta(s^*(w, \mu), w, \mu, \lambda) \left[\int_w^\infty W(x, \mu, \lambda) \frac{\partial}{\partial \mu} \left(\frac{F'(x, \mu)}{1 - F(w, \mu)} \right) \right] dx$$

$$+ \beta(s^*(w, \mu), w, \mu, \lambda) \int_w^\infty W_\mu(x, \mu, \lambda) \frac{dF(x, \mu)}{1 - F(w, \mu)}. \tag{3.12}$$

Hence, Blackwell's conditions also imply that the right-hand side of (3.12) is a contraction map which has as its fixed point the partial derivative function of interest. Therefore, the fact that any sequence of functions obtained by repeated application of the transformation converges to the fixed point, the fact that both the first and the second terms on the right of (3.12) are non-negative if $s^*(\cdot) \geq 0$, and finally an appropriately constructed induction argument imply the desired result. Because $\beta(\cdot)$ is also strictly increasing in the offer arrival parameter when $s^*(\cdot) > 0$, an analogous argument implies that the worker's wealth increases with λ as well. In sum,

$$W_\mu(w, \mu, \lambda) > 0 \quad \text{and} \quad W_\lambda(w, \mu, \lambda) > 0, \quad \text{if and only if } w \leq w^*. \quad (3.13)$$

Of course, $W(w, \mu, \lambda) = w/r$ for all $w > w^*$ by virtue of eqs. (3.6) and (3.8) implies necessity.

That the first term on the right-hand side of (3.12) is positive is implied by the definition of $\beta(\cdot)$ given in (3.10), the fact that $F(w, \mu)$ is decreasing in μ for every w, and the fact that the term in square brackets is positive which is implied by eq. (3.8). The second term is positive because $W(x, \mu, \lambda)$ is increasing in x given μ and because the distribution of acceptable offers is stochastically increasing in μ. Construct the sequence

$$W_\mu^n(\cdot) = T\left(W_\mu^{n-1}(\cdot)\right), \qquad W_\mu^0(w, \mu) \equiv 0,$$

where $T(\cdot)$ is the transformation defined by the right-hand side of (3.12). Every element is positive for all $n > 0$ by induction given $w < w^*$. The fact that $T(\cdot)$ is a contraction implies that the sequence converges to the function of interest. Hence, the fact that every element in the tail is positive and convergence imply (3.13).

Finally, the conditions of (3.13) and eq. (3.8) imply

$$\partial s^*(\cdot)/\partial\mu > 0 \quad \text{and} \quad \partial s^*(\cdot)/\partial\lambda > 0, \quad \text{if and only if } w \leq w^*.$$

Therefore, the hazard in eq. (3.7) in increasing in both the mean wage offer, μ, and the offer arrival parameter, λ, for all wage rates less than or equal to the search reservation wage w^*. Note that the latter implication requires no restriction on the form of the offer distribution function as it does in the standard stopping model which assumes only search while unemployed.

3.2. Learning about the job

In the original search model and the search on the job extension, the job offering a particular package of characteristics must be found but the nature of those characteristics for a located job is known. The consequences of relaxing this assumption have been studied by Jovanovic (1979a, 1979b), Wilde (1979), Viscusi (1979) and Johnson (1978). The principal idea common to this literature is that the worker does not know for sure the future earning stream or some other relevant characteristics of a job at the date of hire. Instead, he or she must spend some time trying it on for size. As more information about the job characteristics is acquired, the decision to stick with it is continually reconsidered. A quit in this framework results as a consequence of a decision that the job is "not a good fit" relative to alternatives available. In short, some important dimensions of jobs are in Hirshleifer's (1973) terminology "experience goods" rather than "inspection goods", as the standard search model supposes. The results drawn from this literature have materially added to the list of hypotheses concerning and explanations for job separation behavior. Furthermore, the analysis represents the first formalization of the "job shopping" explanation for high turnover among the young.

Although the authors' stories vary, Jovanovic assumes that the learning is about productivity on the job while Wilde and Viscusi focus on learning about non-pecuniary job characteristics, the basic formulation of the decision problem is the same. The worker acts as a Bayesian forecaster by using observations to date to make predictions concerning the job's true but unknown characteristics. As new information arrives, the forecast is revised and a quit decision is made. The probability of quitting, then, depends on the information acquired about the job at the time of decision. Formally, the problem is again one of stopping, but now similar to Rothschild's (1974) version of the price search model where the worker must learn about the distribution of offers. As such, its essential features can be illustrated using the machinery we have already developed.

In this section, I have chosen to present Jovanovic's model because of its close relationship to the original wage search model and its focus on wage and turnover dynamics. In Jovanovic's model a worker's future productivity is purely "match specific". Ex ante there is no information that allows a differential prediction concerning the productivity of a given job–worker match. Specifically, a worker's productivities across matches are independent in the sense that performance in one provides no information about productivity on another. In other words, one can view any sequence of realized average future firm-specific productivities as random and independent draws from the same distribution. Were these realizations observable at the time of hire and if the wage rate at each firm were some strictly increasing functions of these realizations, then the original wage search model applies, i.e. the wage–productivity relation and distribution of productivities generate the wage offer distribution. The worker's acceptance decision is the choice of whether or not to continue sampling match specific productivities from this distribution.[11]

---

[11] However, in the formalization presented in Jovanovic and here, the worker is assumed to be able to find new employment opportunities costlessly and instantaneously. This assumption is made for the purpose of focusing the analysis on the learning process. It can be relaxed without changing the essence of the results reported in this section.

Assume that productivity in any job is not immediately observed. Instead, the worker's realized output is observed by both worker and employer and provides a noisy signal for average output over the future tenure of the match. This information is used both to set the current wage and to forecast future earnings for the purpose of making the separation decision. Of course, the conditional predictor of future productivity, given average output to date, becomes increasingly more precise as a consequence of the law of large number. In the limit the worker's average productivity is known with certainty, provided, of course, that he or she has not already decided to leave. As this description suggests, the quit problem is of the "two-armed bandit" variety and shares its properties.[12] Once separated, the worker will not return. Therefore, the probability that the worker will leave even when the true average match specific productivity is higher than any other is positive as a consequence of sampling variation.

Jovanovic maintains the risk neutral and infinite life abstractions that characterize much of the job search literature and assumes that the worker is paid a wage equal to the conditional expected value of his true productivity given all available information to date. Under these assumptions and the assumption that the common distribution from which match specific true productivities are drawn is known, the value of leaving the current job is some constant, V, which represents the discounted future income that the worker can expect were he to try any other job. As indicated by the notation, it is the analogue to the value of search in the original model. The worker quits whenever the value of continuing to work at the job, which will be denoted as a random variable, $W(\cdot)$, to be determined, falls below V. Stopping, then, corresponds to quitting the current job to try another and the probability of stopping is the quit probability. Below we outline the specifics which differ from Jovanovics in order to take advantage of the theoretical apparatus on hand. However, these differences do not violate the spirit of his model; rather they make his results more transparent.

Let $t \geq 0$ denote the worker's tenure on some specific job, and let $\{x(t)\}$ represent the stochastic process generating the time path of realized productivities on the job so long as the worker continues. Imagine that changes in observed productivity occur as random dates over the worker's tenure on the job and that the arrival of new values is a Poisson process characterized by a constant arrival rate η.[13] Further suppose that the new values of productivity are drawn independently from the same and, for simplicity, normal distribution with unknown mean μ, drawn at the time of hire, and known variance σ^2. Following Jovanovic, the worker's true expected productivity over the life of the match is distributed normal with known mean m and variance s.

---

[12] For an introduction, to the "two-armed bandit" problem, see DeGroot (1970). Rothschild (1973) applies the model to a number of economic problems.

[13] One might imagine that the employer monitors the worker's realized productivity from time to time choosing the dates at random.

The stochastic specification is consistent with Jovanovic's except that a continuous jump process with Poisson arrivals of observations on productivity is assumed rather than a Weiner process. The principal advantage of this alternative is that the analysis can be performed using the standard theory of finite sample statistics. Let a sample of n productivity observations be denoted as

$$x_i = \mu + \varepsilon_i, \quad i = 1, 2, \ldots, n. \tag{3.14}$$

At any date such a sample provides the information that the worker has about the unknown mean productivity, μ. Given the assumptions that μ is drawn from a normal with mean m and variance s and that the sequence $\{\varepsilon_i\}$ is i.i.d. normal with zero mean and variance σ^2, the posterior distribution of μ given the sample is distributed normal [see DeGroot [1970]] with mean

$$w(n) = E\{\mu | x_1, \ldots, x_n\} = \left[m/s + \left(\sum_{i=1}^{n} x_i\right)\Big/\sigma^2\right] s(n) \tag{3.15a}$$

and variance

$$s(n) = 1/(1/s + n/\sigma^2). \tag{3.15b}$$

As n becomes large, $w(n)$ converges to the sample mean which is converging to the realized known value of μ, the worker's true average productivity, with probability one.

Following Jovanovic, the statistic $w(n)$ is assumed to be the wage received by the worker given past productivity observations. Given (3.15), it is convenient and permitted to regard the wage and sample size pair as the sample sufficient statistic for the worker's estimation problem. Let $G(w(n+1); w, n)$ represent the conditional distribution of the wage at the next observation of productivity, given that $w(n) = w$. By virtue of equations (3.14) and (3.15),

$$w(n+1) = [s(n+1)/s(n)] w(n) + [1 - s(n+1)/s(n)][\mu + \varepsilon_{n+1}]. \tag{3.16}$$

Therefore, $w(n+1)$ given $w(n) = w$ is distributed normal with mean

$$E\{w(n+1) | w(n) = w\} = w$$

and variance

$$E\{(w(n+1) - w)^2 | w(n) = w\} = [1 - s(n+1)/s(n)]^2 [s(n) + \sigma^2]$$

$$= [s(n+1)/\sigma^2]^2 [\sigma^2 s(n)/s(n+1)]$$

$$= s(n+1)s(n)/\sigma^2$$

by virtue of (3.15b). The properties of subsequent interest are that the variance of $w(n+1)$ is independent of the mean w, is decreasing in the size of the sample of realized values of productivity, and converges to zero as that number, n, tends to infinity. The rational worker, assumed to know all that we do, will use the conditional distribution of the next wage given the current wage to make the predictions of future earnings on the job needed to decide whether or not to quit.

The decision to continue on the job or to try another is made by the worker whenever new information about productivity on the job is obtained, at the time of each arrival of a new realized value of productivity. The decision requires a comparison of the worker's expected present value of future income on any randomly selected alternative job, which we denote as V, and the expected present value of future income given that the worker continues on the current job conditional on the information available about his or her productivity on the current job, the sufficient statistic (w, n). Because there is a possibility that the worker will decide to quit the current job at some future date, the value of continuing is a function of the wage currently earned, the number of realized productivity observations to date, and V. Because a new realization of the productivity process will arrive during the small future time interval dt with probability $\eta\, dt$ by virtue of the Poisson arrival assumption and because that event will induce the worker to choose between the new value of continuing and the value of quitting, the following analogue to eq. (2.6) defines the current value of continuing:

$$rW(w, n, V) = w + \eta \int \{\max[W(y, n+1, V), V]$$
$$- W(w, n, V)\}\, dG(y; w, n). \qquad (3.17)$$

To close the model, we simply note that every job is ex ante identical and that the starting wage in all of them is $w(0) = m$ by virtue of (3.15). Hence,

$$V = W(m, 0, V). \qquad (3.18)$$

In other words, the value of quitting is the expected present value of future earnings on the first day of any new job.

The logic used to obtain (3.17) is the same as that introduced in Section 2. The imputed interest income on the expected wealth associated with working on a job that pays wage w after n productivity observations given that V is the alternative wealth associated with trying another job is equal to the current wage plus the expected capital gain associated with the process generating future wage rates on the current job and the option to quit in the future. The existence of a unique value function $W(\cdot)$, which is continuous in w, and a unique constant V that satisfy (3.18) can be established using a modification of methods outlined earlier.

Furthermore, one can show that the value of continuing is increasing in the current wage, w, and decreasing in the number of productivity realizations to date, n.

That wealth should increase with the current wage earned is intuitively clear. It both represents current earning on the job at hand and is the forecast of earnings on that job in the future. The reason why the value function declines with the sample size is a bit more subtle. Because the worker has the option of quitting to try another job, worker "prefers risk" in a sense quite analogous to that discussed in the case of the wage search model. The existence of the quit option allows the worker to reject low wage realizations on the current job in the future. As a consequence, he prefers dispersion in the future wage because only the higher realizations are relevant. Formally, this preference for risk is reflected in the properties of the value function $W(\cdot)$; it is strictly convex in w. This fact together with the implication from eq. (3.16) that the worker's future wage, conditional on the current wage, has a variance that declines with the sample size to date imply that the value of continuing is a strictly decreasing function of the sample size, n.[14]

These properties of the value function permit a qualitative analysis of the boundary of indifference between quitting and continuing, the set of (w, n) pairs that equate the $W(\cdot)$ and V. The boundary can be characterized in terms of a reservation wage, $w^*(n)$, that is a function of the sample size to date. It solves,

$$W(w^*(n), n, V) = V, \quad n = 0, 1 \dots . \tag{3.19}$$

Since $W(\cdot)$ is increasing in w given n, the worker quits when and if the wage process $\{w(n)\}$ falls below the boundary in the sense that $w(n) \le w^*(n)$. Because $W(\cdot)$ is also strictly decreasing in the sample size, (3.19) implies that the reservation wage increases with n. Finally, the eqs. (3.17) and (3.18) and the definition (3.19) imply

$$w^*(n) = rV - \eta \int_{w^*(n+1)}^{\infty} [W(y; n+1, V) - V] \, dG(y; w^*(n), n) < rV$$

and

$$w^*(0) = m.$$

In sum,

$$m = w^*(0) < w^*(n) < w^*(n+1) < rV, \quad n = 1, 2, \dots . \tag{3.20}$$

[14] Formal proofs of these assertions can be obtained from the author.

Furthermore, the reservation wage converges to rV in the limit as n tends to infinity because the variance of the next wage tends to zero.

The economic reasons underlying these results are easily exposited. First, the reservation wage increases with the sample size because rising precision of the estimate of future wage rates on this job implies a falling chance of quitting a job on which the worker is in fact relatively productive. Second, it converges to the imputed interest income on the wealth attributable to trying another job as the sample size grows because there is no uncertainty about the worker's productivity on this job in the limit and rV represents expected future income when the worker quits. Note that (3.20) also implies that the endogenously determined value of rV exceeds m, the worker's expected prior productivity on every job. It does so because the quit decision modelled is a process of search for a relatively high paying job and because rV is the average future income stream equivalent that can be expected by engaging in the process.

Because the reservation wage increases with the size of the sample of past observations on an individual's productivity and because the sample size and tenure on a job are positively correlated, it is at least intuitively clear that those who remain on a given job for any tenure period of length t or more are those who have experienced a relatively favorable and generally increasing sequence of realized productivities. This implication of a rising wage–tenure profile for those who remain on a job can be formalized as follows. Let $Q(w; n)$ denote the probability distribution over a worker's wage given that the worker is still on the job and that n different productivity values have been observed in the past. It is the conditional distribution of the statistic $w(n)$ defined in eq. (3.15a) given that the sequence of its previous values exceeds the sequence of reservation wage values, i.e.

$$Q(w; n) \equiv \Pr\{w(n) \leq w \mid w(i) > w^*(i), \ i = 1, 2, \ldots, n\}. \qquad (3.21)$$

This distribution improves with n in the sense that higher wage rates are more probable the larger is n, $Q(w; n+1) < Q(w; n)$, as a consequence of the selection process induced by the separation decision. To understand why, first note that the unconditional distribution of the random variable $w(n)$ is normal with constant mean m and variance $s - s(n)$ by virtue of the equations of (3.15). Indeed, the sequence $\{w(n)\}$ converges in distribution to μ which is normal with mean m and variance s. The latter would be the eventual distribution of earnings across workers in a large sample were all to stay on the job indefinitely. However, the separation decision selects to retain on the job those workers whose wage sequence stay above the rising sequence of reservation wage rates. Consequently, the distribution given employment on the job and a sample of productivity observations of size n is roughly speaking the normalized right tail of the unconditional distribution of $w(n)$. The tail elongates as n increases and the left truncation point increases with n.

Since the sample size given tenure t for each worker is distributed Poisson with mean ηt the wage distribution across workers who have attained tenure t is

$$P(w; t) = \sum_{n=0}^{\infty} Q(w; n)\exp(-\eta t)(\eta t)^n/n!. \tag{3.22}$$

The positive correlation between sample size and tenure yields the implication that this family of distributions is stochastically increasing in tenure, i.e.

$$\partial P(w; t)/\partial t = \eta \sum_{n=0}^{\infty} [Q(w; n+1) - Q(w; n)]\exp(-\eta t)(\eta t)^n/n! < 0. \tag{3.23}$$

In words, the faction of those still on the job who receive a higher wage increases with tenure. It follows immediately that the average wage of those who remain on a job,

$$E\{w(t)\} = \int w\, \mathrm{d}P(w, t), \tag{3.24}$$

increases with tenure. This fact implies that the learning about the job hypothesis offers an alternative to the on-the-job training hypothesis for observed on-the-job wage growth.

The dependence of quit rates on the wage earned and tenure attained on the job is another topic of interest in the empirical literature. In this model the probability that the worker quits a job during the short interval $(t, t + h)$ given that the worker's wage at tenure date t is w and the sample size of previous productivity observations is n is the product of the probability that a new observations arrives, ηh, and the probability that the new wage is less than the reservation wage with a sample size of $n + 1$. Hence the instantaneous quit rate is

$$q(w, n) = \eta G(w^*(n+1); w, n). \tag{3.25}$$

Hence the instantaneous quit rate given the wage and tenure, the "hazard rate" for the distribution of completed job spell lengths given the wage, is

$$\phi(w, t) = E\{q(w, n)|w(t) = w\}$$
$$= \sum_{n=0}^{\infty} q(w, n)\exp(-\eta t)(\eta t)^n/n! \tag{3.26}$$

by virtue of the Poisson arrival assumption.

The stylized facts drawn from the literature on empirical quit equations are that the quit rate increases with the wage earned on the job given tenure and decreases with tenure given the wage, holding constant age, work experience, education and other characteristics that are likely to be related to systematic differences in "general" human capital across individuals. By virtue of eq. (3.25), the theoretical quit rate holding sample size constant is decreasing in the wage because the higher the current wage the less likely that any future wage will fall below the reservation wage as a consequence of the positive autocorrelation in the wage process implied by the model. By implication

$$\partial \phi(w, t)/\partial w = \sum_{n=0}^{\infty} \left[\partial q(w, n)/\partial w\right] \exp(-\eta t)(\eta t)^n / n! < 0. \qquad (3.27)$$

Consistency with the other stylized fact, that the conditional quit rate falls given the wage, is not so easily demonstrated. Indeed, such an inference is not true for all wage rates and tenures. However, negative duration dependence is implied for those who remain on the job long enough. To establish these assertions, first note that eqs. (3.26) and (3.25) imply

$$\partial \phi(w, t)/\partial t = \eta \sum_{n=0}^{\infty} \left[q(w, n+1) - q(w, n)\right] \exp(-\eta t)(\eta t)^n / n!, \qquad (3.28a)$$

where

$$q(w, n+1) - q(w, n) = \eta \left[G(w^*(n+2); w, n+1) - G(w^*(n+1); w, n+1)\right]$$
$$+ \eta \left[G(w^*(n+1); w, n+1) - G(w^*(n+1); w, n)\right]. \qquad (3.28b)$$

The change in the quit rate attributable to an increase in the sample size is the sum of two effects corresponding to the two terms on the right-hand side of (3.28b). The first term is the change due to the change in the reservation wage. Because $G(\cdot)$ is a distribution function and the reservation wage increases with the sample size, the effect is always positive but will diminish to zero as n becomes large as a consequence of the convergence of the reservation wage to rV. The second term is the change attributable to the decrease in the variance of the next wage induced by the increase in the sample size. Because $G(\cdot)$ is the normal distribution function, a decrease in variance reduces its value to the left of the mean and increases its value to the right. In other words, the second term is negative if and only if $w \geq w^*(n+1)$. Notice that this condition is always satisfied for wage rates larger than or equal to rV by virtue of (3.20). This fact and convergence of the reservation wage imply that the second negative effect exceeds the first positive effect in absolute value for sufficiently large n. Finally, since the weights on the changes in the conditional quit rate associate with larger value of n increase with tenure in the expression on the right-hand side of (3.28a), the conditional hazard rate must exhibit negative duration dependence for all sufficiently large tenures. Conversely, if w is less than rV, then (3.20) implies that $w < w^*(n+1)$ for all large n. Consequently, even if the condition does not hold for small n, the fact that the weight in the average defined on the right-hand side of (3.28b) on values of the difference associated with large sample sizes increases with t implies a negative duration effect for all large tenures. In sum:

$$\partial\phi(w,t)/\partial t < (>)0, \quad \text{for all large } t \text{ when } w \geq (<)rV. \tag{3.29}$$

A more intuitively meaningful way to express this result is as follows. After an initial period spent learning about productivity, the likelihood of separating from the job decreases with tenure for those who have proven relatively more productive and increases with tenure for those who have proven relatively less productive.

The conclusion (3.29) seems to be in conflict with Jovanovic's (1979a) assertion that the quit rate exhibits negative duration dependence for all large tenure values. This apparent inconsistency is resolved by realizing that his result pertains to the unconditional hazard rate, the theoretical quit rate for the entire subsample of workers who attain tenure t. Formally, the latter is the expectation of the conditional quit rate defined in equation (3.25) taken with respect to the joint distribution of wage rates and sample sizes given that the worker attains tenure t. Specifically:

$$\phi(t) \equiv \sum_{n=0}^{\infty} \left\{ \int q(w,n)\,dQ(w,n) \right\} \exp(-\eta t)(\eta t)^n/n!. \tag{3.30}$$

There are two effects of an increase in tenure on the unconditional hazard:

$$\phi'(t) = \sum_{n=0}^{\infty} \left\{ \int q(w,n+1)\,dQ(w,n+1) - \int q(w,n)\,dQ(w,n) \right\}$$
$$\times \exp(-\eta t)(\eta t)^n/n!$$
$$= \sum_{n=0}^{\infty} \left\{ \int [q(w,n+1) - q(w,n)]\,dQ(w,n+1) \right\} \exp(-\eta t)(\eta t)^n/n!$$
$$+ \sum_{n=0}^{\infty} \left\{ \int q(w,n)\,dQ(w,n+1) - \int q(w,n)\,dQ(w,n) \right\}$$
$$\times \exp(-\eta t)(\eta t)^n/n!.$$

The first is the direct effect on the conditional quit rate of an increase in the sample size averaged over the possible wage rates and sample sizes of worker's who have attained tenure t. As already noted, this effect is negative for w greater than or equal to rV and positive otherwise for large n. Because eqs. (3.20) and (3.21) imply that virtually every worker still on the job will have a wage in excess of rV for n sufficiently large and because n and t are positively correlated, the average will eventually become negative as t increases. The second effect is attributable to "unobserved heterogeneity" in the form of different wage rates that reflect differences in predicted productivity across workers on the job revealed through the learning process and the wage selection process induced by the separation decision. Since workers with lower wage rates but the same sample size quit more rapidly and since the fraction of workers earning higher wage rates rises with the sample size, this effect is negative for all t. In sum, $\phi'(t) < 0$ for all sufficiently large t.

In this review of Jovanovic's model, the fact that the learning about the job hypothesis offers an alternative to the on-the-job training explanation for the observation that wages earned rise with tenure has been emphasized. Although rising productivity attributable to some form of on-the-job training may contribute to the phenomena, as Mincer (1974) and others have long argued, no trend only uncertainty in productivity is needed. Furthermore, to the extent that learning of the outlined form takes place here, any empirical measure of the extent of wage growth overstates the return to on-the-job training. Any empirical attempt to test the learning about the job hypothesis and to measure its contribution to on-the-job wage growth must explicitly model the quit decision responsible for the implied selection in the sequence of wage observations. The papers by Flinn (1973) and Marshall (1983) represent ongoing empirical studies with this purpose.

3.3.   Stochastic models of individual work histories

As we have seen, the original model of search unemployment and its extensions to labor turnover analysis have implications for a worker's labor force experiences. The original model can be used to derive implications for the distribution of completed spells of search unemployment and the distribution of post unemployment earnings. Analogously, the extensions have implications for the nature of the probability distribution over completed job spells lengths and the stochastic nature of time paths of earnings. However, so far the possibility that the worker may either lose his or her job or decide to leave active labor force participation has been ignored. When these possibilities are explicitly treated, the theory can be viewed as a stochastic description of a workers entire labor force participation history. Recent extensions of the theory in these directions is the topic of this section.

Labor economists and the popular press make constant reference to unemployment and participation rates. For a specified population, these statistics describe the distribution at some point in time of the population over three states – nonparticipation, employment, and unemployment. It has long been recognized that if movements among these states by like individuals can be described as a Markov chain, then this distribution converges over time to a steady state which can be completely characterized in terms of the probabilities per period that an individual in the population makes a transition from each to every other state. This model of individual worker histories is the basis for a considerable empirical literature which attempts to understand differences in participation and unemployment rates across populations by studying the differences in the transition probabilities that determine the steady state distribution of workers across states in the Markov model. For example, such an analysis demonstrates that the unemployment rate for young males is higher than that for their older counterparts because their transition probability from employment to unemployment is higher, not because their probability of transition from unemployment to employment is lower. In other words, short employment spells, not long unemployment spells are responsible for the difference.[15]

Of course, there is a close relationship between the search model and the Markov model of the labor force experience of an individual worker over time. In the original model of search unemployment, the probability of finding an acceptable job per period is the worker's probability of making the transition from unemployment to employment per period. In the extensions to turnover analysis, the quit probability per period is the probability of transiting from the worker's current job to a new one. Indeed, Jovanovic's matching theory and the other related work on the job shopping hypothesis provide explanation for why the job spell length are shorter for younger workers. The first rigorous and complete application of the relationship between search theory and the Markov chain model of individual worker histories is contained in a seminal but difficult paper by Lucas and Prescott (1974). In the paper, the authors illustrate how the theory of job search can be used to develop a consistent "equilibrium" theory of the employment and labor turnover experience of the typical individual.

Extensions of this type of analysis to include the labor force participation and hours worked decisions are studied by Burdett and Mortensen (1978) and by Toikka (1976). Subsequent theoretical contributions along these lines designed with empirical estimation in mind include papers by Burdett et al. (1984), Flinn and Heckman (1982b), Coleman (1983), Mortensen and Neumann (1984), Lundberg (1984), and Weiner (1982). Related papers that introduce "aggregate demand" disturbances into a similar theoretical structure include Lippman and McCall (1976b) and Jovanovic (1983). All of these represent efforts on the

---

[15] Examples of this literature include Holt (1970), Hall (1972), Marston (1976), and Clark and Summers (1979, 1982).

research frontier. In this section, a variation on the Lucas and Prescott (1974) model and a simple extension of it is presented. Search unemployment and non-participation are distinguished as a means of introducing the principal ideas and structure that underlies the approach taken in this literature.

In the Lucas and Prescott (1974) formulation the distribution of wage offers represents productivity differentials across different locations (jobs or employers) at a point in time. The authors refer to the locations as "islands" populated at any moment by firms who cannot move among islands and workers who can. On each island, wages are determined competitively, the wage offered is equal to the local marginal product of labor on each island. Hence, the distribution of productivity across islands induces a distribution of wage "offers" across the islands. Although communication among the islands is imperfect in the sense that each worker knows only the current wage on his or her own island, workers know that these differences exist and their extent as described by the wage offer distribution function. This knowledge motivates investment in search as a means of finding an island where labor is more highly rewarded then that currently occupied.

Of course, if the conditions that determine demand on each island were permanent and workers were identical in production, then the search process, even though imperfect, would eventually produce wage rate equalization either because all workers would end up on the island where productivity is highest or, under conditions of diminishing returns to labor, migration would distribute workers across islands in the manner required to equalize marginal productivity. However, it is more realistic to suppose the productivity on each island, though persistent to some extent, changes from time to time due to changes in weather say or to changing conditions of derived demand. In such an economy, individual workers are continually moving from one sector to another in pursuit of wage gains.

At the aggregate level there are always workers who are not employed in such an economy. They are those who are currently on islands where labor productivity happens to be below the opportunity cost of working. However, the unemployed fraction reflects the search and mobility behavior of the workers. The "equilibrium" level of unemployment then depends on the characteristics of the process that generates changes in productivity on the islands, the technology by which workers receive information about alternative earning opportunities, and the motives that workers have to search. Finally, the model also implies that the workers earnings over his or her lifetime can be characterized as a well-specified stochastic process.

Let us suppose that output on each island is produced subject to constant returns using labor as the only input. Output per worker over time, productivity, is assumed to be a stochastic process $\{x(t)\}$ on each island. The productivity processes across islands are identical but independent. Specifically, the process on each is a Poisson arrival process with arrival rate α, which determines the stochastic arrival date of the next value of productivity, and a distribution $F(x)$ from which the next value is drawn. Hence, the process is Markov and F is its stationary distribution in the sense that future values of productivity conditional on the current value of the process converges to F as the future date increases independent of the current value. Furthermore, because productivity processes on other islands are identical and independent, the cross island distribution of productivity converges to F. In the sequel, we assume that the latter convergence has already taken place.

Let w denote the wage currently offered on a particular island. Given the technology and the competitive spot market assumption, w is the current productivity of labor on the island. Given the wage offered, each worker on the island must decide whether to be employed on the island now and/or whether to search for a higher wage elsewhere. For simplicity of exposition, we assume that the cost of search is the same whether employed or not but restrict the worker intensity of search choice to be either zero (no search) or one (search). Let b denote the opportunity cost of working, the output equivalent value of "leisure", and let c denote the cost of search in terms of output as before. When searching, the worker receives information about the wage and employment conditions on some other island with instantaneous probability λdt, where λ is the offer arrival rate. The alternative wage discovered is a random draw from F, the steady state distribution of wage offers across the islands. Upon the arrival of information about the wage offered on another island, the worker must simply decide whether to move to the other island or to stay on that currently occupied.[16]

Let $V(w)$ denote the worker's expected future wealth given an optimal strategy for choosing when to be employed, when to search, and when to move from one island to another where w is the wage paid on the island where the worker is currently occupied. Given the assumption that the cost of search is the same whether employed or not, the worker is currently employed if and only if the wage offered on the island, w, is at least as large as the value of leisure, b. Whether searching or not, the productivity or wage on the worker's current island may change exogenously. Given such a change, the worker re-evaluates both the decision to be employed and the decision to search. If searching, there is a possibility of an arrival of information about employment conditions on another island. This event requires a decision to move or not. Of course, all decisions are made so as to maximize the expected future stream of net income with appropriate account taken of the output equivalent value of leisure. During a short interval of length dt, an exogenous change in the wage offered on the island

---

[16] The specification outlined in this and the previous paragraph deviates from that of Lucas and Prescott (1974) in two respects. First, they allow diminishing returns to labor on each island, and, second, they assume search only while unemployed.

occupied occurs with probability $\alpha\,dt$ and the new wage is a random draw x from the distribution F. The capital gain or loss associated with this event is the expectation of the difference $V(x) - V(w)$. If searching, an alternative wage offer x, also drawn from F, arrives with probability $\lambda\,dt$ during the short future interval of time dt. In this case the worker can choose between $V(x)$, the value of occupying the alternative island, and $V(w)$. In making these comparisons, the future decision to be employed and to search on both the home island and the alternative are assumed to be made optimally.

From this discussion, it follows that the imputed interest income on the worker's wealth given the optimal employment and search strategy can be written as

$$rV(w) = \max_{s \in \{0,1\}} \left\{ \max(w, b) - cs + \lambda s \int \{ \max[V(w), V(x)] - V(w) \}\, dF(x) \right.$$
$$\left. + \alpha \int [V(x) - V(w)]\, dF(x) \right\}, \quad \text{for all } w \in X. \tag{3.31}$$

The $\max(w, h)$ is the worker's current income given the optimal current employment decision. The last two terms on the right-hand side of (3.31) are respectively the expected capital gains (or loss) associated with the arrival of information about the wage on another island and the arrival of a new wage on the worker's current island, respectively. The existence and uniqueness of an optimal search strategy is equivalent to the existence and uniqueness of the value function $V: X \rightarrow R$ that solves the functional eq. (3.31). One can verify that this condition is satisfied by showing that the mapping implicit in (3.31) satisfies Blackwell's (1965) sufficient conditions for a contraction.

It is intuitively obvious and easily demonstrated using the methods presented earlier that

$$V(w) = V(b), \quad \text{for all } w \le b \quad \text{and} \quad V'(w) \ge 0, \quad \text{for all } w \ge b. \tag{3.32}$$

Of course $V(b)$ is the worker's maximal expected wealth when not employed and $V(w)$ for wage rates greater than or equal to the value of leisure is the worker's wealth when employed at such a wage. An implication of (3.32) is that the worker will move to another island only when the wage offered on the alternative x exceeds that on the island currently occupied. Therefore, the solution to the optimal search decision as defined on the right-hand side of (3.31) is

$$s^*(w) = 1, \quad \text{if and only if } \lambda \int_w^\infty [V(z) - V(w)]\, dF(z) \ge c. \tag{3.33}$$

In other words, the worker searches, whether employed or not, if and only if the expected return given the wage currently available exceeds the cost. Since the return to search generally declines with the wage available, the optimal search rule satisfies the reservation property and the reservation wage w^* solves

$$\lambda \int_{w^*}^{\infty} [V(z) - V(w^*)] \, dF(z) = c,$$

provided that $w^* \geq b$. Since in the no search region ($w \geq w^*$), eq. (3.31) implies

$$V(z) - V(w^*) = \{\max[z, b] - \max[w^*, b]\} / (r + \alpha),$$

the search reservation wage is the unique solution to

$$\frac{\lambda}{r + \alpha} \int_{w^*}^{\infty} [z - w^*] \, dF(z) = c, \tag{3.34}$$

which exceeds b if and only if the return to search when unemployed exceeds the cost, i.e.

$$\frac{\lambda}{r + \alpha} \int_{b}^{\infty} [z - b] \, dF(z) \geq c. \tag{3.35}$$

Of course, if (3.35) is not satisfied, no one searches in the model.

Notice that the return to search is decreasing in the frequency with which productivity changes on every island, α. If differences in productivity across islands is purely transistory, which corresponds to the extreme case of $\alpha = \infty$, then there is no incentive to search.

A worker's earnings experience over time can be characterized as a Markov process $\{w(t)\}$ in this model, one defined on X the support of the wage offer distribution F. Let $P(w, t)$ denote the probability that the worker will be on an island that offers a wage less than or equal to w at some future date t. This sequence of c.d.f.s can be derived using procedures found in Feller (1957). The heuristic argument that follows yields the same result. Think of $P(w, t)$ as the fraction of an identical population of workers who are on islands that offer w or less. Since workers only move voluntarily to islands offering a higher wage, the flow of workers into the class of islands offering w or less during the next instant is the exogenous flow of workers on islands whose productivity was larger than w but fell below during the instant. It equals $\alpha \, dt \, F(w)[1 - P(w, t)]$, the product of the probability of an exogenous change in productivity on any island, the probability that the new value is less than or equal to w and the fraction of the population on islands at time t with wage in excess of w. The corresponding exogenous outflow of workers from the set of islands paying less than w is

$\alpha \, dt \, [1 - F(w)] P(w, t)$ for analogous reasons. Finally, the endogenous flow of workers leaving islands paying w or less is made up of those that are searching who obtain information about an island currently paying more than w. This flow is equal to $\lambda \, dt \, [1 - F(w)] P(w, t)$, if $w \leq w^*$, since all workers on such islands are searching, and $\lambda \, dt \, [1 - F(w)] P(w^*, t)$ otherwise, since only the fraction $P(w^*, t)$ of those on islands paying less than w are searching. Since the change in $P(w, t)$ in a time interval of length dt is simply the difference between the inflow and outflow during the interval, the instantaneous time rate of change is given by

$$dP(w, t)/dt = \alpha F(w)[1 - P(w, t)] - (\alpha + \lambda)[1 - F(w)]P(w, t),$$

$$\text{if } w \leq w^*, \quad (3.36a)$$

and

$$dP(w, t)/dt = \alpha F(w)[1 - P(w, t)] - \alpha[1 - F(w)]P(w, t)$$
$$- \lambda[1 - F(w)]P(w^*, t), \quad (3.36b)$$

otherwise.

The stationary distribution associated with this birth and death process with state space X is

$$P^*(w, w^*) = \frac{\alpha F(w)}{\alpha + \lambda[1 - F(w)]}, \quad \text{for all } w \leq w^*, \quad (3.37a)$$

and

$$P^*(w, w^*) = F(w) - (\lambda/\alpha)[1 - F(w)]P(w^*, w^*), \quad \text{for all } w \geq w^*. \quad (3.37b)$$

Of course,

$$P^*(b, w^*) = \frac{\alpha F(b)}{\alpha + \lambda[1 - F(b)]}, \quad (3.38)$$

provided that $w^* \geq b$, the steady state fraction of workers on islands with wage less than or equal to their common reservation wage, is also the steady state unemployment rate for the population.

An alternative direct method of deriving the steady state unemployment rate follows from the observation that each worker's employment experience can be viewed as a Markov chain in continuous time defined on two states, employment and non-employment. If a non-employed worker searches, then the instantaneous transition rate from unemployment to employment is $(\lambda + \alpha)[1 - F(b)]$ and the instantaneous transition rate from employment to unemployment is $\alpha F(b)$. The steady state probability of unemployment associated with such a chain is simply the latter transition rate divided by the sum of the two.

The steady state distribution of earning opportunities across a large sample of identical workers who set the common reservation wage w^* is $P^*(w, w^*)$. The c.d.f. also represents the fraction of each worker's future life when a wage opportunity less than or equal to w will be available given that the worker's reservation wage is w^*. Given the latter interpretation, the role of wage search and in particular the motive for setting the reservation wage can be clearly seen. The searching worker's earnings opportunities in the future are more favorable than the distribution of wage offers on a particular island in the future, which is F, in the sense that $P^*(w, w^*) < F(w)$. In other words, a higher wage is more probable and the degree to which it is more probable increases with the reservation wage, at least for $w > w^*$, when the worker seeks higher wage rates on the other islands.

Models of this type are called "two-state" models of worker experience because the individual worker is either employed or not at any point in time. The non-employment state is search unemployment if condition (3.35) is satisfied and non-participation if it is not. Non-trivial "three-state" extensions of this type of model are presented in the papers by Burdett et al. (1982), Flinn and Heckman (1982b), Coleman [1983], Mortensen and Neumann (1982) and Jovanovic (1983). The extension in all cases is obtained by supposing that a worker's value of leisure is subject to stochastic change over time. We illustrate the basic idea by extending the "island" model in this way along the specific lines contained in Coleman.

Assume that a worker's value of leisure is a stochastic process $\{b(t)\}$ of the now familiar type. New values arrive via a Poisson process with arrival rate β and each new value is a random draw from the stationary distribution of the process, G. The expected duration of any given value $1/\beta$ is a measure of persistence in the worker's value of leisure. The assumption motivates a non-trivial decision when not employed between search unemployment and non-participation, which is defined as the state of being neither employed nor searching. To extend the formal analysis we now need to represent the worker's maximal wealth as a function of both the current wage on the island occupied, w, and the worker's current value of leisure, b. Let $V(w, b)$ represent the function. Now, in addition to the possibility of an endogenously determined arrival of information about the wage paid on another island and an exogenous change in the wage paid on the worker's current home island, there is a possibility of an exogenous change in the worker's value of leisure. It occurs with probability $\beta \, dt$ per period of length dt and yields a new wealth $V(w, y)$, where y is a random draw from G which has support Y. Given such a change, the worker must re-evaluate both his employment and his search decision. The analogue to eq. (3.31) in the extended model is

$$rV(w,b) = \max_{s \in \{0,1\}} \Big\{ \max(w,b) - cs$$

$$+ \lambda s \int \{ \max[V(w,b), V(x,b)] - V(w,b) \} \, dF(x)$$

$$+ \alpha \int [V(x,b) - V(w,b)] \, dF(x) + \beta \int [V(w,y)$$

$$- V(w,b)] \, dG(y) \Big\}, \quad \text{for all } (w,b) \in X \times Y.$$

$$(3.39)$$

In this case,

$$V(w,b) \text{ is strictly increasing in both } w \text{ and } b \text{ everywhere,} \qquad (3.40)$$

because the worker has the option of going to work at wage w in the near future were his value of leisure to fall sufficiently even if the wage is less than the current value of leisure.

As a consequence of (3.40), wealth on an alternative island $V(x,b)$ exceed that on the worker's home island $V(w,b)$ only if the wage offer x exceeds the home island wage w. Therefore, the worker's search strategy satisfies the reservation property but the current reservation wage is a function of the worker's current value of leisure which we denote as $w^*(b)$. The solution to the optimal decision to search or not defined on the left-hand side of (3.39) implies that the contingent reservation wage equates the expected return and cost of search given the current value of leisure. Formally, it is the solution to

$$\lambda \int_{w^*(b)}^{\infty} [V(z,b) - V(w^*(b),b)] \, dF(x) = c. \qquad (3.41)$$

On the no search region $z \geq w^*(b)$, eq. (9) implies:

$$(r + \alpha + \beta)[V(z,b) - V(w^*(b),b)]$$

$$= \max(z,b) - \max(w^*(b),b) + \beta \int [V(z,y) - V(w^*(b),y)] \, dG(y).$$

$$(3.42)$$

By virtue of (3.41) and (3.42) the contingent reservation wage is independent of b

when it is greater than or equal to b since $w^*(b) \geq b$ implies that the first term on the right-hand side of (3.42) is $z - w^*(b)$ and the second term does not directly depend on b. However, when $w^*(b) < b$, then the first term is 0 for $z \leq b$ and $z - b$ otherwise on the region $z \geq b$. This fact and $V(w^*(b), y)$ increasing in its first argument imply that $w^*(b)$ is *decreasing* in b when $w^*(b) < b$. In sum, there exists a constant w^* and a strictly decreasing function $\gamma(b)$ such that

$$w^*(b) = w^*, \quad \text{for all } b \leq w^*, \tag{3.43a}$$

and

$$w^*(b) = \gamma(b) < w^*, \quad \text{for all } b > w^*. \tag{3.43b}$$

Of course, the constant w^* corresponds to the reservation wage in the "two-state" model. It is the wage at which the worker is indifferent to search given employment. The function $\gamma(b)$ determines when the worker searches given that he or she is not employed ($w < b$). If the wage is sufficiently small $w \leq \gamma(b)$, it pays to search but for wage rates on the current island satisfying $b > w > \gamma(b)$, the individual neither works nor searches. In this region, the worker waits instead for productivity on his own island to improve. The size of this region increases with the absolute value of the slope of the function $\gamma(b)$. Note that (3.41) and (3.42) imply that the magnitude of the slope increases as the frequency of change in the value of leisure β decreases. In the limit as β goes to zero, the slope tends to infinity. Of course, the limiting case is the "two-state" model studied earlier.

The analysis above allows one to partition the space of wage and value of leisure pairs, $X \times Y$, into three worker–labor force participation states – employment, unemployed-search, and non-participation. Denote these as E, U and N. Obviously, for this model these are

$$E = \{(w, b) \in X \times Y | w \geq b\}, \tag{3.44a}$$

$$U = \{(w, b) \in X \times Y | w < \min[b, \gamma(b)]\}, \tag{3.44b}$$

$$N = \{(w, b) \in X \times Y | b > w \geq \gamma(b)\}. \tag{3.44c}$$

The significance of these states is obvious. If the worker's current employment opportunity as characterized by the wage on the island occupied and current value of leisure pair lies in E, then employment is preferred. When the pair is in U, the worker chooses to search while unemployed and, when in N, the worker is neither employed nor searching.

Unfortunately, a worker's labor market experience through time cannot be characterized as a simple three-state Markov chain as was true in the two-state version because transitions to and from each of the states depend on the worker's current wage and value of leisure pair. However, it is true that the worker's optimal employment-search strategy induces a stochastic process that characterizes future time paths of the worker's earnings opportunities and values of leisure pairs which is Markov on the state space $X \times Y$. Indeed it is a two dimensional birth–death process extension of the one-dimensional process analyzed earlier. That process has a stationary distribution which depends on the search reservation wage. Using that distribution one can solve in principle for the unemployment and participation rates implied by the model as we did for the unemployment rate in the two-state version.

Jovanovic (1983) incorporates "aggregate" productivity disturbances into the two-state version. Essentially his innovation is to view the wage offered at any island as the product of a local and an aggregate productivity component

$$w = xy, \tag{3.45}$$

where the local component x is generated by a different but identical Markov process on each island and the aggregate component y is generated by a single process which is of course the same for all islands. Were one to view $\{x(t)\}$ as a continuous time jump process with arrival rate α and stationary distribution F which is the independent but identical across islands and $\{y(t)\}$ as the same process on all islands characterized by an arrival rate β and stationary distribution on G, one could easily use the apparatus constructed in this section to analyze a model along the lines that he suggests. Interestingly, one obtains a non-trivial three-state model of worker experience in this case as well because when the local component of productivity is relatively high and the aggregate component is low it pays to wait for aggregate conditions to improve rather than search when unemployed. Jovanovic interprets this third state as laid off rather than not participating with some justification. To the extent that ups and downs in the aggregate productivity component can be interpreted as business cycle variations, the model is consistent with the often observed fact that quits are procyclic and layoffs are counter-cyclic.

The models of the type reviewed in this section are theoretically primitive on the one hand and extremely difficult to empirically estimate and test on the other. Nevertheless, they offer and exemplify a framework capable of producing many suggestive hypotheses about the responses that individual's make to their ever changing work and household environment. There is much room for future research. The identification of the important factors that induce changes in the individual's decision to work and to participate is an open empirical question. Were more known about them and the processes generating changes in them, then the effects of a more realistic analysis of worker response to change and its effect on observed worker histories is possible. The second area for important research is the development of appropriate econometric techniques for estimating and testing models of this type using panel data. One of the obvious problems for estimation is unobservables. Specifically, what does the econometrician use as a measure of either the "wage available" in the case of an unemployed worker or the "current value of leisure" in the models outlined in the section? Are there ways around this problem of incomplete observation or will serious empirical work have to wait for better data?

4. Search equilibrium and the efficiency of unemployment

What does an equilibrium in the labor market look like when worker information about employment opportunities is imperfect and costly? Will an equilibrium under these conditions possess any properties of social optimality? The purpose of this section is to present answers to these questions reported since Rothschild (1973) first seriously raised them.

There are two pertinent existing branches of the literature and a third that seems to be emerging. The first is motivated by Rothschild's question, what is the source of the price dispersion that motivates search? It focuses on the equilibria of pricing games in markets where a well defined homogeneous good is exchanged populated by many price setters who take the prices set by others as given but anticipate the responses of price takers to their own offers and price takers who take the menu of offers as given but search optimally among them as though they knew not who offered which price. The questions in this branch concern conditions for the existence of price dispersion for a homogeneous good. When does the competitive "law of one price" hold? The second branch of the literature, at least its labor economics component, view the source of wage dispersion as job and match specific variations in productivity. The authors ask, are the investments in search that individual workers make socially optimal? Or, in the more provocative language that Prescott (1975) uses, is the "natural rate" of unemployment efficient? The emerging third branch deals with some of the same issues but within the implicit labor contract framework. One of the questions here is whether externalities identified in the second branch of the literature might not be internalized when employers compete by forming reputations concerning their respective wage, recruiting, and layoff policies.

The analysis presented in this section focuses on several specific examples of results found in the second literature for three reasons. First, results presented in the pricing game literature suggest that the single price assumption for a homogeneous good imposes restrictions on the search technology that are not all that severe. In short, were there no real variations in the value of the productivity of an identifiable class of workers across jobs, search theoretic ideas would contribute little to our understanding of the labor market experience of the typical individual in the class. Second, the subject of the second branch of the literature is more pertinent to the field of labor economics. Finally, the budding third branch is better discussed later as a topic for future research. Nevertheless, a short overview of the price setting literature seems appropriate as a preliminary to the main event, if for no other reason than to provide a justification for the author's design of this section.

The literature on the social efficiency of search investment begins with speculation by Phelps (1972), Tobin (1972) and others before them on the existence of congestion effects in the search process. Given the flow of opening, any unemployed individual's probability of finding one is likely to be lower the larger the stock of unemployed, they argue. These authors suggest that the unemployment rate is too high as a consequence. Hall (1972) characterizes the "reserve army" of the unemployed as a common resource which is over utilized by the host of employers that recruit from it with no regard to the impact of their behavior on the other users. In his formal version of the argument, Hall (1976) shows that the result is too little unemployment. The ideas reviewed in this section are derivative of the claim by Lucas and Prescott (1974) that their "island" model of search equilibrium is characterized by an efficient unemployment rate. In their paper and those to be reviewed, worker movements into and out of employment is explicitly specified as a stochastic process generated by an exogenous productivity process and worker search. Agents make individually optimal choices with expectations that are rational in the sense that decision-relevant future events in the economy are expected to occur with probability distributions generated by the model. The long-run outcome is characterized by a statistical balance of the flow of workers into and out of unemployment. "Equilibrium" unemployment is the corresponding steady state stock. The Lucas and Prescott claim for efficiency is the consequence of the fact that there are no external effects present in their model that have an impact on decisions that affect the steady state stock of the unemployed. Such is not the case in the other work reviewed.

Three externalities arising out of different specification assumptions within a model of the general Lucas and Prescott type are entertained. The first specification, due to Diamond (1981), is in a sense Hall's "spare tire" theory of unemployment with the roles of the common resource user and common resource now being played by the worker and vacancies, respectively. The result is analogous. Overutilization implies too few vacancies and, given a fixed number of jobs, too little unemployment. That the searching worker's probability of obtaining information about a job opening is proportional to the vacancy rate is the crucial assumption, valid when the total number of jobs is given and workers search among them at random. Since the vacancy rate declines with the number of workers employed, given a fixed number of jobs, the steady state vacancy rate and with it the welfare of a particular worker increases with the reservation wage chosen by others. Hence, all benefit if all were to raise their reservation wage rates above the equilibrium values because none takes account of the fact that his or her own acceptance decision adversely affects the probability that another will find an opening.

The second effect, pointed out by Jovanovic (1983), can be viewed as a version of musical chairs. Jovanovic imagines that worker productivities across jobs differ but are identical for different workers in the same job. Consequently, it does not matter from a social efficiency point of view who is in which job. Indeed, no one would search in a steady state once the jobs were filled if each were of infinite duration. However, under the assumption that jobs have random finite durations but each one that dies is immediately replaced by a twin somewhere else in the economy, workers who lose their jobs from time to time are motivated to set their reservation wage rates too high by the prospective distributive private gains. The equilibrium unemployment rate is too high, at least when search only by unemployed workers is assumed.

In the third specification, versions of which were formulated independently by Mortensen (1982a, 1982b) and Pissarides (1984), productivity is match specific and revealed only when worker meets job. Wage determination is viewed as a bilateral bargaining process engaged in by each potential pair as they meet. The employer's and worker's reservation wage rates, which reflect, respectively, the value of the opportunity that each has to seek an alternative trading partner, appropriately serve as the "threat or no trade" point in the negotiations. Trade takes place only when the maximum wage that the employer will pay is no less than the minimum that the worker will accept. Presumably, when a surplus exists, they agree to split the difference. But, if such is known to be the bargaining outcome for all possible future job–worker pairs, neither the searching worker nor the recruiting employer takes account of the share of the surplus that their future match mate will enjoy when allocating resources that affect the probability of the meeting. Given that only unmatched agents search at a constant intensity, workers set their reservation wage too low and employers set theirs too high. Consequently, the steady state employment rate is too high. However, if search while matched is feasible and search effort is chosen at a cost, the result is reversed because the private return to search effort is less than the public and because the equilibrium unemployment is inversely related to search effort.

4.1. Equilibrium price dispersion

The story begins with Diamond's (1971) astute observation that there can be no wage dispersion in the equilibrium of a game where employers set wage offers with knowledge of worker search strategies, workers are equally productive with certainty in every job, workers search randomly, sequentially, and without recall among the offers regarded as given, and workers face a positive cost of search. The argument is a simple one. Under these conditions, the stopping wage of every worker is less than the highest wage offer of a disperse distribution whether workers search while employed or not. Therefore, the employer offering such a wage can lower it without affecting either the acceptance decisions of potential employees or the quit decisions of existing ones. Furthermore, for the case of search by unemployed worker's only and workers who are all assumed to have the same value of leisure, which is the case that Diamond considers, the common market wage must equal that just required to induce participation, the value of leisure plus the carrying cost on the search investment required to find the first opening. This conclusion follows from the fact that were a common wage offered in the market, the workers' common reservation wage lies between the offer and the wage required for participation. Notice, however, that the equilibrium market wage is not the "competitive equilibrium" wage in general. Instead, it is the discriminating monopsony wage, that which leaves the workers no surplus, no matter what the demand conditions may be. The problem here is that it does not pay to search if only a single employer out of a host offers an alternative to the equilibrium because no worker knows where the employer is.

Diamond's contribution elicited a flurry of responses, two of the best are by Butters (1977) and Wilde (1977). As Butters observes, a deviant employer has the incentive to advertise to workers where the firm is located if the firm's marginal product of labor exceeds the Diamond equilibrium wage. He then constructs an advertising technology that randomly distributes messages containing both wage offer and location information among the workers at a cost. The result is a non-degenerate equilibrium wage offer distribution. Wilde obtains the same result without a change in the basic information transfer structure by supposing that a random number of different wage offers arrive per period. Within the period, the worker can respond to the highest. In a more recent contribution by Burdett and Judd (1983), the following general characterization is established. If workers receive no more than one offer per period in a sequential search, no recall, discrete time framework, then Diamond's result obtains. If all receive more than one with a positive probability, then a non-degenerate equilibrium wage offer distribution exists with support bounded from above by the value of marginal productivity. Finally, if all workers receive two or more offers per period with probability one, then the only equilibrium distribution is degenerate at the "competitive" wage, i.e. the value of marginal productivity. In short, little price comparison is required to guarantee that the competitive "law of one price" is valid.

Still there is an important information externality implicit in this structure. To make it explicit, suppose that each worker can choose between exactly one or two random wage quotations per period at a cost. If the marginal cost of the second quote is sufficiently small, it would be in the collective interest of all workers for all to purchase two wage quotes since then the common wage offer would equal the common productivity of all the worker's with probability one. However, this outcome is not a non-cooperative equilibrium in the game theoretic sense because when no wage dispersion exists, no individual worker has an incentive to purchase the second wage quote. In this case, Burdett and Judd (1983) establish that a Diamond equilibrium always exists and that multiple non-degenerate equilibria wage offer distributions may exist. The point here is that an individual worker benefits from the investment in search made by others because the nature of the equilibrium depends on their aggregate investment.[17]

4.2.   *Equilibrium unemployment and social efficiency*

For the purposes of forging a simple tool that can be used to illustrate when the equilibrium extent of worker search is and is not socially efficient under the different conditions considered in the literature, it is convenient to think in terms of the following variation on the island theme. In this section, the jobs on any specific island have an uncertain but finite length of life simply described by an exponential distribution with death rate δ. One might think of the distribution as that of the life times of industries, as the distribution of the lengths of time a certain occupation or trade within an industry is useful, or as simply as the random lengths of time required to get a specific job done. Although this distribution can be assumed to take a different functional form and may be in some larger sense endogenous to the economic environment, for the purpose of the illustrations contained here, generalizations of this type matter little. Next, assume that the number of islands where jobs are offered is nonetheless constant over time. Those that die on one day are replaced by others elsewhere. However, the workers on the islands that disappear must move to some other in order to find employment. The third assumption maintained throughout the section is that only unemployed workers search and they do so at a constant search intensity. It is this assumption which is common to the literature and which unfortunately implies that the extent of aggregate investment in search can be measured by the fraction of the labor force not employed. We will attempt to point out how the interpretation of results might change were a more general specification of the search technology allowed. Finally, workers do not discount the future and, therefore, care only about average lifetime net income per period. This last assumption allows one to phrase the social efficiency question in the following terms. Does the amount of search investment determined by the choices of individual workers in response to private motives maximize "steady state" net income per worker? Again, this is just a simplifying devise. However, without it one has to go through the motions of solving a rather tedious dynamic social

---

[17]An earlier demonstration of a similar result is reported in Axell (1977).

welfare problem, that of maximizing aggregate wealth, with very little return in terms of insight per word written on paper.

In our new island economy peopled by infinitely lived workers, those that are unemployed have lost their jobs for "structural" reasons. They are all seeking new locations on some other island – job or industry. As we shall see, the answer to the social efficiency question depends on the interpretation one gives to the wage offer distribution. In this section, the dispersion in wage offers is regarded as a reflection of differences in any worker's job specific productivity at every island. Ex ante, every island is identical from the worker's point of view and every worker appears identical from the employer's. Ex post, as in Jovanovic's (1979) model, a specific worker–job productivity is realized as a draw from the match specific productivity distribution, the same distribution for every worker on every island. However, the samples drawn are independent across islands. Once realized, the worker is offered employment at wage equal to the revealed productivity.

Let $F(w)$ denote the common distribution of match specific productivities or wage offers on every island that is willing to employ workers. Let b denote the common value in output terms that workers place on leisure, c the cost of search in terms of output which is born only when a worker chooses to search, and λ the offer arrival rate when searching. By assumption, offers arrive continually via a Poisson arrival process with frequency λ. A worker's search strategy then is a stopping rule $s(w)$, a function with range equal to the support of the wage offer distribution F and domain equal to either zero, stop, or unity, continue. Only unemployed workers search. Finally, a worker's search strategy maximizes average net income per period over the indefinite future, hereafter referred to as average lifetime income. That strategy will possess the reservation property, i.e. $s(w) = 0$ if and only if $w \geq w^*$. Hence, the only choice to be made is w^*, the value of the worker's reservation wage.

Let $P(w, w^*)$ denote the steady state distribution of future employment opportunities at wage less than or equal to w that the worker will face over his lifetime given that his reservation wage is w^*, where $w = 0$ corresponds to the event of being on an island whose employment opportunities have ended. Because such islands "disappear" but the location of the new islands that replace them are not known to the current occupants, the former are not sampled by searching workers while the latter are no more likely to be found than those already in existence. Under this assumption, the assumption that a worker's productivity in a given job is permanent so long as it lasts and the fact that the worker when searching migrates only to islands where he or she is more productive, the probability of employment at a wage less than or equal to w at the end of the next instant given that the worker's current offer exceeds w is simply $\delta\,dt$, the probability that the worker's current job ends during the next instant. However, if currently offered employment at a wage less than or equal to

w, the probability of employment at a wage that exceeds w at the end of the next short time interval of length dt is $\lambda\,dt\,[1 - F(w)]$ if and only if the worker is searching. Hence, the instantaneous time rate of change in $P(\cdot)$ is

$$dP(w, w^*)/dt = \delta[1 - P(w, w^*)] - \lambda[1 - F(w)]\,P[(w, w^*), \quad \text{if } w \leq w^*, \tag{4.1a}$$

and

$$dP(w, w^*)/dt = \delta[1 - P(w, w^*)] - \lambda[1 - F(w)]\,P(w^*, w^*), \quad \text{otherwise.} \tag{4.1b}$$

Because in the steady state the former probabilistic "inflow" must balance the probabilistic "outflow" by definition, the steady state distribution, given that the worker's reservation wage is w^*, associated with this birth and death process is

$$P(w, w^*) = \delta/[\delta + \lambda[1 - F(w)]], \qquad \text{if } w \leq w^*, \tag{4.2a}$$

and

$$P(w, w^*) = 1 - (\lambda/\delta)[1 - F(w)]\,P(w^*, w^*), \quad \text{otherwise.} \tag{4.2b}$$

The steady state distribution describes the fraction of the indefinite future that a worker who chooses reservation wage w^* will spend on islands where employment is possible at a wage less than or equal to any given value w. Of course, more search as signalled by a larger reservation wage implies a more favorable lifetime distribution of employment opportunities in the stochastic dominance sense, i.e. $P(w, w^*)$ is decreasing in w^* for fixed w, at least for values of $w > w^*$. The fraction of the future that the worker will spend unemployed and searching is given by $P(w^*, w^*)$, the steady state probability of being on an island where the wage is less than his or her reservation wage. Notice that if $w^* = 0$, the worker never searches, then $P(0, 0) = 0$ because eventually jobs on his island disappear.

The worker chooses the reservation wage to maximize own average lifetime income which is defined by

$$y(w^*) = (b - c)P(w^*, w^*) + \int_{w^*}^{\infty} w\,dP(w, w^*). \tag{4.3}$$

Since eq. (4.2b) implies that average lifetime income as expressed in eq. (4.3) can be rewritten as

$$y(w^*) = \left[\delta(b - c) + \lambda\int_{w^*}^{\infty} w\,dF(w)\right] \Big/ [\delta + \lambda[1 - F(w^*)]], \tag{4.4}$$

an interior solution satisfies

$$y'(w^*) = \lambda F'(w^*)[y(w^*) - w^*]/[\delta + \lambda[1 - F(w^*)]] = 0.$$

Consequently, the reservation wage is the maximal average lifetime income per period and solves

$$w^* = b - c + (\lambda/\delta)\int_{w^*}^{\infty}[w - w^*]\,\mathrm{d}F(w) \tag{4.5}$$

if and only if the worker participates $(w^* > b)$ which is equivalent to the condition

$$(\lambda/\delta)\int_{b}^{\infty}[w - b]\,\mathrm{d}F(w) > c. \tag{4.6}$$

Notice that eq. (4.5) is equivalent to the reservation wage equation in the standard model except that δ the probabilistic rate at which any job dies replaces the interest rate. It is in this model the "depreciation rate" applied to the stream of future returns attributable to current search for the next acceptable job.

The social efficiency of the private reservation wage follows by virtue of a simple argument. Since all workers are alike, $P(w, w^*)$ is not only the distribution of a worker's future life over employment opportunities, it also describes the steady state distribution of workers over employment opportunities at a point in time. Hence, the average lifetime income maximization problem is equivalent to the problem of choosing the common reservation wage of all workers to maximize average net steady state output per worker at every date. The resulting socially efficient equilibrium unemployment rate is $P(w^*, w^*)$, where w^* is that chosen privately by each worker. This conclusion would be no different were we to generalize the search technology by allowing a variable search intensity and search on the job in this particular formulation. The argument presented here follows that of Lucas and Prescott (1974), Prescott (1975), and Mortensen (1976). The different types of search externalities whose presence imply that the two problems are not equivalent are introduced in the subsequent sections.

4.3. *Vacancies as a common resource*

In the model presented above, every island was assumed to be able to hire any number of workers at their own realized match specific productivity. In other words, output is produced under constant returns to scale or, equivalently, the derived demand for labor on each island is infinitely elastic. If production were subject to diminishing returns instead, a worker arriving early deprives a later arrival of an employment opportunity at a wage that would be otherwise higher and possibly precludes the latter from a job altogether.

Said another way, suppose the number of jobs on each island at any realized productivity is given and finite, an extreme form of diminishing returns. At any moment in time some of these jobs are open or vacant, others are not. If searching workers do not know where the vacant jobs are and consequently simply search randomly among the islands, then an individual worker's return to search depends on the vacancy rate. However, the steady state vacancy rate is endogenously determined, given the fixed number of jobs assumption, by the acceptance decisions of the other searching workers. An external effect exists. The higher that others set their reservation wage, the higher the vacancy rate, and the higher is the average lifetime income for the individual in question. In short, all benefit from an increase in the common reservation wage. The first formal analysis of the consequences of this external effect is contained in Diamond (1981). The exposition that follows is based on ideas presented in that paper.

To make the point, one only needs to assume that the number of jobs is fixed on each island. Suppose, for simplicity, that there is only one per island. In the aggregate some fraction will be filled and that fraction is a constant in the steady state. Let v denote the steady state fraction of jobs that are vacant. An individual unemployed worker does not know where the vacancies are by assumption and consequently searches randomly among the islands with recognition of the fact that a visit to any one of them will yield an offer with probability v. In other words, each worker anticipates that offers will arrive at rate λv, the product of the frequency of message arrivals from other islands and the probability that the information received communicates that the island in question indeed has an opening. Under these conditions, the distribution of employment opportunities the worker faces over the future given his reservation wage w^* and the vacancy rate v is

$$P(w, w^*, v) = \delta/(\delta + \lambda v)[1 - F(w)], \quad \text{if } w \le w^*, \tag{4.7a}$$

and

$$P(w, w^*, v) = 1 - (\lambda v/\delta)[1 - F(w)] P(w^*, w^*), \quad \text{otherwise}, \tag{4.7b}$$

by virtue of the argument used to derive the eqs. of (4.2). Note that an increase in the vacancy rate, ceteris paribus, improves the distribution, i.e. $P(\cdot)$ is decreasing in v.

The worker chooses his reservation wage to maximize lifetime average income as defined in eq. (4.3) but now with the specification given in (4.7) of the lifetime distribution of employment opportunities. Hence, his choice solves

$$w^* = b - c + (\lambda v/\delta) \int_{w^*}^{\infty} [w - w^*] \, dF(x), \tag{4.8}$$

provided that the solution exceeds b, the participation condition is satisfied. Of course, the chosen w^* for an individual increases with v because an increase in the vacancy rate increases the return to search. To close the model, one may assume, with no loss of generality but considerable gain in notational simplicity, that the number of jobs in the economy is just equal to the number of workers. Hence, in a steady state the vacancy and unemployment rates are equal, i.e.

$$v = P(w^*, w^*, v) = \delta/(\delta + \lambda v [1 - F(w^*)]). \tag{4.9}$$

A search equilibrium is a reservation wage and vacancy rate pair that simultaneously satisfies eqs. (4.8) and (4.9).

Since eq. (4.9) implicitly defines the vacancy rate as an increasing function of the reservation wage, which we denote as

$$v = f(w^*), \tag{4.10}$$

where $0 < f(\cdot) \leq 1$, $f'(\cdot) > 0$, while eq. (4.8) also implies an increasing relationship between the two, the reader can verify that multiple equilibria may exist. But, of course, the important point is that no individual worker takes account of the fact that his choice of a reservation wage affects the vacancy rate that others face. A social planner recognizing this feature of the economy would choose the socially optimal reservation wage w^0 to maximize average steady state net income per worker defined as

$$y(w^0) = \left[\delta(b - c) + \lambda f(w^0) \int_{w^0}^{\infty} w \, dF(w)\right] \Big/ [\delta + \lambda f(w^0)[1 - F(w^0)]], \tag{4.11}$$

the analogue to eq. (4.4) in this case. The necessary first-order condition for an optimal social choice is

$$y'(w^0) = \lambda F'(w^0)[y(w^0) - w^0] / [\delta + \lambda f(w^0)[1 - F(w^0)]]$$
$$+ \lambda f'(w^0) \left[\int_{w^0}^{\infty} w \, dF(w)\right] \Big/ [\delta + \lambda f(w^0)[1 - F(w^0)]]$$
$$- \lambda f'(w^0)[1 - F(w^0)] y(w^0) \Big/ [\delta + \lambda f(w^0)[1 - F(w^0)]] = 0. \tag{4.12}$$

Since the first term is zero at the private choice w^*, i.e. $w^* = y(w^*)$, we have

$$y'(w^*) = \lambda f'(w^*) \int_{w^*}^{\infty} [w - w^*] \, dF(w) / [\delta + \lambda f(w^*)[1 - F(w^*)]] > 0,$$

(4.13)

i.e. a larger reservation wage than any equilibrium value will increase the average lifetime net output of all the workers. Furthermore, since the equilibrium unemployment rate is increasing in the reservation wage, it is "too small". There is not enough search unemployment in this economy because no searching worker takes account of his or her acceptance decision on the vacancy rate that others will face!

The existence of Diamond's externality depends critically on the interpretation of the information arrival process. The specific description of the process given above suggests that the worker randomly makes inquiries among the island regarding whether or not there is an opening and, if so, what the wage would be. This is the standard "search story". Suppose, instead, that the data are supplied by an information service that provides a continual flow of job listings such as the want ads of a newspaper or an employment agency. The cost of search might be interpreted as the cost of subscribing to the service. In this case, if the listing is only composed of vacant jobs and the information is up to date in the sense that the jobs listed are in fact open when the information arrives, then the externality does not exist. The results would be precisely the same as in the original model even when the number of jobs on each island is fixed, provided in the aggregate there are always vacant jobs available.[18] The argument in this section implies that this alternative information transfer mechanism is socially preferred to the random do-it-yourself sampling process, at least at the same average cost per vacant listing, because it eliminates the externality implicit in the latter process. It also suggests the need to model the process by which firms recruit and specifically how they advertise their openings. Of course, the externality reappears in a job advertising model if out of date listings circulate since the vacancy associated with a dated ad may already be filled when the worker responds to it.

4.4. Search as musical chairs

Recently, Jovanovic (1983) has suggested the possible existence of another type of search externality, one which shares features with the well-known children's

---

[18] The argument explains why the equilibrium unemployment rate is socially efficient in the original Lucas and Prescott (1974) model even though diminishing returns to labor on each island is assumed. Specifically, they assume that the flows of searching workers move to the islands where expected marginal productivity is highest.

game. In this model, the wage offer distribution function F represents the distribution of fixed productivities across a given number of jobs or islands. All workers are equally qualified to perform each of these jobs, i.e. productivity is island or job specific not match specific. In the standard perfectly competitive full information model, $1 - F(w)$ would simply constitute the market demand function in this case and the equilibrium wage and employment would be at the intersection with the supply schedule. Instead, workers are uncertain about which jobs offer which wage and jobs die at the exponential rate δ as before. Obviously, there are a limited number of jobs available associated with each wage offer; assume one per island with the aggregate number just equal to the number of participants for simplicity. Finally, to distinguish the externality that arises in this case from the Diamond's, let us suppose that unemployed workers only receive information about jobs that are in fact vacant.

The nature of the externality is already quite obvious given the assumption that the wage offered on each island is simply marginal productivity on that island. There is no social gain associated with having one worker rather than any other in a particular job but there is a private incentive on the part of each to be first in finding the highest paying job. The private incentive to search exceeds the public and there is "too much" search unemployment given the standard model where only the unemployed search.

Again, let $P(w, w^*)$ represent the lifetime distribution of employment opportunities available to a worker given search only when unemployed using the stopping wage w^*. In deriving this distribution, remember that the worker only receives information about the vacant jobs but many of these are going to be jobs that were rejected by other workers. In other words, the sample of vacancies will not be representative of the population of jobs; it will be less favorable because others have picked them over. Indeed, in the steady state each individual is looking for the new "representative" sample of islands that have been born in place of those that have just died. Because of this adverse selection process and the assumption that the worker only receives information about vacancies, we need to characterize the wage offer distribution for vacant jobs before we can derive P, the distribution of employment opportunities over an individual worker's lifetime.

Let $F_1(w, w^*)$ denote the fraction of islands where both a vacancy exists and the wage offer is less than or equal to w given that all workers use w^* as their reservation wage and let $F_2(w, w^*)$ denote its complement so that

$$F(w) \equiv F_1(w, w^*) + F_2(w, w^*), \quad \text{for all } (w, w^*). \tag{4.14}$$

Since no one accepts an offer below the common reservation wage by definition and job deaths are just matched by births in this wage category,

$$F_1(w, w^*) = F(w), \quad \text{for all } w < w^*. \tag{4.15}$$

Now, each worker is receiving information about vacant jobs at arrival rate λ and by assumption there is one unemployed worker per vacancy. These assumptions imply that the instantaneous flow of workers who are informed about any vacancy per period is λ. Hence, the product of λ and the fraction of jobs that offer a wage less than w but greater than or equal to the common reservation wage, $F_1(w, w^*) - F(w^*, w^*)$, is the instantaneous rate at which jobs in this wage category are filled. To keep the fraction $F_1(w, w^*)$ constant for every w, this inflow into the set of jobs that are filled and offer less than w must just balance the deaths of filled jobs that pay less than w since no workers quit. In short, the steady state condition requires

$$\lambda\left[F_1(w, w^*) - F_1(w^*, w^*)\right] = \delta F_2(w, w^*), \quad \text{for all } w \geq w^*.$$

Hence, by virtue of (4.14) and (4.15):

$$F_1(w, w^*) = \left[\delta F(w) + \lambda F(w^*)\right] / [\delta + \lambda], \quad \text{for all } w \geq w^*. \tag{4.16}$$

In other words, the steady state fraction is a mixture of the fraction of newly born jobs that pay less than w and the fraction of all jobs that pay less than the common reservation wage where the relative weight on the latter increases with the information arrival rate relative to the death rate. If no jobs die or information flows are instantaneous, then none of the vacancies is acceptable in the steady state.

The individual worker perceives the conditional distribution of wage offers over vacant jobs to be

$$G(w) = F_1(w, w^*) / F_1(\infty, w^*), \tag{4.17}$$

where $F_1(\infty, w^*)$ is of course the fraction of all jobs that are vacant. The individual worker's choice of reservation wage does not effect G, which is the reason for dropping w^* as an argument in the analysis of the decision problem. Indeed, a worker's lifetime distribution of employment opportunities is precisely analogous to equation (4.2) with G replacing F. Therefore, the reservation

$$w^* = b - c + (\lambda / \delta) \int_{w^*}^{\infty} [w - w^*] \, dG(w), \tag{4.18}$$

i.e. the analogue of eq. (4.5), if the worker participates ($w^* > b$). An equilibrium in this economy is a pair composed of a reservation wage w^* and a vacant job wage offer distribution G that simultaneously satisfy (4.17) and (4.18). To find an equilibrium, simply substitute for G in (4.18) from (4.17) in order to obtain the expression

$$w^* = b - c + (\lambda/\delta) \int_{w^*}^{\infty} [w - w^*] \, dF(w) / [\delta F(\infty) + \lambda F(w^*)]$$

$$= b - c + (\lambda/[\delta + \lambda F(w^*)]) \int_{w^*}^{\infty} [w - w^*] \, dF(w). \tag{4.19}$$

Hence, if all jobs compensated for lost leisure, $F(b) = 0$, workers participate under the same condition as in the original model [see eq. (4.6)]. Furthermore, the equilibrium is unique.

From each individual worker's point of view, the others pollute the set of vacant jobs by leaving those that are unacceptable. Each would benefit if the others were to increase their reservation wage leaving for him or her more acceptable vacant jobs. But, all cannot benefit by increasing their acceptance criterion. The game is a variation on musical chairs! Since $F_1(\infty)$ is both the unemployment rate and the vacancy rate and since $F_2(w)$ is the fraction of both jobs that are filled and pay less than w and workers that are employed and are paid less than w in the steady state by construction, the average income per worker per period given that all used the stopping wage w^0 is

$$y(w^0) = (b - c) F_1(\infty, w^0) + \int_{w^0}^{\infty} w \, dF_2(w, w^0)$$

$$= \left[(b - c)(\delta + \lambda F(w^0)) + \lambda \int_{w^0}^{\infty} w \, dF(w) \right] / [\delta + \lambda],$$

by virtue of eqs. (4.16) and (4.17). But, then the socially optimal reservation wage, the solution to

$$y'(w^0) = \lambda F(w^0)(b - c - w^0)/(\delta + \lambda) = 0, \tag{4.20}$$

is simply the value of leisure less the cost of search. In short, there is no social return to search other than that required to find a job that compensates for forgone leisure. The rest of the private return is motivated by distributional gains. Since $w^* > b - c$ by virtue of (4.18), the equilibrium unemployment rate,

$$P(w^*, w^*) = F(\infty, w^*) = [\delta + \lambda F(w^*)] / [\delta + \lambda], \tag{4.21}$$

is "too high".

4.5. *Wage bargaining and search*

A realistic view of the organization of the labor market suggests that every employer is an island. If so, then the assumption that the wage offer equals marginal product is questionable. In this subsection we consider the consequences of a price determination model that is different from either the pricing game literature reviewed earlier or the simple idea that every island is a Walrasian spot market.

The alternative idea expressed in papers by Mortensen (1982) and by Diamond (1982) is that price determination in a search market context might appropriately be viewed as a bilateral bargaining problem. A "market" at any date in a world where it is costly to find trading partners is typically composed of a single seller negotiating with a single buyer. Of course, each has the option of looking for an alternative, but finding one requires time and resources by construction. The option of not trading and the costs and returns of pursing that option determine for each agent a "threat" or reservation price, a minimal ask price for the seller and a maximal acceptance price for the buyer. If the latter exceeds the former, a bargain will be struck but the actual outcome is indeterminate. How the surplus is divided requires a detailed bargaining theory but is not really the concern here. Whatever the sharing rule, its nature will affect the returns to search of each individual on both sides of the market and, hence, the reservation prices that affect the outcome of every negotiation. An equilibrium for such a market populated by ex ante identical buyers and sellers whose values of exchange are uncertain for each pair until they meet is a specific bargaining outcome rule which determines how the surplus associated with each actual match is divided and an associated individually rational reservation price pair which defines the surplus for each match.

The bottom line in our context is that the wage received by any worker involved in a match is positively related to but less than the match specific productivity. Consequently, the private return to search is less than the social return which implies that there will be "too little" unemployment given the standard stopping model of search unemployment. The surplus that any subsequently met employer would receive were the worker to reject a marginal match now is ignored in the worker's reservation wage calculus. Hence, in the aggregate net output per worker increases given a marginal increase in the common worker reservation wage.

Specifically, let us return to the original model where F is viewed as a distribution of match specific productivities. Suppose further that every employer is an island and that there are no constraints on the number of jobs. However, each job dies at the exponential rate δ. The purpose of these assumptions is to abstract from the two externalities already identified by returning to the original specification but relaxing the assumption that the wage equals match specific productivity. To make the exposition even more similar, we suppose that employers do not recruit. Later we discuss the consequences of relaxing that and other restrictions.

Let x denote a particular match specific realization drawn from F. Under the assumptions, the employer is willing to pay the worker involved a wage up to the value of x since there are no constraints on the number of employees that can be hired and the match specific productivity of each worker is independent of the total number of employees by assumption. Clearly, if x is less than the worker's reservation wage, w^*, there is no bargain possible – the worker continues to search. But if the difference, $x - w^*$, is positive there is a surplus to be haggled over. Suppose that the "going" solution to these bargaining problems in the market is that workers receive the positive constant share θ of the surplus. In other words, the productivity contingent wage is determined by the bargaining outcome rule

$$w(x) = w^* + \theta(x - w^*), \quad 0 < \theta < 1, \tag{4.22}$$

where w^* is to be interpreted as the common worker reservation wage, not necessarily that of an individual worker. The justification for this assumption is that every employer knowing that all workers are identical ex ante views an attempt by any individual to claim a higher reservation wage than that of his or her fellow appropriately as a false threat. Hence, the wage offer is determined as a weighted average of the match specific realized productivity and the common reservation wage.

Equation (4.22) and the distribution of match specific productivity F induce a distribution of wage offers that the worker can expect, which we call G. Formally:

$$\begin{aligned} G(w) &= \Pr\{w(x) \le w\} = \Pr\{x \le w^* + (w - w^*)/\theta\} \\ &= F(w^* + (w - w^*)/\theta), \end{aligned} \tag{4.23}$$

where w^* is dropped as an explicit argument to make the point that no individual worker alone can affect the distribution. The reservation wage choice problem is identical to that formulated originally except that G replaces F as the wage offer distribution. Consequently, the worker reservation wage given the offer distribution is the solution to

$$w^* = b - c + (\lambda/\delta) \int_{w^*}^{\infty} [w - w^*] \, dG(w), \tag{4.24}$$

provided that the participation condition ($w^* > b$) is satisfied. An equilibrium in this model is a wage offer distribution G and a reservation wage w^* that simultaneously satisfy (4.23) and (4.24).

By substituting from (4.22) and changing the variable of integration from w to x, which is equivalent to substituting from (4.23), one finds that the equilibrium common worker reservation wage is the solution to

$$w^* = b - c + (\lambda\theta/\delta) \int_{w^*}^{\infty} [x - w^*] \, dF(x). \tag{4.25}$$

Clearly, the equilibrium reservation wage is unique for every θ and increases with it. But we have already shown in this model that the reservation wage that maximizes net output per worker, call it w^0, is the solution to (4.25) when the worker is paid marginal productivity, $\theta = 1$. Since $w^0 > w^*$ for all $\theta < 1$, there is too little unemployment in equilibrium because workers do not take account of the employer's profit equal to the employer's share of the surplus associated with any match.

When the cost of search is the same whether employed or not and search effort can be chosen by the worker subject to increasing costs, a worker's search effort s^* increases with the worker's share of any surplus, θ, and the equilibrium unemployment rate is

$$P(b, w^*) = \delta / [\delta - s^* \lambda (1 - F(b))]. \tag{4.26}$$

Because the socially optimal amount of search effort, s^0, maximizes net output per worker, s^0 exceeds s^*, the equilibrium unemployment rate is too high. The effect of the externality is to lengthen the expected duration of search in this case.

Of course, if the employer obtains a share of the match specific surplus, then there is an incentive to recruit. Allowing the employer to do so yields a two-sided search model such as those analyzed by Mortensen (1982a, 1982b) and Pissarides (1984). When both sides search, the external effect isolated here is present on both sides of the market. Just as the worker does not take account of the employer's share of the surplus in his search allocation decision, so the employer ignores the worker's share when allocating resources to recruiting. Unemployment is again too high in the simple stopping formulation and too low when both make allocations that affect the meeting rate.

4.6. Implicit labor contracts and search: A future research topic

Contributions to the theory of "reputational" competition among employers known as implicit contract theory has developed into a considerable and insightful literature in recent years. In spite of the intent of its founders, Azariadis (1975) and Baily (1974), most of the literature abstracts from the phenomena search theory is intended to explain, search unemployment and turnover. Conversely, most recent contributors to search theory have ignored the broader implications of implicit contract theory for the determination of wage policies and other job characteristics of interest to workers. It is the opinion of this author that the development of search models set in the context of an implicit contract theory of "personnel policy" determination and, conversely, the study of implicit contract formulations that use search theoretic explanations of the job finding and turnover processes are potentially very fruitful topics for future research. The purpose of this section is to briefly develop a case for this position and then to present an example that illustrates the point.

Implicit contract theory can be regarded as a formulation of the "long run" demand for labor by "reputable" employers in a changing environment characterized by an uncertain future. These are firms that expect to be in business indefinitely and consequently recognize the need to attract workers both now and in the future. Under these conditions, each has an incentive to establish and maintain "labor policies" that both current and prospective employees can depend on even in the face of changing future circumstances. These policies do not explicitly specify what the worker's wage or the probability of layoff will be at every future date. Instead, they embody the contingent rules that the employer will use to determine these variables when that future date arrives. Of course, the predominant application of this idea is the demonstration that equilibrium long run contracts can provide for the efficient sharing of risk between employers and workers, a function that is impossible for a Walrasian spot market for labor services. However, the more general point is that the exchange in the labor market is not simply a trade of labor services for a money wage at a point in time. Instead the labor market promotes the formation of viable employee–employer relationships that are expected to last for some period of time as a consequence of embodied specific capital of a variety of forms. One of those forms arises because of and others such as job-specific training are promoted by the fact that there are costs of forming and finding alternatives to the relationship for both parties. But, of course, the formation and turnover of such relationships is the subject-matter of the related theories of search and matching.

For employers to have an incentive to develop reputations, the workers must necessarily know of them. An understanding of the potential synergy obtained by combining the two approaches requires that one recognize there is no need to suppose imperfect information about policies followed by particular employers in order to find a role for search behavior. Even if perfect information prevails concerning the terms of implicit contracts, a worker at a given date is not likely to know the realized contingencies that prevail at employing firms other than the worker's own or across firms when the worker is not employed. Hence, the role of search for the worker is to find the employer whose circumstances are relatively more favorable to the worker in the short run among those who offer policies or implicit contracts that the worker in question prefers over the long run. Given this structure, competition for workers among employers is a process of setting the terms of one's contract offer to appeal to either the largest number and/or a particular type of worker. Because these ideas are not well developed in the literature, an example follows that illustrates them and their implications for the issues of interest in this paper.

Feldstein's (1976) analysis of the effects of an experience rated UI tax on layoff unemployment is a well-known example of an application of the implicit contract formulation. If UI benefits are taxed like other labor income and the tax used to finance the benefits is fully experience rated in the sense that an employer's tax payments are equal in expected value to the future UI benefits to be collected by the firm's employees, then the unemployment compensation system is neutral in the sense that layoff decisions are invariant to its parameters, say the benefit level. In a recent paper [Mortensen (1983)] I obtained a similar result when the unemployed search and when employers compete in terms of the implicit contracts they offer. The result differs from the standard search theoretic implication that an increase in the UI benefit level increase the expected duration of search whether the UI tax is fully experience rated or not.

A simple way to illustrate the argument is to suppose that each employer's "policy" specifies that any worker who arrives will be hired at some announced non-contingent wage, provided that the realized match specific productivity is above some announced critical value. The worker's decision is to search among those firms offering that policy which maximizes his or her own average lifetime income, a function of the announced wage when employed and the average duration of search implicit in the announced critical productivity value, and then go to work for the first one offering employment. Employers choose among policies which are parameterized by the critical value used to screen workers and the wage paid so as to maximize long-run profit subject to the constraint that the policy chosen yields workers an expected average net income per period no less than that offered by the competition. Finally, expected profits are zero in equilibrium, at least under conditions of constant returns to scale. One can show that the only equilibrium policies are those characterized by a critical employer acceptance productivity exactly equal to what the workers would choose were they simply offered a wage equal to their realized productivity in any match. In other words, the two models have equivalent implications for the equilibrium unemployment rate, at least in the absence of unemployment compensation.

However, given an unemployment compensation scheme in which the employer pays a tax per worker equal to the expected future unemployment benefit per worker, the level of the reservation productivity is independent of the benefit level in the implicit contract formulation but not under the assumption that the wage equals realized productivity less the average UI tax per worker. No individual worker's net wage when employed depends on his own search behavior when unemployed in the latter formulation. Instead, it depends on the average duration of unemployment of all workers which is determined by reservation wage chosen by all the others. For that reason, equilibrium unemployment generally increases with the benefit level. However, the market for implicit contracts internalizes this externality by enforcing an equilibrium with the property that the employer acts as if the UI tax paid depends on the reservation productivity chosen. Specifically, equilibrium contracts that specify a higher reservation productivity must offer a wage that is lower by the amount of the higher tax required to pay the UI benefit received by workers who choose to search among the firms offering that contract when they are unemployed.

This argument is virtually identical to one used by Ramaswami (1983) to show that Hall's congestion externality is also internalized in an implicit contract framework. One obvious question for future research is whether other apparent external effects survive such an analysis.

References

Axell, B. (1977) "Search market equilibrium", *Scandinavian Journal of Economics*, 79:20–40.
Azariadis, C. (1975) "Implicit contracts and unemployment equilibria", *Journal of Political Economy*, 83:1183–1202.
Bartel, A. P. and G. J. Borjas (1981) "Wage growth and job turnover: an empirical analysis", in: S. Rosen, ed., *Studies in labor markets*. Chicago: University of Chicago Press.
Baily, M. N. (1974) "Wages and employment under uncertain demand", *Review of Economic Studies*, 41:37–50.
Barron, J. M. (1975) "Search in the labor market and the durations of unemployment", *American Economic Review*, 65:934–942.
Bellman, R. (1957) *Dynamic programming*. Princeton, N.J.: Princeton University Press.
Benhabib, J. and C. Bull (1983) "The choice of intensity", *Journal of Political Economy*, 91:747–764.
Blackwell, D. (1965) "Discounted dynamic programming", *Annals of Mathematical Statistics*, 36:226–235.
Burdett, K. (1978) "Employee search and quits", *American Economic Review*, 68:212–220.
Burdett, K. (1978) "Search, leisure, and individual labor supply", in: S. A. Lippman and J. J. McCall, eds., *Studies in the economics of search*. New York: North-Holland.
Burdett, K. (1981) "A useful restriction on the offer distribution in job search models", in: G. Eliasson, B. Holmlund and F. P. Stafford, eds., *Studies in labor market behavior: Sweden and the United States*. Stockholm, Sweden: I.U.I. Conference Report.
Burdett, K. and K. L. Judd (1983) "Equilibrium price dispersion", *Econometrica*, 51:955–970.
Burdett, K., N. Kiefer, D. T. Mortensen and G. Neumann (1984) "Earnings, unemployment and the allocation of time over time", *Review of Economic Studies*, LI(4), no. 176.
Burdett, K. and D. T. Mortensen (1978) "Labor supply under uncertainty", in: R. G. Ehrenberg, ed., *Research in labor economics*. Greenwich, Conn.: JAI Press, vol. 2, 109–158.
Burdett, K. and D. T. Mortensen (1980) "Search layoffs, and labor market equilibrium", *Journal of Political Economy*, 88:652–672.
Butters, G. R. (1977) "Equilibrium distributions of sales and advertising prices", *Review of Economic Studies*, 44:465–491.
Chow, Y. S., H. Robbins and D. Siegmund (1971) *Great expectations: the theory of optimal stopping*. Boston, Mass.: Houghton-Mifflin Co.
Clark, K. B. and L. H. Summers (1979) "Labor market dynamics and unemployment: a reconsideration", *Brooking Papers on Economic Activity*, 1:13–72.
Clark, K. B. and L. H. Summers (1982) "Unemployment insurance and labor market transitions", in: M. N. Baily, ed., *Workers, jobs, and inflation*, Washington, D.C.: The Brookings Institution.
Classen, K. P. (1979) "Unemployment insurance and job search", in: S. A. Lippman and J. J. McCall, eds., *Studies in the economics of search*. New York: North-Holland, 191–219.
Coleman, T. S. (1983) "A dynamic model of labor supply under uncertainty", presented at the North American Summer Meeting of the Econometric Society, Northwestern University.
Danforth, J. P. (1979) "On the role of consumption and decreasing absolute risk aversion in the theory of job search", in: S. A. Lippman and J. J. McCall, eds., *Studies in the economics of search*. New York: North-Holland, 109–131.
Diamond, P. A. (1971) "A Model of price adjustment", *Journal of Economic Theory*, 3:156–168.
Diamond, P. A. (1981) "Mobility costs, frictional unemployment, and efficiency", *Journal of Political Economy*, 89:789–812.

Diamond, P. A. (1982) "Wage determination and efficiency in search equilibrium", *Review of Economic Studies*, XLIX: 217–227.

DeGroot, M. H. (1970) *Optimal statistical decisions*. New York, N.Y.: McGraw-Hill, Inc.

Ehrenberg, R. G. and R. L. Oaxaca (1976) "Unemployment insurance, duration of unemployment, and subsequent wage gain", *American Economic Review*, 66:754–766.

Felder, H. E. (1975) "Job Search: an empirical analysis of search behavior of low income workers", Research Memorandum #25, Stanford Research Institute.

Feldstein, M. S. (1976) "Temporary layoffs in the theory of unemployment", *Journal of Political Economy*, 84:937–957.

Feller, W. (1957) *An introduction to probability theory and its applications*. New York: John Wiley & Sons, Inc., vol. 1, 2nd ed.

Flinn, C. J. (1983) "Wages and job mobility of young workers", IRP Discussion Paper #728-83, University of Wisconsin-Madison.

Flinn, C. and J. J. Heckman (1983) "Are unemployment and out of the labor force behaviorally distinct labor force states?", *Journal of Labor Economics*, 1:28–42.

Flinn, C. and J. J. Heckman (1982a) "Models for the analysis of labor force dynamics", in: R. Basmann and G. Rhodes, eds., *Advances in econometrics*. Greenwich, Conn.: JAI Press.

Flinn, C. and J. J. Heckman (1982b) "New methods for analyzing structural models of labor force dynamics", *Journal of Econometrics*, 18;115–168.

Goldberger, A. S. (1980) "Abnormal selection bias", 8006 SSRI Workshop Series, University of Wisconsin, Madison, Wisconsin.

Gronau, R. (1971) "Information and frictional unemployment", *American Economic Review*, 61:290–301.

Gronau, R. (1974) "Wage comparison—a selectivity bias", *Journal of Political Economy*, 82:1119–1144.

Hall, J. R., S. A. Lippman and J. J. McCall (1979) "Expected utility maximizing job search", in: S. A. Lippman and J. J. McCall, eds., *Studies in the economics of search*. New York: North-Holland, 133–155.

Hall, R. E. (1972) "Turnover in the labor force", *Brookings Papers on Economic Activity*: 709–756.

Hall, R. E. (1979) "A theory of the natural unemployment rate and the duration of employment", *Journal of Monetary Economics*, 5:153–169.

Heckman, J. J. and G. Borjas (1980) "Does unemployment cause future unemployment? Definitions, questions and answers from a continuous time model of heterogeneity and state dependence", *Economica*, 47:247–283.

Heckman, J. J. and B. Singer (1982) "The identification problem in econometric models for duration data", in: W. Hildenbrand, ed., *Advances in Econometrics*. Cambridge, U.K.: Cambridge University Press, 39–77.

Hirshleifer, J. (1973) "Where are we in the theory of information?", *American Economic Review*, 87:31–39.

Holt, C. (1970) "Job search, Phillips wage relation, and union influence: theory and evidence", in: E. S. Phelps et al., eds., *Microeconomic economic foundations of employment and inflation theory*. New York: W. W. Norton.

Johnson, W. (1978) "A theory of job shopping", *Quarterly Journal of Economics*, 92:261–277.

Jovanovic, B. (1979a) "Job-matching and the theory of turnover", *Journal of Political Economy*, 87:972–990.

Jovanovic, B. (1979b) "Firm-specific capital and turnover", *Journal of Political Economy*, 87:1246–1260.

Jovanovic, B. (1984) "Matching, turnover and unemployment", *Journal of Political Economy*, 92:108–122.

Jovanovic, B. (1983) "Turnover unemployment and the cycle", mimeo, New York University.

Kasper, H. (1967) "The asking price of labor and the duration of unemployment", *Review of Economics and Statistics*, 49:165–172.

Kalbfleish, J. and R. Prentice (1980) *The statistical analysis of failure time data*. New York: Wiley.

Katz, A., ed. (1977) "The economics of unemployment insurance: a symposium", *Industrial and Labor Relations Review*, 30.

Kiefer, N. and G. Neumann (1979a) "An empirical job search model with a test of the constant reservation wage hypothesis", *Journal of Political Economy*, 87:69–82.

Kiefer, N. and G. Neumann (1979b) "Estimation of wage offer distributions and reservation wages", in: S. A. Lippman and J. J. McCall, eds., *Studies in the economics of search*. New York: North-Holland.

Kiefer, N. and G. Neumann (1981) "Individual effects in a nonlinear model: explicit treatment of heterogeneity in the empirical job search model", *Econometrica*, 49.

Kohn, M. G. and S. Shavell (1974) "The theory of search", *Journal of Economic Theory*, 9:93–123.

Lippman, S. A. and J. J. McCall (1976a) "The economics of job search, a survey", *Economic Inquiry*, 14:155–189 and 347–368.

Lippman, S. A. and J. J. McCall (1976b) "Job search in a dynamic economy", *Journal of Economic Theory*, 12:365–390.

Lippman, S. A. and J. J. McCall, eds. (1979) *Studies in the economics of search*. New York, N.Y.: North-Holland Publishing Company.

Lancaster, T. and S. Nickell (1980) "The analysis of reemployment probabilities for the unemployed", *Journal of the Royal Statistical Society*, Series A, 135:257–271.

Lucas, R., Jr., and E. C. Prescott (1974) "Equilibrium search and unemployment", *Journal of Economic Theory*, 7:188–209.

Lundberg, S. (1981) *Unemployment and household labor supply*, Ph.D. Dissertation, Northwestern University, Evanston, Illinois.

Marshall, R. C. (1983) "The effect of job specific human capital accumulation on wages: a censored regression approach", unpublished paper, University of Virginia.

Marston, S. T. (1976) "Employment instability and high unemployment rates", *Brookings Papers on Economic Activity*, 1:169–210.

Mattila, J. P. (1974) "Job quitting and frictional unemployment", *American Economic Review*, 64:235–240.

McCall, J. J. (1970) "Economics of information and job search", *Quarterly Journal of Economics*, 84:113–126.

Mincer, J. (1974) *Schooling, experience, and earnings*. New York: Columbia University Press.

Mincer, J. and B. Jovanovic (1981) "Labor mobility and wages", in: S. Rosen, ed., *Studies in labor markets*, NBER Conference Report. Chicago: University of Chicago Press.

Mortensen, D. T. (1970) "A theory of wage and employment dynamics", in E. S. Phelps et al., eds., *Microeconomic economic foundations of employment and inflation theory*. New York: W. W. Norton.

Mortensen, D. T. (1983) "A welfare analysis of unemployment insurance: variations on second best themes", *Carnegie-Rochester Series on Public Policy*, 19:67–98.

Mortensen, D. T. (1976) "Job matching and under imperfect information", in: O. Ashenfelter and J. Blum, eds., *Evaluating the labor market effects of social programs*. Princeton, N.J.: Princeton University Press.

Mortensen, D. T. (1970) "Job search, the duration of unemployment, and the Phillips curve", *American Economic Review*, 60:505–517.

Mortensen, D. T. (1982a) "Property rights and efficiency in mating, racing and related games", *American Economic Review*, 72:968–979.

Mortensen, D. T. (1978) "Specific capital and labor turnover", *Bell Journal of Economics*, 9:572–586.

Mortensen, D. T. (1977) "Unemployment insurance and the labor supply decision", in: A. Katz, ed., "The economics of unemployment insurance: a symposium", *Industrial and Labor Relations Review*, 30.

Mortensen, D. T. (1982b) "The matching process as a noncooperative bargaining game", in: J. J. McCall, ed., *The economics of information and uncertainty*. Chicago: NBER, University of Chicago Press.

Mortensen, D. T. and G. Neumann (1984) "Choice or chance? A structural interpretation of individual labor market histories", forthcoming in: G. Neuman and N. Westergaard-Nielsen, eds., *Labor Market Dynamics*. Heidelberg: Springer-Verlag.

Nickell, S. (1979) "Estimating the probability of leaving unemployment", *Econometrica*, 91:39–57.

Parsons, D. O. (1977) "Models of labor turnover, a theoretical and empirical survey", in: R. Ehrenberg, ed., *Research in Labor Economics*. Greenwich, Conn.: JAI Press, vol. 1, 185–225.

Phelps, E. S., et al. (1970) *Microeconomic economic foundations of employment and inflation theory.* New York, N.Y.: W. W. Norton.

Pissarides, C. A. (1984) "Search intensity, advertising, and efficiency", *Journal of Labor Economics,* 2:128–143.

Prescott, E. C. (1975) "Efficiency of the natural rate", *Journal of Political Economy,* 83:1229–1236.

Ramaswami, C. (1983) "Equilibrium unemployment and the efficient job-finding rate", *Journal of Labor Economics,* 1:177–196.

Rothschild, M. (1973) "Models of market organization with imperfect information: a survey", *Journal of Political Economy,* 81:1283–1308.

Rothschild, M. (1974) "Searching for the lowest price when the distribution of prices is unknown", *Journal of Political Economy,* 82:689–711.

Rothschild, M. (1973) "A two-armed bandit theory of pricing", *Journal of Economic Theory,* 9:185–202.

Rothschild, M. and J. Stiglitz (1970) "Increasing risk I: a definition", *Journal of Economic Theory,* 2:225–243.

Salant, S. (1977) "Search theory and duration data: a theory of sorts", *Quarterly Journal of Economics,* 39–58.

Salop, S. C. (1979) "A model of the natural rate of unemployment", *American Economic Review,* 69:117–125.

Salop, S. C. (1973) "Systematic job search and unemployment", *Review of Economic Studies,* 40:191–201.

Seater, J. J. (1977) "A unified model of consumption, labor supply and job search", *Journal of Economic Theory,* 14:349–372.

Stigler, G. J. (1961) "The economics of information", *Journal of Political Economy,* 69:213–225.

Stigler, G. J. (1962) "Information in the labor market", *Journal of Political Economy,* 70:94–104.

Toikka, R. (1976) "A Markovian model of labor market decisions by workers", *American Economic Review,* 66:821–834.

Tobin, J. (1972) "Inflation and unemployment", *American Economic Review,* 62:1–18.

Topel, R. (1983) "On layoffs and unemployment insurance", *American Economic Review,* 73:541–559.

Weiner, S. E. (1982) "A survival analysis of the adult male black/white unemployment rate differential", forthcoming in: G. Neumann and N. Westergaard-Nielsen, eds., *Labor market dynamics.* Heidelberg: Springer-Verlag.

Welch, F. (1977) "What have we learned from empirical studies of unemployment insurance?" in: A. Katz, ed., "The economics of unemployment insurance: a symposium", *Industrial and Labor Relations Review,* 30.

Wilde, L. L. (1979) "An information-theoretic approach to job quits", in S. A. Lippman and J. J. McCall, eds., *Studies in the economics of search.* New York: North-Holland.

Wilde, L. L. (1977) "Labor market equilibrium under nonsequential search", *Journal of Economic Theory,* 16:373–393.

Viscusi, W. K. (1979) "Job hazards and worker quit rates: an analysis of adaptive worker behavior", *International Economic Review,* 20–58.

Chapter 16

THE NATURAL RATE OF UNEMPLOYMENT: EXPLANATION AND POLICY

G. E. JOHNSON and P. R. G. LAYARD*

London School of Economics

1. Introduction and summary

1.1. Aim

In this chapter we deal with unemployment in the long run. We do not bother about the movement of unemployment over the cycle, but only with its average level. In other words, we are looking at what we call the "equilibrium unemployment rate", meaning the level at which the system would settle down if prices and wages were correctly foreseen. This is what Friedman (1968) called the "natural" rate, defining it as "the level that would be ground out by the Walrasian system of general equilibrium equations, provided there is embedded in them the actual structural characteristics of the labor and commodity markets, including market imperfection, stochastic variability in demands and supplies, the cost of gathering information about job vacancies and labor availabilities, the costs of mobility, and so on".

We ask two questions:

(i) What determines the average level of unemployment and its structure?
(ii) What, if anything, can be done to alter it?

1.2. Basic facts

Let us begin with some facts. Figure 16.1 shows the time path of unemployment in the United States, the United Kingdom and Europe. There is an upward trend

*We are deeply grateful for comments to K. Abraham, D. Hamermesh, O. Hart, A. Oswald, C. Pissarides, R. Solow and, above all, R. Jackman whose help and ideas are reflected in many parts of the chapter. A. Newell provided valuable research assistance. The work was partly financed by the U.K. Economic and Social Research Council.

Handbook of Labor Economics, Volume II, Edited by O. Ashenfelter and R. Layard
©Elsevier Science Publishers BV, 1986

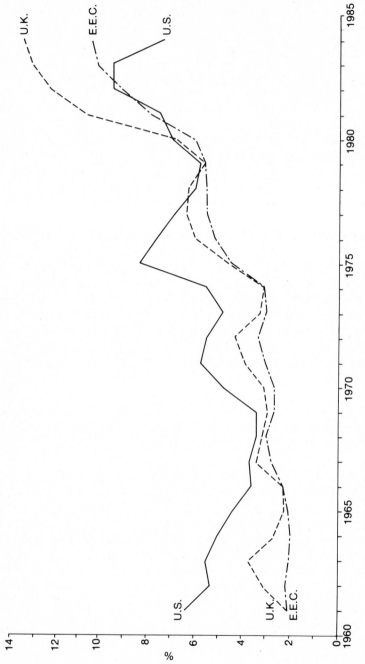

Figure 16.1. Standardized unemployment rates for United States, the United Kingdom and the European Economic Community (EEC), 1961–84 (1984 is an OECD projection). *Sources:* 1961–65: U.S. Department of Labor, Bureau of Labor Statistics (1979) *International Comparisons of Unemployment*, Table F1, p. 157. 1965–84: OECD *Economic Outlook*, July 1984, Table R12, p. 169 and Table 13, p. 43; December 1981, Table R12, p. 142.

in the United States but in Europe there has been an astonishing growth, with unemployment rising in all but one of the last 15 years. We want to throw light on this.

Equally important, we want to explain why the unemployment rates are so different for different groups of people in society. For example, unemployment rates are typically higher for young people than for older people. They are also higher for the unskilled, for blacks and for workers in certain industries (especially construction). These differences are closely related to the different rates of turnover of the different groups.

To explain unemployment we construct three main types of model. The first of these is based on supply and demand, and assumes that without government intervention these are, in the long run, equal. However, even without wage regulation there may be excess supply of labor, and involuntary unemployment may persist due to the wage-setting behavior of monopsonistic firms or of monopolistic unions, or due to bargaining between the two.[1] Thus, our second set of models has wages set by firms; and our third has wages set by unions. At each stage we look not only at the "positive" power of the models to explain unemployment but at their "normative" implications for policy. Not till the final section do we try to explain the upward drift of unemployment, with which we started. Throughout the chapter unemployment is defined as the difference between the total labor force (taken as given) and the number employed.

1.3. Model based on supply and demand

The first model is based on supply and demand. At a given wage only some fraction of the labor force really want to work. This is the effective supply of labor. If the market clears, unemployment is thus simply leisure, voluntarily chosen. If, on the other hand, the government imposes a binding minimum wage, there will be some additional involuntary unemployment.

The model yields some immediate policy insights. It shows, for example, that, if the market clears, unemployment insurance will increase unemployment, as in all our models. Thus, if we consider a rise in the replacement ratio (the ratio of unemployment benefits to net income in work), this will raise unemployment, at given wages. By contrast a rise in wages at a given replacement ratio has an uncertain, and perhaps negligible, effect. Thus, the model does quite well at explaining why high wage groups, with low replacement ratios, have low unem-

---

[1]We do not discuss the literature on implicit contracts between firms and workers which is discussed in the chapters by Parsons and Lilien/Hall. These models generally imply that there is no involuntary unemployment except of new entrants to the labor force. For a critique of these models see Stiglitz (1986).

ployment. It may also help to explain why unemployment has risen in countries where the replacement rate has risen, or benefits become less painful to acquire.

Viewed in the simplest terms, benefits and taxes reduce the efficiency of the economy. The matter is not that simple, however. If one allows for the dynamics of the labor market, one can identify some influences making for too much unemployment in the absence of taxes and benefits, and some influences making for too little unemployment. We remain agnostic on that issue, and do our welfare analysis as though benefits and taxes do create distortions which one would like to off-set. The natural weapon is an employment subsidy. But in a market-clearing model it turns out that no ordinary employment subsidy can affect the level of employment in a market, if it is financed by a tax levied in the same market. The only obvious device that might achieve this is a "marginal employment subsidy". In the short run a marginal employment subsidy (paid only on workers in excess of some non-zero level of employment) would increase employment, even if financed by a tax in the same market. But in the long run (with the real interest rate exogenous), it too would fail.

This is a somewhat gloomy conclusion. However, in practice the economy includes many labor markets, and a subsidy in one market can be financed by a tax in another. If the distortion is worse in one market (say the unskilled) than in another, then we show how a subsidy in the unskilled market, paid for by a tax in the skilled market, can improve efficiency. We also use the two-sector supply and demand model to analyze the role of government training programs. The clearest case is where there is a rigid wage in the unskilled labor market. In that case the increase in social output when a person is trained is not, as is usually assumed, the wage difference between a trained and untrained person. Instead it is the whole of the wage of the trained person, plus the (small) effects of the extra employment of the unskilled induced by the increased employment of complementary skilled labor.

1.4. Models where firms set wages

The problem with the supply and demand model is that it limits the concept of wage rigidity to the case of wages imposed by government. But wages may also be too high due to the actions of monopsonistic firms or monopolistic unions. If wages are set by economic agents rather than impersonal forces one can think of equilibrium unemployment as being determined at the level which makes agents willing to choose for themselves the same level of real wages as generally prevail, rather than trying to run ahead or fall behind.

If firms are the wage-setters, they may set wages above the level consistent with full employment either in order to retain or to attract or to motivate workers.

These considerations give rise to what Stiglitz (1986) and Yellen (1984) call "efficiency-wage" models of unemployment.

The models where firms are concerned with hiring and retaining workers explain clearly why high turnover groups have high unemployment rates. The purpose of the model based on worker motivation is to explain the unemployment increase since 1973. If worker motivation is affected by the real wages people have come to expect, this may help to explain why firms did not sufficiently reduce wages (relative to what they would otherwise have been) after the oil and productivity shocks of the 1970s.

In wage-setting models there is more scope for labor market policy than if demand equals supply. It turns out that if firms are offered a lump-sum subsidy for each worker they employ, financed by a proportional tax on the wage bill in the same market, this will increase employment. The reason is that it is now more expensive for firms to raise wages. Thus, if these models are relevant, employment could be increased by restructuring payroll taxes into a more progressive form. Another policy which can be given the same logical structure is a tax-based incomes policy. If the proceeds of an incremental wage tax are distributed as a per worker subsidy, this has exactly the same effects as a general wage tax used to finance a per worker subsidy. In an efficiency-wage model any of these schemes will increase employment. The same conclusion follows from our third set of models, which involve unions.

1.5. Models with unions

In the first of these the whole economy is unionized. Each firm has its own union, which sets wages in an atomistic fashion to maximize the welfare of its members. In doing so it is strongly influenced by the availability of jobs elsewhere in the economy. The resulting unemployment rate is higher, the less elastic the demand curve for labor in the representative industry. This is because unions will push up wages more when demand is inelastic. It is therefore easy to see why a per worker employment subsidy financed by a proportional wage-bill tax will work – it increases the elasticity of labor demand.

We next develop a model in which there is both a union sector and a non-union sector. In this model an increase in the union mark-up, or a rise in the percentage unionized will increase unemployment. In most European countries the percentage unionized has been rising, while it has fallen in the United States, and this may help to explain the faster rise of unemployment in Europe.

Finally, we examine the question of work-sharing in these models. In the union model, unemployment has to be at whatever level is necessary to stop one group of workers aiming at real wages per hour higher than the prevailing level. In this case legal variations in hours per worker will have no effect on employment. In the model where firms set wages to limit quitting, a limit on hours could even reduce employment.

1.6. Empirical analysis

Finally, we turn to empirical analysis of the equilibrium unemployment rate. First we discuss how to estimate it. The most common approach is through the Phillips-curve wage equation. The equilibrium unemployment rate is that where there is no tendency for inflation to alter nor for real wages to grow at other than their warranted rate. Using this approach, we give very rough estimates of equilibrium unemployment for a number of countries and show how these have increased in the 1970s, especially in Europe. The second approach starts from the assumption that unemployment must be at its equilibrium level unless displaced by unanticipated shocks. Unemployment is therefore regressed on shocks, and its equilibrium level is found by setting the shocks at zero. The two approaches yield similar results.

We then try to explain the secular rise in unemployment, especially in Europe. The influences considered include demographic (compositional) effects, effects of shifts in demand structure, changes in willingness to take jobs, employment protection legislation, productivity and terms of trade effects, tax effects, unions and minimum wages.

2. Some basic facts

We begin with some basic facts. A person is unemployed if he or she has no job and is looking for one. This is the definition used in the U.S. Current Population Survey, from which the regular monthly statistics are taken.[2] In some other countries the regular unemployment statistics are derived from administrative records of unemployed people registered as job-seekers at employment offices (this being usually a condition for obtaining social security).[3] But these figures can be adjusted to a "survey basis" in order to provide a series which attempts to be internationally comparable. Such figures are given in Table 16.1.

---

[2] The exact definition is that the person has no job, has taken active steps to seek for work in the last four weeks and is currently available for work. For definitions in different countries see U.S. Department of Labor, *International Comparisons of Unemployment*, 1978, Bulletin 1979.
[3] In Britain now the monthly statistics are based directly on unemployed people receiving social security.

Table 16.1
Standardized unemployment rates in seven countries.

	1969–73	1974–78	1979–83	1984 (estimate)
Canada	5.6	7.1	9.0	11.1
France	2.5	4.2	7.1	9.2
Germany	0.8	3.2	4.8	7.3
Italy	5.7	6.4	8.4	10.0
Japan	1.2	1.9	2.3	2.5
United Kingdom	3.5	5.3	9.7	13.1
United States	4.9	6.9	7.9	7.4
Major seven countries	3.4	5.0	6.6	7.5

Source: OECD, *Economic Outlook* July 1984, Table R12 (p. 163) and Table 13 (p. 43). The estimates in Table 13 have been adjusted to conform with the standardized data in Table R12.

2.1. Time series

As the table shows, unemployment has drifted steadily upwards in all countries since the 1960s, but the drift has been much more marked in Europe than in the United States or Japan. However, lest one should think of unemployment as something that has grown since the beginning of time, one should remind oneself of the extraordinarily high levels of unemployment in the inter-war years, which have still to be adequately explained. These are shown for the United States and the United Kingdom in Figures 16.2 and 16.3. These figures bring out the enormous variations which have occurred in unemployment, and the tendency for different levels of unemployment to persist for quite long periods following major shocks. In fact over the last century the variation of unemployment over the business cycle has been very small compared with the variation between cycles.[4] Another feature of the record is the strong similarity between the broad swings of unemployment in different countries.

2.2. The duration of unemployment

In order to think about unemployment it is important to know how long people remain unemployed. For consider the following two situations, both of which generate 10 percent unemployment. In the first case 10 percent of the population

---

[4] The standard deviation of the five-year moving average of unemployment in Britain from 1900–82 was 3.52. This compares with the standard deviation of actual unemployment which was 3.86.

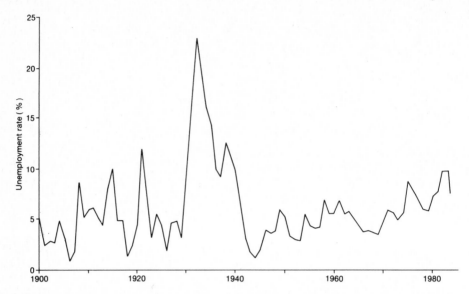

Figure 16.2. Unemployment in the United States. *Source:* 1900–50: The U.S. figures are taken from S. Lebergott, "Annual estimates of unemployment in the United States 1900–1954", in: Universities–NBER, *The Measurement and Behaviour of Unemployment*, Princeton, 1957. Lebergott's rates for 1931–43 have been adjusted for those employed on public works as in M. Darby, *Journal of Political Economy*, 1976. 1950–83: Bureau of Labor Statistics. 1984: Mid-year.

are unemployed the whole time; in the second, everybody is unemployed once a year for one-tenth of the year. The former case could hardly be explained by search unemployment, while the latter might. So what are the facts?

We begin with the basic steady-state identity:

$$\text{stock} = \text{flow} \times \text{average duration},$$

or

$$U = F\bar{d},$$

where U is the unemployment rate, F is the proportion of the labor force becoming unemployed per period and $\bar{d}$ is the average number of periods for which a spell of unemployment lasts. It is fairly obvious why this relationship holds. If all entrants had the same duration (d), then clearly the stock must equal the cohort flow per period times d, since there are d cohorts who have not yet exhausted their duration. Now suppose durations differ between individuals, with a fraction $f(d)$ of the inflow experiencing duration d. The stock at a moment

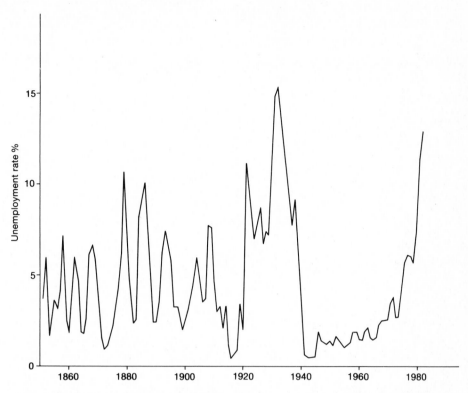

Figure 16.3. Unemployment in the United Kingdom. *Source:* To 1963: C. H. Feinstein, *National Income, Expenditure and Output of the United Kingdom 1855–1965*, Cambridge, 1972. 1963 onwards: Department of Employment Gazette. All figures are adjusted to the basis of unemployment as measured in the 1950s, 1960s and 1970s. 1984 is mid-year.

will include one period's inflow of people who have durations of one period, two periods' inflow of people who have durations of two periods and so on. Hence,

$$U = F\sum_d \mathrm{d}f(d) = F\bar{d}.$$

This is illustrated in Figure 16.4 for the case where three people become unemployed each period and $f(1) = 2/3$ and $f(2) = 1/3$.

One can therefore estimate the average duration of unemployment, by dividing the unemployment rate by the inflow rate. This is done for the United Kingdom in column (7) of Table 16.2. However, these figures are only approximate measures of the duration of all spells of unemployment beginning in a year. For the United States we present exact measures in column (3) based on a detailed

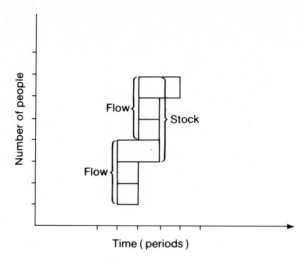

Figure 16.4. Stock = flow$\times\Sigma_d\,df(d)$, i.e. $4 = 3(1(2/3)+2(1/3))$.

study of the "survival rates" of people becoming unemployed. Focusing on 1978, durations were around 1.5 months in the United States and 4 months in Britain. In both Britain and the United States the secular rise in unemployment has been more due to a rise in duration than to a rise in the inflow.

On the basis of these figures one might be tempted to conclude that the bulk of unemployment was accounted for by quite short spells. However, in fact the impression given by the average length of all spells is totally misleading.[5] For, if there is a large number of very short spells, the average lengths of all spells can be quite short, even though most unemployment is accounted for by long spells. To see this, suppose that in a year there were 52 short spells, beginning one a week and lasting one week each, and that there was also one long spell lasting the whole year. The average length of spell would be just under 2 weeks (104/53). But one half of all unemployment would be accounted for by the spell lasting for a year, and the other half by spells lasting a week. To put the same point differently, one could look at the two people unemployed in a particular week and ask: What is their average spell length? The answer is 26.5 weeks – which gives a rather different impression of the nature of unemployment.

How does this paradox arise? The explanation is that in the first statistic (just under 2 weeks) we are including all the spells that *began* in a given time period, whereas in the second statistic (26.5 weeks) we are including every spell that was

---

[5] For discussions of this issue see Clark and Summers (1979) and Akerlof and Main (1980).

Table 16.2
Unemployment, flow and duration.

	United States				Britain (males)			
	Unemploy-ment rate (%) (1)	Flow per month (%) (2)	Average completed duration of all spells (months) (3)	Average completed duration of current spells (months) (4)	Unemploy-ment rate (%) (5)	Flow per month (%) (6)	Average completed duration of all spells (months) (7)	Average completed duration of current spells (months) (8)
1962	5.5	3.8	1.4	6.9	2.3	1.3	1.8	12.6
1963	5.7	3.8	1.5	6.5	3.1	2.0	1.5	13.5
1964	5.2	3.9	1.4	6.2	2.0	1.6	1.3	14.1
1965	4.5	3.7	1.2	5.5	1.8	1.5	1.2	13.8
1966	3.8	3.9	1.0	4.8	1.8	1.1	1.6	12.9
1967	3.8	3.3	1.2	4.1	3.1	1.5	2.0	12.7
1968	3.6	3.4	1.1	3.9	3.2	1.5	2.1	13.2
1969	3.5	3.3	1.1	3.7	3.2	1.6	2.0	19.9
1970	4.9	3.9	1.3	4.1	3.5	1.5	2.3	14.2
1971	5.9	3.7	1.6	5.3	4.5	1.7	2.6	14.2
1972	5.6	3.9	1.4	5.6	5.1	1.7	3.0	16.5
1973	4.9	3.0	1.6	4.7	3.7	1.6	2.3	17.9
1974	5.6	4.3	1.3	4.5	3.6	1.7	2.1	16.7
1975	8.5	4.0	2.1	6.6	5.2	1.6	3.3	14.5
1976	7.7	4.1	1.9	7.4	7.0	1.9	3.6	16.3
1977	7.0	4.2	1.7	6.7	7.2	1.8	3.9	18.1
1978	6.0	4.1	1.5	5.5	7.1	1.8	4.0	18.9
1979	5.8			5.0	6.5	1.4	4.8	21.3
1980	7.0			5.5	8.3	1.5	5.5	19.2
1981	7.5			6.3	13.0	1.5	8.6	18.8
1982	9.5			7.3	15.2	1.6	9.4	23.1
1983	9.5			9.2	16.0	1.7	9.4	26.5

Sources: United States: Akerlof and Main (1980). Column (2) is an estimate of inflow per month and Column (3) of the duration of spells beginning in the period. These columns are based on estimates of cohort survival rates in unemployment. Column (4) is the average uncompleted duration ×2. United Kingdom: Main (1981), Updated for 1979 onwards. To 1970 the methodology is similar to that used for the United States. From 1971 onwards it is as follows: Column (6): Average of inflow and outflow per month. Column (7): Column (5)/Column (6). Column (8): Average uncompleted duration ×2.

current (i.e. in progress) at a point in time. The second measure is bound to be higher than the first because at any particular point in time a long spell is more likely to be in progress than a short spell. This is clear from Figure 16.4. In each period the spells that *began* included one-third of long spells and two-thirds of short spells. But of the spells *current* at a point in time one-half were long and one-half were short. Since we want to understand the unemployment prevailing at a point in time, we should do much better to look at the average duration of current spells (call it $\bar{d}_{cs}$) than of all spells ($\bar{d}$). As we have said, the former exceeds the latter:

$$\bar{d} < \bar{d}_{cs}.$$

Table 16.2 gives data for the average duration of current spells in columns (4) and (8). In the United States the average duration of current spells is about four times as great as that for all spells. In Britain it was never less than a year, even in the 1960s.

Before going any further, it is helpful to introduce one other concept: the "uncompleted duration" of current spells (call it ud_{cs}). Clearly, when we observe a current spell, it is not yet complete. Thus it has two parts: the "uncompleted duration", which has already happened, and the "remaining duration", which is yet to come. If we observe a spell at all, one can see that in a steady state, taking the date of observation as a random variable, we are equally likely to observe it at any point in its length. Thus, on average we shall observe it half way through.[6] In other words, the average uncompleted duration of current spells $(\overline{ud}_{cs})$ equals one half the completed duration of current spells $(\bar{d}_{cs})$:

$$\overline{ud}_{cs} = \tfrac{1}{2}\bar{d}_{cs}.$$

Thus, while $\bar{d}_{cs}$ must exceed $\bar{d}$, there is no logical necessity that the uncompleted duration of current spells should do so. However, as Table 16.2 shows, the uncompleted durations are in fact roughly double $\bar{d}$.

Why is this? To get some insight into these relationships, we can set up as a benchmark the case where the proportion of the unemployed who leave unemployment in a period is the same (ϕ), independently of how long people have been unemployed. In this case the average duration of all spells is $1/\phi$.[7] But the expected remaining duration of unemployment must logically be the same however long the person has been unemployed. It is thus $1/\phi$. But the expected "remaining duration" equals the average "uncompleted duration" $(\overline{ud}_{cs})$, already expired. Hence, for a constant proportion ϕ

$$\overline{ud}_{cs} = \frac{1}{\phi} = \bar{d}.$$

If, as we observe, $\overline{ud}_{cs}$ exceeds $\bar{d}$, this is because on average the proportion finding jobs falls off with duration.

---

[6] For a formal demonstration see Salant (1977).

[7] The simplest proof is that the outflow must equal the probability of leaving *times* the stock: $F = \phi U$. Since $F\bar{d} = U$, $\bar{d} = 1/\phi$.

Table 16.3
Distribution of spells of unemployment: by duration, United States 1974.

	Weeks						
	Under 5	5–10	11–14	15–26	Over 26	All	Average duration
All spells							
Completed duration	63	23	6	6	2	100	$5.6(\bar{d})$
Current spells							
Completed duration	37		20	24	19	100	$19.4(\bar{d}_{cs})$
Uncompleted duration	51	23	8	11	7	100	$9.7(\overline{ud}_{cs})$

Source: Row 1: Akerlof and Main (1980, p. 886). 2: Clark and Summers (1979). 3:
Employment and Training Report of the President, 1982, Table A.35.
Note: Row 2: Figures obtained by rough interpolation.

Does this mean that for a *given* individual the probability also falls with duration? Not necessarily. For suppose that for each individual the probability of finding a job was constant but that this differs between people. If we take a sample of unemployed people, we should inevitably find that those who had been unemployed longer had on average lower probabilities of finding a job. This heterogeneity in the population would produce the illusion of "state dependence": it would give the impression that the probability of finding a job depended on how long you had been in the state of being unemployed. Heckman and Borjas (1980) and Narendranathan, Nickell and Stern (1984) have investigated whether there is true state dependence for individuals, and have found no strong evidence that it exists.

Since we have dealt so far entirely in average durations, it may be useful at this stage to look at some distributions. These are shown for 1974 in Table 16.3. The first row shows the distribution corresponding to $\bar{d}$, the second to $\bar{d}_{cs}$ and the third to $\overline{ud}_{cs}$. The remarkable fact is that in the United States in 1974, although only 3 percent of all spells lasted over 6 months, these accounted for as much as 19 percent of all the unemployment that happened.[8]

If we were to look at a more recent year of course, all these numbers would be higher. To give a wider perspective on the problem we show in Table 16.4 the duration of unemployment in a number of countries in 1979 and 1982. This shows how much shorter the duration of unemployment is in the United States and Canada than in most European countries. An obvious possible explanation of this is that benefits for the unemployed eventually run out or fall sharply in the United States and Canada while they fall off much less in Europe. But

[8] The spells that are current are the spells that "account for" unemployment. Of current spells, 19 percent were to last for over 6 months.

Table 16.4
Long-term unemployment in selected OECD countries:
percent of all current spells with the uncompleted duration shown.

	1979		1982	
	6 months and over	12 months and over	6 months and over	12 months and over
Australia	38	18	39	19
Austria	19	9	20	6
Belgium	75	58	75	59
Canada	16	4	20	5
Finland	42	19	33	11
France	55	30	67	40
Germany	40	20	46	21
Netherlands	49	27	59	32
Norway	8	N.A.	11	N.A.
Sweden	20	7	22	8
United Kingdom	40	24	55	33
United States	9	4	17	8

Source: OECD, Economic Outlook, 1983, July, Table 15, p. 46.

another partial explanation is the greater tendency of Americans to spend time out of the labor force altogether.[9] This brings us to the subject of repeated spells of unemployment.

Some individuals often re-enter unemployment soon after leaving it. Thus due to repeated spells, unemployment affects many fewer people than one might think. In the United States in 1978 only 11 percent of the population experienced unemployment,[10] although the inflow into unemployment in the year equalled 49 percent of the labor force. It is therefore interesting to look at the distribution of individuals unemployed at a point in time, not according to the duration of the current spell, but according to the amount of unemployment they will have over the 12-month period. We then find in the United States that even in high-employment 1974, 42 percent of those unemployed at any particular moment spent over one half the year unemployed.[11] We can also look at spell repetition over a longer period. The average person unemployed at a point in time during the halcyon years 1965–68 spent one-quarter of those 4 years unemployed.[12]

Thus even in the days of much lower unemployment, unemployment was largely accounted for by people who spent a considerable amount of time unemployed. Nowadays durations are even longer.

---

[9] On flows between employment, unemployment, and out of labor force see Marston (1976, 1980) and Keifer and Neumann (1981).
[10] Handbook of Labor Statistics, 1980, p. 97.
[11] Clark and Summers (1979, p. 38).
[12] Clark and Summers (1979, p. 42).

2.3. The structure of unemployment

As is well known, unemployment rates are well above average for
(i)   blacks,
(ii) young people,
(iii) the unskilled,
(iv) people in some industries, like construction, and
(v)   people in some regions.
The first three points are illustrated in Table 16.5.

Table 16.5
Unemployment by age, race and occupation, United States 1978.

	Unemployment rate (%)			Percentage of all the unemployed falling in each category		
	Men	Women	Total	Men	Women	Total
Age and race						
(i) White						
Age 16–19	12.3	14.4	13.3	26	25	25
20–24	7.6	8.3	7.9	23	22	22
25–34	3.7	5.8	4.1	21	23	22
35–44	2.5	4.5	3.3	10	13	12
45–54	2.5	3.8	3.0	10	10	10
55–64	2.6	3.0	2.8	7	5	6
65+	3.9	3.7	3.8	3	2	2
All	4.4	6.2	5.2	100	100	100
(ii) Black						
Age 16–19	34.4	38.4	36.3	28	26	27
20–24	20.0	21.3	20.6	28	28	28
25–34	8.8	11.2	10.0	22	25	23
35–44	4.9	7.6	11.9	9	12	10
45–54	5.0	5.6	5.3	8	7	7
55–64	4.4	5.1	6.0	4	3	4
65+	7.9	4.8	6.5	2	0	1
All	10.9	13.1	11.9	100	100	100
Occupation						
Professional, technical and managerial	1.8	3.5	2.5	11	12	11
Sales and clerical	3.6	5.2	4.7	9	35	22
Craft and kindred	4.6	6.0	4.7	21	2	12
Operatives	6.0	10.2	7.5	24	21	22
Service workers	6.8	7.8	7.3	13	27	20
Laborers	10.0	9.8	10.0	22	4	13
All	4.3	5.7	5.3	100	100	100

Source: U.S. Department of Labor, Bureau of Labor Statistics, *Handbook of Labor Statistics*, December 1980, Tables 31, 32, 35, 36.

Table 16.6
Stock, flow and duration of unemployment: by age.

	Unemployment rate % (1)	Flow per month % (2)	Average completed duration of all spells (months) (3)
United States (whites) 1976			
Teens	17.2	11.5	1.5
20–24	10.9	5.0	2.2
25–59	3.8	1.6	2.4
Britain 1978			
Teens	14.6	3.2	4.6
20–24	8.6	2.8	3.1
25–59	4.3	0.9	5.0

Source: United States: National Commission on Employment and Unemployment Statistics *Counting the Labor Force*, Appendix Vol. 2, p. 150, 1979. We estimate the instantaneous probability of leaving unemployment (on a monthly basis) as $\lambda = -$ the logarithm of the proportion of unemployed persons still unemployed one month later. The average duration $= 1/\lambda$. Column (2) = column (1)/column (3). United Kingdom: *Department of Employment Gazette*, Tables 2.6 and 2.15. Column (3) = column (1)/column (2).
Note: All rates are expressed as a percent of labor force.

It is natural to ask whether these differences in unemployment rates come mainly from differences in durations or in the probability of becoming unemployed. It turns out that the main difference is in the probability of becoming unemployed rather than in the duration. In other words, groups with relatively unstable job attachments have relatively high unemployment rates. Table 16.6 shows this for age-differences in unemployment rates. This stylized empirical fact has been recognized for some time [see Hall (1972) for the United States and Nickell (1980) for the United Kingdom]. It also applies to differences in unemployment by race, occupation and industry. Table 16.7 gives some figures for occupation and industry in the United Kingdom. Column (4) brings out clearly how entry into unemployment is related to the general turnover rate in the group concerned.

2.4. How people become unemployed

The final question is: How do people come to be unemployed?[13] Table 16.8 shows the position in the United States. Not many of the unemployed are there

---

[13] The available data relate to the stock of the unemployed, but there is no evidence of massive differences in the durations of unemployment for people who became unemployed for different reasons [Marston (1976, p. 191) and Layard, Piachaud and Stewart (1978, p. 80)].

Table 16.7
Male unemployment in Britain, 1978.

	Unemployment rate (1)	Flow per month (2)	Average completed duration of unemployment (months) (3)	% of workers taking up present job in last year (4)
Occupations				
Senior and intermediate non-manual	1.8	0.38	4.7	9
Junior non-manual	2.8	0.84	3.3	19
Skilled manual (including foremen)	3.9	0.84	4.7	15
Semi-skilled manual and personal service	6.2	1.30	4.8	20
Unskilled	18.7	3.50	5.4	30
Total	4.2	0.95	4.5	15
Previous industry				
Agriculture	6.2	2.3	2.7	9
Mining	6.4	0.6	10.7	4
Manufacturing	4.5	1.2	3.8	8
Construction	13.2	2.3	5.7	16
Gas, electricity & water	2.5	0.6	4.2	6
Transport	3.9	0.7	5.6	8
Distribution	4.7	1.2	3.9	12
Finance	3.2	0.3	10.7	8
Public administration	4.7	1.2	3.9	7

Source: Unemployment rate (average of figures for available months): Occupation and total: *General Household Survey*, Office of Population Censuses and Surveys, data privately supplied. Industry: Department of Employment Gazette, Table 2.9. Probability of becoming unemployed: Occupation and total: Stern (1982, Table 7), "Unemployment inflow rates for Autumn 1978", London School of Economics, Centre for Labour Economics, Discussion Paper No. 129. Industry: Stern (1982), Discussion Paper No. 129 as above. Duration: Occupation and total: Column (1)/column (2). Industry: Column (1)/column (2). Percentage of workers taking up present job in last year: Occupation and total: Office of Population Censuses and Surveys. Industry: *New Earnings Survey*, 1979, Table 167.

because they quit their previous job – job leavers account for only about 0.8 percentage points of unemployment. By contrast, people who lost their job account for a much larger portion, which fluctuates according to the state of the business cycle. It is never less than three times the number of job leavers and sometimes as high as four times that number. Job losers include people whose job disappears or who are dismissed for personal reasons, but the latter are a minority. The job may disappear either because it was temporary or because of a cut-back in regular work. The rest of the unemployed are people who were not previously in the labor force, either because they had never worked before

Table 16.8
The unemployed by reasons for unemployment: United States.

	Percentage of labor force				
	Lost last job	Left last job	Re-entered labor force	Never worked before	Total unemployed
1974	2.4	0.8	1.6	0.7	5.6
1975	4.7	0.9	2.0	0.9	8.5
1976	3.8	0.9	2.0	0.9	7.7
1977	3.2	0.9	2.0	1.0	7.1
1978	2.5	0.8	1.8	0.9	6.1
1979	2.5	0.8	1.7	0.8	5.8
1980	3.7	0.8	1.8	0.8	7.1
1981	3.9	0.8	1.9	0.9	7.6

Source: Employment and Training Report of the President, 1982, p. 202.

Table 16.9
The unemployed by reasons for unemployment: United States 1979.

	Lost last job	Left last job	Re-entered labor force	Never worked before	All unemployed
Men (20+)	64	14	19	3	100
Women (20+)	37	16	40	6	100
Young people (under 20)	21	12	29	39	100
All	43	14	30	13	100

Source: Employment and Training Report of the President, 1982, Table A-36.

Table 16.10
The unemployed by reasons for unemployment: Britain 1979.

	Lost last job	Left last job	Re-entered labor force	Never worked before	All unemployed
Men (16+)	44	38	10	8	100
Married women	10	38	47	5	100
Other women (16+)	18	37	24	21	100
All	31	38	21	10	100

Source: Office of Population Censuses and Surveys, Labour Force Survey, 1979, Series LFS No. 2. Those giving no reply or other reasons have been excluded.

Table 16.11
Unemployed by reason for leaving last job, Britain 1979.

| | Lost last job | Last job temporary | Percentage of the unemployed left due to: | | | |
			Dissatisfaction	Domestic reasons/ pregnancy/ other	Ill-health	All
Men	48	4	20	8	21	100
Women	26	7	28	30	10	100
All	40	5	23	16	17	100

Source: Office of Population Censuses and Surveys, *General Household Survey 1979.*
Note: The table relates to unemployed people who have previously worked. A tiny number who retired are included in the last column (information on retirement from the *Labour Force Survey*).

(around 0.8 points of unemployment) or because they had worked before but had dropped out of the labor force in the meantime.

This category of re-entrants was nearly a third of all the unemployed in 1979. It was rather less for men but a third for youths and 40 percent for women (see Table 16.9). It raises important difficulties in thinking about the duration of unemployment. For a high proportion of re-entrants to unemployment are in fact people who were unemployed before they left the labor force and have thus a sequence: unemployment, out of labor force, unemployment. We do not really know why they stopped looking for work for a time and were therefore classified as out of the labor force. Some writers, such as Clark and Summers (1979), have stressed that a substantial number of them say that they "want a regular job now", even though they are not looking for one. Others have stressed the weak labor force attachment of the out of work group.[14] But one should at any rate be aware of the fact that nearly a half (45 percent) of all unemployment spells end in withdrawal from the labor force rather than in a job.[15] These spells are roughly the same length as the spells that end in jobs, but the average duration of the two types of spells obviously makes it appear easier to get a job than it really is.

Turning to Britain, Table 16.10 gives information which is directly comparable with the United States. In Britain, a smaller proportion of the unemployed are people re-entering from outside the labor force. And of those who became unemployed directly after a job, almost as many have left their job as have lost it. This contrasts with the United States, where in the same year there were three

[14] Feldstein and Ellwood (1982), Flinn and Heckman (1983).
[15] Nearly half of those who withdrew said in the immediately following month that they "wanted a regular job now".

times as many losing a job as leaving it. In the tables we have been looking at we are not told how re-entrants to the labor force came to end their previous job. However, in Table 16.11 all unemployed people who have ever had a job are asked how the job ended. Again we find that over 50 percent of the time the person left the job of their own accord. But what the data bring out here is the importance of ill-health as a reason for leaving a job. If we exclude those who leave due to ill-health or whose last job was temporary, then about a third of men ended their previous job by their own choice. So did two-thirds of women.

2.5. Conclusion

The key facts we have outlined are thus as follows:

(i) Unemployment has risen steadily over the last 15 years in Europe and to a lesser extent in the United States. It was, however, higher in the Great Depression.

(ii) Most unemployment is accounted for by quite long spells of unemployment, and the concentration of unemployment is even more when one takes into account repeated spells. The majority of the population are practically never unemployed.

(iii) Unemployment is highest among groups with high job turnover – youths, blacks, the unskilled and construction workers.

(iv) In the United States at least two-third of unemployed men lost their last job. The proportion in Britain was almost half and another quarter left it through illness.

Thus, though a part of unemployment is clearly associated with search (especially among the young), a part of it can only be understood by a serious attempt to model the process of labor demand. In the models which follow demand is central, and employment is always determined by the labor demand function and the level of real wages, variously determined.[16]

3. Models based on supply and demand

3.1. The model for one type of labor

Before developing any model, we have to establish one ground rule. Throughout the paper we take the measured labor force (L) as given. We are therefore

---

[16] The same results would follow under monopoly or monopolistic competition, provided product demand elasticities are constant and capital is given.

concerned only with explaining the proportion of the measured labor force which is unemployed (U), and not with explaining the proportion of the total population who participate in the labor force. This is somewhat unsatisfactory for some types of labor, especially married women. But it may not matter much for prime age males, since in many countries nearly all of those who are not incapacitated in fact participate.

To think about different possible causes of unemployment, it is convenient to begin with a simple model of supply and demand. At a given level of real wages and real unemployment benefits a certain fraction of the labor force wants to work. This is the effective "supply of labor", which is less than the total labor force.

If wages are flexible those who want work at prevailing wages will be in work and the remainder will be "voluntarily unemployed". If wages are set above market clearing levels, some of those wanting work will not get it, and they will be "involuntary unemployed". The model thus provides us with a convenient framework for thinking about the effect of benefits upon voluntary unemployment, and the effect of administered wages upon involuntary unemployment. We shall begin in Sections 3.1–3.3 with the market-clearing case.

Before we derive the supply curve, let us first set out the overall model. We shall do it in terms of the employment rate (E), which is one minus the unemployment rate. On the supply side, the employment rate depends on the real wage (W) and other variables (ξ):

$$E = E(W, \xi). \tag{3.1}$$

This may be forward-rising or backwards-bending – a matter we shall discuss later on at some length. In Figure 16.5 we have drawn it forward-rising.

The demand curve for labor comes from the condition that the real wage equals the marginal product of labor. We assume that there is an aggregate production function with constant returns to scale, $Y = F(N, K) = Nf(k)$, where Y is output, N is employment ($= LE$), K is capital and $k = K/N$. Hence the marginal productivity condition is

$$W = F_N(LE, K). \tag{3.2}$$

In the short run, capital is given. There is a downwards-sloping demand curve for labor, as drawn in Figure 16.5. If the market clears, eqs. (3.1) and (3.2) determine E and W.

In the long run it may be better to consider the real interest rate (r) as fixed, either at the world real interest rate or by the Golden Rule – with capital adjusting. In this case we note that under constant returns to scale the marginal

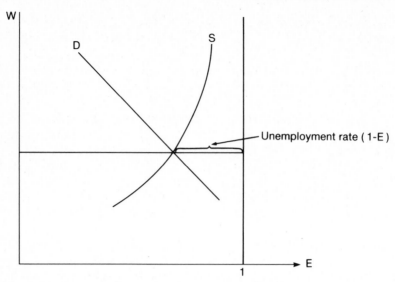

Figure 16.5. Supply and demand model of unemployment: market-clearing.

productivity conditions can be written as

$$W = f(k) - kf'(k) \tag{3.3}$$

and

$$r = f'(k). \tag{3.4}$$

If r is given, the demand price for labor is fixed by (3.3) and (3.4). Unemployment is then determined by the supply relation (3.1).

Thus, in the long run unemployment is independent of the size of the labor force. But in the short run it is interesting to ask how it would respond to a rise in the ratio of capital to the labor force (K/L). If K/L rises, this raises the demand curve in Figure 16.5.[17] Therefore higher wages raise unemployment if the supply curve is backwards-bending, and vice versa.[18]

[17]Equation (3.3) implies that W rises with K/L, for given E, since $f'' < 0$.
[18]

$$\frac{\partial \log E}{\partial \log K/L} = \frac{\alpha \varepsilon / \sigma}{1 + \alpha \varepsilon / \sigma},$$

where ε is the supply elasticity, σ the elasticity of substitution between capital and labor and α is capital's share. The stability conditions require that the denominator be positive. To derive the formula note that the elasticity of demand for labor with capital constant is σ / α (see Chapter 8 by Hamermesh in this Handbook).

Thus, the supply elasticity is a matter of some importance. In the discussion which follows we shall make two alternative assumptions about the derivation of the supply curve. In the first, all workers are identical, and they all choose to be unemployed for a given fraction of the year. In the second, individuals differ in their tastes for work, and some individuals become permanently unemployed while the others are permanently employed. As we have seen, neither of these extreme cases applies – the more concentrated is unemployment, the nearer is the second model to the truth. In any case let us see how the supply curve is derived in each of these cases.

In the first case the representative individual's utility depends on consumption and on the fraction of the year that he spends working (E). He maximizes utility given his budget constraint, and his resulting supply decision will depend on his real wage (W) and the other parameters of his budget constraint (ξ):

$$E = E(W, \xi). \tag{3.1}$$

This may be forward-rising or backward-bending depending on the strength of the substitution and income effects. If each individual chooses to be unemployed for a fraction of the year E and chooses randomly which particular weeks to be employed, the aggregate employment rate at each point in time will be E.

Alternatively, individuals may differ in their tastes for work. We can then offer an alternative derivation of the supply curve which some readers will find more acceptable. In this alternative world we no longer have everybody unemployed for some of the time; rather we have some people unemployed for all of the time. If we can get similar inferences about labor market policy from models at either extreme, we should be on the right track.

So in our alternative model we assume that people differ in their tastes for work. They can choose between working a fixed number of hours per week ($\overline{H}$) or not working at all ($H = 0$). If they work they receive an income W, and if they do not work they get Y_0. Utility (Z) depends on consumption (C) and hours of work (H), with the ith person's utility given by

$$Z_i = Z_i(C_i, H_i). \tag{3.5}$$

Hence the ith person is indifferent between work and unemployment at a reservation wage W_i^* given by

$$Z_i(W_i^*, \overline{H}) = Z_i(Y_0, 0). \tag{3.6}$$

The supply curve of workers is simply the array of workers, starting with the worker with the lowest W^* and working up. Hence, again,

$$E = E(W, \xi). \tag{3.1}$$

The supply curve *must* now be rising in W for given ξ, which was not necessarily the case in our earlier derivation of the supply curve.

3.2. *Supply distortions and employment subsidies with one type of labor*

The preceding model suggests that in the absence of taxes and benefits the equilibrium unemployment rate implied by the intersection of the demand and supply schedules in Figure 16.5 is efficient. There are, however, several distortions that may affect things. First, the government may provide a benefit to unemployed workers. The purpose of this is to compensate people for individual misfortune, but, since individuals have some control over their "fortunes", this is bound to affect the equilibrium unemployment rate. The other distortion on which we shall focus is the income tax, which also drives a wedge between the marginal product of labor and the marginal value of leisure.[19]

We can investigate the effect of these distortions, using first the model where unemployment is the annual holiday and then the model where some of the people are unemployed all of the time. We suppose that the tax takes a linear form:

$$T = W(1-U)t - X, \tag{3.7}$$

where $W(1-U)$ is earnings and X is a positive lump-sum credit, corresponding to the existence of a tax exemption on earnings up to X/t. Benefits are untaxed. Thus, in our first model the budget constraint says that consumption (C) is given by

$$C = (1-U)W(1-t) + BU + X.$$
$$= (1-U)(W(1-t) - B) + B + X. \tag{3.8}$$

The individual's choice set is depicted in Figure 16.6 and his welfare depends on consumption (C) and leisure (U).

Let us first look at the effects of benefits on unemployment. An increase in benefits (B) reduces labor supply (at given W) through an income and substitution effect, assuming leisure is normal. It thus increases unemployment. But the benefits have to be financed. If they are financed by raising the marginal tax rate t, the tax increase on its own may alter unemployment in either direction, but the total package must increase unemployment through a pure substitution effect.

---

[19] For a discussion of taxes and transfers in the supply and demand framework see Hamermesh (1982a).

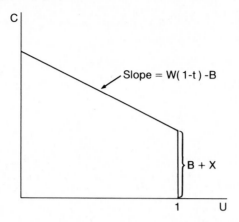

Figure 16.6. Individual budget constraint under benefits and taxes.

Likewise, if the increase in benefits is financed through a reduction in X, unemployment must again increase through a pure substitution effect.[20]

Thus, benefits reduce labor supply, at given wages. And wages may (or may not) raise labor supply, at given benefits; we shall assume they raise it. However, over time benefits and wages tend to grow together. It is therefore interesting to ask how wages affect unemployment if the replacement rate $\rho\ (=B/W(1-t))$ is constant.

To investigate this we begin by writing the budget constraint in general form as

$$C = (1-U)a_1 + a_0. \tag{3.9}$$

Then the Slutzky decomposition for labor supply implies

$$dU = -(1-U)(\varepsilon_s + \varepsilon_I)\frac{da_1}{a_1} - \frac{\varepsilon_I}{a_1}da_0, \tag{3.10}$$

where ε_s is the compensated wage elasticity of labor supply and ε_I is the income effect. Note that $-\varepsilon_I$ is the marginal propensity to spend on leisure out of unearned income $(a_1 dU/da_0)$. ε_s must be positive by the theory of consumer behaviour; ε_I may take any sign but is negative if, as is most likely, leisure is a normal good.

---

[20] We can also imagine a self-financing move to a more progressive tax structure (t up, X up). This again raises unemployment through a substitution effect.

Combining this formula with our actual budget constraint gives

$$dU = -\left((1-U)\varepsilon_s + \left(1-U-\frac{\rho}{1-\rho}\right)\varepsilon_I\right)\left(d(\log W) - \frac{dt}{1-t}\right)$$

$$+ \left((1-U)\varepsilon_s - U\varepsilon_I\right)\frac{d\rho}{1-\rho} - \frac{\varepsilon_I}{W(1-t)(1-\rho)}\,dX. \qquad (3.11)$$

Holding constant the replacement ratio, the effect of wages on unemployment is ambiguous, though it *must* be negative if $\rho \geq 0.5$. As a crude rule of thumb many economists proceed as though labor supply depended only on ρ and not at all on wages.

In the second model (with some people unemployed all the time), increases in benefits again raise unemployment, either on their own or when financed by increases in marginal tax rates (t) or reductions in X.[21] Likewise, higher wages raise employment, for given benefits. But the effect of a rise in wages holding the replacement rate constant is again uncertain.[22]

One reason why we are interested in these effects is, of course, because of their possible welfare significance. If we ignore the insurance argument for unemployment benefit, the efficient thing is to eliminate it. But this may not be desirable because of insurance and equity reasons. In consequence we are left with a distortion in the labor market. Another distortion arises from the need to finance expenditure on public goods. Is there any way in which these distortions could be eliminated? The ideal tax from an efficiency point of view is a lump-sum poll tax (negative X), but this is ruled out on equity grounds.[23]

One might therefore consider a number of other possibilities. The first is a redistribution of taxes between firms and workers. This would have no effect on unemployment, since in a competitive market it makes no difference which side of the market is taxed. The second is an employment subsidy per worker financed by a proportional payroll tax. This too would have no effect, since it would not alter the marginal cost of labor (at given W). For the marginal cost of labor $W(1+q) - h$, where h is the subsidy per worker and q the employment tax rate. If the scheme is self-financing, $NWq - Nh = 0$. So the marginal cost of labor is

---

[21] But a move to a more progressive tax does not affect unemployment so long as benefits are untaxed, since it leaves the average net income of workers unchanged.

[22] For this purpose we have to define the replacement rate as $\rho = B/(W(1-t) + X)$ since the unemployed are unemployed all the time and fall altogether outside the tax system. Thus unemployment rises when W rises if for the marginal worker

$$\frac{\partial}{dW_i}\left[Z_i\left(W_i(1-t) + X, \overline{H}\right) - Z_i\left(\rho\left(W_i(1-t) + X\right), 0\right)\right] > 0.$$

[23] For a full discussion of lump-sum taxation see Atkinson and Stiglitz (1980, Ch. 11).

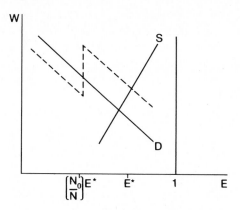

Figure 16.7. A marginal employment subsidy.

unchanged at W. This happens because the marginal cost equals the average cost, which is by definition constant under any self-financing scheme.

So is there any way of reducing the marginal cost of labor while keeping the average cost constant? This is a standard public finance question, to which one standard answer is a two-part tariff. Applied to the labor market, this is known as a marginal employment subsidy. Here a subsidy is paid out for all workers employed, but only for workers above some number N_0. This subsidy in turn is financed by a tax on all workers. Suppose, for simplicity, that the subsidy and tax are both paid on a per worker basis (rather than ad valorem), m being the marginal subsidy and a being the tax. If the scheme is self-financing,

$$m(N - N_0) = aN. \tag{3.12}$$

Hence $a = m(1 - N_0/N)$. For example, if N_0 were 90 percent of N, so that the subsidy were paid only on the last 10 percent of workers, then the marginal subsidy would equal ten times the average tax. As a result, the marginal cost of labor would fall from W to $W - m + a = W - m(N_0/N)$. In the example given, the cost of labor is $W - 0.9m$. In the short run, with capital fixed, this would shift the demand curve to the dotted line illustrated in Figure 16.7. This would tend to offset the distortions arising from the wedge between the marginal product of labor and the marginal value of leisure. If the supply curve is rising, employment will increase.[24]

---

[24](i) One practicable way of operating a marginal employment subsidy is to make N_0 some fraction ϕ of last period's employment. In this case the effective rate of subsidy per worker is $m(\phi\delta + 1 - \phi)$ where δ is the firm's discount rate. If ϕ was approximately unity, the effective subsidy would be δm. To derive this formula, note that, if the wage is constant, the firm maximizes

$$PV = \sum_t [f(N_t) - WN_t + m(N_t - \phi N_{t-1})](1 - \delta)^t.$$

In the long run (with r fixed) the subsidy will tend to lower the wage and will thus do nothing to offset the distortions arising from existing benefits and taxes. Assuming the supply curve is rising, employment will therefore tend to fall.[25] Our conclusion is thus, that in the short run the only labor tax–subsidy scheme that can offset distortions is a marginal employment subsidy, but in the long run no such scheme can offset them.

This requires

$$\partial PV/\partial N_t = (f' - (W - m))(1 - \delta)^t - m\phi(1 - \delta)^{t+1} = 0$$

or

$$f' = W - m(\phi\delta + 1 - \phi).$$

(ii) The subsidy should be set low enough to ensure that the real wage which equated the supply price of labor to the new schedule of demand prices was low enough to ensure positive profit.

(iii) For discussions of marginal employment subsidies, mainly in a more short-run context, see Bishop (1981), Fethke, Policano and Williamson (1978), Layard and Nickell (1980), and OECD (1982).

[25] To see this, we can write the marginal productivity condition as

$$f(k) - kf'(k) = W - m\frac{N_0}{N}.$$

If we allow N_0/N to be a policy variable (θ) we should consider the effective subsidy to be higher the higher θ, since

$$f(k) - kf'(k) = W - m\theta. \tag{1}$$

The other long-run equilibrium condition is the condition of zero profit:

$$f(k) - rk - W = 0. \tag{2}$$

Combining (1) and (2), we have

$$k(f'(k) - r) = m\theta. \tag{3}$$

It follows from (2) and (3) that

$$\frac{dW}{dk} = f'(k) - r = \frac{m\theta}{k} > 0,$$

while from (3)

$$\frac{dk}{d(m\theta)} = 1 \bigg/ \left(kf'' + \frac{m\theta}{k} \right),$$

which is negative for small $m\theta$. Thus, for small (but not zero) $m\theta$, the effect of the subsidy on wages is negative, since

$$\frac{dW}{d(m\theta)} = \frac{dW}{dk} \cdot \frac{dk}{d(m\theta)} < 0.$$

However, this conclusion only holds when we are considering a single labor market, with any scheme self-financing within that market. If we allow for more than one market and use taxes on one group of workers to finance subsidies for another group, we shall find that an appropriate policy can indeed improve the efficiency of the economy. We therefore turn to the case of heterogeneous labor.

3.3. Supply distortions and employment subsidies with many types of labor

In this section we shall show how if there are two types of labor which differ in their labor supply elasticities or in the distortions in their markets, then a simple scheme of taxing one type of labor to subsidize the other will improve the efficiency of the economy. We deal, as before, with the case where wages are flexible.

Assume that aggregate output depends on inputs of two different types of labor (say, the unskilled, the 1's, and the skilled, the 2's) and on capital, according to the linear homogeneous production function

$$Y = G\big(F(N_1, N_2), K \big), \tag{3.13}$$

where F is a constant returns function of N_1 aned N_2. G is written in separable form, i.e. a change in the stock of capital has no impact on the rate of substitution between the two types of labor. (This assumption has no substantive impact on the results that follow; it is extremely convenient for purposes of exposition.) We assume that the capital stock is always in long-run equilibrium in the sense used above, so $G_K = r$, the fixed real interest rate, at all times. This implies that the ratio K/F is fixed and, hence, that $\partial G/\partial F$ is fixed. We choose units such that $\partial G/\partial F = 1$. Thus, the value of labor services will be

$$\frac{\partial G}{\partial F} F(N_1, N_2) = F(N_1, N_2) = N_2 f(N_1/N_2). \tag{3.14}$$

The next step is to determine the two employment levels. The supply condition for each group is given by

$$N_j = E_j\big(W_j(1 - t), \rho_j, X \big) L_j, \quad j = 1, 2, \tag{3.15}$$

where the E_j function was developed above.

We also have the marginal productivity conditions

$$W_1 = f'\left(\frac{N_1}{N_2} \right) \tag{3.16}$$

and

$$W_2 = f\left(\frac{N_1}{N_2}\right) - \frac{N_1}{N_2} f'\left(\frac{N_1}{N_2}\right).$$
(3.17)

We thus have four equations to determine the two employment and wage levels as functions of the tax and transfer parameters, ρ_1, ρ_2, t, and X, and the populations of the two groups, L_1 and L_2. Since the government budget must be in balance, a fifth equation determines any one of the tax and transfer parameters.

We can now ask if there is any way in which labor market policy can improve matters if there are distortions due to these taxes and benefits. The answer is that it can, provided that it is properly *targeted*. Both subsidies (to workers or employers) and preferential public employment can generally increase the efficiency of the economy.[26]

To make our fundamental point as directly as possible, let us simplify the model somewhat. Assume that skilled workers, the 2's, have an inelastic labor supply function[27] and that they pay all the expenses of government through a proportional tax on their incomes. The benefit level for unskilled workers is fixed in real terms at B_1, which, since they pay no taxes, means that $\rho_1 = B_1/W_1$. We shall attempt to undo this distortion by having the government pay firms a subsidy of sW_1 per unskilled employee.

What level of subsidy would be efficient, in the sense of maximizing the value of the national output plus the value of leisure? The maximand is social welfare (Ω), given by[28]

$$\Omega = F(N_1, N_2) - C_1(N_1) - C_2(N_2),$$
(3.18)

where $C_1(N_1)$ is the cost of the leisure foregone by the ith group of workers. Thus, the optimal unemployment rate of unskilled workers is given by

$$\frac{\partial \Omega}{\partial N_1} = F_1 - C_1' = 0.$$
(3.19)

But if supply and demand for unskilled workers are in balance, the wage they receive will equal the marginal cost of working, in terms of leisure and benefits

---

[26] For a fuller treatment of the issues in this section see Johnson (1980) and Jackman and Layard (1980). These papers built on the work of Baily and Tobin (1977).

[27] To be completely rigorous, we need to assume that $\varepsilon_{s2} = \varepsilon_{12} = 0$.

[28] C_i should strictly depend on income as well as leisure, but for our purpose this does not matter as we shall only use the term C_i' and then substitute it out.

foregone $(C_1' + B_1)$:

$$W_1 = C_1' + B_1. \tag{3.20}$$

In addition, firms will equate the marginal product of unskilled workers to their net wage:

$$F_1 = W_1(1 - s). \tag{3.21}$$

Hence, from (3.19)–(3.21) the optimal s is given by

$$s = \frac{B_1}{W_1} = \rho_1 \tag{3.22}$$

Thus, the optimal subsidy is exactly equal to the replacement rate. By following this rule we shall completely offset the distortion and return the economy to a first-best efficient position.

However this possibility of a first-best solution depends on the assumption that the skilled workers have a completely inelastic supply response, so that taxing them to finance the subsidy on the unskilled workers introduces no new distortions. If skilled workers also respond, we have to set the efficiency loss from taxing them against the reduced distortion affecting the unskilled. Even so, provided the skilled are not very responsive, there is bound to be a gain from some level of subsidy on the unskilled.

To show this, we shall assume, for greater generality, that both the unskilled and the skilled receive benefits if unemployed (B_1 and B_2, respectively). In addition both groups pay a proportional income tax at rate t. We now introduce a small employer subsidy at rate s on the unskilled, financed by an employer tax at rate q levied on the skilled. The change in social welfare is given by

$$d\Omega = (F_1 - C_1')dN_1 + (F_2 - C_2')dN_2. \tag{3.23}$$

But the private choices of workers will set C_i' equal to the net return to work, $W_i(1 - t) - B_i$. And the choices of firms will (in the neighborhood of $s = q = 0$) set $W_i = F_i$. Hence,

$$d\Omega = (t_1W_1 + B_1)dN_1 + (t_2W_2 + B_2)dN_2. \tag{3.24}$$

The question is: Under what conditions is this positive?

The supply elasticity of each group (ε_i) is given by[29]

$$dN_i = N_i\varepsilon_i d\log W_i. \tag{3.25}$$

---

[29]Strictly $dN_i = N_i\varepsilon_i(d\log W_i + d\log(1 - t))$. However, we show in a later footnote that if the conditions exist for $d\Omega > 0$ with t constant, then in fact t can be reduced, further increasing welfare.

If we now subsidize the 1's and tax the 2's, W_1 will rise and W_2 fall and we need to know the relationship between these two changes. This is given by the factor-price-frontier equation,[30] which implies that for small q and s

$$W_1 N_1 (\mathrm{d}\log W_1 - \mathrm{d}s) + W_2 N_2 (\mathrm{d}\log W_2 + \mathrm{d}q) = 0. \tag{3.26}$$

But if the subsidy (s) is wholly financed by the tax (q) and both s and q are small

$$W_1 N_1 \, \mathrm{d}s = W_2 N_2 \, \mathrm{d}q, \tag{3.27}$$

so that

$$W_1 N_1 \, \mathrm{d}\log W_1 + W_2 N_2 \, \mathrm{d}\log W_2 = 0. \tag{3.28}$$

Hence using (3.24), (3.25) and (3.28), we can write the change in social welfare as a function of $\mathrm{d}\log W_1$, thus:

$$d\Omega = \left(\frac{tW_1 + B_1}{W_1} \varepsilon_1 - \frac{tW_2 + B_2}{W_2} \varepsilon_2 \right) W_1 N_1 \, \mathrm{d}\log W_1. \tag{3.29}$$

Since a subsidy will raise W_1, making $\mathrm{d}\log W_1 > 0$, the change in social welfare will be positive if

$$\left(t + \frac{B_1}{W_1} \right) \varepsilon_1 > \left(t + \frac{B_2}{W_2} \right) \varepsilon_2. \tag{3.30}$$

There is evidence that groups with high replacement rates tend to have high elasticities of supply, and they also have the high unemployment rates. (This can easily be checked for a Cobb–Douglas utility function.)[31] So if we subsidize these

---

[30] See Chapter 8 by Hamermesh in this Handbook.

[31] Suppose utility is given by

$$Z = \alpha \log C + (1 - \alpha)\log(\gamma - E)$$

$$= \alpha \log[(W(1 - t) - B)E + B] + (1 - \alpha)\log(\gamma - E),$$

$$\frac{\partial Z}{\partial E} = \frac{\alpha(W(1 - t) - B)}{(W(1 - t) - B)E + B} - \frac{1 - \alpha}{\gamma - E} = 0.$$

Hence,

$$E = \alpha\gamma - (1 - \alpha)\frac{\rho}{1 - \rho}, \quad \text{where } \rho = B/W(1 - t),$$

and

$$E \cong \frac{\mathrm{d}E}{\mathrm{d}\log W} = \frac{\mathrm{d}E}{\mathrm{d}\log \rho} = -\frac{(1 - \alpha)\rho}{(1 - \rho)^2}.$$

high unemployment groups, we can improve social welfare. The gain from stimulating their work effort will exceed the losses from the discouragement of the more skilled group.[32]

Notice that there can be no question of subsidizing everybody. For if we gave employers a proportional subsidy at rate s for all workers, financed by a proportional tax on all workers at rate q paid by employers, this would alter nothing. For the cost of the ith type of labor would become $W_i(1 - s + q)$. But if the scheme is self-financing $s = q$. Suppose now that the tax which finances the subsidy is levied on workers rather than firms. This also makes no difference, since in a competitive market the real effect of a tax is the same whether it is levied on buyers or sellers.[33] Thus, in a market that is in equilibrium, targeting is essential for an effective subsidy policy.

---

[32] It remains to check whether income taxes change as a result of the scheme. The budget surplus is given by

$$\Phi = tW_1N_1 - B_1(L_1 - N_1) + tW_2N_2 - B_2(L_2 - N_2).$$

(This omits the employment tax and subsidy which we have already assumed to balance.) Hence, budget balance requires

$$d\Phi = (tW_1 + B_1)dN_1 + (tW_2 + B_2)dN_2 + (W_1N_1 + W_2N_2)dt = 0. \tag{1}$$

But eq. (3.24) gives the condition for social welfare to increase. It follows that, if this condition is satisfied and thus the first two terms in eq. (1) above are positive, we can in fact cut taxes (t), which will further increase social welfare.

[33] To check this in our specific case, we can write the system in simplified form as follows, where $R = W_2/W_1$. First there are the marginal productivity conditions:

$$(1 - s)W_1 = F_1(N_1, N_2),$$
$$(1 - s)W_1R = F_2(N_1, N_2).$$

Then there are the supply conditions:

$$N_1 = N_1(W_1(1 - t)),$$
$$N_2 = N_2(W_1R(1 - t)).$$

And then there is budget balance, where G is expenditure on public goods:

$$(t - s)W_1(N_1 + RN_2) = G.$$

This can be written as

$$(-W_1(1 - t) + W_1(1 - s))(N_1 + RN_2) = G,$$

which gives us five equations in N_1, N_2, $(1 - s)W_1$, $(1 - t)W_1$ and R. If $(1 - s)$ changes, W_1 changes by an equal and opposite proportion and $(1 - t)$ changes by the same proportion.

The same conclusions apply in relation to public employment. Let us assume (to avoid controversy) that the level of government output is fixed and the only issue is how it is to be produced. If government agencies are instructed to minimize the monetary costs of their production, then we simply provide them the same subsidies for employment of the target group that apply in the private sector [see Johnson and Layard (1982)]. If, on the other hand, government agencies are not subsidized or taxed but are instructed to use shadow prices in determining the composition of their employment, then these shadow prices should equal the cost of each type of labor to private sector firms.

3.4. Rigid wages and employment subsidies

A second form of distortion is the case in which the real wage of the unskilled is fixed by law above its market clearing level. This corresponds in the United States to a single minimum wage rate established by law under the Fair Labor Standards Act, and in Britain to the separate occupational wage scales determined by the statutory Wages Councils for certain low-skilled workers. We will represent minimum wages in the context of our model by assuming that the real wage of unskilled workers, W_1, is fixed. [There is some empirical justification for assuming that W_1 is fixed relative to W_2 [Welch (1976)], but the exposition is clearer with W_1 fixed.][34]

Minimum wages are, in a sense, a form of labor market policy. They do affect both the efficiency of and the distribution of welfare in the economy. Consider a variant of the social welfare function (3.18):

$$\Omega = W_1 N_1 - C_1(N_1) + (1 - \omega)(W_2 N_2 - C_2(N_2)), \quad \omega < 1, \tag{3.31}$$

where $C(N_i)$ is the value of forgone leisure. Here social welfare is measured in units of poor people's income. If policy-makers put a greater weight on the income of the unskilled, $\omega > 0$; equal weights imply $\omega = 0$. Taxes and transfers are assumed to equal zero for simplicity. The change in social welfare with respect to W_1 is[35]

$$\frac{d\Omega}{dW_1} = N_1 \left(\omega - \frac{W_1 - C_1'}{W_1} \eta \right), \tag{3.32}$$

where η is the elasticity of demand for unskilled workers. For $\omega = 0$, the case

---

[34] For evidence that wage rigidity has been important mainly in the labor market for black youths, see Johnson and Blakemore (1979).

[35] This follows since $W_2 - C_2' = 0$ and $N_2(dW_2/dW_1) = -N_1$.

where policy-makers are interested solely in efficiency, W_1 is set where the supply and demand functions intersect – which is to say that no minimum is set. For $\omega > 0$, however, there is an overall gain associated with fixing W_1 at some point above its value in competitive equilibrium. It should be pointed out, of course, that there are other instruments of redistribution as well, and wages policy should optimally be chosen at the same time as these other instruments are. This procedure may or may not imply legal minimum wage levels.[36]

Since minimum wages exist in some countries, one can ask if there are any policies that can overcome their implied efficiency cost. Consider an employment subsidy for group 1 workers, financed by a tax on group 2 workers. Assume also that the supply of the latter is fixed. This obviously benefits the unskilled, but the political chances of its being adopted are obviously much higher if it makes skilled workers better off as well – in other words, if it provides a Pareto improvement. Let us see whether this is possible. We shall find that it is, because extra employment of the unskilled raises the marginal product of the skilled workers (assuming they are complementary with the unskilled) and also saves the skilled workers having to finance such high unemployment benefit payments.

For a subsidy rate s on unskilled workers, the proportionate change in their employment is, since W_1 is fixed by assumption, given by[37]

$$d(\log N_1) = \frac{\sigma}{1 - \beta} \frac{ds}{1 - s},$$
(3.33)

where σ is now the elasticity of substitution between the two types of labor, and $\beta = F_1 N_1 / F$ is unskilled labor's share of the wage bill. The change in the skilled wage is

$$d(\log W_2) = (\beta/\sigma)d(\log N_1) = (\beta/(1 - \beta))\,ds/(1 - s).$$

The net income of skilled workers, who pay all taxes, is $\Omega_2 = -sW_1 N_1 + W_2 N_2 - B_1(L_1 - N_1)$, where B_1 is, as before, a benefit paid to unemployed group 1 workers. Thus,

$$\frac{d\Omega_2}{ds} = -W_1 N_1 + N_2 \frac{dW_2}{ds} + (B_1 - sW_1)\frac{dN_1}{ds}.$$
(3.34)

But the first two terms sum to zero since, by the factor-price-frontier equation,[38] $N_1 d(W_1(1 - s)) + N_2 dW_2 = 0$. Hence, $d\Omega_2/ds > 0$ so long as $\rho_1 > s$. Assuming an

---

[36]As a matter of political fact, minimum wages are often introduced to reduce competition between unskilled labor and semi-skilled labor, which is a close substitute for it.
[37]See Chapter 8 by Hamermesh in this Handbook.
[38]See Chapter 8 by Hamermesh in this Handbook.

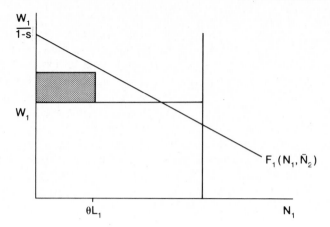

Figure 16.8. A wage subsidy with partial coverage.

interior solution (i.e. one short of full employment), it is thus in the interests of skilled workers to subsidize unskilled employment at a rate equal to the replacement rate.

Let us now consider what is socially efficient. This requires that we choose s to maximize $\Omega_1 + \Omega_2$, where Ω_i is the net income of the ith group of workers. Thus, we need to set

$$\frac{d\Omega_1}{ds} + \frac{d\Omega_2}{ds} = 0. \tag{3.35}$$

Since $d\Omega_1/ds$ is always positive, this requires a higher rate of subsidy.

These principles are all very well in theory, but do they work out in practice? As Johnson (1982) points out, many wage subsidy programs only cover a portion of unskilled workers (e.g. currently unemployed teenagers). So the covered workers are in competition with perfect substitutes for them who are not themselves covered. This can mean that the program has no effect on the total level of unskilled employment. Suppose that only θL_1 of unskilled workers are covered. This position is illustrated in Figure 16.8. The gross wage W_1 is too high to secure full employment of the unskilled, but the subsidy paid (sW_1) would be sufficient to secure full employment, if it was paid in respect to all group 1 workers. But only θL_1 workers are covered. In consequence all the θL_1 workers get employed because they are cheaper than other unskilled labor, but the effective marginal cost of unskilled labor is unchanged. So employment is also unaffected. The distribution of employment has altered so that all the covered workers are employed and their wage is bid up to $W_1/(1-s)$.[39] That is the only effect.

3.5. Training programs

Another form of labor market policy is the provision of subsidized training by the government to selected groups in the population. In terms of the model in this section, an unskilled worker can be "transformed" into a skilled worker by an expenditure of C. This raises by one the number of L_2's, and lowers by one the number of L_1's. The standard approach to the benefit–cost analysis of this activity is to estimate the individual's expected increase in gross earnings due to participation in a training program and assume that this is equivalent to the increase in *GNP* [see Ashenfelter (1978)]. For example, supposing that $U_1 > 0$ and $U_2 = 0$, the expected earnings increase associated with training would be $W_2 - W_1(1 - U_1)$. The estimated net present value per trainee is then

$$V = \frac{1}{r}(W_2 - W_1(1 - U_1)) - C, \tag{3.36}$$

where r is the relevant social discount rate.

Is this procedure correct? Assume, first, the rigid wage model for unskilled workers. Since W_1 is fixed, N_1/N_2 is fixed, which means that $dN_1 = (N_1/N_2)dN_2$. Thus, the change in *GNP* per successful participant in the training program is $(W_2 + W_1(N_1/N_2))dN_2 = (W_2/(1 - \beta))dN_2$. Thus, the true net social present value per trainee is

$$V_s = \frac{1}{r}\frac{W_2}{1 - \beta} - C. \tag{3.37}$$

Instead of subtracting $W_1(1 - U_1)$ from W_2, on the assumption that employment of group 1 workers is reduced, we have in fact to add $W_1 N_1/N_2$ on the assumption that there is some complementarity between group 1 and group 2 workers. If group 1 is small, this addition may be small, but the basic point is that nothing need be subtracted.[40]

One might ask why private individuals do not undertake training at a socially optimal rate. Apart from problems concerning imperfect capital markets, and

---

[39] This problem of limited take-up has a different impact if we are considering the case of a market that is in equilibrium (as in Figure 16.5). Then, assuming that coverage is independent of supply price, it can be shown that the effective wedge between marginal productivity and the marginal value of leisure is reduced by $\theta s W$. The subsidy (s) with take up θ is thus equivalent to a subsidy θs with 100 percent take-up.

[40] In a more general model with several rather than two types of labor and rigid wages in the source market, a quantity is added to observed earnings of the participant so long as trained labor and source labor are complementary. But if, to take an extreme case of substitutability, the training program merely put participants at the head of the queue for a certain type of job, it will have zero gross benefits [see Johnson (1980)]. For evidence on labor–labor substitution, see Hamermesh and Grant (1979).

information, the private value of training is in fact much lower than V_s in (3.37). The private present value of training, assuming that private and social discount rates are equal, is

$$V_p = \frac{1}{r}\left(W_2(1-t) - W_1(1-U_1) - B_1U_1\right) - C. \tag{3.38}$$

This is lower than the conventionally calculated V in (3.36) although they are close for a small tax rate. Thus, the social benefits to the training program outweigh the private benefits, mainly because of the difference between V and V_s. This establishes a strong case for government support for training when there is wage inflexibility in the unskilled labor market. A similar–although not so compelling–case can be made for government intervention in training when wages are flexible and there is relatively more distortion at the low end of the skill distribution [see Jackman and Layard (1980, p. 338)].

Before leaving the issue of training, we need to mention one way in which the existence of training complicates the analysis of unemployment subsidies [Wilson (1982)]. If there is excess supply of unskilled labor there are two possible solutions: one is to encourage the unskilled to become skilled, the other is to increase the employment rate of the unskilled (by subsidies). Obviously if the employment rate of the unskilled increases, the incentive they have to become skilled is reduced. Thus in principle the subsidization of employment and of training should be simultaneously optimized.

From what we have said, the supply and demand model provides a simple framework for analyzing the distortions induced by benefits as well as problems of involuntary unemployment caused by administered wages. But involuntary unemployment may also result from other forms of non-competitive wage-setting and we turn now to these.

4. Models where firms set wages

4.1. Wage-setting models in general

Most models in which wages are set by agents, rather than by impersonal forces, have the same basic structure. There is a labor demand function

$$(1-U)L = N(W), \quad N' < 0. \tag{4.1}$$

Then there is a wage-setting function which, together with the demand function, determines wages and employment. Thus, in the general equilibrium the wage-

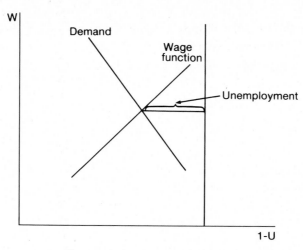

Figure 16.9. Wage-setting models.

setting function replaces the supply function of the market-clearing model. Agents set wages on the basis of the wage they expect others to set (W) and on the basis of the general state of the economy (U). Hence, in the ith firm the wage ($R_i W$) will be

$$R_i W = f(W, U), \quad 1 \geq f_1 > 0; \ f_2 < 0, \tag{4.2}$$

where R_i is the firm's wage relative to a general wage level. But in equilibrium the wage which the representative agent sets must be the same as the general level of wages ($R_i = 1$). If not, agents would be chasing each others' wages upwards (or downwards). Hence, (4.2) becomes

$$W = g(U), \quad g' < 0. \tag{4.3}$$

The model is illustrated in Figure 16.9. To reduce unemployment, wage-setting behavior has to be changed in such a way that the wage function shifts down, and the level of unemployment moves up towards the level which would imply equality of supply and demand.

In this section we consider the case where the wage-setters are firms. Firms may set wages with many objectives in mind: to reduce quitting by their workers, to attract new recruits or to improve the work effort of their workers. This being so, there is no guarantee that the wage set will be such that all who want work at that wage can get it. To investigate this issue, we shall review three models which concentrate in turn on the impact of wages upon quits, hiring and work effort.

In each case we shall assume that the marginal product of labor (in efficiency units) is constant. In fact of course it depends on the real rate of interest, since under constant returns to scale this determines the capital–labor ratio. In the long run the real interest rate is exogenous and in the short run it depends on the overall capital–labor ratio of the economy. To investigate the importance of this issue the reader can easily examine how (if at all) a change endogenizing the marginal product would affect the derivation of the equilibrium rate of unemployment.[41]

4.2. A quitting model of unemployment[42]

Because quitting imposes costs on firms, employers have an incentive to discourage it. The only way they can do this is by trying to raise their relative wages. This may lead in the outcome to a general level of wages that is too high to secure employment of the total labor force.[43]

It is reasonable to assume that the fraction of workers who leave their current employer per period depends negatively on how much he pays, relative to the income they could expect if they left. This expected alternative income can be thought of as $(1-U)W + UB$, where W is the wage paid in the rest of the economy.[44] Thus, the quit rate experienced by the ith firm is $Q(W_i/[(1-U)W + UB])$. It is convenient to denote the relative wage (W_i/W) as R_i and to denote $1/(1 - U(1 - \rho))$ as X, which is exogenous to the firm. So

$$Q_i = Q(R_i X), \quad Q' < 0. \tag{4.4}$$

If workers quit, the firm incurs real costs. These include the cost of hiring the new workers and training them. We shall assume that, if γ is the marginal product of labor, the cost of replacing a quit is $\gamma\theta$. Thus, if N_i is employment, the firm's profit per worker is

$$\frac{\pi_i}{N_i} = \gamma(1 - \theta Q(R_i X)) - R_i W. \tag{4.5}$$

---

[41] In this case the zero profit condition is replaced by the first-order condition for employment. In general this would not affect our qualitative policy conclusions.

[42] This model draws heavily on Pencavel (1972), Stiglitz (1974), Salop (1979) and Calvo (1979). For an efficiency wage model in which the firm does not wish to lower its wage because it will lose its better quality workers, see Weiss (1980).

[43] Note that there would be no problem if workers could be required to deposit a bond which they lost when quitting. Unfortunately, capital market imperfections generally (but not always) prevent this.

[44] We follow Calvo (1979) in abstracting from dynamic considerations.

The firm will choose its relative wage R_i so as to maximize this profit per worker. Hence,

$$\frac{\partial(\pi_i/N_i)}{\partial R_i} = -\gamma\theta Q'(R_i X)X - W = 0. \tag{4.6}$$

Second-order conditions require that $Q'' > 0$. In addition competition will ensure that the firm has zero profit:

$$\gamma(1 - \theta Q(R_i X)) - R_i W = 0. \tag{4.7}$$

We can now examine the general equilibrium of the system. Since all firms are identical the firm's relative wage R_i is unity. Using this and combining (4.6) and (4.7) we find that[45]

$$1 - \theta Q(X) + \theta Q'(X)X = 0. \tag{4.8}$$

This determines X, which is $1/(1 - U(1 - \rho))$. There is only one unemployment rate at which firms will be happy to pay the prevailing wage. If unemployment is lower than that, quitting will be so high that firms will want to raise wages beyond the prevailing level.

This result enables us to see at once how the replacement ratio (ρ) affects the level of unemployment. If the replacement rate is higher, quitting becomes more attractive and, to offset this, unemployment has to be higher.

We turn now to the effect of employment subsidies. Suppose there is a per capita subsidy of h per worker, and also a proportional subsidy to the wage bill at a rate s. This means that the firm's cost per worker falls to $W(1-s)-h$. Note that the two subsidies work very differently, since the value of s to the firm depends on its choice of W_i, whereas the value of the per capita subsidy h does not. We shall find that the proportional subsidy (s) has no effect on unemployment while the per capita subsidy (h) decreases it.

To see this, note first that the firm's profit per worker is now

$$\frac{\pi_i}{N_i} = \gamma(1 - \theta Q(R_i X)) - R_i W(1-s) + h. \tag{4.9}$$

---

[45] This can be written as

$$Q(X) = \frac{1}{\theta(1 + \eta_{QR})},$$

where η_{QR} is the elasticity of the quit rate with respect to R. The higher η_{QR} and θ the higher unemployment.

Maximization of this implies

$$\frac{\partial(\pi_i/N_i)}{\partial R_i} = -\gamma\theta Q'(R_i X)X - W(1-s) = 0, \tag{4.10}$$

while the zero profit condition gives

$$\gamma(1 - \theta Q(R_i X)) - R_i W(1-s) + h = 0. \tag{4.11}$$

In general equilibrium $R_i = 1$ so that we have two equations to solve for $W(1-s)$ and X. Thus, whatever the level of proportional subsidy (or tax) it will be fully passed on into the wage, leaving $W(1-s)$ unchanged. A proportional subsidy or tax will have no effect on unemployment. But a per capita subsidy will reduce unemployment. For setting $R_i = 1$ and subtracting (4.10) from (4.11) we have

$$1 - \theta Q(X) + \theta Q'(X)X = -\frac{h}{\gamma}, \tag{4.12}$$

so that

$$\frac{dX}{dh} = -\frac{1}{\gamma\theta Q''X} < 0. \tag{4.13}$$

Since unemployment is increasing in X, the subsidy reduces unemployment.

This result makes sense. Any proportional tax or subsidy affects equiproportionately the firm's marginal cost from raising its relative wage and the resulting marginal benefit in terms of reduced turnover costs.[46] So it does not affect the equilibrium level of unemployment. By contrast, if one introduces a lump-sum subsidy, this again leaves the marginal cost of raising the relative wage

[46] If $h = 0$ the equilibrium condition (4.12) can be written as

$$W(1-s) = W(1-s)\left(-X\frac{Q'}{Q}\frac{\theta Q}{1-\theta Q}\right)$$

$$= W(1-s)\eta_{QR}\frac{\theta Q}{1-\theta Q},$$

where η_{QR} is the elasticity of quits with respect to the relative wage. The LHS is the marginal cost per worker of raising R, and the RHS is the marginal benefit.

unchanged, but reduces the marginal benefit in terms of reduced costs of turnover.[47] So more quitting will be acceptable and hence lower unemployment.

This finding, that (for a given replacement ratio) per capita subsidies make a difference and proportional subsidies and taxes do not, proves to be very robust to changes of wage-setting models. It is also of relevance to a whole range of policies. It suggests that if governments want to increase employment they should use per capita rather than ad valorem subsidies (even if there were only one type of labor). But subsidies are of course difficult to finance and in practice subsidies on labor often have to be paid for by taxes on labor. So we need also to consider the effect of labor taxes. These are simply negative subsidies, so a proportional tax has no effect on unemployment and a per capita tax is harmful. Thus, a per capita subsidy paid for by a proportional tax would reduce unemployment. Indeed, if the present argument is correct, there would be advantages, in a country with a proportional tax on labor, in restructuring it into a per capita credit plus a higher proportional tax rate – the total net tax take being unchanged.

Another proposal which can be analysed in the present framework is a tax-based incomes policy [see, for example, Jackman, Layard and Pissarides (1984a)]. The idea here is that firms pay a tax per worker proportional to the excess of the wage over a permitted norm (W_0). The firm's tax bill is thus $t(W_i - W_0)N_i$. This is equivalent to a proportional tax t and a per capita subsidy tW_0.[48] In the present model, and those that follow, the proposal would raise employment.

4.3. A model with vacancies and hiring

We can now extend the previous model to include the impact of the firm's wage policy upon the number of workers it can hire, as well as the number who quit. This adds to the realism of our model of the firm. More important, it also enables us to model more explicitly the role of labor market friction in generating

---

[47]Setting $s = 0$, (4.10) and (4.11) give

$$W = (W - h)\left(-X\frac{Q'}{Q}\frac{\theta Q}{1 - \theta Q}\right)$$

$$= (W - h)\eta_{QR}\frac{\theta Q}{1 - \theta Q}.$$

[48](i) If the scheme were to be revenue neutral and employment rose, the extra tax proceeds could be used to provide an additional subsidy.

(ii) In a dynamic context, the effective rate of tax is δt [Jackman, Layard and Pissarides (1986)].

unemployment. The basic friction is this: when workers look for suitable work they often do not find it at once, and when firms look for workers they often have similar difficulty.

We shall begin by discussing this problem of matching, and then revert to the firm's choice of wage level.[49] Each firm will choose a number of workplaces and will have vacancies equal to the shortfall of its actual workforce below its number of workplaces. It will make these vacancies publicly known. Each period unemployed workers will search over these vacancies. We shall assume that an unemployed worker simply wants to get a job, and all jobs pay the same wage. (The case of wage variability is discussed in Chapter 15 by Mortensen in this Handbook.) If during a period an unemployed worker can only visit one vacancy, there is an obvious chance that some other worker will have got there before him. So some workers will remain unemployed. Equally, some vacancies will remain unfilled. It is reasonable to suppose that the proportion of all vacancies filled depends positively on the ratio of the unemployed job-seekers (UL) to the job vacancies on offer (V).[50] This is the average relationship. But the individual firm can increase the probability of filling its own vacancies by raising its relative wage, so the ith firm's probability of filling a vacancy is $P(R_i, UL/V)$. In the long run the firm will have to keep its hirings (PV) equal to its quits (QN). Hence, the firm's flow equilibrium constraint is

$$Q(R_i, U) = P\left(R_i, \frac{UL}{V}\right)\frac{V_i}{N_i}, \quad Q_1, Q_2 < 0; \quad P_1, P_2 > 0. \tag{4.14}$$

At the level of the whole economy, this gives the "U/V relationship" between the unemployment rate (U) and the vacancy rate (V/N):

$$Q(1, U) = P\left(1, \frac{U/(1-U)}{V/N}\right)\frac{V}{N} = h\left(U, \frac{V}{N}\right), \quad Q_2 < 0; \quad h_1, h_2 > 0. \tag{4.15}$$

Since, for given vacancies, higher unemployment reduces quits and increases hirings, vacancies fall when unemployment rises and vice versa. It follows that if we can find out how the vacancy rate is determined, we shall have also determined unemployment.

---

[49] What follows is based on Jackman, Layard and Pissarides (1984).

[50] This follows if workers search randomly over vacancies. Then for a given worker the probability that he visits a given vacancy is $1/V$ and the probability that a given vacancy is visited by no one is $(1 - 1/V)^{UL} \cong e^{-UL/V}$. Thus, the proportion of vacancies filled is

$$P = 1 - e^{-UL/V}$$

[see Hall (1977)].

The key mechanism here is the firm's wage decision. By raising wages the firm can increase its recruitment and lower its quits. However, this is costly and the other way to increase recruitment is to have more vacancies. If vacancies were not costly, the answer would be to increase vacancies without limit. But vacancies are costly. If a firm declares a vacancy it must be willing to fill it, if a suitable applicant comes along. For, if not, its advertisements would lose credibility. And if the firm is going to hire someone it will normally make sense to provide the person with a workplace.[51] This means that, if there is an unfilled vacancy, a capital cost is incurred with no corresponding output. The firm's equilibrium occurs where the cost of a vacancy equals the marginal benefit it derived from a vacancy by not having to offer such high wages.

To derive the appropriate condition we begin with the firm's profit per worker, which is

$$\frac{\pi_i}{N_i} = \gamma - R_i W - \phi\left(1 + \frac{V_i}{N_i}\right). \tag{4.16}$$

Here ϕ is the capital cost per workplace, so that the capital cost per worker is ϕ augmented to allow for the V_i empty workplaces. Using (4.14) the profit per worker can be written as

$$\frac{\pi_i}{N_i} = \gamma - R_i W - \phi\left(1 + \frac{Q_i(R_i, U)}{P_i(R_i, UL/V)}\right). \tag{4.17}$$

The firm chooses its wage so that

$$\frac{\partial(\pi_i/N_i)}{\partial R_i} = -W + \phi\frac{Q_i}{P_i}(\eta_{QR} + \eta_{PR}) = 0 \tag{4.18}$$

when η_{QR} and η_{PR} are the absolute elasticities of Q and P with respect to the relative wage. We can now use (4.18) and (4.14) and the zero profit condition to obtain (with subscripts dropped):

$$\frac{V}{N} = \frac{1}{1 + \eta_{QR} + \eta_{PR}}\left(\frac{\gamma}{\phi} - 1\right). \tag{4.19}$$

Thus the vacancy rate will be higher the higher the marginal product per worker

[51] In a very large establishment it might be worth having more job openings than workplaces, so that in those periods when all jobs were filled some workers would produce nothing. However, one can show that most establishments are too small for this to pay.

(γ) and the lower the cost of a workplace (ϕ). If the response of quits and hires to wages is very strong, then there will be very few vacancies, since it is better to use wages as a way of retaining and recruiting labor. Vacancies only exist due to monopsony power. To determine unemployment, we take vacancies from (4.19) and then use the aggregate U/V relation (4.15) to determine unemployment.

It is easy to see in the model why unemployment might be higher in occupations which have high quit rates.[52] For the vacancy rate will be similar in different occupations if γ/ϕ, η_{QR} and η_{PR} are similar.[53] But suppose the quit function in an occupation is $\psi Q(R_i, U)$ with ψ varying across occupations. Then the U/V relationship (4.15) becomes:

$$\psi Q(1, U) = h\left(U, \frac{V}{N}\right) \tag{4.20}$$

and, holding V/N constant,

$$\frac{\partial U}{\partial \psi} = \frac{q}{h_- - \psi Q_2} > 0. \tag{4.21}$$

We can now examine our various labor market policies. It is easy to check that, as in our pure quits model, a proportional employment subsidy has no effect, while a per capita subsidy lowers unemployment.[54] This is because vacancies are now given by

$$\frac{V}{N} = \frac{1}{1 + \eta_{QR} + \eta_{PR}}\left(\frac{\gamma + h}{\phi} - 1\right). \tag{4.22}$$

In considering the effect of the replacement ratio, we shall now concentrate on its effect on the intensity of search.[55] This is because there is good evidence that the replacement ratio works mainly on the duration of unemployment rather than

---

[52] A similar conclusion follows in Section 4.2 provided we assume that the quit rate if $aQ(\cdot)$ and the cost per quit (θ) is $\theta = a^{-\alpha}$ $(0 < \alpha < 1)$.

[53] In Britain vacancy rates were similar in different occupations in 1978 [Jackman, Layard and Pissarides (1984)].

[54] The profit per worker now is

$$\frac{\pi_i}{N_i} = \gamma + h - W(1-s)R_i - \phi\left(1 + \frac{Q_i}{P_i}\right),$$

and the conclusion follows from the first-order condition and zero profit conditions.

[55] There is also the issue of the effect of UI on the layoff rate, not modelled here [Feldstein (1976)]. The more employers' contributions are experience-rated, the lower will be the lay-off rate.

on the inflow of people into unemployment, either through quitting or layoff.[56] Thus, we shall assume that the probability of filling a vacancy depends not simply on the level of unemployment but on the proportion of the unemployed who search per period. This proportion will fall the higher the replacement ratio, since the cost of not searching is thereby reduced. Thus, if c is the proportion who search per period,

$$c = c(\rho), \quad c' < 0, \tag{4.23}$$

and the U/V relationship is given by

$$Q(1, U) = h\left(cU, \frac{V}{N}\right). \tag{4.24}$$

Thus, if V/N is determined by the behavior of firms, a rise in the replacement ratio, by lowering c, must raise unemployment. (But note that in deriving this result we are assuming that η_{QR} and η_{PR} are independent of unemployment.)

4.4. A model where wages affect morale

We can now consider another factor which employers may take into account when setting their wages – that the wage may affect the morale and efficiency of their workforce. Workers' effort (e) may be affected either by their wage relative to the generally prevailing wage (W) or by the wage relative to what they feel it ought to be (the "expected wage", W_a). We shall explore both these possibilities. The second model provides a possible mechanism by which unemployment could have risen in recent years due to the slowdown in productivity growth.

First we shall suppose that the number of efficiency units of work which a worker does per period is given by

$$e = e\left(\frac{W_i}{W(1-U)+UB}\right) = e(R_i X), \quad e' > 0, \tag{4.25}$$

where $X = 1/(1 - U(1 - \rho))$. Thus, unemployment is a device which disciplines workers.[57]

---

[56] See, for example, Hamermesh (1982b).
[57] For a related, though more complex approach, see Shapiro and Stiglitz (1984).

If γ is the marginal product per efficiency unit, the profit per worker is

$$\frac{\pi_i}{N_i} = \gamma e(R_i X) - R_i W, \tag{4.26}$$

and first-order conditions require

$$\gamma e'(X) X - W = 0, \tag{4.27}$$

with second-order conditions implying $e'' < 0$. Using the zero profit condition, this gives

$$\frac{e'(X) X}{e(X)} = 1. \tag{4.28}$$

Unemployment is determined such that the elasticity of effort with respect to the relative wage is unity. Since $X = 1 - U(1 - \rho)$, the equation determines equilibrium unemployment as a function of the replacement ratio.

This model, as Calvo (1979) points out, is very similar in structure to the quits model and yields the same policy implication – that a proportional employment subsidy has no effect while a per capita subsidy reduces unemployment (by reducing the relative benefit which the firm obtains by increasing its relative wage). If the firm is paid a subsidy per worker equal to $sWR_i + h$, its profit per worker becomes:

$$\frac{\pi_i}{N_i} = \gamma e(R_i X) - RW(1 - s) + h. \tag{4.29}$$

Optimal choice of R_i, together with the zero-profit condition, gives

$$\gamma(e'(X) X - e(X)) = h, \tag{4.30}$$

so that

$$\gamma e''(X) X \mathrm{d} X = \mathrm{d} h. \tag{4.31}$$

Using the second-order condition that $e'' < 0$, we find that $\mathrm{d} X / \mathrm{d} h$ is negative, so that a per capita subsidy reduces unemployment.

The model we have just outlined assumes that morale depends on wages relative to the wage of other workers (W). If the general level of wages fell due to a fall in γ, this would have no effect on unemployment since unemployment is determined by (4.28). Yet many people believe that the increased unemployment of recent years is indeed due to a fall in the rate of productivity growth (and hence of real wage growth). This linkage can be established if we assume instead that worker efficiency depends positively on the actual wage relative to the "expected" wage (W_a) that they consider fair and reasonable.[58] It also depends positively on unemployment, with the morale effect of the relative wage being lower if unemployment is high. Hence,

$$e = e\left(\frac{W_i}{W_a}, U\right), \quad e_1, e_2 > 0, \quad e_{12} < 0. \tag{4.32}$$

If the expected real wage (W_a) only adjusts to actual wags with a lag, this model will explain why a fall in productivity growth leads to a period of transitional unemployment that can be quite prolonged. Unemployment only comes back to its long-run level when the expected wage has converged onto the actual wage.

To explore this, we shall assume for simplicity that γ has been constant for a long time and then falls by a once-for-all jump downwards. We can first analyse the long-run equilibrium of the system for a given γ. If we define R_i as W_i/W_a the firm chooses the wage (R_i) to maximize

$$\frac{\pi_i}{N_i} = \gamma e(R_i, U) - R_i W_a. \tag{4.33}$$

Hence,

$$e_1(R, U) - W_a/\gamma = 0, \tag{4.34}$$

with second-order condition that $e_{11} < 0$. This, together with the zero-profit condition, which is

$$e(R, U) - RW_a/\gamma = 0, \tag{4.35}$$

gives the familiar condition that

$$\frac{e_1(R, U)R}{e(R, U)} = 1. \tag{4.36}$$

In the long run R will be unity, so that eq. (4.36) determines long-run unemployment.[59] Equations (4.34) and (4.35) then determine W_a/γ. But in the

---

[58] This is in the spirit of the empirical specification of the strike model of Ashenfelter and Johnson (1969). The alternative model of Farber (1978) specified the relevant variable as the wage of the firm relative to average wages in the economy (R_i).

[59] The policy conclusions are as for the earlier efficiency wage model.

short-run U and R are determined by eqs. (4.34) and (4.35) as functions of the expected wage (W_a) relative to productivity (γ). By differentiating these two equations logarithmically and solving for the two endogenous variables (U and R), it can be shown that

$$d\log U = \frac{e}{e_2 U} d\log\left(\frac{W_a}{\gamma}\right) \tag{4.37}$$

and

$$d\log R = \frac{e}{e_{11} R^2}\left(1 - \frac{e_{12} R}{e_2}\right) d\log\left(\frac{W_a}{\gamma}\right). \tag{4.38}$$

Thus, if productivity is low relative to the expected wage, unemployment is high ($e_2 > 0$). At the same time the relative wage (R) is low (since by the second-order condition $e_{11} < 0$ and we are assuming $e_{12} < 0$).

We can now examine the adjustment path of the economy to equilibrium, where $R = 1$, as we shall show. This path depends on the process by which wage expectations (W_a) are formed. A plausible assumption is that workers "get used" to the actual real wage rate at some "learning" rate:

$$\frac{d\log W_a}{dt} = \omega(\log W - \log W_a). \tag{4.39}$$

Then suppose that initially the wage was below the expected wage (W_a), so that R was below unity. This would lead to a downward adjustment of the expected wage. But from (4.38) this would lead employers to select a higher R. Thus, if R was initially low, it would tend to rise until it reached unity, when the expected wage would stop adjusting. Similarly, if R was initially too high, it would converge on unity from above.

Now consider the behavior of the economy in the face of a once-and-for-all decline in γ that occurred at time period 0. W_a does not change at once, so [by (4.37)] unemployment increases. At the same time [by (4.38)] the wage falls relative to expectations. This fall in R then [via (4.39)] leads to a downwards adjustment in the expected wage (W_a) which [by (4.37)] starts reducing unemployment. So long as W_a/γ is above its long-run level, unemployment is above its long-run level. But ultimately W_a falls sufficiently; R converges on unity and unemployment on its long-run equilibrium. This path is illustrated in Figure 16.10.

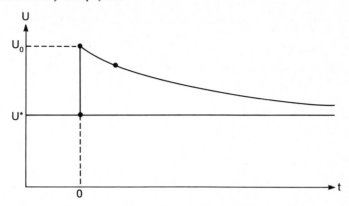

Figure 16.10. Path of the unemployment rate following a productivity shock at $t = 0$.

4.5. Optimality of the natural rate in models where firms set wages

We have not so far discussed whether the equilibrium rates of unemployment derived in this section would be optimal. With the models as we have laid them out it would be impossible to do so, since we have not given explicit expressions for the utility of the participants.

More complex models have been derived by other writers in which these issues are investigated, and the general upshot of the literature is that it is not possible on grounds of pure theory to say whether the equilibrium unemployment rate is above or below the level that is socially efficient. The issue is discussed in relation to an efficiency wage model in Shapiro and Stiglitz (1984) and in relation to a model of job-matching by Mortensen in Chapter 15 of this Handbook.

To illustrate the complexities of the issue we can take the model of matching. In this model a worker's productivity depends on how well he is matched to the job. However, it does not follow that unemployment equilibrium will be optimal, as one can see if one considers all the externalities that occur in the process of labor market flow. First consider a worker's decision to quit his existing firm. This provides an external benefit to other firms and may (depending on contract structures) impose an external cost on his own firm. As regards other job seekers, it benefits them by creating a vacancy and harms them by introducing a competing job-seeker into the pool of unemployed.

Now consider the unemployed worker's decision of whether to accept a job. If he accepts, he imposes an external cost on other potential employers. He also hurts other searchers by reducing vacancies, and helps them by reducing the competition for jobs. Finally, consider an unemployed worker's decision on how hard to search. If he searches harder, he benefits potential employers and hurts competing job-seekers.

Some writers [e.g. Hall (1972) and Diamond (1981)] have focused on the external benefits of having a larger pool of job seekers. But, as Pissarides (1984) points out, when all the possible externalities have been taken into account, it is extremely difficult to say in which direction the balance of the effect lies, nor therefore whether equilibrium turnover unemployment is too high or too low. In any event, as our next section points out, there may be other crucial influences on the unemployment rate which cannot be modelled like this at all.

5. Models with unions

We turn now to consider the role of unions, which may help to throw light on the secular increases in unemployment in some countries.

5.1.   A trade union model with all sectors unionized

The position of unions differs widely between countries. In Britain, about 85 percent of male manual workers have their pay determined by collective bargaining and about 60 percent of all workers are unionized. In the United States the proportions are much smaller. In both countries the union movement is highly decentralized, with separate bargaining for each group of workers. There is no unified national policy on the side of either the unions or the employers. This contrasts sharply with the case in some small countries, like Sweden and Austria, where wages are to a large extent determined by a single national bargain.

In analysing the effect of unions we shall concentrate first on the case, most like the British one, where we shall assume the whole workforce is unionized but in decentralized groups. We shall assume that the unions have the power to determine real wages as they choose (though the solution to a Nash bargaining solution would yield similar qualitative features).[60] We shall also assume that employers have the power to determine employment as they choose (see Chapter 18 by Farber in this Handbook). In other words, management is left to manage, but is subject to the wages set by unions.

In setting wages, unions maximize some objective function, subject to the firm's demand function for labor. Many objective functions have been proposed for unions. Clearly, unions care both about wages and about jobs for their members. Since members continually leave, one might expect the unions to raise wages repeatedly to at least as high as the demand price for the surviving members. But this overlooks the fact that unions cannot prevent other members

---

[60] See Nickell and Andrews (1983), who also assume that employment is determined by employers. Other Nash bargaining models assume bargaining over wages and employment, but this is less realistic.

from continuously joining. In fact therefore the union maximizes the interests of a stable but constantly revolving population. This dynamic problem is analysed reasonably fully in Jackman, Layard and Pissarides (1984b), but here we shall present a much simpler and less rigorous analysis which leads to similar conclusions.[61]

The economy is divided into a number of equal-sized industries. Corresponding to each industry there is a union. Each ith union is concerned with the long-run welfare of a group consisting of M_i people. As a result of the union's choice of wage N_i people will be employed in the industry at a wage W_i, and $(M_i - N_i)$ not employed in the industry. These others will be either unemployed, with probability U, or employed elsewhere in the economy, with probability $(1 - U)$. If unemployed, their net income (including psychic components) is B; if employed, their wage is W. The union's maximand (the welfare of its M_i members) is thus

$$Z_i = N_i W_i + (M_i - N_i)(UB + (1 - U)W)$$
$$= N_i(W_i - UB - (1 - U)W) + \text{constant}. \tag{5.1}$$

The model thus maximizes the sum of the rents (or surpluses) obtained by its members.[62] (Note that the size of the membership M_i, which might appear difficult to determine in advance, does not affect the maximization result.)

Employment in the industry depends on the real wage (W_i): $N_i = N(W_i)$. Thus, if the union maximizes the welfare of it members, this implies:

$$\frac{\partial Z_i}{\partial W_i} = N_i + (W_i - UB - (1 - U)W)N' = 0. \tag{5.2}$$

Turning to the general equilibrium, we set $W_i = W$, so that

$$U(W - B) = -\frac{N}{N'} \tag{5.3}$$

or[63]

$$U = \frac{1}{\eta} \frac{1}{1 - B/W}, \tag{5.4}$$

---

[61] For a related approach see Oswald and Ulph (1982).

[62] We are implicitly assuming $N_i \leq M_i$. Ex post one might expect that M_i would tend to N_i but it would be treated as exogenous when the choice of W_i is made.

[63] In the more rigorous dynamic approach of Jackman, Layard and Pissarides (1984b) the full formula is

$$U = \frac{1}{(\eta(1 - B/W))(1 + r/\lambda)}.$$

where η is the industry-specific elasticity of demand for labor as a function of its own real wage.[64] Thus, the unemployment rate varies inversely with the elasticity of demand for the union's labor. This is exactly what we should expect since $1/\eta$ measures the monopoly power of the union, and the greater this monopoly power the higher the wages and the lower employment. Equally, the higher the replacement ratio the less union members will suffer if the union pushes up wages and reduces employment. Thus a higher replacement ratio will lead to lower employment.

After a negative shock to the general wage level, caused for example by the oil shock, the union might overestimate the general wage level. In this case the perceived value of W would exceed the final wage which was set (W_i), so that $W_i = W(1 - \theta)$, where θ is a positive error factor. In this case

$$U = \left(\frac{1}{\eta} + \theta\right) \frac{1}{1 - B/W}, \tag{5.5}$$

so that the misperception has led to increased unemployment.

If one asks how employment can be raised, the answer is to increase the elasticity of demand for labor with respect to the wage received by workers. One obvious way to do this is by paying employers a per capita subsidy.[65] Equally, a proportional employment tax or subsidy on its own will make no difference.

Thus, suppose the firm is paid $sW_i + h$ per worker. The objective function becomes (with $B = 0$):

$$Z_i = N_i\left(W_i(1 - s) - h\right)\left(W_i - (1 - U)W\right) + \text{constant.} \tag{5.6}$$

First-order conditions imply (with $W_i = W$):

$$N = WUN'(1 - s) = 0 \tag{5.7}$$

---

[64] Even if capital in the whole economy is given, each small industry takes the rental price of capital as given. Hence, η (the elasticity of industry demand for labor with respect to the real wage in units of GNP) is given by the usual Hicksian formula, $(1 - \alpha)\varepsilon + \alpha\sigma$, where α is capital's share, ε is the elasticity of demand for industry output with respect to its relative price and σ the elasticity of substitution between labor and capital.

[65] Suppose the elasticity with respect to the firm's wage cost is

$$\frac{dN}{d(W - h)} \frac{W - h}{N} = \eta.$$

Then the elasticity with respect to the worker's wage is

$$\frac{dN}{dW} \frac{W}{N} = \frac{dN}{d(W - h)} \frac{W - h}{N} \frac{W}{W - h} = \eta \frac{W}{W-h}.$$

and

$$U = \frac{1}{\eta}\left(1 - \frac{h}{W(1-s)}\right). \tag{5.8}$$

Thus, once a lump-sum subsidy has been paid, a proportional subsidy will also raise employment.

It is interesting to ask whether employment would rise as a result of our familiar self-financing tax/subsidy scheme consisting of a per capita subsidy financed by a proportional tax. Suppose that the per capita subsidy equalled a fraction (h^*) of the ex post wage. Then clearly the tax rate ($-s$) would have to equal (h^*). Hence,

$$U = \frac{1}{\eta} \frac{1}{1+h^*}. \tag{5.9}$$

So a subsidy equal to say 20 percent of the wage should reduce unemployment by about 16 percent. This line of thought suggests that, if unions matter, one should increase the progressivity of employment taxes.

5.2. A queue model of unemployment

The preceding model may be relevant in some countries, but in many only a fraction of the workforce is unionized. To analyse this type of situation we need a model with two sectors, one unionized and the other competitive [Hall (1975)]. We shall initially take the union wage (W_U) and the competitive wage (W_c) as given, with the union wage exceeding the competitive wage, so that there is a positive mark-up (m) with

$$\frac{W_U}{W_c} = 1 + m > 1. \tag{5.10}$$

This mark-up generates a queue of people wanting union jobs. Assuming that the skill requirements of union and non-union jobs are the same, the queue will build up until people are indifferent between joining the queue and working in the competitive sector. This process will generate an equilibrium unemployment rate, which will be higher the higher the mark-up and the higher the percentage unionized.[66]

---

[66] One can also get this result from a model in which the unskilled labor market clears but the supply of labor is elastic. This proposition is put forward in Minford (1983) – our own formalization would be that given in Jackman, Layard and Pissarides (1984a).

To establish this, we begin with the flow equilibrium of the union sector. We assume that a proportion Q of union workers leave their jobs per unit time (either to retire or to join the unemployment pool). And we assume that the probability of a unemployed worker finding a union job per unit time is the job-finding rate ϕ. Thus, if N_U is union employment and J is the number of unemployed job-seekers, flow equilibrium requires

$$\frac{J}{N_U} = \frac{Q}{\phi}. \tag{5.11}$$

But the job-finding rate (ϕ) has to be such that people are indifferent about whether or not to join the queue. We assume that it is impossible to get a union job unless you are previously unemployed,[67] but that non-union jobs can be got for the asking. We can thus compute the present values of not searching for a union job and of searching, and then set them equal. The present value of not searching is simply the present value of a non-union job, held continuously:

$$V_c = \int_0^\infty W_c e^{-\delta t}\, dt = \frac{W_c}{\delta}, \tag{5.12}$$

where δ is the discount rate. The present value of being unemployed is

$$V_U = \int_0^\infty \left(e^{-\phi t} B + (1 - e^{-\phi t}) W_U \right) e^{-\delta t}\, dt$$

$$= \frac{1}{\phi + \delta} B + \frac{\phi}{(\phi + \delta)\delta} W_U. \tag{5.13}$$

If the queue is in equilibrium, people are indifferent about whether to join, so that $V_U = V_c$ and thus

$$\phi = \frac{\delta(1 - B/W_c)}{(W_U/W_c) - 1} = \frac{\delta(1 - \rho)}{m}. \tag{5.14}$$

So

$$\frac{J}{N_U} = \frac{Qm}{\delta(1 - \rho)}. \tag{5.15}$$

---

[67]Similar results could be got from the less extreme assumption that it was easier to get a union job if unemployed than if working in the non-union sector.

This is the ratio of the unemployed to unionized employment. It is higher the higher the union mark-up.

The ratio of unemployment to the *total* labor force obviously depends in addition on the fraction of workers who are unionized (P). To be specific, if $P = N_U/N$, the overall unemployment rate is, by definition,

$$U = \frac{J}{\frac{N_U}{P} + J} = \frac{1}{\frac{N_U}{J}\frac{1}{P} + 1}. \tag{5.16}$$

Hence, using (5.15):

$$U = \frac{1}{\frac{\delta(1-\rho)}{QmP} + 1}. \tag{5.17}$$

The higher the percentage unionized, the higher the general unemployment rate.

The model we have been discussing is widely used to explain urban unemployment in the Third World [Harris and Todaro (1970)].[68] Here the "high wage" sector is the "organized" sector, which includes the public sector and the modern parts of the private sector. The wages in this sector may be high due to union activity or other reasons. The "low wage" sector is the informal sector together with the rural economy.

Finally, it is interesting to ask how the union mark-up is determined. The union maximizes the rents of its members, so its objective function is

$$Z_i = N(W_i)(W_i - W_c) + \text{constant}. \tag{5.18}$$

Maximization implies that, after setting $W_i = W_U$, the relative trade union mark-up is given by

$$\frac{W_U}{W_c} - 1 = \frac{1}{\eta - 1}, \tag{5.19}$$

where η is the sector-specific elasticity of demand for labor in the representative unionized sector. Thus, the greater union power (the lower η), the higher the mark-up and the higher unemployment.

---

[68]A similar model has also been used by Mincer (1976) to show how unemployment will respond to the level of minimum wages and to the proportion of the workforce "covered".

If a subsidy of $Ws + h$ is paid to all firms, this will reduce the mark-up to

$$\frac{W_U}{W_c} - 1 = \frac{1}{\eta \Big/ \left(1 - \dfrac{h}{W(1-s)}\right) - 1}.\tag{5.20}$$

Hence, unemployment will fall.

5.3. Work-sharing

We can now analyse a policy that is increasingly commonly proposed as a way of reducing unemployment: namely work-sharing.[69] In its simplest form this can be represented as an exogenous reduction in weekly hours per worker. The argument is that, if hours per worker were reduced, employment would increase. This argument is of course tautologically correct, provided total man-hours do not fall in equal proportion to the fall in hours per worker.

Clearly, there is one model where this assumption is correct. This is the model of Section 3 where the real hourly wage is fixed by government. But few wages fall into this category. Even if hourly wages are "rigid" in the sense of not clearing the market, wage-setters may well change them in response to external circumstances. So let us analyse the effects of work-sharing in our union wage-setting models.

We shall begin with the trade union model of Section 5.1. We modify our earlier analysis, letting W be hourly wages and H hours per worker. We assume that hours are set nationally – for example by law or by a national agreement between workers and employers.

The demand for labor in the ith sector is now a demand for man-hours, given by[70]

$$N_i H = f(W_i).\tag{5.21}$$

Ignoring benefits,[71] we can write the individual union's maximand as

$$\begin{aligned}
Z_i &= N_i W_i H + (M_i - N_i)(1 - U)WH \\
&= HN_i(W_i - W(1 - U)) + \text{constant} \\
&= f(W_i)(W_i - W(1 - U)) + \text{constant}.
\end{aligned}\tag{5.22}$$

---

[69] For an empirical discussion see Ehrenberg and Schumann (1982).

[70] If there is one-shift working and capital hours are KH the demand function is $N_i H / K_i H = f(W_i)$. In this case W determines N and hours reduction cannot increase employment, even if hourly wages remain constant.

[71] We are implicitly ruling out any change in ρ due to changes in wages.

Hence, if the union selects the optimal wage,

$$\frac{\partial Z_i}{\partial W_i} = f' + (W_i - (1 - U)W)f = 0. \tag{5.23}$$

In general equilibrium $W_i = W$, so that

$$U = \frac{f}{f'W} = \frac{1}{\eta}. \tag{5.24}$$

Thus, the unemployment rate is independent of hours of work. If hours are reduced, workers force up hourly wages to a level where exactly the same number of people are employed as before. The same level of unemployment as before is needed to make workers willing to accept the prevailing wage.

Turning to the queue model of unemployment, a change in hours would have no effect on the trade union mark-up, for reasons similar to those in the preceding model. So the unemployment rate would not change.

The finding in the quits model is even more remarkable. If γ is the hourly output per worker and $\theta\gamma$ is the cost per quit, the profit per worker is

$$\frac{\pi_i}{N_i} = \gamma(H - \theta Q(R_i X)) - R_i WH.$$

$$= \left[\gamma\left(1 - \frac{\theta}{H}Q(R_i X)\right) - R_i W\right]H. \tag{5.25}$$

This is exactly the same expression as our original one [eq. (4.2)] except that θ has been replaced by θ/H. Thus, unemployment is determined by

$$1 - \frac{\theta}{H}(Q(X) - Q'(X)X) = 0. \tag{5.26}$$

Hence,

$$\frac{\partial X}{\partial H} = -\frac{1}{\theta Q''X} < 0. \tag{5.27}$$

So a fall in hours will raise X and thus actually raise unemployment. In effect lower hours add to the relative cost of quitting, so that higher unemployment is needed to offset this cost and reduce quits.

A similar conclusion follows from the vacancies model. The profit per worker now becomes

$$
\begin{aligned}
\frac{\pi_i}{N_i} &= \gamma H - R_i W H - \phi\left(1 + \frac{V_i}{N_i}\right) \\
&= \left(\gamma - R_i W - \frac{\phi}{H}\left(1 + \frac{V_i}{N_i}\right)\right) H.
\end{aligned}
\tag{5.28}
$$

So a reduction in hours is just like a rise in the cost of a workplace. Accordingly it reduces vacancies [as can be seen by replacing ϕ by ϕ/H in (4.16)] and raises unemployment (through the U/V curve).

With the efficiency–wage model the effect of an hours reduction is to leave unemployment unchanged. For the firm's maximand becomes:

$$
\frac{\pi_i}{N_i} = H\gamma e(R_i X) - R_i W H,
\tag{5.29}
$$

where $H\gamma$ is the marginal product per efficiency hour. Clearly, hours do not affect equilibrium unemployment.

Our conclusion is that those who advocate work-sharing have in mind a particular form of rigid wage, which is not particularly common. If instead one thinks of unemployment as being in equilibrium when wage-setters have no incentive to change their wages, then one is unlikely to conclude that unemployment can be reduced by reductions in hours per worker.

6. Empirical analysis of the time series

6.1. *Estimates of the equilibrium unemployment rate*

We can finally use the framework of thought we have developed to throw light on the reasons for the secular increase in the long-run unemployment rate. Each of the models we have discussed implies which variables (X) should empirically be found to determine the equilibrium unemployment rate. In other words,

$$
U^* = U^*(X).
\tag{6.1}
$$

According to the model in question, X could include the replacement rate, propensities to quit, unionization rates, the union mark-up and any recent changes in underlying real wage growth. Of course in the short run the level of unemployment will not always be at this equilibrium rate, so that we can usefully think of the actual rate as given by

$$U = U^*(X) + (U - U^*(X)), \tag{6.2}$$

where the term in brackets is the disequilibrium component.

There are two well-established approaches to the estimation of U^*, which have a good deal in common, though their derivation differs sharply.[72] The first approach is the Phillips curve approach in which intended real wages appear as the dependent variable, and their growth is affected by the extent to which unemployment differs from its equilibrium level. High employment leads to an above average growth in intended real wages, for the simple reason that high employment is associated with an abnormally low real wage, and an abnormal upward adjustment is therefore needed. Thus, if g is the perceived underlying growth of real wages, the Phillips curve could be written as

$$\Delta w - \Delta p^e = g^* - \gamma(U - f(Z)), \tag{6.3}$$

where w and p are the logs of nominal wages and prices and Z is all the X variables except the perceived underlying real wage growth (g^*) and the actual underlying real wage growth (g).

We can use (6.3) to compute the equilibrium rate of unemployment that would hold when real wage growth was at its trend level g. In such a case unemployment must be

$$U^* = f(Z) + \frac{g^* - g}{\gamma}. \tag{6.4}$$

If we can find a way of modelling price expectations, we can estimate (6.3). One could use rational expectation estimates of price expectations, though in practice over the ranges of inflation so far experienced in Western countries, adaptive expectations often may be a reasonable approximation to rational expectations.[73]

Many thousands of Phillips curve regressions have been published and many more estimated but not published. They are subject to notorious difficulties, discussed at length in Santomero and Seater (1978). They often prove unstable over different time periods due to our inability to include proper measures of all the Z variables. In practice few researchers have included any Z variables, and instead have proxied them by a time trend. For illustration we can examine a

---

[72] There are also many more experimental approaches: see, for example, the structural approach of Nickell and Andrews (1983) and Layard and Nickell (1986a, 1986b).

[73] If a variable consists of an unobservable permanent part generated by a Markov process, plus a transitory error, the rational forecast uses adaptive expectations.

simple Phillips curve of this kind run for a number of countries. In this, expected changes in prices are proxied by a weighted average of lagged prices and lagged wages. Thus, the equation estimated is

$$\Delta w = \beta + \alpha \Delta p_{-1} + (1 - \alpha)\Delta w_{-1} - \gamma \log U + \delta t, \tag{6.5}$$

where t is time (1970 = 0). We shall discuss later the reasons for the time trend

Table 16.12

Wage equations. A = Using unemployment; B = Using vacancies.

		Constant	$(\dot{p} - \dot{w})_{-1}$	$\log U$	$\log V$	$t/100$	D.W.	S.E.
Australia	A	−0.29 (2.9)	1.26 (5.0)	−0.064 (3.2)		0.35 (2.3)	1.8	0.041
	B	0.29 (4.3)	1.41 (6.1)		0.073 (4.2)	0.33 (2.7)	1.9	0.036
Austria	A	−0.14 (2.5)	0.99 (4.8)	−0.055 (3.6)		−0.16 (2.7)	1.6	0.023
	B	0.32 (4.8)	0.98 (5.3)		0.055 (4.2)	−0.13 (2.4)	1.8	0.021
Belgium	A	−0.21 (3.8)	0.54 (2.7)	−0.053 (4.1)		0.23 (2.6)	1.4	0.022
	B	0.24 (5.1)	0.16 (0.1)		0.041 (5.0)	0.09 (1.5)	2.2	0.020
Canada	A	−0.16 (3.6)	0.42 (2.1)	−0.056 (4.1)		0.08 (1.5)	1.3	0.016
	B	0.31 (4.1)	0.41 (2.0)		0.050 (3.6)	−0.21 (3.5)	1.7	0.016
Finland	A	−0.13 (1.3)	0.03 (0.1)	−0.027 (1.3)		0.15 (1.0)	2.0	0.029
	B	0.20 (1.7)	0.28 (0.8)		0.027 (1.6)	−0.19 (1.6)	2.0	0.028
France	A	−0.42 (1.8)	0.19 (0.6)	−0.076 (1.8)		0.68 (1.7)	2.3	0.026
	B	0.22 (1.7)	0.53 (1.2)		0.029 (1.7)	−0.14 (1.4)	2.4	0.026
Germany	A	−0.04 (1.0)	0.91 (3.8)	−0.023 (3.1)		−0.09 (1.1)	1.8	0.025
	B	0.20 (4.1)	0.88 (3.9)		0.033 (3.3)	−0.11 (1.4)	1.9	0.025
Japan	A	−0.27 (1.5)	0.29 (1.0)	−0.071 (1.6)		−0.03 (0.2)	1.7	0.040
	B	−1.49 (4.6)	0.53 (2.5)		0.170 (4.5)	−0.03 (0.4)	2.3	0.030
Netherlands	A	−0.20 (2.3)	0.86 (3.4)	−0.051 (3.1)		0.20 (1.4)	1.8	0.032
	B	0.17 (2.9)	0.72 (2.8)		0.034 (2.3)	0.02 (0.1)	1.8	0.035
Norway	A	−0.10 (1.1)	0.57 (2.4)	−0.033 (1.5)		−0.08 (1.0)	1.8	0.029
	B	0.23 (2.1)	0.62 (2.6)		0.032 (1.8)	−0.13 (1.6)	1.9	0.029
New Zealand	A	−0.20 (2.0)	0.45 (1.7)	−0.025 (2.3)		0.31 (1.5)	1.6	0.040
	B	−0.02 (0.2)	0.18 (0.6)		−0.020 (0.6)	−0.32 (1.2)	1.7	0.046
Sweden	A	−0.20 (2.1)	0.88 (4.4)	−0.061 (2.7)		−0.08 (1.0)	1.6	0.028
	B	0.30 (3.2)	1.06 (4.9)		0.046 (2.1)	−0.25 (1.9)	1.6	0.027
Switzerland	A	−0.05 (2.0)	0.86 (2.5)	−0.009 (3.1)		0.00 (0.1)	1.3	0.021
	B	0.12 (1.3)	−0.04 (0.1)		0.019 (1.3)	−0.00 (0.0)	1.8	0.023
United Kingdom	A	−0.36 (2.8)	0.89 (3.0)	−0.075 (3.1)		0.52 (2.5)	1.7	0.036
	B	0.25 (3.4)	0.80 (2.7)		0.074 (3.1)	0.17 (1.4)	1.9	0.036
United States	A	−0.10 (3.1)	0.34 (2.4)	−0.034 (3.4)		0.03 (1.0)	2.2	0.011
	B	0.31 (3.8)	0.36 (2.6)		0.39 (3.6)	−0.09 (2.8)	2.4	0.010

Sources: For sources see Grubb, Jackman and Layard (1983).
Notes: 1. The estimated equations were:

$$(A) \quad \dot{w} - \dot{w}_{-1} = \alpha(\dot{p} - \dot{w})_{-1} - \beta \log U + \delta t + \text{constant},$$

$$(B) \quad \dot{w} - \dot{w}_{-1} = \alpha(\dot{p} - \dot{w})_{-1} + \gamma \log V + \delta t + \text{constant}.$$

2. The t-statistics are in parentheses (absolute values).
3. The period of estimation was, A: 1957–83, B: 1957–83, in all cases except for United States and New Zealand (1961–83), and Finland, Canada and Sweden (1963–83).
4. w is mainly hourly earnings in manufacturing and p the consumption deflator.

Table 16.13
Estimated equilibrium unemployment (U^*) and various growth rates.

	U^* (1983)	U^* (1973)	$g_{u|v} \times 100$	$g_u \times 100$
Australia	7.1 (1.8)	2.7 (0.4)	1.4 (0.8)	5.5 (1.6)
Austria	2.6 (0.4)	1.4 (0.2)	−0.0 (0.5)	−3.0 (1.2)
Belgium	7.6 (1.3)	3.2 (0.3)	2.5 (1.2)	4.4 (1.1)
Canada	8.5 (1.1)	5.4 (0.5)	6.2 (0.7)	1.4 (0.8)
Finland	5.4 (2.3)	3.0 (1.1)	9.1 (0.8)	5.5 (2.7)
France	8.1 (1.2)	3.1 (0.3)	9.7 (0.6)	8.9 (0.9)
Germany	3.5 (1.4)	0.8 (0.3)	2.4 (0.9)	−3.9 (4.2)
Japan	1.8 (0.5)	1.3 (0.3)	3.4 (1.5)	−0.4 (1.7)
Netherlands	7.0 (1.7)	1.7 (0.3)	3.1 (1.1)	4.0 (2.1)
Norway	2.9 (1.2)	1.5 (0.4)	1.3 (0.3)	−2.3 (2.8)
New Zealand	1.4 (0.9)	0.3 (0.1)	8.1 (7.9)	12.3 (4.4)
Sweden	2.9 (0.5)	1.4 (0.2)	0.4 (0.9)	−1.2 (1.5)
Switzerland	0.3 (0.3)	0.0 (0.0)	−38.8 (66.5)	0.4 (6.5)
United Kingdom	6.5 (1.3)	2.7 (0.4)	3.9 (0.5)	7.1 (5.6)
United States	6.9 (1.0)	5.3 (0.4)	3.8 (0.3)	0.9 (0.9)

Note: Standard errors in parentheses.

but for the moment it is enough to document it. As Table 16.12 makes clear, the effect of the changing Z variables reflected in the trend is to raise unemployment in some countries but not all. We can in fact look in Table 16.13 at the natural rates implied in 1980 and in 1970. In computing these we have calculated the equilibrium unemployment rate from

$$\log U^* = \frac{\beta - \alpha \overline{\Delta(w-p)} + \delta t}{\gamma}, \qquad (6.6)$$

where $\overline{\Delta(w-p)}$ is the average rate of growth of real wages over the preceding 5 years. Needless to say the calculation is extremely crude and subject to wide margin of error.

As can be seen, the change in $\log U$ is

$$\log U_{80}^* - \log U_{70}^* = 10 \frac{\delta}{\gamma} - \frac{\alpha}{\gamma} \left(\overline{\Delta(w-p)}_{80} - \overline{\Delta(w-p)}_{70} \right). \qquad (6.7)$$

The first part is the effect of the time trend. The second shows the effect of the fall in the underlying rate of real wage growth. The slow-down of productivity growth has been one of the main economic changes in the last 10 years and it appears not to have been significantly reflected in a shift in the constant term (β) in the Phillips curve.[74] This has been an important cause of the increase in

[74] Grubb, Jackman and Layard (1982).

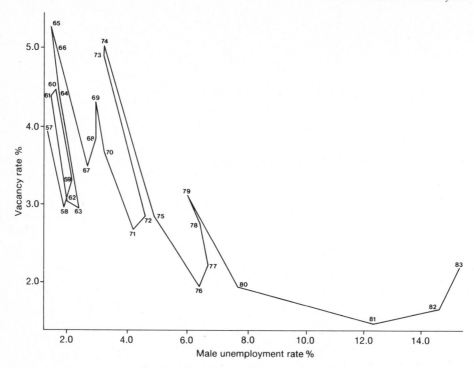

Figure 16.11. Vacancies and male unemployment (United Kingdom). *Source*: Jackman, Layard and
Pissarides (1984).

unemployment between 1970 and 1980. But the time trend has generally been
more important, and we need to consider what may have caused it. Attempts to
include the replacement ratio in time series regressions have generally been
inconclusive (see below). But this does not mean that the unemployed may not
have become less eager for work for other reasons.

To throw light on this, one might ask whether unemployment has risen at a
given level of vacancies. As Figures 16.11 and 16.12 show, this has indeed been
the case in Britain and to a lesser extent in the United States. To summarize the
data we estimated the following equation:

$$\log U = a_0 + a_1 \log U_{-1} + a_2 \log V + a_3 t. \tag{6.8}$$

Table 16.13 shows in column (3) the annual percentage increases in unemployment at a given level of vacancies. This was in some countries as large as the total
effect of time on the equilibrium level of unemployment [shown in column (4)].
We shall discuss later what factors could have increased the level of unemploy-

Figure 16.12. Help-wanted index and prime-age male unemployment (United States). *Source*: Medoff and Abraham (1982) "Unemployment, Unsatisfied Demand for Labor, and Compensation Growth, 1956–80", in: M. N. Baily, ed., *Workers, Jobs, and Inflation*, p. 67, Figure 3.

ment at given vacancies. At this stage we can simply complete our discussion of the Phillips curve by noting in Table 16.12 (row *B*) that the rate of wage inflation is explained just about as well by vacancies as by unemployment.

The equilibrium approach

The second way of estimating the natural rate of unemployment is based on the idea that deviations from the natural rate occur because workers are induced to supply an amount of labor different from that they would supply in perfect foresight equilibrium. In the long run the supply curve is vertical, but in the short run workers can be induced to supply more labor if they think real wages are above their trend level. This can only happen if they are confused over the price level. The position is illustrated in Figure 16.13. The trend level of real wages is $(w - p)^*$. *S* indicates the short-run supply that would originate at a given *perceived* real wage. If real wages were correctly perceived unemployment could never deviate from U^*. But if actual prices exceed expected prices ($p - p^e > 0$), then labor supply as a function of the actual real wage will be higher than that indicated by *S*. Instead it is given by *S'*. Since employment is determined by the equality of supply and demand, and demanders always correctly perceive the real wage, unemployment can only fall below U^* if workers believe that prices are lower than they are. This gives us the famous "Lucas supply curve" [Lucas

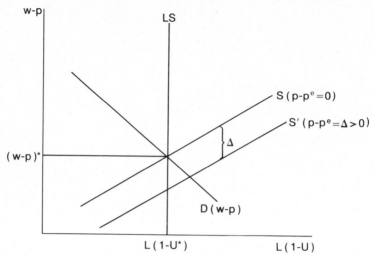

Figure 16.13. The Lucas supply curve.

(1973)]:

$$U = U^* + \beta(p - p^e).$$ (6.9)

This is surprisingly similar to the Phillips curve in its empirical implications since if there is a constant mark-up of prices on wages ($\Delta p - \Delta w = g^*$), (6.3) implies:

$$p - p^e = -\gamma(U - f(Z)).$$ (6.10)

All that has happened is a reversal of the causal relationship. However, in practice, those who believe in the Lucas supply curve then generally proceed to assume that ($p - p^e$) is a function of demand shocks, which yields the function:

$$U = U^* + \beta(\text{shocks}).$$ (6.11)

The most straightforward example of this approach is Barro (1978). The shock variable in (6.11) is unanticipated money growth, and the estimated equilibrium unemployment rate in year t is simply the calculated value of $U(t)$ with all the relevant shock terms sets equal to zero. Barro selected two labor market variables to explain movements in U^* in the United States over time: $MINW$, the ratio of the federal minimum wage to average hourly earnings times the proportion of workers covered by the $FLSA$, and MIL, the ratio of armed forces personnel to the male population aged 16–44. (Barro reports that he also experimented unsuccessfully with an unemployment compensation variable, the equivalent of our ρ.) Based on a regression on annual data for 1946–73 (in which the value of *MIL* is set equal to zero for the years in which there was not a military draft), he presents estimates of values of U^* for each year. For example, in 1955 $U^* = 4.0$ percent, in 1975 $U^* = 6.5$ percent.

6.2. Explanation of changes in the equilibrium unemployment rate

We can now proceed to examine more systematically the main possible explanations that have been offered for the rise in the natural rate in the major Western countries in the last 15 years. The issues here are still very unsettled, but there is *some* evidence. We offer it mainly in the hope of stimulating further work on these crucial questions.

6.2.1. Changes in the composition of the labor force

A first possible explanation of changes in the natural rate is simply that the composition of the labor force has shifted towards groups with higher long-run unemployment rates. This is essentially a matter of arithmetic, and can be readily checked out in countries like the United States where sufficiently disaggregated data series exist. For the period 1951–79 we regressed the measured unemployment rate of each of 32 demographic groups (8 age groups, male/female, white/non-white) on unanticipated money growth and its lagged value as well as a time trend. The predicted values of the equilibrium unemployment rate for each demographic group (found by setting unanticipated money growth equal to zero) for 1955 and 1979 are shown in Table 16.14. Also reported are the sum of the estimated coefficients on unanticipated money growth terms, which is a measure of the cyclical sensitivity of the group's unemployment rate, and the *t*-value of the estimated time trend.

The estimated overall natural rate by this procedure, $U^* = \sum U_i \phi_i$, the weighted average of the estimates for the 32 subgroups, is 4.2 percent for 1955 and 6.4 percent for 1979.[75] The change in the overall rate can be decomposed into three parts: (i) that due to changes in the composition of the labor force $\sum U_{i55}^* \Delta \phi_i$; (ii) that caused by changes in group equilibrium rates, $\sum \phi_{i55} \Delta U_i^*$; and (iii) the interaction of (i) and (ii), $\sum \Delta U_i \Delta \phi_i$. These equal 1.2, 0.5, and 0.5, respectively, which means that without a change in labor force weights the natural rate in 1979 would have been 5.4 percent, without an increase in individual group natural rates the overall rate would have been 4.7 percent in 1979.

---

[75] It is interesting to point out that the Phillips curve estimates of U^* for these periods are of about this magnitude. See Perloff and Wachter (1979) and Nichols (1983). These studies are more detailed and reliable than the illustrative figures shown in our Table 16.13.

Table 16.14
Estimated natural rates of unemployment for 32 demographic groups
in the United States, 1955 and 1979 (Estimated standard errors in parentheses).

Group	Age	$\hat{U}_i^*$ (55)	$\hat{U}_i^*$ (79)	Unanticipated money	t-value of time trend	$\Delta\phi_i$
White	16–17	12.2 (0.4)	18.1 (0.6)	−107.2 (28.3)	7.1	0.004
males	18–19	10.6 (0.6)	13.3 (0.7)	−161.5 (36.6)	2.7	0.008
	20–24	6.5 (0.5)	8.9 (0.7)	−116.2 (34.0)	2.4	0.027
	25–34	2.9 (0.3)	4.2 (0.3)	−67.0 (16.9)	2.7	−0.013
	35–44	2.5 (0.2)	2.8 (0.2)	−51.8 (11.7)	0.8	−0.049
	45–54	2.9 (0.2)	2.7 (0.2)	−58.0 (11.7)	−0.5	−0.036
	55–64	3.5 (0.2)	2.9 (0.2)	−63.8 (10.8)	−1.8	−0.024
	65+	3.5 (0.2)	3.8 (0.2)	−60.6 (10.2)	1.0	−0.019
Black	16–17	15.3 (0.9)	41.2 (1.2)	−181.4 (58.3)	15.3	0.000
males	18–19	15.5 (1.0)	32.4 (1.2)	−297.2 (61.6)	9.4	0.000
	20–24	11.0 (0.9)	17.9 (1.1)	−237.1 (57.8)	4.2	0.003
	25–34	7.9 (0.6)	8.5 (0.7)	−205.8 (37.6)	0.5	0.001
	35–44	6.6 (0.4)	5.4 (0.5)	−170.7 (27.3)	−1.6	−0.003
	45–54	6.3 (0.4)	5.0 (0.5)	−150.2 (27.4)	−1.8	−0.002
	55–64	6.8 (0.4)	4.9 (0.5)	−178.5 (23.7)	−2.7	−0.001
	65+	6.1 (0.4)	7.0 (0.5)	−189.2 (26.4)	1.2	−0.001
White	16–17	12.0 (0.4)	18.5 (0.5)	−109.6 (26.2)	8.5	0.007
females	18–19	8.8 (0.4)	14.7 (0.5)	−95.0 (25.1)	8.1	0.008
	20–24	5.3 (0.3)	9.2 (0.4)	−74.0 (17.6)	7.7	0.026
	25–34	4.6 (0.4)	5.8 (0.5)	−59.4 (25.5)	1.6	0.037
	35–44	3.8 (0.2)	5.0 (0.2)	−53.8 (12.3)	3.4	0.004
	45–54	3.3 (0.2)	4.1 (0.3)	−49.6 (12.6)	2.2	0.002
	55–65	2.6 (0.2)	3.4 (0.3)	−47.4 (12.7)	0.3	−0.007
	65+	2.6 (0.2)	4.2 (0.2)	−39.0 (12.0)	4.4	−0.001
Black	16–17	19.1 (1.2)	46.6 (1.5)	−228.5 (76.4)	12.4	0.001
females	18–19	21.1 (1.0)	38.7 (1.2)	−182.8 (61.6)	9.8	0.001
	20–24	12.2 (0.6)	21.3 (0.8)	−209.4 (39.6)	7.9	0.005
	25–34	8.4 (0.3)	11.5 (0.4)	−146.1 (18.9)	5.7	0.006
	35–44	6.3 (0.3)	7.7 (0.4)	−126.5 (21.9)	2.2	0.001
	45–54	4.6 (0.3)	5.4 (0.3)	−92.1 (16.2)	1.8	0.001
	55–64	4.0 (0.2)	4.4 (0.3)	−77.2 (14.6)	0.9	0.001
	65+	3.2 (0.2)	3.5 (0.4)	−70.5 (18.3)	0.6	0.000

These results only show which groups increase their equilibrium unemployment rates; they obviously do not tell us anything about *why* these increases occurred. It is interesting to note that the increases in U^* are concentrated among the younger groups and for women; the estimated equilibrium rates for men over age 35 fell slightly during the sample period. Attempts to "explain" the trend with various X variables (such as Barro's minimum wage and military variables, the value of the union/non-union wage differential, a demand "shock" variable, and the like) were subject to difficulties similar to those noted for the aggregate unemployment equation.[76] But then the U.S. group-specific natural rates have not risen greatly. The main puzzle relates to Europe.

6.2.2. Structural shifts

We shall therefore review in turn the main reasons why the unemployment rate (standardized for compositional shifts) may have risen. An obvious possibility, which is widely believed by the general public, is that there have been shifts in the pattern of labor demand that have been inadequately matched by changes in the pattern of labor supply. These lead to falls in employment in the declining sectors that are not fully offset by rises in employment in the expanding sectors. The obvious major cause in recent years for changes in the pattern of demand is the change in the real price of oil.

Unfortunately, it is difficult to measure shifts in labor demand as such. But assuming that there is no change over time in the flexibility of supply, shifts in demand can be approximately measured by shifts in employment. In Table 16.15 we compute for a number of countries an index of the shift in the pattern of employment across industries This starts from the annual net change in the structure of employment, which is a highly cyclical variable. To smooth the series we show its 5-year moving average. Only in Belgium is there any evidence of a rise after the early 1970s. In Germany, the United Kingdom and the United States there was a rise in the late 1960s, but not thereafter. Thus, except in Belgium, there is absolutely no evidence of unusual disturbances in the mid to late 1970s.[77] Evidently demand shifts caused by the energy shock were not particularly strong, compared to earlier demand shifts. So there is no reason to suppose that we are suffering from an "increased pace of change" or from "increased structural imbalance" across industries. By contrast, in the inter-war period there was massive turbulence in the industrial structure. In the United States the index averaged 3.2 between 1924 and 1939 compared with 2.8 between 1900 and 1910 and 1.7 since 1950. Similarly, in Britain an index based on two-digit industries averaged 4.4 between 1924 and 1939 compared with 2.1 since 1950. This may help to explain inter-war unemployment, but not the current episode.

There are other dimensions of structural imbalance. If there are massive shifts of employment between regions this can cause dislocation [Medoff (1983)]. In the

---

[76] For an interesting attempt to explain differential trends by race in the employment situation of young workers, see Ellwood and Wise (1983).

[77] If the tale is recalculated excluding the agricultural sector, this conclusion is not altered. The same is true in the United Kingdom if it is recalculated for 26 two-digit industries. It is also true in the United States if it is recalculated for 20 two-digit manufacturing industries and 11 other sectors (data on this and on inter-state shifts kindly supplied by K. Abraham).

Table 16.15
Annual percentage changes in the structure of employment: Five-year moving averages.

	By industry							By region	
	Belgium	France	Germany	Italy	Netherlands	United Kingdom	United States	United Kingdom	United States
1953	1.8				1.5	1.1	1.9		
1954	1.7				1.6	1.0	1.7	0.6	
1955	1.4				1.3	1.0	1.9	0.5	1.2
1956	1.7				1.3	0.9	2.3	0.6	1.4
1957	1.8	2.0		4.3	1.3	1.0	1.7	0.6	1.3
1958	1.9	1.9		4.2	1.3	1.1	1.8	0.6	1.2
1959	2.0	1.9		3.8	1.4	1.2	2.1	0.6	1.2
1960	2.1	1.7	2.5	3.4	1.4	1.4	1.9	0.6	1.1
1961	1.9	1.8	2.7	3.1	1.4	1.5	1.4	0.6	0.9
1962	1.7	2.0	2.5	3.2	1.5	1.4	1.4	0.6	0.8
1963	1.6	2.1	2.3	2.9	1.6	1.4	1.2	0.5	0.9
1964	1.7	2.1	2.2	2.7	1.6	1.5	1.0	0.5	0.8
1965	1.9	2.2	2.2	2.4	1.9	1.6	1.2	0.4	0.8
1966	1.9	2.2	1.8	2.7	2.0	1.5	1.2	0.4	0.8
1967	1.9	2.2	2.0	2.5	2.0	1.6	1.2	0.4	0.8
1968	1.8	2.0	2.1	3.0	2.0	1.6	1.6	0.4	0.8
1969	1.8	2.1	2.9	2.6	2.0	1.8	1.9	0.5	0.9
1970	1.7	2.1	2.8	2.8	2.1	1.9	1.7	0.5	1.1
1971	1.7	2.0	2.7	2.5	1.9	2.1	1.6	0.6	1.2
1972	1.7	2.0	2.6	2.4	1.9	2.0	1.7	0.6	1.3
1973	2.1	2.1	2.8	2.1	1.9	2.4	2.1	0.7	1.4
1974	2.2	2.1	2.1	2.3	2.1	2.3	1.8	0.7	1.4
1975	2.3	2.1	2.0	2.1	2.0	1.9	1.9	0.7	1.2
1976	2.5	2.1	2.0	2.0	1.9	1.6	2.0	0.5	1.3
1977	2.7	2.0	1.8	2.0	1.9	1.6	1.9	0.5	1.3
1978	2.5	1.7	1.4	1.7	1.9	1.4	1.4	0.5	1.2
1979	2.6	1.6	1.4	2.0	2.0	1.8	1.5	0.6	1.3

Sources: United States: (a) By industry (i) 1901–70: *Historical Statistics of the United States – Colonial times to 1970 – Part 1* – Table D127–141. (ii) 1970–81: U.S. Department of Labor, *Employment and Earnings*, May 1982 – Table B-1. (b) By region *Employment and Training Report of the President*, 1982 – Table D-1. United Kingdom: Department of Employment Gazette. Others, OECD, *Labor Force Statistics*.

Notes: The index is a centred five-year average of $\Sigma|e_{i,t} - e_{i,t-1}|$, where e_i is the percentage share of the ith sector in total employment. The industrial sectors are the usual ISIC sectors, except that sectors 8 and 9 have been aggregated. Each index covers the whole labor force, except that the United States excludes agriculture. The regional breakdown involves 10 regions in the United States and 8 in the United Kingdom (we exclude Northern Ireland).

United States the index of shifts in employment between regions rose in the early 1970s but it has not risen since (see Table 16.15). The same is true of an index based on shifts between states.

To investigate the impact of structural shifts on unemployment one approach is to look directly at evidence on the match in the pattern of vacancies and unemployed analysis by industry or region. A reasonable index of structural mismatch is got by comparing the share of unemployment and the share of vacancies in each sector. If there was no structural mismatch, one might expect these shares to be the same in each sector. So an index of mismatch is provided by $\frac{1}{2}\Sigma_i|u_i - v_i|$, where u_i is the percentage of the unemployed and v_i the percentage of the vacancies, and $|\cdot|$ indicates absolute value. This index suggest no increase in mismatch in the 1970s, either by industry, region or skill, in Britain, France or Germany.[78]

The evidence we have been examining so far relates to secular movements in structural unemployment. However, Lilien (1982a, 1982b) has argued that there are short-term movements of structural unemployment which account for much of the short-run movements of unemployment. He calculated an employment variation index, σ, equal to the weighted standard deviation of employment growth rates across 11 two-digit industries in the United States. He then estimated a Barro-type regression of the following form:

$$U = \alpha_0 + \alpha_1 U_{-1} + \alpha_2 t + \alpha_3 \sigma + \sum_{i=0}^{M} \beta_i DMR_{-i} + e, \qquad (6.12)$$

where DMR is the unanticipated rate of money growth. The results [his equation (1), Table 3] for the 1948–50 period include $\hat{\alpha}_0 = 0.276$, $\hat{\alpha}_1 = 0.489$, $\hat{\alpha}_2 = 0.056$ and $\hat{\alpha} = 53.9$, the last coefficient with a t-value in excess of five.

Lilien's interpretation of this model is that structural demand shifts (along with unanticipated money) are a precipitating cause of the business cycle. Our interest in his model concerns its implications about the natural rate. σ varies over the sample period from 0.0133 to 0.0583, which implies a range in the steady-state unemployment rate of $(\alpha_3/(1-\alpha_1))\times 0.045 = 4.7$ percentage points. Thus, policies that are designed to facilitate the adjustment of the labor force between industries and areas (retraining programs, occupational information, relocation allowances, and the like) might have a tremendous potential payoff. It is important, therefore, to examine the robustness of Lilien's results very carefully.

One can obviously question whether the Lilien model has correctly modelled the direction of causation between U and σ. Suppose that, when unemployment is

---

[78] For Britain see Jackman, Layard and Pissarides (1984).

high, the reduction in employment in cyclically-sensitive industries is large but that growth in employment across industries is fairly even in economic recoveries. This is precisely what his series (and the modified series in the 1983 paper) *looks like* – high values in 1954, 1958, 1961, 1970, 1971, and 1975. This alternative hypothesis about the determination of employment variation implies that

$$\sigma = \beta_0 + \beta_1 U + \beta_2 U_{-1} + u. \tag{6.13}$$

Using Lilien's data for 1949–79, one obtains OLS estimates of $\hat{\beta}_1 = 0.75(0.15)$ and $\hat{\beta}_2 = -0.78(0.15)$ with $R^2 = 0.52$ and $D.W. = 1.97$. Equations (6.12) and (6.13) imply that U and σ are jointly determined, and the two equations should be estimated simultaneously. The problem, however, is that (6.12) is not identified [i.e. there are no exogenous variables in (6.13) that do not appear in (6.12)]. All the other macro variables that we could reasonably expect to influence σ turned ou* to have no impact. To get around this problem one can remove U_{-1} from (6.12), which is the original Barro specification. The resultant OLS estimate of the coefficient on σ is still positive and significant, $\hat{\beta}_3 = 33.2(12.2)$, but the $2SLS$ estimate is negative and statistically insignificant. The $2SLS$ estimate of (6.13), on the other hand, is little different from the OLS estimate. Thus, although the test is far from perfect, the evidence favors the alternative interpretation of Lilien's result: variation in industry employment is a result rather than a cause of variations in unemployment. Further strong evidence in favor of this view comes from the fact that, when σ is high, vacancies tend to be low rather than high as the Lilien interpretation implies [Abraham and Katz (1984)]. We shall not therefore follow Lilien in thinking of the equilibrium unemployment rate as something that fluctuates up and down from year to year.

6.2.3.   Willingness to take jobs

We come now to a third explanation of the secular rise in unemployment – that the unemployed have become less willing to take the jobs that are available. The prima-facie argument in support of this view comes from the trend increase in unemployment at a given level of vacancies that we have already documented above (Table 16.13). Clearly, the U/V curve can shift out for a number of reasons. First it could shift out due to increases in structural mismatch. We have cast some doubt on this hypothesis for the United States and Britain, but the question clearly needs investigating for a wide range of countries. Another possible factor is employment protection legislation. This is discussed in the next section, but is unlikely to be a major explanatory variable. Another possibility is that the statistical series of vacancies do not reflect actual vacancies in a way that is consistent over time. For most countries the series is the number of vacancies registered with the public employment services, while for the United States and Canada it is the "help-wanted index" of newspaper advertisements for jobs.[79] Clearly, a change in the role of the public employment service (or of newspaper ads) can throw off the series, unless an adjustment can be made to allow for this. Such an adjustment has been made in the figures presented above for Britain,[80] but it would be desirable to do it for other countries. Failing this, the results must be interpreted with caution. All one can say is that, if there has been no major increase in mismatch, nor a major impact of employment protection, and if the time series are sound, then in many countries the unemployed must have become less willing to take the available jobs.

Why could this be? The reason most commonly given is an increase in replacement ratio. This has indeed increased in a number of countries, due either to better benefits or wider coverage. But the increases generally occurred in the 1950s and 1950s, rather than more recently. Many time-series studies have tried including the replacement ratio as a variable in an unemployment function or a wage equation. The results vary wildly, depending on what other variables are included and what period is studied. This is illustrated by Metcalf, Nickell and Floros (1982) in their comment on Benjamin and Kochin's (1979) argument that inter-war unemployment was high largely because of high replacement rates. It also emerges in the comparison of Minford's (1983) and Layard and Nickell's (1986a) work on the effects of replacement rates in post-war Britain.

Better estimates of the effect of benefits can be obtained from cross-sectional studies. Most work has concentrated on the effect of benefits on the durations of unemployment, holding constant all other labor market conditions so far as possible. In a study of a cohort of people unemployed in Britain in 1979 Narendranathan, Nickell and Stern (1985) found that the elasticity of duration with respect to benefits was around 0.3. In a U.S. interstate study Ehrenberg and Oaxaca (1976) found an elasticity of around unity.[81]

Given these estimates and the history of replacement rates, it seems unlikely that increases in the replacement ratio have accounted for much of the secular rise in European unemployment. There is, however, circumstantial evidence that the administration of benefits has become much less strict and whole categories of people (such as students) who formerly did not consider taking benefits now do so. This and other changes in the work ethnic cannot easily be quantified or explained, but they may be important influences on the level of unemployment.

---

[79]Abraham (1984) shows that in Wisconsin and Minnesota actual vacancies increased at least as much as the index.

[80]Jackman, Layard and Pissarides (1984).

[81]See also Solon (1983) and Hamermesh (1977).

6.2.4. Employment protection legislation

In Europe the costs of firing have increased greatly in the last fifteen years. Required redundancy payments have increased, advance notice of redundancy has been lengthened, and the right to claim unfair dismissal strengthened. This has naturally made employers more choosy about who they appoint, and this too may have shifted out the U/V curve.

6.2.5. The productivity slowdown and changes in the terms of trade

An important change that has affected all industrialized countries has been the fall in the rate of productivity growth since 1973 (or earlier in the case of the United States). This has reduced the feasible growth of real wages. In addition, for two decades up to 1973 the industrialized countries benefited from a steady fall in the price of imported raw materials relative to the price of their own output, but this stopped after the first oil shock. Both these changes reduced the feasible rate of growth of real wages (g). If target real wages (g^*) do not adjust fully, this will, according to eq. (6.4), raise equilibrium unemployment. We have already given estimates of the role of this variable. Our equation of course assumed that "expectations" have not so far adapted to reality. This is because it is difficult to estimate the process of adaptation. However, there must have been some adaptation. Our model of Section 4.3 offers an interpretation of this process which provides some insight into why the adaptation might be slow. Even if people correctly perceive reality, it may take some time for them to adjust psychologically and accept the fairness of wages lower than they would earlier have considered fair.[82]

6.2.6. Tax effects

Another set of forces that require workers to accept lower real wages are tax increases. In most countries there have been secular increases in employers' labor taxes, in employees' tax on earnings and in indirect taxes. If employees do not accept this implied fall in real take-home pay then employment will be reduced. Clearly, there could be transitional problems along the lines discussed above, but what of the long run? In our earlier models a proportional employers' tax was fully passed back into wages, though a per worker tax was not. There has been surprisingly little work investigating these effects. Nor is much known about responses to changes in employees' taxes or indirect taxes, which in our models

---

[82] For an elegant market-clearing analysis based entirely on misperception, see Brunner, Cukierman and Meltzer (1980). But misperception does not seem a plausible explanation of a really slow adaptation.

Table 16.16
Union membership as a percentage of employees in employment

	Belgium	France	Germany	Italy	Netherlands	Sweden	United Kingdom	United States
1950			38		44	59	45	31
1955			40		44	64	46	33
1960	62	24	37	55–60	42	68	45	31
1965	62	23	36	55–60	40	69	45	28
1970	66	22	36	50–55	39	72	50	27
1975	75	23	39	50–55	44	82	53	25
1980	76[a]	28	40	60[a]	44	83	57	22

Sources: Germany, Sweden, United Kingdom, United States: G. S. Bain and R. Price, *Profiles of Union Growth*, Blackwell, Oxford, 1980 (updated for 1980). Belgium, France, Italy: Eurostat, *Social Indicators of the E. C., 1960–1978*. 1980 figure for France from INSEE. Eurostat stress that figures for these three countries should be taken as rough guides only. Netherlands: *Netherlands Statistical Yearbook*.
[a]1978 figures.

would have no effects unless they affected the replacement ratio. Clearly, empirical work on these issues is urgently needed.[83]

6.2.7. Unions

The influences we have so far considered could all affect unemployment if wages were set by firms (or even in most cases if they were set by supply and demand). However unions play an important part in many labor markets, especially in Europe, where they often have a profound influence on the pay of non-union as well as union members.

Our earlier models showed that increases in trade union membership and in the trade union wage mark-up would both increase unemployment. Table 16.16 gives some figures on union membership, which show how this generally rose in Europe during the 1970s and fell in the United States. As regards the mark-up, the evidence suggests that this has risen fairly steadily in Britain since the early 1960s [Layard and Nickell (1986a)], while in the United States it fell during the 1960s and rose in the 1970s to a level of higher than in 1960 [Johnson (1983)].

As so often, attempts to estimate union employment effects from time-series produce results that vary wildly with the specification. Minford (1983) finds strong effects of unions and benefits in Britain, but his estimates of the process of wage formation make no allowance for the influence of productivity. Layard and Nickell (1986a) find that union effects via the increased mark-up may have

---

[83] For attempts see Knoester (1983) and Layard and Nickell (1986a).

increased unemployment in Britain by around 3 percentage points over the last 20 years.

6.2.8. Minimum wages

Perhaps the most studied cause of unemployment is minimum wages. These only affect a small proportion of the labor force in any country – mostly young people and, to a lesser extent, women. Their effect in the United States has been fairly clearly demonstrated,[84] and variations in minimum wages do account for a small portion of the rise in the U.S. equilibrium unemployment rate. In most other countries, however, the secular rise in unemployment has also affected adult male workers, which requires a more general explanation along the lines we have suggested.

6.2.9. Aggregate demand

Finally, we must refer to the short run, since nobody knows how short it is. Clearly aggregate demand can drive the level of employment away from its equilibrium level for quite a number of years. The United States had a prolonged demand-led boom in the 1960s, and Europe appears to be in a prolonged demand-led slump in the 1980s.[85] An important issue is what determines employment in the short run, but this topic is covered in other chapters of this Handbook. Our own inclination is to think that in the short run employment depends directly not only on real factor prices (as in the perfect competition model) but also on aggregate demand variables (as in imperfect competition models). However, in equilibrium the net effect of aggregate demand influences is itself endogenous,[86] and our earlier models give an adequate insight into the basic influences affecting aggregate unemployment.

---

[84] For a survey see Brown, Gilroy and Kohen (1982).

[85] Layard, Basevi, Blanchard, Buiter and Dornbusch (1984).

[86] A reasonable model might be:

$$\text{employment:} \quad N = f_1\left(\frac{W}{P}, D\right);$$

$$\text{price:} \quad \frac{P}{W} = f_2(D, W - W^e);$$

$$\text{wage:} \quad \frac{W}{P} = f_3(N, P - P^e),$$

where D is a demand shift which depends on say real interest, fiscal variables, world trade, and competitiveness. In the long-run $W - W^e = P - P^e = 0$. So there is a natural rate of N, W/P and D. This model is estimated for the United Kingdom in Layard and Nickell (1986a). See also Layard and Nickell (1986b) for a more recent analysis, which distinguishes between the short-run and long-run natural rates of unemployment.

To conclude, economists cannot claim to have answered all the questions with which we began this chapter. But the questions are among the most important which people expect economists to answer. We hope this survey will stimulate more efforts to solve them.

References

Abraham, K. G. (1984) "What does the help-wanted index measure", mimeo, Massachusetts Institute of Technology.

Abraham, K. G. and L. F. Katz (1984) "Cyclical unemployment: sectoral shifts or aggregate disturbances?", Working Paper No. 1579-84, Massachusetts Institute of Technology, Alfred P. Sloan School of Management.

Akerlof, G. A. and B. G. M. Main (1980) "Unemployment spells and unemployment experience", *American Economic Review*, 70:885–893.

Ashenfelter, O. (1978) "Estimating the effect of training programmes on earnings with longitudinal data", *Review of Economics and Statistics*, 60(1).

Ashenfelter, O. and G. E. Johnson (1969) "Bargaining theory, trade unions, and industrial strike activity", *American Economic Review* 59(1).

Atkinson, A. B. and J. E. Stiglitz (1980) *Lectures on public economics*. McGraw-Hill.

Baily, M. N. and J. Tobin (1977) "Macroeconomic effects of selective public employment and wage subsidies", *Brookings Papers on Economic Activity*, 2:511–541.

Barro, R. J. (1978) "Unanticipated money, output, and the price level in the United States", *Journal of Political Economy*.

Benjamin, D. L. and L. A. Kochin (1979) "Searching for an explanation of unemployment in inter-war Britain", *Journal of Political Economy*, 87(3).

Bishop, J. (1981) "Employment in construction and distribution industries: the impacts of the new jobs tax credit", in: S. Rosen, ed., *Studies in Labor Markets*. NBER.

Brown, C., C. Gilroy and A. Kohen (1982) "The effect of the minimum wage on employment and unemployment", *Journal of Economic Literature*, 10:487–528.

Brunner, K., A. Cukierman and A. H. Meltzer (1980) "Stagflation, persistent unemployment and the permance of economic shocks", *Journal of Monetary Economics*, 6:467–492.

Calvo, G. (1979) "Quasi-Walrasian theories of unemployment", *American Economic Review*, 69(2).

Clark, K. B. and L. H. Summers (1979) "Labor market dynamics and unemployment: a reconsideration", *Brokkings Papers on Economic Activity*, 1:13–72.

Diamond, P. A. (1981) "Mobility costs, frictional unemployment, and efficiency", *Journal of Political Economy*, 89:798–812.

Ehrenberg, R. G. and R. L. Oaxaca (1976) "Unemployment insurance, duration of unemployment and subsequent wage gain", *American Economic Review*, 66(5).

Ehrenberg, R. G. and P. L. Schumann (1982) *Longer hours or more jobs?*. Cornell University.

Ellwood, D. and D. Wise (1983) "Youth employment in the 70's: the changing circumstances of young adults", in: R. R. Nelson and F Skidmore, eds., *American families and the economy*. Washington, D.C.: National Acad. Press.

Farber, H. S. (1978) "Bargaining theory, wage outcomes, and the occurrence of strikes", *American Economic Review*, 68:262–271.

Feldstein, M. (1976) "Temporary layoffs in the theory of unemployment", *Journal of Political Economy*, 84:937–957.

Feldstein, M. and D. T. Ellwood (1982) "Teenage unemployment: what is the problem?", in: R. B. Freeman and D. A. Wise, eds., *The youth labor market problem*, University of Chicago Press.

Fethke, G. C., A. J. Policano and S. H. Williamson (1979) "Macroeconomic implications of employment tax credit policy", *Southern Economic Journal*, 46:513–527.

Flinn, C. J. and J. J. Heckman (1983) "Are unemployment and out of the labor force behaviorally distinct labor force states?", *Journal of Labour Economics*, 1:28–42.

Friedman, M. (1968) "The role of monetary policy", *The American Economic Review*, 58:1–17.

Grubb, D., R. A. Jackman and P. R. G. Layard (1982) "Causes of the current stagflation", *Review of*

Economic Studies, 49:707–730. Reprinted (1983) in: C. A. Greenhalgh, P. R. G. Layard and A. J. Oswald, eds., *The causes of unemployment*. Clarendon Press.

Grubb, D., R. A. Jackman and P. R. G. Layard (1983) "Wage rigidity and unemployment in OECD countries", *European Economic Review*, 21(1/2).

Hall, R. E. (1972) "Turnover in the labour force", *Brookings Papers on Economic Activity*, 3:709–756.

Hall, R. E. (1975) "The rigidity of wages and persistence of unemployment", *Brookings Papers on Economic Activity*, 2:301–350.

Hall, R. E. (1977) "An aspect of the economic role of unemployment", in: G. C. Harcourt, ed., *Microeconomic foundations of macroeconomics*.

Hamermesh, D. S. (1977) *Jobless pay and the economy*. Johns Hopkins.

Hamermesh, D. S. (1982a) "Transfers, taxes and the NAIRU", in: Lawrence Meyer, ed., *The supply-side effects of economic policy*. Boston: Kluwer Nijoff.

Hamermesh, D. S. (1982b) "The interaction between research and policy: the case of unemployment insurance", *American Economic Review Proceedings*, 72:237–241.

Hamermesh, D. S. and J. Grant (1979) "Econometric studies of labour–labour substitution and their implications for policy", *Journal of Human Resources*, 14(4).

Harris, J. and M. Todaro (1970) "Migration, unemployment and development. A 2-sector analysis", *American Economic Review*, 55:126–142.

Heckman, J. J. and G. J. Borjas (1980) "Does unemployment cause future unemployment? Definitions, questions and answers from a continuous time model of heterogeneity and state dependence", *Economica*, 47:247–285.

Jackman, R. A. and P. R. G. Layard (1980) "The efficiency case for long-run labour market policies", *Economica*, 47:331–349.

Jackman, R. A., P. R. G. Layard and C. Pissarides (1984) "On vacancies", revised, mimeo, London School of Economics, Centre for Labour Economics.

Jackman, R. A., P. R. G. Layard and C. Pissarides (1986) "Policies for reducing the natural rate of unemployment", in: J. L. Butkiewicz, K. J. Koford and J. B. Miller, eds., *Keynes' economic legacy*. Praeger.

Johnson, G. E. (1980) "The theory of labour market intervention", *Economica*, 47:309–329.

Johnson, G. E. (1982) "Allocation and distributional effects", in: R. H. Haveman and John L. Palmer, eds., *Jobs for disadvantaged workers, the economics of employment subsidies*. Brookings.

Johnson, G. E. (1983) "Unionism in a macroeconomic context: an exploratory analysis", mimeo, University of Michigan.

Johnson, G. E. and A. Blakemore (1979) "The potential impact of employment policy for reducing the unemployment rate consistent with non-accelerating inflation", *American Economic Review*, 69:119–130.

Johnson, G. E. and P. R. G. Layard (1982) "Efficient public employment with labour market distortions", in: R. Haveman, ed., *Public finance and public employment*. Detroit: Wayne State University Press.

Keifer, N. M. and G. R. Neumann (1982) "Wages and the structure of unemployment rates", in: M. N. Baily, ed., *Workers, jobs and inflation*. Brookings.

Knoester, A. (1983) "Stagnation and the inverted haavelmo effect, some international evidence", *De Economist*, 131:548–583.

Layard, R., G. Basevi, O. Blanchard, W. Buiter and R. Dornbusch (1984) "Europe: the case for unsustainable growth", CEPS Papers No. 8/9, Centre for European Policy Studies.

Layard, P. R. G. and S. J. Nickell (1980) "The case for subsidising extra jobs", *Economic Journal*.

Layard, P. R. G. and S. J. Nickell (1986a) "Unemployment in Britain", *Economica*, Supplement, 53:S121–S170.

Layard, P. R. G. and S. J. Nickell (1986b) "The performance of the British labor market", Discussion paper no. 249, London School of Economics, Centre for Labour Economics.

Layard, P. R. G., D. Piachaud and M. Stewart (1979) *The causes of poverty*, Background Paper No. 5, Royal Commission on the Distribution of Income and Wealth, HMSO, 1978.

Lilien, D. M. (1982a) "Sectoral shifts and cyclical unemployment", *Journal of Political Economy*, 777–793.

Lilien, D. M. (1982b) "A sectoral model of the business cycle", MRG Working Paper No. 8231, University of Southern California, Department of Economics.

Lucas, R. E. (1973) "Some international evidence on output–inflation trade-offs", *American Economic Review*.

Main, B. G. M. (1981) "The length of employment and unemployment in Great Britain", *Scottish Journal of Political Economy*, 28(2).

Marston, S. T. (1976) "Employment instability and high unemployment rates", *Brookings Papers on Economic Activity*, 1.

Marston, S. T. (1980) "Voluntary unemployment", in: National Commission on Unemployment Compensation, *Unemployment compensation: studies and research*, Vol. II, 431–438. Washington, D.C.

Medoff, J. L. (1983) "U.S. labor markets: imbalance, wage growth, and productivity in the 1970s", *Brookings Papers on Economic Activity*, 1:87–128.

Metcalf, D., S. J. Nickell and N. Floros (1982) "Still searching for an explanation of unemployment in inter-war Britain", *Journal of Political Economy*.

Mincer, J. (1976) "Unemployment effects of minimum wages", *Journal of Political Economy*, 84:S87–S105.

Minford, P. (1983) "Labour market equilibrium in an open economy", *Oxford Economic Papers*, 35(4). Reprinted (1983) in: C. A. Greenhalgh, P. R. G. Layard and A. J. Oswald, eds., *The causes of unemployment*. Clarendon Press.

Narendranathan, W., S. Nickell and J. Stern (1985) "Unemployment benefits revisited", *Economic Journal*, June.

Nichols, D. A. (1983) "Macroeconomic determinants of wage adjustment in white-collar occupations", *Review of Economics and Statistics*, 65:203–213.

Nickell, S. J. (1980) "A picture of male unemployment in Britain", *Economic Journal*, 90:776–795.

Nickell, S. J. and M. Andrews (1983) "Unions, real wages and employment in Britain 1951–79", *Oxford Economic Papers*. Reprinted (1983) in: C. A. Greenhalgh, P. R. G. Layard and A. J. Oswald, eds., *The causes of unemployment*. Clarendon Press.

OECD (1982) *Marginal employment subsidies*.

Oswald, A. J. and D. T. Ulph (1982) "Unemployment and the pure theory of the trade union", Discussion Papers in Economics, No. 30, University College, London.

Pencavel, J. H. (1972) "Wages, specific training, and labor turnover in U.S. manufacturing industries", *International Economic Review*, 13(1).

Perloff, J. M. and M. L. Wachter (1979) "A production function—Non-accelerating inflation approach to potential output", *Journal of Monetary Economics*, 10(Supplement):113–163.

Pissarides, C. (1984) "The allocation of jobs through search: some questions of efficiency", *Economic Journal*, Dec.

Salant, S. W. (1977) "Search theory and duration data: a theory of sorts", *Quarterly Journal of Economics*, 91:39–58.

Salop, S. C. (1979) "A model of the natural rate of unemployment", *American Economic Review*, 69:117–125.

Santomero, A. A. and J. J. Seater (1978) "The inflation–unemployment trade-off: a critique of the literature", *Journal of Economic Literature*, 16:499–544.

Shapiro, C. and J. Stiglitz (1984) "Equilibrium unemployment as a worker discipline device", *American Economic Review*.

Solon, G. (1983) "Work incentive effects of taxing unemployment benefits", mimeo, University of Michigan.

Stern, J. (1982) "Unemployment inflow rates for autumn 1978", Discussion Paper No. 129. London School of Economics, Centre for Labour Economics.

Stiglitz, J. E. (1974) "Wage determination and unemployment in LDCs", *Quarterly Journal of Economics*, 88:194–227.

Stiglitz, J. E. (1986) "Theories of wage rigidity", in: J. L. Butkiewicz, K. J. Koford and J. B. Miller, eds., *Keynes' economic legacy*. Praeger.

Weiss, A. (1980) "Job queues and layoffs in labour markets with flexible wages", *Journal of Political Economy*, 88:523–538.

Welch, F. (1976) "Minimum wage legislation in the United States", in: O. Ashenfelter and J. Blum, eds., *Evaluating the labour market effects of social programs*, 1–38. Princeton University Press.

Wilson, J. D. (1982) "The optimal public employment policy", *Journal of Public Economics* 17:241–258.

Yellen, J. L. (1984) "Efficiency wage models of unemployment", *American Economic Review*, 74:200–205.

Chapter 17

CYCLICAL FLUCTUATIONS IN THE LABOR MARKET

DAVID M. LILIEN

University of California, Irvine

ROBERT E. HALL

Stanford University

1. Introduction and scope

Every few years the U.S. economy, and similar economies around the world, enters recessions. Though the macroeconomic event triggering the recession will differ from one episode to the next, the responses of the labor market are generally quite similar. As total output declines, a characteristic set of changes occurs. During the expansion, these changes are reversed, though the cycle in the labor market often lags behind the cycle in output and some other indicators.

In this chapter we examine facts and theories related to cyclic fluctuations in the labor market. In the process, we review and summarize, selectively, a good deal of research by macroeconomists and labor economists.

We organize our examination of the facts about cyclical fluctuations by starting with annual variations in total hours of work. In an economy unperturbed by sudden new developments, or one where a smoothly functioning price system could absorb all shocks, annual hours would grow smoothly along with the population. But in the U.S. economy, hours fluctuate around their growth path; they tend to track the business cycle. People work harder in booms than in slumps. We decompose fluctuations of annual hours into a number of components. When total hours of work are higher, people tend to spend fewer hours looking for work and fewer hours in non-work activities. The two together account for the bulk of cyclical changes. But there are important changes in the hours of workers within the framework of their continuing jobs. Weekly hours fall during a recession. A larger fraction of workers are cut involuntarily to part-time schedules as well.

We look behind these fluctuations in hours of work with a view to appraising the quantitative importance of phenomena identified in recent research. One

Handbook of Labor Economics, Volume II, Edited by O. Ashenfelter and R. Layard
©*Elsevier Science Publishers BV, 1986*

important issue is the distribution of employment adjustments. When annual hours fall by 3 percent, is it because an added 3 percent of workers do not work at all that year, or because everybody works a week or two less during the year? The answer is that extended periods of unemployment and non-work for individuals are an important part of the process. It is true that employment adjustments are distributed widely across the labor force, but most of them generate relatively little unemployment. The quantitatively important source of unemployment is long spells.

We also take a special look at the difference between unemployment and joblessness. Some of the unemployed have not lost their jobs; they are temporarily laid off and expect to return to their jobs in a few weeks. It is true that a reasonably large fraction of workers who are laid off return, eventually, to their original jobs. However, the contribution of temporary layoffs to total unemployment is quite small. The biggest jump in unemployment in a recession comes from workers who have unambiguously lost their jobs and are seeking new ones.

The bulk of the chapter looks at theories that try to explain cyclical fluctuations in the labor market. Generally, the theories do not tackle the explanation of the finer grain of the process – most treat annual hours as the variable of interest.

At the outset, we introduce a distinction between the two major ingredients of a successful theory of cyclical fluctuations: an *economic mechanism* and a *driving force*. The three mechanisms that have been prominent in recent thinking are, first, the Keynesian hypothesis of unilateral employment determination by the firm; second, the intertemporal substitution mechanism; and, third, the job search mechanism. The driving forces we consider are real shocks and misperceptions about the state of the economy.

Thinking about cyclical fluctuations in the labor market has been as strongly influenced as almost any area of macroeconomics by the hypothesis of rational expectations. However, the hypothesis is not divisive. On the contrary, as the implications of rational expectations have been clarified over the past decade, the surviving theories of fluctuations have embodied the hypothesis. One of the most important consequences has been a diminution of the role of misperceptions as a driving force and an upsurge of interest in real driving forces.

Important models of labor market fluctuations have emerged that combine one or another mechanism and the moving force of misperceptions. The oldest of these, the Phillips curve, rests on the premise that wages are predetermined and employers determine employment unilaterally by equating the marginal revenue product of labor to the wage. Misperceptions in setting the wage in advance create departures of employment from equilibrium. Though the Phillips curve view has not answered some important criticisms from other schools, it remains the dominant mode of thinking among practical macroeconomists. The upsurge of interest in labor market contracts has helped support some of the ideas about the Phillips curve, most notably the hypothesis that employers set employment unilaterally.

The search model explains fluctuations in unemployment in terms of misperceptions by the unemployed or by employers about the prevailing level of the wage in the market. Because the most important dimension of fluctuations seems to be between work and non-market activities, rather than between work and intensive job search, the search model never achieved much importance in practical thinking. More generally, research on job search has developed into a major field of its own, but has not focused on explaining aggregate fluctuations.

Intertemporal substitution models hypothesize that employment fluctuates according to a mechanism in which temporarily high real interest rates or temporarily high real wages are mistakenly perceived by workers. Again, this type of model has not achieved much practical importance. There seems to be little basis for well-informed workers to make the mistake of thinking that real wages are temporarily high, because the stochastic process of real wages has only a small transitory component. Though perceived real interest rates probably fluctuate quite a bit, empirical work based on their influence on labor supply has reached negative conclusions.

Real shocks have been married to intertemporal substitution and job search to yield cyclical models as well. As we mentioned earlier, professional interest has shifted in this direction as the rational expectations hypothesis has circumscribed the theoretical role of perception errors. Shifts in productivity or in product demand have been proposed as real driving forces in connection with the intertemporal substitution mechanism. As with the intertemporal substitution model with perception errors, the empirical evidence has not so far been favorable.

Real shocks have been combined with ideas about job search in recent work. If the nature of the shock is a change in the composition of product demand, the response in the job market may involve shifting workers from one sector to another, which involves temporarily lower levels of employment and higher unemployment. Empirical research suggests that this consideration may have been important in the fluctuations of the 1970s, though it cannot explain all of the labor market movements of the postwar era.

2. The nature of employment fluctuations

2.1. Fluctuations in total annual hours of work

A basic question about cyclical fluctuations in the labor market is the following: How large are fluctuations in total hours of work and how are they distributed between changes on the job and movements into and out of the labor market?

Over the postwar period, several long-term trends, including increasing labor force participation of women, decreasing participation of men, earlier retirement,

Table 17.1
Means and standard deviations of detrended measures of
hours of work, 1956–1983.

Detrended series	Mean	S.D.
Annual hours per capita (16 +)	1168.2	33.2
Annual hours (all workers)	2053.6	14.8
Annual hours (full-time workers and workers on part-time schedules for noneconomic reasons)	2066.1	11.9
Unemployment rate (percent of labor force)	6.1	1.5
Per capita hours lost to unemployment time	75.5	18.2
Labor force participation rate	60.6	0.4
Percent of labor force on part-time schedules for economic reasons	3.2	0.7
Per capita hours lost to part-time schedules for economic reasons	7.1	3.6

Source: See Table 17.2.

and the changing age composition of the population, were occurring at the same time as the shorter-term fluctuations in labor market aggregates that we are interested in. For that reason we have detrended the aggregates to isolate short-run fluctuations. We regressed all variables on two trend variables and the unemployment rate of males aged 25–54. The first trend variable is a simple time trend running over the entire period from 1956 through 1983. The second is set at zero before 1968 and follows a simple time trend from 1968 to 1983. The detrended series were then calculated by subtracting the estimated trend from the actual series after normalizing the two trend variables to zero in 1972. Thus, the resulting hours series can be interpreted as reflecting fluctuations in normalized 1972 hours.

Tables 17.1 and 17.2 examine variations in hours of work per capita over the business cycle. Because we are concerned about cyclical shifts in the size of the labor force, we define per capita relative to the potential working population (those 16 and older) rather just those who are classified as being in the labor force. A significant fraction of hours variation stems from changes in the size of the labor force. Our calculations also sidestep the question as to how successful the BLS measure of labor force participation is in distinguishing between unemployment and non-participation [see Clark and Summers (1979)]. These tables give no indication of the distribution of hours fluctuations among individuals.

A line in Table 17.2 should be read in the following way. Take the total deviation in annual hours from trend; say, 24.6 hours in 1956. Of this, 15.7 hours

Table 17.2
Dimensions of variation in hours per capita.

Year	Detrended annual hours per capita		Deviation in annual hours per capita attributable to deviations of:					
			Employment			Hours/employed worker		
	Total	Deviation from average	Total employment	Unem- ployment	Labor force participation	Total hours	Full time	Involuntary part time
1956	1192.8	24.6	15.7	11.1	4.8	8.8	4.9	3.8
1957	1176.0	7.7	9.5	10.0	−0.1	−1.8	−3.5	1.6
1958	1135.8	−32.4	−20.8	−20.7	−0.3	−11.4	−9.6	−1.5
1959	1160.0	−8.2	−5.0	−2.2	−2.7	−3.1	−1.9	−1.1
1960	1165.1	−3.1	−0.2	−2.3	2.1	−2.6	0.1	−2.6
1961	1150.1	−18.1	−13.0	−15.6	2.2	−4.6	−0.2	−4.1
1962	1163.3	−4.9	−6.9	−0.5	−6.5	2.3	5.5	−3.1
1963	1166.0	−2.2	−6.8	−0.4	−6.6	5.0	3.3	1.6
1964	1174.6	6.4	2.9	6.8	−3.8	3.7	1.5	2.1
1965	1199.9	31.7	16.4	16.0	0.6	15.3	12.4	2.7
1966	1217.6	49.4	34.8	26.0	8.9	14.3	11.3	2.7
1967	1227.8	59.6	45.2	26.4	18.6	14.0	10.3	3.5
1968	1223.9	55.7	42.9	30.3	12.4	12.6	9.0	3.3
1969	1221.3	53.1	45.5	31.5	13.7	7.7	4.1	3.3
1970	1190.5	22.3	25.9	13.2	12.2	−2.8	−6.3	3.4
1971	1164.1	−4.1	2.2	1.4	0.2	−5.5	−8.7	3.1
1972	1168.6	0.4	2.9	6.1	−3.7	−1.8	−5.0	3.1
1973	1181.2	13.0	13.0	15.7	−3.3	1.0	−1.3	2.2
1974	1166.9	−1.3	5.2	6.3	−1.7	−5.6	−6.8	1.1
1975	1116.7	−51.5	−38.5	−28.8	−9.8	−13.5	−12.7	−0.6
1976	1130.1	−38.1	−29.7	−18.8	−11.0	−8.5	−8.3	−0.1
1977	1147.9	−20.3	−15.8	−10.3	−5.7	−4.2	−4.7	0.5
1978	1180.0	11.8	6.9	2.3	4.1	5.7	4.5	1.2
1979	1186.1	17.9	12.6	5.3	6.6	6.2	5.5	0.7
1980	1153.7	−14.5	−10.0	−10.8	1.0	−4.6	−2.3	−2.2
1981	1141.7	−26.5	−21.3	−16.0	−4.7	−5.8	−0.5	−5.1
1982	1100.9	−67.3	−54.2	−42.0	−10.1	−16.3	−6.3	−9.6
1983	1107.2	−61.0	−59.4	−40.0	−17.3	−4.5	5.7	−9.7

Source: Raw data are from U.S. Bureau of Labor Statistics, *Employment and Earnings*. All series are detrended by the authors.
Notes: Components do not sum to total due to interaction terms. The column labeled "Full time" includes workers on full-time and part-time schedules for noneconomic reasons.

occurs in connection with fewer people being at work – there were 11.1 extra hours per year per person of unemployment and 4.8 extra hours spent out of the labor market. The rest of the reduction, 8.8 hours, is reduced time during weeks of work. Of the 8.8, 4.9 takes the form of lower hours for people still considered full time (that is, reduced overtime and the like) and 3.8 is lower hours for people involuntarily on part time.

Between 1956 and 1983, hours of work per capita (normalized as described at the 1972 age composition and trend participation rates) averaged 1168 hours per year. In a typical week 60.5 percent of the population was in the labor force, of which 93.9 percent were employed. The employed worked an average of 39.5 hours. Of these 3.2 percent were constrained to part-time schedules for economic reasons; the average hours of full-time and voluntary part-time workers were 39.7 hours.

Annual fluctuations in hours of work are not terribly big. The standard deviation in annual hours is only 2.9 percent of the normal level of hours. Even in 1975 and 1982–83, the two lowest points for detrended employment since the Great Depression, annual per capita hours were down by only 50.6 hours and 69.1 hours, respectively, or by about 4.3 percent and 5.9 percent of normal labor market hours. Between 1966 and 1969 per capita hours averaged 55.3 hours or 4.7 percent above normal hours.

In a study of the data for any given month, it is apparent that hours fluctuations associated with the business cycle are not spread relatively evenly among the working population through the use of work sharing and shorter work weeks for most workers but instead are concentrated as unemployment for a few workers. Because private compensation for workers on layoff is relatively rare in the United States, reductions in hours of work through unemployment introduce considerable variation in weekly and monthly earnings. Whether annual earnings are more variable than they would be with complete work sharing depends on the distribution of unemployment within the labor force. If unemployment is distributed evenly among all workers, then it amounts to no more than a slightly different pattern of work sharing. We will return to this issue in the next section. In the typical recession no more than a fourth of aggregate hour reductions stem from changes in weekly hours on full-time jobs. In 1975, employed full-time workers and workers on voluntary part-time schedules worked 26 minutes a week less than their normal (trend) hours including normal overtime. This amounts to a 1.1 percent deviation from trend and approximately a fourth of the total deviation in per capita hours from trend.

The biggest component of the variation in hours is fluctuations in the level of employment. In 1975, for example, per capita hours were 4.3 percent below trend. The detrended employment rate (the ratio of employed persons to the adult aged population) was 54.9 percent compared to the trend of 56.8 percent. That is to say, employment per capita was roughly 1.8 percentage points or 3.2 percent below trend; this accounted for roughly 74 percent of the total decline in per capita hours. Similar patterns occurred in other years. Fluctuations of the employment rate account for between 75 and 80 percent of the below trend hours in 1982–83 and the above trend hours in 1967–69.

There are several reasons why the bulk of hours reductions take the form of periodic nonemployment rather than shorter full time schedules.

(1) Imperfect experience rating of unemployment insurance subsidizes hour reductions that take the form of unemployment [see Feldstein (1976)].

(2) Fixed costs of work in the form of commuting and setup costs make it more economical for workers to stay home rather than working short hours.

(3) Production technologies may make it infeasible or expensive to shorten the work week. High startup and shutdown costs in manufacturing industries encourage less frequent plant shut downs lasting several weeks rather than the frequent ones associated with shorter shifts. Feldstein and others have modeled this by allowing number of employees and hours per employee to enter the production function separately.

(4) Shifts of demand between sectors of the economy necessitate labor reallocation. Employees must depart firms with contracting demand and be hired by firms with expanding demand. Efficiency calls for separations rather than hour reductions in these situations. Informational problems may yield separation rates in excess of what is efficient [Hall and Lazear (1984)]. Lilien (1982a, 1982b) argues that part of what we label cyclical fluctuations is in fact slow adjustment to intersectoral shifts of demand.

So far, we have stressed the cyclical fluctuations in hours of work per capita. Although data on work hours are not entirely free of problems, there is no important conceptual ambiguity about defining and measuring hours. Table 17.2 also makes the distinction between unemployment and not in the labor force, with respect to hours not spent at work. That distinction is a notoriously difficult and ambiguous one, although it is obviously important. In the U.S. data, the distinction is made almost purely on the basis of job-seeking activity. Of those people not working during the survey week, those who have taken any specific step to look for work within four weeks of the survey count as unemployed. Those who have not looked in the past four weeks are out of the labor force.

Table 17.2 shows that hours fluctuations associated with changes in labor force participation were unimportant in the contractions of 1957–58 and 1961, but became a significant part of the story of labor market fluctuations starting with the expansion of the 1960s. In 1967, when total hours of work per capita were almost 60 hours per year above trend, about 19 of those hours were associated with a bulge in the fraction of the population who were in the labor force. Similarly, the strong contractions of 1975 and 1982 saw important declines in labor force participation.

Table 17.2 does not try to describe the process of temporary layoffs, which some authors have stressed as a mechanism for cyclical fluctuations in hours of work. Part of the reduction in employment that occurs in a recession is not a consequence of job loss. When demand slackens, workers in manufacturing are sometimes put on temporary layoff. They retain their jobs and can usually expect to return to work in a few weeks or months. In the automobile industry, reduced hours per year are frequently brought about by cycling a large fraction of workers through periodic one-week layoffs. We will have more to say about this process later in this section.

2.2. *Concentration of unemployment*

The fact that the majority of hours fluctuations stem from fluctuations of employment, not hours per week, in itself tells us little about how evenly hours reductions are distributed among workers or whether they bear most severely on a particular group of workers.

Until recent decades, the economist's image of unemployment was largely an outgrowth of the Great Depression. The view was of a relatively stagnant stock of job-seekers. Unemployment was viewed as an extreme hardship for the few who would not find jobs until the economy recovered from recession. In the 1960s and 1970s the view of unemployment changed radically. Better unemployment data, including spell duration data and labor turnover data, along with relatively low unemployment rates, changed the perception of unemployment to that of a short-term state occupied by workers at various times during their working careers. As a general matter, thinking about unemployment began to focus on the role of turnover.

Labor turnover data indicate that flows into unemployment are quite high. In manufacturing industries almost 4.5 percent of workers depart their jobs each month. Similarly, duration data show that most unemployment spells are quite short. BLS data on the duration of incomplete unemployment spells indicate a mean spell duration of 12.5 weeks on the average from 1956 to 1983. Kaitz (1970) and others have shown that these BLS duration figures grossly overstate the duration of completed unemployment spells because the CPS samples workers rather than spells.

The new view of the labor market was one where workers frequently left jobs, either voluntarily or involuntarily, suffered short duration spells of unemployment and quickly became reemployed. To the extent that most workers were viewed as suffering some but not much unemployment, the burden of aggregate fluctuations was spread among a large base, not concentrated on a few individuals.

More recently, a new middle ground between these two extreme characterizations is being argued. While it is recognized that (a) most unemployment spells are very short and (b) most jobs do not last long, it also recognizes two other important facts.

(1) Most unemployment time is spent in spells of long durations or sequences of repeated spells of unemployment. A small fraction of individuals suffer the majority of unemployment time.

(2) Most workers are in jobs that will last for quite a number of years.

The pioneering work that showed that the stochastic process governing the labor market had all of these characteristics was Clark and Summers (1979). Their most important point was that a minority of workers have low job-finding rates when they are looking, even though most job-seekers have about a 50 percent chance of departing unemployment each month. The unsuccessful minority contribute the bulk of unemployment. In 1974, only 2.4 percent of the labor force had more than 6 months of unemployment, but that group accounted for over 40 percent of all unemployment. By contrast, in a simple Markoff model that generated the same unemployment rate, that group would account for only 8 percent of total unemployment. In the Markoff model, all job-seekers would face the same monthly probability of success. It is the unequal distribution of job-finding probabilities that makes unemployment so concentrated.

Clark and Summers also examine the concentration of unemployment and non-work over longer time spans. They show that over a four-year period, 40 percent of all unemployment is experienced by people who are out of work for a full year or more. Again, if everybody had the same probabilities of finding work when looking and losing work when working, the concentration of unemployment and non-work would be vastly lower.

Closely related to their central conclusion is Clark and Summers' finding that successful job search is a relatively unimportant contributor to unemployment. In 1974, only 28 percent of unemployment was associated with spells of 2 months or less ending in re-employment. Almost half of all unemployment – 47 percent – came from spells ending in withdrawal from the labor force rather than success in finding work.

We can summarize the current state of thinking about turnover in the following way. The unemployed are neither a stagnant mass of people who will not work until the economy improves nor are they exclusively a group of job-seekers on the verge of finding new work. Disproportionately, they are people who have trouble finding and holding jobs. They cycle from brief jobs to extended periods of job search and equally extended periods out of the labor force. Mixed in are people who are making normal job changes and have high probabilities each month of finding new work. In terms of flows through unemployment, the latter group is dominant. But in terms of the stock of the unemployed at any one time, those with poor experience are dominant.

2.3. Layoffs and rehires

Feldstein (1972) called attention to the importance of layoffs and rehires in the response to fluctuations in demand. The process has two aspects. First, in contractions, layoffs rise relative to rehires, so that the number of workers on layoff rises. The reverse happens in expansions. Second, and less intuitive, is that a continual process of recurrent layoffs is one of the ways that work sharing operates during a period of sustained slack. In the auto industry, as we men-

Table 17.3
Unemployment by reason.

Year	Total unemployment	Involun- tary	On layoff	Lost job	Quit or entered
1967	3.8	1.6			2.2
1968	3.6	1.4			2.2
1969	3.5	1.2			2.3
1970	4.9	2.2			2.7
1971	5.9	2.8			2.9
1972	5.6	2.4			3.2
1973	4.9	1.9			3.0
1974	5.6	2.4			3.2
1975	8.5	4.7			3.8
1976	7.7	3.8	1.1	2.7	3.9
1977	7.1	3.2	1.0	2.2	3.9
1978	6.1	2.5	0.7	1.8	3.4
1979	5.8	2.5	1.2	1.3	3.4
1980	7.1	3.7	1.4	2.3	3.4
1981	7.6	3.9	1.3	2.6	3.7
1982	9.7	5.7	2.1	3.6	4.0

tioned earlier, one-week layoffs occurring every few weeks or months are a common adaptation to low demand. Because of the second influence, both layoffs and rehires continue at high rates after the economy has reached its trough.

Table 17.3 presents data from the U.S. household survey on reasons for unemployment. Until 1976, the survey did not distinguish between layoffs and other reasons for involuntary departure from work. The column labeled "involuntary" includes workers who had unambiguously lost their jobs, together with those on layoff, who retain some claim on their jobs. Most, but not all, workers on layoff are rehired eventually. Note that the bulk of cyclical fluctuations occur in the involuntary category. For example, between 1974 and 1975 total unemployment rose by 2.9 percentage points. Of this, 2.3 points were in the involuntary category and only 0.6 in the category of unemployment due to earlier quit, entry, or re-entry to the labor force. The involuntary category remains high well into the expansion (in 1976 and 1977, for example), thanks to the relation between the level of unemployment and the amount of layoff–rehire turnover.

The data in Table 17.3 make it clear that layoffs are not the major contributor to unemployment, even in a deep recession. In 1982, when total unemployment rose 2.1 percentage points, the layoff contribution rose by only 0.8 points. And even this included a fraction who in fact had lost their jobs permanently.

Clark and Summers (1979) examined the role of temporary layoffs in total unemployment. From unpublished data from the household survey, they found that temporary layoffs (those where the individual expected to return to work within 30 days) accounted for only 13 percent of the unemployment of males

Table 17.4
Layoffs and rehires.

Year	Layoff rate	% ending in rehire[a]	Unemployment ending in rehire[a]	Manufacturing total	Unemployment job losers
1965	1.4	0.70	1.7	4.0	N/A
1966	1.2	0.68	1.3	3.2	N/A
1967	1.4	0.65	1.4	3.6	2.1
1968	1.2	0.68	1.3	3.3	1.9
1969	1.2	0.63	1.1	4.4	1.8
1970	1.8	0.60	1.6	5.6	3.7
1971	1.6	0.70	1.8	6.8	4.7
1972	1.1	0.75	1.5	5.6	3.5
1973	0.9	0.71	1.1	4.3	2.4
1974	1.5	0.64	1.6	5.7	3.6
1975	2.1	0.78	3.3	10.9	8.4
1976	1.3	0.74	1.8	7.8	5.4

[a] Estimated by Lilien (1979) from labor turnover data and are not strictly comparable to CPS unemployment data

aged 25–39. Even that number is probably an overstatement for the labor force as a whole. Adult men are more likely to be employed in the manufacturing industries where temporary layoffs are most important. Furthermore, not all of those expecting to return actually returned.

Table 17.4 summarizes results from Lilien's (1979) study of the layoff–rehire process. It shows that about three-quarters of layoffs end in rehire. Moreover, the percentage of layoffs that end in rehire increases in recessions – in the slack market of 1975, 78 percent of layoffs resulted in rehire rather than job change. But layoffs ending in rehire contribute only a small fraction of total unemployment, either in terms of averages or marginal changes occurring in recessions.

3. Theories of employment and unemployment fluctuations

A theory of cyclical movements of employment and unemployment combines an *economic mechanism* with a *driving force*. The economic mechanism may be as simple as standard supply and demand, or it may involve more elaborate considerations. There are three mechanisms that stand out in the literature on employment fluctuations.

(1) *Employment is chosen unilaterally by the firm, given a predetermined wage.* This is a central concept of Keynesian thinking: recently work on labor contracts has provided a sound economic rationale for what earlier seemed to be an arbitrary but realistic assumption.

(2) *Intertemporal substitution.* Workers are fairly flexible about the timing of their work from one year to the next. When they perceive that the rewards to

greater effort are strong, they will work more. Employment is higher and unemployment is less.

(3) *Search*. Unemployment is more than simple joblessness. The unemployed are making use of their time searching for the best available jobs. They balance the cost of forgone wages against the benefits of better job matches. Fluctuations in unemployment occur as changes take place in the perceived benefits of search.

The two driving forces that have figured in thinking about fluctuations are as follows.

(1) *Real shocks* – shifts in the real level and composition of demand. Examples are changes in government purchases, in investment demand, and in productivity.

(2) *Misperceptions* about the state of the economy. The wage in an employment arrangement with a predetermined wage may be set too high and bring excess unemployment. Workers may underestimate the current reward to work and so choose to work too little. Or, they may overestimate wages and adopt a search strategy that leaves them unemployed too long.

3.1. *Economic mechanisms*

Before describing the economic mechanisms that have prominent roles in the literature on employment fluctuations, it will be useful to indicate why the simplest model of supply and demand does not seem attractive as a mechanism capable of explaining the observed movements of employment. In the simple competitive labor market model, wages and employment are determined at the intersection of labor demand and labor supply curves. At the equilibrium level of employment, the marginal value of labor services in production is just equal to the value workers place on alternative uses of their time. Competitive markets yield an equilibrium that is efficient. Equilibrium in the competitive model can be perturbed by shifts in the demand for products and in labor productivity, and by changes in the value of workers' time. The resulting perturbations to employment are efficient.

The problem with the simple competitive model is that it interprets the observed employment-wage combinations as points on a simple, static labor supply curve. A glance at the data for the United States and many other economies shows large movements of employment occurring at the same time that the real wage remains unchanged. There are two possible explanations within the simple model. First, the labor supply schedule may be highly wage elastic. But a large literature on labor supply contradicts that view. Static labor supply is only slightly wage elastic, and then only for workers with major non-work alternatives. The second potential explanation is that shifts of the labor supply schedule may be a principal driving force in the economy, so that the observed wage–employment combinations are on an elastic labor demand schedule. In the second view, the typical recession occurs because people have decided not to work as hard as usual. That view has no important support in the literature, to our knowledge.

Because the simple supply and demand model cannot plausibly generate the observed pattern of co-movement of wages and employment, students have reached for more exotic economic mechanisms. In the rest of this section, we will comment on the mechanisms briefly. We will not lay out complete models until we have discussed the driving forces in the next section.

3.1.1. *Predetermined wages and unilateral employment determination*

In the simple Keynesian model the assumption of wage determination in markets is replaced with the assumption of a predetermined wage. Given the wage, firms choose the level of employment unilaterally. Excess supplies and demands may exist. In the case of excess supply of labor, the value of workers' time in production exceeds the value workers place on their own time. Workers are constrained in that at the market wage rate they wish to sell more of their services than they are able to.

The predetermined wage–unilateral employment mechanism is plainly capable of explaining the facts of employment fluctuations. It is not embarrassed by the observed pattern of employment and wages. The notion that employment decisions are made by management alone rings true in an economy where the great bulk of increases in unemployment occur because of job losses that generally appear to be regretted by the workers involved. Its continuing popularity among practical macroeconomists is understandable.

Recent thinking about employment contracts has helped clarify the circumstances when the predetermined wage–unilateral employment mechanism works well. The issue was first investigated in Calvo and Phelps (1977); they looked at what they called an "employment-contingent" contract. Later work by Hall and Lilien (1979) established the following result. Suppose that the firm faces stochastic demand, but the variable perturbing demand is not public knowledge and cannot serve as the basis of a contract contingency. Suppose further that the opportunity cost of workers' time is predictable and that workers and the firm are risk neutral. Then it is optimal to predetermine the wage to equal the opportunity cost and to let management choose the level of employment through unilateral profit maximization. The predetermined wage–unilateral employment contract is optimal because it brings a level of employment that equates the marginal revenue product of labor to the opportunity cost of labor's time.

More generally, the literature on labor contracts [see, for example, Azariadis (1982) and Grossman and Hart (1981) as well as the two papers just cited] argues that totally efficient employment contracts are impossible. Even in the case just mentioned, if firms are risk averse, fully efficient employment-contingent contracts are not feasible and "next best" incentive-compatible contracts will yield overemployment in periods of high demand and underemployment in low demand. Hall and Lilien show that even when firms and workers are risk neutral, totally efficient incentive-compatible contracts are not feasible when both the marginal revenue product of labor and the opportunity cost of labor time are subject to independent shocks that are not public knowledge. On the grounds that demand fluctuations are more frequent and volatile than fluctuations in the value of workers' time, they argue that approximately efficient employment contingent contracts specifying nominal wage schedules may be written that yield efficient adjustments to demand shocks. However, unforeseen fluctuations in the value of workers' time that are not accounted for by cost of living indexing will yield inefficiencies in employment determination and under- or overemployment. Thus, there will be a need for periodic contract renegotiation to correct for these fluctuations that are not handled by the approximately efficient contract.

To summarize, the large literature on incentive-compatible contracts provides a justification for employment relationships where the wage is predetermined, possibly by an indexing formula. Because of bilateral information asymmetries, employment relations governed in this way may yield less than totally efficient outcomes.

3.1.2. *Intertemporal substitution*

Lucas and Rapping (1969) first developed the intertemporal substitution model. Its prominence is not so much the result of empirical verification, but because of the important role it plays in equilibrium business cycle models [see, for example, Lucas (1975)]. The basic idea of the intertemporal substitution hypothesis is that current leisure and future leisure are close substitutes. Its proponents argue that while lifetime labor supply may be relatively wage inelastic, short-run labor supply will be highly elastic because workers are close to being indifferent to the timing of leisure. Consequently, workers will allocate lifetime hours so that they work more hours in periods where the return to their labor is higher and fewer hours when the return is lower.

Maximization of a simple two-period utility function,

$$U = U(c, c^*, h, h^*),\qquad\qquad(1)$$

subject to the intertemporal budget constraint,

$$c + \frac{1}{1+r}c^* = wh + \frac{1}{1+r}w^*h^* + A, \tag{2}$$

yields the labor supply function:

$$h = F(w, w^*, r, A), \tag{3}$$

with

c, c^* = current and future consumption,
h, h^* = current and future work,
w, w^* = current and future real wages,
r = real interest rate,
A = assets.

The assumption of a high degree of substitutability between current and future leisure implies that labor supply responds strongly positively to an increase in either the current real wage or the real interest rate, everything else held constant.

If we now give this simple two period model a multi-period interpretation by calling starred variables the normal values for the future, the supply function can be given by the following interpretation. Temporarily lower than normal real wage rates, or low real interest rates (which imply low purchasing power of today's wages in terms of future consumption) induce workers to shift consumption of leisure from future periods to the current period when it is relatively cheap. A recession will be a time when hours of work are low because workers perceive low real wages or a low real interest rate. Similarly, in periods of temporarily high wages or high interest rates, workers delay their consumption of leisure because it is unusually expensive; then a boom occurs.

Employment fluctuations due to intertemporal substitution result from movement in perceived real variables. The same mechanism is at work whether the perceptions are correct or not. In the Lucas–Rapping model errors in perceiving real wages and real interest rates were the driving force. In more recent models of the real business cycle, there are genuine movements of the variables as well.

Despite the widespread adoption of the intertemporal substitution model by equilibrium business cycle theorists, relatively little empirical work has gone into testing its implications. Lucas and Rapping provide some support for the theory by estimating an annual model with data from 1930 to 1965 under the assumption of adaptive expectations of unknown future variables. Their estimates, however, ignore the effects of interest rates and because of the time period of estimation and the assumption of adaptive expectations are of somewhat limited value in explaining recent labor market fluctuations.

In order to know whether the sensitivity of labor supply to intertemporal considerations is large enough to explain the observed fluctuations of unemployment, it is necessary to know the driving forces in the economy. If fluctuations in product demand are the main driving force, then all the burden of intertemporal substitution effects must operate through real interest rates, not real wages. This point, due originally to Stanley Fischer, is elaborated in Hall (1980). If an increase in product demand (say, because the government is buying more in wartime) stimulates output, and the capital stock is fixed, it is necessarily the case that the real wage *falls*. Real wages can play a role in the explanation of employment fluctuations if temporary changes in productivity are an important driving force, but not if product demand is the force.

Macro evidence provides little support for intertemporal substitution. Altonji (1982) provides two tests of the model. In the first he attempts to duplicate the basic Lucas–Rapping model using essentially the same data updated to 1976 but with far greater attention to econometric issues and the modeling of expectations for future wages and real interset rates. His estimates of the effect of current and future wages on labor supply are either significantly estimated with the wrong sign or are insignificantly different from zero. The same is generally true of expected real interest rates.

One of the weaknesses of Altonji's initial estimates is that they are conditional on assumptions about the way expectations of future wages and real interest rates are formed. Arguing that the life cycle model underlying the intertemporal substitution model also has implications about consumption, Altonji notes that consumption embodies agents' expectations of the determinants of well-being. He reformulates his model using consumption to proxy for expectations. The results sustain his general rejection of intertemporal substitution.

Recently Mankiw, Rotemberg and Summers (1982) (MRS) have carried out an investigation of intertemporal substitution in the framework of modern finance theory. Their results are unambiguously unfavorable, especially for labor supply. First, they find that employment responds *negatively* to a variable that combines intertemporal incentives from real wages and real interest rates; the intertemporal substitution model absolutely requires this response to be positive. Second, they find that consumption and employment move together, whereas the intertemporal substitution model requires that they move in opposite directions – when people are better off, they should consume more and work less.

MRS note that their results are biased if shifts in consumer behavior are an important driving force in the economy. Hall (1984) shows that these shifts are probably quite important, though not of the same magnitude as shocks from investment. However, when he corrects for the bias caused by consumer shifts, the results still do not show a strong enough negative relation between employment and consumption to fit the intertemporal substitution model. Further, Hall (1980) used a method for estimating the response of labor supply to intertemporal incentives that avoids the bias in MRS. His results have the right sign, but it is not clear that the magnitude of the response is large enough to make intertemporal substitution an important part of the explanation of employment fluctuations.

3.1.3. Search theory

The first significant effort to create a microeconomic foundation for unemployment theory occurred in the late 1960s. High levels of labor turnover and generally short duration of unemployment over the 1960s led to models characterizing unemployment as a job-search process. The unemployed were not viewed as a stagnant stock of displaced workers, but rather as in a state virtually all workers pass through in their transitions between jobs.

Phelps' (1970) model emphasized the role of firms' recruitment policies in labor markets characterized by high labor turnover. Imperfect information on the part of workers leads to an upward sloping supply curve of labor to the firm in the short run giving what Phelps calls "dynamic monopsony power". Firms set wages for some period in the pursuit of an optimal recruitment policy which considers not only the effect the wage rate will have in recruiting new workers but also the incentives it gives existing workers to quit their jobs. Given the demand for their products, firms attempt to set their wage rates optimally relative to expectations of other wages.

Search models of the type proposed by Mortensen (1970a, 1970b) emphasize the behavior of job seekers. Workers who become unemployed are viewed as facing a distribution of wages of potential job prospects. It would not generally be optimal for them to accept the first job offer they receive; a better job might be offered if they continue searching. Workers have perceptions of the wage distribution. They are modeled as choosing an optimal reservation wage and accepting the first job paying the reservation wage or more. In determining the optimal reservation wage, workers face the obvious tradeoff: the higher the reservation wage the longer it is likely to take to find a job and the longer the worker can expect to remain unemployed. The lower the reservation wage, the lower is the expected wage the worker will receive once employed.

When workers correctly perceive the distribution of wages, their unemployment is efficient in the sense that workers are following optimal strategies, and are voluntarily choosing to remain unemployed by turning down wage offers less than their reservation wage. The unemployment that exists in search equilibrium when agents correctly perceive the distribution of wages is simply the natural rate. If the unemployed as a group misperceive the distribution, they will set reservation wages above or below the efficient level, and unemployment will be above or below the natural rate.

3.2. The driving forces of the economy

3.2.1. Real forces

The driving forces that are real, as against misperceptions with nominal origins, can be divided into aggregate and sectoral. The aggregate real shift that figures most prominently in the literature about the real business cycle is in productivity. In a year of abnormally high productivity, people will work harder than usual. They will schedule their vacations in times of low productivity. This is straightforward theory, but there is little evidence that important, temporary fluctuations in productivity take place in the United States or any other economy.

Shifts in product demand are also potentially important driving forces. Temporary increases in government purchases in wartime should set off a characteristic response which will include an increase in total employment, in almost any theory. A similar response should occur if investment or net exports rise exogeneously.

Shifts in world relative prices are another important real driving force that has received much attention since the two oil price shocks of the 1970s. Unless labor supply is more responsive to a permanent decline in real wages than is indicated by the evidence, higher oil prices or other import prices should not have a major impact on the level of employment or physical output. Instead, when the price of a commodity rises where the United States is a net importer, consumption should fall and net exports and investment rise by about the same amount.

The most likely avenue for a shift in world relative prices to influence U.S. employment levels is by mistake, through a wage-setting mechanism that is not designed to deal with such shifts.

At the level of individual sectors, shifts in the composition of demand can be an important driving force. If the movement of workers among sectors takes time, as search ideas suggest, then periods of rapid change in composition will be periods of diminished employment and higher unemployment as well.

3.2.2. Errors and misperceptions

Few economists hold that all of the ups and downs of employment are the smooth accommodation of the economy to real driving forces. Such a view would leave no room for the possibility that bad monetary policy was a cause of recessions, for example. Rather, most accounts of the driving forces behind employment fluctuations stress the roles of mistakes and misperceptions.

In a situation where the wage is predetermined and management chooses employment unilaterally, employment is vulnerable to errors in setting the wage. The failure of wages to respond to current conditions is at the heart of the Keynesian analysis of economic fluctuations and leads directly to its policy prescriptions. Recent contract theory has revealed the critical issues in this line of thought. Mistakes in setting the wage are costly to the two parties to the employment bargain – the total cost of a major recession in terms of forgone output may be hundreds of billions of dollars. Consequently, we might expect a great deal of care in the design of wage-setting formulas to try to minimize errors by using every available piece of reliable information. In practice, wages seem to be linked only to the cost of living; otherwise they do not respond to current information at all. Gigantic mistakes seem to occur without any corresponding effort to avoid them.

In models where intertemporal substitution is the economic mechanism bringing employment fluctuations, errors in perceiving the real wage and real interest rates give rise to movements in employment. In Lucas and Rapping (1969), workers overestimate the real wage in booms and underestimate it in recessions. In Lucas (1972), a monetary expansion creates the mistaken impression of high real interest rates so people work harder than they should or they would if they knew what was really happening.

In search theories, misperceptions about the prevailing wage level cause firms or workers to adopt strategies that bring employment or unemployment levels different from the optima. A worker who is unaware that a recent monetary expansion has raised the average level of wages will set a reservation wage that is too low and will find a job sooner than expected and sooner than is optimal. If the same thing is happening to most job-seekers, unemployment will fall below its normal level.

3.2.3. Rational expectations and perception errors

As we stressed in the introduction, rational expectations has had a strong influence on recent thinking about labor market fluctuations, but it is not a divisive issue. On the contrary, virtually all current thinking incorporates the hypothesis of rational expectations fully. Because rational expectations strongly circumscribes the magnitude and duration of perception errors, its ascendancy has made economists concerned with issues of employment fluctuations redouble their efforts to identify plausible economic mechanisms and driving forces.

According to rational expectations, economic agents should use all available information in forming their perceptions about current economic conditions and expectations about the future. Because perception errors are costly to both sides of the employment bargain, the two sides have substantial incentives to undertake information gathering and processing to avoid those costs. A model that involves avoidable perception errors, especially those that are persistent over months and years, seems unattractive in the light of the rational expectations hypothesis.

When the mechanism of employment fluctuations is the predetermined wage and unilateral employment determination, perception errors enter the picture through the wage-setting process. The formula that sets wages ought to use all available reliable public information about the opportunity cost of workers' time. A theory is manifestly implausible if it rests on the hypothesis that wages are held stubbornly at a given level without consideration for observed conditions, and that this process has repeated itself for recession after recession even though it is obvious that indexing wages to unemployment, nominal GNP, and other public variables would drastically reduce deadweight loss.

Rational expectations strongly limits the role of perception errors in models based on intertemporal substitution. In Lucas's (1972) classic paper, only very strong assumptions about the unavailability of information gives a rational expectations equilibrium where misperceptions create employment fluctuations. The economy in that paper would have no aggregate fluctuations at all if somebody just published a financial section in a newspaper. *Any* additional piece of information about contemporaneous monetary developments would eliminate the fluctuations Lucas describes.

Similarly, unemployment fluctuations in search models occur only as long as misperceptions exist. In an economy where job-seekers talk to their employed friends in bars and at cocktail parties, mistakes about the current level of wages should not last too long. Learning the level of prevailing wages is of paramount importance to the searcher. A theory is unappealing if it invokes a casual theory of information acquisition and builds from it a model of fluctuations that cost the people involved hundreds of billions of dollars.

3.3. Specific models of employment fluctuations

In this section we examine the major recent models of employment fluctuations, with a view to describing the economic mechanisms that bring the fluctuations and the driving forces behind them.

3.3.1. The Phillips curve

Modern thinking about employment fluctuations began with the Phillips curve. Phillips curve doctrine has two important elements.

(1) From Keynes, it takes the assumption that the observed wage–employment combination is a point on the labor demand curve but not necessarily a point on the labor supply curve. Unemployment can occur when the wage is too high; the level of unemployment is the difference between supply and demand.

(2) The Phillips curve itself describes a gradual process of equilibration. If unemployment is high, the wage falls. If too low, the wage rises. Ultimately, supply and demand are brought to equality and excess unemployment disappears.

Phillips (1958) documented an inverse relationship between British inflation and unemployment. Well before Phillips' paper appeared, economists recognized the existence of some kind of inflation–unemployment tradeoff. Fisher (1926) is an early example. Phillips and others [for example, Lipsey (1960)] provided a theoretical underpinning in terms of relatively simple disequilibrium paradigms where excess demand for labor leads firms to compete with each other in attracting workers, thus bidding up wages, and excess supply of labor leading to reduced pressure on employers to raise wage levels. Though the empirical generalization of the Phillips curve became popular soon after the publication of Phillips' original paper, little formal micro theoretical foundation was provided for the curve until the late 1960s.

3.3.2. Shifts in the Phillips curve under sustained inflation

Friedman (1968) and Phelps (1967) launched the line of thought that more clearly identified employment and unemployment fluctuations with perception errors. Their arguments were based on simple implications of labor market equilibrium. In their view, there exists a natural rate of unemployment in the economy necessary to accomplish the continuous process of labor allocation within the economy. Variations of factors such as the demand for their products or the cost of inputs to production lead to labor turnover as firms continually adjust the sizes of their labor forces. In good times or bad there will always be some firms trying to expand their employment while other firms are contracting. Moreover, the process of workers seeking better jobs or moving up career ladders leads to further labor turnover. Together these factors cause about 3 percent of employed workers to leave jobs (either voluntarily as quits or involuntarily as layoffs) for new ones every month within the U.S. economy. Because it takes time for separated workers to locate new jobs, some unemployment is unavoidable. See Lucas and Prescott (1974) and Hall (1979) for examples of models of the natural rate.

The natural rate is the normal unemployment rate that results from this process of labor allocation when workers and firms correctly perceive the levels and rates of change of price and wages. In the long run, as people adjust to changing inflation patterns, unemployment will tend to this natural rate, but in the short run agents may suffer from misperceptions. Unemployment can be driven below the natural rate by an increase in demand, which will cause prices to rise faster than people anticipate. Similarly, a recession occurs when demand is less than expected; unemployment rises above the natural rate and inflation drops below its expected level.

Friedman and Phelps' modification of the Phillips curve led a number of investigators, including Gordon (1971), to add expected inflation to the right-hand variables in the Phillips curve. The foundation for this specification was still a loosely based disequilibrium adjustment theory. Most researchers thought of expected inflation as just another explanatory variable in the Phillips curve. But moving expected inflation to the left-hand side, so that the Phillips curve became a relation between unexpected inflation and the departure of unemployment from the natural rate, called attention to the importance of misperceptions in explaining unemployment fluctuations.

The emergence of the concept of the natural rate of unemployment also clarified a possible role for real driving forces in unemployment fluctuations. Any influence that raised the fraction of the labor force that was looking for work in any given month, either through layoffs or quits, would raise unemployment through the natural rate.

In earlier thinking, the unemployment rate was something chosen by macro policy and by other determinants of aggregate demand, more or less without restriction. The natural rate hypothesis strongly circumscribed fluctuations in unemployment relative to earlier theories. Unemployment could rise or fall only through negative or positive surprises or through changes in the natural rate. In particular, macro policy could keep the unemployment rate below the natural rate only by creating a continuing sequence of inflationary surprises.

3.3.3. Misperceptions and search

The Friedman–Phelps modification of the Phillips curve was a plausible assertion about wage adjustment, but it lacked a detailed theoretical foundation. A particularly awkward question was the following: When are the expectations formed that shift the Phillips curve? Why do not people read the newspaper and update their beliefs about inflation as soon as the cost of living index is announced? Without more theoretical structure, questions like these could not be answered.

The search theory, as propounded in the Phelps volume (1970) and elsewhere by Phelps, Mortensen, and others, argued that misperceptions on the part of job-seekers could explain the relation between unemployment fluctuations and inflationary surprises.

In the version of the model developed by Phelps, when employers face excess demand for labor, they try to raise their relative wage so as to attract more workers. Each tries to raise his own wage by more than the amount he expects average wages to rise. If most firms in the economy face excess demand for labor, then most firms will be setting their own wages above expected inflation, and average wages will rise by more than expected.

Other versions of search theory, including Mortensen's (1970), stress the role of job-seekers. When searchers misperceive the distribution of wages, they incorrectly set reservation wages and unemployment deviates from the natural rate. If job-seekers underestimate the level of wages in the economy, they set their reservation wages below the optimal reservation wage and find jobs quickly.

Unemployment falls below the natural rate. When workers overestimate the level of wages they set their reservation wage too high and remain unemployed longer than is optimal. Unemployment exceeds the natural rate. Nevertheless, unemployment is optimal subject to the imperfect information workers have. It is inefficient only relative to the unattainable standard of perfect information.

Search models have greatly enhanced our understanding of labor market dynamics and the determinants of the natural rate of unemployment in particular. However, they face serious limitations in explaining the actual pattern of fluctuations over the cycle. Neither can explain why firms would choose to lay off workers rather than lower wages. The failure to explain layoffs is particularly troublesome when trying to explain unemployment fluctuations. As we showed in Table 17.1, virtually all of the increase in unemployment during recessions comes from involuntary job-losers and labor force reentrants. Unemployment of voluntary job-leavers is relatively small and non-cyclical. To explain unemployment fluctuations, we must explain layoffs. It is hard to argue that the long-term unemployment (see Section 2.3) that makes up the majority of cyclical increases in unemployment has much to do with optimal search behavior. There is little to indicate that job search is considerably more efficient when workers are unemployed – Mattila (1974) finds that over 60 percent of workers who quit jobs find employment while still on their old jobs. And it is unconvincing to argue that job-seekers choose to remain unemployed for such long intervals because of mistakes in evaluating the distribution of wages in the economy.

Search models were the first attempts to explain more deeply why the observed combination of employment and wage is a point on the demand function and not on the supply function. Research in the Phillips curve line has never come to grips with this issue and even today many writers seem unaware of its importance. In search theory, firms set their offered wages so as to maximize profit. In this sense, they are on their labor demand schedules. Job-seekers set their reservation wages so as to maximize expected earnings over working and non-working hours. In so doing, they anticipate spending a certain amount of their time searching and the rest working. They are on their supply functions for both activities. Unemployment is an outcome of a considered choice about the allocation of time. Unemployment is the difference between the total amount of time committed by workers to the labor market and the amount of time spent working. By making unemployment the result of a decision about the use of time, the search theory avoids the arbitrary assumption of earlier models that the supply of hours of work exceeds the demand.

3.3.4. Misperceptions and intertemporal substitution

Lucas and Rapping (1969) and later Lucas (1972) developed a different line of argument to provide the needed theoretical background for the natural rate proposition. Again, their models are driven by misperceptions of price and wages.

However, instead of the work-search margin that is distorted in the search theory, it is the margin between work now and work later that provides the economic mechanism of these models.

The second paper presents the full development of rational expectations and is embedded in a general equilibrium framework. In it, workers mistakenly work too hard when a monetary expansion occurs because they are unable to distinguish the jump in prices from the one that would occur if there were a local disturbance. In the case of a local disturbance, the incentive for current work is genuinely high. The only hint that workers have about a local disturbance comes from the price level, which is also influenced by purely monetary expansion. They have to hedge their bets. When prices rise, they work somewhat harder. If they were sure it was a local shock, they would work even harder. If they knew it was a monetary shock, they would work only a normal amount.

In Lucas's model, and in other models based on the intertemporal substitution mechanism, it is perception errors in the real interest rate that drive employment fluctuations. Although perception errors in the real wage seemed to be important in Lucas and Rapping, they do not seem a likely candidate for driving aggregate fluctuations, for the reason mentioned in Section 3.1.2: it seems unlikely that disturbances would push the real wage in the right direction to explain observed fluctuations.

As we noted earlier in Section 3.1.2, research has not so far documented the influence of expected real interest rates on labor supply. As a result the intertemporal substitution mechanism driven by errors in expected real interest rates suffers from defects in both its elements. First, it is no more than a theoretical possibility that expected real rates (correctly or incorrectly forecast) influence labor supply; it depends on the intertemporal elasticity of substitution. Second, it is not clear that the public makes significant errors in forecasting real rates that are in the direction needed to explain the observed fluctuations in employment.

3.3.5.   Contracts and errors in setting wages

Where search theory emphasizes labor market turnover and job changing, contract models of wage and employment determination start from the presumption that workers and firms maintain long-term relationships. Search theory claims to say something about unemployment among the jobless; contract theory deals with fluctuations of hours of work and with the type of unemployment brought by temporary layoffs. Since workers stay with firms through periods of fluctuating demand, employment and wage determination need not respond directly and instantaneously to market forces. Rather, firms and workers enter into contracts that specify, in advance, wage rates and hours of employment or rules for determining wages and employment, conditional on the level of demand. Contract theory has made at least one solid contribution – it explains why the unilateral determination of employment by firms may be desirable.

The pioneering contract models of Azariadis (1975), Baily (1974), and D. Gordon (1974) explained long-term employment contracts as optimal risk-sharing relationships between risk-neutral firms and risk-averse workers. They demonstrated that in a world of stochastic product demand a firm could offer workers a fixed wage–variable employment contract that allowed for the possibility of periodic spells of temporary layoff unemployment. Such a contract could dominate the spot market. Workers and firms enter into contracts bilaterally, but individual unemployment spells are involuntary for the worker ex post; they are chosen unilaterally by the employer under the rules of the contract. It should be noted that these results depend heavily on the assumption that firms do not compensate workers while unemployed [see Akerlof and Miyazaki (1980)].

Other models invoke different reasons for long-term employment relationships such as the development of firm specific skills and heavy turnover cost, but still yield unilateral layoffs as an efficient response to demand fluctuations. Feldstein (1976) showed that even with the assumption of risk-neutral workers, the incentives given by imperfect experience rating in the unemployment compensation system encourages the use of temporary layoffs. Weiss (1980) shows that when workers within the firm receive the same wage despite differences in productivity, wage reductions may encourage high productivity workers to quit. Because of selection problems layoffs can in some circumstances be more desirable than wage reductions.

When contract theory was first introduced, much hope was held out that it would provide a microeconomic foundation for the predetermined wage–unilateral employment view of the business cycle. Unlike search models, it explained unilateral employment determination by employers and explained why firms might not reduce wages in the face of falling demand. Furthermore, most workers do maintain long-term relationships with firms. Hall (1982) estimates that the typical worker is holding a job which has lasted or will last about 8 years. Over a quarter of workers are holding jobs which will last 20 years or more.

Contract theory offered hope of providing a justification for the basic Phillips curve setup discussed at the beginning of this section. Suppose a contract had the form that the firm could choose the level of employment subject to a wage dictated by the contract. Suppose, further, that the contract can make the wage respond only imperfectly and with a lag to the relevant variables. Then employment fluctuations will occur very much as described by the predetermined wage–unilateral employment model which is still the foundation of the bulk of practical macroeconomics.

Despite initial optimism Barro (1977) pointed out that these early microeconomic contract models were not capable of explaining the effects of purely monetary disturbances on real output. ABG models can explain why optimal risk-sharing contracts might specify rigid real wages, but they cannot explain the failure of money wages (and prices) to fall in response to a drop of aggregate demand nor can they justify a contract that specifies money wages several periods in advance as in Fischer (1977) or Phelps and Taylor (1977). Such a contract ignores public information about the price level that all agents know. While the rigid money wage models can explain aggregate fluctuations, they have obvious problems. Presetting nominal wages has imposed huge costs on firms and workers. Why do they not make wages respond to national and local variables like unemployment, nominal GNP, sensitive prices, and other relevant indicators?

An efficient contract between a firm and a group of workers will set employment at the point where the marginal revenue product of labor equals the marginal opportunity cost of time. Contract models can explain aggregate fluctuations of employment in response to shifts in terms of trade or shifts of labor productivity (both of which affect the aggregate real MRP of labor). No contract model to date, however, provides a foundation for money wage rigidity.

The large literature on incentive compatible contracts provides a justification for employment relationships that yield less than totally efficient outcomes [see Hart (1983) and his references]. When one or both parties to an employment contract is risk averse, the optimal second-best contract compromises between employment efficiency and insurance. In some conditions, employment will exceed the efficient level, and in others, it will fall short. So far, these theoretical considerations have not been incorporated in any convincing account of the occasional episodes of severe unemployment in the U.S. economy.

3.3.6. *Intertemporal substitution and real shocks*

A number of recent papers, including Kydland and Prescott (1982) and King and Plosser (1982), have developed the theoretical proposition that real driving forces are capable of creating fluctuations in employment through intertemporal substitution. The force whose effect most obviously operates in this way is a shift in demand. Suppose that investment demand rises, or government purchases rise. Then the real interest rate will rise to clear the output market. Not only does a higher real interest rate make consumers and investors defer purchases, but it also makes workers offer more current labor services. In the new equilibrium, employment and output are above normal if intertemporal substitution in labor supply occurs. The accommodation of higher product demand takes the form partly of higher product supply and partly deferral of other components of demand.

The theoretical models of employment fluctuations as the response through intertemporal substitution to real driving forces are airtight as theory. It is very much an open question whether the response of labor supply to real interest rates is strong enough, and the changes in real interest rates big enough, to make this explanation of employment fluctuations an important part of the story empirically. As we noted earlier, work by Altonji (1982) and Mankiw, Rotemberg and Summers (1982) has generally reached negative conclusions about the empirical success of the intertemporal substitution mechanism.

3.3.7. Sectoral shifts as real driving forces

There is a tendency in macroeconomics to view aggregate fluctuations as resulting from aggregate shocks. Recently, Lilien (1982a, 1982b) has argued that this view ignores a major source of aggregate fluctuations: the slow adjustment to intersectoral shifts of labor demand. In this view the natural or frictional rate of unemployment is not constant as in most macroeconomic models but varies with the degree of required labor reallocation in the economy. Periods of rapid technological change in production or dramatic shifts of domestic product demand require unusually large movements of labor between labor market segments. If for whatever reasons labor is slow to adjust to these shifts of labor demand unemployment increases.

A long tradition explains unemployment in terms of structural or market imbalance. The basic hypothesis is that mismatching of jobs and workers raises both vacancies and unemployment. The Beveridge Curve, the locus of unemployment–vacancy combinations at various levels of demand, shifts outward when mismatching is high [see, for example, Holt (1970)]. Some have viewed these structural imbalances primarily in the dimension of skills. The primary motivation for the manpower programs of the 1960s and 1970s was to bring skill levels in the labor force into line with the composition of labor demand, thereby reducing the rate of unemployment.

Lilien's work suggests a slightly different view. Structural imbalances are the transitory result of slow labor market adjustment to rapid shifts in the composition of employment demand. He argues more specifically that during the 1970s the decline in military purchases, shifts in relative prices, particularly oil prices, increased foreign competition in manufactured goods, and movements toward more automated manufacturing production led to dramatic shifts of the demand for labor out of manufacturing industries and into the service, retail trade, finance, insurance and real estate industries. Between 1970 and 1981 manufacturing's share of total employment fell from 29 percent to 22 percent, a 24 percent decline in share. Over the same period the shares of service, retail trade and finance–insurance–real estate grew by 31 percent, 11 percent and 19 percent, respectively. Service industry employment grew in every year of the 1970s despite three major recessions and record declines in manufacturing employment. In contrast to the 1970s, employment grew relatively uniformly throughout the 1960s; manufacturing's share of employment declined by only 6.1 percent between 1958 and 1969.

Lilien argues that much of the increased unemployment of the 1970s as well as the cyclical pattern of unemployment was the result of the slow movement of labor out of declining and into expanding sectors of the economy. He labels fluctuations due to intersectoral demand fluctuations as shifts of the natural rate of unemployment because they are not associated with the level of aggregate labor demand but rather the composition of demand.

Lilien presents two somewhat different theoretical models of the role of sectoral demand shifts. His 1982 paper emphasizes the role of turnover and is not dissimilar in structure to the equilibrium search model of Lucas and Prescott (1974). Shifts of product demand or labor productivity lead some firms to expand employment while other firms lay workers off. Unemployment results because it takes time for workers displaced from shrinking firms to find jobs in expanding firms. Holding aggregate demand constant, the level of unemployment is positively related to the magnitude of intersectoral demand shifts.

Lilien (1982b) examines the consequences of slow labor mobility in a model where that employment is set efficiently within labor market sectors, that is, employment is set at the point of equality of the marginal revenue product of labor and the opportunity cost of labor. However, labor flows are too slow to equate the marginal revenue product of labor among sectors. Shifts of sector specific product demand or labor productivity (through the introduction of new technology) temporarily widen the gap between sectors in the MRPL until labor flows from low to high MRPL sectors, but until equality is restored aggregate employment is depressed. Basic convexity properties (decreasing marginal productivity of labor in production and decreasing marginal utility of leisure) imply that employment hours fall by more in firms with declining product demand than hours rise in firms with growing product demand. As time passes, labor flows out of low MRPL sectors to high MRPL sectors and normal employment is restored.

These two approaches are consistent. The first emphasizes flow equilibrium conditions while the latter emphasizes the determinants of stock employment equilibrium. They have identical implications for aggregate fluctuations, so we will briefly examine the simpler turnover model.

At the level of the firm, hiring consists of two components: an aggregate component and a firm specific component. Ignoring quit behavior and letting h be firm net hiring or the rate of change of employment at the firm, we decompose h into two factors:

$$h = H + e,$$

where H is the aggregate rate of change in employment and represents the component of hiring that is common to all firms and e is a firm-specific component distributed among firms with variance $\sigma(t)$. The innovation here over equilibrium unemployment models like Lucas and Prescott's is that $\sigma(t)$ is not assumed to be constant in all periods.

Assuming that when $h < 0$ firms lay workers off and when $h > 0$ firms hire new workers, we derive the aggregate relations:

$$H = A - L,$$
$$L = g(H, \sigma(t)),$$
$$A = H + g(H, \sigma(t)),$$

where L is aggregate layoffs, A is aggregate accessions, and $0 > g_1 > -1$ and $g_2 > 0$. Increases in the dispersion of hiring conditions as measured by σ lead to both greater L and A holding H constant.

Assuming that the duration of unemployment is influenced by aggregate demand or money illusion, $X(t)$, as in equilibrium search models and that the aggregate labor force is constant, so that H is equal to negative the change in unemployment, Lilien derives a dynamic unemployment equation of the form:

$$U(t) = f(U(t-1), \sigma(t), X(t)).$$

This equation has the form of an equilibrium Phillips curve where the natural rate of unemployment is a function of σ, and $X(t)$ represents expectation errors in wages or prices.

Lilien estimates several versions of the layoff and unemployment equations above using the observed dispersion of industry employment growth rates as a proxy for σ and a measure of unanticipated money growth as a measure of $X(t)$. During the 1960s intersectoral demand shifts account for relatively little unemployment fluctuations, while aggregate demand as measured by unanticipated monetary growth explains the bulk of unemployment. In marked contrast, σ explains a major fraction of unemployment fluctuations in the 1970s and relatively less is explained by money growth.

Lilien interprets these results as indicating that the sources of aggregate fluctuations in the 1970s were fundamentally different from the 1960s. In the 1960s most fluctuations were deviations from the natural or equilibrium unemployment rate induced by fluctuations of aggregate demand. In the 1970s most fluctuations were movements of the natural rate induced by exogenous shifts in the composition of employment demand.

Several criticisms have been made of this interpretation of the data. Abraham and Katz (1984) and Lilien (1982b) point out the inappropriateness of using dispersion in employment growth rates as a measure of exogenous sectoral shifts that are not influenced by the level of aggregate demand. If some sectors are more cyclically sensitive than others we might expect dispersion in growth rates to result from movements of aggregate demand. Shifts of demand always affect manufacturing employment more than service employment, so that movements of aggregate demand (increases or decreases) will tend to be associated with increased dispersion in employment growth rates.

Lilien (1982b) attempts to create a proxy for σ that does not suffer from this bias. Industry employment growth rates are decomposed into a component that measures the industries' normal response to aggregate conditions and a component that measures industry specific factors. He finds that aggregate labor market conditions and industry specific conditions are of roughly equal importance in explaining the typical industry's employment growth over time. He also finds that the dispersion of industry specific effects accounts for virtually none of the variance of unemployment of prime age males during the 1960s, but between 50 and 60 percent of the variance of unemployment through the 1970s.

Abraham and Katz (1984) point out another criticism of Lilien's interpretation of the data. If the sectoral shift–structural unemployment model of unemployment is correct, vacancies as well as unemployment should be increasing functions of σ when the level of aggregate demand is controlled for. However, when a proxy for vacancies, help-wanted advertising, is regressed on σ and unanticipated money, vacancies appear to be negatively related to σ. They interpret this as indicating that Lilien's σ variable is simply measuring shifts of aggregate demand. It may be, however, that different industries have different tendencies to use help wanted advertising and that the help wanted index cannot be used as a consistent measure of vacancies during periods of structural change. Also, if wages rise quickly in expanding demand sectors, there is no reason to believe that increases in σ will lead to increased vacancies. Within an equilibrium framework we might expect short-run increases in unemployment in declining sectors and higher wages in expanding sectors.

While Abraham and Katz's analysis casts some doubt on Lilien's σ as a proper empirical measure of the short-run dispersion of demand shocks, vacancy data generally support the hypothesis of increased labor market imbalance during the 1970s. Medoff (1983) presents both cross-section and time-series evidence that both unemployment and vacancies increased significantly during the 1970s.

Medoff also points out other dimensions of intersectoral shifts. While Lilien emphasizes shifting industrial patterns of labor demand, Medoff emphasizes geographic shifts. The 1970s were characterized by dramatic shifts of employment out of the Northeast and Middle Atlantic regions towards the Southwest and Pacific regions. Of course these are the same shifts described by Lilien. The states experiencing declining employment had heavy manufacturing industrial bases.

Evidence that these geographical shifts were at least partially demand driven comes from the fact that help-wanted advertising measures of vacancies grew at an annual rate of 6.2 and 4.9 percent per year in the Southwest and Pacific, respectively, and declined by 3.4 and 1.3 percent per year in the Northeast and Middle Atlantic states.

Research on sectoral shifts raises an important question: Why does it take so long for labor to adjust to intersectoral demand shifts? Lilien finds that the intensity of intersectoral shifts as measured by σ influence unemployment for up to two years in quarterly equations and somewhat longer in annual equations.

One possibility is that workers cannot tell instantaneously whether reduced demand at the level of the firm represents a temporary cyclical phenomenon or a permanent shift in the firm's permanent level of demand. It may pay workers to incur heavy mobility costs as well as loss of firm specific skills if they know demand reductions are permanent, but not if they are temporary cyclical fluctuations. Thus, workers continue to search within their industry and region until convinced that demand will not recover.

Hall (1975) provides another explanation that may be particularly relevant to explaining the effect of declining manufacturing employment. He presents a two-sector model with one high-wage and one low-wage sector. The high-wage sector has administered wages that adjust only slowly to demand. Even when wages adjust quickly to clear the competitive (low)-wage sector unemployment exists as workers prefer to remain unemployed with a chance of getting a job in the high-wage sector. In terms of our recent experience declining employment has been primarily in high-wage manufacturing jobs, while employment has been expanding in low-wage service jobs. Given the low wages on alternative jobs, an unemployed auto or steel worker may have a strong incentive to wait for re-employment within the industry, even if the probability of recall is quite low.

4. Conclusions

Employment in the United States shows important cyclical fluctuations, both in the amount of work performed by workers on their jobs and in the fraction of the population holding jobs. Macro and labor economists have been interested in explaining these fluctuations for many years. Microeconomic criticism of the standard Keynesian view of employment determination has sharpened and improved that view. In addition, new theories have captured attention. In our view, however, no single theory has been completely successful in explaining the facts of cyclical fluctuations on the basis of a fully articulated microeconomic analysis and a satisfactory econometric model. We look forward to much additional progress in this field of research.

The Keynesian analysis posits that firms choose employment unilaterally subject to a predetermined wage. Because the choice does not take account of the marginal value of workers' time, the employment level may be inefficient. It is precisely the monumental inefficiency of widespread unemployment during cyclical contractions that makes Keynesians call for corrective government action. Although most practical economists take as given the unilateral determination of employment by firms, it was not until the flowering of contract theories of employment that a good justification was offered for that hypothesis. Contract theories have demonstrated that it makes sense for the firm to choose employment unilaterally when the level of product demand is private information to the firm. But theoretical work has not made the other steps that would be necessary to provide a complete foundation for standard macroeconomic models of cyclical employment fluctuations. In particular, the theory seems to predict that employment contracts would be indexed to a number of observable indicators that convey information about the current marginal value of labor's time, such as the unemployment rate.

Equilibrium models of employment fluctuations provide the most serious intellectual competition to the standard macro model today. Two versions are under active development. One invokes cyclical changes in product demand (say, from investment or the government) which bring changes in real interest rates to clear the output market. When the real interest rate is high, people work harder and employment rises, because there is an incentive to work now and consume later. Or, along the same lines, a temporary increase in productivity again creates an incentive to work harder. However, empirical testing of this type of model has reached negative conclusions.

A second version of the equilibrium model notes that the movement of workers from one sector to another takes time and resources. Periods of rapid structural change will be periods of lower employment and output, and higher unemployment, because a larger fraction of the labor force will be in transit from one sector to another. Empirical work on this idea has been successful in linking measures of structural change to the unemployment rate. The result is not a complete, unitary model of cyclical fluctuations, however. The model still attributes part of the fluctuations of employment to purely nominal influences, and does not have a theory to explain why those influences have real effects.

Two other hypotheses enjoyed an earlier vogue in the literature on employment fluctuations. Search theory dealt specifically with unemployment, treating it as one of the uses of time chosen by rational economic agents. Changes in relative prices will change the amount of unemployment, according to this line of thought. Though search theory is still an active area of research, as this Handbook shows, few economists still look to its mechanisms for much of the explanation of observed fluctuations. First, it has nothing to say about the shift of labor resources from employment to non-market activities that is an important part of the cycle. Second, the concentration of unemployment among a fairly small group of people with low levels of average employment casts doubt on the relevance of the theory in the first place.

Theoretical work of the 1970s put a great deal of emphasis on the role of perception errors as a driving force for cyclical fluctuations in employment. Here, too, recent thinking has moved in other directions. Rational expectations makes it clear that perception errors are tightly circumscribed. If cyclical fluctuations involving millions of jobs and hundreds of billions of dollars in output are just the result of misunderstandings that could be cleared up by better financial reporting, then there is a monumental and inexplicable failure for markets in information to operate. Certainly Lucas's fully worked out model along this line rests explicitly on an assumption about lack of information that does not transplant in any obvious way to the U.S. economy. The economy has a flourishing industry providing just the sort of information ruled out in the model.

We see likely progress in two areas. There is much more work to be done in following up the theory of labor contracts with empirical work. Further work on the equilibrium cycle based on sectoral shifts or related influences seems promising.

References

Abraham, Katherine G. and Lawrence Katz (1984) "Cyclical unemployment: sectoral shifts or aggregate disturbances?", M.I.T. Working Paper.

Akerlof, George and Hajime Miyazaki (1980) "The implicit contract theory of unemployment meets the wage bill argument", *Review of Economic Studies*, 47:321–338.

Altonji, Joseph G. (1982) "The intertemporal substitution model of labour market fluctuations: an empirical analysis", *Review of Economic Studies*, 49:783–824.

Azariadis, Costas (1975) "Implicit contracts and underemployment equilibria", *Journal of Political Economy*, 83:1183–1202.

Baily, Martin Neil (1974) "Wages and employment under uncertain demand", *Review of Economic Studies*, 41:37–50.

Barro, Robert (1977) "Long term contracting, sticky prices, and monetary policy", *Journal of Monetary Economics*, 3:305–316.

Calvo, Guillermo and Edmund S. Phelps (1977) "Employment contingent wage contracts", in: K. Brunner and A. Meltzer, eds., *Stabilization of the domestic and international economy*, Carnegie–Rochester Conference Series on Public Policy. Amsterdam: North-Holland.

Clark, Kim B. and Lawrence H. Summers (1979) "Labor market dynamics and unemployment: a reconsideration", *Brooking Papers on Economic Activity*, 13–60.

Feldstein, Martin (1976) "Temporary layoffs in the theory of unemployment", *Journal of Political Economy*, 84:191.

Fischer, Stanley (1977) "Long-term contracts, rational expectations, and the optimal money supply rule", *Journal of Political Economy*, 85: 191–205.

Fisher, Irving (1926) "A statistical relation between unemployment and price changes", *International Labour Review*, 12:785–792. Reprinted in *Journal of Political Economy*, 81:496–502.

Friedman, Milton (1968) "The role of monetary policy", *American Economic Review*, 58:1–17.

Gordon, Donald (1974) "A neo-classical theory of Keynesian unemployment", *Economic Inquiry*, 12:431–459.

Gordon, Robert J. (1971) "Inflation in recession and recovery", *Brookings Papers on Economic Activity*, 105–158.

Grossman, Sanford and Oliver Hart (1981) "Implicit contracts, moral hazard, and unemployment", *American Economic Review*, 71:301–307.

Hall, Robert E. (1975) "The rigidity of wages and the persistence of unemployment", *Brookings Papers on Economic Activity*, 301–335.

Hall, Robert E. (1979) "A theory of the natural unemployment rate and the duration of unemployment", *Journal Monetary Economics*, 5:153–169.

Hall, Robert E. (1980) "Labor supply and aggregate fluctuations", in: K. Brunner and A. Meltzer, eds., *On the state of macroeconomics* Carnegie–Rochester Conference Series on Public Policy. Amsterdam: North-Holland.

Hall, Robert E. (1980) "Employment fluctuations and wage rigidity", *Brooking Papers on Economic Activity*, 1:91.

Hall, Robert E. (1982) "The importance of lifetime jobs in the U.S. economy", *American Economic Review*, 73:716.

Hall, Robert E. (1983) "The wage adjustment process", unpublished manuscript.

Hall, Robert E. (1984) "The role of consumption in aggregate fluctuations", in: Robert J. Gordon, ed., *The proceedings of the National Bureau Conference on Business Cycles*.

Hall, Robert E. and Edward P. Lazear (1984) "The excess sensitivity of quits and layoffs to demand", *Journal of Labor Economics*, 2:233–257.

Hall, Robert E. and David M. Lilien (1979) "Efficient wage bargains under uncertain supply and demand", *American Economic Review*, 69:868–79.

Hart, Oliver D. (1983) "Optimal labour contracts under asymmetric information: an introduction", *Review of Economic Studies*, 3–35.

Holt, Charles C. (1970) "Job search, Phillips' wage relation and union influence: theory and evidence", in: Edmund S. Phelps et al., ed., *Microeconomic foundations of employment and inflation theory*. New York: Norton.

Kaitz, Hyman B. "Analyzing the length of spells of unemployment", *Monthly Labor Review*, 93:11–20.

King, Robert G. and Charles I. Plosser (1982) "The behavior of money, credit, and prices in a real business cycle", Working Paper, University of Rochester.

Kydland, F. and Edward C. Prescott (1982) "Time to build and aggregate fluctuations", *Econometrica*, 50:1345–1370.

Lilien, David M. (1980) "The cyclical pattern of temporary layoffs in U.S. manufacturing", *Review of Economics and Statistics*.

Lilien, David M. (1982a) "Sectoral shifts and cyclical unemployment", *Journal of Political Economy*, 90:777–793.

Lilien, David M. (1982b) "A sectoral model of the business cycle", USC-MRG Working Paper.

Lipsey, Richard G. (1960) "The relation between unemployment and the rate of change of money wage rates in the United Kingdom, 1862–1957: a further analysis", *Economica*, 27:1–31.

Lucas, Robert E., Jr. (1972) "Expectations and the neutrality of money", *Journal of Economic Theory*, 4:103–124.

Lucas, Robert E., Jr. (1975) "An equilibrium model of the business cycle", *Journal of Political Economy*, 85:113–144.

Lucas, Robert E., Jr. (1976) "Econometric policy evaluation: a critique", *Journal of Monetary Economics*, 2:19–46.

Lucas, Robert E., Jr. and Edward C. Prescott (1974) "Equilibrium search and unemployment", *Journal of Economic Theory*, 7:188–209.

Lucas, Robert E., Jr. and Leonard A. Rapping (1969) "Real wages employment and inflation", *Journal of Political Economy*, 77.

MaCurdy, Thomas E. (1981) "An empirical model of labor supply in a life cycle setting", *Journal of Political Economy*, 89:1059–1086.

Mankiw, N. Gregory, Julio Rotemberg and Lawrence H. Summers (1982) "Intertemporal substitution in macroeconomics", Working Paper 898, National Bureau of Economic Research.

Mattila, J. Peter (1974) "Job quitting and frictional unemployment", *American Economic Review*, 64:235–239.

Medoff, James L. (1983) "U.S. labor markets: imbalance, wage growth, and productivity in the 1970s", *Brookings Papers on Economic Activity*, 1:87–120.

Mortensen, Dale T. (1970a) "A theory of wage and employment dynamics", in: Edmund S. Phelps et al., eds., *Microeconomic foundations of employment and inflation theory*. New York: Norton.

Mortensen, Dale T. (1970b) "Job search, the duration of unemployment and the Phillips curve", *American Economic Review* 60:847–862.

Phelps, Edmund S. (1967) "Phillips curves, expectations of inflation, and optimal unemployment over time", *Economica (NS)*, 34:254–281.

Phelps, Edmund S. (1970) "Money wage dynamics and labor market equilibrium", in: Edmund S. Phelps et al., eds., *Microeconomic foundations of employment and inflation theory*. New York: Norton.

Phelps, Edmund S. et al. (1970) *Microeconomic foundations of employment and inflation theory*. New York: Norton.
Phelps, Edmund S. and John Taylor (1977) "Stabilizing power of monetary policy under rational expectations", *Journal of Political Economy*, 85:163–190.
Phillips, A. W. (1958) "The relation between unemployment and the rate of change of money wage rates in the United Kingdom, 1862–1957", *Economica*, 25:283–299.
Weiss, Andrew (1980) "Job queues and layoffs in labor markets with flexible wages", *Journal of Political Economy*, 88:526–538.

PART 5

THE INSTITUTIONAL STRUCTURES
OF THE LABOR MARKET

Chapter 18

THE ANALYSIS OF UNION BEHAVIOR

HENRY S. FARBER*

Massachusetts Institute of Technology

1. Introduction and overview

There is a large literature documenting the observed differences between the
union and nonunion sectors in the U.S. economy. It is well known that union
workers earn between 5 and 25 percent more than nonunion workers with the
same observable characteristics, with the precise figure depending both on the
occupation, industry, and other characteristics of the worker and on the level of
aggregate economic activity.[1] There are also important differences between union
and nonunion jobs in many other dimensions. Some of these are: (1) nonwage
benefits make up a significantly larger share of total compensation in the union
sector than in the nonunion sector [Freeman (1981)]; (2) the structure of
compensation in the union sector is such that the variance of earnings is lower
than in the nonunion sector both overall and for workers in particular occupations and industries [Freeman (1980b), Bloch and Kuskin (1978)]; (3) quits from
union jobs occur at lower rates than quits from nonunion jobs [Freeman
(1980a)]; (4) the layoff rate and cyclical swings in employment are larger in the
union sector than in the nonunion sector [Medoff (1979)]; (5) formal mechanisms
for settling disputes between employers and their employees, often with arbitration as the ultimate recourse, are more common in unionized establishments;[2] (6)
the role of seniority in determining the order of layoffs and preference for
promotion is greater in the union sector [Abraham and Medoff (1984, 1985)];

*The first version of this chapter was written while the author was a Fellow at the Center for
Advanced Study in the Behavioral Sciences. The author received support for this research from the
National Science Foundation under Grants BNS-76-22943, SES-8207703, and SES-8408623 and from
the Sloan Foundation as an Alfred P. Sloan Research Fellow. Comments by David Card, Roger Noll,
Andrew Oswald, and John Pencavel on related research are gratefully acknowledged.

[1] Lewis (1963) presents the first detailed empirical examination of the union–nonunion wage
differential. Freeman and Medoff (1981a) and Lewis (1986) and elsewhere in this volume present
recent surveys of the vast literature on this topic.
[2] Card (1983) presents an interesting theoretical analysis of the role that grievance arbitration might
play in the collective bargaining relationship.

Handbook of Labor Economics, Volume II, Edited by O. Ashenfelter and R. Layard
©Elsevier Science Publishers BV, 1986

and (7) the working setting is more rigidly structured in the union sector [Duncan and Stafford (1980)].

Overall, there has been a tremendous amount of effort devoted to measuring the observed differences between union and nonunion jobs, and it is fair to say that this effort has been successful. However, there has been less success in understanding the reasons for these differences, and there is quite a bit of controversy about what these differences mean.[3] Are they accurate measures of the *effects* of unions, are they biased estimates of the effects, or are they statistical artifacts? How can these estimates be used to predict union response to changing economic conditions? Without a complete understanding of union behavior and how the outcomes of collective bargaining are determined it is difficult to answer these questions.

There is a substantial body of economic research, largely theoretical but with a recent empirical component, on the analysis of union behavior. It is the purpose of this chapter to survey this literature selectively and to place it in perspective so that analysts may begin to answer questions raised by the descriptive research on labor unions and to understand the role that unions play in the economy. The emphasis throughout is on work that is operational in the sense that it has an empirical component or is amenable to empirical implementation. No attempt is made to be exhaustive in reviewing the literature. The primary focus is on fitting the existing work into a coherent conceptual framework and on suggesting some directions for further research. In order to keep the analysis and discussion tractable, the presentation will be restricted for the most part to a discussion of the determination of wages and employment as these have been the focus of the vast majority of earlier research.[4]

In the next section, the stage is set with a working definition of a labor union and a brief description of the economic modus operandi of labor unions in the American economy. A number of examples of unions in various industries within the United States are presented in order to highlight the role that market and legal/political constraints play in determining the environment within which unions operate. It is argued that there are three actors or sets of actors that must be considered in any model of the operation of the union sector: (1) the firm; (2) the members of the union; and (3) the leaders of the union. As is appropriate for an economic model, it is to be assumed that individuals (leaders as well as

---

[3] The most attention has been paid to interpreting estimates of the union–nonunion wage differential. Does it actually measure the "effect" of unions on wages? Does unionization affect the wages of nonunion workers? Do unions organize the "better" workers? The extensive literature on this topic includes work by Lewis (1963), Rosen (1969), Schmidt and Strauss (1976), Lee (1978), Freeman and Medoff (1981a, 1981b), and Freeman (1984). See also the surveys by Lewis (1986) and elsewhere in this Handbook.

[4] Of course this is at least partly because wages and employment are more easily quantifiable and measurable than such things as the particular terms of a grievance settlement procedure or a seniority preference provision.

members) have well-defined objective functions that they are maximizing. In addition, it is assumed that the firms are profit-maximizers.

While the union members and their leaders may be maximizers, it does not necessarily follow that the union, as an organization, has a well-defined objective function. The famous debate between Ross (1948), who took the position that unions cannot be analyzed fruitfully as maximizing a well-defined objective function, and Dunlop (1944), who argued the opposite, is recounted briefly. Basically, it is concluded that Dunlop was right in that it is fruitful to analyze labor unions as maximizing a well-defined objective function but that the internal structure of the union and its political process, emphasized by Ross, are important determinants of the objective function.

In order to continue with the analysis of union behavior the structure of bargaining needs to be considered carefully. In this context the structure of bargaining refers to the set of issues that are determined directly through the bargaining process.[5] Two polar examples of bargaining structure that have played a prominent role in the literature on wage and employment determination are discussed in Section 3. The first is where the parties bargain only over the wage leaving the firm to determine employment according to the labor demand schedule. The second is where the parties bargain over both the wage and the employment level. The optimal wage/employment outcomes of the union and the firm are derived in each of these cases. The more realistic intermediate case, where work rules and the like provide partial control over employment, is also addressed briefly.

Section 3 also contains a discussion of the efficiency of labor contracts as it is related to the bargaining structure. It has been argued that efficiency is strongly affected by the degree to which the parties bargain (either explicitly or implicitly) over employment as well as wages.[6] It is concluded that if only the wage is negotiated and the employer is free to set employment then a bargain will never be efficient. On the other hand, if both the wage and employment are bargained then the contract could be efficient. It is further argued that problems of asymmetric information and incentive compatibility make it likely that most unions can bargain over the wage but that they can control employment imprecisely at best. Thus, it is concluded that labor contracts are not likely to be efficient in most cases.[7]

---

[5] Bargaining structure often has a different meaning in the industrial relations literature than that used here. In that context bargaining structure refers to the scope of the bargaining unit (the group of workers that bargain together). The scope of a bargaining unit can be defined by such things as industry, occupation, and location. The determinants and implications of bargaining structure defined this way is an interesting and important problem, but its analysis is beyond the scope of this chapter.

[6] See, for example, Hall and Lilien (1979), McDonald and Solow (1981), Brown and Ashenfelter (1986), and MaCurdy and Pencavel (1986).

[7] Of course, this issue can only be settled empirically. A discussion of some attempts to do just that [Brown and Ashenfelter (1986), MaCurdy and Pencavel (1986)] are contained in Section 5. See also Abowd (1985).

Given an objective function for the union, the profit function of the firm, the structure of the bargain, and the constraints posed by the economic environment, it is necessary to specify the process by which the parties bargain and reach agreement. This is the focus of Section 4. The general framework for collective bargaining between the union and the firm is that they attempt to reach agreement, but if they do not agree then there is a strike where the union withholds its labor. The workers suffer the loss of wages and the firm suffers loss of output and profits. These costs of disagreement provide the incentive for the parties to reach agreement. A complete analysis of the bargaining process is beyond the scope of this study, but some simple models that have proven useful in empirical work are presented briefly.[8]

In Section 5 a number of empirical studies that implement models of the outcomes of collective bargaining and that are consistent with the general framework are presented and discussed. These studies, though restricted to a small number of industries, present fairly clear evidence regarding systematic variation in the wage/employment bargains struck by unions and employers. The interpretation that is given to these results is that labor unions weight employment relatively heavily compared to wages in reaching an agreement. An alternative interpretation is that employers resist union wage demands successfully, resulting in what appears to be a relatively high weight on employment when, in fact, the union would have preferred higher wages and less employment. With regard to the efficiency of labor contracts, some seemingly conflicting empirical results are reconciled and conclusions are drawn regarding the extent to which unions in one setting can control employment in addition to wages.

While much is learned from these studies, the sort of ad hoc objective function for a labor union proposed by Dunlop and characteristic of most of the studies reviewed in Section 5 misses a central feature of labor unions: their basically political nature. In order to understand the behavior of labor unions fully it is necessary to follow Ross's lead in considering the political process that a union uses to make decisions. Given an understanding of the internal operation of the union, it is possible to derive an objective function for a union from the preferences of the members and leaders that can be used for the empirical investigation of union behavior. Because such a model is derived from the behavior of individual economic agents in a consistent fashion, it will be more likely to yield reliable predictions regarding the effects of changes in important economic variables on union behavior.

The development and empirical implementation of a general political/economic model of union behavior is no simple task, particularly since unions differ in the institutional framework governing the political process. All that are fixed across different settings are the preferences of the workers and some general

---

[8]See Chapter 19 by Kennan in this Handbook for a more detailed discussion of strikes.

principles relating worker preferences and the political process to the objective function of the union. The agenda for future research on union behavior must include theoretical and empirical analyses of these principles. The final sections of this chapter contain preliminary discussions of three problems that are central to this effort. These discussions are meant to illustrate our current understanding of these problems and to suggest directions for further research rather than to present complete solutions.

Section 6 focuses on an issue that is central to the analysis of union behavior and that has been neglected by virtually all researchers: the determination of the size of the union. The size of the union determines who the voting membership are and what their preferences over various wage–employment combinations are. It is argued that the size and composition of the union depend crucially on the rule used for the allocation of scarce union jobs among the membership (random, worksharing, seniority, productivity, etc.) and whether the union can restrict membership.

In Section 7 the problem of heterogeneity in preferences among workers is discussed in the context of a very simple model of union behavior, where a single issue is being decided (wages) and the democratic process operates perfectly. The central issue is how the diverse preferences of the workers are reconciled into a coherent objective function for the union. The median voter model of preference aggregation, its limitations, and its implications for union behavior are discussed with heterogeneity in a number of dimensions, including seniority and productivity. The dynamic implications of the median voter formulation for the size of the union are also addressed.

In Section 8 the union leadership is introduced as an entity capable of pursuing its own goals. This is achieved through relaxation of the assumption of perfect democracy. First, the polar opposite of the perfect democracy model is considered by assuming that the leadership of the union is a dictatorship constrained only by the possibility that workers will leave the union and by the behavior of the employer.[9] Second, a more realistic intermediate case is discussed where there are costs that must be borne by an insurgency and where the ultimate success of an insurgency is uncertain. A model of leadership behavior is discussed where the leadership is attempting to maximize a well-defined objective function (e.g. employment, dues revenues) subject to the constraints of attracting members [a membership function as in Dunlop (1944)], a labor demand function, and the probability of a successful insurgency. This probability is modeled as a function of the preferences of the members, the policies adopted by the leadership, and the costs (monetary and otherwise) of an insurgency. It is concluded that the leadership will generally adopt a position close to that preferred by the median

---

[9] The classic reference for this model of union behavior is Lewis (1959). Dunlop (1944) discusses the "membership function" as a constraint on union behavior.

voter unless the costs of an insurgency are very high. Thus, the oft-cited median voter model of union behavior may be of descriptive significance in a broader range of settings than is suggested by its rather stringent set of underlying assumptions.

2. Setting the stage

For the purposes of the discussion here, a labor union can be considered to be a group of workers who bargain collectively with employers regarding the terms and conditions of employment.[10] These workers will generally not bargain themselves but will have as agents union leaders who are elected as representatives of the workers both in the bargaining and in the administration of the contract. While the union will obviously be concerned with a wide range of employment related issues, virtually all economic research on the behavior of unions has focused on the determination of wages and employment. Thus, the discussion here will concentrate on these dimensions of union behavior, and other issues will be discussed largely as they are relevant to understanding union wage and employment policy.

It is useful at this point to make clear the conception of the general mode of operation of a labor union in the American economy that is at least implicit in most economic research on labor unions. Unions are fundamentally organizations that seek to create or capture monopoly rents available in an industry. These rents could come from product market imperfections or from regulation of the industry. Alternatively, the union could organize a significant portion of the labor in a competitive industry and act as a monopolist in the sale of labor, creating and capturing rents from the product market. Entry by low cost nonunion firms would be prevented by the threat to organize new entrants.

Good examples of unions which have historically operated in each of these modes are easy to find. The United Automobile Workers (UAW) is a union that thrived in the past on its ability to exploit market imperfections that existed in the American automobile industry and to ensure that the entire industry was organized. Recently, they are having considerable difficulty maintaining their position due to the increased competitiveness of the automobile industry that resulted from the shift in preferences of American consumers toward types of automobiles that are produced in other parts of the world. However, workers in

---

[10] Note that this definition excludes such cartels as the organizations of doctors, lawyers, barbers, or other tradesmen who organize in order to further their own interests through mechanisms other than collective bargaining.

other countries are not unionizable by the UAW so that the UAW can no longer control the supply of labor in the automobile industry broadly defined.[11]

Another example is the airline industry.[12] The various unions in that industry were able to achieve high wages with little resistance from the airlines because the airlines knew that fares and routes were regulated and that the regulatory agency would pass through any increases in costs to the flying public. All airlines flying a particular route were required to offer the same fare. The primary harm to the airlines from high wages resulted from the likelihood that fewer people and less freight would fly at higher prices as consumers switch to other modes of transportation. However, this sort of intermodal substitution is certainly more difficult for consumers than substitution among airlines. With the recent deregulation of the airline industry, new entrants who are nonunion can undercut the prices of the established union airlines resulting in substitution of nonunion airlines for union airlines by fliers. Once again, the unions no longer control the supply of labor in their industry. Note that exactly the same analysis can be applied to the International Brotherhood of Teamsters (IBT) with regard to the recent deregulation of the trucking industry.[13]

A final example concerns the United Mine Workers (UMW) and the bituminous coal industry. This industry was characterized by a fragmented and competitive product market. The product was differentiated largely on the basis of location, as coal has a very high weight to value ratio making transportation relatively expensive. The UMW organized virtually the entire industry in key locations so that these firms as a group had local market power. The union exercised that market power by raising wages uniformly. New entry by large firms was discouraged by the threat of unionization of the new entrants. The changing (declining) role of coal in the economy and the rise of strip mining has reduced the ability of the UMW to make a credible threat of organization upon entry of new firms. The result has been a declining position for the UMW within the coal industry.[14]

These examples have been selected to highlight the importance of the market and institutional constraints within which unions operate. They truly set the bounds on what unions are able to achieve. Essentially, the tradeoff is one of wages versus employment. In situations where the union is able to gain market power by one means or another, they may be able to raise wages without substantial consequences for employment. On the other hand, as the examples

---

[11]See H. Katz (1984a, 1984b) for more detailed analyses of the history and problems of the UAW and the automobile industry.

[12]Kahn (1980) presents a description of collective bargaining in the airline industry.

[13]See Levinson (1980) for a description of collective bargaining in the trucking industry.

[14]See Farber (1978b, 1978c) for a more detailed analysis of the wage policy of the UMW and its long-term implications.

show, such market power may be a fragile thing. An important focus of this study is the analysis of how a labor union that is faced with a given set of constraints makes decision regarding its wage and employment policy.

The wage–employment outcomes of collective bargaining are determined by the behavior of three actors: (1) the firm; (2) the union workers/members; and (3) the union leaders. The first step towards an economic analysis of bargaining outcomes is defining the objectives of each of these actors. It is straightforward to model the firm as a profit-maximizer. The union members can be assumed to have standard utility functions of the sort usually used in the analysis of individual behavior. For the purpose of this analysis, workers' utility is assumed to be a function of income/consumption.[15] That the union leaders have an objective function that deviates in any way from the objectives of the union as a whole is a relatively controversial and undeveloped notion.[16] Most analysts have ignored any independent role for the preferences of union leaders and have considered the union to be a reflection of the members preferences alone.[17] Nonetheless, it seems reasonable that union leaders have well defined objectives and that they are constrained by the political process of the union.[18]

Early debate over the behavior of labor unions revolved around the issue of whether it is useful to model unions as having a coherent objective function that they attempt to maximize. This debate can be interpreted as turning on the relative importance of economic and political considerations in the determination of union wage policy. The relevant economic considerations are the constraints imposed by the labor market and employer response to the wage bargain (the labor demand schedule). The relevant political considerations are the way in which the preferences of the workers, the preferences of the union leaders, and the market constraints interact to yield the wage policy (objective function) of the union as a whole.

Ross (1948, p. 8) took the position that the wage policy of unions "...is not to be found in the mechanical application of any maximization principle". Ross goes on to argue (p. 14) that "...the typical wage bargain (with certain significant exceptions) is necessarily made without consideration of its employment effect". Ross claims further (p. 14) that the economic environment in the collective

---

[15] It is standard in labor economics to have utility be a function of leisure (the complement of hours of work) as well as of income. Leisure is ignored here as not being central to the analysis of union behavior. Little is lost through this simplifying assumption. Oswald (1982) presents an analysis of union objectives where leisure is an explicit argument in the workers' utility functions.

[16] At this point it is impossible to be explicit about the objectives of the union as a whole. Indeed, this depends crucially on the preferences of workers *and* leaders as well as on the political process that governs the union.

[17] Exceptions to this are Ross (1948), Berkowitz (1954), Atherton (1973), Martin (1980), and Faith and Reid (1983).

[18] Some possible maximands for the leaders are the size of the union, dues revenues, and dues revenues net of the costs of running the union.

bargaining relationship operates "...at the second remove... [I]t generates political pressures which have to be reckoned with by the union leader". Indeed, these internal political pressures are central to understanding the behavior of unions in Ross's framework. These pressures have two sources. The first is differences in interests between necessarily heterogeneous workers. The second, and perhaps more important in Ross's estimation, is the difference in interests between the workers and the union leaders. Ross is not clear on the precise nature of the interests of the workers, but he argues (p. 16) that organizational survival is the "...central aim of the leadership".

In contrast to Ross's view of union behavior is the view, taken by Dunlop (1944, p. 4) and most economic analysts since, that "[a]n economic theory of a trade union requires that the organization be assumed to maximize (or minimize) something". While he goes on to say that the standard case is one of wage bill maximization subject to the constraint imposed by the labor demand function, the force of his argument is that union behavior is amenable to analysis using the economist's standard tools of optimizing behavior. Indeed, much subsequent work on the behavior of unions has been aimed at presenting alternatives to the wage bill as the appropriate maximand for the union.[19]

It is clear that a truly useful analysis of union behavior must address both economic and political factors. It seems appropriate to consider the union as a whole to be attempting to maximize a well-defined objective function constrained by product and labor market considerations. It is likely that the behavior of *both* the leadership and the rank-and-file are affected by labor and product market considerations as they affect employment and the size of the union. At the same time the political considerations are central in determining exactly how the preferences of the workers and the preferences of the leaders interact with each other and with the economic environment to yield the objective function for the union.

3. The structure of bargaining and the efficiency of labor contracts

Two types of bargaining structures will be considered. The first type is where the union and the employer bargain over the wage leaving the employer free to set employment. The second type is where the union and the employer bargain over both the wage and employment. These are polar cases of a more general model where the parties bargain over the wage and some aspects of employment. For

---

[19] The list of such studies is too numerous to detail here. Some of the more influential work includes that of Fellner (1949), Simons (1944), Cartter (1959), and Pen (1959). Surveys of the literature are contained in Atherton (1973) and Oswald (1985). Recently some empirical work has emerged that implements models of union wage determination in order to investigate the nature of the union objective function. This work is discussed in more detail in Section 5.

example, it may be the case that the parties agree on a set of work rules that specify manning requirements or minimum crew sizes. Such work rules do not actually control the level of employment. They are closer to a specification of the capital–labor or output–labor ratio.

Consider first the preferences of the employer. Let the firm's profits be a function of wages and employment holding product market conditions and the cost of capital constant. This function is

$$\pi = \pi(W, L), \tag{1}$$

where W is the wage rate and L is the level of employment. A higher wage raises costs which will make the employer, who faces a downward sloping demand curve for the product, raise price and reduce output. Thus, profits are monotonically declining in the wage ($\pi_W < 0$). With regard to employment, there is a unique optimum level of employment conditional on the wage. Partially differentiating the profit function with respect to L and setting the result (π_L) equal to zero yields the familiar downward sloping demand curve for labor. This relationship,

$$L = L(W), \tag{2}$$

defines the profit-maximizing employment level at any wage. As the wage rises employment will fall not only because of the reduction in output caused by higher prices but also because the employer can substitute capital for labor in the production process.

It is useful to ask what the isoprofit curves of the employer look like in wage–employment space. Their slope is simply

$$\frac{dW}{dL} = -\frac{\pi_L}{\pi_W}. \tag{3}$$

While π_W is always negative, the sign of π_L depends on the values of W and L. The labor demand function was derived by setting $\pi_L = 0$, and it is clear that π_L is negative (positive) if the wage–employment pair lies above (below) the labor demand schedule. Thus, each isoprofit curve is concave from below and has zero slope at the point where it crosses the labor demand schedule. Curves closer to the horizontal (L) axis represent higher profit levels. Figure 18.1 contains a representation of isoprofit curves with these properties along with the associated labor demand schedule.

While it seems that the firms would prefer a wage that is as low as possible, it is constrained by the need to attract workers to the firm. Assuming that the workers have alternative jobs available at a wage W_a, the employer must pay at

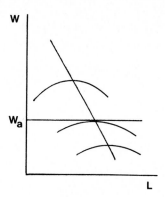

Figure 18.1

least that much or no workers will accept employment with the firm. Thus, the optimal wage from the firm's point of view is W_a and the optimal employment level is $L(W_a)$. In terms of the isoprofit diagram in Figure 18.1, this pair is defined by the tangency between an isoprofit curve and a horizontal line at W_a. No isoprofit line yielding more profit will allow the firm to pay the wage (W_a) required to attract workers. This is precisely the outcome that would occur in a competitive labor market with no union. Note further that this wage–employment pair is optimal from the employer's standpoint regardless of the structure of the bargain.

In order to begin the discussion of the union's behavior, all questions of how the union's objective function is derived from the preferences of the workers and union leaders through the political process are deferred until later. Assume that the union has a well-behaved objective function of the form

$$U = U(W, L),$$
(4)

where both W and L have a positive effect on union utility. Consider first the case where the parties bargain only over the wage and leave the employer to select the level of employment. In this case the optimal wage (W^*) from the union's point of view results from maximization of this objective function with respect to wages subject to the constraint implied by the labor demand function. Transformation of the first-order condition for a maximum yields:

$$\frac{U_W}{U_L} = -L'(W),$$
(5)

which implies that the optimum is where the union's marginal rate of transforma-

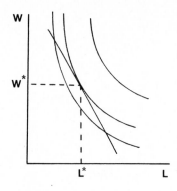

Figure 18.2

tion of employment for wages is equal to the slope of the labor demand schedule. The union has negatively sloped indifference curves in wage–employment space, and the highest indifference curve the union can reach when constrained by the labor demand schedule is that one which is tangent to the labor demand schedule. This is illustrated in Figure 18.2.

In the case described here, where bargaining takes place only over the wage rate and the employer has discretion over employment, the bargaining conflict is apparent in the firm wanting to pay a wage W_a to the workers while this is the absolute minimum that the union can accept and still remain in existence (attract members).[20] It must be true that the optimal wage from the union's point of view is larger than W_a.

In the case where the employer and the union bargain over both the wage and the level of employment, the employer will prefer the same combination $[W_a, L(W_a)]$ as in the earlier case. However, the optimal wage–employment bargain from the union's point of view is affected by the structure of the bargain. The union would like as high a wage and employment level as possible. The question is what the constraints on these values are. Clearly, the union cannot force the employer to continue operation with negative profits or profits less than some minimum. Denote this minimum profit level by π_0. The problem for the union is to maximize its utility with respect to W and L subject to the constraint that

$$\pi \geq \pi_0, \tag{6}$$

where the profit function is defined in eq. (1). On this basis the optimal

---

[20] If there are costs of union membership, then the minimum survival wage required by the union will be higher than W_a by the amount necessary to cover these costs.

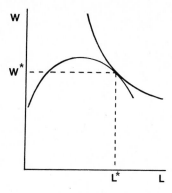

Figure 18.3

wage–employment bargain from the union's point of view is defined implicitly by the equality of the union's marginal rate of substitution of employment for wages and the employer's marginal rate of substitution of employment for wages along with the minimum profit constraint defined in eq. (6). The first condition is

$$\frac{U_W}{U_L} = \frac{\pi_W}{\pi_L}. \tag{7}$$

Geometrically, the optimum is defined by the tangency between an indifference curve of the union and the firm's isoprofit line denoting profits of π_0. This is shown in Figure 18.3.

Aside from the obvious difference in the most preferred bargains from the union's point of view as a function of the structure of the bargain, there is another aspect of the problem that is highlighted. It is clear that where the parties bargain over both the wage and employment the most preferred position of the union is efficient in the sense that neither the firm nor the union can be made better off without making the other party worse off.[21] However, where the parties bargain only over the wage the most preferred position of the union is not efficient.

An important lesson can be drawn from this. Bargaining over the wage alone will not generally permit an efficient outcome.[22] In this case the union is acting as

[21] Note that this is only one possible definition of efficiency given the political nature of the union. What is at issue is efficiency regarding the profit function of the firm and the objective function of the union as a whole. The preferences of the workers and the union leaders are considered only indirectly through the union objective function. There may be important distributional consequences within the union that would suggest different definitions of efficiency.

[22] This notion has a long history. See, for example, Leontief (1946) and McDonald and Solow (1981).

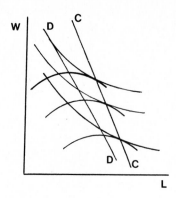

Figure 18.4

a simple monopolist and the standard sort of inefficiency arises. The employer will act conditionally on the bargained wage and select an employment level that is on the firm's labor demand schedule. The locus of efficient bargains (the contract curve) is derived in a straightforward fashion as the set of tangencies between the union's indifference curves and the firm's isoprofit curves. Recall that the labor demand schedule is the locus of points that lie on isoprofit curves at points of zero slope in wage–employment space. Thus, if the indifference curves of the union are downward sloping everywhere in wage–employment space then no tangency between isoprofit and indifference curves will lie on the labor demand schedule and a simple wage bargain can never be efficient. Figure 18.4 contains a graphic representation of the contract curve (CC) along with the labor demand schedule (DD).[23]

If the parties can bargain over employment (either explicitly or implicitly) as well as the wage, then *any* wage–employment outcome is feasible. This includes inefficient as well as efficient bargains. The economist's presumption is that where enough policy instruments exist for an efficient outcome the outcome will, in fact, be efficient. However, given our relative lack of understanding of the bargaining process, the efficiency of labor contracts must remain an empirical question. The conclusion is that bargaining over both wages and employment is a necessary but not sufficient condition for an efficient labor contract.

Do unions and employers bargain over employment as well as wages? There are examples of declining industries or industries/occupations with declining

[23] Note that the contract curve can have any slope. It is drawn in Figure 18.4 with a negative slope for no particularly compelling reason. The shape of the contract curve will be discussed further in Section 5.

employment as a result of technological change where employment guarantees have been negotiated. However, it is difficult to think of examples of industries with stable or growing employment where such guarantees have been negotiated.[24] The more common situation is either no control over employment or the negotiation of work rules that attempt to control the capital–labor or labor–output ratio. One well-known example is the set of work rules which existed for many years in the longshoring industry and specified minimum crew sizes and sometimes included the requirement that workers actually handle individual pieces of cargo regardless of the technology in use.[25] If fully effective, work rules could lead to an efficient outcome depending on the nature of the technology and the product demand function. It is an empirical issue as to whether work rules in a particular situation are a sufficient instrument to remedy the inefficiency inherent in the standard wage contract.[26]

Why do virtually no labor contracts specify an efficient combination of wages and employment? A convincing argument can be made that efficient labor contracts are not feasible. Consider two types of efficient contracts. The first is an incentive compatible efficient contract where the employer, left to his own devices, would hire the efficient quantity of labor. This form of an efficient contract would specify that workers be compensated directly by employers at some wage rate which would imply a level of employment consistent with the labor demand schedule. In order to ensure "enough" employment, this wage rate is likely to be low in the sense that the union needs more revenue at that employment level to yield an efficient outcome. The firm would then, as a supplement to wage payments, make a lump-sum payment to the union which is *not* contingent on employment. The union leaders would then have to distribute the lump-sum payment to the members of the union. Two political problems for the union arise. First, the union may not have any mechanism to restrict membership so that anyone may claim a share of the lump-sum payment.[27] More

[24] Oswald (1984) presents evidence regarding the extent of explicit and implicit agreements concerning employment in ongoing collective bargaining relationships based on examination of a sample of contracts and a survey of large unions. The results are consistent with the view that bargaining over employment is uncommon.

[25] With the advent of containerized cargo, the requirement that workers actually handle each piece of cargo resulted in "stripping and stuffing" where each container was unpacked and repacked on the dock. The result was a reduction in both the quantity of shipping and employment in the ports where the union maintained such rules. The unions were forced to modify their rules in the end.

[26] Some attempts at tests of the structure of the bargain by Brown and Ashenfelter (1986) and MaCurdy and Pencavel (1986) are discussed in Section 5.

[27] The problems that arise in such a distribution are identical to those that arose recently when the government of Alaska wanted to make lump-sum distributions to their residents from royalties received for North Slope oil. At first they established a rather lengthy residence requirement for eligibility, but new arrivals challenged this in court and won. A much shorter requirement was imposed, and a much smaller royalty was paid to many more individuals.

importantly, the internal political process of the union may be such that those members with a controlling voice are those members who will be employed even when the wage rate is considerably above the efficient wage. These members would prefer an inefficient bargain with a higher wage and no lump-sum transfer unless the union would make larger lump-sum payments to these workers. However, it is likely that the union will have difficulty finding a stable mechanism for making different lump-sum payments to different members. These considerations suggest that the political process that governs the union may preclude incentive compatible efficient contracts.[28]

One could argue that efficient contracts that are not incentive compatible are feasible. This is the second type of efficient contract. In this type of contract the wage is set above the opportunity wage so that no lump-sum payments are required and the employment level is set (either explicitly or implicitly) at the efficient level where the value of marginal product of labor is less than the wage rate. However, the employer left to his own devices would prefer to reduce the level of employment. Clearly, the employer will either have to be entirely precluded from adjusting the size of the workforce or have to be monitored very closely. Neither of these options is likely to be feasible. Given that demand will vary over time and that it would be exceptionally costly to the firm not to be able to adjust the size of the workforce in response to demand shifts, the firm will require some discretion in setting employment. In addition, it is likely that shifts in demand will be very difficult for the union to monitor so that the employers will have the opportunity to "cheat" on any labor agreement by reducing employment and output below the efficient level while claiming that there has been a demand shift. In more formal terms, there is asymmetric information regarding the state of product demand, and this will force the use of incentive compatible contracts.[29]

Overall, incentive compatible efficient contracts, where workers are paid in addition to compensation received on the basis of work performed, may not be feasible due to the political difficulties involved for the union in making the additional payments. On the other hand, incentive incompatible efficient contracts, which specify both the wage rate and the level of employment, may be precluded due to the asymmetric information held by the firm regarding the state of demand. We are likely to be left with inefficient labor contracts of the type generally observed, where the wage rate is determined through collective bargain-

---

[28] Consistent with this argument is the fact that it is difficult (if not impossible) to think of examples of unions (or firms) compensating workers on any basis other than time worked or output.

[29] Chatterjee (1982) presents a formal analysis of the difficulty in reaching efficient contracts where there is uncertainty. Grossman and Hart (1981) and Hart (1983), among others, present models of implicit contracts with asymmetric information more generally that are relevant to the arguments made here.

ing and the level of employment is set by the employer who is constrained to some extent by work rules.[30]

4. The bargaining problem

The discussion in the previous section highlighted the most preferred outcomes of the union and the firm. These objectives are to some extent in opposition to each other, and the observed outcomes will not in general be precisely the most preferred outcome of either party. Some further structure is needed to specify how the preferences of the parties are translated into bargaining outcomes. In virtually all private sector collective bargaining relationships in the United States, if the parties cannot reach agreement on the terms of the contract a strike occurs. The workers lose income and the firm sacrifices output and profits. Fundamentally, disagreement imposes costs on both parties so that there is an incentive for the parties to reach agreement.[31]

The bargaining problem is essentially one of the determination of price in bilateral monopoly. It is well known that the solution to this problem is indeterminate in the most general case. An early determinate solution that has been widely cited is that proposed by Zeuthen (1930) as extended by Harsanyi (1956). This solution is based on the notion of sequential concessions made by the parties until agreement is reached. The key to the model is an ad hoc process that determines which of the two parties will concede at any point. The details are not important here except to say that the solution has the property that it maximizes the product of the incremental utilities of the parties.[32] While the ad hoc concession rule is not convincing, the model is widely cited due to the fact that the solution is identical to the axiomatic model of bargaining outcomes derived by Nash (1950, 1953) so that Zeuthen seems to provide a process justification for the later "rigorous" Nash model.

The Nash model is probably the best known model of bargaining outcomes, and it has served as the basis for much work on axiomatic bargaining models.

[30] Virtually all existing applied work proceeds under the assumption that unions bargain over wages and the employer selects the employment level without any work rule constraints. Although analysis of union decision-making regarding work rules is an important area for future research, the discussion in succeeding sections of this chapter does not take formal account of work rules.

[31] This framework is directly applicable to collective bargaining in the private sector in the United States where the right to strike over economic issues in the setting of the terms of a collective bargaining agreement is largely unrestricted. In the public sector many jurisdictions have laws that prohibit some or all categories of public sector employees from striking. However, many of these jurisdictions have provided for arbitration of unresolved labor disputes involving public employees. Farber and Katz (1979) argue that arbitration imposes costs on the parties that have a similar effect in inducing agreement that the costs of a strike do. See also Crawford (1979) and Farber (1980a, 1981a).

[32] The incremental utility of a party is the difference between the utility of the proposed settlement and the utility if the parties failed to agree (the threat point).

Essentially, a set of properties (axioms) that a solution should have are proposed, and the set of solutions that satisfy these axioms is derived. To the extent that the axioms are reasonable, the solution has appeal. Without going into any detail, the important axioms of the Nash model are (1) the solution should be Pareto efficient; (2) the solution should be symmetric in that if the sets of incremental utilities of the parties are symmetric then the incremental utilities of the two parties at the solution should be equal; (3) the solution should be independent of irrelevant alternatives in the sense that if all of the feasible outcomes of game A are contained in the set of feasible outcomes of game B and if the solution of game B is a feasible outcome of game A, then it will also be the solution of game A; and (4) the solution should be unaffected by linear transformations of the utilities of the parties.[33] The strong result of Nash is that the only feasible solution that satisfies all of these axioms is the outcome that maximizes the product of the incremental utilities of the parties.[34]

The important point to note is that the Nash model and most other axiomatic models are normative rather than positive. They prescribe what an outcome *ought* to look like, and they are best considered prescriptions for arbitrators rather than a description of the likely outcomes of collective bargaining. Nonetheless, there have been some attempts to "test" the Nash–Zeuthen solution in the sense of seeing if actual negotiated agreements are consistent with the Nash model. A relatively crude empirical implementation of the model using aggregate data was done by De Menil (1971). Variables representing bargaining factors were found to be important, but little could be said about the precise form of the solution. Hamermesh (1973) implemented a test of the Zeuthen–Nash solution using disaggregated data, and he was not able to reach a definitive conclusion regarding whether the observed outcomes were consistent with the predictions of the model. A problem that Hamermesh recognized with his analysis is that the test is based on the extent to which outcomes "split-the-difference" between the initial offers of the parties.[35] This approach has two problems: (1) the initial offers are subject to manipulation of the parties so that they are not good indicators of the threat point and (2) there is the implicit assumption that the utility functions of the parties are linear. Svejnar (1980) points out some of the problems with attempts to test the Zeuthen–Nash model, and he suggests an alternative that does not rely on information on the initial offers of the parties. However, it does require an explicit assumption regarding the form of the union's objective function. Indeed,

---

[33] See Luce and Raiffa (1957) for a clear discussion of the Nash model and its axioms. Bishop (1963) and Roth (1979) present recent surveys of axiomatic bargaining models. Svejnar (1983) presents a generalization of Nash's model that relaxes the symmetry constraint.

[34] In the case of symmetric utilities, this solution has the property that it results in each party receiving an equal utility increment from the threat point.

[35] Bognanno and Dworkin (1975) and Bowlby and Shriver (1978) implement similar tests using disaggregated data.

a requirement of any implementation of the Zeuthen–Nash or any other particular solution to the bargaining problem is that a specification of the union's objective function must be assumed. The test then proceeds conditionally on this utility function. Most of the existing studies use a very simple assumption regarding the union utility function. The union is usually assumed to be a rent-maximizer or to have a linear utility function. However, as is discussed in the next section, the existing evidence regarding union objective functions is not consistent with this view.[36]

An important weakness of the axiomatic models of bargaining is that they generally do not admit the possibility of strikes.[37] There exists a body of literature that attempts to derive a determinate solution to the bargaining problem while at the same time admitting the possibility of a strike. These studies tend to rely on notions of relative bargaining power, bluffing, threats, investment, asymmetric information, uncertainty, and learning to explain the outcomes of collective bargaining. This literature is far too vast to survey here, but suffice it to say that most of the models do not have both the union and the firm behaving in ways fully consistent with optimizing behavior.[38] For example, while both parties may be attempting to optimize well-defined objective functions, a determinate solution might be derived by imposing ad hoc rules for predicting the behavior of the other party or for learning about important facts.

Two models of industrial disputes that have been widely cited and have served as the basis for much further analysis are those of Hicks (1964) and Ashenfelter and Johnson (1969) (A–J). The Hicks model is well known for presenting a graph in wage–strike space of an upward sloping employer "concession schedule" and a downward sloping union "resistance curve". It is the intuitive appeal of this diagram which seems to mirror the concession process that leads to agreement, rather than the precise behavioral underpinnings of the model that accounts for the popularity of the Hicks model.[39] The union resistance curve gives "...the length of time [the workers] would be willing to stand out rather than allow their remuneration to fall below the corresponding wage" [Hicks (1963, p. 142)]. This

---

[36] It should be pointed out that all of the evidence discussed in the next section regarding union objective functions rely on arbitrary assumptions regarding the solution to the bargaining problem.

[37] The game theoretic models of bargaining that allow noncooperative behavior or mixed strategies in repeated games do allow for strikes. However, the notion of mixed strategies in this context is not terribly appealing. Fudenberg, Levine and Ruud (1983) and Tracy (1987) present interesting empirical analyses of a game theoretic model of bargaining outcomes with noncooperative behavior that admits strikes.

[38] See Chapter 19 by Kennan in this Handbook. Examples of models of the sort described here include Pen (1952), Bishop (1964), Cross (1965), Shackle (1957), Hicks (1963), Ashenfelter and Johnson (1969), and Johnston (1972). Bishop (1963) and Coddington (1968) presents surveys of some of this work.

[39] Hicks does not interpret the diagram as representing concessionary behavior. It is, in his view, an ex ante representation rather than a dynamic view of the concession process. See Comay, Melnik and Subotnik (1974) for an attempt at empirical estimation of employer and union concession schedules. Farber (1980b) presents a more detailed discussion of Hicks's model than there is room for here.

curve is downward sloping because the sacrifice involved in accepting a lower wage is larger so that workers will be willing to endure a longer strike to avoid such a reduction. The employer concession schedule is defined more precisely by Hicks. It is the sequence of wage–strike pairs such that "...the expected cost of the stoppage and the expected cost of concession...just balance" [Hicks (1963, p. 141)]. This is upward sloping by construction because at a higher wage the cost of concession is higher and a longer strike is also more costly. Clearly, the employer concession schedule is based on equality of total costs rather than the sorts of marginal considerations that would signify an optimizing model. While it may seem natural to interpret the intersection of the resistance curve and the concession schedule as the likely outcome of bargaining, there is no reason to think that this will be true.

Ashenfelter and Johnson (1969) develop what could be considered a logical reformulation of the Hicks model. They argue that the union has a "concession schedule" in wage–strike space that is downward sloping and represents the minimum wage (increase) acceptable to the union after a strike of a given length. It is downward sloping because it is likely that the privations endured by the workers as a strike wears on will reduce their militancy and make them willing to settle for less.[40] The innovation in the A–J model is that the employer is modeled as being a maximizer of the present discounted value of profits subject to the constraint implied by the union concession schedule. Essentially, the employer determines the optimal strike length by equating the *marginal* cost of continuing a strike (marginal forgone profits) with the *marginal* benefit of continuing a strike (marginal decrease in the present value of the wage bill). The model explains not only the optimal strike length but also the wage outcome and whether a strike occurs at all. A number of important results can be derived from this model, and Ashenfelter and Johnson use the model to help specify and interpret the estimates of an aggregate time series regression analysis of strike activity in U.S. manufacturing.[41] Farber (1978a) implements a structural version of the model using microeconomic data on individual bargains both across firms and over time.[42] The strength of the A–J model is that it allows the firm to act in a manner fully consistent with profit-maximization while yielding a determinate and plausible analysis of the outcome of collective bargaining. The weakness of

---

[40]Ashenfelter and Johnson claim that an important element of their model is that the union leadership plays a central role both in mediating between the employer and the rank and file and in helping to enlighten the rank and file regarding what is a realistic demand. However, this does not seem central to their analysis.

[41]Pencavel (1970) presents a similar analysis for Great Britain.

[42]See Farber (1977) and Farber (1981b) for other microeconomic analyses using the A–J model. Hamermesh (1970) presents an early analysis of the outcomes of collective bargaining using microeconomic data though without an explicit model of the process by which the agreement is reached. Farber (1980b) presents an extension of the A–J model that introduces uncertainty about the union concession schedule and derives the optimal set of offers for the firm to make in this situation.

the A–J model is that the behavior of the workers/union is naive and not derived from an optimizing model of individual or union behavior.

As should be clear from the discussion in this section, there is a long way to go toward a realistic and empirically tractable model of the outcomes of collective bargaining that allows for fully rational behavior on the part of all the actors. Progress has been made generally by denying full rationality at some point in the bargaining process and by assuming particularly simple forms for the union objective function. The latter is crucial because it seems that without a specification of the union objective function it is not possible to identify the process that leads to a particular bargaining outcome. At the same time, what led to the discussion in this section is that it does not seem possible to identify the objectives of the union without specifying, a priori, the process that leads to a particular bargaining outcome. Indeed, for the investigations of union objectives surveyed in the next section, this dilemma is "solved" by assuming a very simple bargaining rule: the union can impose whatever settlement it wishes.

5. Empirical investigations of union objectives

There has recently been great interest in estimating models of union behavior based on maximization by unions of well-defined objective functions. Some of these, including studies by De Menil (1971), Rosen (1970), and Nickell and Andrews (1983), use aggregate data to estimate reduced form models of wage–employment determination in the union sector. While interesting in their own right, these studies are limited in the degree to which they can shed light on the nature of union objectives and the process by which agreement is reached. More interesting in this regard are some recent studies using disaggregated data that focus on the nature of the union objective function as it affects wage and employment determination. These studies include Farber (1978b, 1978c), Dertouzos and Pencavel (1981), Carruth and Oswald (1983), Pencavel (1984a, 1984b), Brown and Ashenfelter (1986), and MaCurdy and Pencavel (1986). What these studies have in common is that they focus on particular industries and they solve (avoid?) the difficult problem of the solution to the pure bargaining problem in similar ways. Farber (1978b, 1978c) and Carruth and Oswald (1983) analyze the objectives of unions in the U.S. and British coal industries, respectively. All of the other studies focus on the objectives of the International Typographer's Union (ITU) in its relationships with American newspapers. All of the studies assume that the union can impose whatever settlement it wishes on the firm so that the observed wage outcome represents the outcome that is most preferred by the union. The studies differ in what they assume about the structure of the bargain and in the extent to which the union objective function is derived from the preferences of the members and the political process within the union.

The conceptual underpinnings of this literature date at least to the work of Dunlop (1944), Leontief (1946), Fellner (1947), and Cartter (1959), all of whom present models of union behavior where the union attempts to maximize a well-defined objective function. In this early work the firm is assumed to maximize profits and the structure of the bargain is assumed to be such that the parties bargain over the wage while the employer is free to set employment according to the labor demand function of the firm/industry. Thus, the union is assumed to be a utility-maximizer with respect to wages subject to the constraint embodied in the labor demand function. Dunlop (1944) argued that the appropriate maximand for the union is the wage bill although he entertained some alternatives, including rent-maximization.[43] The others are less explicit about the particular maximand. No attempt is made in this early literature to derive the union objective function from the preferences of the individual workers or the political process within the union.[44]

Oswald (1982) presents a model of a "utilitarian" union that has an objective function that looks very much like rent (in utility units) maximization. In this model all of the workers within the union are assumed to be identical (a common assumption) and the utility function of the union is simply the sum of the utilities of the individual workers. There is no explicit political model presented that would yield such a simple form for the union objective function. However, the empirical studies of Farber (1978b), Carruth and Oswald (1983), and Brown and Ashenfelter (1986) are based on empirical specifications that are more or less consistent with a utilitarian union. For this reason, it is worth considering in a bit more detail. Its objective function is

$$V = LU(W_u) + (M - L)U(W_a),$$
(8)

where V is the union objective function, $U(\cdot)$ is the utility function of the representative worker as a function of the wage rate, L is union employment, M represents the membership of the union, W_u is the union wage, and W_a is the opportunity wage of the workers.[45] Essentially, L of the union members will be earning W_u and $M - L$ will be earning W_a. The union objective function can be rewritten as

$$V = L[U(W_u) - U(W_a)] + MU(W_a).$$
(9)

[43] The wage bill is defined as the product of employment and the wage rate while rents are defined as the product of employment and the difference between the union wage and the opportunity wage of the workers.

[44] More recently, Atherton (1973) attempted an extension of the early literature to account for individual preferences and the internal politics of the union, but the results are not entirely successful.

[45] Consideration of the determination of the size of the union is deferred to Section 6. For the time being M is considered to be exogenously determined.

Clearly, the last term is simply a constant from the standpoint of union wage–employment policy. The relevant maximand is $L[U(W_u) - U(W_a)]$. If the individual utility function is linear in wages then maximization by a utilitarian union is simply rent-maximization. If the utility function is linear and the opportunity wage available to the workers is zero then objective function is the wage bill. Given a nonlinear individual utility function, the objective function is rents in utility terms rather than dollar terms. If the alternative utility is zero then the union objective function is simply "total" utility.[46]

Another general form for the union objective function that has been used as the foundation of some of the recent empirical work [Dertouzos and Pencavel (1981), Pencavel (1984a)] is a modified Stone–Geary utility function. This objective function has the form

$$V = \alpha[W_u - W^*]^\delta [L - L^*]^\gamma. \tag{10}$$

The relative value of δ and γ is an indicator of the relative importance of wages and employment in union objectives. The quantities W^* and L^* can be interpreted as the absolute minimum wage and employment levels that the union can tolerate. One interpretation of W^* is as the opportunity wage of the workers [Pencavel (1984a)]. This is because it is unlikely that a union can survive if it negotiates a wage below the opportunity wage of the workers. There is no equally clear interpretation for L^*. This model also has some interesting special cases. If $\delta = 1$, $\gamma = 0$, and $W^* = 0$, then the objective is wage-maximization [Simons (1944)]. If $\delta = 1$, $\gamma = 1$, $L^* = 0$, and $W^* = W_a$, then the objective is rent-maximization. Finally, if $\delta = 1$, $\gamma = 1$, $W^* = 0$, and $L^* = 0$, then the objective is the wage bill. The advantages of the Stone–Geary utility formulation include its tractability and flexibility. Its disadvantage for the purposes of this analysis is that there is no pretense of its being derived from the preferences of the individual workers through the political process that governs the union.

A final objective function that has been used [Pencavel (1984a, 1984b)], but which will not be presented here in any detail, is the augmented addilog utility function. Again, this is a relatively flexible functional form that has many interesting special cases. It shares advantages and disadvantages with the Stone–Geary, though it is probably a bit less tractable in estimation and a bit more flexible.

How are the models implemented, and what is found when the models of union behavior are implemented using disaggregated data? It is worth going through a number of the empirical studies in some detail paying particular

---

[46]Assuming that the individual utility can be normalized, one could define $U(W_a) = 0$ for a single value of W_a. However, as W_a changed over time, $U(W_a)$ would differ from zero.

attention to assumptions regarding the structure of the bargain, the specification of the union objective function, and the central findings.

Farber (1978b) estimates a model of wage and employment determination in the bituminous coal industry in the United States in the period from 1948 to 1973. It is argued that the United Mine Workers (UMW) had cartelized the industry and could impose whatever wage it wished on the essentially competitive firms in the industry who would be free to set the employment level according to the labor demand schedule. It is further assumed that all of the members of the union are identical except that they are of different ages so that they prefer different mixes between wages and fringe benefits in the compensation package. A median voter argument is used to derive the optimal mix in the compensation package as that preferred by the median aged member of the union.[47] Each worker is assumed to have the same probability of having a union job so that the expected utility of a given worker is

$$E(U) = \frac{L}{M} U(T_{ui}) + \left[1 - \frac{L}{M}\right] U(T_a), \tag{11}$$

where L is union employment, M is the membership of the union, T_{ui} is the total compensation per manhour of the ith worker on the union job, and T_a is the alternative compensation level per manhour available to each worker. Essentially, total union compensation is a weighted average of the wage and per capita expenditures on fringe benefits where the weights are a function of the age of the worker. The quantity L/M represents the probability that a worker will be employed on a union job.

Farber argues that the union will act as if it is maximizing the expected utility of the median aged member of the union subject to the constraint imposed by the industry labor demand function. Thus, the level and mix of compensation will be set so as to maximize $E(U)$ as defined in eq. (11) substituting T_{um} for T_{ui}, where m is the index of the median aged member. Given the assumption of exogeneity of the size of the union (M), multiplication of the expected utility in eq. (11) by M yields exactly the utilitarian objective function proposed by Oswald in eq. (8). In other words, Farber's objective function for the UMW would be the same as the objective function of a utilitarian union that had all members with preferences identical to those of the median aged member. Farber assumes that each individual had a constant absolute risk aversion utility function, and a measure of average hourly earnings elsewhere in the U.S. economy was used as a proxy for T_a. On this basis the first-order conditions for the optimal level and mix of

---

[47]This analysis raises important issues of how to deal with multiple objectives for a labor union. Blair and Crawford (1981) show that the median voter equilibrium proposed by Farber does not exist in general. The problem of aggregation of heterogeneous preferences and the median voter model in particular are discussed in Section 7.

compensation were derived. The model is implemented using Full Information Maximum Likelihood (FIML) to estimate the first-order conditions directly, the labor demand function, and a set of other relationships defining the labor and product markets for coal.

The central result of Farber's research on the UMW with regard to the union's objective function is that the workers appear to be quite risk averse, with a coefficient of relative risk aversion of 3.0 or more. Even if one does not accept the literal interpretation of the model, this result suggests that the union places substantial weight on employment in setting its compensation policy. The special case of risk neutrality, where the coefficient of relative risk aversion is zero and which would imply that the union is maximizing rents, is strongly rejected. In other words, the UMW seems to have placed more weight on employment relative to compensation than rent-maximization would imply.

Carruth and Oswald (1983) develop and estimate a model of the wage policy of the National Union of Mineworkers (NUM) in Great Britain over the period from 1950 to 1980. They adopt a utilitarian objective function for the NUM where all of the members of the union are identical with constant relative risk aversion utility functions. The union is assumed to maximize this objective function with respect to the wage rate subject to the constraint imposed by the labor demand function.[48] Government unemployment benefits are used as a proxy for W_a. The model is implemented using FIML to estimate the two-equation system consisting of the labor demand schedule and a first-order condition for a maximum of the union objective function.

The central finding with regard to the union objective function of Carruth and Oswald is that they find a significant degree of relative risk aversion (a coefficient of relative risk aversion of about 0.8), though less risk aversion than seems to be implicit in the compensation policy of the UMW in the United States. This difference in results may be due to the fact that Carruth and Oswald used government unemployment benefits to measure the alternative income available to workers while Farber used an actual earnings measure which is bound to be larger than unemployment benefits.[49] Such a systematic difference in alternative income measures is likely to produce the observed difference in the degree of risk aversion even if preferences are, in fact, identical. Nonetheless, even the lower degree of risk aversion found by Carruth and Oswald implies a greater weight on employment relative to wages than would be implied by rent-maximization.

---

[48] The source of the labor demand function in this case is a bit different than in the standard case. The British coal industry was nationalized over the entire period under investigation. The National Coal Board (NCB) was set up to run the industry. It is not clear exactly what the objectives of the NCB were so that it is difficult to argue that the sort of labor demand schedule a profit-maximizing firm would have is appropriate for the British coal industry over this period.

[49] Carruth and Oswald do find that alternative wages as measured by earnings elsewhere in the economy are a significant determinant of union wage policy, but it enters the worker's objective function in an ad hoc fashion. It is not clear how to interpret this result.

Dertouzos and Pencavel (1981) explore the wage policy of the International Typographical Union (ITU) in their relationships with newspapers in a number of American cities in the period from 1946 to 1965. The union local in each city negotiates its own bargain, and it is argued that within each city the members of the union are homogeneous. It is further argued that the union has a long and important democratic tradition so that there is little conflict between the goals of the leaders and the goals of the rank and file. On this basis, Dertouzos and Pencavel argue that the objective function of the union is that of a leader who "...is assumed to integrate the welfare of all the union members" (p. 1167). There is no discussion of exactly how this integration takes place. It is assumed that the union objective function derived in this fashion is of the Stone–Geary form described in eq. (10).[50] The union maximizes this objective function with respect to wages and employment subject to the constraint imposed by the labor demand function. The model is estimated by specifying a labor demand function along with the reduced form wage equation derived from the first-order condition for a maximum of the objective function. The estimates presented are derived using FIML on this system of two equations.

The wage bargains struck by the *Cincinnati Post* with the ITU are examined in detail by Dertouzos and Pencavel. They find that the union placed a large weight on employment relative to wages. In the notation of eq. (10), they estimated a value of γ greater than the value of δ. They are able to reject the special cases, imbedded in the Stone–Geary formulation, of rent-maximization and wage-bill-maximization. They also carry out somewhat less detailed analyses of the wage bargains struck by the ITU in a number of other cities. The key result is that preferences seem to vary substantially across cities. More specifically, the weight on employment relative to wages as well as the minimum acceptable wage (W^*) and employment (L^*) levels are quite variable.

Pencavel (1984b) extends his earlier work with Dertouzos on the wage policy of the ITU to consider an addilog objective function for the union.[51] This has the advantage of being flexible and yielding a particularly simple form for the marginal rate of substitution that is equated to the slope of a particular specification for the labor demand schedule at the optimum. This relationship is solved for the wage and estimated directly using nonlinear two-stage least squares (NLTSLS) where employment is treated as endogenous along with the wage. Once again, Pencavel finds substantial variation in preferences across different locals of the ITU. Tentative evidence is found that the larger locals have an objective function that may approximate rent-maximization. The others seem to

---

[50] Pencavel (1984a) presents a further analysis of similar data using the Stone–Geary objective function and the same set of assumptions.

[51] Pencavel (1984a) presents a further analysis of ITU wage policy using the addilog objective function.

place relatively more weight on employment. Wage-bill-maximization is rejected in all cases.

The set of studies that have been discussed thus far [Farber (1978b, 1978c), Carruth and Oswald (1983), Dertouzos and Pencavel (1981), and Pencavel (1984a, 1984b)] all find that implicit in the union wage policies that were examined is a wage–employment policy that puts a relatively high weight on employment. Both the rent-maximization hypothesis and the wage-bill maximization hypothesis are rejected in virtually every situation. Of course only a very few different settings have been examined: mineworkers in the coal industries in the United States and Great Britain and typesetters in the newspaper industry in the United States. Given the great differences that exist across industries both in the characteristics of workers and in the structure and institutions of collective bargaining, great care should be exercised in generalizing these results to other settings. This is particularly true in light of the evidence presented by Pencavel and Dertouzos (1981) and Pencavel (1984a, 1984b) that even within the ITU there is great variation across locals in the objective function of the union.

While the studies discussed above have focused on the nature of union objectives, a pair of studies by Brown and Ashenfelter (1986) (B–A) and by MaCurdy and Pencavel (1986) (M–P) have focused on the issue of the efficiency of labor contracts. Recall that it was argued in Section 3 that an efficient contract would not be possible if all that was bargained over was the wage. Thus, an investigation of efficiency is, at least in part, an investigation of the structure of the bargain. Do unions and firms bargain over wages alone? Do they bargain over both wages and employment? If they bargain over wages and work rules, are the work rules sufficient to ensure that the outcome would be efficient? Both the B–A and the M–P studies use data on wages and employment from the ITU. The two studies use very different approaches to the problem and they come to essentially opposite conclusions.

Brown and Ashenfelter specify a union objective function that is the expected utility of the representative worker where each worker has the same utility function and the same probability of working on a union job. This is identical to the objective function used by Farber (1978b) and described above in eq. (11).[52] It is also observationally equivalent to the utilitarian utility function proposed by Oswald (1982). The general form of the efficiency condition is contained in eq. (7) as the equality of the union's marginal rate of substitution of employment for wages and the employer's marginal rate of substitution of employment for wages. Assuming, as B–A do, that the profit function is simply the difference between revenues and labor costs, the efficiency condition is

$$V_W/V_L = (W - R_L)/L, \tag{12}$$

[52] Wages are substituted by Ashenfelter and Brown for the measure of total compensation used by Farber.

where $V(W, L)$ is the union objective function, and R_L is the marginal revenue product of labor. In the specific case of the utility function used by B–A the efficiency condition is

$$[U(W) - U(W_a)]/U_W(W) = W - R_L, \tag{13}$$

where $U(\cdot)$ is the utility function of the representative worker. If the workers are risk neutral so that the $U(\cdot)$ is linear, then the efficiency condition reduces to the equality of the marginal revenue product of labor with the alternative (opportunity) wage ($R_L = W_a$). In this case the union objective function is rent-maximization, and employment is set at the same level it would be in the absence of the union. This is the key property used by the B–A analysis because it suggests that employment will not be a function of the actual wage (W) but only of the alternative wage (W_a) so that the contract curve (the set of efficient settlements) is vertical.[53] Brown and Ashenfelter go on to argue that this condition will be approximately true for more general utility functions. However, it is clear that it can only be exactly true if the union utility function is a monotonic transformation of total rents. This is

$$V(W, L) = g([W - W_a]L), \tag{14}$$

where $g(\cdot)$ is an increasing function of its argument.

Brown and Ashenfelter base their test of the efficiency of the wage–employment bargains of the ITU on a test of whether employment is a function of the actual wage as opposed to the alternative wage. Of necessity, the validity of this test is conditional on the validity of the assumption that the union is maximizing rents (or some monotonic transformation of rents). Their empirical analysis suggests rather strongly that employment is significantly affected by the actual wage even after controlling for the alternative wage. This would seem to be strong preliminary evidence for a conclusion that contracts in the newspaper industry between the ITU and their employers are not efficient. However, it may be that rent-maximization is a sufficiently bad approximation to union objectives in the industry that a vertical contract curve is not appropriate.

MaCurdy and Pencavel set up two models. The first is the labor demand curve equilibrium model (LDEM) where a union sets the wage so as to maximize its objective function subject to the constraint imposed by the labor demand schedule of the firm. This is clearly not efficient. The second model is the contract curve equilibrium model (CEM) where the parties set wages and employment so that the general efficiency condition [eq. (7)] is satisfied. They derive the standard equilibrium condition in the LDEM model where the factors of production (including labor) are employed such that the ratio of their prices is equal to the ratio of their marginal products. They further show that the equilibrium condi-

---

[53]This is consistent with the vertical contract curve suggested by Hall and Lilien (1979).

tion in the CEM model is identical to that in LDEM model with the exception of an additional term in the former representing the marginal rate of substitution (MRS) of the union objective function. This term has the effect of making the ratio of the wage to the price of other factors exceed the ratio of marginal products in an efficient bargain.[54] The empirical test of the two models proposed by M–P is essentially a test of the importance of the "additional term" in the equilibrium condition implied by the CEM model.

In implementing their test, M–P assume that the MRS implicit in the union objective function is a nonlinear function of employment and a set of union (local) and time dummy variables. Some special cases of the MRS are integrated to derive the associated utility functions, and it is argued that the form selected is sufficiently general to admit a wide range of objective functions. MaCurdy and Pencavel find that the LDEM model is rejected by the data in the sense that the variables that make up the additional term seem to be important. They further argue that the CEM is supported by their data largely because the estimated MRS implies a quasi-concave objective function for the union. However, they agree that a rigorous test of the CEM model is not possible without making more restrictive assumptions regarding the form of the union objective function and its associated MRS. The conclusion to be drawn is that in the case of the ITU the wage–employment bargain is not characterized properly by a union selecting a wage to maximize its objective function subject to the constraint imposed by the labor demand schedule. One must be agnostic as to whether the contract is, in fact, efficient.

What do the results of the B–A and the M–P studies imply for the structure of the bargain? It seems clear that the simple LDEM model that is the null hypothesis of the M–P study is not appropriate in the ITU case. At the same time the B–A results, though limited due to the restrictive functional form, suggest that labor contracts in the ITU case are not efficient. This is consistent with the M–P results which cannot, in fact, distinguish between different departures from the LDEM model. A reasonable interpretation would be that the structure of the ITU's bargains is that the parties negotiate over wages and a set of work rules. However, there is no presumption that these work rules are sufficient to force the bargain to be efficient. The union has, at best, partial control over employment. A final note of caution is that the structure of the bargain, including the particular work rules, is situation specific, and there is little, if anything, in these studies that provides convincing evidence on the efficiency of labor contracts or the validity of the LDEM model outside the ITU's relationship with the newspaper industry.

It is useful to ask if there is anything general that has been learned from existing empirical studies of union objectives. Optimists would answer in the

[54] This condition reflects the property of an efficient contract that the employer would prefer to hire less labor at the given wage. The equilibrium is off the labor demand curve.

affirmative that they have learned it is generally true that unions are sensitive to the employment consequences of their wage policies and that they put substantial weight on employment relative to wages. They would concede that the precise relative weighting is context specific. However, the pessimist would argue that such strong conclusions are unwarranted for at least two reasons. The first is that the assumption underlying all of the studies, that the union can impose whatever settlement it wishes on the parties, may well not be appropriate. The researcher ignores the bargaining problem through use of this assumption at the peril of misattributing moderation in wages to union preferences as opposed to employer resistance in bargaining. This would make it seem as if the union was putting a higher weight on employment relative to wages than is, in fact, the case. All of the results regarding rejection of the rent-maximization hypothesis and the high relative weight put on employment would be called into question. However, as mentioned in the previous section on the bargaining problem, it may not be possible to identify the form of the solution to the bargaining problem without assuming something about the structure of the union objective function. An interesting and important agenda for future research is a careful exploration of exactly how much a priori structure has to be put on objectives and/or the bargaining process in order to learn something useful from bargaining outcomes about both union objectives and the bargaining process.

The second reason for pessimism regarding any general conclusions that can be drawn from these studies is based on the likelihood that while workers may have similar preferences in different contexts, the structural, institutional, and political characteristics that govern collective bargaining are sufficiently variable that the union objective functions will differ considerably across contexts. What this suggests is that in order to model union behavior more generally, the process by which the individual preferences are aggregated into an objective function for the union *must* be considered carefully. Unfortunately, the studies surveyed here shed relatively little light on the relationships between worker preferences, the structural features of a union, the political process, and the union objective function.

There are at least three important issues that must be addressed in order to derive a union objective function from the preferences of the workers and the political process of the union in a consistent manner: (1) the determination of the size and composition of the union; (2) heterogeneity in preferences among the membership; and (3) reconciliation of conflicting goals of the membership and leadership.[55] These problems are interrelated, and how one problem is addressed

---

[55]Another important issue relates to the conceptual problems introduced by a bargaining structure where the parties bargain over more than one issue (e.g. wages *and* employment). Farber (1978b, 1978c) attempts to handle multiple objectives of the UMW in the context of a median voter model, but Blair and Crawford (1981) point out some problems with Farber's analysis. Voting equilibria with multiple issues exist where some special conditions regarding the preferences of the workers are met. However, these cases are not intuitively appealing [see Riker (1980)]. This general problem will not be discussed further here.

depénds on how the others are addressed. All of the empirical research surveyed in this section embodies a set of implicit or explicit assumptions regarding these issues. In the succeeding sections each problem is discussed briefly in turn in order to indicate why they are important and to suggest potential avenues for analysis.

6. Size and composition of the union

It is commonplace to model the objective of a union as a function of wages and the level of employment. However, it is the *membership* of the union at the time the collective bargaining agreement is negotiated that participates in the decision-making process. While the level of employment implied by the agreement may be indistinguishable from the ex post membership, the ex ante membership (at the time of negotiation) is likely to be very different.[56] Thus, the role that the level of employment plays in the union objective function is not at all clear from the perspective of how that objective function might be derived from the preferences of the workers through whatever political process governs the union. The relationships among membership, employment, and how workers evaluate potential wage–employment bargains require further examination.

The decision of a worker regarding union representation has been modeled as a utility-maximizing decision based on a comparison by the worker of the utility on a union job and on a nonunion job.[57] Union wage–employment policy is directly relevant to the decision of an individual regarding whether to join a union because it affects how a potential member values a union job. The importance of the wage is obvious. The level of employment is relevant to the extent that union employment is related to the worker's evaluation of the likelihood of getting a scarce union job and sharing in the advantages of unionization. Thus, an important factor in determining the size and composition of the union is how scarce union jobs are allocated among the membership. In discussing allocation schemes it is assumed that the parties negotiate over the wage and that the employer is free to set the level of employment.

Note that whether a union job is scarce depends in part on the mechanism used to allocate union jobs. Lewis (1959) made a distinction between the allocation rules used by what he called boss-dominated and employee-dominated unions. He argued that boss-dominated unions allocate jobs using the price

---

[56] It is likely that membership and coverage by a collective bargaining agreement are not the same thing even ex post. In states with Right-to-Work laws workers are not required to join a union or pay dues as a condition of employment. L. Katz (1983) presents evidence regarding the prevalence of covered-nonmembership in states with and without Right-to-Work laws. Lunsden and Peterson (1975), Warren and Strauss (1979), Wessels (1981), Ellwood and Fine (1983), and Farber (1984) present analyses of the effect of Right-to-Work laws on the extent of unionization.

[57] See, for example, Lee (1976), Farber and Saks (1980), Abowd and Farber (1982), and Farber (1983a).

mechanism. For example, the level of dues might be adjusted so as to eliminate the excess demand for union jobs. On the other hand, employee-dominated unions allocate jobs with nonprice mechanisms such as random assignment, jobsharing, seniority, nepotism, and the like. In the boss-dominated union most of the advantages of unionization are realized by the leadership, while in an employee-dominated union most of the advantages of unionization are left for at least part of the membership. Evidence consistent with the employee-dominated model is presented by Abowd and Farber (1982) and Farber (1983a) who find that there is excess demand by workers for union jobs. Thus, the discussion of allocation rules here revolves around nonprice mechanisms. Any analysis of boss-dominated unions is more properly deferred until the discussion of the reconciliation of the preferences of the membership and leadership in Section 8.

A simple job allocation rule is one which allows the jobs to be allocated randomly so that each member has the same probability of having a job after the wage is determined.[58] This rule implies that each member has a probability of employment equal to the ratio of labor demand to existing union membership (L/M). Assuming that if a worker is not employed on a union job then the worker will work on an alternative job at W_a, the representative worker's expected utility is

$$E(U) = \frac{L}{M} U(W_u - C) + \left[1 - \frac{L}{M}\right] U(W_a), \tag{15}$$

where union employment (L) is an inverse function of the union wage and C represents the cost of continued union membership. The expected utility of individual members is inversely related to the size of the membership because as the union grows each worker has a smaller probability of being selected in the lottery for union employment. However, it is straightforward to demonstrate that the most preferred wage of each worker is *not* affected by the size of the union (M).

Workers will make their choice regarding union membership on the basis of a comparison of $E(U)$ and $U(W_a)$. The condition for preferring union membership is that

$$\frac{L}{M} U(W_u - C) + \left[1 - \frac{L}{M}\right] U(W_a) > U(W_a), \tag{16}$$

and it is clear that all workers will prefer union membership as long as $W_u - C$ is greater than W_a. Thus, the union will expand, which implies a dilution of the

---

[58] This is the rule that is explicit in the work of Farber (1978b, 1978c) and Brown and Ashenfelter (1986).

benefits of unionization. Where workers differ in their alternative wage only those workers with alternative wages below $W_u - C$ will desire union membership and the marginal member of the union will be indifferent between union membership and employment at the alternative wage.[59]

One possible alternative to a random assignment for the allocation of jobs would be an equal sharing of available work so that all members are guaranteed at least some work. A somewhat more complicated objective function for each worker is required because implicit in worksharing is the notion that hours are variable. Assume that all workers have identical preferences defined over income (Y) and the fraction of the standard workday (or week, month, year) worked (H). Represent these preferences by the function

$$U = U(Y, H),$$ (17)

where income has positive marginal utility and hours of work (the complement of leisure) has negative marginal utility.[60] The representative worker's utility on a union job is

$$U_u = U(W_u H - C, H),$$ (18)

where H represents the fraction of time worked with pure worksharing which is simply the ratio of labor demand to union membership ($H = L/M$). Net income on the union job is the product of the fraction of time worked and the wage rate less the cost of union membership (C).

The size of the membership has important effects on the level of utility in the worksharing model, though in an ambiguous fashion. An increase in the membership means less income which reduces utility. On the other hand it means more leisure which increases utility. Note that it would normally be expected that a larger membership would mean more division of the "spoils" of unionization and less utility. However, that is not necessarily the case here because it is assumed that workers are not free to set their hours at the optimal level for a given wage. Their hours are completely determined by the wage rate through the labor demand schedule and the size of the union. Unlike random assignment, the optimal wage is not independent of the size of the union where there is worksharing. Workers make their choice regarding union membership on the basis of a comparison of U_u and $U(W_a)$. The condition for preferring union membership is that

$$U(W_u H - C, H) > U(W_a, 1),$$ (19)

[59] The implications of heterogeneity in the alternative wage for union policy is discussed further in Section 7.

[60] Implicit in the random assignment model is that employers hire workers for a fixed number of hours which is the same both in union employment and in alternative jobs. Thus, there was no need to consider the labor–leisure tradeoff explicitly.

noting that on the alternative job the worker will work standard hours (full time). If workers are identical and union work was full time, all workers would desire union representation as long as $W_u - C$ was greater than W_a. What this suggests is that at a given wage the size of the union will expand so that the degree of worksharing makes workers indifferent between union membership and employment on the alternative job. If workers are heterogeneous in their alternative wage, then only those workers with low alternative wages will desire union membership and the size of the union will expand so that the marginal worker (the worker in the union with the highest alternative wage) is indifferent between union employment and working full time at the alternative wage.

Two factors limit the settings in which random assignment and worksharing schemes are feasible. The first factor is highlighted by the previous discussion regarding the dilution of the benefits of unionization if the union is open to anyone who wishes to join. On this basis, it is clear that neither random assignment nor worksharing is likely to be feasible unless the union has an effective mechanism for excluding workers from union membership and eligibility for union work. The second factor is based on the fact that it is likely that worksharing is more easily implemented over periods longer than a week or month through rotation of workers through jobs. This sort of worksharing can be accomplished by periodically reallocating jobs, perhaps randomly. Thus, there is an element of worksharing even in random allocation schemes. On this basis, random assignment or worksharing is likely to be found only where workers have long-run attachments to the union rather than to the employer. If workers had long-run relationships with particular employers, then the initial draw from the lottery for union jobs in a random assignment scheme would have long-run implications that preclude workers from having additional chances at attaining a union job and sharing in the work.

Examples of industries that are appropriate for random assignment or worksharing are the hiring hall industries best exemplified by the construction trades.[61] These unions historically have had effective mechanisms to limit membership through stiff skill requirements that could be met through apprenticeship programs which allowed only limited enrollment. In addition, construction jobs are necessarily of limited duration, and the workers have long-run attachments to the union. Job referrals from union run hiring halls can be interpreted as a mechanism for explicit worksharing.[62]

The key to understanding the job allocation system in most union settings is that workers have *job rights*. Workers who are employed in particular positions are not forced to share those jobs with anyone else. Nor are they required to

---

[61] See Haber (1945) and Mills (1980) for descriptions of collective bargaining in the Construction Industry.

[62] While dated, Haber (1945) presents examples of hiring halls enforcing work sharing through referrals.

enter a lottery to keep their job. In this context workers who are not already working on a union job have little incentive to join a union and pay dues because joining gives them no rights to share in the advantages of unionization. The union will be composed of workers who are employed at a given time, and it is these workers who will make decisions regarding future wage–employment policy. The way most union contracts outside the hiring hall industries are structured, the employer has complete discretion in hiring when employment is growing.[63] However, once the worker is hired (and is past some relatively short probationary period) the worker has a right to the job. Since wage increases will generally imply a decline (or smaller increase) in employment, it is crucial to specify how scarce union jobs are allocated when all workers have rights to their jobs.

Perhaps the most widely used rule for the allocation of union jobs is based on accumulated seniority [Abraham and Medoff (1984)]. Those workers who are more senior have priority. If there is a decline in employment then the workers are laid off in inverse order of seniority.[64] Consider the case where workers have identical preferences and alternative wages and differ only in their position in the seniority hierarchy. Index workers by their position in the seniority hierarchy so that worker i is the ith most senior worker.[65] If there are L workers employed at a given wage, the Lth most senior worker is just on the margin of being employed. All workers with less seniority than the Lth worker have no seniority and are equivalent from the standpoint of not having union employment. The utility of each of the L union workers is $U(W - C)$, while all other workers have utility $U(W_a)$.

There are two important implications of the seniority job allocation scheme that are relevant for the discussion here. The first is that the issue of excludability versus nonexcludability of potential members is not important. Since all workers with zero seniority do not have a right to a union job, they represent no threat to dilute the benefits of unionization to the existing workers. In fact, this may be one reason why seniority rules are so popular. The second important implication of the seniority job allocation rule is that workers of different seniority levels will have systematically different preferences regarding optimal union wage–employment policy. Workers with more seniority will generally prefer higher wages because their jobs are well protected by a buffer of less senior workers. The less senior workers are likely to prefer lower wages because they are more vulnerable

[63] Depending on whether or not there is a union security clause in the contract and whether or not there is a Right-to-Work law in existence, these new workers may or may not be required to join the union or pay dues.

[64] Laid off workers often retain for a limited period of time rights to the jobs that they held. If there is a subsequent increase in hiring after layoff then the employer may be required to offer the new jobs to laid off workers in seniority order (the last laid off are the first recalled).

[65] This notation is due to Blair and Crawford (1984) who present a concise analysis of union wage behavior where there is uncertainty about labor demand and seniority is used to allocate jobs.

to layoffs in employment declines. In the simplest possible static model where there is no uncertainty about labor demand, each worker will prefer the wage that puts that worker just on the margin of being employed. In other words, the ith most senior worker will prefer a wage such that labor demand is just equal to i. In a more complicated model where there is uncertainty about labor demand [Blair and Crawford (1984)], the optimal wage for each worker is likely to be a monotonic function of seniority but not with such a simple relationship. If the workers are risk averse, then it seems likely that they will prefer a wage such that the expected employment level implies a buffer of less senior workers.

The discussion in this section makes clear the important role of employment in determining the value to individual workers of union wage policy. More importantly, it suggests that the job allocation mechanism implies structural restrictions on how employment enters individuals' evaluations of union policy that ought to be exploited in generating an objective function for the union as a whole. While individual preferences regarding wage–employment policies under various job allocation schemes are relatively clear, nothing further can be said about how the union as a whole will behave with respect to wage–employment policy without specifying the political process that governs the union.

7. Heterogeneity in preferences among workers

If all workers have identical preferences regarding the appropriate union wage–employment policy, then the preference aggregation problem is trivial. Assuming that there is perfect democracy so that the leadership cannot pursue its own goals independently, the union objective function will accurately reflect the objectives of the representative member. However, the assumption of homogeneous preferences is untenable in general, and the preferences of workers with regard to the optimal wage–employment policy will differ along a number of dimensions. The most important differences are likely to be: (1) workers having different labor market alternatives and (2) workers having different amounts of seniority as it affects their job security through the job allocation system. The risk associated with any wage–employment policy will vary systematically along both of these dimensions. It is likely that workers with better labor market alternatives and with more seniority will prefer higher wages.[66] Clearly, some mechanism must be provided to aggregate the disparate preferences of the members into a coherent union objective function.

The problem of preference aggregation is not unique to the analysis of union behavior. It arises in the context of public choice at all levels: How does a

---

[66] This claim is based on an implicit model where union labor demand is uncertain and workers are employed at their alternative wage if they do not have a union job. Blair and Crawford (1984) present such a model where preferences vary by seniority.

political process take the disparate preferences of individuals and translate them into public policy?[67] In the context of this study, what is the political process that prevails within labor unions? It is perhaps a measure of how far analysis of this problem has yet to go that the only truly operational model of aggregation of individual preferences into a coherent objective function for a democratic organization is the median voter model.

The median voter model was first formulated by Black (1948) and Arrow (1950). Assume that individual preferences are a function of only a single variable (e.g. wages), the quantity of which is to be determined through some sort of voting mechanism. Assume further that each individual's preferences are single peaked in this dimension so that there is only a single relative maximum in utility defined over the entire range of possible outcomes. A sufficient condition for this is that the utility function be globally concave. Assume further that the individuals' most preferred outcomes are distributed across the voting population in a well-defined fashion. Under a set of reasonable conditions, it can be shown that the median most preferred outcome is the only position that will defeat all other positions in any sequence of pairwise elections. Thus, a candidate who adopts this position cannot be defeated in a pairwise election. This is called a *voting equilibrium*. The median voter is defined as that voter for whom half of the other voters have most preferred outcomes that are lower and half have most preferred outcomes that are higher. More importantly, it can be shown that if any of the basic assumptions of the model fails then no position will exist that can defeat all other positions. In such a case the outcome will depend on the order in which the various options are presented for voting and control of the agenda becomes crucial. From the standpoint of the discussion here, the most important assumptions are (1) single peaked preferences; (2) a single issue being decided; (3) no imposition of outcomes other than through voting (nondictatorship); and (4) pairwise elections.

As a simple illustration of the median voter approach to the analysis of union wage policy consider the case where workers differ in their productivity and hence in the alternative wage (W_a) available to them. Assume that jobs are allocated randomly and that the size of the union is fixed. Each worker's expected utility is defined in eq. (15). It is straightforward to show both that these preferences are single peaked under standard conditions regarding the utility and labor demand functions and that the optimal wage of each worker is a monotonically increasing function of W_a. Thus, the conditions for a voting equilibrium are satisfied, and the objective of the union is to provide the wage that maximizes the expected utility of the worker with the median alternative wage.

---

[67]See Buchanan and Tullock (1962) for an early discussion of problems of public choice in a broader context. There is a large body of literature on public choice that is beyond the scope of this chapter to review. Some examples from this literature include Downs (1957), Arrow (1963), Plott (1967), Fishburn (1973), and Riker (1980).

What are the implications of this outcome? First, as one would expect, unions with higher median skill levels will have higher optimal wages. More importantly, the optimal wage depends only on the median skill level and not on any other characteristics of the distribution. If the distribution is skewed so that there are some members with very low alternative wages, these workers will have a particularly large advantage from unionization. On the other hand, if the distribution is skewed so that there are some members with very high alternative wages, these workers will have a particularly small advantage from unionization. In fact, the alternative wage for these high productivity workers may be larger than the equilibrium union wage so that the high productivity workers will leave the union. The result will be a drop in the median alternative wage and a reduction in the union wage. This cycle will be repeated until at some point an equilibrium will be reached in both the size of the union and the union wage.

The implications of this model are consistent with two types of observations. First is the well-known standardization of rates within industrial unions resulting in a large union–nonunion wage differential for unskilled workers and a smaller union–nonunion wage differential for skilled workers in this sector.[68] Second is the set of internal political problems that exist in unions, such as the United Automobile Workers (UAW), with a skewed skill mix. For example, the skilled tradesmen within the UAW have historically been unhappy with their relative lack of influence on union wage policy. They have felt that they could do better if they negotiated on their own.

The UAW example also shows the limits of the median voter formulation. The UAW must accommodate the high-skilled workers in order to keep them in the union and in support of union policy. While beyond the scope of this analysis, it is likely that the bargaining position of the UAW would be weaker without the support of skilled workers crucial to the production process. In fact, it could be argued that the strategy of bargaining over percentage increase in wages rather than over wage levels themselves is in part an attempt to maintain historic differentials between workers of differential skill levels.[69]

If the union uses seniority to allocate jobs then the most preferred wage of any particular worker will depend on that worker's seniority. In a static context where there is no uncertainty about labor demand, each worker will prefer a wage such that the worker is the least senior worker employed. Preferences are single peaked

---

[68] Many studies have documented the standardization of rates across skill levels within the union sector through the estimation of cross-section earnings functions. See, for example, Bloch and Kuskin (1978), Freeman (1980b), and Lewis (1984). Even these studies exaggerate the variation in union rates for particular jobs within establishments because the estimates are made with very crude skill measures across establishments. Farber and Saks (1980) present evidence that can be interpreted as workers perceiving that unions standardize wage rates within establishments. See Webb and Webb (1920) for an early and insightful discussion of the importance of the standard rate.

[69] See H. Katz (1984b) for a more detailed discussion of the influence of skilled workers within the UAW.

and the median voter equilibrium is to set the wage so that the median seniority worker is the least senior worker employed. This version of the median voter model implies a shrinking union over time. If there are initially M members, then the union will have as an objective the optimal wage of the $(M/2)$th worker. The optimal wage of this worker has the property that the worker is now the least senior worker employed in the union firm. The result is that the new membership of the union is $M/2$. When it is time to renegotiate the contract, the $(M/4)$th worker is the median worker. The optimal wage of this worker will be higher yet so that this worker is the least senior worker employed. The union will again reduce its size by half, and this process will repeat itself until there are at most a handful of workers in the union.[70]

Of course, unions do not shrink out of existence so that there must be an element missing from this model. One element is that the union may not be able to achieve its objectives in bargaining due to employer resistance. The result will be a lower wage, more employment, and a larger union than desired. Another element is foresight on the part of the current median member. This worker must recognize that pursuing the wage policy described above will result in a loss of the union job in the following period as effective control of the union passes to a more senior (or more skilled) worker. A more conservative wage policy may delay the time until the job is lost, but the only wage policy that will preserve the median member's control is to set the wage so that the entire initial membership is employed.

An important consideration, neglected thus far, that will limit the shrinkage of the median voter controlled union where jobs are allocated on the basis of seniority is uncertainty about the demand for labor. In this situation, the worker with median seniority does not know with certainty the wage that will make the worker the least senior employee. It is worthwhile developing this model more fully following the analysis of Blair and Crawford (1984). Let

$$L(W) = G(W) + \mu, \tag{20}$$

where $G(W)$ represents the systematic part of the labor demand function and μ represents a random element affecting labor demand with zero mean. The probability that a worker with seniority rank i will be employed on the union job ($EMP_i = 1$) at the wage W is

$$\begin{aligned}
\Pr[EMP_i = 1] &= \Pr[L(W) > i] \\
&= \Pr[\mu > i - G(W)] \\
&= 1 - F(i - G(W)),
\end{aligned} \tag{21}$$

---

[70] Heterogeneity in alternative wages does not affect the thrust of this argument.

where $F(\cdot)$ represents the cumulative distribution function of μ. The expected utility of worker i at union wage W is

$$EU_i(W) = U(W_{ai}), \qquad W - C < W_{ai},$$
$$EU_i(W) = \{1 - F(i - G(W))\}U(W - C) + F(i - G(W))U(W_{ai}),$$
$$W - C \geq W_{ai}, \quad (22)$$

where C represents the (dues and other) costs of unionization and W_{ai} represents the alternative wage of worker i. Assuming that $W - C \geq W_{ai}$, it is straightforward to derive the optimal wage for a worker with seniority i. Blair and Crawford (1984) derive sufficient conditions on the utility function and the distribution of μ for the preferences of the workers to be single peaked.[71]

If all workers have the same alternative wage the median voter is the member with the median seniority level. This worker's seniority index is $i = M/2$. Note that the allocation rule could be defined over almost any dimension without altering the optimal wage at all. If the alternative wage varies across workers the situation is somewhat more complicated because the most preferred wage of each worker depends not only on seniority but also on the alternative wage. A voting equilibrium still exists, but it is not clear who the member with the median most preferred wage is. Workers with more seniority will certainly prefer a higher wage as will workers with a higher alternative wage. However, unless the distributions of seniority and alternative wages have the same rank ordering, the individual optimal wages will be monotonic in neither seniority nor the alternative wage. Preferences are still single peaked and a voting equilibrium exists, but, without information on the joint distribution of seniority and the alternative wage, it is impossible to predict whose preferences will prevail.

The dynamic implications of the median voter model with uncertain labor demand for the size of the union are difficult to derive precisely. Blair and Crawford (1984) show that the optimal wage of a given member declines as the worker's risk aversion increases. This is relevant here because it implies that risk averse workers prefer to set the wage so as to provide a cushion of low seniority workers who will be laid off first in the event of an unfavorable realization of the labor demand uncertainty (μ). Thus, where there is uncertainty about labor demand, the median voter controlled union will not shrink to the same point as it would were there no uncertainty.[72]

The median voter model as derived here is a very powerful tool for aggregating the preferences of union members into a coherent objective function for the union as a whole. However, its applicability is limited due to the restrictive set of

---

[71] In addition to the usual conditions regarding the concavity of $U(\cdot)$, the sufficient conditions include a labor demand function concave in the wage rate and demand uncertainty (μ) with a nondecreasing hazard rate. The hazard rate of μ is defined as $f(x)/(1 - F(x))$. Many common distributions, including the normal, have this property.

[72] The median voter controlled union could even grow where there is uncertainty if there is an unexpectedly large realization of labor demand.

assumptions required. The most stringent of these for the purpose at hand are that only a single issue be decided and that there is perfect democracy. While the analysis of union behavior with multiple issues is not considered formally, the next section contains a discussion of the implications of conflicting goals of the union leadership and membership for the determination of union objectives.

8. Conflicting goals of membership and leadership

The median voter model discussed in the previous section had as a basic assumption that the union was perfectly democratic in the sense that the leadership would be defeated immediately and costlessly if they strayed at all from the voting equilibrium wage. Thus, the issue of leadership goals as distinct from membership goals was not relevant. In fact, the members might as well vote for wage levels rather than for leaders. Of course, the assumption of perfect democracy is no more valid for labor unions than it is for other political institutions. Union leaders are free within certain limits to pursue their own goals. Many analysts, including Ross (1948), Berkowitz (1954), and Atherton (1973), have recognized the importance of imperfections in the democratic process and the concomitant consideration of the distinct goals of the leadership. Ashenfelter and Johnson (1969) develop a model of the outcome of collective bargaining that they argue is consistent with the view that the leadership and the rank and file have distinct expectations and objectives. More recently, Faith and Reid (1983) reformulated the problem as a principal–agent problem where the union leadership acts as the agent for the membership. The case where there is a perfectly operating democracy (as it is called here) is the case of no malfeasance in the principal–agent nomenclature. Similarly, the case of imperfectly operating democracy is a situation where malfeasance on the part of the agent is possible.

A major problem with the analysis of union behavior where the leadership has some freedom to pursue its own goals (malfeasance) is that very little is known about what these goals might be or how they might be analyzed in a systematic fashion. Ross (1948, p. 16) argues for "…the primary importance of organizational survival as the central aim of the leadership". However, beyond this there is very little analysis, and saying that the primary goal of the leadership is to survive is really to say nothing at all about the goals of the leadership. It is obvious that the organization must survive if the leadership is to have a vehicle to pursue whatever its true aims are.[73]

It is not possible here to provide a theory of the objectives of union leadership. However, it is possible to gain some insight into union behavior by examining the

---

[73]An exception to this is that a union leadership may destroy the union slowly over time so as to fully exploit its "capital", either on their own behalf or on behalf of the current members, before their inevitable departure. Leaders have finite lifetimes while organizations have (at least conceptually) infinite lifetimes.

constraints acting on the union leadership. The primary constraint on the union leadership is that they remain in power because otherwise they would not be able to pursue their objectives, whatever they might be. This is more than an empty formalization. Essentially, limits will be set on how far the leadership can deviate from the interests of the membership, perhaps as reflected in a voting equilibrium. These limits will depend crucially on the friction in the democratic process. It may be that in some cases the limits turn out to be sufficiently loose that the leadership can maximize their objective function without regard to the constraints of the political process (dictatorship). In other cases it may be that the leadership is severely constrained by the political process and the need to answer to the rank and file.

It is worth developing a simple version of this model more formally in order both to consider the potential of this approach and to highlight some of the difficulties in an analysis of this sort. Assume that the leadership is interested in having as large a union as possible. This objective for the leadership may be rooted in the desire to maximize the dues income of the union where dues are levied on a per capita basis. As before, the members get utility solely from their wage income net of dues payments, and the union bargains with the employer over the setting of a single wage for all workers. Workers may differ in their alternative wage, and job allocation is on the basis of seniority if the net wage is such that the number of members who desire jobs is greater than the number of available jobs. Maximization of membership in this context is identical to maximization of employment where members who are not employed leave the union. The analysis proceeds conditional on a given dues level.[74]

If the democratic process in the union is operating perfectly, so that no malfeasance is possible, then the wage will be set at the voting equilibrium defined by the optimal wage of the median individual. The other extreme is the case where the leadership is completely unconstrained by the political process. In this situation the leadership is constrained by two relationships. The first is the labor demand function of the employer ($L(W)$). This is a declining function of the wage rate, and it represents the maximum level of employment/membership at a given wage. The second constraint is a membership function of the sort proposed by Dunlop (1944). This is an increasing function of the wage rate net of dues, and it represents the number of members who want union jobs at a given wage.

The membership function can be derived formally from the distribution of alternative wages among the members. Let i index worker's rank on the basis of their alternative wage where $i = 1$ represents the highest alternative wage. An individual will desire a union job if the wage (W) net of the costs of unionization

---

[74] The case where the leadership is interested in maximizing dues income directly and sets both the wage and the dues level to that end is considered below.

(C) is greater than the alternative wage (W_{ai}). More formally, a worker will desire a union job if $W - C \geq W_{ai}$. The membership function is

$$M(W - C) = M_0 \Psi(W - C), \tag{23}$$

where M_0 represents the initial size of the union and $\Psi(\cdot)$ represents the cumulative distribution function of W_{ai} among the initial membership. This is clearly an increasing function of the wage rate.

Because the union cannot coerce workers to join and cannot coerce the employer to hire workers, the quantity of employment at a given wage rate is

$$H(W, C) = \min[L(W), M(W - C)]. \tag{24}$$

Given the negative slope of $L(W)$ and the positive slope of $M(W - C)$, the wage rate that maximizes employment is defined by the intersection of the labor demand and membership functions. This relationship is

$$L(W) = M(W - C). \tag{25}$$

Note that there is no job allocation problem because the number of members is equal to the number of jobs. The union will be composed of the least skilled workers among the initial membership, and all of the original members who have alternative wages greater than $W - C$ will take jobs at their alternative wage.

Now suppose that the union leadership is interested in maximization of dues revenues directly and that they can set the dues level as well as the wage. The objective function for the union leadership is

$$V(W, C) = CM(W - C), \tag{26}$$

which is maximized subject to the constraint that only those workers who are employed become/remain members of the union. This constraint, embodied in eq. (25), is simply that the membership of the union is equal to the labor demand of the employer. Without deriving the explicit relationships defining the optimal wage–dues pair, it is clear that at any wage rate the union leadership will raise dues to the point where the increase in dues revenues from existing members is just offset by the loss of dues revenues as membership declines. Once again, there is no job allocation problem because the number of members is equal to employment, and the union is composed of the least skilled workers.

In both the case of the membership-maximizing union leadership and the case of the dues-revenue-maximizing union leadership, the marginal worker will be indifferent between union employment and the alternative job $(W_{ai} = W - C)$, and all of the inframarginal workers get a positive wage advantage from unionization equal to $W - C - W_{ai}$. This result is very similar to that derived by Lewis (1959) for his conception of a "boss-dominated" union. Lewis argued that the union leaders monopsonize the supply of labor and extract from the members all of the rents so that the members are indifferent between union employment and nonunion employment. However, he did not consider the possibility that different workers get different benefit from unionization so that a single wage and dues level cannot extract all rents. If the union leadership could set different wages or dues levels for different workers it would act as a perfectly discriminating monopsonist buying labor from workers at their reservation price. Thus, the model developed here is an extension of Lewis's boss dominated union with heterogeneous workers.

It is impossible to determine whether the wage net of dues $(W - C)$ that an employment- or dues-maximizing union leadership sets will be higher or lower than a perfectly democratic union with a voting equilibrium would set. Detailed information on the labor demand function, the distribution of alternative wages, and the preference function of the union members would be required. However, the fact that there are likely to be more workers willing to work at the union wage than the union employer is willing to hire at that wage suggests that dues revenue and employment could be increased by some combination of increasing the dues level and reducing the wage in order to induce the employer to hire more workers.[75] This is consistent with the notion that the net wage set by a dues-revenue-maximizing union leadership with no political constraints would be below that implied by a voting equilibrium. Certainly, it is clear that it would only be by accident that an unfettered leadership would set wages and dues equal to that which would arise out of a perfectly operating democratic union.[76]

The perfectly operating democratic union and the completely unfettered leadership-run union are two extreme views that are unlikely to be a perfect reflection of any real union. The attractiveness of the two types of models presented thus far is not their congruence with the operation of actual labor unions, but it is the ease with which these models can be operationalized. Indeed, virtually all empirical work on the behavior of labor unions surveyed in Section 5 at least pays lip service to the model of the perfectly democratic union. While no one has attempted to analyze union objectives as the result of an unfettered leadership pursuing its own goals, this would certainly be feasible. It is an open question as to the relative empirical performance of these two extreme models.

---

[75] See Abowd and Farber (1982) and Farber (1983a) for discussions and estimation of models of the determination of the union status of workers where there are queues for union jobs. Raisian (1981) presents evidence suggesting the the levels of dues and fees in most unions do not offset the union–nonunion wage differential.

[76] The role that dues play in a perfectly democratic union has not been considered directly to this point. Essentially, this is a dimension in addition to wages that the members have preferences over, assuming that the level of union services (grievance handling, etc.) is a direct function of dues revenues in a democratic union. This raises all of the complicated problems of a multiple issue voting process.

While it is impossible to characterize completely a model of union behavior with a "somewhat" imperfect democracy, it is useful to at least lay out the barest outlines of such an approach. Consider the case where the leaders are elected through a process that is both costly and uncertain. By costly it is meant that potential candidates or insurgent groups must spend time and/or money in attempt to defeat the current leadership.[77] In addition, it is not certain ex ante whether the insurgency will succeed. As before, assume that workers differ in their alternative wages, that jobs are allocated based on seniority when there are more members than union jobs, and that dues are fixed. If there is a perfect democracy then the voting equilibrium is where the wage is set at the level that maximizes the utility of the median member (the member with the median optimal wage) as derived above. Without a perfect democracy the union leadership has some freedom to pursue its own goals constrained by the knowledge that as they stray farther from the goals of the membership they are more likely to be defeated. For the purpose of this discussion characterize the leadership goal as maximization of dues revenues which, with fixed dues, is identical to employment/membership maximization.

At the voting equilibrium wage (W_m) only the median member feels that this is an optimal outcome. All other members feel that there is some other wage that would make them better off. The essence of the voting equilibrium is that W_m is the only wage for which there does not exist some other wage that more than half the members prefer. Suppose that the leadership deviates from W_m in their pursuit of dues-revenue-maximization (or any other goal) and that they set the wage at W_B. Note that W_B may be greater or less than W_m. In this situation there is a set of wages, including W_m, of which all the elements are preferred by at least half the workers to W_B.

If there are more workers who would like a job at W_m than the employer is willing to hire, then the membership/dues-maximizing union leadership will attempt to set the wage below W_m so as to induce the employer to hire more workers. In this situation all of the members of the union with optimal wages above W_m will be worse off and all of the members with optimal wages below W_B will be better off. Some of the group of workers whose optimal wage is between W_B and W_m will be better off and some will be worse off. The important question is whether those workers who are worse off find it in their interest to form a coalition to defeat the leadership. It seems reasonable that what the coalition can offer a worker is a reduction in the distance (where the metric is expected utility) between the union wage and the worker's optimal wage. The larger the reduction in distance the more the worker will value the coalition. Denote this value function by $H(W, W_i, W_B)$, where W_i, the optimal wage of the ith worker, embodies all of the information about the individual including the level of seniority and the alternative wage.

---

[77]At certain times and in certain unions the costs of mounting an insurgency have been much higher and more immediate.

The *total* gain to the coalition net of the costs of formation of the coalition is

$$H = \sum H(W, W_i, W_B) - K, \tag{27}$$

where the summation is over all members of the potential coalition and K represents the costs of formation of the coalition.[78] There is likely to be uncertainty on the part of the incumbent leadership about the ultimate net gain of a coalition. Given that a coalition will be formed only where the net gain is positive the incumbent leadership will be uncertain as to whether a particular coalition will, in fact, form. The leadership can compute a distribution for the total gain for each possible coalition, and from this they can compute the probability that at least one coalition will form. The central feature of this model (conjecture at this point) is that coalitions will be more likely to form the larger is the total gain to the members of the coalition. It is certainly true that the incumbent leadership can influence the total gain from any coalition by manipulating W_B which implies that they can influence the probability that at least one coalition will form. Since the benefit from leadership is also a function of W_B, the incumbents can compute the expected benefit from leadership as a function of W_B as the product of the probability that no coalitions form and the benefit from continued leadership. On this basis they can compute the value of W_B that maximizes the expected benefit from leadership. This is the wage that the union will set where there is "imperfect" democracy.

Although they are not demonstrated formally here, there is a pair of substantive results that emerge from this model. First, the existing leadership will deviate more from the voting equilibrium position where insurgencies are more costly (K is larger). Lower costs make insurgencies more likely, and the leadership will compensate for this with a more popular wage policy. Second, the position promised by the insurgency (and delivered by the union if K is small) will be relatively close to the voting equilibrium position. This is more difficult to make intuitive, but consider a union with three members. The optimal wages of the three workers are W_1, $W_2 = 2W_1$, and $W_3 = 3W_1$. The voting equilibrium wage is clearly W_2, but a union leadership may not feel bound to provide this wage. If the leadership provides a wage that deviates only slightly from W_2, say W_B slightly lower, then an insurgency could promise an improvement to the last two workers but not to the first. However, the maximum to improvement to the last two members (at some wage slightly higher than W_B) will be relatively small. The insurgents cannot raise the wage very far above W_B without losing member 2 to the incumbents. The small gain is not likely to cover the cost K of forming the insurgency. On the other hand, if the leaders set the wage at a very high level, say $W_B = W_3$, then there will be substantial gain to the insurgency. Any wage lower

---

[78] This will be true whether coalitions are organized by aspiring leaders out for personal gain or by groups of workers who will share the gain.

than W_3 is preferred by both member 1 and member 2, and the gain is likely to be quite substantial. For example, the voting equilibrium position (W_2) is a dramatically different position from W_3 that members 1 and 2 are both likely to prefer strongly to $W_B = W_3$. Of course, these conclusions rest on strong (but reasonable) assumptions about the expected utility functions of the members. Overall, unless the barriers to an insurgency are very high the existing union leadership will set the wage relatively close to the voting equilibrium so as not to encourage insurgencies.

The conclusion that even with imperfect democracy a union is not likely to stray far from the voting equilibrium has important implications for evaluating the recent popularity of a casual sort of median voter model to describe union behavior. The use of the median voter concept in this area has ranged from formal use as a voting equilibrium [Farber (1978b), Blair and Crawford (1984)] to more widespread use as a general description of unions as organizations that satisfy "average" members while labor markets cater to "marginal" workers [Freeman and Medoff (1979, 1983), Freeman (1980a, 1981), Medoff (1979)]. It is clear that a pure median voter equilibrium exists only under very special conditions that are unlikely to be met in the context of labor unions. However, the argument made in this section provides a more general justification for the approximate descriptive validity of the median voter concept.

The discussion in this section demonstrates the power of even relatively simple models of the goals of members and leaders to generate testable implications regarding union behavior. Clearly, a fruitful area for further theoretical and empirical research relates to the problems of aggregation of individual preferences, particularly where workers are heterogeneous and the democratic process is not perfect. More specifically, with further work it may be possible to isolate the institutional features of particular unions that affect the ease with which insurgencies can form and their effect on union wage–employment policies.

Overall, the research surveyed in this chapter illustrates the substantial progress that has been made in the analysis of union behavior. At the same time, there remains an extensive agenda for further research that needs to be addressed before economists can claim a real understanding of union behavior.

References

Abowd, John M. (1985) "Collective bargaining and the division of value of the enterprise", mimeo.
Abowd, John M. and Henry S. Farber (1982) "Job queues and the union status of workers", *Industrial and Labor Relations Review*, 35(3).
Abraham, Katharine G. and James L. Medoff (1984) "Length of service and layoffs in union and nonunion work groups", *Industrial and Labor Relations Review*, 38:87–97.
Abraham, Katharine G. and James L. Medoff (1985) "Length of service and promotion in union and nonunion work groups", *Industrial and Labor Relations Review*, 38:408–420.
Arrow, Kenneth J. (1950) "A difficulty in the concept of social welfare", *Journal of Political Economy*, 58:328–346.

Arrow, Kenneth J. (1963) *Social choice and individual values*. New York: Cowles Foundation Monograph.

Ashenfelter, Orley and George Johnson (1969) "Bargaining theory, trade unions, and industrial strike activity", *American Economic Review*, 59:35–49.

Atherton, Wallace N. (1973) *The theory of union bargaining goals*. Princeton, New Jersey: Princeton University Press.

Berkowitz, Monroe (1954) "The economics of trade union organization and administration", *Industrial and Labor Relations Review*, 7.

Bishop, Robert L. (1963) "Game-theoretic analyses of bargaining", *Quarterly Journal of Economics*, 77:559–602.

Bishop, Robert L. (1964) "A Zeuthen–Hicks theory of bargaining", *Econometrica*, 32:410–417.

Black, Duncan (1948) "On the rationale of group decision making", *Journal of Political Economy*, 56:23–34.

Blair, Douglas H. and David L. Crawford (1984) "Labor union objective is and collective bargaining", *Quarterly Journal of Economics*, 99:547-566.

Bloch, Farrell E. and Mark S. Kuskin (1978) "Wage determination in the union and nonunion sectors", *Industrial and Labor Relations Review*, 31:183–192.

Bognanno, Mario F. and James B. Dworkin (1975) "Comment: who 'wins' in wage bargaining?", *Industrial and Labor Relations Review*, 28:570–572.

Bowlby, Roger L. and William R. Schriver (1978) "Bluffing and the 'split-the-difference' theory of wage bargaining", *Industrial and Labor Relations Review*, 31:161–171.

Brown, James N. and Orley Ashenfelter (1986) "Testing the efficiency of employment contracts", *Journal of Political Economy*, 94:540–587.

Buchanan, James M. and Gordon Tullock (1962) *The calculus of consent: logical foundations of constitutional democracy*. Ann Arbor: The University of Michigan Press.

Card, David E. (1983) "Arbitrators as lie detectors", Working Paper No. 172, Princeton University, Industrial Relations Section.

Carruth, Alan A. and Andrew J. Oswald (1983) "Miner's wages in post-war Britain: an application of a model of trade union behavior", mimeo, University of Kent.

Cartter, Allan M. (1959) *Theory of wages and employment*. Homewood, Illinois: Irwin.

Chatterjee, Kalyan (1982) "Incentive compatibility in bargaining under uncertainty", *Quarterly Journal of Economics*, 97:717–726.

Coddington, A. (1968) *Theories of the bargaining process*. London: Allen and Unwin.

Comay, Yochanan, Arie Melnik and Abraham Subotnik (1974) "Bargaining yield curves and wage settlements: an empirical analysis", *Journal of Political Economy*, 82:303–313.

Crawford, Vincent P. (1979) "On compulsory arbitration schemes", *Journal of Political Economy*, 87:131–160.

Cross, John G. (1965) "A theory of the bargaining process", *American Economic Review*, 55:67–94.

De Menil, George (1971) *Bargaining: monopoly power versus union power*. Cambridge, Massachusetts: Massachusetts Institute of Technology Press.

Dertouzos, James N. and John H. Pencavel (1980) "Wage and employment determination under trade unionism: the international typographical union", *Journal of Political Economy*, 89:1162–1181.

Downs, Anthony (1957) *An economic theory of democracy*. New York: Harper and Row.

Duncan, Greg J. and Frank P. Stafford (1980) "Do union members receive compensating wage differentials?", *American Economic Review*, 70:355–371.

Dunlop, John T. (1944) *Wage determination under trade unions*. New York: Macmillan Co.

Ellwood, David T. and Glen Fine (1983) "Effects of right-to-work laws on union organizing", National Bureau of Economic Research Working Paper no. 1116.

Faith, Roger L. and Joseph D. Reid Jr. (1983) "The labor union as its members' agent", *Research in Labor Economics*, 2(supplement):3–25.

Farber, Henry S. (1977) "The determinants of union wage demands: some preliminary empirical evidence", *Proceedings of the thirtieth annual winter meeting of the industrial relations research associations*, 303–310.

Farber, Henry S. (1978a) "Bargaining theory, wage outcomes, and the occurrence of strikes", *American Economic Review*, 68:262–271.

Farber, Henry S. (1978b) "Individual preferences and union wage determination: the case of the United Mine Workers", *Journal of Political Economy*, 86:923–942.

Farber, Henry S. (1978c) "The United Mine Workers and the demand for coal: an econometric analysis of union behavior", *Research in Labor Economics*, 2.

Farber, Henry S. (1980a) "An analysis of final-offer arbitration", *Journal of Conflict Resolution*, 24.

Farber, Henry S. (1980b) "An analysis of Hicks's theory of industrial disputes", mimeo, Massachusetts Institute of Technology.

Farber, Henry S. (1981a) "Splitting-the-difference in interest arbitration", *Industrial and Labor Relations Review*, 35:70–77.

Farber, Henry S. (1981b) "Union wages and the minimum wage", *Report of the Minimum Wage Study Commission*, Vol VI.

Farber, Henry S. (1983a) "The determination of the union status of workers", *Econometrica*, 51:1417–1437.

Farber, Henry S. (1983b) "Worker preferences for union representation", *Research in Labor Economics*, 2(supplement):171–205.

Farber, Henry S. (1983c) "The union status of jobs: some preliminary results", mimeo, Massachusetts Institute of Technology.

Farber, Henry S. (1984) "Right to work laws and the extent of unionization", *Journal of Labor Economics*, 2:319–352.

Farber, Henry S. and Harry C. Katz (1979) "Interest arbitration, outcomes, and the incentive to bargain", *Industrial and Labor Relations Review*, 33:55–63.

Farber, Henry S. and Daniel H. Saks (1980) "Why workers want unions: the role of relative wages and job characteristics", *Journal of Political Economy*, 88:349–369.

Fellner, William (1949) *Competition among the few.* New York: Alfred A. Knopf.

Fishburn, Peter (1973) *The theory of social choice.* Princeton, New Jersey: Princeton University Press.

Freeman, Richard B. (1980a) "The exit–voice tradeoff in the labor market: unionism, job tenure, quits, and separations", *Quarterly Journal of Economics*, 94:643–673.

Freeman, Richard b. (1980b) "Unionism and the dispersion of wages", *Industrial and Labor Relations Review*, 34:3–23.

Freeman, Richard B. (1981) "The effect of trade unionism on fringe benefits", *Industrial and Labor Relations Review*, 34:489–509.

Freeman, Richard B. (1984) "Longitudinal analyses of the effects of trade unions", *Journal of Labor Economics*, 2:1–26.

Freeman, Richard B. and James L. Medoff (1979) "The two faces of unionism", *The Public Interest*, 57:69–93.

Freeman, Richard B. and James L. Medoff (1981a) "The impact of collective bargaining: illusion or reality", in: J. Stieber, R. B. McKersie and D. Q. Mills, eds., *U.S. industrial relations 1950–1980: a critical assessment*. Madison, Wisconsin: Industrial Relations Research Association.

Freeman, Richard B. and James L. Medoff (1981b) "The impact of the percentage organized on union and nonunion wages", *Review of Economics and Statistics*, 561–572.

Freeman, Richard B. and James L. Medoff (1983) "The impact of collective bargaining: can the new facts be explained by monopoly unionism?", *Research in Labor Economics*, 2(supplement):293–332.

Fudenberg, Drew, David Levine and Paul Ruud (1983) "Strikes and wage settlements", Department of Economics Working Paper No. 249. University of California, Los Angeles, mimeo.

Grossman, Sanford J. and Oliver D. Hart (1981) "Implicit contracts, moral hazard, and unemployment", *American Economic Review*, 77:301–307.

Haber, William (1945) "Building construction", in: *How collective bargaining works.* New York: The Twentieth Century Fund, 183–228.

Hall, Robert E. and David M. Lillian (1979) "Efficient wage bargains under uncertain supply and demand", *American Economic Review*, 69:868–879.

Hamermesh, Daniel S. (1970) "Wage bargaining, threshold effects, and the Phillips curve", *Quarterly Journal of Economics*, 84:501–517.

Hamermesh, Daniel S. (1973) "Who 'wins' in wage bargaining?", *Industrial and Labor Relations Review*, 26:1146–1149.

Harsanyi, John C. (1956) "Approaches to the bargaining problem before and after the theory of games", *Econometrica*, 24:144–157.

Hart, Oliver D. (1983) "Optimal labor contracts under asymmetric information: an introduction", *Review of Economic Studies*, 50:3–36.

Hicks, John (1963) *The theory of wages*. London: MacMillan.

Johnston, Jack (1972) "A model of wage determination under bilateral monopoly", *Economic Journal*, 82:837–852.

Kahn, Mark L. (1980) "Airlines", in: G. Somers, ed., *Collective bargaining: contemporary American experience*. Madison, Wisconsin: Industrial Relations Research Association, 315–372.

Katz, Harry C. (1984a) "The U.S. automobile collective bargaining system in transition", *British Journal of Industrial Relations*, 22:205–217.

Katz, Harry C. (1984b) *Shifting gears: changing labor relations in the U.S. automobile industry*. Cambridge, Massachusetts: Massachusetts Institute of Technology Press, in press.

Katz, Lawrence (1983) "Union status and the union–nonunion wage differential: the issue of membership vs. coverage", Massachusetts Institute of Technology mimeo.

Lazear, Edward P. (1983) "A competitive theory of monopoly unionism", *American Economic Review*, 73:631–643.

Lee, Lung-Fei (1978) "Unionism and wage rates: a simultaneous equations model with qualitative and limited dependent variables", *International Economic Review*, 19:415–433.

Leontief, Wasily (1946) "The pure theory of the guaranteed annual wage contract", *Journal of Political Economy*, 54:76–79.

Levinson, Harold M. (1980) "Trucking", in: G. Somers, ed., *Collective bargaining: contemporary American experience*. Madison, Wisconsin: Industrial Relations Research Association, 99–150.

Lewis, H. Gregg (1959) "Competitive and monopoly unionism", in: P. Bradley, ed., *The public stake in union power*. Charlottesville, Virginia: University of Virginia Press, 181–208.

Lewis, H. Gregg (1963) *Unionism and relative wages in the United States*. Chicago: University of Chicago Press.

Lewis, H. Gregg (1986) *Union relative wage effects: a survey*. Chicago: University of Chicago Press.

Luce, R. Duncan and Howard Raiffa (1957) *Games and decisions*. New York: John Wiley & Sons, Inc.

Lunsden, Kieth and Craig Peterson (1975) "The effect of right-to-work laws on unionization in the United States", *Journal of Political Economy*, 83:1237–1248.

Martin, Donald L. (1980) *An ownership theory of the trade union*. Berkeley: University of California Press.

MaCurdy, Thomas E. and John Pencavel (1986) "Testing between competing models of wage and employment determination in unionized labor markets", *Journal of Political Economy*, 94:S3–S39.

McDonald, Ian M. and Robert M. Solow (1981) "Wage bargaining and employment", *American Economic Review*, 71:896–908.

Medoff, James L. (1979) "Layoffs and alternatives under trade unions in U.S. manufacturing", *American Economic Review*, 69:380–395.

Mills, D. Quinn (1980) "Construction", in: G. Somers, ed., *Collective bargaining: contemporary American experience*. Madison, Wisconsin: Industrial relations Research Association, 49–98.

Mincer, Jacob (1976) "Unemployment effects of minimum wages", *Journal of Political Economy*, 84:S87–S104.

Nash, John F. (1950) "The bargaining problem", *Econometrica*, 18:155–162.

Nash, John F. (1953) "Two person cooperative games", *Econometrica*, 21:128–140.

Nickell, Stephen J. and M. Andrews (1983) "Trade unions, real wages, and employment in Britain 1951–79", *Oxford Economic Papers* (New Series), 35(supplement):183–206.

Oswald, Andrew J. (1982) "The microeconomic theory of the trade union", *Economic Journal*, 92:576–596.

Oswald, Andrew J. (1984) "Efficient contracts are on the labor demand curve: theory and facts", Paper No. 178, Princeton University, Industrial Relations Section.

Oswald, Andrew J. (1985) "The economic theory of trade unions: an introductory survey", *Scandanavian Journal of Economics*, 87:160–193.

Pen, Jan (1952) "A general theory of bargaining", *American Economic Review*, 42:24–42.

Pen, Jan (1959) *The wage rate under collective bargaining*. Cambridge, Mass.: Harvard University Press.

Pencavel, John (1970) "An investigation into industrial strike activity in Britain", *Economica*, 37:239–256.

Pencavel, John (1984a) "The empirical performance of a model of trade union behavior", in: J. Rosa, ed., *The economics of labor unions: new directions*. Kluwer-Nijhoff Publishing Company.

Pencavel, John (1984b) "The tradeoff between wages and employment in trade union objectives", *Quarterly Journal of Economics*, 99:215–231.

Plott, Charles (1967) "A notion of equilibrium and its possibility under majority rule", *American Economic Review*, 57:787–806.

Raisian, John (1981) "Union dues and wage premiums", U.S. Department of Labor mimeo.

Riker, William H. (1980) "Implications from the disequilibrium of majority rule for the study of institutions", *American Political Science Review*, 72:432–446.

Rosen, Sherwin (1969) "Trade union power, threat effects, and the extent of organization", *Review of Economic Studies*, 36:185–196.

Rosen, Sherwin (1970) "Unionism and the occupational wage structure in the United States", *International Economic Review*, 11:269–286.

Ross, Arthur M. (1948) *Trade union wage policy*. Berkeley and Los Angeles: University of California Press.

Roth, Alvin (1979) *Axiomatic models of bargaining*. New York: Springer-Verlag.

Schmidt, Peter and Robert P. Strauss (1976) "The effect of unions on earnings and earnings on unions: a mixed logit approach", *International Economic Review*, 17:204–212.

Shackle, G. L. S. (1957) "The nature of the bargaining process", in: J. Dunlop, ed. *The theory of wage determination*. London: MacMillan.

Simons, Henry C. (1944) "Some reflections on syndicalism", *Journal of Political Economy*, 52:1–25.

Svejnar, Jan (1980) "On empirical testing of the Nash–Zeuthen bargaining solution", *Industrial and Labor Relations Review*, 33:536–542.

Svejnar, Jan (1983) "Bargaining power, fear of disagreement, and wage settlements: empirical evidence from U.S. industry", mimeo, Cornell University.

Tracy, Joseph S. (1987) "An emprical test of an asymmetric information model of strikes", *Journal of Labor Economics*, 5, forthcoming.

Warren, Ronald L. and Robert P. Strauss (1979) "A mixed logit model of the relationship between unionization and right-to-work legislation", *Journal of Political Economy* 87:648–655.

Webb, Beatrice and Sidney Webb (1965) *Industrial democracy*, 1920 reprint edition. New York: Augustus M. Kelley.

Wessels, Walter J. (1981) "Economic effects of right-to-work laws", *Journal of Labor Research*, 2:55–76.

Zeuthen, Frederik (1930) *Problems of monopoly and economic warfare*. London: Routledge and Kegan Paul.

Chapter 19

THE ECONOMICS OF STRIKES

JOHN KENNAN*

The University of Iowa

1. Introduction

There is no commonly accepted economic theory of strikes. The main obstacle is that if one has a theory which predicts when a strike will occur and what the outcome will be, the parties can agree to this outcome in advance, and so avoid the costs of a strike. If they do this, the theory ceases to hold. This might be called the "Hicks Paradox", since it is implicit in Hicks's (1963) theoretical discussion of strikes. To state the point in another way, strikes are apparently not Pareto optimal, since a strike means that the pie shrinks as the employer and the workers argue over how it should be divided. If the parties are rational, it is difficult to see why they would fail to negotiate a Pareto optimal outcome.

Hicks suggested two possible explanations for strikes: either the union is trying to maintain a "reputation for toughness", or there is private information on at least one side of the bargaining table:

> Weapons grow rusty if unused, and a Union which never strikes may lose the ability to organise a formidable strike, so that its threats become less effective. The most able Trade Union leadership will embark on strikes occasionally,... in order to keep their weapon burnished for future use....
>
> Under a system of collective bargaining, some strikes are more or less inevitable for this reason; but nevertheless the majority of actual strikes are doubtless the result of faulty negotiation. ...Any means which enables either side to appreciate better the position of the other will make settlement easier; adequate knowledge will always make a settlement possible [Hicks (1963, pp. 146–147)].

An intriguing feature of the Hicks Paradox is that empirical studies generally agree that strike activity is to some extent predictable. In particular, it is

*I thank Dan Hamermesh, Alan Harrison, George Neumann, Barry Sopher and Neil Wallace for helpful comments. I am also grateful to the Editors for their patient encouragement.

Handbook of Labor Economics, Volume II, Edited by O. Ashenfelter and R. Layard
©*Elsevier Science Publishers BV, 1986*

generally found that strikes are procyclical: in the expansionary phase of the business cycle, strikes increase, and when the economy contracts, strikes decrease. As Ashenfelter and Johnson (1969) observe:

> It is not apparent how the propensity of either or both of the parties to (a) miscalculate the intentions of the other or (b) act irrationally would be systematically related to any of the conceptually observable variables in the system (p. 36).

This chapter is essentially a study of Ashenfelter and Johnson's observation. Specifically, the prospects for constructing a theoretical explanation of strike activity will be examined, and the evidence that strikes are systematically related to other economic variables will be reviewed. The literature in this area is voluminous and the quality of the papers is not uniform; thus complete coverage here is neither feasible nor desirable. There is no discussion of strikes in the public sector, but this topic is treated elsewhere in Chapter 22 by Ehrenberg and Schwarz in this Handbook. Neither is there any discussion of arbitration; a good introduction to this topic can be found in Ashenfelter and Bloom (1984).

2. Are strikes mistakes?

2.1. A Basic pie-splitting model

Collective bargaining is basically concerned with the division of rents which may be collected jointly by the workers and the firm's owners. A strike reduces the pie which will eventually be divided between the two sides, so a strike is a collective mistake. The strike continues only as long as each side believes that there is more to be gained by continuing the strike than by settling at the terms which are currently acceptable to the other side. Since the pie is shrinking, there is a sense in which these beliefs are inconsistent: both sides expect to win, but there can be at most one winner.

Consider Figure 19.1. A fixed pie is to be divided between "One" and "Two". One expects to get x eventually, and so is willing to concede $\pi - x$ now: this is the point labeled A. Two expects y and concedes $\pi - y$: this is B. The points A and B are inconsistent, so bargaining continues and the pie shrinks. Finally, agreement is reached at C.

As the diagram is drawn, it appears that both players made mistakes, ex post. If One had foreseen the outcome, A^* would have been a rational initial bargaining position, while B^* would have been rational for Two. Then a Pareto optimal agreement could have been reached at a point like C^*. On the other hand, each side can blame the other: given that One was insisting on A, if Two

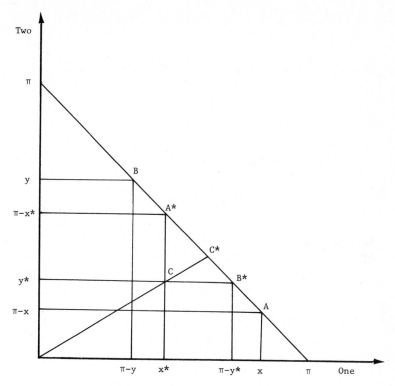

Figure 19.1. Division of a shrinking pie.

had offered B^* it would have been rejected. Similarly, both sides can claim victory: the outcome C is better for One than the pre-strike offer B, and C is better than A for Two.

2.2. *An escrow model*

As a point of reference, it is useful to consider examples of bargaining processes which achieve a Pareto optimal outcome, by providing alternatives to the use of a strike in case agreement on a new contract is not reached before the old contract expires. Marceau and Musgrave (1949) proposed the idea of a "statutory strike", in which production continues as if an agreement had been reached, but both the workers and the employer are subjected to fines which are roughly equal to the costs that they would bear during a strike. They suggested that the fines could be paid into a trust fund which could either become part of government revenue or be divided between the parties when an agreement is finally reached. In either case, the pie would not shrink as the union and the firm argue as to how to divide it. A practical difficulty with this scheme is that the appropriate fines would be difficult to calculate, and any proposed figures would undoubtedly promote further conflict.[1]

Instead of having a third party impose fines, it might be possible to achieve a similar effect through a kind of Vickrey auction. Suppose that a union and an employer are attempting to negotiate a new contract. As the expiration date of the old contract approaches, the union is demanding, say, $15 an hour, and the employer is offering $12 an hour. Instead of launching a strike, the two sides set up an escrow account with their local banker. Business goes on as usual, and the workers receive a wage of $12 an hour (the amount offered by the employer). The employer pays a wage of $15 an hour (the amount demanded by the union), with $12 going to the workers, and $3 going into the escrow account. Negotiations continue, and after a week (40 hours) the union reduces its demand to $14, and the employer increases its offer to $12.50. By this time, the escrow account contains $120 for each worker. The banker pays each worker $20 (40 hours at 50¢ an hour), and pays the employer $40 per worker, leaving a balance of $60 per worker, which is the amount still in dispute (40 hours @ $1.50). Work goes on, with the workers receiving $12.50 an hour, and the employer paying $14 an hour. When a new contract is finally signed, the escrow account contains enough money to make the wage increase retroactive to the expiration of the old contract.

This is a variation on the observation that if the eventual settlement after a strike had been applied at the outset, everyone would have been better off. The escrow model can be used to keep strike theories honest: if the parties are embroiled in the Cross (1969) bargaining mechanism, for example, would they not gladly switch to the escrow mechanism? In practice, escrow accounts are apparently not used, but retroactive agreements are common: the union allows the employer to act as banker.

The escrow model draws attention to a commonly held opinion about strikes: that the function of a strike is to impose costs on the employer or on the union, and so promote agreement. If this is so, the escrow model misses the point, since (absent liquidity constraints) no costs are imposed on either side. A variant of the

---

[1]See Sosnick (1964) for a discussion of objections to the statutory strike proposal, as well as a review of other related schemes. McCalmont (1962) describes an attempt to implement this proposal during a bus strike in Miami in October 1960. The bus company and its employees agreed that bus service would continue as usual during the strike, but the company would not collect bus fares, and the workers would not be paid. The company terminated this arrangement after four days, on the pretext that bus drivers were accepting tips from the passengers, contrary to the agreement. The strike then continued for a further 29 days. This was hardly a test of the statutory strike, however, since the arrangement made both the company and the workers worse off than they would be in a conventional strike.

Marceau–Musgrave scheme, which does impose costs on each side, has been suggested by Blackorby and Donaldson (1983): instead of being paid into an escrow account, the difference between the employer's last offer and the union's last demand is collected by the government. Blackorby and Donaldson proposed that if the parties have not reached agreement by some deadline, the negotiations will be cut off, and the government will impose a contract in which the employer pays the workers' last demand, and the workers receive the employer's last offer. It would probably be better, however, to let negotiations continue, as in the escrow scheme, and let the government collect the current difference between the parties until agreement is reached. This is an unusual tax proposal: the tax may introduce a distortion, but if so the distortion *promotes* Pareto optimality.

3. Two bargaining models

Bargaining theory contains very few interesting propositions that can be tested empirically [Hamermesh (1973, p. 1146)].

There is a large literature on bargaining which will not be dealt with here. Instead, two very well-known models will be discussed briefly.[2]

3.1. The Nash model

When two parties can do better by cooperating than by acting independently, a bargaining problem arises, involving the division of the gains from cooperation (the "pie"). Nash (1950) proposed an ingenious solution for such problems, which predicts that the parties will act so as to maximize the product of their utility gains from cooperation. Nash's argument was quite simple, and can be presented in the context of the pie-splitting problem illustrated in Figure 19.1, where two parties ("One" and "Two") divide a fixed sum of money π, with the understanding that if they cannot agree on a division each party gets nothing.

It is assumed that each party would rather have more money than less, and these preferences are represented by increasing utility functions $U(x)$ and $V(y)$, with $U(0) = V(0) = 0$. Then the triangle in Figure 19.1 can be transformed into the utility-possibility set F shown in Figure 19.2. It is assumed that F is convex. A special point N is now singled out by the property that the utility product uv is greater at N than at any other point in F. Change units so that both One and Two obtain 1 unit of utility at N, and re-draw the utility-possibility set in these new units, as shown in Figure 19.3. The point which maximizes the utility

---

[2] For more detailed discussions of bargaining see Luce and Raiffa (1957), Bishop (1963), Cross (1969), Harsanyi (1977), Roth (1979) and Myerson (1984b).

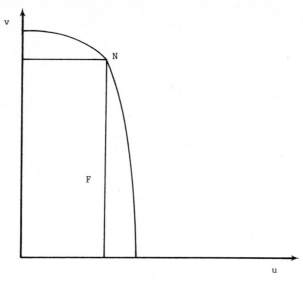

Figure 19.2.

product is invariant under this change of units, so the utility-possibility frontier is tangent to the rectangular hyperbola $uv = 1$ in Figure 19.3. The common tangent generates a triangle T which intersects each axis at 2 utils.

The core of Nash's theorem can now be seen. Suppose the parties could bargain over T rather than F. Nash assumed that if the utility-possibility set is symmetric about the 45° line then the outcome must be on the 45° line, since there is no reason to expect one bargainer to do better than the other. He also assumed that the outcome must be Pareto optimal, so if the parties were to bargain over T the result would be the point N. Then, assuming independence of irrelevant alternatives, N must also be the outcome for F. This outcome can be traced back through Figure 19.2 to give a particular split of the pie in Figure 19.1.

Nash's result is essentially an intuitive argument about symmetry. As is usual with such arguments, the result depends on where the symmetry principle is invoked. For example, the triangle in Figure 19.1 is also symmetric, but if the principle is invoked here rather than in Figure 19.3, the result is a 50–50 split of the pie. Moreover, if preferences are represented by different increasing utility functions, the Nash solution will generally be different. Nash pinned things down by using von Neumann–Morgenstern utility functions which register the degree of risk aversion of each bargainer. This seems quite arbitrary. What risks are involved? If, as Luce and Raiffa (1957) suggest, the Nash solution is to be

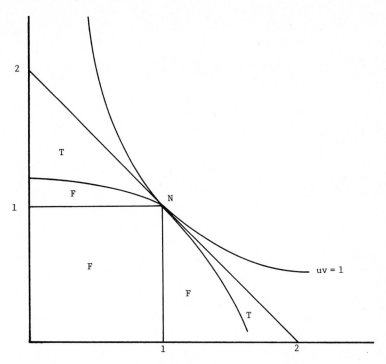

Figure 19.3.

regarded as a fair arbitration scheme, why should an arbitrator penalize one of the bargainers who is found to be more risk averse?[3]

A related criticism of the Nash solution appeared in Crawford and Varian (1979). Since the more risk-averse player loses in Nash's game, an intelligent player will pretend to be risk neutral, or even risk loving. Nash assumed complete information, which includes the assumption that the players' von Neumann–Morgenstern utility functions are common knowledge. Crawford and Varian (1979) assumed that each player can report any utility function which is not risk loving, and that the Nash game is then played as if it were common knowledge that these reports were truthful. The result is that each player will pretend to be risk neutral, so the pie will be split 50–50. Although this is a silly game (since each player, while lying through his teeth, is supposed to believe that the other

---

[3] See Luce and Raiffa (1957, pp. 129–130) for an argument defending this aspect of the Nash solution. Harsanyi (1977, p. 145), on the other hand, argued that the Nash model should not be interpreted as a model of arbitration: in particular, fairness should not be considered except to the extent that the players themselves attach value to it.

player is George Washington) it clearly illustrates that the Nash solution depends crucially on the unrealistic assumption of complete information.

Roth and Malouf (1979) gave an interesting example of a "binary lottery game" which further illustrates the Nash solution. Consider two single-prize lotteries, each with 100 equal-chance tickets. Suppose One and Two bargain over the division of 100 lottery tickets, with the understanding that tickets assigned to One are good for lottery One, and tickets assigned to Two are good for lottery Two. Thus, if the agreement gives 30 tickets to One and 70 to Two, then One will have a 30 percent chance of winning lottery One, while Two will have a 70 percent chance of winning lottery Two. Assume that each bargainer has a von Neumann–Morgenstern utility function in which zero tickets means zero utility. Then, for each player, expected utility is proportional to the number of tickets received, so the Nash model predicts an equal split of the tickets. If the prize in lottery One is increased by a million dollars the Nash model implies that the outcome of the bargaining process will not change. This prediction is implausible, and it has been refuted in experimental tests by Roth and Malouf (1979) for the case where both players know both prizes.[4]

3.2. The Cross model

An interesting but ultimately unsuccessful attempt to evade the Hicks Paradox was made by Cross (1965, 1969). Cross considered a pie-splitting model in which each side maximizes a discounted sum of utility flows by making a continually changing series of "final" demands. A canonical version of this model will be presented here.

Suppose that Two initially demands q_2, but One believes that this demand will be reduced at the rate of r_2 dollars per time-period, so that One could obtain the entire pie by waiting q_2/r_2 periods. Then to obtain q dollars One must wait until Two has conceded $q + q_2 - \pi$, so One's problem is

$$\max_q U(q)\exp\left(-\frac{a}{r_2}[q + q_2 - \pi]\right), \tag{1}$$

where U is One's utility function, and a is One's rate of time preference. Since q_2 and π enter the objective function only through a multiplicative constant, it is evident that the optimal demand does not depend on either the size of the pie or the demand made by the other side, but only on the gain from waiting (r_2) relative to the cost of waiting (a). Similarly, Two's demand will depend only on

---

[4]A good review of experimental evidence bearing on the Nash model may be found in Roth and Malouf (1979). Some more recent work is discussed in Roth and Schoumaker (1983).

the rate at which One is expected to concede (r_1) relative to Two's rate of time preference (b). Thus, for example, if we observe initial demands of \$60 and \$70 when the pie is \$100, we should also observe initial demands of \$60 and \$70 when the pie is \$950000. This remarkable prediction surely damns the Cross model, unless the anticipated concession rates r_1 and r_2 are somehow tied to the size of the pie.

At the outset each party expects to stand fast while the other concedes. To reconcile these contradictory expectations a model of learning is introduced in which One revises the estimate r_2 of Two's concession rate in light of the actual concessions made by Two over time. Assume that each party learns at the same rate according to an adaptive expectations rule. Then

$$\dot{r}_2 = \alpha[-\dot{q}_2 - r_2] \tag{2}$$

and

$$\dot{r}_1 = \alpha[-\dot{q}_1 - r_1], \tag{3}$$

where the dot notation denotes a time derivative, and α is a parameter representing the speed at which the parties learn. Assume that each party is an income-maximizer, and that the rates of time preference are equal. Then it can easily be shown that the optimal demands are $q_1 = r_2/a$ and $q_2 = r_1/a$. Substitute these in the learning equations to obtain a pair of differential equations in q_1 and q_2:

$$a\dot{q}_1 = \alpha[-\dot{q}_2 - aq_1] \tag{4}$$

and

$$a\dot{q}_2 = \alpha[-\dot{q}_1 - aq_2]. \tag{5}$$

The model can easily be solved by introducing a variable $Q = q_1 + q_2$ to denote the sum of the demands, and a variable $D = q_1 - q_2$ to denote the difference in the demands. Then by adding and subtracting eqs. (4) and (5) one obtains:

$$(a + \alpha)\dot{Q} + a\alpha Q = 0 \tag{6}$$

and

$$(a - \alpha)\dot{D} + a\alpha D = 0. \tag{7}$$

These Equations can be solved separately. Eq. (6) gives

$$Q(t) = Q_0 e^{-\lambda t}, \tag{8}$$

where λ is $a\alpha/(a + \alpha)$, and Q_0 is the sum of the initial demands, reflecting the initial beliefs about concession rates. Thus, the sum of the demands declines exponentially, and agreement is reached at t^*, when $Q(t^*) = \pi$. The solution of eq. (7) is

$$D(t) = D_0 e^{-\mu t}, \tag{9}$$

where μ is $a\alpha/(a - \alpha)$, and D_0 is the difference of the initial demands. Cross assumed (arbitrarily) that the time preference rate a exceeds the learning rate α, which implies that the difference of the demands also declines exponentially, and less rapidly than the sum. Since $D(t)$ does not change sign, whoever makes the larger initial demand will end up with more than half of the pie.[5] In other words, if One expects Two to concede rapidly, while Two expects One to concede slowly, then One will obtain more than half of the pie.

The Cross model has two fatal flaws. First, the bargainers do not behave rationally. At any given moment, each acts as if all future concessions will be made by the other, even though this is manifestly unrealistic in light of the bargaining history so far. Second, the model has no empirical content unless another model is adjoined which explains how each party forms an initial estimate of the other's concession rate. In applications, therefore, the model degenerates into a series of ad hoc speculations about, say, the effect of variations in the unemployment rate on the firm's beliefs about the rate at which workers will moderate their demands. There is no question that such beliefs are important in practical negotiations. The problem is that the Cross model does not add anything to the "war stories" found in the descriptive literature on bargaining and strikes. For example, it is misleading to claim that the Cross model provides "insight" into the bargaining process, by showing that a union may wish to make some concession but be deterred by the prospect that management will infer weakness and become intransigent. One does not need a model to predict this kind of behavior, and it is foolish to expect that an irrational model can be used to sharpen the prediction in some way.

The real value of the Cross model is that it posts a "cul de sac" sign on an otherwise plausible avenue of research. By working through the model one is led to appreciate the futility of attempting to build a two-sided model of rational bargaining and strikes in which each side continually revises its subjective expectations about the behavior of the other. This clears the way for a discussion of several alternative theoretical models, to be discussed in the next two sections.

---

[5] Provided that neither party demands more than the entire pie initially, it is easy to show that both demands will remain positive until a settlement is reached.

4. Escaping the Hicks paradox

4.1. The Ashenfelter and Johnson model

Hicks (1963) offered many useful observations on the economics of strikes, but his attempt to build a formal model led to hopeless confusion. Although the behavior of the employer in Hicks's model was governed by the usual rules of profit maximization, the description of workers' behavior consisted of a series of conjectures regarding the psychology of the "working man".[6] Ashenfelter and Johnson (1969) ingeniously turned this aspect of Hicks's model to advantage. By ignoring the question of whether workers behave rationally, they obtained a remarkably simple and useful model which determines the incidence and duration of strikes, as well as the terms of settlement. This model can be summarized quite easily.

Consider a profit-maximizing firm which sells output at a fixed rate, Q, and at a fixed price, P, and which employs a fixed number of workers, M. A new contract is negotiated which increases the old wage rate, W, by the proportion y so that the new wage is $(1 + y)W$. The union will strike if the firm does not offer an increase of at least y_0. Then as the strike goes on, the union will modify its position so that the required wage declines along an exponential "resistance curve":

$$y(S) = y_* + (y_0 - y_*)e^{-\tau S}. \tag{10}$$

Here y_* is the lowest conceivable wage increase (which might be negative) and S is the duration of the strike.

The firm seeks to maximize the present discounted value of profits, which accrue at the rate $(PQ - WM)$. The highest conceivable wage increase is

$$y_b \equiv \frac{(PQ - WM)}{WM}. \tag{11}$$

Thus, if the wage increase is y_b, the firm will just break even. It can easily be shown that the firm's optimal policy is to set a target y_T, and settle as soon as the

---

[6] For example: "...some new level [of wages] may easily invoke a special attachment – because it has been granted elsewhere, and is therefore considered fair, or because it has been paid at some earlier period, or for some similar reason. ... More or less sentimental considerations of this sort evidently have a large influence on the willingness to hold out for a given rate of wages" (p. 153).

Also: "...in an industry whose methods are very flexible, ...the workman always feels his job to be insecure because of the progress of invention. It is not difficult for him to get some rudimentary idea that he is more likely to be displaced if he becomes more expensive" (p. 158).

union is willing to accept this wage increase. The target is a weighted average of y_b and y_*, with weights depending on how rapidly the union concedes (as measured by τ), relative to the firm's cost of waiting (measured by the interest rate r):

$$y_T \equiv (1-\lambda)y_* + \lambda y_b, \tag{12}$$

where

$$\lambda \equiv \frac{r}{\tau + r}.$$

If $y_0 \leq y_T$ the firm grants the wage increase y_0, and no strike occurs. Otherwise, y_0 does not influence the terms of settlement, but only the duration of the strike. Any change which increases y_T or which reduces y_0 will decrease the probability of a strike. Thus, if the firm becomes more profitable (so that y_b increases) or if the union becomes more aggressive (i.e. either the sticking point y_* increases, or the rate of concession decreases) then a strike becomes less likely, provided that the union's initial demand is held constant.

This model was used by Ashenfelter and Johnson (1969) to run interference for an ad hoc regression of strike frequency on the aggregate unemployment rate, a distributed lag of real wage changes, and the ratio of profits to total compensation. They argued that λ and y_* should not vary much in time-series regressions, so that variations in strike incidence can be explained through variations in y_0 and y_b. The unemployment rate and lagged real wages were introduced as determinants of y_0. The direct effect of profits through y_b is partly masked by an indirect effect through y_0.

Unfortunately, the empirical content of the Ashenfelter and Johnson model comes almost exclusively from intuitive guesses about the determinants of the workers' resistance curve, rather than from any analysis of rational economic behavior. No matter how reasonable such guesses might seem, they are open to a serious theoretical objection. For example, Farber (1978) hypothesized that the resistance curve will have a more rapid rate of decay (τ) if the union's strike fund is low, or if the unemployment rate is high. This seems plausible only because it seems to be consistent with rational behavior by workers. Yet if workers were rational in this model, they would set $y_0 = y_b$ and $\tau = 0$, and so obtain the whole pie. In other words, workers could obtain large wage increases if they would just read the *American Economic Review* (or this Handbook).

Although the theoretical interpretation of the results may be open to question, the Ashenfelter–Johnson model has proved very successful in explaining aggregate data on strike frequency. The empirical applications of the model will be discussed in Section 7.2 below.

4.2. The joint cost theory

Reder and Neumann (1980) and Kennan (1980a) have proposed the simple theory that strike activity is inversely related to its cost. What matters is the sum of the costs to both parties, since costs which are incurred by one side can be shifted to the other side by making a more generous bargaining proposal. Reder and Neumann (1980) argued that negotiation is expensive, so that it will not be optimal to reach agreement in advance to cover all contingencies which might arise over the life of a contract, or of a bargaining relationship. Those contingencies which would otherwise be most likely to lead to expensive strikes will, however, be covered by an advance agreement: a "protocol". Strikes should still be viewed as mistakes in this theory. After all, even if an issue arises which is not covered in the protocol, there is no reason why this issue could not be resolved without a strike. The point is that the likelihood of a mistake can be reduced or eliminated if the issue is covered by a protocol, and since the protocol covers the more expensive strike possibilities it follows that strikes will be less likely when they are more costly. Kennan (1980a) argued that this is in any case an attractive behavioral hypothesis, even if the bargaining process is treated as a "black box".

An attractive feature of the joint cost theory is that it makes straightforward predictions about the economic determinants of strike frequency and duration. Consider, for example, the effect of public subsidies such as the payment of welfare benefits to workers who are on strike. In the Ashenfelter and Johnson (1969) model one must make a guess as to how these payments will affect the union's resistance curve in order to obtain any prediction about strike activity. In the Cross model one must guess the effect of the subsidy on each party's expectations about the other party's concession rate. The joint cost theory, on the other hand, simply predicts that if strikes are subsidized, strike activity will increase.

In Kennan (1980b) the joint cost theory was used to analyze the implications of New York and Rhode Island statutes which allow workers to collect unemployment insurance benefits while on strike, after a waiting period of seven or eight weeks. The theory first predicts that these statutes will affect strike activity only to the extent that the UI system subsidizes workers and employers, through imperfect experience rating, or interest-free loans, or preferential tax treatment. Since the UI system does in fact provide such subsidies, the theory predicts that strikes which last through the waiting period will be further prolonged by the payment of UI benefits. Some empirical support was found for this prediction.[7]

---

[7]After the waiting period, the hazard function (i.e. the conditional probability of settlement within the next day, as a function of duration so far) was found to be significantly lower in New York and Rhode Island than in other states which do not allow UI payments. This supports the theory, but it was also found that the hazard function is significantly higher in New York and Rhode Island before the waiting period is up, and the theory does not explain why this should be so.

4.3.   The wimp theory

Given the difficulty of constructing a strike theory which avoids the Hicks Paradox, it is hardly surprising that some rather desperate hypotheses have been put forward. The most spectacular of these is due to Kerr and Siegel (1954):

> If the job is physically difficult and unpleasant, unskilled or semiskilled, and casual or seasonal, and fosters an independent spirit (as in the logger in the woods), it will draw tough, inconstant, combative, and virile workers, and they will be inclined to strike. If the job is physically easy and performed in pleasant surroundings, skilled and responsible, steady, and subject to set rules and close supervision, it will attract women or the more submissive type of man who will abhor strikes. Certainly the bull of the woods and the mousy bank clerk are different types of people and can be expected to act differently. Certainly, also, the community is more sympathetic with striking miners coming out of the ground than with school teachers abandoning their desks (p. 195).

The reader, being a submissive type, will presumably not be offended by this theory.

5.   Private information theories of strikes

Recently Hayes (1984), Morton (1983), Fudenberg, Levine and Ruud (1983) and Tracy (1984) have shown that the theory of exchange with private information can provide a theoretically complete model of strikes. The basic point is that although strikes are not Pareto optimal ex post they may be Pareto optimal ex ante, in the sense that every alternative leaves either the union or the employer worse off in some contingency which cannot be ruled out on the basis of the information which is common to both sides.

A representative of this class of models, due to Hayes (1984), will first be described briefly.[8] These models involve noncooperative games in which the union makes proposals which the employer must accept or reject. This gives the union an arbitrary bargaining advantage. A broader theory based on a cooperative game will be outlined in Sections 5.2–5.5.

5.1.   The Hayes model

Hayes (1984) analyzed a situation in which the firm knows more about the demand for its product than the union does. The state of the product market is

---

[8]Although the Hayes (1984) paper was the first published paper in this class, a very similar paper was written independently and contemporaneously by Morton (1983).

either good or bad and the union makes two alternative proposals, one directed at the good firm and the other at the bad firm. Specifically, one proposal involves a high wage with no strike, while the other concedes a lower wage after a strike of some duration. The ending date of the contract is fixed, so that the effective duration of the contract is reduced by the length of the strike. The proposals are designed so that the good firm will find it more profitable to grant the high wage immediately, while the bad firm prefers to take the strike in order to achieve a lower wage. Thus, as Morton (1983) pointed out, the union can be viewed as a price-discriminating monopolist selling labor to a firm with an unknown demand price. Alternatively, the union's policy could be viewed as a nonlinear pricing scheme: the firm is allowed to buy a large quantity of labor at a high price, or a smaller quantity at a lower price. Under reasonable assumptions about the union's objective function, Hayes (1984) showed that the union may achieve higher expected utility by striking in the bad state. If the good state is viewed as unlikely, on the other hand, the union does better by offering just one contract, with no strike.

The Hayes model and the other models in this class are leader–follower models in which the union plays the role of leader. In the basic version of the model Hayes (1984) assumed that the union could set the wage, while the employer was free to choose the number of workers hired; an alternative version was then analyzed in which the union could set both the wage and the level of employment. There is no good reason why the union should be given the role of leader. If anything, since the firm has an informational advantage, it would be more natural to let the firm lead. If the firm is allowed to lead, however, it will set the wage equal to the union's reservation wage (regardless of the state) and the union can do no better than to accept, so strikes will not occur. The best solution to this problem is to consider a cooperative model of bargaining, in which the union and the firm are treated symmetrically.

5.2 A simple cooperative model

Suppose a firm and a union bargain over the division of a "pie" of fixed size. The firm knows the size of the pie, but the union does not. There are two states, good and bad, with pies π_g and π_b, respectively. The union assesses the probability of the good state as p. Following Myerson (1984a), the two sides bargain over a *mechanism* which assigns a (possibly random) outcome for each state. A binding agreement on the mechanism must be reached before the firm reveals its information.

Although the union has no way to verify statements made by the firm about the size of the pie, it can strike to reduce the pie by some fraction. Let γ be the fraction of the pie remaining after a strike, and assume that γ can be made to take any value between 0 and 1, by varying the duration of the strike.

A mechanism works as follows: the firm first claims that the state is good or bad. The union then reduces the pie to $\gamma_g \pi$ or $\gamma_b \pi$ and receives a payoff x_g or x_b, according to the claim made by the firm. The firm receives the difference between the reduced pie and the union's payoff. Thus a mechanism μ may be defined as a 4-tuple $(x_b, x_g, \gamma_b, \gamma_g)$.

Nothing is lost by requiring that the mechanism is incentive compatible: the state claimed by the firm is true. Indeed, if the mechanism were such that the firm always lies, it could be modified by interchanging the outcomes in the two states: then the firm would always tell the truth and the modified mechanism would be equivalent to the original one. If the firm only lies in one state, on the other hand, the union's payoff is independent of the true state, and if the mechanism is modified so as to deliver this payoff to the union in both states, the firm no longer has an incentive to lie.

The firm's incentive-compatibility constraints can be described by listing the payoffs received by the firm in each state, depending on whether it lies or tells the truth:

	truth	lie
good state	$\gamma_g \pi_g - x_g$	$\gamma_b \pi_g - x_b$
bad state	$\gamma_b \pi_b - x_b$	$\gamma_g \pi_b - x_g$

Incentive compatibility means that truth is a dominant strategy in this payoff matrix, which reduces to the condition:

$$(\gamma_g - \gamma_b)\pi_b \le x_g - x_b \le (\gamma_g - \gamma_b)\pi_g,$$

where the first inequality keeps the "bad" firm honest, and the second inequality keeps the "good" firm honest. Since $\pi_b < \pi_g$, the incentive-compatability condition requires $\gamma_g \ge \gamma_b$, and $x_g \ge x_b$. Thus, incentive compatability means either $\gamma_g = \gamma_b$ with $x_g = x_b$ or

$$\pi_b \le \frac{x_g - x_b}{\gamma_g - \gamma_b} \le \pi_g.$$

Following Harris and Townsend (1981) and Myerson (1984a), a Pareto ordering of incentive-compatible mechanisms is established by treating the good-state firm and the bad-state firm as separate agents. In this ordering, a mechanism μ is dominated by an alternative μ^0 only if the firm prefers μ^0 to μ in both states, and the union also prefers μ^0 to μ. An incentive-compatible mechanism is *incentive efficient* (IE) if it is not dominated in this sense by any other incentive-compatible mechanism. That is, μ is IE if there is no other incentive-compatible mechanism

$\mu^0 = (x_b^0, x_g^0, \gamma_b^0, \gamma_g^0)$ such that

$$px_g^0 + (1-p)x_b^0 \geq px_g + (1-p)x_b,$$
$$\gamma_g^0 \pi_g - x_g^0 \geq \gamma_g \pi_g - x_g$$

and

$$\gamma_b^0 \pi_b - x_b^0 \geq \gamma_b \pi_b - x_b,$$

with at least one strict inequality among these three.

This definition of efficiency seems appropriate when the firm's private information is available before bargaining begins. A stronger definition can be obtained by treating the firm as a single agent which maximizes expected profit, given the probability p. This would be appropriate in case the firm has no private information at the time the mechanism is selected, but it is known that the firm will receive private information before the mechanism is implemented. In this case the mechanism could be regarded as a "protocol" in the sense of Reder and Neumann (1980).

It is easy to show that $\gamma_g = 1$ for any efficient mechanism. Otherwise, suppose $\gamma_g = 1 - \delta < 1$. Define a new mechanism μ^0 with $\gamma_g^0 = 1$, $\gamma_b^0 = \gamma_b + \delta$, $x_g^0 = x_g$ and $x_b^0 = x_b$. This mechanism satisfies the incentive-compatibility condition; also μ^0 increases the firm's payoff by $\delta \pi_g$ or $\delta \pi_b$, while it does not change the union's payoff, so μ^0 is Pareto superior to μ.

Next, if γ_b can be increased without violating the incentive-compatibility constraint, the bad-state firm will be made better off, and the union and the good-state firm will be unaffected. It follows that the right-hand inequality in the incentive-compatibility condition will bind:

$$x_g - x_b = (1 - \gamma)\pi_g,$$

where γ means γ_b from now on. The firm's payoff is therefore $\gamma\pi - x_b$, where π is π_g in the good state and π_b in the bad state. The union's (expected) payoff is $(1 - \gamma)p\pi_g + x_b = p\pi_g - p\pi_g\gamma + x_b$. To keep the bad firm in the game x_b cannot exceed $\pi_b\gamma$.

The set of potentially efficient mechanisms can now be illustrated by Figure 19.4, which shows the admissible combinations of x_b and γ, with the understanding that x_g is determined by the incentive-compatibility condition. The set of feasible mechanisms is the set of points in the smaller triangle, with vertices N, S, F. To see whether all of these are incentive efficient, consider a movement from any point (γ, x) inside the triangle to another point $(\gamma + \delta, x + d)$ inside the triangle. Let ΔV_g, ΔV_b and ΔU denote the resulting changes in payoff for the

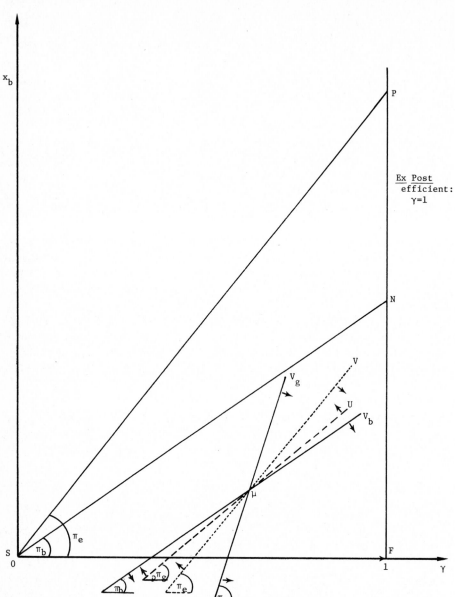

Figure 19.4. Preferences over mechanisms.

good firm, the bad firm and the union, respectively. Then

$$\Delta V_g = \pi_g \delta - d, \qquad \Delta V_b = \pi_b \delta - d, \qquad \Delta U = -p\pi_g \delta + d.$$

Is it possible to choose δ and d so that each of these three changes is nonnegative? If so

$$\pi_g \delta \geq d \geq p\pi_g \delta \quad \text{and} \quad \pi_b \delta \geq d \geq p\pi_g \delta.$$

The first set of inequalities implies $\delta > 0$, and the second set then implies $\pi_b > p\pi_g$.

The set of incentive-efficient mechanisms therefore depends on whether π_b is greater than $p\pi_g$. If so, efficiency requires $\gamma = 1$, which means that there will be no strikes. If not, any point in the smaller triangle in Figure 19.4 represents an efficient mechanism, which means that strikes *may* occur in the bad state.

5.3. Gains from negotiating in advance

Suppose the mechanism is chosen before the firm knows the state, but not implemented until after the firm knows the state. This enlarges the set of feasible mechanisms, since it is no longer irrational for the firm to accept a mechanism which gives negative profits in the bad state, provided that the expected profit, π_e, is positive. The triangle N, S, F of feasible contracts in Figure 19.4 is replaced by the steeper triangle P, S, F. In this context, an incentive-compatible mechanism μ is efficient if there is no other incentive-compatible mechanism μ^0 such that

$$px_g^0 + (1-p)x_b^0 \geq px_g + (1-p)x_b$$

and

$$p\left(\gamma_g^0 \pi_g - x_g^0\right) + (1-p)\left(\gamma_b^0 \pi_b - x_b^0\right) \geq p\left(\gamma_g \pi_g - x_g\right) + (1-p)\left(\gamma_b \pi_b - x_b\right),$$

where at least one of these inequalities is strict.

If the parties agree to a mechanism before the firm knows the state the chosen mechanism will be Pareto optimal, ex post: strikes will not occur. To show this, suppose $\mu = (x_b, \gamma)$ is an efficient mechanism with γ less than 1. The union's expected utility under this mechanism is $U = (1-\gamma)p\pi_g + x_b$. Consider a new mechanism $\mu^0 = (x_b^0, \gamma^0)$ with $x_b^0 = U$ and $\gamma^0 = 1$ (so that the firm guarantees U to the union, regardless of the state). The firm's expected profit under μ is $V = \gamma\pi_e - x_b$, while under μ^0 the firm expects $V^0 = \pi_e - x_b - p(1-\gamma)\pi_g$. Thus, the firm's gain under μ^0 is $(1-\gamma)(\pi_e - p\pi_g) = (1-\gamma)(1-p)\pi_b$, which is positive.

Thus, if only one side receives private information, and if bargaining takes place before this information is available, strikes will not occur. This is very similar to the Hall and Lilien (1979) result that efficient contracts can be found which deliver the same level of utility to workers in each state of nature, so that workers have no further interest in learning the firm's information.[9] The private information theories of strikes developed in Fudenberg, Levine and Ruud (1983), Hayes (1984), Morton (1983a) and Tracy (1984) are all based on one-sided models in which the firm knows the state and the union does not. The results apply only in cases where opportunities for negotiating in advance either did not exist, or have been passed over. One possible interpretation, following Reder and Neumann (1980), is that contingencies which are regarded as likely, ex ante, are covered by prior negotiation, so that strikes occur only when an unlikely event occurs.

5.4.   *Implementation of strike mechanisms*

It has been shown that $p\pi_g > \pi_b$ is a necessary condition for strikes to occur. This is equivalent to the condition that the union prefers the southwest vertex (S) of the triangle N, S, F in Figure 19.4 to the northeast vertex (N). The vertices represent mechanisms which could be implemented as non-negotiable demands made by the union, where the point S means that the union demands π_g while N represents a demand of π_b. The firm can do no better than to accede unless the union demands more than π, so the good firm will accept both S and N, while the bad firm will accept N and reject S. Thus, the union's expected payoffs are $p\pi_g$ for S and π_b for N. Clearly, if $p\pi_g < \pi_b$ the union will prefer the no-strike mechanism N to the strike mechanism S. Although these are just two of many possible strategies, it has been shown that the union's preferences over these two completely determine whether strikes will occur.

This raises a potentially interesting question. In a general model of collective bargaining with private information on the firm's side one could define a mechanism N which gives the union the same wage regardless of the state of nature, this wage being such that the firm could just break even in the worst state. Suppose that N yields a higher payoff for the union than any other mechanism which can be implemented by having the firm react to a non-negotiable demand. Is it then true that strikes will never occur (that is, that strikes are not incentive efficient)?

Fudenberg, Levine and Ruud (1983), Hayes (1984), Morton (1983a) and Tracy (1984) all model the bargaining process as a noncooperative game, in which the

---

[9]It seems likely that this result can be extended to the case where private information is received on both sides, although it may be necessary to introduce a risk-neutral third party into the model.

union is given the right to make demands, which the employer must accept or reject. In the model presented here, assuming that the necessary condition for strikes is satisfied, this implies that the outcome will be at S, since S maximizes the union's expected utility, over the set of IE mechanisms. This solution is arbitrary. At the other extreme, if the employer had the right to make offers which the union must accept or reject, the outcome would be the point F, at the southeast vertex of the triangle in Figure 19.4. Myerson's (1984a) "neutral bargaining solution" would split the difference between these two extremes, so that $x_b = 0$, $\gamma = \frac{1}{2}$: the employer gets half of the pie in both states, with the other half being destroyed in the bad state, and given to the union in the good state.[10]

5.5. Empirical implications

There is an obvious problem in extracting empirical implications from private information models, since some of the relevant data are not available, by definition. In the model considered here, for example, strikes occur only in the "bad" state. This does not mean that the model is refuted by the observation that strike activity is procyclical. The problem is that the state of the business cycle is public information: the union does not need to use the strike mechanism to find out whether the economy is up or down. A particular firm's private information must refer to how this firm is doing relative to the economy in general. The interpretation of private information is further restricted by the existence of publicly audited earnings reports, and by public trading of the firm's stock. Moreover, it is not enough for the firm to have information at the time of bargaining which the union will not acquire until later. In this case, contracts can be made contingent on the state, as announced by the firm, with a heavy deferred penalty if the firm is subsequently caught in a lie. This forces the firm to reveal its information, and the strike mechanism is unnecessary.

Suppose now that there are many independent bargaining pairs, each playing the game analyzed above. Each firm reports its private information to a statistical agency run by the government, and this agency publishes an average of these data, while keeping individual reports confidential. In this way, the proportion of "good" firms (p) is common knowledge, as in the model, and this proportion will vary with the state of the economy. In fact, a recession can be identified with a low value of p.

If changes in p do not alter the mechanism selected by the parties, then a "recession" will be associated with an unusually large number of "bad" firms, and therefore with an unusually large number of strikes. This result would hold locally, for example, if Myerson's Neutral Bargaining Solution is used to de-

---

[10] Note that this solution is locally insensitive to the probabilities of the states.

termine the mechanism. On the other hand, if p falls by a large amount, the critical inequality $p\pi_g > \pi_b$ will be reversed, so that any mechanism involving a strike becomes inefficient. Thus, the model is capable of explaining procyclical variations in strike activity in an intuitively appealing way. If the parties agree to a mechanism which includes a strike in the bad state, then the union takes a gamble which pays off in the good state, and which is costly in the bad state. In the extreme case (point S in Figure 19.4) the union wins the whole pie in the good state, and gets nothing in the bad state. Now if it is known that the good state is unlikely to be true, then the union will not wish to take this gamble. The union may still threaten to strike, but this threat can be bought off at the expense of a relatively small concession in wages (x_b).

This intuitive argument is hardly new. For example, Pigou (1927) argued that unions take a more aggressive bargaining position when the economy is strong, and that this increases the number of strikes.[11] A. similar argument can be applied to the firm, however, suggesting that the union's increased demands may be offset by concessions made by the firm, so that the number of strikes might increase or decrease. In the private information model presented here, however, any concessions which the firm might make are built into the mechanism. In any case, strikes occur only in bad firms which are not in a position to make concessions. When the union knows that most firms are doing well, it is reluctant to believe that its own firm is doing badly, and this leads to a strike.

6. Early empirical studies of strike activity

The empirical study of strikes is more than one hundred years old. For example, Bevan (1880) presented a detailed discussion of British strike statistics (which he compiled himself), covering 2352 strikes over the years 1870–79. Substantial studies were published around the turn of the century by Huebner (1905), Meyer (1907) and Simiand (1907). In 1911, Henry L. Moore (of Columbia University) published a collection of econometric studies of wage determination, which included a lively essay on the relationships between strikes and wages (complete with correlation coefficients and contingency tables). Subsequently, a large and unwieldy empirical literature has emerged, with contributions by economists, industrial relationists, sociologists, and political scientists. A comprehensive review of this literature will not be attempted here.[12] Instead, I will discuss the extent to which these studies establish empirical regularities which an economic theory of strikes might be expected to explain. Particular attention will be given to the evidence underlying the main "stylized fact" in this area: that strike activity varies procyclically.

---

[11]See below.
[12]A useful discussion of some of this material can be found in Shalev (1980).

Winners and losers

No strike has ever been lost, and there can be no defeat for the labor movement.

However disastrous the day of battle has been, it has been worth its price, and only the scars remain to bear testimony that the movement is invincible and that no mortal wound can be inflicted upon it [Debs, (1904, p. 12)].

As with any other kind of game or fight, the first question that comes to mind in regard to a strike is "who won?"; next, "what was the score?". These questions were taken seriously in the early days of strike statistics. Officials in government statistical bureaus called the plays, judging whether each strike was settled on terms favorable to the union (a Win), or to the employer (a Loss), or whether a compromise was reached. Empirical scholars pointed out that this classification was so impressionistic as to be almost meaningless, and then got down to the serious business of analyzing the results. As Ross and Hartman (1960) put it, "Picking the winner of a strike is notoriously difficult, but the attempt has been made in a number of countries, and the statistical results are sufficiently similar to invite attention" (p. 55).

The most interesting result of this kind was that, in the judgment of presum--ably knowledgeable observers, unions were much more likely to win when strikes were short. For example, Meyer (1907, pp. 243–244) reported that for both France and Germany (1899–1904) the workers won about 29 percent of those strikes lasting less than a week, and less than 5 percent of those lasting more than 100 days; the percentages of both union losses and of compromises increased with duration. Moore (1911, p. 119) presented similar figures. Using U.S. data for the period 1927–36, Peterson (1938, p. 77) reported that while workers won 40 percent of all strikes lasting less than two weeks, they won only 22 percent of strikes lasting more than 3 months. Edwards (1981, p. 47) confirmed these results, using U.S. data for 1881–94 and 1927–41, and Knowles (1952, pp. 256–258) obtained a qualitatively similar result for Britain (1911–38).

These studies uniformly agreed that unions are substantially less likely to win long strikes than short strikes. Since the studies were based on several large and distinct data sets, the results do indeed "invite attention". In fact, it is tempting to argue that the results support the Ashenfelter and Johnson (1969) model, in which a long strike occurs when the employer refuses to settle until the workers have made substantial reductions in their wage demands. Similarly, one might claim that the facts support private information models in which a long strike convinces the workers that the firm is relatively unprofitable, and that they should accept a relatively low wage. On the other hand, a more prosaic interpretation of the data is available. In any empirical study, it is important to distinguish three types of strikes: those involving negotiation of a new wage level, those involving disciplinary or administrative disputes, and those involving union organization. Generally, "administrative" strikes are much shorter than either of the other two types. Therefore, if unions are more likely to win administrative strikes (which seems plausible), and if all three types of strikes are aggregated together (as was the case in the studies cited), then it will be found that unions win a disproportionate share of short strikes.

A closely related question has been considered in more recent work on the relationship between strikes and wage increases. Riddell (1979) analyzed 2284 Canadian labor contracts covering the period 1953–73, and found that contracts involving a strike were associated with significantly larger wage increases than contracts reached without a strike. In addition, longer strikes were associated with significantly larger wage increases than shorter strikes. Similarly, Gramm (1984) analyzed 932 strikes involving at least 1000 workers in U.S. manufacturing, and found (after controlling for a number of other variables) that strike incidence and duration were both positively associated with wage increases. One could make a prima facie case against both the Ashenfelter–Johnson model and the private information model based on these findings, since the data include only contract strikes. On the other hand, it is important to ask why strikes occurred in some negotiations and not in others, and why the duration of strikes varied across different bargaining pairs. In the Ashenfelter–Johnson model, for example, there is no reason to expect that variations in profitability across firms (as reflected in the breakeven level y_b) will trace out a resistance curve which is fixed across unions. If the variation in strike incidence and duration is due entirely to vertical shifts in the union's resistance curve (i.e. equal changes in y_0 and y_*) then strike incidence and duration will both be positively related to wage changes.

In addition to the results on the relationship between strike duration and the probability of a union victory, some results are also available on the relevance of the state of the economy, and on strike size (number of workers involved). Citing a five-country study by Forchheimer (1948), Ross and Hartman (1960, p. 55) asserted that "larger strikes were less successful [from the union's point of view] than smaller strikes". This might be explained by "the importance of being unimportant" in determining the elasticity of labor demand [Hicks (1963, pp. 242–246)]. In fact, however, Forchheimer's interpretation of the data was "that compromises prevail relatively in larger disputes, and that complete workers' victories are more frequent in small disputes" (1948, p. 294). This is consistent with evidence presented by Meyer (1907) for Germany and France (1899–1904) showing that as the size of the strike increases, the proportion of outright victories by either side decreases, in favor of compromise outcomes (1907, pp. 52, 120).

There is no apparent relationship between the unemployment rate and the unions' batting average in Knowles' data (1952, p. 259). Griffin (1939, pp. 90–92), on the other hand, identified nine "business troughs" in the period 1891–1927, and found that the percentage of worker victories decreased in each case.

7. Cyclical fluctuations in strike frequency

The study of cyclical fluctuations in strikes seems to have been initiated in 1921 by Hansen's note in the *American Economic Review*. Taking wholesale prices as "representative of the business cycle", Hansen looked for correlations between the number of workers involved in strikes and the wholesale price index, using annual data for the period 1881-1914. Prices fell by 28 percent over the first 16 years of this period (1881-97), and a weak negative correlation between prices and the number of strikers was found for these years (after correction for trend). From 1898 to 1914, on the other hand, prices gradually returned to the 1880 level, and a positive correlation was found for this period.

Although Hansen's note is now quite famous (at second hand) among labor economists, it is an unconvincing piece of empirical work which was, quite rightly, ignored by his contemporaries. The next mention of cyclical fluctuations in the literature occurred in a different context, when Pigou (1927) examined the possibility that strikes play a causal role in business cycles.

Pigou's opening statement is worth quoting at length, if only as a fine example of how qualifying clauses may be used to keep the reader in his place:

> It seems plain that, whenever the number of men involved in industrial disputes is larger than usual, this must make *pro tanto* for a decline in the prospects of profit elsewhere, and so in aggregate industrial activity, and that, whenever the number so involved is smaller than usual, there is *pro tanto* an impulse toward industrial expansion. For a shortage of the goods produced by one industry, if it lasts long enough to trench seriously upon, not to say to exhaust, accumulated stocks, is bound to lessen the yield, in terms of things in general, of work done in other industries. In view of these considerations there can be little doubt that industrial disputes – or rather excesses and deficiencies in industrial disputes as against the average – are a genuine cause of industrial fluctuations [Pigou (1927, pp. 50-51)].

Pigou looked at data for 1894-1913 "to gauge how important this cause is". He found that the number of days lost by persons involved in stoppages averaged about one day per annum for each worker in the industrial population. He pointed out that stoppages are typically short, and that they are followed by a compensatory effect, so that the loss of output during the strike overstates the true effect of the strike on production. He found no positive correlation between the number of persons involved in strikes and the unemployment rate for 1894-1913, and concluded

> On the whole body of evidence, however, it seems reasonable to conclude that, in recent times at all events, industrial disputes have not played any significant part in causing industrial fluctuations (p. 52).

Pigou noticed an apparent negative correlation between unemployment rates and strike activity, and speculated as to its interpretation:

> ...there is reason to suspect that prosperity in a sense causes disputes, because it stimulates workpeople to try to force a rise of wages more strongly than depression stimulates employers to try to force a fall. ... Moreover, it must be remembered that any compensatory expansion, that takes place after the close of a dispute in the industry where it has occurred, enters into our unemployment figures, though the contraction during the dispute itself in this industry does not (p. 52).

This suggestion of a statistical basis for procyclical variations in strike activity has apparently been forgotten in the literature (although something similar appears in Neumann and Reder (1984), where it is noted that the Commerce Department takes pains to purge the effects of strikes from output data).

Griffin (1939) reviewed U.S. strike data for the period 1880–1937. He concluded:

> ...strikes have continued to oscillate in accordance with two factors... The first is the business cycle which, whether measured by prices or wages, has been reflected in the rise and fall of strikes. ... The second factor is the political climate... (p. 204).

Griffin argued that cycles in the number of strikes corresponded quite closely with cycles in general economic activity, over the period 1880–1937. Using annual data on strikes, and business cycle data compiled by Willard L. Thorp of NBER, he identified 15 peaks in strike activity over this period, and found that 10 of these corresponded to years of general recession or depression.

Knowles (1952) presented graphs showing a rather substantial positive relationship between the number of strikes and the level of wages and prices in Britain, and a slightly less impressive negative relationship between strikes and the unemployment rate. Both Griffin and Knowles placed particular emphasis on the period around 1921. In the United States wholesale prices fell by about 35 percent in 1921. The number of strikes fell from 329 in 1920 to 231 in 1921 and 107 in 1922; a great many of these strikes were against wage decreases, and the number of successes was unusually low. In Britain also wholesale prices fell substantially in 1921, the unemployment rate rose to about 14 percent (from about 3 percent in 1920) and the number of strikes fell by more than 50 percent relative to 1920. Here, too, strikes were largely aimed at avoiding decreases in wages [Knowles (1952, p. 314)].

7.1. Applications of the Burns–Mitchell method

The most convincing evidence of procyclical fluctuations in strike activity was originally developed by Jurkat and Jurkat (1949), and subsequently amplified by

Rees (1952), O'Brien (1965) and Weintraub (1965). Earlier studies used charts and linear correlation coefficients to summarize the relationship between strikes and business activity. The results suggested a positive relationship, but the evidence was weak. Yoder's (1940) interpretation was that

> This analysis would appear to justify the conclusion that, while business conditions are reflected in strikes, there is no simple pattern of covariation. ... If monthly data are correlated, the measure for the 276 months from 1915 through 1937 is $r = 0.16$ (1 percent limit: 0.15).[13] From these calculations it is apparent that no significant covariation in month-to-month or year-to-year fluctuations can be depended upon (p. 234).

Jurkat and Jurkat (1949) applied the Burns–Mitchell–NBER tools for business-cycle analysis to monthly strike data for the period 1915–38. The results were much sharper than the results obtained from essentially the same data set by Yoder (1940), who used more conventional statistical methods. According to Burns and Mitchell (1946), the period contained six business cycles, each of which was divided into nine phases, corresponding to expansion followed by contraction. Phase 1 in the Burns–Mitchell scheme includes three months centered at the initial trough of the cycle, and Phase 5 includes three months centered at the peak. Phase 9 includes three months centered at the terminal trough of the cycle, and this period coincides with Phase 1 of the next cycle. The expansionary Phases 2, 3, and 4 are defined by splitting the months between Phase 1 and Phase 5 into three periods of equal length, and the contractionary Phases 6, 7 and 8 are defined in the same way, between Phases 5 and 9. Thus although Phases 1, 5 and 9 always last exactly three months, the lengths of the intermediate phases vary from cycle to cycle, and the expansionary phases do not generally have the same length as the contractionary phases.

In studying cyclical fluctuations in strikes, the relevance of the Burns–Mitchell analysis is simply that it divides the period under study into subperiods corresponding to alternating phases of the business cycle.[14] On the null hypothesis that strikes are not related to the business cycle, the rate of strike activity should be more or less randomly distributed over these subperiods. On the alternative hypothesis that strikes are procyclical, the number of strikes should be lowest in periods designated as Phase 1, progressively higher in Phases 2, 3 and 4, highest in Phase 5, and progressively lower in Phases 6–9. Rather than examining the number of strikes directly, however, the NBER liturgy recommends the use of index numbers, in which the average number of strikes per month in each cycle serves as the base (which implies that the base of the index changes from one

---

[13] This overstates the significance of the estimated correlation coefficient, since there is no allowance for serial correlation; see Granger and Newbold (1977, pp. 202–214). Thus, Yoder's results are even weaker than he thought.

[14] This assumes, quite reasonably, that data on strikes do not influence the procedure by which business cycle peaks and troughs are identified.

Table 19.1
Burns–Mitchell analysis of U.S. strikes, 1915–80.

Trough Peak Trough (month/year)	Phases of the "reference cycle"								
	1 Trough	2	3 Expansion	4	5 Peak	6	7 Contraction	8	9 Trough
Jurkat and Jurkat (1949)									
1/15 8/18 4/19	31	53	121	122	101	101	118	91	86
4/19 1/20 9/21	76	95	129	99	96	97	74	67	40
9/21 5/23 7/24	111	114	73	100	138	113	104	95	80
7/24 10/26 12/27	106	111	123	105	91	81	82	66	67
12/27 6/29 3/33	79	76	78	103	113	98	97	123	128
3/33 5/37 5/38	41	70	80	113	232	202	130	115	107
Average, 1915–38	74	87	101	107	129	115	101	91	85
Rees (1952)									
5/38 2/45 10/45	74	71	99	119	115	127	132	153	161
10/45 11/48 10/49	147	124	100	84	80	92	97	87	77
Weintraub (1966)									
10/49 7/53 8/54	72	102	106	109	110	96	78	75	71
8/54 7/57 4/58	88	103	110	100	98	91	85	78	79
4/58 5/60 2/61	83	113	109	94	95	91	86	88	88
Average, 1938–61	93	102	105	101	100	99	96	96	95
2/61 12/69 11/70	75	80	92	118	110	129	151	140	120
11/70 11/73 3/75	97	96	94	98	103	113	124	100	93
3/75 1/80 7/80	101	109	105	96	95	83	67	56	75
Average, 1961–80	91	95	97	104	103	108	114	98	96
Average, 1915–80	84	94	102	104	113	108	102	94	91

cycle to the next). This means that changes in the level of strike activity from one cycle to the next are irrelevant, so that, for example, any trend in the number of strikes is assumed to follow a step function, with steps at each cyclical trough.

The results of the Jurkat and Jurkat (1949) study are shown in the first 7 rows of Table 19.1. To illustrate the procedure, consider the entries for Phase 9 of the third cycle, and Phase 1 of the fourth cycle, namely 80 and 106. These entries both refer to the three-month period June–August 1924, in which there were 252 strikes (after seasonal adjustment), or 84 per month. The average number of strikes per month from September 1921 to July 1924 was 105, and 84 is 80 percent of this. Similarly, 84 is 106 percent of 79, which was the average number of strikes per month in the fourth cycle.

The punch line of the Jurkat and Jurkat (1949) analysis is shown in row 7 of Table 19.1, which is a simple average of the strike indices shown in rows 1–6. The movements in the indices for individual cycles seem irregular, but when the data are averaged over six cycles, the pattern of strike activity fits the business cycle *perfectly*. Even though the Burns–Mitchell techniques involve a substantial amount of data manipulation, with virtually no formal statistical foundation, I can think of no reason why the perfect fit obtained in this case should be considered spurious. On the other hand, the statistical significance of the result is difficult to assess. Suppose, for example, that artificial time series were generated by an ARMA (1,1) model, and substituted for the strike series which produced Table 19.1. How often would the artificial series give a perfect fit?

A reasonable conjecture is that a perfect fit should occur by accident no more than once in 64 tries. A perfect fit means that the direction of change is "right" 8 times out of 8. If the first six changes are right, however, the last two will probably follow, since the index for Phase 9 is the same as the index for Phase 1, except for trend correction, and an appropriately weighted average of the index numbers is 100. Thus, the relevant probability is approximately the probability of six heads in six tosses of a fair coin, which is 1 in 64.

Table 19.1 also summarizes the results obtained by Rees (1952) and by Weintraub (1966), covering five additional business cycles over the period from May 1938 to February 1961. One could argue that these results continue to show procyclical fluctuations in strikes, but the fit is less impressive than it was for the earlier period. The last section of Table 19.1 reports estimates[15] for three cycles between February 1961 and July 1980, and again the fit is doubtful. The last row of the table shows, however, that when all 14 cycles between 1915 and 1980 are averaged, the fit is perfect.

In recent years, the Burns–Mitchell method of analyzing business-cycle data has gone out of style, in favor of multivariate regression analysis. This seems unfortunate in the present context. The Burns–Mitchell view of the business cycle was that it could be summarized by the movement of a single index of economic activity.[16] In principle, the advantage of regression models is that they allow the separate influences of several explanatory variables to be disentangled. If the question of interest is whether strikes are procyclical, however, then estimates of regression coefficients miss the point. One must somehow use the regression coefficients to simulate the response of strikes to the typical pattern of co-movements in the explanatory variables over the course of the business cycle. Thus, for example, a negative regression coefficient associated with the unemployment rate does not necessarily mean that strikes are procyclical, if the

---

[15] I am grateful to Wang Xing-he for his very able assistance in carrying out these calculations.

[16] For a modern treatment of business cycles from this point of view, see Sargent and Sims (1977) and Litterman, Quah and Sargent (1984).

regression also includes variables such as prices, wages and profits which may vary systematically with the cycle.

It would be very useful to apply the Burns–Mitchell procedure to separate data series for contract and noncontract strikes. Even if we (tentatively) accept the evidence that strikes are procyclical, we do not know whether this means that the incidence of strikes at contract expiration varies with the state of the economy, or whether it means that a strong economy tends to produce a number of trivial strikes which do not involve contract negotiations, and which might be viewed as little more than spontaneous holidays.

7.2   Empirical applications of the Ashenfelter–Johnson model

The first systematic multiple regression analysis of fluctuations in strike activity appeared less than 20 years ago. Ashenfelter and Johnson (1969) specified a regression equation which was vaguely associated with the theoretical model discussed in Section 4.1 above, and estimated this equation using U.S. data on the number of strikes beginning in each quarter, for the period 1952:1 to 1967:2. A strong negative (i.e. procyclical) relationship was found between strikes and the unemployment rate, and a strong negative relationship was found between strikes and lagged real wage changes; the effect of profits was negligible. When nominal wage and price changes were allowed to enter the regression as separate explanatory variables, each variable was highly significant, and the coefficients were of comparable magnitude and opposite sign. Pencavel (1970) obtained essentially identical results for U.K. quarterly data covering the period 1950:1 to 1967:2. Abbott's (1984) careful and detailed analysis of Canadian data further illustrates the impressive out-of-sample performance of the Ashenfelter–Johnson regression.[17]

Farber (1978) argued that the Ashenfelter–Johnson theoretical model should be tested against micro data. Indeed, given an appropriate stochastic addendum, the theory leads to a strong econometric model of bargaining settlements, strike incidence and strike duration. Farber analyzed data for ten bargaining pairs in U.S. manufacturing industries, covering 80 contracts and 21 strikes over the period 1954–70. In the econometric specification, the unemployment rate was supposed to influence the union's resistance curve through both the concession rate τ and the sticking point y_*, while lagged real wage changes were supposed to influence only y_*. The model was tested against the data on strike incidence: the

---

[17]Turkington (1975) applied a version of the Ashenfelter–Johnson model to quarterly data for New Zealand covering the period 1958:3 to 1971:4. He included a measure of vacancies in addition to the unemployment rate, and he decomposed the real wage change variable into its nominal wage and price components. Lagged price changes and the unemployment and vacancy rates were found to have the expected effects, while profits had a significant negative effect on strikes.

duration data were discarded. The empirical results were weak. The unemployment rate was barely significant in the equation for τ, and neither the unemployment rate nor the real wage change variable was significant in the equation for y_*.

Although Farber (1978) provided a good illustration of the potential empirical applications of Ashenfelter and Johnson's (1969) theoretical model, his empirical results suffered from lack of data: 17 regression coefficients were estimated, using data on just 21 strikes in 80 contracts. Farber (1981) analyzed an extended data set containing 159 contracts signed over the period 1954–79. Here the unemployment rate was not allowed to influence either τ or y_*, but it was allowed to influence y_0. Empirically, however, it turned out that unemployment was not a significant determinant of y_0. An important feature of this specification is that the effect of the unemployment rate on strike duration is closely tied to its effect on strike incidence. To see this, note that a change in y_0 has no effect on the firm's target wage y_T, so that an increase in y_0 must increase the probability of a strike. If y_0 was already above y_T before the increase, then the strike (which would have occurred even when y_0 was low) is prolonged, since the firm must wait longer before the target is reached. Finally, if y_0 was originally below y_T and is then raised above it, there will be a short strike which would not have occurred otherwise. The problem here is that in addition to the evidence of procyclical fluctuations in strike incidence, there is some evidence (to be discussed below) of countercyclical fluctuations in duration. Thus, it would be desirable to have a model in which the unemployment rate is allowed to act independently on incidence and duration.[18]

8. Measurement without theory

The literature on industrial disputes has been marked to a major degree by lack of careful analysis of evidence and statistics and has shown a tendency to rely upon the repetition of a set of generalizations handed down from author to author and preserved with a care that their complete lack of objective verification did not warrant [Griffin (1939, p. 182)].

There has been a great deal of empirical work using aggregate data to measure the determinants of strike activity. Most of the papers are written according to a standard formula. First there is a "theory" section containing an impressionistic

---

[18] Farber (1981) also estimated a "reduced-form" Tobit model of incidence and duration, using a larger data set containing 209 contracts and 34 strikes. This model turned out to have essentially no explanatory power, and in particular the unemployment rate was not significant. If there are variables which move incidence and duration in opposite directions, however, the Tobit model is clearly inappropriate. Tracy's (1984) econometric specification is more flexible, from this point of view: he combined a logit model of incidence with a proportional hazards model of duration, conditional on incidence.

discourse on the factors that make strikes more or less likely to occur. Then these theoretical factors are reduced to a set of imperfectly measured proxy variables. Finally, regression results are obtained which provide suspiciously impressive support for the theoretical insights of the first section. The empirical results are often presented in the breathless style of an encyclopedia salesman.

Despite the bombast, the empirical results of these studies seem quite uncontaminated by theoretical restrictions, so they might be regarded as a mine of information on the facts to be explained. Paldam and Pedersen (1982) surveyed 15 studies using quarterly and annual data for Australia, Britain, Canada, New Zealand and the United States. They tabulated results of regressions with the number of strikes as dependent variable, and various independent variables including the unemployment rate, the inflation rate, and the rate of change of real or nominal wages. When "insignificant" regression coefficients were ignored, a uniform pattern emerged, indicating that strikes are negatively related to the unemployment rate, and to recent real wage increases, and positively related to the inflation rate. Even though the tests of significance in these studies are generally polluted by serial correlation, the uniformity of results is impressive.

Paldam and Pedersen (1982) proceeded to analyze annual data for 15 countries (including the five mentioned above) by regressing the number of strikes per year on the unemployment rate (U) and on contemporaneous changes in the real or nominal wage rate $(DRW$ and $DW)$. In regressions including U and DRW, the U-coefficients were mixed, but the DRW coefficients were negative for just two countries (including the United States), and positive for the other thirteen. When nominal instead of real wages were used, the U-coefficients were again mixed, and the DW coefficients were all positive, except for one or two countries where strike activity is negligible in any case (Holland, Norway).[19]

A serious deficiency in these results is that no trend terms were included in the regressions. In addition, since many countries were considered, the data analysis for each country was necessarily superficial. Very detailed and careful analyses of postwar quarterly data for the United States, Britain[20] and Canada have been reported by Ashenfelter and Johnson (1969), Pencavel (1970) and Abbott (1984), respectively, and in each of these studies a significant negative relationship was found between strikes and the unemployment rate, and between strikes and lagged real wage increases. Although Paldam and Pedersen (1982) confirmed

---

[19] Very similar results were reported for two overlapping sample periods: 1953–72 and 1956–75. In a related study, Pedersen (1982) analysed data for 23 countries covering the inter-war period 1919–39. His regression results matched the Paldam and Pedersen (1982) postwar results quite closely: the regression coefficient on DW was positive in 16 of 18 countries. Again, no trend term was included in the regressions. It would be useful to extend the Paldam–Pedersen analysis to include current and past inflation rates; the high degree of serial correlation found in the strike series also warrants attention.

[20] An extensive study of British strikes over the period 1946–73 has recently been published by Durcan, McCarthy and Redman (1983). Unfortunately, this volume came to my notice too late to be given the attention it apparently deserves.

these results for the United States, they reported quite different results for Britain and Canada. It is essential that the conflicts in these results be resolved if any progress is to be made toward general agreement on the facts to be explained.

Paldam and Pedersen (1982) reported an almost uniformly positive relationship between strike activity and the rate of wage inflation (without controlling for trend). Kaufman (1981) also reported a significant positive relationship between strikes and inflation in quarterly data for U.S. manufacturing, over the period 1954–75. Unfortunately, while Kaufman's regressions did include a trend variable, he failed to control for seasonality, so that the results are difficult to interpret. Although there is no convincing theory which predicts a relationship between inflation and strikes, it seems intuitively reasonable that such a relationship might exist. For example, inflation might disrupt the established wage structure, as Paldam and Pedersen (1982) suggest, or it might increase the degree of uncertainty as to the size of the pie. In any case, correlations between inflation rates and strike activity should surely be included near the top of the list of the desirable stylized facts.

Paldam and Pedersen (1984) examined several potential explanations for trends in strike activity, using annual data for 18 countries over the period 1919–79. In some countries (Holland, Germany, Switzerland, Scandinavia and Austria) the level of strike activity declined enormously over this period. One theory is that strong labor movements reduce conflict levels. As Paldam and Pedersen (1984) pointed out, this theory does a good job of explaining the trends in some countries, but it fails to explain Germany, Holland and Switzerland, where strike activity is very low, but the union movement is weak.

9. The incidence of contract strikes

9.1. Measuring strike incidence

Strikes are rare. Pigou's (1927) estimate that the average industrial worker spends one day a year on strike (see above) gives the right order of magnitude.

The natural way to measure the incidence of (contract) strikes is to count contract expirations, and then ask what proportion led to a strike. There is a serious difficulty with this when data on contracts and on strikes are collected separately, as is the case in the United States, since a laborious (and not always successful) matching effort is required.[21]

---

[21] The quality of the U.S. strike data has deteriorated further in recent years. Prior to 1982, the Bureau of Labor Statistics collected data on all work stoppages involving at least 6 workers. Because of budget cuts implemented in 1982, however, the U.S. data are now restricted to work stoppages involving at least 1000 workers.

The best available information on strike incidence is contained in the data on Canadian labor contracts, where the occurrence or nonoccurrence of a strike is recorded for each contract negotiation. These data have been analyzed by Riddell (1979), Dussault and Lacroix (1980), Swidinsky and Vanderkamp (1982) and Gunderson, Kervin and Reid (1985). The incidence of strikes in Canadian manufacturing over the period 1967–75 was estimated as 13.5 percent (222 strikes in 1641 contracts) by Swidinsky and Vanderkamp (1982). An incidence estimate of 15.7 percent (383 strikes in 2437 contracts) was reported by Gunderson, Kervin and Reid (1985), referring to all industries other than construction over the period 1971–83.

Despite the difficulties involved in matching contract data with strike data for the United States, several data sets have been assembled which include contracts reached both with and without strikes. Farber (1978) obtained data on contracts and strikes for 10 bargaining pairs covering the period 1954–70; this data set was extended in Farber (1981) to cover 19 pairs over the period 1954–79 (18 of these pairs were in manufacturing industries).[22] The incidence of strikes in Farber's (1981) data was 16 percent (34 strikes in 209 contracts); the average strike duration was 43 days. Mauro (1982) constructed a similar data set, covering 14 bargaining pairs[23] over various periods, starting between 1952 and 1959, and ending between 1974 and 1978. The incidence of strikes here was 23 percent (34 strikes in 149 contracts).

Gramm (1985) matched strikes and contract expirations involving 1000 workers or more for the period 1971–80. The incidence of strikes in this data set (which is not restricted to manufacturing) was 13.3 percent (801 strikes in 6046 contracts). Tracy (1984) matched strikes and contracts for manufacturing industries over the period 1973–77. Coverage was restricted to contracts involving 1000 workers or more, and organizational and sympathy strikes were excluded. Tracy's estimate of strike incidence was 11.5 percent (242 strikes in 2113 contracts)[24] with considerable variation across different two-digit industries.[25]

In the United States most labor contracts last for three years. If about 15 percent of all contract negotiations lead to strikes, which last about 40 days, on average, then the average U.S. worker who is involved in collective bargaining spends about two days a year striking over contract terms. Contract strikes account for about 50 percent of all U.S. strikes [Kennan (1980a)]; strikes

---

[22] Fudenberg, Levine and Ruud (1983) used a subset of these data.

[23] Five of these pairs are included in Farber's (1981) data.

[24] Tracy's empirical analysis of the determinants of strike incidence and duration is based a subsample of 1319 contracts. The incidence of strikes in the subsample was apparently 15 percent (Table 6, p. 20b), which is quite different from the 11.5 percent figure for the entire data set. According to data published by BLS [U.S. Department of Labor (1981)] there were 27612 strikes over the period 1973–77, of which 11784 (43 percent) were in manufacturing. Of the manufacturing strikes, 677 (6 percent) involved 1000 workers or more.

[25] Clearly, we should encourage a merger of the Gramm and Tracy data sets.

involving organization or recognition of a union account for another 10 percent, approximately, and the duration of these strikes is similar to the duration of contract strikes. The remaining strikes (40 percent), including strikes during the term of a contract, typically last less than a week. Taking all these strikes together, it seems safe to say that the average worker involved in bargaining spends less than three days a year on strike. According to Freeman and Medoff (1979), only about 30 percent of U.S. wage and salary workers are covered by collective bargaining agreements. So to indicate the appropriate order of magnitude, it can be said that a typical U.S. worker spends less than one day on strike every year.

I know of no estimates of strike incidence for countries outside North America. No doubt this is largely because of institutional differences; for example, labor contracts in Britain or Australia are much less formal than in North America. Paldam and Pedersen (1982) provided some broader international comparisons for the period 1948–75. They reported 150000 days lost per million inhabitants for the United States, which would mean about 1.5 days for each worker covered by collective bargaining, or about half a day for each wage and salary worker. The corresponding figure for Britain was 57000 days per million inhabitants, and of the 17 industrial countries covered, only Italy (180000) had a higher figure than the United States.

9.2. Cyclical fluctuations in strike incidence

The empirical studies discussed in Section 7 above contain fairly convincing evidence of procyclical fluctuations in the frequency of strikes. This does not necessarily imply that strike incidence is procyclical. First, the strike frequency variable in these studies includes wildcat and other strikes in addition to contract strikes. Second, the frequency variable does not control for variations in the number of contract expirations;[26] this is potentially of considerable importance, since the bargaining calendar is quite irregular.

Unfortunately, the studies which have used micro data do not provide reliable measures of cyclical variations in strike incidence. The main problem is that the micro data sets do not have many observations in the time dimension, so that it is difficult to estimate cyclical effects. Tracy's (1984) data, for example, cover just 5 years. He used one-step-ahead forecasts of state and industry employment levels to measure variations in economic conditions. Most of the variance in these variables is presumably cross-sectional.

It would apparently be possible, however, to get a time series of at least 20 years for Canada, by splicing data for 1964–75 used by Dussault and Lacroix

---

[26] Kaufman (1981) is a partial exception.

(1980) with data for 1971–83 used by Gunderson, Kervin and Reid (1985). In the meantime, perhaps the best that can be done is to crudely splice the results of these studies. Dussault and Lacroix (1980) reported a positive relationship between strike incidence and an index of vacancies; the relationship was significant for the private sector as a whole, but of marginal significance for manufacturing. Gunderson, Kervin and Reid (1985) reported a significant negative relationship between strike incidence and a measure of "demand deficient" unemployment, for private industries other than construction. On the basis of these studies one might tentatively conclude that procyclical fluctuations in strike frequency are due, at least in part, to procyclical fluctuations in the incidence of contract strikes.

10. The duration of strikes

10.1. Hazard function estimates

By comparison with the large number of empirical studies of strike frequency, there has been very little econometric work on duration. There is, however, a small but informative statistical literature on strike duration, which was apparently started by Horvath (1968). The aim here was to characterize the probability distribution from which strike durations are drawn and, in particular, to investigate the hazard function associated with this distribution. Horvath (1968) showed that the Weibull distribution, with a downward-sloping (log-linear) hazard function, gives a good fit to data on all U.S. strikes ending in 1961.[27] Horvath's estimated distribution fits very well for the period 1953–74 also, but it conceals very large differences between the distributions for contract and noncontract strikes [Kennan (1980a)]. Lancaster (1972) found that the inverse Gaussian distribution gave a good fit for data on British strikes beginning in 1965, but Newby and Winterton (1983) have shown that this too conceals large differences between the distributions for "official" and "unofficial" strikes.

Horvath's estimates imply that the remaining life expectancy of strikes *increases* with strike age. Thus, given two strikes, A and B, which are currently in effect, and given that B has already been going on for a long time, while A has just recently begun, strike A will probably end before B. This is largely due to heterogeneity in the population of strikes. In particular, the probability of settling a contract strike is generally less than 4 percent per day, while the corresponding probability for a strike during the term of a contract may be as high as 40 percent per day.

---

[27]For good measure, Horvath showed that the Weibull distribution explains the duration of wars equally well.

In light of recent interest in the analysis of duration data drawn from mixtures of heterogeneous distributions [see, for example, Heckman and Singer (1984)], it is worth asking whether the high degree of heterogeneity in the strike duration data can be detected by estimating mixed-distribution models. On this question, the evidence is strikingly mixed. Morrison and Schmittlein (1980) re-analyzed Horvath's and Lancaster's data, using a model which allows for heterogeneity by mixing Weibull distributions according to a gamma distribution. They found that the strike data were "consistent with a relatively homogeneous population (in terms of mean strike duration)" (p. 237).[28] On the other hand, Newby and Winterton (1983) estimated Weibull, log-normal and inverse Gaussian distributions, using data on strikes in Britain over the period 1966–73, and found that none of these gave a satisfactory fit. "However, mixed distributions did provide a satisfactory fit with the proportions corresponding roughly to the proportions of official and unofficial strikes" (p. 64). Unfortunately, the details of these estimates were not reported, so it is impossible to determine why the mixed distribution model worked in this case, and failed in the Morrison and Schmittlein (1980) analysis.[29]

A serious limitation of the duration models described above is that they impose arbitrary (and probably false) restrictions on the shape of the hazard function. The Weibull distribution has a monotonic hazard function, and the hazard rate for both the log-normal and inverse Gaussian distributions rises initially, reaches a peak, and then falls toward some asymptotic value [Lancaster (1972), Kalbfleisch and Prentice (1980)]. According to estimates presented in Kennan (1985), the most likely hazard function for strike duration is basically U-shaped. This could presumably be generated by some mixture of upward-sloping hazard functions, but this imposes heterogeneity, rather than allowing the data to speak for themselves. Moreover, the gamma mixture of Weibulls used by Morrison and Schmittlein (1980) generates an inverted U-shaped aggregate hazard function.

It is difficult to find an economic explanation for the apparent decline in strike hazard rates over the first few months [Kennan (1980a)]. This suggests that it may be worthwhile to analyze mixtures of distributions with increasing hazard functions, in order to characterize the conditions under which the aggregate hazard function will be U-shaped. Unless further restrictions are forthcoming from

[28] Similarly, although Horvath did not consider mixture distributions, he observed that "the strike data...constitute a homogeneous population" (p. 26).

[29] One possibility, suggested (in another context) by Heckman and Singer (1984), is that the two-point mixture distributions (presumably) used by Newby and Winterton (1983) are more flexible than the gamma distribution. In particular, the gamma distribution cannot give a good approximation to a bimodal distribution corresponding to the classification of strikes by contract status. Morrison and Schmittlein (1980) recognized this, and presented estimates for a two-point mixture of exponential distributions, using Horvath's data. They found, however, that this model gave a much poorer fit than a gamma mixture of exponentials, which was dominated in turn by a gamma mixture of Weibulls.

economic theory, however, this analysis seems unlikely to yield substantive results.

10.2. *Cyclical fluctuations in duration*

In order to measure cyclical fluctuations in strike duration, Kennan (1985) analyzed the influence of industrial production on the hazard function, using data on contract strikes in U.S. manufacturing involving 1000 workers or more, over the period 1968 through 1976. Given the short duration of most strikes, it seems reasonable to associate a fixed value of industrial production with each strike. First, seasonal and trend components were removed from monthly data on industrial production in manufacturing (measured in logs), by taking the residual from a regression on time, time squared and monthly dummies. Then each strike was assigned the residual value of industrial production for the month in which the strike began.

Hazard functions were estimated for the two disjoint subsamples obtained by classifying strikes according to whether industrial production was above or below its mean (in the month when the strike began).[30] Statistically significant counter-cyclical variations were found in the duration of strikes. The shape of the estimated hazard function was stable across the two samples: for example, in each case the hazard rate reached a minimum after about three months. The countercyclical variation in hazard rates was substantial, particularly in the first two months or so. For example, the mean duration of strikes when industrial production was high was 37.2 days, as compared with a mean duration of 52.3 days when industrial production was low.[31] On the other hand, the number of high-industrial production strikes was 325, as compared with only 241 low-industrial production strikes. This is consistent with the evidence discussed above, showing that the frequency of strikes varies procyclically.

Thus, an intriguing empirical regularity appears. The incidence and duration of contract strikes move in opposite directions over the business cycle: incidence is procyclical, and duration is countercyclical.[32] If this regularity holds up under more detailed econometric analysis it should provide a powerful screening device

---

[30] These hazard functions were estimated using a generalized version of the beta-logit model discussed by Heckman and Willis (1977); see Kennan (1985) for details.

[31] These results were based on a limited data set. Harrison and Stewart (1985), however, have analyzed a comprehensive set of data on Canadian contract strikes in manufacturing for the years 1971–80, and they also found significant countercyclical movements in duration.

[32] A very early piece of evidence on this can be found in Bevan (1880). During the boom years of 1872 and 1873 there were 343 and 365 strikes, respectively, by Bevan's count; the duration of the average strike was 20 days in 1872 and 21 days in 1873. A severe recession occurred in 1879; the number of strikes was 308 (excluding December) and the average strike duration was 27 days.

for alternative theories of strikes. For example, it is difficult to see how the joint cost theory can explain opposite movements in incidence and duration.[33]

So far, only Tracy (1984) has attempted to confront a serious economic theory of contract strikes with data on both incidence and duration. Tracy's theoretical model is a variant of the Hayes model discussed in Section 5.1 above, leading to the prediction that strikes are more likely when the pie is relatively small, or when the union is more uncertain about the size of the pie. It is difficult to sort out the cyclical pattern in Tracy's empirical results, because the set of explanatory variables includes many competing cyclical indicators, and because the data cover only five years. If one argues that cross-section and time-series variations in economic conditions have similar effects on strike activity, then the dominant cyclical variable appears to be a measure of the one-step-ahead forecast of employment for the state in which the bargaining pair is located. The effect of this variable is robust under various alternative specifications: the effect on strike incidence is significantly positive, and the effect on duration is significantly negative. Under Tracy's interpretation of the private information model, any variable which has a positive effect on incidence should also have a positive effect on duration, so the theory cannot explain the opposing cyclical movements in incidence and duration. As was argued in Section 5.5 above, however, the empirical implications of the private information theory are subtle, in general, and some version of this theory might well provide a plausible explanation of the facts.

11. The seasonality of strikes

There is a high degree of seasonal variation in strike activity. Yoder (1938) analyzed data on U.S. strikes beginning between January 1927 and December 1936, and found a statistically significant pattern. The average number of strikes beginning in May was 139 percent of the annual average, while the number beginning in December was 52 percent of the annual average (Table VI, p. 693). The amplitude of these variations was an order of magnitude greater than the amplitude of seasonal variations in general business activity. Yoder (1940, p. 231) cited estimates by Kuznets showing that business activity peaks in the spring and fall months at about 105 percent of the annual average, with troughs in the summer and winter at about 95 percent.

Griffin (1939) showed that the seasonal pattern found by Yoder held also for U.S. data covering the period 1915–26. Moreover, a remarkably similar pattern was reported by Knowles (1952, pp. 157–159) for British data covering the

---

[33] On the other hand, it seems quite easy to rig the Ashenfelter–Johnson model to explain these empirical results, but this is hardly a virtue of the model.

period 1919–39. Here too the number of strikes peaked in May and fell off drastically in December, and the amplitude of the British seasonal fluctuations was also much greater than the amplitude of seasonal fluctuations in business activity.

Even though these seasonal fluctuations are regular and very large, no serious effort has been made to explain them. Griffin (1939) implied that the question is not worth thinking about:

> The seasonal movement of strikes is in general determined by two elements, first the already-existing pattern of business, and second the greater capacity for resistance on the part of employees in the early summer and late summer as opposed to spring and winter. Here, as elsewhere, the weather shapes the affairs of men (p. 54).

Given that seasonal variations in strikes are very much larger than seasonal variations in business activity, the "pattern of business" explanation is implausible. The weather is of course a good candidate to explain seasonal variations, but I know of no attempt to test this explanation. For example, it would be interesting to know whether the seasonal pattern in San Diego is similar to the pattern in Chicago. It is not true that the seasonal pattern in the southern hemisphere is a mirror image of the northern pattern. Geare (1972) showed that the seasonal trough in New Zealand occurs in December, at 41 percent of the annual average, so it seems fair to say that Christmas has a much more important effect on strikes than the weather.

Both Knowles (1952, p. 160) and Geare (1972, p. 326) suggest that strikes are timed so as not to interfere with vacations.[34] Alternatively, strikes might be regarded as a substitute for vacations. Of course, one must be careful about analyzing the optimal timing of strikes, since if the argument is taken too far, the optimal time may be never. Still, it may be sensible in some contexts to take the occurrence of strikes as given, and build a cost-minimizing theory of timing.

Ashenfelter and Johnson (1969) suggested that seasonality in strikes is caused by seasonality in contract expirations. Indeed, it is evident from casual inspection of the BLS *Bargaining Calendar* [U.S. Department of Labor (1980)] that there are huge seasonal variations in the number of contracts expiring by month. If this is the explanation for seasonality in strikes, then one should not expect to find a seasonal pattern in strikes occurring during the term of a contract. Flaherty (1983), however, reported very substantial seasonal variation in such strikes, in U.S. quarterly data for the period 1961–77. More direct evidence was given by Gramm (1985), who tabulated the incidence of contract strikes by month for the U.S. over the period 1971–1980 (Table 19.2). These figures show clearly that the

---

[34] See also Durcan, McCarthy and Redman (1983, p. 213).

Table 19.2

	Jan.	Feb.	Mar.	Apr.	May	June	July	Aug.	Sept.	Oct.	Nov.	Dec.
Negotiations	374	328	614	677	644	735	542	617	546	418	289	263
Strikes	57	48	131	82	71	111	71	53	65	49	48	15
Incidence (%)	15.2	14.7	21.3	12.1	11.0	15.1	13.1	8.5	11.9	11.7	16.6	5.7

seasonality of U.S. strikes cannot be explained by seasonality in the bargaining calendar. For example, the average incidence was 21.3 percent (131 strikes in 614 negotiations) in March, as compared with only 5.7 percent (15 strikes in 263 negotiations) in December.

12. Strikes and stock prices

When a labor contract involving a publicly-owned firm is negotiated, the stock market must assess the implications of the negotiations for the value of the firm. This means that stock market data are a potentially rich source of information about the economic role of labor contracts, and in particular about the economics of strikes. This point was first recognized by Neumann (1980), who analyzed the excess returns to a sample of firms involved in strikes over the period 1967–75. Using standard methods from the finance literature, Neumann (1980) first estimated what the market value of each firm would have been on each day within three weeks of the starting and ending dates of the strike, if the strike had not in fact occurred. The difference between the actual market value and this estimated value (the "excess return") was attributed to the effects of the strike.

A major finding of Neumann's (1980) analysis was that (on average) excess returns were significantly negative on the day when a strike began, and significantly positive on the day when it ended. Excess returns were also negative for the days immediately preceding the beginning of the strike. One implication is that although strikes may be predictable to some extent, they cannot be predicted perfectly. If strikes are exogenous events the results also imply that strikes are costly to the firm, and in fact Neumann (1980) estimated the cost of an average strike as about 0.9 percent of the value of the firm. The private information theory suggests an interesting alternative interpretation, however. If the managers of the firm have information which is not fully understood by the stock market, then the theory implies that strikes will occur when the managers believe that the firm is overvalued by the market. In this case the occurrence of a strike reveals new information which decreases the market value of the firm, but one cannot infer anything about the cost of the strike.

There is certainly room for further work in this area. Starting with a complete set of contract negotiations it would be very useful to compare changes in market value for those firms which reach agreement without a strike with the corresponding changes for firms which become involved in a strike. A detailed analysis of the relationship between market value and strike duration would also be of interest. Finally, a systematic analysis of stock market data using a private information model of strikes could lead to substantial advances in both theoretical and empirical knowledge.

13. Experimental analysis of strikes

Experimental data provide a potentially rich source of information about strike behavior. So far, very little work has been done in this area. It is true that there is a large experimental literature on bargaining, but this is of limited relevance. In the bargaining literature, Pareto optimality is taken for granted and the investigation centers on the division of the pie. In studying strikes, however, the question of interest is, under what circumstances is a bargaining pair more or less likely to reach an agreement on the Pareto frontier?

Malouf and Roth (1981) reported an experiment involving binary lottery games (as described in Section 3.1 above) where the share of the pie which could be achieved by one player was constrained. A total of 90 lottery tickets was available to be divided, and it was stipulated that Two could receive no more than M of these tickets (each player received $5 for sure, and a player who received x tickets would have an x percent chance of winning an extra $5). When M was set to 90 it was found that the players almost always agreed to an equal division, with each receiving 45 tickets. This is a well-established result in the experimental literature: when a bargaining game is symmetric, "strikes" do not occur, and the outcome is an equal split of the pie. When M was set to 40 or 50, however, a significant number of strikes was observed, even though in the latter case an equal split was still feasible. Malouf and Roth (1981) concluded that asymmetry in a bargaining situation appears to be a prerequisite for strikes. Although bargaining between workers and firms involves obvious asymmetries, it is not clear how one could say that one bargaining situation is more asymmetric than another, so as to predict when a strike is more likely to occur.

Coursey (1982) reported an experiment in which each bargaining pair played a repeated bilateral monopoly game with a limited time (128 seconds) allowed for negotiation in each period. The buyer did not know the seller's supply curve, nor did the seller know the buyer's demand curve. In 146 periods involving seven bargaining pairs there were 47 "strikes". Coursey (1982) claimed that the strikes were caused by the time limit, but since this was fixed for all of the reported plays of the experiment the claim is moot. In any case it is difficult to find a convincing analog for the time limit in practical collective bargaining situations.

The joint cost and private information theories of strikes are natural candidates for experimental analysis.[35] In fact the expected payoff from carefully specified experimental studies is probably larger than the expected payoff from any other applied studies of strikes, given the present state of the literature.

14. Conclusion

The economic analysis of strikes begins with the "Hicks Paradox": it is impossible to build a bargaining model in which each side behaves optimally but the outcome is not Pareto optimal. This paradox can be circumvented in several ways. Ashenfelter and Johnson (1969) assumed that only one side behaves optimally. The joint cost theory proposed by Reder and Neumann (1980) and by Kennan (1980a) treats bargaining as a black box, and assumes that there is a tendency toward Pareto optimal outcomes which is stronger when strikes are more expensive. Finally, the private information theory is based on the idea that strikes are Pareto optimal after all, when incentive-compatibility constraints are taken into account.

It is difficult to assess the extent of empirical knowledge on economic aspects of strikes. We do know that strikes are rare, which is perhaps contrary to popular belief. In addition, we know that strikes are systematically related to economic variables, although these relationships are not well understood, nor have they been precisely measured. There is persuasive although not conclusive evidence that the frequency and (more importantly and more doubtfully) the incidence of strikes are positively related to general cyclical movements in the economy. There is also some recently developed evidence that strike duration is negatively related to the cycle. There are very large seasonal movements in strike activity which we do not understand. Beyond this, there is a disorganized mass of empirical work which may contain some useful pieces of information.

As to the prospects for future research, three topics stand out. First, the private information theory should be systematically developed, with particular emphasis on empirical implications. Second, detailed econometric analysis of micro-data on contracts reached with and without strikes should prove very useful, particularly if these data cover substantial periods of time. Finally, the development of empirically useful theoretical hypotheses should be stimulated by experimental simulations of the circumstances under which strikes are more likely to occur.

---

[35]Some preliminary results for the joint cost theory have been reported by Sopher (1985).

References

Abbott, Michael G. (1984) "Specification tests of quarterly econometric models of aggregate strike frequency in Canada", in: Ronald G. Ehrenberg, ed., *Research in labor economics*, vol. 6, 177–250.

Ashenfelter, Orley and David E. Bloom (1984) "Models of arbitrator behavior: theory and evidence", *American Economic Review*, 74:111–124.

Ashenfelter, Orley and George E. Johnson (1969) "Bargaining theory, trade unions and industrial strike activity", *American Economic Review*, 59:35–49.

Bevan, G. Phillips (1880) "The strikes of the past ten years", *Journal of the Statistical Society*, 43:35–54.

Bishop, Robert L. (1963) "Game-theoretic analyses of bargaining", *Quarterly Journal of Economics*, 77:559–602.

Blackorby, Charles and David Donaldson (1983) "A suggestion for reducing the social costs of labour disputes without biasing the outcome", Discussion Paper No. 83-01, Department of Economics, University of British Columbia.

Burns, Arthur F. and Wesley C. Mitchell (1946) *Measuring business cycles*. New York: National Bureau of Economic Research.

Coursey, Don (1982) "Bilateral bargaining, Pareto optimality, and the empirical frequency of impass", *Journal of Economic Behavior and Organization*, 3:243–259.

Crawford, Vincent P. and Hal R. Varian (1979) "Distortion of preferences and the Nash theory of bargaining", *Economics Letters*, 3:203–206.

Cross, John G. (1965) "A theory of the bargaining process", *American Economic Review*, 55:67–94.

Cross, John G. (1969) *The economics of bargaining*. New York: Basic Books.

Debs, Eugene V. (1904) *Unionism and socialism; a plea for both*. Terre Haute: Standard Publishing Co.

Durcan, J. W., W. E. J. McCarthy and G. P. Redman (1983) *Strikes in post-war Britain: a study of stoppages of work due to industrial disputes, 1946–73*. London: Allen & Unwin.

Dussault, Francois and Robert Lacroix (1980) "Activite de Greve: un test des hypotheses explicatives traditionnelles", *Canadian Journal of Economics*, 13:632–644.

Edwards, Paul K. (1981) *Strikes in the United States 1881–1974*. New York: St. Martin's Press.

Farber, Henry S. (1978) "Bargaining theory, wage outcomes and the occurrence of strikes: an econometric analysis", *American Economic Review*, 68:262–271.

Farber, Henry S. (1981) "Union wages and minimum wages", *Report of the minimum wage study commission*, Vol. VI, 105–134.

Flaherty, Sean (1983) "Contract status and the economic determinants of strike activity", *Industrial Relations*, 22(1):20–33.

Forchheimer, K. (1948) "Some international aspects of the strike movement", *Bulletin of the Oxford University Institute of Statistics*, 10:9–24 and 294–304.

Freeman, Richard B. and James L. Medoff (1979) "New estimates of private sector unionism in the United States", *Industrial and Labor Relations Review*, 32(2):143–174.

Fudenberg, Drew, David Levine and Paul Ruud (1983) "Strike activity and wage settlements", NBER Conference on the Economics of Trade Unions.

Geare, A. J. (1972) "Seasonal influences on strike intensity in New Zealand", *The Journal of Industrial Relations*, 14:323–329.

Gramm, Cynthia L. (1984) "The impact of strike incidence and length on negotiated wage settlements: U.S. micro-level evidence", Unpublished Working Paper, University of Iowa.

Gramm, Cynthia L. (1985) "New U.S. industry, union, and time series estimates of the propensity to strike during contract negotiations", Unpublished Working Paper, University of Iowa.

Granger, C. W. J. and Paul Newbold (1977) *Forecasting economic time series*. New York: Academic Press.

Griffin, John I. (1939) *Strikes: a study in quantitative economics*. New York: Columbia University Press. (reprinted by AMS Press, 1968).

Gunderson, Morley, John Kervin and Frank Reid (1985) "Logit estimates of strike incidence from Canadian contract data", unpublished paper, University of Toronto.

Hall, Robert E. and David M. Lilien (1979) "Efficient wage bargains under uncertain supply and demand", *American Economic Review*, 69(6):868–879.

Hamermesh, Daniel S. (1973) "Who 'wins' in wage bargaining", *Industrial and Labor Relations Review*, 26:1146–1149.

Hansen, Alvin H. (1921) "Cycles of strikes", *American Economic Review*, XI:616–621.

Harris, Milton and Robert M. Townsend (1981) "Resource allocation under asymmetric information", *Econometrica*, 49:33–64.

Harrison, Alan and Mark B. Stewart (1985) "Cyclical fluctuations in strike duration", preliminary draft.

Harsanyi, John C. (1977) *Rational behavior and bargaining equilibrium in games and social situations*. New York: Cambridge University Press.

Hayes, Beth (1984) "Unions and strikes with asymmetric information", *Journal of Labor Economics*, 2.

Heckman, J. and B. Singer (1984) "A method for minimizing the impact of distributional assumptions in econometric models for duration data", *Econometrica*, 52:271–320.

Heckman, James J. and Robert J. Willis (1977) "A beta-logistic model for the analysis of sequential labor force participation by married women", *Journal of Political Economy*, 85:27–58.

Hibbs, Douglas A., Jr. (1976) "Industrial conflict in advanced industrial societies", *The American Political Science Review*, 70:1033–1058.

Hicks, J. R. (1963) *The theory of wages*, 2nd edn. London: Macmillan.

Horvath, W. J. (1968) "A statistical model for the duration of wars and strikes", *Behavioral Science*, 13:18–28.

Huebner, Grover G. (1905) "The statistical aspect of the strike", in: Wisconsin Bureau of Labor Statistics, Twelfth Biennial Report, 73–147.

Jurkat, Ernest H. and Dorothy B. Jurkat (1949) "Economic function of strikes", *Industrial and Labor Relations Review*, 2(4):527–545.

Kalbfleisch, J. D. and R. L. Prentice (1980) *The statistical analysis of failure time data*. New York: John Wiley.

Kaufman, Bruce E. (1981) "Bargaining theory, inflation, and cyclical strike activity in manufacturing", *Industrial and Labor Relations Review*, 34:333–355.

Kaufman, Bruce E. (1982) "The determinants of strikes in the United States, 1900–1977", *Industrial and Labor Relations Review*, 35:473–490.

Kennan, John (1980a) "Pareto optimality and the economics of strike duration", *Journal of Labor Research*, 1:77–94.

Kennan, John (1980b) "The effect of unemployment insurance payments on strike duration", in: *Unemployment compensation: studies and research*. National Commission on Unemployment Compensation, Vol. 2.

Kennan, John (1985) "The duration of strikes in U.S. manufacturing", *Journal of Econometrics*.

Kerr, Clark and Abraham Siegel (1954) "The interindustry propensity to strike—an international comparison", in: Arthur Kornhauser, Robert Dubin and Arthur M. Ross, eds., *Industrial Conflict*. New York: McGraw-Hill.

Knowles, Kenneth G. J. C. (1952) *Strikes: a study in industrial conflict*. Oxford: Basil Blackwell.

Lancaster, Tony (1972) "A stochastic model for the duration of a strike", *Journal of the Royal Statistical Society*, A135:257–271.

Litterman, Robert B., Danny Quah and Thomas J. Sargent (1984) "Business cycle analysis with unobservable index models and the methods of the NBER", unpublished paper.

Luce, R. Duncan and Howard Raiffa (1957) *Games and decisions*. New York: John Wiley & Sons.

McCalmont, David B. (1962) "The semi-strike", *Industrial and Labor Relations Review*, 15:191–208.

Malouf, Michael W. K. and Alvin E. Roth (1981) "Disagreement in bargaining", *Journal of Conflict Resolution*, 25(2):329–384.

Marceau, Le Roy and Richard A. Musgrave (1949) "Strikes in essential industries: a way out", *Harvard Business Review*, 27:286–292.

Mauro, Martin J. (1982) "Strikes as a result of imperfect information", *Industrial and Labor Relations Review*, 35:522–538.

Meyer, Maximilian (1907) *Statistik der Streiks und Aussperrungen im In und Auslande*. Leipzig: Verlag.

Moore, Henry L. (1911) *Laws of wages*. New York: MacMillan.

Morrison, D. G. and D. C. Schmittlein (1980) "Jobs, strikes and wars: probability models for duration", *Organizational Behavior and Human Performance*, 25:224–251.

Morton, Sanford (1983) "The optimality of strikes in labor negotiations", Discussion Paper No. 83/7. New Orleans, LA.: Tulane University.

Myerson, Roger (1984a) "Two-person bargaining problems with incomplete information", *Econometrica*, 52(2):461–488.

Myerson, Roger (1984b) "An introduction to game theory", CMSEMS Discussion Paper No. 623, Northwestern University.

Nash, John F., Jr. (1950) "The bargaining problem", *Econometrica*, 18:155–162.

Neumann, George R. (1980) "The predictability of strikes: evidence from the stock market", *Industrial* and *Labor Relations Review*, 33(4):525–535.

Newby, Martin and Jonathan Winterton (1983) "The duration of industrial stoppages", *Journal of the Royal Statistical Society*, A146:62–70.

O'Brien, F. S. (1965) "Industrial conflict and business fluctuations: a comment", *Journal of Political Economy*, LXXIII(6):650–654.

Paldam, Martin and Peder J. Pedersen (1982) "The macroeconomic strike model: a study of seventeen countries, 1948–1975", *Industrial and Labor Relations Review*, 35:504–521.

Paldam, Martin and Peder J. Pedersen (1984) "The large pattern of industrial conflict—a comparative study of 18 countries 1919–79", *International Journal of Social Economics*.

Pedersen, Peder J. (1982) "Industrial conflicts in the inter-war years—a quantitative reappraisal", Memo 1982-2, Institute of Economics, University of Aarhus.

Pencavel, John H. (1970) "An investigation into industrial strike activity in Britain", *Economica*, 37:239–256.

Peterson, Florence (1938) "Review of Strikes in the United States", *Monthly Labor Review*, 46:1047–1067.

Peterson, Florence (1971) *Strikes in the United States, 1880–1936*, U.S. Bureau of Labor Statistics, Bulletin No. 651. Originally published in 1938; republished by Scholarly Press, St. Clair Shores, MI, 1971.

Pigou, Arthur C. (1927) *Industrial fluctuations*. London: MacMillan.

Reder, Melvin W. and George R. Neumann (1980) "Conflict and contract: the case of strikes", *Journal of Political Economy*, 88:867–886.

Reder, Melvin W. and George R. Neumann "The cost of strikes and the inter-industry wage structure", unpublished manuscript.

Rees, Albert (1952) "Industrial conflict and business fluctuations", *Journal of Political Economy*, 60:371–382.

Riddell, W. Craig (1979) "The effects of strikes and strike length on negotiated wage settlements", Research Paper 79-9, Department of Economics, University of Alberta.

Ross, Arthur M. and Paul T. Hartman (1960) *Changing patterns of industrial conflict*. New York: John Wiley and Sons.

Roth, Alvin E. (1979) *Axiomatic models of bargaining*, Lecture Notes in Economics and Mathematical Systems, No. 170. Berlin: Springer-Verlag.

Roth, Alvin E. and Michael W. K. Malouf (1979) "Game-theoretic models and the role of information in bargaining", *Psychological Review*, 86:574–594.

Roth, Alvin E. and Francoise Schoumaker (1983) "Expectations and reputations in bargaining: an experimental study", *American Economic Review*, 73:362–372.

Sargent, Thomas J. and Christopher A. Sims (1977) "Business cycle modeling without pretending to have too much a priori economic theory", in: Christopher A. Sims, ed., *New methods in business cycle research*. Minneapolis: Federal Reserve Bank of Minneapolis.

Shalev, Michael (1980) "Trade unionism and economic analysis—the case of industrial conflict", *Journal of Labor Research*, 1:133–173.

Shorey, John (1977) "Time series analysis of strike frequency", *British Journal of Industrial Relations*, 15(1):63–75.

Shorter, Edward and Charles Tilly (1971) "The shape of strikes in France, 1830–1960", *Comparative Studies in Society and History*, 13:60–86.

Simiand, Francois (1907) *Le salaire des ouvriers des mines de charbon en France*. Paris: Edouard Cornely.

Sopher, Barry (1985) "Bargaining and the total cost theory of strikes: an experimental study", unpublished paper, University of Iowa.

Sosnick, Stephen H. (1964) "Non-stoppage strikes: a new approach", *Industrial* and *Labor Relations Review*, 17:73–80.

Stern, Robert M. (1978) "Methodological issues in quantitative strike analysis", *Industrial Relations*, 17(1):32–42.

Swidinsky, Robert and John Vanderkamp (1982) "A micro-econometric analysis of strike activity in Canada", *Journal of Labor Research*, III(4):455–471.

Tracy, Joseph S. (1984) "Contract negotiations and strikes", Seminar Paper, Centre for Labour Economics, LSE.

Turkington, D. J. (1975) "Strike incidence and economic activity in New Zealand", *New Zealand Economic Papers*, 9:87–106.

U.S. Department of Labor, Bureau of Labor Statistics (1980) *Bargaining Calendar*. Annual publication, e.g. Bulletin 2059.

U.S. Department of Labor, Bureau of Labor Statistics (1981) *Analysis of Work Stoppages*. Annual publication, e.g. Bulletin 2092.

Weintraub, Andrew R. (1966) "Prosperity versus strikes: an empirical approach", *Industrial* and *Labor Relations Review*, 19(1):231–238.

Yoder, Dale (1938) "Seasonality in strikes", *Journal of The American Statistical Association*, 23:687–693.

Yoder, Dale (1940) "Economic changes and industrial unrest in the United States", *Journal of Political Economy*, XLVIII:222–237.

Chapter 20

UNION RELATIVE WAGE EFFECTS

H. GREGG LEWIS*

Duke University

1. The union/nonunion wage gap

This chapter surveys empirical studies of the *union / nonunion relative wage differential*, or wage *gap* as Mincer [72][1] has termed it, in the United States for the period 1967–79. For an individual worker the *wage gap* is the excess of his wage if unionized (covered by a collective bargaining agreement) over his wage if nonunion (not so covered), given his working conditions.

In recent years the wage gap usually has been estimated by fitting wage equations to cross-section, individual-worker data on wages, union status (union or nonunion), and other variables supposedly controlling for differences among workers in working conditions and worker quality. Most of these equations are encompassed in their form by eq. (1):

$$W = a_n + a_{nx}x + U\left[(a_u - a_n) + (a_{ux} - a_{nx})x\right] + e, \tag{1}$$

where W is the natural logarithm of a worker's wage, x is a set of variables characterizing the worker and his employment, U is the union status of the worker (equal to unity if unionized and zero if nonunion), e is a residual reflecting left-out variables, and the a's are the *estimated* coefficients of the equation. Eq. (1) may be rewritten and sometimes has been fitted as two separate

---

*This chapter is a much condensed version of a larger study surveying recent (1964–82) empirical work on union relative wage effects in the United States. The report of the larger study, available now (Jan. 1984) only in the draft manuscript of the book [62a], contains the documentation for many of the assertions made in this chapter. In preparing this book manuscript I have benefited from comments of members of labor workshops at the University of North Carolina, North Carolina State University, Duke University, Appalachian State University, University of South Carolina, Princeton University, University of Pennsylvania, University of Chicago, and the National Bureau of Economic Research (Cambridge), from my Duke colleagues, especially George Tauchen, and most of all from the authors of the studies that I have used, especially Richard Freeman, James Medoff, Wesley Mellow, and Jacob Mincer.

[1] Citations are by number to the numbered references at the end of this chapter.

Handbook of Labor Economics, Volume II, Edited by O. Ashenfelter and R. Layard
©Elsevier Science Publishers BV, 1986

equations:

$$W_i = a_i + a_{ix}x + e_i \begin{cases} i = \mathrm{u}, & \text{if } U = 1; \\ i = \mathrm{n}, & \text{if } U = 0. \end{cases} \tag{2}$$

Frequently the fitted equations contain few or no cross-product or interaction terms Ux between union status U and other right-hand variables x. When there are no such cross-product terms, eq. (1) becomes

$$W = a_\mathrm{n} + a_x x + (a_\mathrm{u} - a_\mathrm{n})U + e \tag{3}$$

and eqs. (2) become

$$W_i = a_i + a_x x + e_i \begin{cases} i = \mathrm{u}, & \text{if } U = 1; \\ i = \mathrm{n}, & \text{if } U = 0. \end{cases} \tag{4}$$

Measurement errors in the dependent wage W variable or in the classification of workers by union status U and nonrandom sampling in the underlying data set of course may lead to biased estimates of the wage equation (1) – see Section 4. Furthermore, since residual variance is by no means usually negligible and selection of workers by union status U is surely not random, the left-out variables (e's) also may lead to bias, a fact that econometricians not only have noticed, but have tried to overcome – see Section 2.

Assume, however, that the residuals in eq. (1) are well behaved and that the equation has been estimated without bias. Then an unbiased estimate of the wage gap, conditional on or given x, is

$$M \equiv E(W_\mathrm{u} - W_\mathrm{n}|x) = a_\mathrm{u} - a_\mathrm{n} + (a_{\mathrm{u}x} - a_{\mathrm{n}x})x. \tag{5}$$

Of course, if the wage equation contains no cross-product terms Ux, as in (3), $M = a_\mathrm{u} - a_\mathrm{n}$, the coefficient of U in (3). Define $\hat{W}$ as $E(W|x, U)$, the expected value of W in (1) conditional on x and U. Then the wage gap M is the partial derivative of $\hat{W}$ with respect to union status U. Thus, the presence of the union status variable U on the right-hand side of the wage equation, either explicitly as in (1) and (3), or implicitly as in (2) and (4), is critical for estimating the wage gap.

In the specification of the wage equation (1) the dependent variable W is measured in natural logarithmic units. Therefore, the wage gap M also is measured in these log units and throughout this chapter the reported estimates will be in these units. To translate the gap M so measured into a percentage difference, simply perform this calculation: $100(e^M - 1)$.

Equation (5) allows for the possibility that the wage gap M depends on the characteristics x of workers and their employments. Indeed, if the gap is not generally zero, it would be quite surprising to find that it does not vary somewhat systematically across the labor force. Section 3 presents evidence on this variation.

Let $\bar{x}$ denote the means of the right-hand variables x among workers included in the fitting of the wage equations (1). Then, from (5), the estimate of the mean wage gap among included workers is

$$\overline{M} = a_u - a_n + (a_{ux} - a_{nx})\bar{x}. \tag{6}$$

Of course if the fitted wage equation contains no interaction terms Ux of union status with other right-hand variables, as in eq. (3), then the estimated mean wage gap is simply $a_u - a_n$, the coefficient of union status U in the wage equation. The central task of this chapter is to estimate the mean wage gap $\overline{M}$ for the U.S. work force as a whole for the period 1967–79. This is the subject of Sections 5 and 6.

Wage gaps versus wage gains

I turn now from the concept of a union-induced wage *gap* to that of a union-induced wage *gain*. There is, of course, an obvious sense in which the wage gap for a worker measures a wage gain: if for him the wage gap is greater than zero, the expected value of his wage would be higher if he were unionized than if he were nonunion. In what follows, however, the wage *gain* concept is quite different from that of a wage *gap*.

Imagine a hypothetical U.S. economy differing from the existing one in its laws regarding unions and collective bargaining. In particular, in this hypothetical economy "anti-trust" laws long have made unions powerless to affect wages. Such an economy might have unions and collective bargaining, but they would be compatible with competition in the labor market. I think that it is this contrast between competitive and monopoly unions that I and numerous others have had in mind when we referred to the contrast between the "absence" of unionism and its "presence". In this hypothetical economy a worker paid a wage W in the presence of the existing unionism would be paid a wage V where V like W is measured in logarithmic units. His unionism-induced *absolute* wage *gain* A is the expected value of the excess of his wage W in the "presence" of unionism over his wage V in the "absence" of unionism:

$$A_i \equiv E(W_i - V | x, y) \begin{cases} i = u, & \text{if } U = 1; \\ i = n, & \text{if } U = 0. \end{cases} \tag{7}$$

Notice that for each worker there is a pair of absolute gains one of which is actual and the other potential. For example, if the worker is nonunion, his actual absolute gain is A_n and his potential absolute gain is A_u. Notice also that his wage gap M is the same as the excess $A_u - A_n$ of his potential absolute gain over his actual absolute gain.

There is also a *relative* wage *gain* concept. I denote by a superscript "a" the all-worker (both union and nonunion) mean of the actual values of a variable.

Thus, A^a is such a mean of the absolute gains A. The *relative* wage *gain R* of the worker then is

$$R_i \equiv A_i - A^a \begin{cases} i = \mathrm{u}, & \text{if } U = 1; \\ i = \mathrm{n}, & \text{if } U = 0. \end{cases} \tag{8}$$

For relative gains as for absolute there is a pair of gains, one actual and one potential. Thus, for a nonunion worker his actual relative gain is R_n, his potential relative gain is R_u, and his wage gap M is the excess $R_\mathrm{u} - R_\mathrm{n}$ of his potential gain over his actual gain.

Thus, the wage *gap* for a worker is the excess of $\hat{W}_\mathrm{u}$ over $\hat{W}_\mathrm{n}$ or of A_u over A_n or of R_u over R_n. The wage *gain* for a worker, on the other hand, is the excess of his expected wage (absolute or relative, actual or potential) in the presence of unionism over its counterpart (absolute or relative) in the absence of unionism. The wage *gap* therefore is similar to the wedge produced by a payroll tax between the before-tax wage and the after-tax while the wage *gain* is similar to the difference between either the before-tax wage or the after-tax wage, given the tax, and the wage that would be paid in the absence of the tax.

We now have a large stock of empirical wage equations (1) fitted to data for recent years and thus in the presence of unionism. From these equations and related data we can calculate wage gaps (5). Can we also calculate from these same equations and the related data absolute or relative wage gains?

Write the counterpart of (1) in the absence of unionism as

$$V = b + b_x x + e_v. \tag{9}$$

This equation cannot be fitted to recent data because V cannot be observed in the presence of unionism. The coefficients of (9) in that sense are unknown. But if wage *gains* are to be calculated from (1), the coefficients of (9) must be inferred, somehow or other, from those of (1). In the general equilibrium of the economy in the presence of unionism the relative wages of workers depend upon their union status, on whether the working force is 5 percent, 20 percent, or 50 percent unionized and on which categories of workers are unionized, as well as on the effectiveness of labor unions in achieving wage gains for their workers. That is, the coefficients (the a's) in the fitted cross-section wage eq. (1) depend on the extent of unionism in the economy as a whole and by categories of workers. If these latter are non-negligibly changed, the coefficients in (1) will change, making it impossible to infer (9) from (1) and, therefore, making it impossible to estimate wage *gains* from (1). For this reason the "union relative wage effect" estimates surveyed in this chapter are for the wage *gap*, not the wage *gain* concept and the two should not be confused.

2. Micro, OLS, CS and other estimates of the wage gap

When the wage eqs. (1) or (2) are fitted to cross-section (CS), individual-worker (or micro) data by ordinary least squares (OLS), I term both the wage equations and the wage gap estimates derived from them as *Micro, OLS, and CS*. Most of the wage gap estimates yielded by recent (1964–82) empirical studies of wage differentials are of this type and, indeed, the remaining sections of this chapter survey *only* these Micro, OLS, and CS estimates.

Universally in the fitted wage equations underlying these estimates the unexplained or residual wage variances were *not* negligible, indicating that important wage-explanatory variables were omitted from the right-hand side. These omissions would not be worrisome if, conditional on the right-hand variables (other than U), the union status selection process were random.

However, most students of unionism, I think, would argue that union status selection is not random and that therefore Micro, OLS, and CS wage gap estimates may suffer from serious "selectivity" or left-out variables bias. I have strong priors on the direction of the bias. Let a union through collective bargaining impose on an employer higher wages for his workers than he otherwise would pay them with worker quality and quality of working conditions not tightly specified in the collective bargaining agreement. The higher wages will lengthen the queue of the applicants for the unionized jobs including some applicants of greater productiveness than otherwise would have applied. At the same time the employer has an incentive to evade the increase in his labor costs by employing workers of greater quality. The evasions will take time and will be impeded by the costs of screening for worker quality, imperfect substitution in production among worker qualities, and employment constraints in the collective bargaining agreement. Nevertheless, higher wages, I argue, eventually will lead to a higher quality work force. All of this would not matter, of course, if the available data permitted approximately perfect control for worker quality in wage equations. But the data do not permit such control. Hence, my priors are that the Micro, OLS, and CS wage gap estimates are biased upward – the omitted quality variables are positively correlated with union status U.

The likelihood that Micro, OLS, and CS wage gap estimates are selectivity biased has not escaped the notice of econometricians and recently a substantial number of papers have appeared that use techniques designed to reduce this bias. Broadly speaking these papers fall into two groups according to the technique used.

(1) Simultaneous equations (SE) studies that postulate a system of equations consisting of at least the wage equation (or pair of equations by union status) and an equation or equations determining union status.[2] The equation system then is fitted to the cross-section, individual-worker data.

---

[2] In some SE studies the equation system contains not only wage and union status equations, but also other equations such as one for worker mobility.

(2) Panel studies that use longitudinal data, thus permitting wage comparisons "before and after" unionization.

2.1. The SE estimates

In a majority of the SE studies the estimation method is one in which the union status equation first is fitted (by OLS, logit, or probit) to data on union status and the exogenous variables in the equation system. The predicted value $\hat{U}$ (or a curvilinear function $h(\hat{U})$ of $\hat{U}$) of the union status variable U is then calculated for each worker from the fitted union status equation and is entered on the right-hand side of the wage equation in place of (or in addition to) the observed union status variable in fitting the wage equation. In the other SE studies the parameters of the equation system are estimated by three-stage least squares or by maximum likelihood methods.

The wage gap estimates from the SE studies are surveyed in detail in Lewis [62a, ch. 4]. For most of these SE estimates there are corresponding Micro, OLS, and CS estimates with which the SE estimates may be compared. The simultaneous equations estimates are much more dispersed than the OLS estimates. They are not consistently smaller than the OLS estimates or consistently larger. Furthermore, a substantial fraction of the SE estimates are, I think, preposterously large or outlandishly negative. There is also considerable evidence in the set of SE estimates that they are sensitive to the econometric specification of the equation system, the method of fitting the system to the data, and to the data set used. From the practical point of view of estimating the mean wage gap in the work force, the SE estimates are, I think, considerably less reliable than their OLS counterparts, and I have ignored them.

The selectivity bias problem is one of omitted variables, a lack of information. I admire the ingenuity that has gone into the development of simultaneous equations econometrics to deal with this problem. Yet in the present context, the techniques are not working. In order to make them work satisfactorily, I think that we need to know much more than we do about the economics of trade unionism.

2.2. The panel estimates

The key feature of panel data is that the same set of individuals, the "panel", is observed at more than one date. Thus, panel data consist of a cross-section of individual-worker time series. All of the panel studies explicitly exploit this time-series aspect of panel data. The problem which the panel studies attempt to solve is the same as that faced in the "simultaneous equations" studies: omitted wage-explanatory variables that are correlated with the included union status variable in the wage equation.

Central to the treatment of this problem in the panel studies is the notion that a worker's position in the wage distribution, as measured by his relative wage, though subject to life-cycle and transitory variations, tends to persist over time. A considerable part of the permanent or fixed component of his relative wage, as well as the life-cycle and transitory components, undoubtedly can be captured by right-hand variables such as schooling, age, experience, and other commonly-used right-hand variables. But even after controlling for these variables, a substantial part of the permanent relative wage component may remain in an unobserved (to the econometrician) fixed effect portion of the error term in the wage equation. This portion of the error term, fixed for each worker, but varying across workers, undoubtedly includes effects of omitted worker quality and working conditions variables likely to be correlated with the union status or workers. It may be eliminated, of course, by comparing the relative wage of each worker at one date with *his* relative wage at another date. Thus, write the relative wage equation at the individual worker level at date t as follows:

$$W_t = a_t + a_{xt}x_t + \overline{M}_t U_t + e^f + e_t, \tag{10}$$

where e^f is the fixed (time-invariant) part of the error term and e_t is the remaining part. (The other symbols have their usual meanings.) Then if t' is a date different from t,

$$W_{t'} - W_t = a_{t'} - a_t + a_{xt'}x_{t'} - a_{xt}x_t + \overline{M}_{t'}U_{t'} - \overline{M}_t U_t + e_{t'} - e_t. \tag{11}$$

Not surprisingly, the fixed effect error e^f does not appear in (11). Thus, if the remaining error $e_{t'} - e_t$ in (11) were uncorrelated with union status $(U_{t'}, U_t)$ and if $U_{t'}$ were not equal to U_t for all workers, unbiased estimates of the wage gaps $\overline{M}_{t'}$ at date t' and $\overline{M}_t$ at date t could be obtained by regressing $W_{t'} - W_t$ on $x_{t'}$, x_t, $U_{t'}$, and U_t.

What I have just described is not exactly the procedure followed in any of the panel studies, though for several of the studies the description does not err seriously, and for all of them contains the key ingredients of the panel studies: eliminating fixed effects by one or another type of differencing across time within worker. The panel wage gap estimates are reviewed, study by study, in Lewis [62a, ch. 5]. There is much agreement among the studies that panel estimation procedures lead to reduced, but on average positive, wage gap estimates. That is, the studies suggest that wage gap estimates from wage *level* equations fitted by least squares to *cross-section* micro-data are upward biased. This suggestion is in accord with my priors.

Nevertheless, I do not regard this evidence from the panel studies as settling definitively this question of bias. If union status were a permanent characteristic of workers ($U_{t'} = U_t$, for all $t' \neq t$ and all workers), then, as suggested by (11), the panel estimation procedures used in the studies would have failed to yield wage gap estimates. All of the studies thus rely heavily on accurate distinction in the panel data between union status changers and nonchangers and on observing a substantial number of changers. Unfortunately, data from the panel studies show that the fraction of workers who changed union status typically was small and strongly suggest that appreciable fractions of those *reported* as changing status really experienced no status change. Such inaccuracy in the status change data is very likely to lead to serious downward bias in wage gap estimates from panel data. Indeed, I have presented empirical evidence in Lewis [62a, ch. 5] showing that misclassification of workers by union status may account for most, perhaps all, of the differences between the panel wage gap estimates and the corresponding Micro, OLS, and CS estimates.

Furthermore, the panel wage gap estimates display a disconcertingly large sensitivity to the choice of dates or period to which the estimates pertain. This, too, may be a consequence of date-to-date variation in the fraction of workers misclassified by union status, an aspect of measurement error that I have not been able to explore. Alternatively, it may be the result of substantial nonrandom selectivity among workers changing status. That the fraction of workers who experienced union status change was small makes it possible that this fraction was a quite nonrandom sample of all workers. The nonrandomness of union status selection and associated worker mobility makes the possibility a worrisome likelihood. Thus, in this present survey of wage gap estimates, I ignore the panel estimates except for noting their suggestion that the Micro, OLS, and CS estimates are upward biased. However, I have been unable to obtain from either the panel or the SE studies an estimate of the magnitude of this upward bias.

2.3.   Macro estimates[3]

Return to the wage equation (3), interpret it as a Micro, OLS, and CS wage equation, but modify its format slightly as follows:

$$W = a + a_x x + a_x^* x^* + a_U^* U^* + \overline{M} U + e,$$ (12)

where x^* and U^* are the means of x and U in the industry (or geographic area or occupation, etc.) in which a worker is employed and $\overline{M}$ is the estimated wage gap. I term U^* as an extent of unionism variable.

---

[3] What follows under this heading is a summary of Lewis [62b].

The union status variable U is a *micro* concept of collective bargaining coverage. For each worker it distinguishes between two states: unionized and nonunion. Its presence on the right-hand side of wage equations such as (12) permits the estimation of the wage gap $\overline{M}$. Extent of unionism U^*, whether measured by industry, occupation, locality, etc., is a group or *macro* concept of union status or collective bargaining coverage. There is a strong presumption, I think, that in the general equilibrium of the economy in the presence of unionism, the relative wage of each worker depends not only on his union status, sex, color, schooling, experience, and like variables, but also on the extent of unionism in the whole work force and the distribution of workers by union status among work force sectors. This argues for the presence on the right-hand side of Micro wage equations of extent of unionism variables characterizing this distribution, though it does not, of course, settle the question of the proper specification of these variables.

We now have a substantial stock of Micro wage equations that include extent of unionism variables. The estimated coefficients a_U^* of these variables often are numerically large, of uncertain sign, with values that are sensitive to the way U^* is measured, the specification of the wage equation, and the data set used. The large dispersion of the estimated a_U^* argues against any simple "threat" or "spillover" interpretation of the wage effects picked up in the data by these coefficients. Indeed, I am not by any means convinced that these estimated wage effects are mostly effects of *unionism* rather than mostly effects of left-out variables correlated with the included U^* variables.

Until about 1965 there were no large random samples with broad coverage of the U.S. work force containing information on wages and numerous worker and employment characteristics that also classified workers by their union status U. In the absence of the union status data, either one or the other of two alternative procedures were followed in the earliest of the post-1963 studies and in numerous later studies emulating them.

(1) The wage equation (12) or similar equation was fitted to individual-worker data on W, x, x^*, and U^* *omitting* union status U. I write the fitted wage equation as

$$W = c + c_x x + c_x^* x^* + c_U^* U^* + e', \tag{13}$$

where by the omitted-variable theorem

$$c_U^* = a_U^* + \overline{M} b_{UU^*}, \tag{14}$$

where b_{UU^*} is the partial regression coefficient of union status U on extent of unionism U^* in a regression that also includes x and x^* on the right-hand side.

(2) The wage equation (12) or similar equation, thought of as pertaining to individual workers, was aggregated by industry (or geographic area, etc.) across individual workers and the resulting equation was fitted to observations on the industry (or area, etc.) aggregates. Assume that the aggregation is by industry and denote the industry mean of a variable by an asterisk (*) superscript. Then the aggregation of (12) by industry is

$$W^* = a + (a_x + a_x^*)x^* + (a_U^* + \overline{M})U^* + e^*. \tag{15}$$

Since (12) has been fitted by OLS, the residual e is uncorrelated across the individual-worker observations with the industry means x^* and U^*. Therefore, the industry mean residual e^* in (15) also is uncorrelated with the industry means x^* and U^* in (15) provided only that each industry observation is weighted by the number of covered workers employed in the industry. Hence, if (15) were fitted by employment-weighted least squares, the coefficient of the extent of unionism variable U^* would be exactly equal to the sum $a_U^* + \overline{M}$ of the coefficients a_U^* for U^* and the wage gap $\overline{M}$ for the union status dummy variable U in the underlying Micro equation.

I term eqs. (13) and (15) as *Macro* equations and the fitted coefficients of U^* in these equations as *Macro* estimates. It is clear from (13), (14), and (15) that these Macro estimates contain a mixture in uncertain ratio of the wage gap $\overline{M}$ and a separate extent of unionism effect a_U^*. In Lewis [62b] I survey the post-1963 Macro estimates and present the results of experiments that I hoped might yield empirical regularities by which I could separate $\overline{M}$ from a_U^* in the Macro estimates. The experiments were unsuccessful. Hence, in the remainder of this chapter I ignore the Macro estimates as well as those from the SE and panel studies.

3. Variation in the wage gap across the U.S. work force[4]

This section is the first of four that survey the union/nonunion wage gap estimates derived from the Micro, OLS, and CS wage equations provided by a large number of empirical studies that have appeared since 1963. The focus of this section is on the question: Does the union/nonunion wage gap vary across the work force by characteristics of workers and their work places and, if so, by how much?

Consider first the following pair of Micro, OLS, and CS wage equations fitted separately by sex:

$$W_i = a_i + a_{ix}x + M_iU + e_i; \quad i = m, f, \tag{16}$$

---

[4]This section is a summary of Lewis [62a, ch. 7].

where the subscript *i* denotes the sex (m = male, f = female) of a worker. Deriving the wage gap *M*'s from the fitted equations involves no more than reading the equations[5] and calculation of the gap difference $M_m - M_f$ by sex only a subtraction.

Notice that the pair of equations (16) may be written as a single equation:

$$W = U\left[M_f + (M_m - M_f)D\right] + a_f + (a_m - a_f)D + a_{fx}x$$
$$+ (a_{mx} - a_{fx})Dx + e_f + (e_m - e_f)D. \tag{17}$$

In (17) the wage gap $M = M_f + (M_m - M_f)D$ depends upon sex *D* and the wage gap difference by sex, $M_m - M_f$, is the partial derivative of the wage gap *M* with respect to *D*.

Alternatively, suppose that a single wage equation of the following form has been fitted to data:

$$W = a + a_x x + a_D D + U\left[b + b_D D\right] + e. \tag{18}$$

This equation, of course, is the simplified version of (17) that contains no interactions *Dx*. The estimated wage gap *M* is $b + b_D D$ whose partial derivative with respect to sex *D* is the estimated gap difference $M_m - M_f$ and is equal to the coefficient b_D of the interaction term *UD* in the wage equation.

For some studies the retrieval of estimated gap *differences* was as simple as the preceding paragraphs suggest. But in numerous other studies additional calculations were required. First, wage equations comparable to (16) often were fitted separately by sex *and color* (Black workers versus White) yielding four wage gap estimates by sex and color. To obtain wage gap figures by sex for both colors combined I calculated the employment-weighted[6] mean of the wage gap estimates by color within each sex.[7] Second, in the separate equations by sex (16) the union status variable *U* often was interacted with some or all of the *x*'s as in (19):

$$W_i = a_i + a_{ix}x + U\left[b_i + b_{ix}x\right] + e_i; \quad i = m, f. \tag{19}$$

The estimated wage gap M_i, for $i = m, f$, then was calculated as $b_i + b_{ix}\bar{x}$, where $\bar{x}$ is the mean of *x* over the observations to which the equation was fitted. Third, in some wage equations the dependent wage variable was the wage e^W measured in

---

[5] However, in some instances wage equations were incompletely reported and were obtained in correspondence with study authors.

[6] The employment weights almost always came from the sample data to which the equations were fitted with appropriate adjustments for oversampling of Black workers in some of the underlying data files.

[7] A similar procedure was followed in a few studies in which the wage equations were fitted separately by sex, color, and some other right-hand variables.

its natural units rather than the wage W in logarithmic units. The required calculation then involves two steps. First proceed as though the dependent variable were W rather than e^W. Then divide the resulting wage gap or wage gap difference estimate by the mean of e^W over the covered observations.

The same procedure as for sex was followed for all of the qualitative or discrete variables describing workers and work places such as color and region and for continuous variables, such as years of school completed, treated as discrete variables. For continuous variables treated as continuous rather than discrete the procedure was essentially the same.

(1) For each wage equation that includes the union status variable U on the right-hand side[8] the estimated wage gap M is the partial derivative of $W = \ln e^W$ with respect to U. (If the left-hand wage variable is e^W rather than W, divide the partial derivative of e^W with respect to U by the mean of e^W to obtain M.) In general this partial derivative M will depend on some or all of the right-hand variables. I use years of school completed, denoted by S, as an example. That is $M = M(S,$ other variables).

(2) The wage gap difference per year of school completed then is the partial derivative $\partial M/\partial S$ of M with respect to S. If this second derivative also depends on right-hand variables, evaluate it at the means of these variables over the observations covered in fitting the equation.

(3) If S enters the wage equation as a quadratic, the curve relating M to S may be U-shaped or inverted U-shaped. If so, note the shape and calculate the value of S at which M is a minimum or maximum.

In summary, the estimates of wage gap *differences* are second partial derivatives $\partial^2 W/\partial U\partial x$ calculated from Micro, OLS, and CS wage equations, where each x is a right-hand control variable in the equation.

Wage gap estimates from Micro, OLS, and CS wage equations are subject to several potentially serious sources of bias, namely the left-out variables bias already discussed and some others that are the subject of the next section. Although this does not imply that the estimates of wage gap *differences* presented here also are seriously biased, I strongly suspect that some of them are. Thus, I regard the estimates of wage gap differences presented here as quite tentative.

I turn now to these estimates of wage gap differences by sex, color, marital status, major industry, major occupation, region, city size, years of school completed, age, labor market experience, seniority, public versus private employment, and establishment or firm size. The number of studies in which these estimates are based is so large that I cannot present in a few pages here the full study-by-study detail underlying each of the gap difference estimates. For that detail see Lewis [62a, ch. 7].

---

[8]When the wage equations are fitted separately by union status U, first write the pair of equations as a single equation that explicitly includes U on the right-hand side.

By sex. Estimates of the male-minus-female gap difference drawn from 39 studies for recent (1967–79) years shows that: (1) the sign of the mean gap difference is ambiguous and (2) the numerical magnitude of the difference is close to zero.

The Micro, OLS, and CS wage gap estimates that I have retrieved from recent studies are disproportionately for male workers who have comprised roughly 60 percent of the U.S. work force. Let M_m, M_f, and $\overline{M}$ denote the overall mean wage gap for male workers, female workers, and all workers, respectively. Then if the conclusion of the preceding paragraph is correct, the sign of $M_m - \overline{M} \simeq 0.4(M_m - M_f)$ is ambiguous and its numerical magnitude is close to zero.

By color. Estimates of the Black- (or nonwhite-) minus-White wage gap difference were retrieved from 46 different studies. The evidence on the overall mean Black–White gap difference is somewhat murky. Estimates from Current Population Survey data suggest a negligible difference. But estimates from other data sources points rather strongly to a positive difference of the order of magnitude of 0.05–0.10, except for young men. More precisely, the central tendency of the estimates based on Survey of Economic Opportunity (SEO) or Michigan Survey Research Center data was about 0.06, the corresponding figure for National Longitudinal Survey (NLS) data for older men was 0.12, and that for NLS data for young men was −0.045. Since Black workers comprise about 10 percent of the male work force in the United States, a mean Black–White gap difference for males of 0.10 implies that the mean wage gap for *all* males is about 0.01 larger than the mean wage gap for *White* males.

By marital status. This wage gap difference is the excess of the mean wage gap for married workers (both spouse present and spouse absent) over that for workers in all other marital status categories. Nine studies provided estimates of this gap difference. In eight of the nine studies the gap difference estimate was negative and the mean over the nine studies was about −0.1.

By major industry. Seventeen studies provided estimates of the excess of the wage gap in nonmanufacturing over that in manufacturing. In 16 of the 17 studies the excess was positive and the central tendency of the excess was about 0.11. Since manufacturing workers comprise only about one-fourth to one-third of the U.S. work force, an excess of 0.11 of nonmanufacturing over manufacturing implies that the wage gap in manufacturing was about 0.07–0.08 *below* the mean wage gap for all workers.

Ten studies yielded estimates of the gap difference between contract construction and other nonmanufacturing. In all 10 of these studies the gap in construction was larger than that in other nonmanufacturing. The mean excess was about 0.13. Thus, there is little room for doubting that the wage gap in construction is exceptionally high.

By major occupation. I have calculated the estimated excess of the wage gap for blue-collar workers over that for white-collar workers from 19 studies. In every case the excess was positive and among estimates for both sexes the mean excess was about 0.10. Thus, wage gap estimates for blue-collar workers will overstate the mean wage gap for both blue- and white-collar workers taken together. Since white-collar workers recently have comprised about half of the U.S. work force, this overstatement amounts to about 0.05.

Within the blue-collar category, the wage gap estimates for both craftsmen and service workers tended to be below corresponding gap estimates for operatives; for craftsmen (22 studies), however, the mean difference was only -0.01 and for service workers (14 studies) the mean difference was -0.05. For laborers (21 studies), on the other hand, the wage gap estimates tended to exceed those for operatives; the mean difference was 0.04.

By region. The estimates of wage gap differences by region come from Micro, OLS, and CS wage equations (in 19 studies) containing regional dummy variables and their interactions with union status U. In the majority of such equations the regional detail was no finer than that of the four Census geographic divisions and in some instances the contrast was simply between the South and the non-South.

For each of the Northeast, North Central, and West regions the signs of the estimated gap differences (excess over South) were disproportionately negative. However, the estimates showed little or no wage gap difference between the West and North Central regions and for both of these regions the excess of the South wage gap was small, 0.02–0.03. The outlier is the Northeast region whose estimated wage gap was well below that in other regions.

By city size. The commonly used microdata files do not permit the size (population) of the "city" in which a worker resides to be treated as a continuous rather than discrete variable. The May Current Population Surveys (CPS), for example, distinguish among (1) residence in the central city of a Standard Metropolitan Statistical Area (SMSA), (2) residence in an SMSA but not in the central city, and (3) residence outside an SMSA. (The CPS also identifies the 98 largest SMSAs so that among these SMSAs population distinctions can be made.) As a consequence, most of the Micro, OLS, and CS wage equations contain little detail on wage gap differences across communities of different size.

I have drawn 22 estimates (from 14 different studies) of the excess of the wage gap in SMSAs over that in other places. Only 2 of the 22 estimates were positive, but few of the estimates were as small as -0.10. The mean excess was about -0.05 (after eliminating a few outliers). About two-thirds of the U.S. work force resides in an SMSA. Hence, the mean wage gap for this urban work force will tend to understate the economy-wide wage gap by about 0.02.

By years of school completed. Almost all of the Micro, OLS, and CS wage equations surveyed in this chapter included both years of school completed S and either years of age A or years of labor market experience E among the right-hand variables and often these variables were interacted with the union status variable U. Typically the resulting wage gap M was a linear function of schooling S and a quadratic function of age A or experience E. From equations in which schooling S and age A were paired, both being treated as continuous rather than discrete variables, I calculated the partial derivative of the wage gap M with respect to schooling S (in years).

More frequently, however, it was experience E rather than age A that was entered in the wage equation together with schooling S. Usually, experience E in these equations was defined as age A minus schooling S minus a constant. For all equations in which both S and E were treated as continuous variables I calculated two partial derivatives of M with respect to S, one in which age A was held constant and the other which held experience E constant. Fortunately, the two partial derivatives differed negligibly.

Much to my surprise, I discovered that the estimates of wage gap differences by schooling differed substantially according to the sources of the microdata used in fitting the wage equation. In particular, the estimated derivatives of M with respect to S were considerably closer to zero in wage equations fitted to Current Population Survey (CPS) data than in other wage equations. All (18) of the CPS estimates (from 10 studies) were negative, except two for young males, and only 3 of the 18 estimates of the gap difference per year of schooling were as small as -0.03. The central tendency of the CPS estimates was about -0.02 to -0.01 per year of schooling.

There were 17 estimates (12 studies) from wage equations fitted to data sources other than the CPS. All of these estimates were negative, only 4 of the 17 estimates were as low *numerically* as 0.02, and most of the estimates were in the range -0.04 to -0.02.

Thus, there is a strong presumption that the wage gap falls as schooling rises, but the magnitude of the decline in the gap per year of schooling is indicated rather imprecisely. The CPS estimates suggest that the difference per year is about -0.015; other data sources put the difference at about -0.03, about twice as large numerically. In the U.S. work force the mean years of school completed is between 12 and 13 and the standard deviation is between 2.5 and 3.0. Hence, a two standard deviation difference (say, 5.5) in years of schooling, centered about the mean, leads to a wage gap difference of about 0.08 according to the CPS estimate and about 0.16, according to the estimate from other data sources.

By experience, age, and seniority. Twenty-one studies provided 27 estimates of wage gap differences by years of experience. In 19 of the 21 studies (25 of 27 estimates) the estimated wage gap was a quadratic function of experience and in 22 of these 25 estimates the wage gap–experience profile was U-shaped with a minimum that in 16 of the 22 U-shaped profiles was at 25–30 years of experience. The typical profile was moderately steep at zero years of experience: in the majority of the profiles (12 of 22) the slope at $E = 0$ ranged from -0.08 to -0.16 per decade and the mean slope at $E = 0$ over all 22 profiles was -0.12 per decade.

Embedded in the wage gap–*experience* profiles, of course, are wage gap–age profiles for given years of schooling. Thus, the picture of the typical wage gap–*age* profile implied by the preceding paragraph is one of U-shape with a minimum at about 45 years of age and a slope at age 18 of about -0.12 per decade. In 4 studies (6 estimates) the wage gap was expressed as a quadratic function of age rather than experience. The estimated wage gap–age profiles from these studies strongly resemble the typical *age* profile implied by the *experience* profiles of the preceding paragraph.

In several studies matching wage equations were fitted separately by age group permitting the separate estimation of the wage gap for each of the age groups. The estimated gap differences by age are broadly consistent with the picture of the wage gap–age profile that I have just given. And all of the evidence suggests rather strongly that wage gap estimates drawn from wage equations fitted to the data for young males will tend to overstate the mean wage gap for males of all ages.

There is considerably less evidence on wage gap differences by seniority or tenure on the current job or with the current employer than for the gap differences by age or experience. Furthermore, the evidence for seniority is less clear than that for age or experience. Twelve studies provided 15 estimates of the wage gap–seniority function. In 4 of the 15 estimates the wage gap was expressed as a linear function of seniority and all of these linear profiles were negatively inclined. Of the 11 remaining profile estimates, 6 were U-shaped and moderately steep at zero seniority, 1 was negatively inclined at all levels of seniority and moderately steep, 1 was positively inclined, another was flat, and 2 had the shape of an inverted U. Thus, the preponderance of the evidence is that the wage gap is a declining function of seniority at least at low levels of seniority.

By public versus private employment. Here there were eight studies and all agreed that the larger wage gap is for privately employed workers. The private minus public gap difference derived from one study was only 0.02, but in the other seven studies the difference ranged from 0.08 to 0.16 and averaged about 0.13. Since government workers recently have comprised about one-fifth of the U.S. work force, this gap difference implies that wage gap estimates confined to the private sector will overstate the all-employee mean wage gap by about 0.025.

By establishment or firm size. Six studies provided estimates of the partial derivative of the wage gap with respect to the size of the employing firm or establishment. All of these estimates, except two, pertain to manufacturing workers. All of the estimated partial derivatives with respect to employer size that I have calculated from these studies were negative, indicating that the wage gap declines as firm or establishment size increases.

An overview of the wage gap variation. Let $\hat{W}_u(x)$ be the expected wage of a worker, conditional on his measured personal and workplace characteristics x, if he is in unionized status, and $\hat{W}_n(x)$ his corresponding wage if he is nonunion status. His expected wage *gap* then is $M(x) \equiv \hat{W}_u(x) - \hat{W}_n(x)$. The findings of this section rather strongly reject the notion that the union/nonunion wage gap $M(x)$ does not depend upon the x's – that is, that $M(x)$ is a constant.

Question: Can the variations in $M(x)$ with the x's described here be characterized in some simple way – simpler, that is, than reciting the findings of this section, x by x? For example, several authors of studies used in this section have noted that if x is a "human capital" variable such as schooling, age, experience, and seniority, the union profile, $\hat{W}_u(x)$, of the wage related to x is flatter than the corresponding nonunion profile $\hat{W}_n(x)$ – that is, $\partial M(x)/\partial x$ has a sign that is opposite to that of $\partial \hat{W}_n(x)/\partial x$. For ease of reference I term this hypothesis as the "F" (for flattening) hypothesis. This hypothesis holds for schooling, age, experience, and seniority. But does it hold in general for other right-hand x's in the wage equations?

I first consider other variables x for which the hypothesis holds – i.e. for which the hypothesis is an apt characterization of the way $M(x)$ varies. $\hat{W}_n(x)$ rises and $M(x)$ falls with both city size and firm or establishment size. $\hat{W}_n(x)$ is larger and $M(x)$ is smaller for married workers than for workers in other marital status, for manufacturing workers than for nonmanufacturing workers, for workers in the West region than for workers in the South, for white-collar than for blue-collar for craftsmen than for operatives, for operatives than for laborers, for government workers than for private.

However, there are several variables for which the hypothesis does not correctly describe the variation in $M(x)$. $\hat{W}_u(x)$ is markedly higher for males than for females but the wage gap difference by sex is close to zero. $\hat{W}_n(x)$ is higher and so is $M(x)$ for construction workers than for nonmanufacturing workers, for operatives than for service workers. $\hat{W}_n(x)$ differs little between the Northeast and North Central regions but $M(x)$ is substantially lower in the Northeast. Indeed, in general the F-hypothesis does not perform very well in characterizing wage gap differences by region, industry, and occupation. $\hat{W}_n(x)$ is larger, but not by much, for White workers than for Black or non-White workers. If the F-hypothesis is correct, then $M(x)$ should be smaller, but not by much, for White workers. This is close to the findings reported above from *CPS data*. However, if the CPS data are ignored, $M(x)$ is substantially lower for White workers.

Thus, though the F-hypothesis performs better than its opposite in describing wage gap variations, I do not regard it as correctly describing some important components of these variations.

4. Micro, OLS, and CS estimates: Data problems[9]

Micro, OLS, and CS wage gap estimates, I have argued, are subject to potentially serious upward bias stemming from correlation of omitted right-hand variables with the union status variable U. This is the union status selectivity problem

---

[9] This section is a summary of Lewis [62a, ch. 6].

previously discussed. But this selectivity is not the only source of possible bias. In this section I examine estimate errors arising from four types of imperfections in the data rather than from failure to observe unobservables: (1) the omission of fringe benefits in the dependent wage variable; (2) the use of a weekly or annual wage instead of an hourly wage; (3) misclassification of workers by union status; and (4) nonrandomness by design in some of the micro-data sets.

4.1.   *Errors resulting from the omission of fringe benefits*

In the most commonly used household surveys (the CPS, NLS, SEO, and PSID[10]) the wage measures that may be routinely calculated from the data are the more or less conventional ones of hourly, weekly, and annual earnings. All of these wage measures surely exclude employer expenditures for fringe benefits that are not paid directly to workers and hence do not show up promptly in worker pay envelopes. Indeed, some of the wage measures derived from household survey data and used in wage gap estimation probably omit some employer fringe expenditures that are paid directly to workers.

Denote by e^W the reported or measured wage concept, e^F is that for the omitted employer expenditures for fringe benefits, and $e^C = e^F + e^W$ is that for total employee *compensation*. Then $M_C - M_W = a(M_F - M_W)$, where M_W is the measured wage gap, M_F is the corresponding gap for the omitted fringes, M_C is the compensation gap and $a = e^F/e^C$. (The M's, of course, are measured in natural logarithmic units.)

I have derived estimates of $M_C - M_W$ from 19 different studies. (For the detailed estimates see Lewis [62a, ch. 6].) There is great agreement among these studies that in recent years $M_C - M_W$ was positive and small, but not negligible. From these studies I estimate that for the work force as a whole $M_C - M_W$ was about 0.028 except when the measured wage concept was that of annual earnings or annual average hourly earnings for which my estimate is about 0.020.

4.2.   *Weekly or annual wage and the hours gaps*

For an individual worker let W be his hourly wage or earnings, $W1$ his weekly wage, $W2$ is annual wage, $H1 = W1 - W$ his weekly hours worked, $H2 = W2 - W$ his annual hours worked, and $H3 = H2 - H1$ his annual weeks worked, where the wage W and hours H concepts are measured in natural logarithmic units. In a

---

[10] CPS is short-hand for Current Population Surveys, NLS for National Longitudinal Surveys, SEO for Survey of Economic Opportunity, and PSID for Panel Study of Income Dynamics. These and other *household* surveys rarely attempt to get data on employer fringe benefit expenditures.

substantial fraction of the studies from which I have drawn wage gap estimates the dependent wage variable was $W1$ or $W2$ rather than W. Clearly, if unionism produces a union/nonunion differential or *gap in hours worked*, then *wage* gaps estimated from $W1$ or $W2$ will differ from the corresponding wage gap estimated from the hourly wage W. In particular, $M_{W1} - M_W = M_{H1}$ and $M_{W2} - M_W = M_{H2} = M_{H1} + M_{H3}$, where each M denotes the union/nonunion gap in the subscripted variable.

I have calculated hours gap estimates from 13 studies – see Lewis [62a, ch. 6]. These studies indicate that typically the hours gaps M_{H1}, M_{H2}, and M_{H3} were negative and not negligible in size. Among the studies with at least moderately broad worker coverage, the mean estimate of M_{H1}, the hours per week gap, was about -0.016 and that for M_{H2}, the hours per year gap, about -0.030. These estimates of M_{H1} and M_{H2} in turn are consistent with the estimates of M_{H3}.

4.3. Errors from union status misclassification

The union status questions in the large sample surveys underlying most of the Micro, OLS, and CS wage gap estimates are simple ones. There is good reason therefore to expect that in these surveys only a small fraction of the surveyed workers were misclassified by their union status. The evidence we have on the extent of misclassification is consistent with this expectation – see Mellow and Sider [70], for example. Although even a small fraction of misclassified workers may lead to large bias in wage gap estimates obtained by panel techniques (see Section 2 above), the corresponding bias in Micro, OLS, and CS wage gap estimates is likely to be small, but perhaps not negligibly small, and of uncertain sign. At present we have too little empirical evidence to estimate the size of the bias in the cross-section wage gap estimates.

4.4. Nonrandomness in the NLS, SEO, and PSID data sets

The National Longitudinal Surveys (NLS) and a portion (the so-called "nonrandom half") of the Survey of Economic Opportunity (SEO) and of each of the surveys of the Panel Study of Income Dynamics (PSID) were not random samples of the U.S. population that they were designed to cover. In particular, in all of these surveys the relative frequency of Black workers was much higher than in the corresponding U.S. population. This nonrandomness probably leads to a negligible problem of bias in Micro, OLS, and CS wage gap estimates if the underlying wage equations are fitted separately by color to the data. Then the only problem is to use the appropriate *population* weights in averaging the Black and White gap estimates, which I have uniformly attempted to do.

However, Micro, OLS, and CS wage equations often were fitted to the combined data for both Black and White workers (without a color * union status interaction variable). Then the resulting wage gap estimate is an average of underlying separate gap estimates by color in which the Black gap estimate is heavily overweighted *unless* in fitting the wage equation each observation is weighted by the reciprocal of its sampling probability. Such weighting, however, seldom was done.

Consider the following pair of wage equations that differ only in that one includes and the other excludes a union status * color interaction variable (both fitted by OLS without population weights):

$$W = a + a_x x + a_b B + a_u U + a_{ub} UB + e \tag{20}$$

and

$$W = A + A_x x + A_b B + A_u U + e', \tag{21}$$

where $B = 1$ for a Black worker and is zero otherwise, U is the union status dummy variable, the x's are other right-hand variables, and the a's and A's are the estimated coefficients. The first equation (20) provides separate wage gap estimates by color: $\overline{M}_b = a_u + a_{ub}$, $\overline{M}_w = a_u$, so that $\overline{M}_b - \overline{M}_w = a_{ub}$ and the overall wage gap estimate is $\overline{M} = B^* \overline{M}_b + (1 - B^*) \overline{M}_w = a_u + a_{ub} B^*$, where B^* is the appropriate *population* weight for Blacks. The second equation (21) yields only an estimate A_u of the mean wage gap $\overline{M}$ for both Blacks and non-Blacks combined. This estimate A_u presumably overweights $\overline{M}_b$ relative to $\overline{M}_w$ and the overweighting bias is $A_u - (a_u + a_{ub} B^*)$.

It follows from the left-out variable theorem applied to (20) and (21) that

$$A_u = a_u + a_{ub} b_{UB,U}, \tag{22}$$

where $b_{UB,U}$ is the coefficient of U in a regression of UB on U, B, and the x's. I know of no estimates of this coefficient. I think it is likely, however, that $b_{UB,U}$ is approximated well by the coefficient $b'_{UB,U}$ of U in a regression of UB on U and B *without the* x's:

$$b'_{UB,U} = \overline{B}J; \quad J \equiv \frac{\overline{U}_b(1 - \overline{U}_b)(1 - \overline{B})}{\overline{U}(1 - \overline{U})(1 - \overline{B}) - (\overline{B})(\overline{U}_b - \overline{U})^2}, \tag{23}$$

where $\overline{B}$ is the mean of B in the sample data, $\overline{U}_b$ is the mean of U among Black workers in the sample, and $\overline{U}$ is the mean of U among all workers in the sample. Then the bias from overweighting of Blacks is approximately

$$\text{bias} = (\overline{B}J - B^*)a_{ub} = (\overline{B}J - B^*)(\overline{M}_b - \overline{M}_w). \tag{24}$$

Several of the studies covered in Section 3 provided estimates of $\bar{B}$, $\bar{U}_b$, and $\bar{U}$ from which $\bar{BJ}$ can be calculated. These estimates of $\bar{BJ}$ ranged from 0.27 to 0.37, averaged 0.31, and there were no systematic differences by data source. The population weight B^* for Black wage and salary workers was close to 0.10 in all of the data sources. Hence, I estimate that $\bar{BJ} - B^*$ in (24) was approximately 0.21. The estimates of $\bar{M}_b - \bar{M}_w$ from Section 3 differ by data source: PSID and SEO, about 0.06; NLS Young Men, about -0.045, and NLS Mature Men, about 0.12. My estimates of the bias from overweighting of Blacks then are: PSID and SEO, 0.012; NLS Older Men 0.024; and NLS Young Men, -0.009.

5. Adjusting the Micro, OLS, and CS wage gap estimates[11]

The focus in this section and the next is on the *mean* union/nonunion wage gap in the U.S. work force as a whole in recent years. As in Sections 3 and 4, the basic estimation inputs are fitted Micro, OLS, CS wage equations and related numbers reported in (or obtained by correspondence with the authors of) a large number of empirical studies of wage differentials in the United States. Since the focus in this section and the next is on the overall mean wage gap, I have ignored in this section and the next empirical studies in which the worker coverage was quite narrow – e.g. nurses, police, firefighters, and even sectors as large as that of contract construction.

For each broad coverage Micro, OLS, and CS wage equation I first calculated the unadjusted estimates of the mean wage gap. The calculation procedures were spelled out in Section 3. These unadjusted estimates are then adjusted for nonrandomness in the underlying data files, differences in the left-hand wage variable, incomplete worker coverage, and finally for "incompleteness" in the set of right-hand variables. The resulting adjusted estimates are presented by data source and date in Section 6.

5.1. Adjusting for nonrandomness in the SEO, NLS, and PSID data files

In Section 4 I noted that in the National Longitudinal Surveys (NLS), and a portion (the so-called "nonrandom half") of each of the 1967 Survey of Economic Opportunity (SEO) and the Panel Study of Income Dynamics surveys the proportion of Black workers was much higher than in the U.S. population. Such nonrandomness, I judge, is not a serious problem if the wage equations provide separate wage gap estimates by color. Then the only problem is to use appropriate *population* weights in averaging the Black and White wage gap estimates.

---

[11] This section is a summary of Lewis [62a, ch. 8].

However, in frequent instances wage equations were *not* fitted separately by color, there were no union status * color interactions, and in fitting the wage equations each observation was *not* weighted by the reciprocal of its sampling probability. Then the wage gap estimate is an average of underlying estimates by color in which the Black estimate is heavily overweighted. On the basis of my estimates in Section 4 of the resulting bias I have made the following adjustment.

Adjustment 1. Overweighting of Blacks
  PSID and SEO: subtract 0.012 from wage gap estimate.
  NLS Mature Men: subtract 0.024 from the wage gap estimate.
  NLS Young Men: add 0.009 to wage gap estimate.

5.2. *Adjusting for differences in the dependent wage variables*

I take as my *standard* specification of the dependent variable in the wage equation the natural logarithm of a worker's *compensation* per hour worked. In almost all of the Micro, OLS, and CS wage equations surveyed in Section 6, however, the dependent variable differed from this standard in one or more respects.

First, the wage concept typically was one that omitted most or all of the employer expenditures for fringe benefits. The findings presented in Section 4 indicate that omissions of the fringe items biases mean wage gap estimates downward by about 0.028, unless the wage concept used was that of *annual earnings* or annual average hourly earnings for which the downward bias was a bit smaller, 0.020. Hence, the adjustments for omission of fringe expenditures are:

Adjustment 2. Omission of fringes
  (a) Add 0.028, except when
  (b) wage concept is that of annual earnings or annual average hourly earnings; then add 0.020.

Second, in several studies weekly or annual earnings rather than an hourly wage measure were used. If unionism yields a union/nonunion gap in hours worked, then wage gap estimates based on weekly or annual earnings will differ from those based on hourly wages. The estimates given in Section 4 indicate that the hours *per week* gap was about -0.016 and the hours *per year* gap about -0.030. Hence, in Section 6 I make hours gap adjustments as follows:

Adjustment 3. Hours gap adjustment
  (a) Wage gap estimates from weekly earnings: add 0.016.
  (b) Wage gap estimates from annual earnings: add 0.030.

Fourth, in a minority of wage equations the dependent wage variable was expressed in its natural units e^W rather than in logarithmic units W. For each such equation I have calculated the wage gap estimate in logarithmic units by first calculating the gap estimate in the natural units of the wage variable e^W and then divided this estimate by the mean of e^W. Does this procedure itself produce biased estimates? Fortunately, in five studies ([3], [83], [104]–[106]) matching pairs of wage equations were fitted in which the equations differed only in the dependent variable, e^W (arithmetic) in one and W (logarithmic) in the other. In all five of these studies the wage gap estimates from the arithmetic e^W equations were lower than the corresponding gap estimates from the logarithmic W equations. The differences ranged from 0.012 to 0.030 and averaged 0.023. Therefore, in Section 6 I adjust the wage gap estimates from arithmetic equations upward by 0.023.

Adjustment 4. Arithmetic dependent variable
  Add 0.023 to wage gap estimate

5.3. *Adjusting for incomplete worker coverage*

The findings of Section 3 strongly suggest that incomplete coverage of the U.S. work force in fitted wage equations may lead to significantly biased estimates of the U.S. mean wage gap. The wage equations surveyed in Section 6 vary substantially in the categories of workers they cover. Many of them, for example, pertain only to males, frequently only to White male wage and salary workers of specified ages, industries, occupations, etc. I have amassed too little information to adjust each wage gap estimate for incompleteness in all of its detail of the worker coverage in the underlying wage equation. On the other hand, Section 3 does provide a basis for making some adjustments for incomplete worker coverage. These adjustments are listed below.

Adjustment 5. Omission of Blacks
  SEO and PSID (and other Michigan) data: add 0.006
  NLS Mature Men: add 0.012
  NLS Young Men: subtract 0.004

Adjustment 6. Omission of nonmanufacturing
  Add 0.07 to 0.08 to estimated gap for manufacturing

Adjustment 7a: Subtract 0.05 from gap estimates for blue-collar workers, for omission of white-collar workers

Adjustment 7b: Add 0.05 to gap estimates for white-collar workers for omission of blue-collar workers

Adjustment 8: Omission of non-SMSA workers
  Add 0.02 to estimated wage gap

The four NLS panels were designed to cover workers of specified ages. In particular, the NLS panel for Young Men covers only workers who were 14–24 years old in 1966, that for Mature Men only males who were 45–59 in 1966. Thus, even when these Panels are combined, males who were 25–44 or 60 and over in 1966 were omitted. There are numerous wage gap estimates based on wage equations fitted to these NLS data for men. Therefore, I am reluctant to ignore them in forming my judgment of the size of the all-worker mean wage gap. However, in the light of the findings reported in Section 3, with respect to variation in the wage gap with age, there is a considerable likelihood that these NLS-based estimates will be misleading unless they are adjusted for age omissions.

Consider first the Young Men 14–24 in 1966. The earliest estimates for this panel are for 1969 when these men were 17–27, the latest are for 1971 when they were 19–29. The findings of Section 3 strongly suggest that the wage gap for such young men was above the all-worker mean wage gap, but the amount of the excess cannot be estimated from the information given there. Fortunately, there are two studies, one by Holzer [48] and the other by Mincer [72] that contain useful information. These two studies support the following age adjustments (but none for the NLS Mature Men):

Adjustment 9. Age adjustment for NLS Young Men
   Subtract 0.08 from wage gap estimate

Adjustment 10. Omission of workers < 25 years old
   Add 0.03 to wage gap estimate

In many of the studies covered in Section 6, the fitted wage equations covered only workers in private employment. In Section 3 I estimated that exclusion of government workers would tend to increase the estimated all-worker mean wage gap by about 0.025. Hence:

Adjustment 11. Omission of government workers
   Subtract 0.025 from wage gap estimates

5.4. Adjusting for differences in the set of right-hand variables

I turn now to differences in gap estimates produced by differences in the list of right-hand (RH) variables. All of the commonly used data sets for individual workers contain information on the worker's union status, sex, color, schooling, labor market experience or age, and place of residence and almost universally these variables were included on the right-hand side. In the sparsest of wage equation specifications these were the only right-hand variables. However, these data sources also identify the worker's industry and occupation, sometimes in considerable detail, marital status, worker class (public versus private employer, self-employed versus wage and salary worker), and distinguish between part-time and full-time workers. Moreover, some of the micro-data sources provide information on the worker's health status, veteran status, number of dependents, seniority, size of the employing firm or establishment, and on some nonpecuniary aspects of his work and workplace. Thus, the wage equations underlying the wage gap estimate surveyed in the next section differ considerably in the list of RH variables and undoubtedly some of the differences in the gap estimates are produced by differences in the list of wage-explanatory variables.

Fortunately several of the studies covered in Section 6 reported experiments on the wage gap effects of adding RH variables. The details are reported in Lewis [62a, ch. 8]. On the basis of these experiments I make the following adjustments:

Adjustment 12. Omission of occupation as a RH variable
  Add 0.01 to wage gap estimate

Adjustment 13. Omission of industry as a RH variable
  Subtract 0.02 from wage gap estimate

Adjustment 14. Omission of extent of unionism by industry
  Subtract 0.01 from wage gap estimate

6. The adjusted Micro, OLS, and CS gap estimates

The goal of this section is to estimate the overall mean union/nonunion wage gap for the U.S. work force in recent years, especially the decade of the 1970s. Unadjusted and adjusted wage gap estimates by data source and year retrieved from 108 different studies are presented here.

The upshot of this survey is a set of numbers, one for each year in the period 1967–79. These numbers presumably are estimates of the mean union/nonunion wage gap in the whole U.S. work force. However, because I am convinced that Micro, OLS, CS wage gap estimates tend to be upward biased, I present these numbers as *upper limit* estimates of the overall mean gap.

6.1. Adjusted estimates from CPS data

I consider first the wage gap estimates derived from Micro, OLS, and CS wage equations fitted to Current Population Survey data, usually in May of each year, 1970–79. I have more gap estimates from this source than from any other. The CPS offered much larger sample sizes than the NLS and the University of Michigan surveys; in contrast to the SEO, provided union status information for

Table 20.1
Estimates of the mean wage gap from CPS data.

Line no. (1)	Year (2)	Study no. (3)	Wage gap estimate		Adjustments (6)
			Unadjusted (4)	Adjusted (5)	
1	1979	[7]	0.049	0.127	2, 7b
2	1979	[68, 69]	0.077	0.105	2
3	1978	[48]	0.138	0.156	2, 14
4	1978	[67]	0.176	0.194	2, 14
5	1978	[68, 69]	0.172	0.200	2
6	1978	[91]	0.175	0.193	2, 14
7	1978	[102]	0.174	0.192	2, 8, 13, 14
8	1977	[67]	0.188	0.206	2, 14
9	1977	[70]	0.150	0.168	2, 14
10	1976	[8]	0.192	0.210	2, 14
11	1976	[35]	0.18	0.18	2, 11
12	1976–78	[48]	0.225	0.168	2, 7a, 8, 9, 11
13	1975	[10]	0.168	0.186	2, 14
14	1975	[32]	0.205	0.158	2, 7a, 11
15	1975	[36]	0.122	0.145/0.155	2, 6, 7a, 11
16	1975	[66]	0.181	0.194/0.204	2, 6, 7a, 11, 14
17	1975	[82]	0.113	0.161/0.171	2, 6, 7a
18	1975	[96]	0.208	0.206	2, 13, 14
19	1975	[101]	0.190	0.188	2, 13, 14
20	1974	[32]	0.188	0.141	2, 7a, 11
21	1974	[36]	0.106	0.129/0.139	2, 6, 7a, 11
22	1974	[82]	0.136	0.184/0.194	2, 6, 7a
23	1973	[10]	0.148	0.166	2, 14
24	1973	[14]	0.106	0.129	2, 10, 11, 14
25	1973	[32]	0.197	0.150	2, 7a, 11
26	1973	[36]	0.110	0.133/0.143	2, 6, 7a, 11
27	1973	[56, 98–100]	0.21	0.21	2, 13, 14
28	1973	[66]	0.160	0.173/0.183	2, 6, 7a, 11, 14
29	2973	[81]	0.155	0.128	2, 11, 13, 14
30	1973	[82]	0.148	0.196/0.206	2, 6, 7a
31	1973	[89]	0.107	0.145	2, 8, 14
32	1973	[90]	0.182	0.155	2, 11, 13, 14
33	1973	[91]	0.128	0.146	2, 14
34	1973–78	[5]	0.243	0.227	2, 3, 7a, 14
35	1973–76	[50]	0.112	0.150	2, 8, 14
36	1973–75	[4]	0.112	0.191/0.201	2, 3, 6, 11, 14
37	1973–75	[18]	0.103	0.166/0.176	2, 6, 11, 14
38	1973–75	[48]	0.148	0.121	2, 7a, 8, 11
39	1971	[45]	0.112	0.146/0.156	2, 3, 6, 7a, 13, 14
40	1970	[83]	0.140	0.093	2, 7a, 11

Notes:

Line 4. Comparable unadjusted estimate for 1977 was 0.192.

Line 5. Comparable unadjusted estimate for 1979 was 0.126.

Line 8. Unadjusted estimate is based on employer responses to wage, industry, occupation, and union status questions. Corresponding estimate based on worker responses was 0.173.

Line 12. Pertains to 16–24 year old males. Comparable unadjusted estimate for 1973–75 was 0.224.

Lines 16, 17, 22, 28, 30 pertain to workers paid by the hour. No adjustment was made for this coverage restriction.

government as well as private workers; in contrast to the NLS and the nonrandom portions of the SEO and the PSID, the CPS did not over-sample Blacks; the CPS was not restricted in coverage to particular age groups as in the NLS.

Table 20.1 reports unadjusted and adjusted mean wage gap estimates based on CPS data, 1970–1979, from 30 different studies. I have excluded from this table and from other tables in this section numerous Micro, OLS, and CS estimates that pertain to small sectors of the economy (construction workers, hospital employees, teachers, etc.). Moreover, for studies (or groups of similar studies involving the same author) providing more than one unadjusted mean gap estimate, I have chosen what I regarded as the single best estimate, sometimes a mean of several estimates. In making this choice I preferred broad to narrow coverage of workers, long to short lists of right-hand variables in the wage equation, and more to fewer interactions among the right-hand variables, especially interactions involving the union status variable. Furthermore, for some studies the wage gap estimates given in column 4 are based on wage equations supplied to me by the study author in correspondence rather than on equations reported in the author's study.

The studies identified by number in column 3 are listed in the references at the end of this section. Similarly, the adjustments made in going from column 4 to column 5, which are listed by number in column 6, are those discussed in Section 5 and are described in the Appendix.

Turn first to the estimates for 1973 on lines 23–33. The mean of the 11 *adjusted* estimates (after replacing ranges by their midpoints) is 0.159 and the median is 0.150. (The corresponding averages of the 11 unadjusted estimates are: mean 0.150, median 0.148.) However, the estimates on lines 28 and 30 are based on wage equations in which the worker coverage was restricted to those paid by the hour. On the basis of experiments reported to me in correspondence by Wesley Mellow I judge that the effect of such a coverage restriction is to bias wage gap estimates upward substantially. Hence, discard the estimates on lines 28 and 30. The mean of the 9 remaining *adjusted* estimates is 0.152 and the median is 0.146; the averages of the 9 *unadjusted* estimates are: mean 0.149, median 0.148. The standard deviation of the 9 adjusted estimates was 0.023, that for the unadjusted estimate was 0.038. This comparison of standard deviations indicates that the adjustments made to the unadjusted estimates have reduced the dispersion among the estimates substantially, at least for the 1973 CPS figures.

The best of the 1973 CPS estimates, in my judgment, are those based on the Ashenfelter study (no. [10] on line 13), the Bloch–Kuskin study (no. [14] on line 24), and the Sahling–Smith study (no. [91] on line 33). The mean of the adjusted estimates on these 3 lines is 0.147. Hence, I tentatively fix 0.147 as the *upper bound* to the overall mean wage gap for 1973.

There are only three CPS-based wage gap estimates for 1974 (see lines 20–22) and one (line 22) of these is tainted for my purposes by restriction of coverage to workers paid by the hour. The mean of the other two adjusted gap estimates (after replacing the range on line 21 by its midpoint) is 0.138 or 0.009 below the tentative figure of 0.147 for 1973. What evidence is there in addition to this comparison that the mean wage gap fell by about 0.009 between 1973 and 1974? Six studies provide matching estimates for 1973 and 1974: nos. [32], [36], and [82] using CPS data (Table 20.1) and nos. [72], [76], and [78] using PSID data (Table 20.3). The excess of the 1973 estimate over the matching 1974 estimate for each of the six studies is: no. [32]: 0.009; no. [36]: 0.004; no. [72]: 0.009; no. [78]: 0.009; no. [82]: 0.012; no. [76]: −0.023. The figure −0.023 from no. [76] is an outlier. The mean of the other five figures is 0.009. Thus, I accept 0.138 tentatively as my upper bound estimate for 1974.

Table 20.1 contains seven wage gap estimates for 1975 (lines 13–19) but two of these are made doubtful by coverage restricted to workers paid by the hour for which I made no adjustment. The mean of the other five adjusted estimates is 0.178. However, the three best studies for 1975, in my judgment, are nos. [10], [32], and [36] for which the mean of the adjusted estimates is 0.165 or 0.018 above my tentative bound for 1973. Seven studies, nos. [10], [32], [36], [66], and [82] using CPS data (Table 20.1) and nos. [72] and [78] using PSID data (Table 20.3) provide matching estimates for 1973 and 1975. The 1975 minus 1973 estimate differences from these studies are: no. [10]: 0.020; no. [32]: 0.008; no. [36]: 0.012; no. [66]: 0.04; no. [72]: 0.024; no. [78]: 0.015; no. [82]: −0.035. The last of these differences (−0.035) is clearly an outlier. The means of the other six differences is 0.017. Hence, I accept 0.165 tentatively as the upper bound estimate for 1975.

The mean of the tentative upper bound figures for 1973, 1974, and 1975 is 0.150. Three studies – see lines 36–38 in Table 20.1 – fitted wage equations to the pooled CPS for 1973–75. The mean of the adjusted estimates on lines 36–38 is 0.163 or 0.013 above the mean (0.150) of the tentative upper bounds for 1973–75. Hence, these three studies suggest that these bounds may be a bit too low.

There are no CPS-based estimates for 1972, one for each of 1970 and 1971, and none before 1970. Hence, I first extrapolate my tentative upper bound estimate for 1973 to the years 1970–72 with the help of studies [72], [76], and [78] based on PSID data (Table 20.3) for 1970–73 and then check these extrapolations against the CPS-based estimates for 1970 and 1971 shown on lines 39 and 40 of Table 20.1. The estimate differences from the three PSID studies are:

Study no.	1973 minus 1972	1973 minus 1971	1973 minus 1970
[72]	0.007	0.013	0.039
[76]	0.021	−0.006	0.016
[78]	0.035	−0.009	0.022
Mean	0.021	−0.001	0.026

Hence, my extrapolations (1973 = 0.147) are: 1972 = 0.126, 1971 = 0.148, and 1970 = 0.121. The CPS-based estimate on line 39 of Table 20.1 for 1971 is 0.151, which is close to the extrapolation. On the other hand, the corresponding estimate for 1970 on line 40 is 0.093, which is almost 0.03 below the extrapolation for that year. Nevertheless, I tentatively fix the upper bound for 1972 at 0.13, for 1971 at 0.15, and for 1970 at 0.12.

The adjusted wage gap estimates on lines 3–12 indicate that the mean wage gap in 1976–78 was higher than that in 1973–75. The smaller and, I think, better of the two estimates for 1976 is 0.18 which is 0.03 above the upper bound I have set for 1973–75. This is quite consistent with the excess of the 1976 over the 1973–75 wage gap estimates shown in PSID-based studies [72] and [78] (see Table 20.3). Hence, I fix the tentative upper bound for 1976 at 0.180, which makes the average upper bound for 1973–76 equal to 0.158, a bit above the adjusted estimate for 1973–76 from study no. [50] on line 35 of Table 20.1.

The two estimates for 1977 on lines 8 and 9 average 0.008 below the corresponding average for 1976, lines 10 and 11. A decline of this amount from 1976 to 1977 is consistent with the mean of the 1976–77 changes estimated in studies [72] and [78] (Table 20.3). Therefore I put the tentative upper bound for 1977 at 0.172.

The mean of the five adjusted wage gap estimates for 1978 (lines 3–7, Table 20.1) is the same as that for the two 1977 estimates (lines 8–9, Table 20.1) which suggests an upper bound for 1978 the same as that (0.172) for 1977. Other evidence on the change in the wage gap from 1977 to 1978 and from 1973–78 is mixed. Study [67] (Table 20.1, lines 4 and 8) shows a decline of 0.012 from 1977 to 1978. Study [72] (Table 20.3) shows an even larger decline (0.043) from 1977 to 1978. But CPS-based study [91] (Table 20.1, lines 6 and 33) shows a large increase 0.047 from 1973 to 1978. Thus, with considerable uncertainty I put the upper bound for 1978 at 0.172 the same as for 1977. Notice that if the upper bounds are put at 0.172 in 1977 and 1978 and 0.180 in 1976, the mean 0.175 of these three bounds is above the wage gap estimate 0.168 from study [48] on line 12.

I regard the estimates on line 2 from the Mellow studies [68] and [69] as the best of the CPS-based wage gap estimates. The unadjusted estimate is derived from a wage equation (actually six wage equations fitted separately by union status and firm size) with no worker coverage restrictions other than the usual ones and more importantly the most complete (for CPS-based studies) list of right-hand variables. In particular, only this wage equation and that underlying the estimates on line 1 included seniority and firm-size as right-hand variables.

Notice that the estimates on line 2 are 0.095 lower than the corresponding estimates on line 5. About half of this difference is accounted for by the date difference: 1979 on line 2, 1978 on line 5. The rest of the difference is attributable to the inclusion of seniority and firm size as right-hand variables in the line 2, but not the line 5 equations. Thus, if I were to accept the adjusted estimate 0.105 on line 2 as the 1979 upper bound, I would have to set the upper bounds for 1970–78 about 0.02 lower than I have put them. Instead, to be conservative in the upper bound estimates, I put the 1979 upper bound at 0.126 as suggested by line 5 (see the line 5 note).

In summary: on the basis of the CPS-based estimates (with some help from PSID estimates) I have fixed the following upper bounds to the overall mean wage gap for 1970–79 (after rounding):

$$1970 = 0.12, 1971 = 0.15, 1972 = 0.12, 1973 = 0.15, 1974 = 0.14,$$
$$1975 = 0.16, 1976 = 0.18, 1977 = 0.17, 1978 = 0.17, 1979 = 0.13,$$

whose 10-year mean is 0.15. The mean excess of the adjusted estimates on lines 1–40 of Table 20.1 over the corresponding upper bounds just listed is 0.013 and the standard deviation of these differences is 0.026.

6.2. Adjusted estimates from 1967 SEO data

Table 20.2 reports unadjusted and adjusted wage gap estimates derived from 16 different studies in which wage equations were fitted to 1967 Survey of Economic Opportunity data. The means and medians of the adjusted and unadjusted figures are all equal to 0.13. The standard deviation (0.027) of the adjusted estimates is about two-fifths lower than that (0.044) for the unadjusted estimates.

The best of the Table 20.2 estimates, in my judgment, are those on lines 1, 2, 3, and 11 from three Ashenfelter studies and one by Oaxaca. The mean of these four estimates is 0.11. This mean is 0.04 below the tentative upper bound I have fixed for 1973 and thus is broadly consistent with estimates from Ashenfelter's study No. [10] (see line 2 and the line note) that the mean wage gap in 1967 was appreciably below that in 1973. Hence, I put the tentative upper bound for 1967 at 0.11.

6.3. Adjusted estimates from the PSID data

Table 20.3 reports unadjusted and adjusted wage gap estimates retrieved from 25 studies in which the underlying Micro, OLS, and CS wage equations were fitted to the University of Michigan Panel Study of Income Dynamics data for one or another year or period during 1967–78.The primary purpose of this tabulation is to check the upper bounds I have tentatively fixed for 1967 and 1970–79. Column 6 shows for each year or period the values of these bounds.

Since I have not yet fixed bounds for 1968 and 1969 I first attend to that task. I estimate the bound for 1969 by extrapolation of that (0.15) for 1971 with the help of eight studies ([72], [76], [78], and [87] in Table 20.3 based on PSID data, and

Table 20.2
Estimates of the mean wage gap from 1967 SEO data.

Line no. (1)	Study no. (2)	Wage gap estimates		Adjustments (5)
		Unadjusted (3)	Adjusted (4)	
1	[9]	0.107	0.100	2, 11, 14
2	[10]	0.118	0.111	2, 11, 14
3	[11]	0.067	0.096	2, 5, 8, 11
4	[16]	0.195	0.168	2, 11, 13, 14
5	[31]	0.138	0.144	1, 2, 14
6	[37]	0.133	0.091	2, 7a, 13
7	[40]	0.189	0.162	2, 11, 13, 14
8	[41]	0.103	0.131	2, 8, 12–14
9	[58]	0.137	0.105	2, 7a, 14
10	[65]	0.201	0.174	2, 11, 13, 14
11	[79]	0.128	0.141	2, 8, 11, 14
12	[80]	0.166	0.159	2, 8, 11, 13, 14
13	[93]	0.060	0.088	2–4, 11–14
14	[94]	0.103	0.131	2–4, 11–14
15	[97]	0.098	0.122	2, 5, 14
16	[104]	0.198	0.141	2, 7a, 11, 14

Note to line 2. Comparable CPS estimates (adjusted) for 1973 = 0.166, for 1975 = 0.186.

[27], [60], [62], and [72] in Table 20.5 based on NLS data for Mature Men) that provided comparable estimates for both 1969 and 1971. In these eight studies the excess of the 1971 over 1969 estimate is:

Table 20.3	Table 20.5
[72] = 0.044	[27] = 0.039
[76] = 0.037	[60] = 0.032
[78] = 0.052	[62] = 0.032
[87] = 0.010	]72] = 0.030

The figure from study [87] is an outlier. The mean of the other seven figures is 0.038. Hence, I put the 1969 upper bound at 0.11.

There are only three studies ([72], [76], and [78] in Table 20.3) that provide estimates for 1968 along with comparable estimates for 1967 or 1969–71 and they disagree sharply with respect to placing the 1968 gap relative to that in 1967 or in 1969–71. Hence, I arbitrarily fix the gap for 1968 at 0.11 as in 1967 and 1969.

The mean excess of the adjusted estimates in column 5 over the bound in column 6 is 0.028 over the 25 lines of the table. The corresponding standard deviation is 0.059. Notice, however, that seven lines, 16–21 and 23, have an author (Raisian) in common. When these seven lines are combined and treated as one line, the mean excess (over 19 lines now) is 0.021 and the standard deviation

Table 20.3
Estimates of the mean wage gap from PSID data.

Line no. (1)	Study no. (2)	Year (3)	Gap estimate		Bound (6)	Adjustments (7)
			Unadjusted (4)	Adjusted (5)		
1	[13]	1967	0.251	0.271	0.11	2, 10, 13, 14
2	[47]	1967	0.157	0.177	0.11	2, 12, 14
3	[74]	1970	0.190	0.188	0.12	1, 2, 14
4	[34]	1971	0.150	0.190	0.15	2, 10, 14
5	[52]	1972	0.134	0.144	0.12	2, 14
6	[108]	1972	0.198	0.204	0.12	2, 5, 12–14
7	[55]	1973	0.106	0.106	0.15	2, 12–14
8	[64]	1973	0.208	0.208	0.15	2, 12–14
9	[73]	1973	0.133	0.139	0.15	2, 5, 12–14
10	[44]	1974	0.107	0.137	0.14	2, 3, 12–14
11	[1]	1975	0.073	0.073	0.16	2, 12–14
12	[22]	1975	0.19	0.20	0.16	2, 5, 12–14
13	[2]	1976	0.076	0.076	0.18	2, 12–14
14	[84]	1976	0.191	0.172	0.18	2, 5, 11–14
15	[63]	1967–73	0.11	0.13	0.12	2, 3, 14
16	[76]	1967–74	0.180	0.170	0.13	2, 13, 14
17	[85]	1967–74	0.163	0.157	0.13	1, 2, 3, 13, 14
18	[86]	1967–74	0.236	0.214	0.13	1, 2, 13, 14
19	[77]	1967–77	0.204	0.194	0.14	2, 13, 14
20	[78]	1967–77	0.204	0.204	0.14	1, 2, 14
21	[88]	1967–77	0.219	0.207	0.14	1, 2, 12–14
22	[72]	1968–78	0.134	0.150	0.14	2, 5, 14
23	[87]	1969–71	0.177	0.142	0.13	2, 11, 13, 14
24	[24]	1970–71	0.050	0.071	0.13	1, 2, 4, 14
25	[25]	1970–71	0.209	0.229	0.13	2, 10, 13, 14

Notes:

Line 16. Unadjusted estimate in column 4 is the mean of separate yearly estimates as follows: 1967 = 0.199, 1968 = 0.235, 1969 = 0.143, 1970 = 0.158, 1971 = 0.180, 1972 = 0.153, 1973 = 0.174, 1974 = 0.197.

Line 18. Estimate in column 4 is the mean of 4 separate estimates.

Line 20. Unadjusted estimate in column 4 is the mean of yearly figures as follows: 1967:0.207, 1968 = 0.204, 1969 = 0.165, 1970 = 0.186, 1971 = 0.217, 1972 = 0.173, 1973 = 0.208, 1974 = 0.199, 1975 = 0.223, 1976 = 0.242, 1977 = 0.220.

Line 22. Estimate in column 4 is the mean of three estimates from three different wage equations fitted to pooled 1968–78 data. Quite different estimates by year from a fourth wage equation are: 1968 = 0.026, 1969 = 0.040, 1970 = 0.055, 1971 = 0.081, 1972 = 0.087, 1973 = 0.094, 1974 = 0.085, 1975 = 0.118, 1976 = 0.125, 1977 = 0.130, 1978 = 0.087.

Line 23. Estimate in column 4 is the mean of yearly figures as follows: 1969 = 0.174, 1970 = 0.173, 1971 = 0.184.

is 0.064. The corresponding figures for the CPS data in Table 20.1 are 0.013 for the mean and 0.026 for the standard deviation and for the 1967 SEO data in Table 20.2 the mean excess is 0.019 and the standard deviation is 0.027. The best of the estimates in Table 20.3, in my opinion, is that on line 22 from the Mincer study. The adjusted figure 0.150 from the Mincer study for the period 1968–78 is 0.01 above the corresponding bound. Thus, I do not regard the PSID-based estimates in Table 20.3 as seriously challenging the upper bounds I have tentatively set. There is a suggestion that the upper bounds perhaps are about 0.01 too low.

6.4. Adjusted estimates from other Michigan Survey Research Center (SRC) data

Table 20.4 summarizes the unadjusted and adjusted wage gap estimates I have calculated from wage equations in 14 studies that were fitted to Survey Research Center survey data other than the PSID. The survey used on lines 1–6 of the table was the 1972–73 Quality of Employment Survey about which there is some ambiguity evidenced in the studies with respect to the date of the dependent wage

Table 20.4
Estimates of the mean wage gap from other SRC data.

Line no. (1)	Study no. (2)	Year (3)	Gap estimates		Bound (6)	Adjustment (7)
			Unadjusted (4)	Adjusted (5)		
A. Quality of employment survey						
1	[3]	1973	0.20	0.14	0.15	2, 5, 7a, 12–14
2	[4]	1973	0.101	0.119	0.15	2, 14
3	[43]	1973	0.145	0.179	0.15	2, 5, 10, 13, 14
4	[49]	1973	0.109	0.133	0.15	2, 3, 8, 13, 14
5	[71]	1973	0.120	0.146	0.15	2, 3, 5, 13, 14
6	[107]	1973	0.115	0.125	0.15	2, 14
7	[28]	1977	0.202	0.220	0.17	2, 14
8	[30]	1977	0.264	0.272	0.17	2, 12–14
B. Survey of working conditions						
9	[21]	1969	0.110	0.133	0.11	2, 4, 12–14
10	[43]	1969	0.070	0.104	0.11	2, 5, 10, 13, 14
11	[105, 106]	1969	0.108	0.098	0.11	2, 3, 7a, 14
C. Survey of consumer finances						
12	[42]	1968	0.153	0.151	0.11	2, 13, 14
13	[51]	1965–66	0.285	0.243	n.a.	2, 7a, 12–14
14	[103]	1966	0.152	0.185	n.a.	2, 4, 14
D. Time use survey						
15	[26]	1976	0.174	0.132	0.18	2, 7a, 12–14

Note: Line 5 is the mean of six estimates.

Table 20.5
Estimates of the mean wage gap from NLS data.

Line no. (1)	Study no. (2)	Year (3)	Gap estimates		Bound (6)	Adjustment (7)
			Unadjusted (4)	Adjusted (5)		
A. Young men						
1	[6]	1969	0.259	0.170	0.11	2, 4, 7a, 9, 14
2	[20]	1969	0.193	0.130	0.11	1, 2, 9, 12–14
3	[38]	1969	0.203	0.140	0.11	1, 2, 9, 12–14
4	[57]	1969	0.287	0.224	0.11	1, 2, 9, 12–14
5	[60]	1969	0.214	0.142	0.11	2, 9, 12–14
6	[72]	1969	0.21	0.13	0.11	2, 5, 9, 12–14
7	[73]	1969	0.167	0.091	0.11	2, 5, 9, 12–14
8	[20]	1970	0.188	0.125	0.12	1, 2, 9, 12–14
9	[39]	1970	0.163	0.100	0.12	1, 2, 9, 12–14
10	[19, 20]	1971	0.190	0.127	0.15	1, 2, 9, 12–14
11	[53]	1971	0.209	0.127	0.15	2, 9, 13, 14
12	[60, 62]	1971	0.224	0.152	0.15	2, 9, 12–14
13	[72]	1971	0.22	0.14	0.15	2, 5, 9, 12–14
14	[29]	1970–71	0.279	0.216	0.13	1, 2, 9, 12–14
15	[17]	1966–71, 1973	0.177	0.104	0.125	1, 2, 9, 13, 14
B. Mature men						
16	[6]	1969	0.165	0.156	0.11	2, 4, 7a, 14
17	[27]	1969	0.129	0.133	0.11	2, 5, 13, 14
18	[54]	1969	0.122	0.116	0.11	1, 2, 14
19	[60, 62]	1969	0.129	0.137	0.11	2, 12–14
20	[61]	1969	0.123	0.141	0.11	2, 14
21	[72]	1969	0.05	0.07	0.11	2, 5, 12–14
22	[27]	1971	0.168	0.172	0.15	2, 5, 13, 14
23	[46]	1971	0.061	0.056	0.15	1, 2, 12, 13
24	[53]	1971	0.149	0.147	0.15	2, 13, 14
25	[60, 62]	1971	0.161	0.169	0.15	2, 12–14
26	[72]	1971	0.08	0.10	0.15	2, 5, 12–14
27	[95]	1971	0.142	0.140	0.15	2, 13, 14
C. Young women						
28	[53]	1971	0.151	0.149	0.15	2, 13, 14
29	[75]	1972	0.124	0.132	0.12	2, 12–14
30	[92]	1973	0.160	0.168	0.15	2, 12–14
D. Mature women						
31	[53]	1971	0.111	0.109	0.15	2, 13, 14
32	[75]	1972	0.126	0.134	0.12	2, 12–14

Notes:
Lines 2, 8. Column 4 is the mean of three estimates.
Lines 10, 15. Column 4 is the mean of four estimates
Lines 12, 18, 19, 25. Column 4 is the mean of two estimates.
Line 15. Column 6 is the mean of bounds for 1967–71 and 1973.

variable. Some of the studies report the date as of 1972, others 1973, and still others do not report the date. I have put the date at 1973 on the basis of correspondence with one of the authors.

The mean excess of the adjusted estimates in column 5 over the bound in column 6 on the 13 lines of the table for which I have estimated the column 6 bound is 0.007 and the standard deviation of these differences is 0.039. The estimate of line 8, I think, is an unacceptable outlier. When it is discarded, the mean excess is -0.001 and the standard deviation is 0.029. The best of the adjusted estimates in Table 20.4, I judge, is that on line 6, which is 0.025 below the corresponding upper bound. Thus Table 20.4 suggests to me that perhaps I have set the upper bounds a bit too high.

6.5. *Adjusted estimates from the National Longitudinal Surveys*

I have unadjusted and adjusted wage gap estimates from 20 studies in which wage equations were fitted to data from the National Longitudinal Surveys. These estimates are presented in Table 20.5.

From the point of view of estimating the overall mean wage gap in the U.S. work force all four of the NLS panels suffer from strong age restrictions on

Table 20.6
Estimates of the mean wage gap from other sources.[a]

Line no. (1)	Study no. (2)	Year (3)	Gap estimates		Bounds (6)	Adjustments (7)
			Unadjusted (4)	Adjusted (5)		
1	[23]	1967–72	0.116	0.101/0.111	0.12	6, 7a, 11–13
2	[32]	1967–72	0.160	0.085	0.12	7a, 11, 12, 14
3	[33]	1967–72	0.173	0.108	0.12	7a, 11, 12
4	[36]	1967–72	0.119	0.124/0.134	0.12	6, 7a, 11, 12
5	[7]	1977	0.053	0.131	0.17	2, 7b
6	[12]	1977	0.118	0.178	0.17	7b, 8, 14
7	[59]	1978	0.13	0.14	0.17	2, 12–14

[a]*Sources*:
Lines 1–4. U.S. Bureau of Labor Statistics: *Employer Expenditures for Employee Compensation* (EEEC) surveys. In these surveys the observations are for establishments rather than individual workers.
Lines 5–6. A sample of 96 large establishments in 13 large SMSAs appearing in both the Bureau of Labor Statistics EEEC surveys and their *Area Wage Surveys*.
Line 7. Rand *Health Insurance Study*.

Line notes:
Line 4. Figure in column 4 is the mean of two estimates.
Line 7. The survey covered only 6 locations (cities or counties). No adjustment was made for this coverage restriction.

worker coverage and from over-sampling of Black workers. Furthermore, I have been able to adjust for the age restriction only for the panel of Young Men and crudely at that.

Nevertheless, the adjusted estimates in column 5 of Table 20.5 offer no more serious a challenge to the upper bounds (column 6) than the adjusted estimates based on CPS data in Table 20.1. The mean excess of the adjusted estimates over the corresponding bounds across the 32 lines of Table 20.5 is 0.008 and the standard deviation of the differences is 0.038. The corresponding figures for Table 20.1 are 0.013 for the mean and 0.026 for the standard deviation. Furthermore, when the outliers on lines 4, 14, 21, 23, and 26 of Table 20.5 are ignored, the mean excess is 0.009 and the standard deviation drops to 0.023.

6.6. Adjusted estimates from other sources

There remain seven studies in which the wage gap estimates are based on data sources other than those already covered in previous sections. The estimates from these studies are shown in Table 20.6. The mean excess of the adjusted estimates over the previously set upper bounds is −0.016 and the standard deviation is 0.018. Thus, these studies suggest that I may have set the upper bounds a bit too high.

6.7. Upper bounds for the overall mean wage gap

In the preceding pages of this section I have set a tentative upper bound on the overall mean wage gap for each of the years 1967–79, a period that covers almost all of the years for which Micro, OLS, and CS wage gap estimates are available. In fixing these bounds I have given preference to estimates (1) based on CPS data and (2) derived from wage equations with long lists of right-hand variables including interactions of union status with other right-hand variables. Furthermore, I have taken account of the information provided by several studies on date to date changes in the mean wage gap.

As a last check on these upper bounds I have sorted the adjusted gap estimates in Tables 20.1 to 20.6 by year instead of data source and for each year I have calculated the mean, standard deviation, and range. In making these calculations I have not excluded any of the estimates for 1967–79 reported in these tables and have given equal weight to each of the estimates. The results of these calculations appear in Table 20.7. Column 3 reports the number of estimates, column 4 the mean, column 5 the standard deviation, column 6 the range of the adjusted estimate, and column 7 the upper bound I have tentatively fixed for each year.

Table 20.7
Adjusted mean wage gap estimates by year.

Line no. (1)	Year (2)	No. of estimates (3)	Mean estimate (4)	Estimate S.D. (5)	Estimate range (6)	Tentative bound (7)	Period mean (8)
1	1967	20	0.14	0.04	0.09/0.027	0.11	
2	1968	4	0.15	0.07	0.03/0.22	0.11	
3	1969	20	0.13	0.04	0.05/0.22	0.11	
4	1970	8	0.13	0.05	0.06/0.19	0.12	
5	1971	18	0.14	0.04	0.06/0.22	0.15	
6	1972	7	0.14	0.03	0.09/0.20	0.12	
7	1973	24	0.15	0.03	0.10/0.21	0.15	
8	1974	7	0.15	0.04	0.09/0.20	0.14	
9	1975	11	0.17	0.04	0.07/0.22	0.16	
10	1976	7	0.16	0.05	0.08/0.24	0.18	
11	1977	8	0.19	0.05	0.13/0.27	0.17	
12	1978	7	0.17	0.04	0.09/0.20	0.17	
13	1979	2	0.12	–	0.11/0.13	0.13	
14	1967–79	143	0.15	0.04	0.07/0.22	0.14	
15	1967–72	4	0.11	0.02	0.08/0.13	0.12	0.14
16	1967–74	2	0.18	–	0.16/0.21	0.13	0.14
17	1967–77	1	0.21	–	–	0.14	0.15
18	1968–78	1	0.15	–	–	0.14	0.15
19	1970–71	3	0.17	–	0.07/0.22	0.14	0.14
20	1973–75	3	0.16	–	0.12/0.20	0.15	0.16
21	1973–76	1	0.15	–	–	0.16	0.16
22	1973–78	1	0.23	–	–	0.16	0.17
23	1976–78	1	0.17	–	–	0.16	0.17

Notes:

Line 14 is the 1967–79 mean (or total in column 3) of the yearly figures on lines 1–13.

Lines 15–23. The estimates in columns 4, 5, and 6 come from wage equations fitted to pooled data for several years without union status * year interactions. (There is no duplication between lines 1–13 and lines 15–23.) The figures in column 7 are appropriately dated means of the yearly bounds on lines 1–13. The figures is column 8 similarly are appropriately dated means of yearly means given in column 4 of lines 1–13.

Refer especially to line 14 which shows unweighted means across lines 1–13 of the 13 yearly figures for 1967–79. Notice that the 13-year mean of the adjusted estimates in column 4 is only 0.01 above the corresponding mean of the bounds in column 7. (That this column 4 mean 0.15 is a bit higher than that 0.14 for column 7 is not surprising given that in deriving column 7 from the underlying adjusted estimate I gave much greater weight to some estimates than to others.) Furthermore, the simple correlation across lines 1–13 between columns 4 and 7 is 0.74 and there is a moderately good simple correlation 0.50 between the first differences of columns 4 and 7.

In my judgment Tables 20.1 to 20.7 strongly support my estimates of the mean wage gap in column 7 of Table 7. Hence, I now drop the adjective "tentative" I have used to describe these figures. I have much more confidence, of course, in their 1967–79 average 0.14 than in the individual yearly figures which range from 0.11 to 0.18.

I describe these estimates of the U.S. mean wage gap, all derived from Micro, OLS, and CS wage equations, as "upper bounds" because I believe that in general such estimates suffer from *upward* bias resulting from the omission of right-hand variables correlated with the union status variable. I do not rule out the possibility that during 1967–79 the U.S. mean wage gap averaged as high as 0.14, but I suspect that the average was lower. By how much? I wish that I knew.

Appendix: Identification of adjustments in Tables 20.1–20.6: Adjustments to wage gap estimates

Adj. no. (1)	Adjustment amount (2)	Adjustment for (3)
1	−0.012	Overweighting Blacks in PSID and SEO
1	−0.024	Overweighting Blacks in NLS Mature Men
1	+0.009	Overweighting Blacks in NLS Young Men
2	+0.028	Omission of fringes, except when wage concept is
2	+0.020	that of annual earnings or annual average hourly earnings
3	+0.016	Hours gap, weekly earnings dependent
3	+0.030	Hours gap, annual earnings dependent
4	+0.023	Arithmetic dependent variable
5	+0.006	Omission of Blacks, SEO and Michigan data
5	+0.012	Omission of Blacks, NLS Mature Men
5	−0.004	Omission of Blacks, NLS Young Men
6	+0.07 to +0.08	Omission of nonmanufacturing
7a	−0.05	Omission of white-collar workers
7b	+0.05	Omission of blue-collar workers
8	+0.02	Omission of non-SMSA workers
9	−0.08	Age exclusions, NLS Young Men
10	+0.03	Omission of workers < 25 years of age
11	−0.025	Omission of government workers
12	+0.01	Omission of occupation variable
13	−0.02	Omission of industry variable
14	−0.01	Omission of extent of unionism by industry

References

[1] Abowd, John M. and Henry S. Farber (1978) "Relative wages, union membership, and job queues: econometric evidence based on panel data", Mimeographed. Cambridge: Massachusetts Institute of Technology.

[2]   Abowd, John M. and Henry S. Farber (1982) "Job queues and the union status of workers", *Industrial and Labor Relations Review*, 35:354–367.
[3]   Allen, Steven G. (1978) "Work attendance and earnings", Mimeographed. Raleigh: North Carolina State University.
[4]   Allen, Steven G. (1981) "How much does absenteeism cost?", Mimeographed. Raleigh: North Carolina State University.
[5]   Allen, Steven G. (1981) "Trade unions, absenteeism, and exit-voice", Mimeographed. Raleigh: North Carolina State University.
[6]   Andrisani, Paul J. and Andrew I. Kohen (1977) "The effects of collective bargaining as measured for men in blue-collar jobs", *Monthly Labor Review*, 100:46–49.
[7]   Antos, Joseph R. (1983) "Union effects on white collar compensation", *Industrial and Labor Relations Review*, 36:461–479.
[8]   Antos, Joseph R., Mark Chandler and Wesley Mellow (1980) "Sex differences in union membership", *Industrial and Labor Relations Review*, 33:162–169.
[9]   Ashenfelter, Orley (1972) "Racial discrimination and trade unionism", *Journal of Political Economy*, 80(Part I):435–464.
[10] Ashenfelter, Orley (1978) "Union relative wage effects: new evidence and a survey of their implications for wage inflation", in: R. Stone and W. Peterson, eds., *Econometric contributions to public policy*. New York: St. Martins Press.
[11] Ashenfelter, Orley and Michael K. Taussig (1971) "Notes on documentation of 'alternative estimates of union–nonunion wage differentials'", Mimeographed. Princeton: Princeton University.
[12] Atrostic, B. K. (1981) "Alternative compensation measures: effects on estimates of wage and compensation differentials", Mimeographed. Washington, D.C.: U.S. Bureau of Labor Statistics.
[13] Blinder, Alan S. (1973) "Wage discrimination: reduced form and structural estimates", *Journal of Human Resources*, 8:436–455.
[14] Bloch, Farrell E. and Mark S. Kuskin (1978) "Wage determination in the union and nonunion sectors", *Industrial and Labor Relations Review*, 31:183–192.
[15] Borjas, George J. (1979) "Job satisfaction, wages, and unions", *Journal of Human Resources*, 14:21–40.
[16] Boskin, Michael J. (1972) "Unions and relative real wages", *American Economic Review*, 62:466–472.
[17] Brown, Charles, (1980) "Equalizing differences in the labor market", *Quarterly Journal of Economics*, 94:113–134.
[18] Brown, Charles and James Medoff (1978) "Trade unions in the production process", *Journal of Political Economy*, 86:355–378.
[19] Chamberlain, Gary (1978) "On the use of panel data", Mimeographed. Madison: University of Wisconsin.
[20] Chamberlain, Gary (1982) "Multivariate regression models for panel data", *Journal of Econometrics*, 18:5–46.
[21] Cohen, Malcolm S. (1971) "Sex differences in compensation", *Journal of Human Resources*, 6:434–447.
[22] Da Vanzo, Julie and James R. Hosek (1980) "Does migration increase wage rates?—an analysis of alternative techniques for measuring wage gains to migration", Rand Working Draft No. WD-566-2-NICHD.
[23] Donsimoni, Marie-Paule (1981) "Union power and the American labor movement", *Applied Economics*, 13:449–464.
[24] Duncan, Greg J. (1974) "Nonpecuniary work rewards", in: James N. Morgan, ed., *Five thousand American families — patterns of economic progress*. Ann Arbor: Institute for Social Research, Vol. II.
[25] Duncan, Greg J. (1977) "Paths to economic well-being", in: Greg J. Duncan and James N. Morgan, eds., *Five thousand American families — patterns of economic progress*. Ann Arbor: Institute for Social Research, Vol. V.
[26] Duncan, Greg J. and Frank P. Stafford (1980) "Do union members receive compensating wage differentials?", *American Economic Review*, 70:355–371.

[27] Duncan, Gregory M. and Duane E. Leigh (1980) "Wage determination in the union and nonunion sectors: a sample selectivity approach", *Industrial and Labor Relations Review*, 34:24–34.
[28] Ehrenberg, Ronald G. and Paul L. Schumann (1981) "Compensating wage differentials for mandatory overtime", NBER Working Paper No. 805.
[29] Farber, Henry S. (1980) "Unionism, labor turnover, and wages of young men", *Research in Labor Economics*, 3:33–53.
[30] Farber, Henry S. (1983) "Worker preferences for union representation", *Research in Labor Economics*, 2(Supplement):171–205.
[31] Fechter, Alan E. and Charles O. Thorpe, Jr. (1977) "Labor market discrimination against the handicapped: an initial inquiry", Working Paper 3610-1, The Urban Institute.
[32] Freeman, Richard B. (1980) "Unionism and the dispersion of wages", *Industrial and Labor Relations Review*, 34:3–23.
[33] Freeman, Richard B. (1981) "The effect of unionism on fringe benefits", *Industrial and Labor Relations Review*, 34:489–509.
[34] Freeman, Richard B. (1981) "Troubled workers in the labor market", NBER Working Paper No. 816.
[35] Freeman, Richard B. and James L. Medoff (1981) "The impact of collective bargaining: illusion or reality", in: Jack Stieber, Robert B. McKersie and D. Quinn Mills, eds., *U.S. Industrial Relations 1950–1980: a critical assessment*. Industrial Relations Research Association.
[36] Freeman, Richard B. and James L. Medoff (1981) "The impact of the percentage organized on union and nonunion wages", *Review of Economics and Statistics*, 63:561–572.
[37] Gay, Robert S. (1975) "The impact of unions on relative real wages: new evidence on effects within industries and threat effects", Ph.D. Dissertation, University of Wisconsin–Madison.
[38] Griliches, Zvi. (1976) "Wages of very young men", *Journal of Political Economy*, 84(Part 2):569–585.
[39] Griliches, Zvi. (1978) "Earnings of very young men", in: Griliches, Krelle, Krupp and Kyn, eds., *Income distribution and economic inequality*. Frankfurt: Campus Verlag.
[40] Hall, Robert E. (1971) "Prospects for shifting the Phillips curve through manpower policy", *Brookings Papers*, 3:659–701.
[41] Hall, Robert E. (1973) "Wages, income, and hours of work in the U.S. labor force", in: Glen G. Cain and Harold W. Watts, eds., *Income maintenance and labor supply*. Chicago: Markham.
[42] Hamermesh, Daniel S. (1975) "The effects of government ownership on union wages", in: Daniel S. Hamermesh, ed., *Labor in the public and nonprofit sectors*. Princeton: Princeton University Press.
[43] Hamermesh, Daniel S. (1977) "Economic aspects of job satisfaction", in: Orley C. Ashenfelter and Wallace E. Oates, eds., *Essays in labor market analysis: in memory of Yochanan Peter Comay*. New York: Wiley.
[44] Heckman, James J. and George R. Neumann (1977) "Union wage differentials and the decision to join unions", Mimeographed. Chicago: University of Chicago.
[45] Hirsch, Barry T. and Mark C. Berger (1982) "Union membership and wage determination in manufacturing: the effects of concentration, capital intensity, and firm size", Mimeographed. Lexington: University of Kentucky.
[46] Hirsch, Werner Z. and Anthony M. Rufolo (1982) "Determinants of municipal wages: some tests of the competitive wage hypothesis", *Research in Urban Economics*, 2:309–327.
[47] Hoffman, Saul D. (1977) "Discrimination over the life-cycle: a longitudinal analysis of black–white experience–earnings profiles", Ph.D. Dissertation, University of Michigan.
[48] Holzer, Harry J. (1982) "Unions and the labor market status of white and minority youth", *Industrial and Labor Relations Review*, 35:392–405.
[49] Hyman, David N. and Robert M. Fearn (1978) "The influence of city size on labor incomes", *Quarterly Review of Economics and Business*, 18:63–73.
[50] Johnson, George E. (1982) "Inter-metropolitan wage differentials in the U.S.", University of Michigan Institute of Public Policy Studies Discussion Paper No. 171.
[51] Johnson, George E. and Kenwood C. Youmans (1971) "Union relative wage effects by age and education", *Industrial and Labor Relations Review*, 24:171–179.

[52] Johnson, William R. (1978) "Racial wage discrimination and industrial structure", *Bell Journal of Economics*, 9:70–81.

[53] Jones, Ethel B. (1982) "Union/nonunion differentials: membership or coverage?", *Journal of Human Resources*, 17:276–285.

[54] Kalachek, Edward and Fredric Raines (1976) "The structure of wage differences among mature male workers", *Journal of Human Resources*, 11:484–506.

[55] Kenny, Lawrence W. (1978) "Male wage rates and marital status", Mimeographed. Gainesville: University of Florida.

[56] Kiefer, Nicholas M. and Sharon P. Smith (1977) "Union impact and wage discrimination by region", *Journal of Human Resources*, 12:521–534.

[57] Lazear, Edward (1976) "Age, experience, and wage growth", *American Economic Review*, 66:548–558.

[58] Lee, Lung-Fei (1978) "Unionism and wage rates: a simultaneous equations model with qualitative and limited dependent variables", *International Economic Review*, 19:415–433.

[59] Leibowitz, Arleen (1981) "Fringe benefits in employee compensation", Mimeographed. Santa Monica: The Rand Corporation.

[60] Leigh, Duane E. (1978) "An analysis of the interrelation between unions, race, and wage and nonwage compensation", Final Report prepared for the Employment and Training Administration, U.S. Department of Labor, under Research and Development Grant No. 91-53-77-06.

[61] Leigh, Duane E. (1978) "Racial discrimination and labor unions: evidence from the NLS sample of middle-aged men", *Journal of Human Resources*, 13:568–577.

[62] Leigh, Duane E. (1980) "Racial differentials in union relative wage effects: a simultaneous equations approach", *Journal of Labor Research*, 1:95–114.

[62a] Lewis, H. G. (1982–84) *Union relative wage effects: a survey*. Mimeographed. Durham: Duke University.

[62b] Lewis, H. G. (1983) "Union relative wage effects: a survey of macro estimates", *Journal of Labor Economics*, 1:1–27.

[63] Lillard, Lee A. and Robert J. Willis (1978) "Dynamic aspects of earnings mobility", *Econometrica*, 46:985–1012.

[64] Linneman, Peter (1982) "The economic impacts of minimum wage laws: a new look at an old question", *Journal of Political Economy*, 90:443–469.

[65] Lucas, R. E. B. (1977) "Hedonic wage equations and psychic wages in the returns to schooling", *American Economic Review*, 67:549–558.

[66] Medoff, James L. (1979) "Layoffs and alternatives under trade unions in U.S. manufacturing", *American Economic Review*, 69:380–395.

[67] Mellow, Wesley (1981) "Unionism and wages: a longitudinal analysis", *Review of Economics and Statistics*, 63:43–52.

[68] Mellow, Wesley (1982) "Employer size and wages", *Review of Economics and Statistics*, 64:495–501.

[69] Mellow, Wesley (1983) "Employer size, unionism, and wages", *Research in Labor Economics*, 2(Supplement):253–282.

[70] Mellow, Wesley and Hal Sider (1983) "Accuracy of response in labor market surveys: evidence and implications", *Journal of Labor Economics*, 1:331–344.

[71] Miller, Frederick H., Jr. (1982) "Wages and establishment size", Ph.D. Dissertation, University of Chicago.

[72] Mincer, Jacob (1983) "Union effects: wages, turnover, and job training", *Research in Labor Economics*, 2(Supplement):217–252.

[73] Mincer Jacob and Linda Leighton (1981) "The effects of minimum wages on human capital formation", In: Simon Rottenberg, ed., *The economics of legal minimum wages*. Washington, D.C. and London: American Enterprise Institute for Public Policy Research.

[74] Moore, William J. (1980) "Membership and wage impact of right-to-work laws", *Journal of Labor Research*, 1:349–368.

[75] Moore, William J., Douglas K. Pearce and R. Mark Wilson (1981) "The regulation of occupations and the earnings of women", *Journal of Human Resources*, 16:366–383.

[76] Moore, William J. and John Raisian (1980) "Cyclical sensitivity of union/nonunion relative wage effects", *Journal of Labor Research*, 1:115–132.

[77]   Moore, William J. and John Raisian (1981) "Unionism and wage rates in the public and private sectors: a comparative time series analysis", Mimeographed. Washington, D.C.: U.S Bureau of Labor Statistics.

[78]   Moore, William J. and John Raisian (1983) "The level and growth of union/nonunion relative wage effects, 1967–77", *Journal of Labor Research*, 4:65–79.

[79]   Oaxaca, Ronald (1973) "Male–female wage differentials in urban labor markets", *International Economic Review*, 14:693–709.

[80]   Oaxaca, Ronald (1975) "Estimation of union/nonunion wage differentials within occupational/regional subgroups", *Journal of Human Resources*, 10:529–537.

[81]   Olson, Craig A. (1981) "An analysis of wage differentials received by workers on dangerous jobs", *Journal of Human Resources*, 16:167–185.

[82]   Pearce, James E. (1980) "Trade unionism, implicit contracting, and the response to demand variation in U.S. manufacturing", Research Paper No. 8003, Federal Research Bank of Dallas.

[83]   Podgursky, Michael J. (1980) "Trade unions and income inequality", Ph.D. Dissertation, University of Wisconsin–Madison.

[84]   Polachek, Solomon W. (1981) "Unionization of the white collar worker", Mimeographed. Chapel Hill: University of North Carolina.

[85]   Raisian, John (1979) "Skill acquisition and associated cyclic variability in hours, weeks, and wages", Mimeographed. Houston: University of Houston.

[86]   Raisian John (1979) "Cyclic patterns in weeks and wages", *Economic Inquiry*, 17:475–495.

[87]   Raisian John (1983) "Union dues and wage premiums", *Journal of Labor Research*, 4:1–18.

[88]   Raisian, John and Elaine Donovan (1980) "Patterns of real wage growth 1967–77: who has prospered?", BLS Working Paper No. 104.

[89]   Roback, Jennifer (1982) "Wages, rents, and the quality of life", *Journal of Political Economy*, 90:1257–1278.

[90]   Ryscavage, Paul M. (1974) "Measuring union–nonunion earnings differences", *Monthly Labor Review*, 97:3–9.

[91]   Sahling, Leonard G. and Sharon P. Smith (1983) "Regional wage differentials: has the South risen again?", *Review of Economics and Statistics*, 65:131–135.

[92]   Sandell, Steven H. and David Shapiro (1980) "Work expectations, human capital accumulation, and the wages of young women", *Journal of Human Resources*, 15:335–353.

[93]   Schmidt, Peter (1978) "Estimation of a simultaneous equations model with jointly dependent continuous and qualitative variables: the union-earnings question revisited", *International Economic Review*, 19:453–465.

[94]   Schmidt, Peter and Robert P. Strauss (1976) "The effect of unions on earnings and earnings on unions: a mixed logit approach", *International Economic Review*, 17:204–212.

[95]   Shapiro, David (1978) "Relative wage effects of unions in the public and private sectors", *Industrial and Labor Relations Review*, 31:193–203.

[96]   Smith, D. Alton (1980) "Government employment and black/white relative wages", *Journal of Human Resources*, 15:77–86.

[97]   Smith, Robert S. (1973) "Compensating wage differentials and hazardous work", Department of Labor, Office of Evaluation Technical Analysis Series Paper No. 5.

[98]   Smith, Sharon P. (1976) "Government wage differentials by sex", *Journal of Human Resources*, 11:185–199.

[99]   Smith, Sharon P. (1976) "Are postal workers over- or underpaid?", *Industrial Relations*, 15:168–176.

[100] Smith, Sharon P. (1977) "Government wage differentials", *Journal of Urban Economics*, 4:248–271.

[101] Smith, Sharon P. (1977) *Equal pay in the public sector: fact or fantasy.* Princeton: Industrial Relations Section, Princeton University.

[102] Smith, V. Kerry (1983) "The role of site and job characteristics in hedonic wage models", *Journal of Urban Economics*, 13:296–321.

[103] Stafford, Frank P. (1968) "Concentration and labor earnings: comment", *American Economic Review*, 58:174–181.

[104] Thaler, Richard and Sherwin Rosen (1975) "The value of saving a life: evidence from the labor market", in: Nestor E. Terleckyj, ed., *Household production and consumption*. New York: National Bureau of Economic Research.

[105] Viscusi, W. Kip (1978) "Wealth effects and earnings premiums for job hazards", *Review of Economics and Statistics*, 60:408–416.

[106] Viscusi, W. Kip (1980) "Union, labor market structure, and the labor market implications of the quality of work", *Journal of Labor Research*, 1:175–192.

[107] Wessels, Walter J. (1981) "Economic effects of right to work laws", *Journal of Labor Research*, 2:55–75.

[108] White, Halbert (1981) "Consequences and detection of misspecified nonlinear regression models", *Journal of the American Statistical Association*, 76:419–433.

Chapter 21

SEGMENTED LABOR MARKETS

PAUL TAUBMAN and MICHAEL L. WACHTER*

University of Pennsylvania

1. Introduction and summary

The segmented labor market (SLM) approach is typically identified with a group of economists who argue that the neoclassical apparatus provides an inadequate or incomplete description of the labor market and leaves unexplained most of the major labor market policy issues. In particular, the neoclassical model is viewed as not providing adequate explanation of the distribution or dispersion of wages (and, as a consequence, income) across workers, the incidence of unemployment, and the causes of discrimination.

The SLM literature itself ranges over a broad spectrum of viewpoints that share a common hypothesis that labor markets are segmented and that problems of income distribution, unemployment, and discrimination are a result of that segmentation. Some models and research that carry the SLM label are clearly different from neoclassical research. Others, however, are close to the borderline, where a demarcation becomes fuzzy. The factors that are stressed as causing segmentation as well as the permeability of the barriers that separate the segments are the central issues that differentiate the research in this area.

A distinctive feature of SLM research is that it is primarily motivated by concern over policy issues. The SLM studies tend to attack both positive and normative questions together: Are there segmented labor markets? If so, what can be done to deal with them?

Although there are important differences between Marxian oriented policy solutions and those favored by non-Marxian SLM researchers, all share a belief that the wage and income distributions are unfairly tilted against the poor and that greater government involvement is needed to rectify the solution. The private sector market is viewed as either not working or yielding solutions that are unacceptable on normative grounds. In pursuing policy issues, less stress is

*The research underlying this chapter was supported by grants from the General Electric Foundation and the National Institutes of Health.

Handbook of Labor Economics, Volume II, Edited by O. Ashenfelter and R. Layard
©*Elsevier Science Publishers BV, 1986*

placed on conventional tax and transfer policies to alter the income distribution and more attention is given to industrial policies that shift the distribution of economic market power.

Given the differences within the SLM literature, we have selected to highlight the major points that are shared by most of the models in this area. We shall use the neoclassical model as a point of reference, although this may be a disservice to that portion of the literature that is based on alternative methodologies (e.g. the Marxian approach).

Neoclassical models also recognize that labor markets are segmented. Geographical and biological, especially age, factors cause labor inputs to be imperfect substitutes for each other. In addition, preference functions are assumed to vary as a function of variables such as age. Labor market institutions, such as labor unions, and government laws, such as restrictions on in-migration, also cause market segmentation. The SLM literature, however, tends to stress other causes of segmentation.

Distinguishing between the SLM and neoclassical literatures is thus useful. Methodological as well as substantive differences exist. In addition, researchers themselves often use the SLM label to describe their work. We do not attempt to assess whether there is a distinctive SLM model that can be interpreted as an alternative paradigm to the neoclassical model. Instead, for the purposes of this Handbook we highlight the specific conceptual and empirical hypotheses that arise from a focus on segmentation. As will be seen, many of these hypotheses can be integrated into the neoclassical apparatus.

Our reading of the SLM literature suggests that the major conceptual difference between the neoclassical and SLM literature can be described in the following manner: the thrust of neoclassical economics is the study of maximizing behavior on the part of individuals and firms. In this approach, endogenous changes in the tastes of individuals and details on the institutional framework of markets are largely ignored. The SLM, on the other hand, focuses specifically on the development of institutional constraints and on the determinants of endogenous tastes. Based on this approach, the SLM literature typically eschews the equilibrium analysis associated with neoclassical economics in favor of historical analysis. That is, labor market problems are viewed in a dynamic context, where maximizing behavior, to the extent that it does exist, is unimportant for the market outcomes that are of the greatest concern. Thus, historical dynamism overwhelms any tendency toward labor market equilibrium.

Some researchers, operating within neoclassical ground rules, do treat tastes and institutions as endogenous, while taking profit-maximizing behavior as given. Examples are habit formation in economic demography, scarring effects in unemployment, and labor market contracting in industrial relations. Although these models depart from standard neoclassical models in treating tastes and institutions as endogenous, they all share the maintained assumption of profit- and utility-maximizing behavior on the part of firms and individuals.

The central empirical hypothesis of the SLM approach is that the labor market segmentation that exists does not correspond to skill differentials in the labor market. For expositional purposes in describing this hypothesis, it is useful to use the dual labor market version of the SLM theory.

The dual labor market is characterized by two sectors: a high wage primary sector that is composed of firms with internal labor markets and a low wage secondary sector that is composed of firms that hire from the external or spot market. Since the workers in the two sectors have, at least initially, similar skills, the jobs in the high wage sector can be fairly classified as "good" jobs, while those in the secondary sector can be classified as "bad" jobs.[1]

Much of the SLM literature is devoted to exploring the reasons why the markets are segmented along lines where the observed wage differentials are not a result of underlying skill differentials. Why is it that mobility between these sectors is severely limited so that excess demand pressures cannot compete away the wage differential? That is, what are the causes of market segmentation and how quantitatively important are those factors to the distribution of wages and unemployment?

The SLM develops a number of themes in answering these questions. First, the internal labor market in the primary sector does not function along profit-maximizing lines. Rather, institutional rules are substituted for market processes. As a result, competitive pressures to equalize wage differentials are absent. Second, labor unions play a positive role in the primary sector. Rather than being viewed as artificially raising wages and restricting employment, labor unions are credited with "positive feedback", which improves workers' productivity. Third, a different reward and incentive system exists across the segmented labor markets. Specifically, the wage mechanism is different across sectors so that otherwise comparable individuals achieve different outcomes. The result is underemployment for those "good" workers dead-ended in "bad" jobs. Finally, bad jobs create negative feedback. The learning-by-doing in the secondary sector is thus equivalent to negative general training where individuals are "scarred" by working.

The SLM model as a theory, however, is incomplete, with important links missing. This is partly a result of its tendency to rely on historical and descriptive analysis. As a consequence, in our discussion of the model below, we are forced to assume some of the missing equilibrium linkages that tie the model together. together.

In the SLM literature causes of segmentation are typically divided into two categories: those that emanate from the high wage sectors and those that arise from the low wage sectors of the labor market. An alternative categorization

---

[1] The seminal paper in this literature is Doeringer and Piore (1971). In the early literature, see also Gordon (1972) and Harrison (1972). The literature through 1975 was surveyed by Cain (1976) and Wachter (1974).

distinguishes between pre-market (or supply) and market (i.e. in-market or demand) causes of segmentation.[2]

Empirical work has concentrated on three issues. The first is whether the primary and secondary sectors yield different returns to schooling and different years of work experience profiles. Differences exist though it is difficult to divide occupations between the two sectors. Moreover, as indicated below, especially in the section on job training, the differences may be irrelevant. The second issue is whether bad jobs convert good workers to bad workers. Proving causation is very difficult here, though some estimates of scarring are available. The third issue is whether there are any large groups of people who are trapped in low paying jobs. Most of the evidence from lengthy longitudinal samples suggests substantial intertemporal mobility in earnings except for the groups of poor blacks and the wealthy. The former may fit the theory, the latter does not.

In Section 2 the SLM model of the internal labor market of the primary sector of the economy is explored, and the SLM model of the secondary or low wage sector of the economy is introduced. In Section 3 the secondary sector model is analyzed in more detail. In Section 4 the findings in the empirical literature that are relevant to the testable hypotheses of the SLM are surveyed.

2. The internal labor market

The term "internal labor market" refers to the set of rules and institutions that govern the allocation and pricing of labor within the firm. Although all firms have an industrial relations system to some extent, whether explicit or implicit, most researchers seem to reserve the term for those internal labor markets that have well-developed institutional characteristics. Since most of these firms are in the high wage sectors of the economy, the internal market terminology is frequently associated with the practices of high wage firms. In this chapter we follow the convention of identifying the internal labor market with primary sector firms.

To what extent and through what mechanism do the internal labor markets of the primary sector contribute to segmentation? Several explanations have been offered to answer these questions. First, the SLM (or, more specifically, the dual labor market) hypothesis is that the internal labor market does not function along profit-maximizing lines. Rather, institutional rules are substituted for market processes. As a result, competitive pressures to equalize wage differentials are absent.[3] Second, a relevant Marxian interpretation is that the internal labor

---

[2] See Ryan (1981).
[3] The internal labor market in the SLM literature is developed by Doeringer and Piore (1971).

market serves as a process for de-skilling the wage force.[4] Third, the neoclassical version is that the internal labor market represents an efficiency response to externalities, in particular those created by job-specific training.[5]

2.1. Historical antecedents

Disagreements as to how best to characterize the functioning of the labor market have been a long-standing dispute between neoclassical and institutional oriented economists. Although the historical arguments do not strictly parallel the schools of thought existing today, there are interesting differences that seem to have persisted over time. An example is provided by the differences in the views of Adam Smith and John Stuart Mill with respect to wage determination. Smith, as the forerunner of the neoclassical school, emphasized the workings of the marketplace. Just as today's neoclassical economists recognize the existence of labor unions and nonpecuniary factors, Smith provided the arguments for wage differentials based on "compensating differentials".

John Stuart Mill, on the other hand, tended to argue that the institutional realities of the marketplace were too prevalent and important to be characterized as mere departures from otherwise competitive markets. Not unlike the secondary labor markets of today, the agricultural labor markets of the 1800s could be viewed as reasonably competitive. To Mill, however, many of the important primary, nonagricultural labor markets were better characterized as being composed of "noncompeting groups". Due to such factors as guild or local laws and customs, supply and demand conditions in the labor market were not relevant. Within these groups, wage levels and the allocation of labor were determined by the institutional rules and customs of the day.

The American institutionalist school of thought in the early 1900s built upon this tradition. Their argument was that the equilibrium analysis of the day, largely following the work of Marshall, did not apply to labor markets. In a world of large scale immigration, labor markets consisted of entrepreneurs, who set the rules of the game, and a group of undifferentiated, largely unskilled workers. The subsequent theory of monopsony captured some but by no means all of the concerns expressed in the labor market writings of Thornton Veblin, W. C. Mitchell, and Henry Commons.

The institutionalist tradition was maintained during the 1950s and 1960s by the industrial relations literature. The notion of "balkanized" labor markets was advanced by Kerr (1954) to describe market segmentation that existed across firms and industries. The work by Dunlop (1957), Hildebrand (1963), Livernash

[4] See, in particular, Braverman (1974).
[5] See, for example, Williamson, Wachter, and Harris (1975).

(1957), and Ross (1958), among others, developed the notion of job clusters, wage contours, orbits of coercive comparisons, and pattern (collective) bargaining. These concepts presented details on the workings of internal (to the firm) employment relationships. They also sketched out the degree to which certain firms and industries seemed to follow each other, while seemingly ignoring others, in setting their wages and conditions of employment.

The industrial relations researchers were interested in describing the rich diversity of rules and customs that could be found and did not specifically address the degree to which these institutions fit into or conflicted with neoclassical theory. Their argument was largely that the textbook model of labor markets functioning as "spot" markets was not relevant.

For the industrial relations specialists, the neoclassical models were guilty of omission rather than commission. Specifically, they tended to view the neoclassical spot labor market as largely irrelevant to the central issues that they wished to explore. They left unanswered the question as to whether the neoclassical model could be expanded upon to explain the observable institutional realities. Differences in methodology, however, did lead to contentiousness between the neoclassical and industrial relations camps.

The SLM model of the 1970s and 1980s draws heavily upon such industrial relations research and institutionalist theories. Researchers, such as Doeringer and Piore, used the internal labor market construct as a building block for their theory that labor markets were segmented in a way that conflicted with the neoclassical apparatus. Thus, they argued that what may have been methodological disagreements were now, in fact, theoretical differences. Other researchers differed, however, and claimed that the internal labor market could be interpreted as the institutional detail through which neoclassical labor markets functioned. Before exploring these conflicting hypotheses, it is worth noting briefly the institutional realities of the internal labor market that are shared by the various schools of thought.

2.2. Internal labor markets

A representative firm in the high wage labor market governs its labor relations through the use of an internal labor market. The internal labor market consists of a set of structured employment relationships within a firm, embodying a set of rules, formal (as in unionized firms) and informal, that governs all jobs and their interrelationships. These rules cover the content and wages attached to each job, the organizational structure that ties jobs together, entry requirements for new hires, and the opportunities for promotion and job-specific training. Since the full set of rules is necessarily part of an "implicit labor contract", a grievance procedure is frequently used to complete the governance structure.

As a consequence of technological consideration and/or the functioning of the set of rules governing the internal market, most jobs within the firm are unique and thus separate and distinct from any external labor market. New workers are used principally to fill specially designated entry jobs, which exist at various levels of the organization structure. Other jobs are linked to entry jobs through promotion ladders and, hence, are filled from within.

Idiosyncratic jobs buffer the internal market from external wage pressures. Workers already in a firm have an advantage over outsiders and thus a degree of monopoly power that is either a result of job-specific training or job rights based on the implicit labor contract. The discrepancy between the workers' opportunity wage and internal labor market wage also gives the firm monopoly power over the worker.

The major differences among the schools of thought on internal labor markets relate to: (1) the degree to which the rules governing the internal market reflect efficiency considerations; (2) the distribution of the above monopoly power between firms and workers; and (3) the nature of restrictions on the number of primary sector jobs that are created.

The SLM model argues that the internal labor market should be viewed as substituting rules for markets. The assignment of individuals and wages to jobs is specifically done in a way that bears little relationship to a competitive market solution to the same problem. In addition, and for reasons that can only be understood by analyzing the historical development of these markets, too few primary sector (or good) jobs are created.

The differences between the SLM and the neoclassical interpretation of the internal labor market are stressed by Piore:

> The [neoclassical] convention has been to assume that factors such as the internal rules of the firm or the internal psychology of the individual are either very stable or so tightly constrained by the market that references to the latter will explain their variability. It is at this point that I think that the whole attempt to encompass notions of labor market stratification within conventional theory begins to break down.[6]

In the SLM literature, labor market problems are viewed in a dynamic context and the historical dynamism is viewed as overwhelming any tendency toward equilibrium. The topical orientation of this type of analysis has its closest neoclassical counterpart in economic history, which searches for the invisible hand of market forces behind historical developments. The efficiency explanation of internal labor markets offered below can be viewed as illustrating this latter type of analysis.

---

[6] Piore (1983, p. 26).

Empirical support for the SLM view of internal labor markets is typically based on field research in specific internal labor markets and historical studies of the evolution of these types of markets. See, for example, Wilkinson (1981) and Osterman (1984) for edited collections of essays on the evolution of specific internal labor markets.

The analysis in these essays places considerable stress on specific historical events and disequilibrium processes. The view is that these markets are in a constant state of evolution which overrides market pressures toward equilibrium. Labor unions, government policies that intervene in the market, and other such institutional events determine the outcome. Competitive market forces, on the other hand, are viewed as largely irrelevant.

For example, in an investigation of labor relations practices of large firms in the early 1900s, Jacoby (1982) argued that few of the practices associated with internal labor markets predated labor unions. Consequently, he claimed that the internal labor market should not be interpreted as developing in response to market pressures for more efficient employment relationships. Data limitations, however, make it difficult to identify the pre-labor union internal labor market practices that were not made explicit. Absent labor unions, managers of the manufacturing assembly lines of the early 1900s could both utilize elements of today's internal labor markets while maintaining discretion. Hence, it is possible the impact of labor unions was less to initiate the processes of the internal market and more to regularize them.[7]

2.3. The question of allocative efficiency

The SLM literature views internal labor market jobs to be better than jobs in the secondary sector. That is, the rules and customs that set wages in that market set them higher than comparable jobs in the spot (or secondary) market. This raises major questions as to allocative efficiency. Is the number of primary sector jobs artificially reduced below what efficiency considerations would dictate? What is the process through which the economy produces too few good jobs?

Answering these questions is not a simple task. Since many of the SLM researchers view themselves as working outside the neoclassical framework, they frequently do not indicate how or where their model diverges from the neoclassical model. As a consequence, the explanation provided here is based on our own interpretation of the SLM model.

---

[7]More generally, historical methodology that seeks to identify the specific forces that determine historical outcomes is likely to be biased against finding in favor of "the invisible hand". The alternative approach, utilized by neoclassical oriented economic historians, is to decide whether the outcomes and existing institutions are compatible with market drive efficiency forces.

The first issue seems noncontroversial and, in the neoclassical model, perhaps even redundant. Given the *high* wages, not only would there be too few jobs in the high wage sector, but also the "high" wages would be the cause of the problem.

In the SLM, however, the firm may not be fixing the wage–employment decision on the basis of a neoclassical, downward sloping demand curve for labor. This frees the high wages from bearing the onus of causing the misallocation of resources. This conclusion of the existence of too few good jobs is based on the observation that there are many more good workers than good jobs. The result of the shortage of jobs is the need to allocate those jobs among workers. In the SLM model, the allocation of labor among good jobs is done in an arbitrary manner. That is, the jobs are not filled on the basis of whatever skill differences are observable.

The above discussion answers the question as to how the high-wage jobs are allocated. The factors that determine the size of the primary sector, according to the SLM model, are largely a consequence of exogenous technological and historical economic development. In fact, there is a considerable literature on the historical evolution of internal labor markets in different industries. This, however, does not provide much insight for understanding the model within a neoclassical framework.

Although the SLM omits important linkages in its description of the general equilibrium properties of its systems, there are ways of filling in these gaps. For example, in the economic development literature there is a "dual model" corresponding to the modern and traditional sectors. The modern sector has some similarities to the SLM's primary sector, and the traditional sector can be compared to the secondary sector. Taking this approach, a hybrid of the SLM and dual model in the economic development literature might suggest the following interpretation.[8]

First, the size of the "modern" or primary sector would be determined by the size of the capital stock. The wage level in the primary sector would be determined by labor unions, government minimum wage policy, or social custom. (As an alternative, a high wage policy might be adopted by firms whose cost structure is such that it is profitable to pay a higher wage than that found in the secondary sector. This might result from a high turnover cost or for other reasons that lead the firm to desire to have a queue of workers readily available.)

Second, positing low or zero (where the technology is Leontief) elasticities of substitution among factors would mean that the wage itself has little or no allocative effect on the level of employment. Employment in the high wage sector would then be determined on a first-come basis to immigrants pulled away from the subsistence wages paid in the secondary sector.

[8] Harris and Todaro (1970); and Kelley, Williamson and Cheetham (1972).

Third, unemployment in this type model would be determined by the size of the wage differentials between the high and low wage industries. Workers queue for jobs in the high wage sector as long as the expected value of waiting is greater than the wage rate in the secondary sector. The value of queuing is a function of the probability of being hired into a primary job, the length of time waiting to be hired, the amount of time expected to be working in the primary sector, and the value of any government transfer assistance programs that might be available while unemployed.

The above type hybrid model is a reasonable approximation to a number of the general equilibrium type implications of the SLM model. Other features of the SLM model, however, are missed by the above model. Of particular importance is the role played by negative feedback effects.

The issue of "negative feedback" is crucial to the SLM story.[9] Although it is explored in some depth in the next section, it is introduced here because it provides a separate answer to the question of how workers are allocated between the primary and secondary sectors. Indeed, in a historical context, it could even be useful in explaining the size of the primary sector.

The argument is the following. Although workers in the secondary sector may initially be as good as workers in the primary sector, a process of divergence eventually molds the workers to their jobs. Hence, the allocation of labor may, ex post, be justified. That is, the direction of causality is assumed to run from job to worker quality. The SLM literature is quite explicit on this point, at least as it refers to low wage jobs molding the workers initially trapped in that sector to the skill and behavioral requirements of those jobs. (The literature is less definite with respect to high wage jobs creating high wage workers.)

2.4.   The role of labor unions

The above considerations lead the neoclassical and SLM literatures to different assessments of the influence of labor unions. In terms of the SLM model, labor unions play an integral and positive role. Specifically, they are one of the agents in the economy that encourages positive or, at least, avoids negative feedback between job and worker quality. In addition, since the size of the primary sector is largely dictated by technological considerations, where wage differentials or relative factor costs are unimportant, labor unions' wage premiums do not have the role of spoiler in terms of the number of good jobs. That employment in the heavy industry base of the unionized sector has been on a long-run decline is attributed to other factors.

---

[9] The importance of negative feedbacks has been stressed by Vietorisz and Harrison (1973).

Although we do not explore in detail the Marxian version of the SLM, one aspect of that literature is useful to the issues raised in this section. The notion that internal labor markets are part of the "good" jobs in the economy is not shared by all SLM researchers. In fact, as mentioned above, there is a growing literature on internal labor markets in different industries and countries that uses the internal labor market designation generically to refer to the employment relationship without differentiating between primary and secondary type markets.

In the Marxian literature, the internal labor market is explored for its function in determining the power relationship between employers and employees. Where labor unions are present, the workers are viewed as having some degree of power in dealing with employers. The same type of internal labor market, absent labor unions, however, may represent a way of imposing hierarchical corporate structure on workers.

Indeed, an important subset of the SLM research on internal labor markets investigates the efficiency of that type of market in "de-skilling" workers. The internal labor market provides the firm with an organizational structure which subdivides skills and narrows the expertise that any single worker or group of workers can acquire. To prevent workers from organizing against de-skilling, firms are viewed as contracting out work to nonunion or secondary market firms. In this model, the size of the primary sector is not determined by the available capital stock and the array of factor prices; rather, it is determined by the firms' political-economic power to manipulate their economic environment. Given the power exercised by firms, the distinction between primary and secondary firms is blurred, and primary sector jobs simply could not become too attractive.[10]

The neoclassical alternative to the SLM or Marxian vision is that the internal labor market represents an efficiency response to externalities inherent in the employment relationship and those externalities and market imperfections foreclose atomistic market solutions [Wachter (1974) and Williamson, Wachter and Harris (1975)]. Several arguments have been advanced. First, large-scale internal markets (compared to spot or external markets) develop to take advantage of scale economies with respect to capital and information indivisibilities. Second, nonseparabilities among workers require an organizational framework to bring the appropriate groups of workers together. Third, pervasive job specificity exists, which creates firm-specific human capital which in turn poses problems similar to bilateral monopoly. The internal labor market functions to economize on those transactions costs by encouraging joint maximization on the part of both firms and workers.

Once an internal labor market exists to represent the employment relationship, the issue of whether the rules represent efficiency considerations is largely one of

---

[10] See, in particular, Braverman (1974). Other references include Edwards (1979) and Gordon, Edwards and Reich (1982).

whether firms maximize profits. In this view the presence of, for example, labor unions and government regulations does not negate the model. Rather, such institutions should be viewed as posing added constraints on the ability of firms to deal with employment-related externalities and to influence the outcome of firm–worker bargaining.

Since the transactions costs argument draws upon the SLM research on internal labor markets, it is worth elaborating briefly on its main arguments. The existence of a bilateral monopoly problem between the firm and individual workers yields the likelihood of suboptimal outcomes. The purpose of the internal labor market is to neutralize this issue by encouraging joint maximization. Accomplishing this aim involves minimizing bargaining and turnover costs, encouraging workers to exercise their specific knowledge, and ensuring that investments of idiosyncratic types are undertaken without risk of exploitation by either side. Hence, contrary to the SLM argument, important features of the employment relationship encourage efficiency.

Issues concerning the origin of internal labor markets, however, need not influence the allocative function of these markets. For example, the observation that the specific wage rates that are attached to any of the jobs internal to the firm can be arbitrary does not indicate a departure from efficiency considerations. The human capital as well as the institutional labor relations literatures have long recognized that single-period wage rates on any individual job can be arbitrary. Efficiency concerns only constrain the expected present value of an intertemporal stream of earnings across jobs that are part of promotion ladders.

The term "good jobs" is not defined in the neoclassical model. Adam Smith's compensating differentials are presumed to be working; hence, wage rates are set so as to offset nonpecuniary factors. To the extent that the neoclassical models borrow from John Stuart Mill's noncompeting groups, however, the term is defined. Good jobs in the neoclassical–Mill sense refer to jobs that are paid more than that dictated by competitive market forces. Since these jobs represent a departure from competitive norms, there is broad agreement among neoclassical economists that there are too *many* good jobs for purposes of efficiency. On the other hand, there are too *few* good jobs given the number of workers who have the human capital requirements to fill them.

As indicated above, it is on this issue that the neoclassical and SLM models differ in their assessment of labor unions. In the neoclassical model, it is the process of labor union wage determination that creates both the existence and scarcity of good jobs. That is, labor unions by artificially raising wages restrict the number of jobs that would otherwise exist in the unionized sector. In addition, by restricting the number of jobs in the unionized sectors, unions are likely to increase the labor supply that is available in the nonunion sector. The result is a secondary sector wage that is both below the high union wage as well as below the equilibrium wage that would exist in an economy without labor unions.

Although the above considerations lead the neoclassical and SLM literatures to different assessments of the influence of labor unions, the neoclassical interpretation of the functioning of the internal labor market does open an avenue for labor unions to have a positive feedback on worker productivity and wage rates.

As indicated above, job-specific training creates firm-specific or idiosyncratic jobs that introduce problems of bilateral monopoly between workers with idiosyncratic skills and their employers. Absent institutional arrangements, workers and firms will invest too little in this type of training for fear of not realizing their investment. In addition, since incumbent workers have a productivity advantage over external candidates, the incumbents can work below potential and still have a cost edge over outsiders [Riordan and Wachter (1982)].

By creating an appropriate governance structure, the internal labor market can minimize the transactions costs imposed by the above bilateral monopoly concerns. Workers and firms can thus be encouraged to maximize jointly, i.e. to invest in the optimal amount of job-specific training and to work at full potential.

The degree to which internal labor markets succeed in economizing on transactions costs determines the size of the "surplus" that is created and can be shared by the parties to the bilateral monopoly. In this regard, there is a potential feedback between the structure of the employment relationship and the productivity of the work force. To the extent that labor unions aid in economizing on transactions costs, they contribute positively to the size of the surplus and, hence, to the degree of positive feedback [Freeman and Medoff (1984)].

3. The secondary sector

The policy issues that provide a focus for the SLM literature largely involve the functioning of the secondary labor market. With the exception of the Marxian interpretation, the primary sector firms and their internal labor markets are judged as having outcomes that are normatively viewed as being satisfactory. As such they can serve as a standard or point of comparison when analyzing the secondary sector labor market.

The basic hypothesis of the SLM with respect to the secondary market is that wage levels in the secondary market are lower than in the primary sector, even after correcting for ability. Noncompeting groups mean that significantly different opportunities and rewards are accorded to otherwise comparable people. The SLM translates this hypothesized empirical observation into three major conclusions.

(1) The different reward structure within sectors implies that segmented labor markets can be identified in terms of differences in their wage determination mechanisms. In other words, it is possible to draw one or more demarcation lines through the industrial wage structure. Statistically speaking, to explain wages or mobility within each sector would indicate that the underlying data between

sectors could not have been drawn from the same population. These wage discrepancies between primary and secondary sectors are taken to mean that underutilization in the secondary sector is pervasive.

(2) The large wage differentials between sectors could not occur in a market system where investment in human capital was available to and worked for all of the workers. Specifically, the secondary sector either does not reward human capital or provides a significantly lower rate of return on additional units of human capital than is found in the primary sector. Moreover, it tends to encourage rather than discourage employee turnover.

(3) There exists a negative feedback between early labor market experience and later behavior; that is, bouts of unemployment and/or employment in the secondary sector increase the likelihood of future unemployment and/or low wage employment. Employment in the secondary sector, rather than contributing positive on-the-job training, imparts negative human capital. The presence of negative persistence effects or scarring is a crucial theoretical building block of the SLM model. It contributes to economic dualism or, at least, imparts a high variance to interindustry wages and unemployment. The negative feedback also helps to cement the lack of mobility between sectors.

The above three effects could be created by a number of different factors. Pre-market factors, especially biological differences related to age and ability, are the elements stressed in the neoclassical model as leading to income differentials among individuals. Pre- and in-market discrimination is also one of the methods through which markets are segmented. The SLM researchers agree that these factors contribute to segmentation.

The SLM model, however, strongly argues that observable segmentation is not due primarily to pre-market forces or to discrimination. That is, segmentation would still occur absent discrimination and age effects. Specifically (capitalist) economic systems seem to require or, at least, to function more smoothly in the presence of a secondary sector.

3.1. Finding the demarcation line that distinguishes sectors

Perhaps the central hypothesis of the SLM literature is that different reward and incentive systems exist across the segmented labor markets. Specifically, the wage mechanism is different across sectors so that otherwise comparable individuals achieve different outcomes. The result is underemployment for those "good" workers dead-ended in "bad" jobs.

The identification of segmented labor markets poses conceptual and empirical difficulties. In order for differential reward mechanisms to exist across sectors, labor mobility must be limited. With mobility, sectoral convergence would occur as firms and workers bid away systematic sector differences.

As noted above, a conceptual difficulty with the SLM notion of underemployment is the lack of a mechanism that explains the barriers to mobility that keep good workers in bad jobs. The institutionally fixed minimum wage, whether imposed by labor unions or the government, is an integral feature of the neoclassical description of wage rigidity contributing to underemployment.

The SLM, however, if it is to be differentiated from the neoclassical description of the problem, must rest on other factors. The Marxian versions of the SLM have an answer in the form of the class struggle in which the capitalists conspire to impose occupational and earnings immobility on workers. The difficulties of having large numbers of employers successfully conspire together have been the standard criticism of this model. The Marxian answer is that the conspiracy can be enforced by social custom, as may be the case with racial discrimination, and need not involve an organized conspiracy.

The non-Marxian versions of the SLM, by eschewing the conspiracy theory, face the difficult problem of constructing a distinct cause of segmentation. As will be developed below, the negative feedback hypothesis appears to be the most promising candidate, at least on a theoretical level, for explaining segmentation.

The empirical, as well as the theoretical, problem of identifying the sectors of the economy where wage outcomes differ has been an ongoing difficulty for SLM researchers. The major issue is to identify the distinctive sectors of the economy where the variance in wage outcomes does not reflect purely compensating differentials. The relevant empirical literature, spawned by the dual market characterization, has sought to identify primary and secondary sectors. An unresolved problem for this literature has been to develop an appropriate methodology so that the hypotheses concerning industrial dualism could be statistically tested.

Typically, the approach has been to make an a priori determination as to which sectors are part of the secondary and which part of the primary labor market. Wage equations, or equations for other labor market variables (e.g. employment instability), estimated for the two sectors could then be tested to determine whether the observations for each sector could have been generated by the same population. A finding that the two sectors could not have been generated by the same population could be interpreted to imply the presence of dualism.

Examples of this type of research are Wachtel and Betsy (1972) and Oster (1979). Wachtel and Betsy estimated alternative wage equations for primary and secondary sectors. They found that "demand" variables, including industry concentration ratios, were significant in differentiating among sectoral wage mechanisms. Oster used factor analysis and found that a series of industry-specific variables, such as firm size, concentration ratio, industry total receipts, industry total assets, depreciable assets per production worker, and unionization, all contributed positively to the first-factor loading. He interpreted this to support the existence of a core–periphery dualism where the above industry variables defined the core industries.

These methodologies – if used as evidence to support the existence of labor market segmentation – have a number of important weaknesses. The central concern is that structural differences between sectors in wage determination, employment, or other labor market processes are not a hypothesis confined to the SLM literature. The variables mentioned above, relating to the presence or absence of labor unions and differences in industry and firm product market structure, are all included in neoclassical empirical work on sectoral differences.

The difficulty in isolating specific hypotheses with respect to the sign or the magnitude of variables exemplifies the difficulties in constructing an SLM hypothesis that is different from the standard neoclassical empirical model. Based on these difficulties in constructing distinguishable hypotheses, we conclude that, at least to date, the SLM hypothesis has not generated a testable empirical hypothesis for identifying demarcation boundaries for segmented labor markets.[11]

The unsupportive empirical results, of course, do not doom the hypothesis. Part of the problem undoubtedly rests with the quality of the data. The SIC codes were not drawn along lines suggested by the SLM theory, so that distinction across sectors are determined as much by data availability as by the theory.

The recent SLM literature, reflecting the disappointing empirical results concerning dualism and the inherent data limitations, has moved away from a literal interpretation of the SLM hypothesis. Specifically, bimodality or demarcation lines across industrial sectors and the distinction between good and bad jobs are no longer viewed as necessary features of the hypothesis. Rather, stress is to be placed on alternative hypotheses that do not have as a prerequisite the identification of dichotomies across industrial lines.

Ryan (1981), in a summary analysis of the SLM literature, states that, "A failure to find bimodality and a distinct frontier between the segments does not, however, mean the absence of segmentation... As segmentation remains large, in-market segmentation is still in evidence." Indicating that strict duality is used more as a heuristic device, he continues that, "Jobs located toward the lower tail

---

[11] It is worth noting that even if one or more unique variables could be identified that could test the SLM hypothesis, complications would remain. For example, some differences in coefficients might satisfy the theory while others might not. In addition, significant differences might be found across sector equations for "neutral" variables for which the SLM had no specific hypotheses. These differences, however, could not be simply ignored when the neutral variables had a nonzero covariance with the key variables (for which the theory did have a prediction).

These empirical methodology problems have not been resolved to the satisfaction of the different intellectual camps. Indeed, a limitation of interpreting the literature in this area is the lack of attention that is given to constructing rigorous tests of the theory.

Empirical work that is critical of the SLM includes Leigh (1976) and Dickens and Lang (1983). The latter paper provides support for market segmentation, but the underlying basis of the argument is neoclassical.

of the [wage distribution] may be classed as secondary and the rest as primary using an arbitrary frontier" (p. 7).

This shift away from a literal interpretation of duality has made the SLM hypothesis more understandable in a neoclassical framework. It has also shifted research away from the rather sterile search for demarcation lines.

3.2. The impact of human capital

The central policy interest of the SLM models concerns the distribution of wage income (and to a lesser extent family income) across individuals. This issue focuses research attention on the rewards to human capital and the resulting mobility in the wage and income distribution over the life cycle.

The SLM literature argues that human capital is largely irrelevant (or at least less relevant) to individual wages in the secondary sector. The causes of low rates of return to education in the secondary sector can be attributed to a number of factors. The mechanisms through which they work are largely related to "taste" formation effects. First, as argued by Bowles and Gintis (1976), the purpose of school is related to the process of socialization. Schools help to mold students into their "proper" place in the economic hierarchy. For students from low income families, schooling conditions them to accept jobs in the secondary sector of the economy. Second, as suggested in the Marxian interpretation, employers are interested in de-skilling their work force. In order to forestall unionization, employers encourage turnover. Consequently, they hire workers without much prior screening and provide little subsequent on-the-job training. Finally, negative feedback effects trap workers into bad jobs. As will be discussed below, individuals who take jobs that have the array of characteristics associated with low wages and unstable positions become acclimatized to that type of work. In so doing, they acquire bad work habits and become unsuited to work in the primary sector.

The hypothesized low or zero rates of return to experience or investment in on-the-job training in the secondary sector mean that secondary workers exhibit a flat profile of earnings across age groups. Note that tests of this hypothesis do not first require the separation of industrial sectors. This is an advantage in that attempts to draw a priori demarcation lines through the industrial sector, as indicated above, have not proved successful. Tests of the human capital version of segmentation, however, still require the utilization of a dichotomization across occupational lines. Here again, the lines are admittedly drawn in an arbitrary fashion.

The use of occupational rather than industrial demarcations, however, creates new methodological problems. Two related problems need to be mentioned. First, human capital theory does not suggest that all types or levels of schooling yield age–earnings profiles with the same slope. In fact, it very clearly argues the reverse. Some occupations can be expected to have distinctively flatter profiles than others. Specifically, the human capital model is compatible with individuals "choosing" experience–earnings profiles that are perfectly flat or upwardly sloped. The observation that some individuals have flat experience–earnings profiles thus contains no information on the rate of return to education or training that is available to those individuals.

The original SLM hypothesis is that workers in some industrial sectors receive both lower wages and lower returns to post-employment human capital acquisition than workers in other sectors. This would require that identical occupations in different industries yield differently sloped age–earnings profiles. The difficulty, of course, is to control for individual-specific or heterogeneity effects.

The second problem involves "truncation bias". Specifically, any attempt to divide or truncate samples may create subsamples that violate underlying assumptions concerning the distribution of the error term component or the assumption that the error term is independent of the presumed independent variables in the analysis. The truncation bias problem is sufficiently endemic to this issue that some elaboration of the issue is useful.[12]

In studying segmented labor markets, a natural research strategy is to divide the labor market into separate segments. The segments can then be tested to see whether they emerge from the same underlying population. This approach, however, contains implicit assumptions, which if not valid, substantially weaken one's ability to confirm the SLM hypothesis and to distinguish it from neoclassical alternatives. In a sense these assumptions revolve around truncation (or censoring).

Censoring is defined as not including information on observations above a ceiling or below a floor. Truncation is the elimination of such observations from the sample. While the treatment and consequences of these two processes are not identical, we shall treat them as one. When we divide a sample into various occupations and estimate within occupation regressions for earnings on a set of independent variables, we are assuming that we have a random draw of the population or, put another way, that the independent variables are not correlated with the error term in the equation. If the error term in part measures an individual's abilities and talents that are rewarded in the marketplace, however, bias will result.

For example, Taubman and Wales (1974) and Sewell and Hauser (1975) suggest that wages on first jobs are not well correlated with measures of intelligence but that over time employees and employers are sorted into appropriate jobs and that intelligence is rewarded. Suppose that this same pattern over time holds for many skills and traits. Then one would expect those workers

---

[12] This issue was stressed by Cain (1976).

in poor jobs with little experience to be drawn from the full spectrum of abilities but that over time the more able workers would leave the poor jobs (if there is mobility) and the least able would drop out of the job market. If there is such mobility, a comparison of more and less experienced workers in a given occupation would compare people with different ability levels and not measure the pure effect of experience.

Attempts to test the hypothesis concerning the unimportance of secondary market human capital tend to find some support for this contention. Cross-sectional equations tend to find that "experience" variables are statistically significant in all sectors of the economy but have smaller coefficients in the low wage sectors.

McNabb and Psacharopoulos (1981) estimate earnings functions separately for those in low and high status occupations.[13] This splitting creates some truncation at least indirectly related to education and earnings, which should bias education coefficients downward and upward in the low and high status groups, respectively.[14] The authors, while aware of this problem, make no corrections. Nevertheless, they find that education and years of work experience are significant, with more human capital leading to higher earnings in both groups. The effects tend to be different in the two sectors. This may be due to the truncation or to the nature of the sectors. It is not, however, inconsistent with neoclassical theory, which often poses choices between flatter and steeper (but intersecting from below) profiles.

The SLM literature has generally agreed on the application of human capital theory to the primary sector. Instead, it has argued forcefully only against its application to the secondary sector. Recent work, however, suggests that a different approach might prove to be rewarding. In particular, studies by Abraham and Medoff (1982) have argued that the positively sloped age–earnings profiles of many industrial workers do not reflect returns to increments in human capital; rather, they interpret their results as indicating a pure return on seniority. Thus, the positively sloped age–earnings profiles of high wage sector employees reflect higher lifetime earnings premiums rather than a higher return on human capital.

If these results prove robust, they can be interpreted to suggest that the lower coefficient on age in secondary sector wage equations reflects the "true" return on experience. Consequently, the ability of workers to advance their position

---

[13] Low is below 30 on the Goldthorpe and Hope scale, which is an English socioeconomic index scale that runs from 0 to 100. The cutoff point chosen is arbitrary.

[14] The truncation effect will definitely cause a negative bias if there is only one independent variable or if all independent variables are normally distributed [see Cain (1976)]. The bias arises for the following reason. At each education level, there is a distribution of earnings that depends partly on occupation. People with much education who are in low paying jobs are "losers". Within a low wage rate occupation, those with low education are a random draw from that stratum. Therefore, dividing by occupation causes one to compare a random draw with "losers".

through education is limited in all sectors. Lifetime earnings, therefore, largely reflect the luck of the draw, i.e. success in being hired off the queue to high wage sector firms.

3.3. Negative feedback effects

The pivotal hypotheses of the SLM literature concern the tendency of markets to allocate "bad" jobs to "good" workers. To an important extent the SLM model relies on a negative feedback mechanism between early labor market experience and future labor market behavior to explain this phenomenon. The low wage sector workers start out as having the same human capital as high wage sector workers, but they are eventually molded to their jobs. That is, bad jobs create low quality workers. This is in contrast to neoclassical markets creating low wage jobs in response to relative prices signaling the availability of low quality workers.

The SLM is perhaps most at variance with standard textbook, neoclassical labor market models in its emphasis on negative feedbacks. Although feedback mechanisms have long been an important concept in sociological and psychological models, they have received only limited attention in labor economics. This is not only because they involve endogenous tastes but also because of difficulties in testing for their presence.

Rather than viewing individuals as maximizing an unchanging utility function subject to market constraints, the feedback mechanism allows for shifts in the utility function in response to changes in the constraints. In a standard, static individual-maximizing model, the supply of labor, for example, depends upon relative prices in the current period. The parameters of the system are assumed to be constant over time.

When feedback effects are present, individuals are actually "changed" by their experience. In terms of individuals' static demand and labor supply function, the "experience dependency" effects appear as supply "shocks". The parameters of the utility function now become functions of the (lagged values of the) experience variables that cause behavior to change.

Feedback effects can take a wide variety of forms. In general they can be described as creating "experience" dependent effects. That is to say, experience in one period creates persistence effects that last into later periods. Stated in this form, it becomes clear that the human capital model can itself be viewed as a feedback model. Specifically, the introduction of durable goods, into an otherwise purely static model, creates persistence events. The accumulation of human capital or any other durable good means that past events will influence current behavior.

The difference between the SLM literature and the human capital, durable goods type case largely involves the type of feedback that is being discussed. The

SLM is more concerned with negative feedbacks and with feedbacks that specifically have their effect by altering the preference function.

A good example of the SLM type effect is that presented by Bowles and Gintis (1976) with respect to education. As mentioned above, their argument is that the real role of schooling is to socialize students into the capitalist work environment. Thus, individuals are molded into the preference function that best fits the hierarchical capitalist–worker system. The socialization effects of institutions are typically ignored by economists or quantitative sociologists because of the difficulties in stating the relevant hypothesis in a statistically testable form.

Empirical testing of feedback effects is a difficult problem, but one that is currently receiving some attention. An interesting model which relates to the specific type phenomena discussed in the SLM literature and one which has been tested quantitatively involves the notion of labor market "scarring". The scarring model has been utilized, for example, to investigate the causes of youth unemployment and low wages. The hypothesis is that bouts of youth unemployment have long-term or persistent effects on the wages and employment rates of the affected individuals.

Models of this type fit into the form of equations referred to as income generating equations. Before analyzing the scarring version of this model, it is useful briefly to indicate its relationship to the more traditional income generating models.

4. Models of earnings mobility over the life cycle

The segmented labor market model is not the only model which predicts some stability of earnings power for some or all occupations or individuals. In this section we sketch out several such models. Since versions of each of these models predict immobility or segmentation, some empirical evidence can be consistent with all these models. There are some predictions, however, that can be used to distinguish some versions of these models. The testing of these specific hypotheses typically has such data requirements that are very difficult to satisfy.

The four basic models we shall examine are the permanent income model, the Markov model, the human capital model, and the negative feedback model. In all of them, we shall ignore changes over time arising from economy macroeconomic development.

4.1. The permanent income model

The permanent income model is originally due to Friedman and Kuznets (1945) and was popularized by Friedman (1957).

A permanent income model is described by

$$Y_t = Y_p + Y_{vt},\tag{1}$$

where Y_t is measured income in year t, Y_p is long-run, permanent income, and Y_{vt} is transitory income in year t.

The permanent income model assumes that there is some long-run constant (or slowly changing) level of income[15] for each individual that depends on his ability level, but that in each period a person realizes a particular draw of transitory and thus observed income. If Y_t is averaged over sufficiently long time periods, its observed value will approach Y_p and individuals will be placed or segmented at a particular point in the distribution. Year to year, of course, individuals will bounce around.

If the permanent income model is correct, then those observed with low earnings in time t consist primarily of two groups – those with a low Y_p and near zero values of Y_v and those with near average values of Y_p and very low values of Y_v. If Y_p altered slowly, the change over time in Y_t will be small if Y_v is small in both years but large if Y_v is a large negative number in t but returns to its expected value of 0 in $Y_{v,t+j}$. In the latter case, the observed change in earnings will be large and there will appear to be mobility. The use of annual data in a permanent income world can thus give rise to an impression of less segmentation than truly exists. To estimate true segmentation, it is necessary to use an instrument (variable) correlated with Y_p, but not $Y_{v,t}$ to obtain predicted values of Y_t, or to average Y_t over enough t so that the $(1/T)\sum_j Y_{v,t-j}$ approaches 0.

It is still the case, however, that immobility in the permanent income model framework is based on heterogeneity factors, such as ability and (permanent) tastes, which are assumed to be homogeneous initially in the SLM models.

4.2. The Markov model

A Markov model is described by

$$Y_t = Y_{t-1} + w_t,\tag{2}$$

where w_t is an error or innovation in year t.

A major distinction between the Markov and permanent income model is that in the former, the current error random term (w_t) is built into the wage base forever, while in the permanent income model $Y_{v,t}$ is not built in and the wage always centers about Y_p. While Markov models can generate stable income distributions, no one's position is segmented.

---

[15] Hall (1978), however, models Y_p as subject to updating via a Markov process.

The permanent income model assumes that $Y_{v,t}$ and $Y_{v,t-j}$ are uncorrelated, at least after one year (since business cycle effects can spill over). As long as the expected value of $\sigma_{Y_v}^2$ is constant over time, then the permanent income model implies that $R_{Y_t Y_{t-j}}^2$ is a constant for all j. Assume that the Markov process is first order, i.e. $E(w_t, w_{t-j}) = 0$, $j \neq 0$. Equation (2) can be rewritten as

$$Y_t = \sum_{j=0}^{T} w_{t-j}. \tag{2a}$$

Then the expected value of $R_{Y_t Y_{t-j}}^2$ is given by

$$E\left(R_{Y_t Y_{t-j}}^2 \right) = \sum_{j}^{T} \left(w_{t-j}^2 \right) \bigg/ \left(\sum_{0}^{T} w_{t-j}^2 \right). \tag{2b}$$

Contrary to the permanent income model, the closer j is to 0 the larger the R^2 in the Markov model. This difference lets us distinguish between the two models. Hart (1976), using annual data from England, concluded that the permanent income model is inappropriate and that the Markov model is a better representation.

There is an alternative way to compare these two models which combines data from several years and avoids the problem of classifying partially by transitory income. An equation describing the evolution of earnings over time can be specified for the ith person as

$$Y_{it} = a_i + b_t + u_{it}, \tag{3}$$

$$u_{it} = \rho u_{it-1} + z_t. \tag{4}$$

In eq. (3), a_i is the individual-specific effect that depends on a person's talents and abilities; b_t are year effects which incorporate work experience, age, cohort and secular trends (their separate effects can sometimes be found by imposing some arbitrary identification assumptions); and u_{it} is the random error which in (4) follows a first-order autocorrelation pattern in which z_t is white noise.

A way to estimate the model is to lag eq. (3) one period, and to substitute $Y_{it-1} - a_i - b_{t-1} - Z_{t-1}$ for u_{it-1}. This yields:

$$Y_{it} = a_i(1-\rho) + b_t - \rho b_{t-1} + \rho Y_{it-1} - \rho z_{it-1}. \tag{5}$$

Assuming a, b, and u are uncorrelated, we can use panel data to calculate the proportion of the variance of Y_{it} that is attributable to each source, i.e. σ_a^2/σ_Y^2, σ_b^2/σ_Y^2, and $\sigma_u^2\sigma_Y^2$. If people are permanently stratified, we would expect σ_a^2/σ_Y^2 to be large. "Large" is a subjective term. We can test to see if σ_a^2 differs from 0 or from σ_Y^2, but intermediate cases require judgment and experience. Of course, if the distinction between primary and secondary markets is that the former has growth potential and the latter does not, then in eq. (3) a and b are positively correlated. In this instance we should in principle calculate the model separately for the two labor groups, but if their division is unknown, this tack is impractical.

A basic implication of the segmented labor market literature is that some people get locked into poorly paid jobs with irregular employment fairly early in their careers. As noted earlier, it has proved difficult to agree empirically on which occupations are good and which are bad. Low wages or earnings can be calculated and can be used as a proxy for good or bad.[16] To examine the hypothesis that those observed with low earnings at a point of time are to remain at the bottom of the distribution, repeated observations on earnings are necessary and certain statistical problems must be overcome. Unfortunately, a large data set with earnings measured accurately over long periods of time is not available. Instead, evidence must be obtained from samples deficient in some respect.

Markov drift can be difficult to distinguish from the scarring suggested by negative feedback effects. In fact, higher order Markov processes can mimic any endogenous feedback effect. The solution to the problem involves sufficiently lengthy longitudinal data so that the error properties of the system can be separately identified.

4.3. The human capital model

The human capital model provides the third major dynamic model for earnings. The driving force in this model is investment in on-the-job training, I_t. For simplicity, assume all such training is general, i.e. can be used equally well in many occupations. Then a trained individual will be paid his marginal product by all employers, including the one who trained him, because he is equally valuable to all. Since the training employer cannot pay a trained person less than his marginal product, the employee pays for the training by receiving a wage during training that falls short of his marginal product by his training costs. This is explained in detail in Mincer (1975), who derives the following set of nonstochastic equations for *annual* earnings:

$$Y_{it} = Y_{it-1} - I_t + rK_t, \tag{6}$$

where I_t is investment in on-the-job training, K_t is accumulated investment $= \sum I_t$, and r is the rate of return on prior training investments.

---

[16] There is at least one such European sample based on school children in Malmo, Sweden. This is described most extensively in Fagerlind (1975) and has been analyzed by several economists.

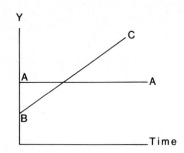

Figure 21.1. Hypothetical wage–experience profiles.

Mincer (1975) argues that I_t in general will decrease with age, such as

$$I_t = A e^{-bt}. \tag{6a}$$

Mincer further argues that if the labor market offers equally skilled individuals the choice of AA or BC in Figure 21.1, then wage rates will adjust so that the present discounted value of the two streams are equated.

It is important to note that human capital theory does not require profiles to follow BC. It is perfectly legitimate in the human capital world to observe an individual choosing AA since he can consume the same amount in each year as with BC, provided he can borrow or lend at a fixed interest (as is assumed in this model). Thus, the human capital model is consistent with no mobility or complete mobility in annual earnings over long time periods.

The human capital model describes how earnings and wage rates vary over time and with age. Users of this model usually assume that there are no age effects that occur because of changes of skills or wage rates that arise solely from aging. It is possible, for example, for mental and physical skills to deteriorate for physiological reasons or for people to choose to work less because of age-related diseases. Similarly, union rules on seniority can affect wages. There is a scarcity of evidence to distinguish the work experience and exogenous age change models.

4.4. The negative feedback model

The final immobility model is drawn from the part of the SLM model that argues that working in a bad job exposes an individual to poor work habits and causes him to adopt some of these habits.

Human capital formation is, with respect to most data sets, indistinguishable from positive job-related feedback effects. Indeed, if human capital formation is not restricted to follow rigid rules, e.g. an exponential trend, it cannot be separately identified from on-the-job feedback effects. For example, in its extreme form, the SLM can be interpreted as viewing negative feedback as negative on-the-job training. Previous work experience (in bad jobs) *reduces* future income.

4.5. Empirical results

Testing models of this kind generally requires the use of panel data. The reason is that individual differences in behavior, or heterogeneity, must be differentiated from experience dependent behavior. Specifically, in an equation of the form

$$Y_{it} = b_t X_{it} + c_t Y_{it-1} + d_{it} + u_{it},$$

Y is the person in a particular state during period t, X is a vector of exogenous variables, d is an individual constant, and u is a random component. In this model d is the control for individual heterogeneity and c is the test of experience dependence.

Even using panel data, very strong assumptions or a very rich data set (e.g. observations for individuals over an extended period of time) are needed to isolate experience dependent effects. For example, individual behavior, even absent scarring, tends to exhibit inertia. An individual who is employed in a given job today or is unemployed today is more likely to be in that state in the next period, if only because of the difficulty or inertia in shifting between states.

The problem of isolating scarring effects becomes even more difficult in a model where individual behavior is nonstationary. Life-stage effects (due to maturation or pure aging), however, mean that nonstationarity will be present. Although life-stage effects are frequently ignored in economic modeling, they cannot be ignored in models that attempt to identify endogenous or systematic shifts in preferences. It is important to recognize that the SLM researchers are quite specific in indicating that the negative feedback effects they are studying are quite different from biologically caused shifts in preferences.[17]

Due to the difficulties inherent in the problem, the literature on persistence effects has tended to confuse a number of phenomena including pure inertia, age, nonstationary related preferences, and scarring. Early work tended to ignore these distinctions and, in attributing persistence effects to scarring, imparted a serious upward bias to their estimates. More recent work, including that of Ellwood (1982), Chamberlain (1982), and Heckman (1978), is clear in distinguishing among these different effects. Data limitations, however, force them

---

[17]Piore, for example, is very clear in making the distinction between scarring type effects and changes in preferences that are associated with growing older.

either to the conclusion that scarring effects are underidentified or that their estimates of scarring are upper limit estimates.

Ellwood, for example, concludes that employment persistence among the young is due in large part to differences in tastes and abilities of individuals (i.e. heterogeneity). He does, however, find some significant part of employment behavior can be attributed to prior work experience or the lack thereof. The magnitude of the latter effect was a three-week employment loss for a six-month gap in employment in the previous year. He also found that early work experience had a large impact on wage growth. In this case, however, it was particularly difficult to separate heterogeneity from true dependence.

An alternative explanation of people persisting in low income jobs is that those with very limited resources cannot afford to invest in extensive job search.

Again, without empirical definitions of the primary and secondary markets, it is difficult to test this proposition directly. The negative income tax (NIT) experiments, however, provide some interesting indirect evidence. An NIT is a program which pays an individual or family a basic grant of money per time period (G) and then reduces this amount by p cents $(0 < p < 1)$ for each dollar earned until the grant falls to zero. NIT experiments generally are based on low income groups, e.g. family earnings in the previous year being no more than one and one-half times the poverty level.

Several experiments have been designed to test the effect of various combinations of G and p on labor force behavior, fertility, marital stability, etc. These studies reach their conclusions based on comparisons of different p and G combinations given to experimental subjects and to controls whose p and G are both zero.

Robbins, Tuma and Yaeger (1978), who use the Seattle and Denver Income Maintenance Experiment data, find that the controls with no guaranteed income are more likely to remain employed and to spend less time out of the labor force. However, West (1979) concludes that the NIT has little effect on wage rates received. It seems the NIT leads to more leisure rather than to better jobs. Moreover, these results suggest that an income protection mechanism that could offset the behavior learned on poor jobs does not have such consequences.

Most, though not all, of the empirical studies on income mobility have not been designed to examine or distinguish among the models described above. We believe, however, that these studies do shed some light on the issues.

Schiller (1977) provides some extremely important data for our purposes.[18] He uses the Longitudinal Employer Employee Data (LEED), a 1 percent random sample of the Social Security Administration's files, which apply to about 90 percent of the labor force in any one year and which contain quarterly earnings in employment covered by (subject to) Social Security tax. In this sample, the

---

[18] We do not endorse his tests of all the models he examines.

annual earnings of people truncated at the taxable ceiling are estimated from information on quarterly patterns.

His analysis is based on 74 227 males who were 16–49 years old in 1957, had at least $1000 in earnings in 1957, and had positive earnings in 1971. He reports (p. 932) that the correlation (R) between an individual's earnings (converted to his rank in his age cohort's earnings distribution) in 1957 and 1971 is 0.15, which is rather small, though, of course, he has made only crude adjustment for years of work experience or age.

His detailed analysis covers movement of individuals within the earnings distribution of their own age cohort. For each five-year age cohort, he arranges people by the level of their earnings and divides into 20 intervals, each having the same percentage of people in the cohort. These groupings are called ventiles (for one-twentieth).[19] This division into age cohorts can be considered as a rough adjustment for age or work experience; subsequent adjustment by regression of earnings on age within each of the five-year groups would have been even better. Note that since he uses observed earnings in 1957 as his classifying variable, he is partly arranging by 1957 transitory earnings.

Schiller presents two measures of mobility: the percentage of a 1957 ventile that moved less than two ventiles, which he labels "immobile", and the mean algebraic change in ventile position, which is an average of an ordinal measure. He finds that on average 29 percent moved less than two ventiles up or down. The groups with the largest percentage of immobility are those in the top 10 percent of the earnings distribution in 1957, who had 42 and 48 percent immobile. Looking at the bottom of the 1957 distributions, those in the third and fourth ventiles in 1957 (the $1000 floor eliminates the first two ventiles) have 35 and 33 percent remaining within two ventiles in 1971. His other mobility measure is the mean algebraic change. In this sample he finds regression toward the mean, i.e. those at the bottom moving up and those on top moving down over time.[20] Note that this may be due to classifying by Y_t rather than Y_p in 1955, though this tendency is found throughout the 1957 distribution and not just at the extremes where atypical transitory income would most likely be found.

Schiller also subdivides his sample by race into white and black subsamples. The average immobility rate is 29 percent for whites and 30 percent for blacks. The immobility rate is distributed differently for the two groups, with blacks more likely to remain at the bottom and less likely remain at the top. For blacks, 47 percent of those in the third ventile from the bottom in 1957 have not moved more than two ventiles. That is perhaps the strongest evidence of earnings immobility, but it surely is partly due to discrimination.

---

[19] For this calculation he includes those with less than $1000 in 1957, or without earnings in 1971.

[20] Some of his results may occur because he classifies by 1957 earnings. As argued earlier, some of those at the bottom are there because of large negative transitory income which is not expected to be repeated in 1971. Moreover, those at the very top or bottom can not rise or fall more, and this induces some regression toward the mean.

Schiller's results are substantiated by several other studies that use similar techniques. The National Longitudinal Survey (NLS) commenced in 1966 with surveys of young men (14–24), middle age women, and older men (45–59). The first and last groups will be our main interests. Kohen, Parnes and Shea (1975) rank families by family income in 1966, and then break the distribution into 16 successive categories, most of which span $1000 but which are larger for higher income groups (see pp. 157, 158). They then calculate what percentage of men are in the same category in 1969.[21] They do the analysis separately for older and younger blacks and whites. Among older whites, about one-half are in a higher class in 1969. There is no strong tendency for the percentage in a higher class to vary with starting income. There is a slight tendency for those in higher 1966 earnings positions to have a decrease in their rank over the three-year period. For older blacks, there is more variability and less upward mobility. Those at the top and bottom are less likely to move up. Blacks with at least $9000 are more likely to move down by 1969.

For younger whites, those at the bottom in 1966 sustain much larger increases with decreases concentrated among those with at least $9000. For younger blacks, there are very strong upward movements with downward movements concentrated among those few with at least $7000 in 1966.

Taubman (1975) presents similar information from the NBER–TH sample which contains men who were born between 1917 and 1924 and volunteered for an army training program for bombardiers, navigators, and pilots in 1943. The sample only contains people with at least a high school diploma and in the top half of the IQ distribution. Thus, it is unlikely to have many people in poor jobs.

These men have been surveyed several times. Directly reported earnings data are available for 1955–56 and 1968–69. Taubman reports that R^2 between 1955 and 1969 earnings is less than 0.2. He ranks the men and divides into 10 deciles. He finds that over the 14 year period, from 39 to 64 percent of the men fall within the same or neighboring decile as in 1955 (p. 120).[22] He also finds that the mean compound annual growth rate is highest for those in the bottom decile in 1955 and lowest for those in the top decile in 1955 (p. 122). For high school graduates, the group in this sample most likely to be in SLM, the compound growth rates are highest for the bottom decile, lowest for the top two deciles, and roughly constant for those in between (p. 125). The results for the top and bottom deciles are explicable in terms of Friedman's Permanent Income Hypothesis.

These studies shed some light on earnings stability over various time periods. They indicate that there is substantial mobility in earnings over long periods of time and that the mobility is largely unaffected by level of earnings or age in the

---

[21] It appears that no correction was made for inflation or increases in work experience.

[22] Roughly, the sample covers the top half of the earnings distribution; hence, deciles here are close to Schiller's ventiles.

first survey period. The major exceptions to this conclusion are poor blacks and wealthy whites who tend to remain where they are.

Other studies examine mobility in different ways. Diamond et al. (1976) also use Social Security records. They drew a sample of men and calculated the correlation of earnings in a year with earnings in year $t - j$ and $t + j$, where j runs from 1 to 14. They made these calculations separately for people initially age 20, 30, and 40. They found that the R^2 declines uniformly as j increases forward or decreases backward in each of the three age groups.

There are several other longitudinal studies that contain direct reports of earnings or wage rates. The direct reporting and the lack of censoring of the data are distinct advantages over the studies based on Social Security data. These studies suffer, however, two major disadvantages. Most of the panels are only now approaching 20 years' duration and many studies are based on 10 or fewer observations per person. Moreover, panels, which are expensive per person to maintain over long periods, have relatively few respondents. Usually it is not possible to study separately people who are poor, have low wages, or are in the secondary labor market.

Chamberlain (1982) constructs a latent variable model in which he replaces b_t in eq. (3) with b_i and lets both a_i and b_i have individual-specific effects modeled as unobserved components. Using the National Longitudinal Survey, he estimates that those young men with a high value of a_i will have a low growth rate in earnings and vice versa. This is not in accord with the SLM hypothesis, but is in accord with a human capital model with investment in on-the-job training.

Lillard (1983) estimated a more general model in which he explains both life cycle wages and labor supply developments. He uses 11 years of the Michigan Panel of Income Dynamics for white male heads of households who were not disabled, retired, or full-time students. His model is similar to Chamberlain's with the average wage rate and its rate of growth allowed to have individual-specific components. He finds (pp. 192, 193) that these specific components are positively correlated. This is in accord with the SLM. The results may differ from those in Chamberlain because he is examining residuals for young men early in their career, while Lillard is looking at men at ages 18–54. Most of Lillard's observations are, on average, late in the men's careers. Such a difference in pattern for the young and old is in accord with Mincer's on-the-job training theory.

Lillard and Willis (1978) estimated eqs. (3) and (4) using the Michigan Panel Study of Income Dynamics, which is a nationwide random clustered sample of 5000 families that began in 1968.[23] Using six years worth of data, they calculate that for whites and blacks σ_a^2/σ_Y^2 are 70 percent and 80 percent, respectively.

---

[23] The full PSID contains an oversampling of blacks. Lillard and Willis reduce the black sample to nationwide proportions.

Equation (4) is a very simple process. It is possible to use much more complicated processes. MaCurdy (1981) generalizes substantially this equation in the model. He also uses the Michigan Panel but a version containing several additional years of observations. He concludes that there are no permanent earnings. Using the same sample but different techniques, Bhargava and Sargan (1983) reach the opposite conclusion.

The Dual Labor Market hypothesis is at times tied to the idea that if parents are poor, then their children are likely to be poor. This concern is part of the broader issue of the degree of social mobility in a society. Social mobility is generally defined by the size of R, the intergenerational correlation in earnings, income or wealth. R can range from -1 to $+1$ with 0 being complete mobility. Behrman and Taubman (1984) have recently summarized the scant available evidence. They conclude that the U.S. based studies indicate that the R for earnings or income in this century is on the order of magnitude of 0.2–0.3, which they argue is small. Two caveats are in order. First, the correlations are based on "noisy" annual earnings rather than lifetime earnings. Second, the conclusions are based on only a few studies, many of which are not a random draw from populations of interest.

Of course, R could be small, but poor people could be very immobile. The Behrman–Taubman paper does present cross-classifications which suggest that their lowest earning parents have children scattered over the children's distribution, but the sample they use probably does not include many poor parents.

The studies we have examined contain most of the available data for the United States. Those studies that use longitudinal studies that span more than a few years convey an image of substantial mobility – though Lillard and Willis are an exception.

Those studies that span 14 or more years and which rely mostly on Social Security data are consistent with an ever decreasing correlation in earnings as the time period j between Y_t and Y_{t-j} lengthens. This confirms the notion of mobility over time for the population as a whole. The few studies that calculate mobility separately for people with different characteristics or initial earnings levels indicate that such mobility is found nearly everywhere with the major exceptions being poor blacks and wealthy whites. The former may be indicative of SLM though the latter are not. Except for poor blacks, the mobility information is not in accord with the SLM model. The permanent income model also does not fare well. The human capital model has not been subject to tests of this sort, except in Taubman (1975) who finds some weak evidence against it.

4.6. Demand structures and chance versus ability

Another element in the SLM literature is the idea that there exists a hierarchy of jobs. The best paying or good jobs are filled by people who have the best signals or credentials and have wage rates that do not adjust to excess supply. The types of signals that are thought to be most used are education, race, and sex. This part of the literature at times suggests that (marginal) productivity is associated with positions and not with the people in the positions. Thus, Thurow and Lucas (1972) have argued that redistribution of people across occupations would not affect output and that an elementary school graduate would function as well as a college graduate in a high level executive position. Jencks (1972) has also argued that the distribution of income is largely determined by luck.[24]

If luck is thought to operate like a game of chance, then there are some testable hypotheses. For example, if the game of life is viewed as one in which one bets all one's wealth or one's salary each period and receives a random return denoted u_t, then the evolution of the natural log of earnings over time will be a first-order Markov process:

$$\ln Y_t = \ln Y_{t-1} + \ln(1 + \mu_t) = \ln Y_0 + \sum_j \ln(1 + \mu_{t-j}).$$

Suppose that Y_0 were determined by the signals given above or by ability denoted X. Then $R^2_{Y_t X}$ would decline as people age. The available evidence, which is surveyed in Behrman, Hrubec, Taubman and Wales (1980), indicates that the opposite occurs.

An additional piece of evidence on the ability versus luck issue is found in the literature on twins and other kin groups.[25] It is always possible to divide the factors that determine an individual's earnings capacity into the genes with which he is endowed and the environment with which he is provided. Let the marketplace value of the person's genes equal G, the marketplace value of the skills acquired from schooling, health care, etc. equal N, and luck equal u. Let the observed earnings capacity or phenotype be denoted by Y. Then it is always true that

$$Y = f(G, N, u).$$

Identical twins have exactly the same G and share some, though not all, N. Thus, the correlation of earnings of identical twins provides a lower bound estimate of the contribution of ability to the variance in Y, and its complement is an upper bound estimate to the contribution of luck.[26]

---

[24] This particular conclusion is drawn from a well-known early study by Jencks. In later work, which draws on better samples, some of which was developed by Jencks and colleagues, he substantially modifies this conclusion.

[25] This material is drawn from Behrman, Hrubec, Taubman and Wales. A criticism of the estimate of G is given by Goldberger.

[26] Goldberger's criticism cited above does not apply to this point.

Behrman, Hrubec, Taubman and Wales calculate this R to be about 0.56 for a group of 1020 pairs of white male veterans about 50 years old. This estimate has not been adjusted for measurement error, for schooling, or for compensating differentials for nonpecuniary job differences. Thus, late in their careers, the identical twins have similar earnings, and post-conception luck does not dominate the distribution of earnings.

References

Abraham, K. G. and J. L. Medoff (1982) "Length of service and the operation of internal labor markets", *Proceedings of the Industrial Relations Research Association*, December:308–318.

Behrman, J., Z. Hrubec, P. Taubman and T. Wales (1980) *Socioeconomic success: a study of the effects of genetic endowments, family, environment, and schooling*. Amsterdam: North-Holland.

Behrman, J. and P. Taubman (1984) "The intergenerational correlation in earnings: some estimates and test of Becker's equilibrium generational model", Mimeographed, University of Pennsylvania.

Bhargava, A. and J. D. Sargan (1983) "Estimating dynamic random effects models from panel data covering short time periods", in: A. B. Atkinson and F. A. Cowell, eds., *Panel data on incomes*. London: London School of Economics.

Bowles, S. and H. Gintis (1976) *Schooling in capitalist America: educational reform and the contradictions of economic life*. New York: Basic Books.

Braverman, H. (1974) *Labor and monopoly capital*. New York: Monthly Review Press.

Cain, G. G. (1976) "The challenge of segmented labour market theories to orthodox theory: a survey", *Journal of Economic Literature*, 14:1215–1257.

Chamberlain, G. (1982) "Panel data", Mimeographed, University of Wisconsin.

Clark, K. B. (1980) "The impact of unionization on productivity: a case study", *Industrial Labor Relations Review*, 33:451–469.

Diamond, P., et al. (1976) *Consultant panel on social security: report to Congressional Research Service*. Washington, D.C.: Government Printing Office.

Dickens, W. T. and K. Lang (1983) "A test for dual labor market theory", Working Paper No. 172, University of California, Berkeley.

Doeringer, P. B. and M. J. Piore (1971) *Internal labor markets and manpower analysis*. Lexington, Mass.: D. C. Heath.

Dunlop, J. T. (1957) "The task of contemporary wage theory", in: G. W. Taylor and F. C. Pierson, eds., *New concepts in wage determination*. New York: McGraw-Hill.

Edwards, R. C. (1979) *Contested terrain*. New York: Basic Books.

Ellwood, D. T. (1982) "Teenage unemployment: permanent scars or temporary blemishes?", in: R. B. Freeman and D. A. Wise, eds., *The youth labor market problem: its nature, cases, and consequences*. Chicago: University of Chicago Press (NBER).

Fagerlind, I. (1975) *Formal education and adult earnings*. Stockholm: Almquist and Wicksell.

Freeman, R. B. and J. L. Medoff (1984) *What do unions do?*. New York: Basic Books.

Friedman, M. (1957) *A theory of the consumption function*. Princeton, N.J.: Princeton University Press.

Friedman, M. and S. Kuznets (1945) *Income from independent professional practice*. New York: Columbia University Press.

Goldberger, A. (1979) "Methods and models in the IQ debate", *Economica*, 46:327–347.

Gordon, D. M. (1972) *Theories of poverty and underemployment*. Lexington, Mass.: D. C. Heath.

Gordon, D. M., R. C. Edwards and M. S. Reich (1982) *Segmented work, divided workers: the historical transformation of labor in the United States*. Cambridge: Cambridge University Press.

Hall, R. (1978) "Stochastic implications of the life cycle–permanent income hypothesis: theory and evidence", *Journal of Political Economy*, 86:971–987.

Harris, J. R. and M. P. Todaro (1970) "Migration, unemployment and development: a two-sector analysis", *American Economic Review*, 60:126–142.

Harrison, B. (1972) *Education, training and the urban ghetto*. Baltimore: Johns Hopkins University Press.

Hart, P. (1976) "Dynamics of earnings", *Economic Journal*, 86:551–565.

Heckman, J. (1978) "Simple statistical models for discrete panel data developed and applied to test the hypothesis of true state dependence against the hypothesis of spurious state dependence", *Annales de l'INSEE*, 30–31:227–270.

Hildebrand, G. H. (1963) "External influences and the determination of the internal wage structure", in: J. L. Meij, ed., *Internal Wage Structure*. Amsterdam: North Holland, 260–299.

Jacoby, S. M. (1982) "The development of internal labor markets in American manufacturing firms", Working Paper No. 42. Los Angeles, Calif.: UCLA Institute of Industrial Relations.

Jencks, C. (1972) *Inequality: a reassessment of the effect of family and schooling in America*. New York: Basic Books.

Jencks, C. (1979) *Who gets ahead? The determinants of economic success in America*. New York: Basic Books.

Kelley, A. C., J. G. Williamson and R. J. Cheetham (1972) *Dualistic economic development: theory and history*. Chicago: University of Chicago Press.

Kerr, C. (1954) "The Balkanization of labor markets", in: essays by E. W. Bakke et al., *Labor mobility and economic opportunity*. Cambridge, Mass.: Technology Press of MIT.

Kohen, A. I., H. S. Parnes and J. R. Shea (1975) "Income instability among young and middle-aged men", in: J. D. Smith, ed., *The personal distribution of income and wealth*. New York: Columbia University Press (NBER).

Leigh, D. E. (1976) "Occupational advancement in the late 1960s: an indirect test of the dual labor market hypothesis", *Journal of Human Resources*, 11:155–171.

Lillard, L. (1983) "A model of wage expectations in labor supply", in: A. B. Atkinson and F. A. Cowell, eds., *Panel data on incomes*. London: London School of Economics.

Lillard, L. and R. Willis (1978) "Dynamic aspects of earnings mobility", *Econometrica*, 46:985–1012.

Livernash, E. R. (1957) "The internal wage structure", in: G. W. Taylor and F. C. Pierson, eds., *New concepts in wage determination*. New York: McGraw-Hill.

MaCurdy, T. (1981) "The use of time series process to model the error structure of earnings in a longitudinal data analysis", Working Paper No. E-81-5. Stanford, Calif.: Hoover Institute, 1981.

McNabb, R. and G. Psacharopoulos (1981) "Further evidence on the relevance of the dual labor market hypothesis for the U.K.", *Journal of Human Resources*, 16:442–448.

Medoff, J. L. and K. G. Abraham (1980) "Experience, performance, and earnings", *Quarterly Journal of Economics*, 95:703–736.

Medoff, J. L. (1981) "Are those paid more really more productive: the case of experience", *Journal of Human Resources*, 16:186–216.

Mill, J. S. (1900) *Principles of political economy*. New York: Colonial Press, 2 vols.

Mincer, J. (1975) *Schooling, experience, and earnings*. New York: Columbia University Press.

Oster, G. (1979) "A factor analytic test of the theory of the dual economy", *Review of Economics and Statistics*, 61:33–39.

Osterman, P. (1975) "An empirical study of labor market segmentation", *Industrial and Labor Relations Review*, 28:508–523.

Osterman, P. (1977) "Reply", *Industrial and Labor Relations Review*, 30:221–224.

Osterman, P., ed. (1984) *Internal labor markets*. Cambridge: MIT Press.

Piore, M. J. (1973) "Fragments of a 'sociological' theory of wages", *American Economic Review, Papers and Proceedings of the Eighty-Fifth Annual Meeting*, 63:377–384.

Piore, M. J. (1983) "Labor market segmentation theory: critics should let the paradigm evolve", *Monthly Labor Review*, 106:26–28.

Reich, M. S., D. M. Gordon and R. C. Edwards (1973) "A theory of labor market segmentation", *American Economic Review, Papers and Proceedings of the Eighty-Fifth Annual Meeting*, 63:359–365.

Riordan, M. H. and M. L. Wachter (1982) "What do implicit contracts do?", *Proceedings of the Industrial Relations Research Association*, 291–298.

Robbins, P., N. Tuma and K. Yaeger (1978) "Effects of the Seattle and Denver income maintenance experiments on changes in employment status", Research Memorandum. Menlo Park, Calif.: SRI International.

Ross, A. M. (1958) "Do we have a new industrial feudalism?", *American Economic Review*, 48:903–920.

Ryan, P. (1981) "Segmentation, duality, and the internal labor market", in: F. Wilkinson, ed., *The dynamics of labour market segmentation*. London and New York: Academic Press, 3–20.

Schiller, B. R. (1977) "Relative earnings mobility in the United States", *American Economic Review*, 67:926–941.

Sewell, W. and R. Hauser (1975) *Education, occupation, and earnings: achievement in the early career*. New York: Academic Press.

Smith, A. (1937) *The wealth of nations*. New York: Modern Library.

Taubman, P. (1975) *Sources of inequality of earnings*. Amsterdam: North Holland.

Taubman, P. and T. Wales (1974) *Higher education and earnings*. New York: McGraw-Hill.

Thurow, L. C. and R. E. B. Lucas (1972) *The American distribution of income: a structural problem*. Washington, D.C.: Joint Economic Committee.

Vietorisz, T. and B. Harrison (1973) "Labor market segmentation: positive feedback and divergent development", *American Economic Review, Papers and Proceedings of the Eighty-Fifth Annual Meeting*, 63:366–376.

Wachtel, H. M. and C. Betsy (1972) "Employment at low wages", *Review of Economics and Statistics*, 54:121–129.

Wachter, M. L. (1974) "Primary and secondary labor markets: a critique of the dual approach", *Brookings Papers on Economic Activity*, (3):637–680.

West, R. W. (1979) "The impact of the Seattle and Denver income maintenance experiments on wage rates and earnings", SRI Technical Memorandum. Menlo Park, Calif.: SRI International.

Wilkinson, F., ed. (1981) *The dynamics of labour market segmentation*. London and New York: Academic Press.

Williamson, O. E., M. L. Wachter and J. E. Harris (1975) "Understanding the employment relation: the analysis of idiosyncratic exchange", *Bell Journal of Economics*, 6:250–278.

Chapter 22

PUBLIC-SECTOR LABOR MARKETS

RONALD G. EHRENBERG and JOSHUA L. SCHWARZ*

Cornell University

1. Introduction

Why does the study of public-sector labor markets in the United States warrant a separate chapter in this *Handbook of Labor Economics*? One reason is that federal, state, and local governments are differentiated from most (but not all) private-sector employers in that profit maximization is unlikely to be an objective of governmental units. As such, labor-market models based upon the assumption of profit-maximization are clearly inappropriate for the government sector; alternative models must be developed.

A second is that employment expanded more rapidly between 1950 and 1975 in the state and local government (SLG) sector than in any other sector of the economy, increasing from 9.1 percent to 15.5 percent of total nonagricultural payroll employment. Indeed, the absolute number of SLG employees almost tripled during this period, rising to nearly 12 million. Although the share of SLG employment has declined slightly since 1975, the absolute number of SLG employees has continued to rise. The growing importance of the sector suggests that attention should be directed to analyses of it.

A third is that the pattern of unionization and the laws governing collective bargaining, dispute resolution, and wage determination differ between the public and private sectors. In contrast to the declining fraction of private-sector workers who are union members, union membership is growing rapidly in the public-sector in both absolute and percentage terms.

*Ehrenberg is Irving M. Ives Professor at Cornell University and Research Associate at the National Bureau of Economic Research. Schwarz is an Assistant Professor of Industrial Relations at the University of Minnesota. Our research was partially supported by a National Science Foundation grant to Ehrenberg. Without implicating them for what remains, we are grateful to John Burton, David Lipsky, Robert S. Smith, Sharon Smith and the editors for commenting on sections of the paper and/or discussing ideas with us. An earlier version, Ehrenberg and Schwarz (1983b) contains more extensive discussions of a number of topics.

Handbook of Labor Economics, Volume II, Edited by O. Ashenfelter and R. Layard
©Elsevier Science Publishers BV, 1986

One factor that influenced the growth in public-sector unionization was changing public attitudes and legislation governing bargaining in the public-sector. Unlike the private sector where the rights of workers to organize and bargain collectively have been guaranteed since the National Labor Relations Act, laws governing bargaining in the public-sector are of much more recent vintage. Executive Order 10988 issued by President John F. Kennedy in 1962 legitimized collective bargaining in the federal sector for the first time, providing federal workers with the rights to join unions and bargain over working conditions – but not wages. While this executive order has been modified several times since then, most federal employees' wages are still not determined by the collective bargaining process.[1] Instead, they are determined via comparability legislation, first passed in 1962, which ties the wages of most federal civilian workers to the results of government surveys of wages of "comparable" private workers, subject to possible Presidential or Congressional modification.[2] The influence of federal unions on wages operates primarily through the political pressure they can exert on the President and Congress to approve wage increases that the surveys suggest are warranted.

Favorable state legislation for SLG employee collective bargaining began with a 1959 law in Wisconsin; prior to that date collective bargaining was effectively prohibited in the state and local sector. By the late 1970s most industrial states had adopted statutes that permitted SLG employees to participate in the determination of their wages and conditions of employment, although not all employees in each state were covered by the laws.[3] While these statutes were being adopted, and at the same time that employment and unionization were growing in the SLG sector, SLG employees' earnings also started to rise relative to the earnings of private sector employees and continued to do so through 1970.

The growth in the relative earnings position of SLG employees during the 1960s, coupled with the growing strength of public-employee unions, their increased militancy, and the trend towards allowing SLG employees to bargain over wage issues, led to fears that inflationary wage settlements would continue in the sector and aggravate the financial problems faced by state and local governments. These fears were explicitly based upon the belief that many public services are essential and this implied that the wage elasticity of demand for public employees was very inelastic. To many, the logical conclusion was that, in the absence of market constraints that would limit the wage demands of public

[1] There were some major exceptions – namely, postal workers and employees of federal government authorities, such as the Tennessee Valley Authority. In each of these cases the prices of the services produced (mail delivery, hydroelectric power) can be raised to cover the cost of the contract settlement, unlike other federal agencies.

[2] See Sharon Smith (1977a) for a more complete description of the comparability process in the federal sector.

[3] See Schneider (1979) for a more complete discussion of the evolution of laws governing bargaining in the public-sector.

employees, limitations should be placed on the collective bargaining rights of these groups.[4]

Although by 1981 eight states did grant the right to strike in one form or another to selected employee groups, most continued historic prohibitions against strikes.[5] The states that prohibited strikes, however, often provided assistance to local governments and unions in settling contract disputes, with a number of states adopting forms of binding arbitration as the terminal stage in their impasse procedures. How these alternative institutional arrangements operate and affect economic outcomes is, of course, worthy of discussion.

A final reason why public-sector labor markets warrant separate treatment is that they represent an area toward which much of our public policy has recently been directed. To take one example, during the decade of the 1970s attempts were made to reduce unemployment by means of public service employment (PSE) programs. Established under the Emergency Employment Act of 1971 and the Comprehensive Employment and Training Act (CETA), the federal government provided funds under these programs to SLGs to increase their employment levels, in the hope that the availability of extra public-sector jobs would provide job opportunities for the unemployed. By 1978, 569 000 individuals were reported employed on PSE program funds; these employees comprised some 3.3 percent of total SLG employment.[6] To take another example, growing concern over the fiscal condition of state and local governments and the increased state and local tax burden borne by taxpayers led to the passage of expenditure- and tax-limitation legislation in a number of states in the late 1970s. The most notable was the enactment of Proposition 13 in California, which drastically reduced local property taxes and limited the ability of all governmental units in the state to increase their revenues.

The unique nature of the agents in public-sector labor markets (nonprofit organizations), the institutional arrangements governing these markets, and the public policies that have been directed towards them, all suggest that research relating to them warrants separate treatment in this Handbook. The discussion that follows is structured along topical lines, but a common thread that runs throughout is the effects of unions and the institutional arrangements for dispute resolution in the sector.

We begin with a discussion of the research on wage determination in the state and local government (SLG) sector. Although our focus is on attempts to estimate union/nonunion wage and total compensation differentials and to explain why such differentials appear to be smaller than their private sector counterparts, we also emphasize the importance of various characteristics of the

---

[4] See Wellington and Winter (1969).
[5] For more details, see Kochan (1979).
[6] The PSE was terminated, however, in the early 1980s.

environment in which bargaining takes place. This discussion is followed by a discussion of the research on the effects of unions on productivity.

The long section that follows analyzes the research relating to dispute resolution in the SLG sector. It first discusses normative models of different impasse procedures (conventional arbitration, final-offer arbitration, the right to strike) and then the empirical research on the determinants of the use of the various procedures. Finally, it discusses studies of the effects of the availability and the use of the various procedures on wage and nonwage outcomes.

Given the variety of institutional arrangements that determine compensation in the public-sector, it is natural to ask whether (a) they generate settlements that leave "comparably qualified" workers performing "comparable" work in the public and private sectors receiving roughly equal total compensation and (b) they result in less gender and race discrimination than occurs in the private sector. Answers to such questions are of more than academic interest and the next two sections evaluate the research on them.

The literature on wage determination in the SLG sector is based, at least implicitly, on some notion of the forces that affect the demand for labor in the public-sector. In Section 8 we explicitly focus on studies of public-sector labor demand that have sought to provide estimates both of wage elasticities of demand for various categories of SLG employees and of the net job creation effects of PSE programs. The former studies are important because they shed light on the question of whether the market forces that constrain union power in the private sector would exist in the public-sector if the same institutional rules governed collective bargaining in both sectors. The latter are important because they address the issue of "fiscal substitution"; to what extent were PSE funds used to hire SLG employees who would have been hired (in the aggregate) even in the absence of the program? A final section then summarizes some of the main points in the chapter.

Both space and time constraints have caused us to limit the scope of our survey and three omissions warrant special mention. First, except in passing, we have limited our discussion to public-sector labor markets in the United States and ignored studies of other countries.[7] Second, our discussion is limited to nonmilitary employees; we have ignored the important literature on military manpower and compensation problems.[8] Third, in the main, we have not discussed the research relating to the compensation of elected and appointed "top" government officials and managers.[9]

---

[7]For example, on the public/private pay comparability issue alone one could cite Layard et al. (1982) for Great Britain, and Gunderson (1980) for Canada.
[8]See, for example, Binkin and Kyriakopoulos (1981).
[9]See, for example, Hartman and Weber (1980) and Goldstein and Ehrenberg (1976).

2. Wage determination in the state and local government sector[10]

Several features distinguish studies of the effects of collective bargaining on SLG employees' wages from similar studies of union wage effects in the private sector. First, the unit of observation in the public-sector studies is typically an individual bargaining unit where, in the presence of collective bargaining, the same negotiated union wage scale covers nonunion employees as well as union employees. In contrast, private-sector studies tend to use either individual workers or industry aggregates as the units of observation.

Second, in an attempt to control for the forces other than collective bargaining that might influence wages, public-sector studies tend to stress economic, demographic, and political variables relating to the geographic area that the bargaining unit is in, while typically ignoring the personal characteristics of the public employees. In contrast, the private-sector studies stress the personal characteristics of employees and only occasionally incorporate characteristics of the employer or the industry (e.g. establishment size, concentration ratios, capital/labor ratios).

Finally, because public-sector studies tend to utilize bargaining unit data, their focus is often on how various characteristics of the environment in which bargaining takes place (e.g. city size, form of government, formal parity agreements) influence the effects of collective bargaining. In contrast, although a few private-sector studies have looked at how the structure of collective bargaining (multiemployer, union competition, etc.) affect union/nonunion wage differential estimates, most have stressed how these differentials vary with individual worker characteristics (e.g. race, sex, age, education, occupation).

Most studies of the effects of collective bargaining on SLG employees' wages are based explicitly, or implicitly, on a rather simple conceptional framework. Based upon a utility maximizing model of government behavior, the demand for public employees is specified to be a function of the wage costs of public employees (W) and a vector of sociodemographic and economic variables (Z) that represent the determinants of both the fiscal capacity (or ability to pay) of residents of the jurisdiction and the relative preferences of the community for various public services. Similarly, the supply of public employees is specified to be a function of the wages paid to public employees and another vector of sociodemographic and economic variables (V), that reflect alternative wages in the private sector and those forces that influence applicants' relative nonpecuniary preferences and qualifications for public-sector employment. In the absence of imperfections in the labor market, one can then solve for the market

---

[10] This section owes much to previous surveys including Lipsky (1982), Mitchell (1979), and Flanagan and Mitchell (1982).

clearing wage. However, given the presence of unions and political and institutional forces (e.g. form of government, monopsony power, parity agreements), which may be represented by a vector of variables (X), the actual wage equation to be estimated is specified as

$$W_i = F(Z_i, V_i, X_i, U_i) + \varepsilon_i,$$ (1)

where the ith subscript is used to denote a bargaining unit, U_i is some measure of collective bargaining (to be discussed shortly) and ε_i is a random error term.

Tables 22.1 and 22.2 present a nonexhaustive survey of studies published between 1970 and 1983 that estimate equations similar to eq. (1). The former contains estimates for public school teachers, while the latter focuses on various categories of noneducational employees. Most of the studies use individual bargaining units as the units of observation, although some of the early teacher studies used statewide data, one study of hospital employees did some analyses using SMSA-wide data, and several studies use data on individuals from the *Current Population Survey*. In the main they are cross-section studies in which the extent of unionization or collective bargaining coverage is taken as exogenous. However, a number of the studies allow the unionization variable to be endogenous, in the context of models that seek to control for selection bias.[11] In addition, at least one of the studies [Ichniowski (1980)] performs some analyses

[11] In spite of the dramatic growth of public-sector collective bargaining over the last 25 years, relatively few studies have been conducted on the determinants of the growth of public-sector unionization over time or on why collective bargaining coverage in the sector varies across areas. This is surprising because the laws governing bargaining in the SLG sector differ across states and are continuously evolving.

A number of studies have estimated probit union coverage, or existence of a union contract, equations using cross-section data in the context of models that seek to control for selection bias in union outcomes equations. See, for example, Cain et al. (1981), Bartel and Lewin (1981), and Ehrenberg, Sherman and Schwarz (1983). The latter found that the probability of observing a union in a municipal public library was significantly related to the laws in the state governing collective bargaining for municipal employees. In particular, a law prohibiting strikes reduced the probability of observing a union, while one providing mediation or fact-finding services in the event of an impasse, increased the probability.

This study illustrates a type of natural experiment one can perform to analyze the effects of state laws on union coverage. A second type is found in Ichniowski (1982a) who used panel data and found that the number of years since a public-sector bargaining law was passed in a state significantly was associated with the probability of observing a union contract for police in a city.

A final study, Moore (1978), sought to explain both aggregate time-series (1919–70) and interstate (1970) variation in teachers' unions membership. For some specifications of his cross-section work, he found that the presence of a mandatory bargaining law for public employees was associated with teacher union membership.

One senses from these studies that state laws governing public-sector bargaining are significantly associated with union membership and collective bargaining coverage. However, an unresolved issue is the direction of causation; no one has seriously studied whether public-sector union strength influences laws governing public-sector bargaining. Room is clearly present here for more work, possibly involving Granger causality tests.

Table 22.1
Estimated union/nonunion earnings differentials for public school teachers: Selected studies.

Study	Year	Coverage[a]	Outcomes	Union variable	Estimated earnings differential
Baird and Landon (1972)	1966–67	national (D)	starting salary	(1,0) negotiations held	4.9%
Kasper (1970)	1967–68	national (S)	average salary	proportion of teachers or districts with union representation	0
Frey (1975)	1964–65 to 1969–75	New Jersey (D)	starting salary	(1,0) formal contract	0–1.4%
Lipsky and Drotning (1973)	1967–68	New York (D)	B.S. min., plus various steps in salary schedule	(1,0) formal contract	0–3%
Hall and Carroll (1973)	1968–69	Illinois (D)	average salary	(1,0) formal contract	1.8%
Thornton (1971)	1969–70	national (D)	B.A. min. and max. M.A. min. and max.	(1,0) formal negotiations	0–5% save for M.A. max. which was > 20%
Balfour (1974)	1969–70 1970–71	national (S)	average salary	% of teachers and/or districts covered by agreements	0%
Chambers (1977)	1970–71	California (D)	(1) starting salary (2) increments	(1,0) formal contract	(1) 5.7–12.2% (2) 0%
Moore (1976)	1970–71	Nebraska (D)	average secondary/ average elementary salary	(1,0) formal negotiations	negative
Zueike and Frohreich (1977)	1972–73	Wisconsin (D)	variety of salary variables	index of comprehensiveness of negotiations	negative
Gustman and Segal (1977)	1972–73	national (D)	minimum salary, maximum salary, number of steps between min. and max.	(1,0) formal agreement	0 on min. or max., but reduce number of steps
Holmes (1976)	1974–75	Oklahoma (D)	average salary	(1,0) any union activity	7%
Gallagher (1978)	1976–77	Illinois (D)	variety of measures	(1,0) presence of collective bargaining	1–4.5%
Schmenner (1973)	1962–70	9 large cities (D)	B.A. min. salary	% union members (1,0) formal agreement	12–14% 6–9%
Baugh and Stone (1982)	(1) 1974 and 1975 (2) 1977 and 1978	national (C)	annual earnings	(1,0) union member (1,0) union or employee association member	0–7% 12–22%

[a] D = school district level data; S = state level data; C = individual data from the CPS.

Table 22.2

Estimated union/nonunion earnings differentials noneducational employees: Selected studies.

Study	Year	Coverage	Outcomes	Union variable	Estimated earnings differential[a]
Ashenfelter (1971)	1960–66	firefighters	(1) average hourly wage (2) annual hours (3) annual salary	(1,0) any union members	(1) 2–10% (2) −3 to −9% (3) 0
Freund (1974)	1965–71	noneducational employees	% change in average weekly earnings	% union members	0
Fottler (1977)	1966, 1969, 1972	hospital employees	average weekly	% union members	4–8%
Ehrenberg and Goldstein (1975)	1967	10 categories noneducational employees	average monthly earnings	% represented by a union	2–16%
Schmenner (1973)	1962–70	police and firefighters in 9 large cities	minimum salary	% union members (1,0) formal bargaining	15% 0
Ehrenberg (1973b)	1969	firefighters	hourly and annual minimum, maximum and average salary	(1,0) some union members (1,0) formal contract	0 2–18% primarily due to lower hours
Shapiro (1978)	1971	noneducational (individual data)	hourly pay	(1,0) union member	0–20%
Cain et al. (1981)	1973–76	hospital employees (1) individual data (2) by hospital (3) by SMSA	hourly pay hourly compensation	(1) (1,0) union membership (2) (1,0) organized (3) % organized	on wages– 0–10%, on fringes some-what larger
Ehrenberg (1980)	1973	police firefighters	minimum, maximum annual and hourly salary	(1,0) formal negotiations	3–10%

Study	Year	Group	Dependent variable	Union measure	Effect
Bartel and Lewin (1981)	1973	police	minimum, maximum average annual salaries and hourly wage	(1,0) written contract	6% / 10–21%[a]
Edwards and Edwards (1982a, 1982b)	1974	sanitation	average hourly wage	(1,0) any union members	10–17% / 10–11%
Victor (1979)	1975	(1) police (2) fire (3) sanitation	average hourly earnings	% organized / (1,0) any union members / (1,0) written contract	(1) 7–12% (2) 9–13% (3) 7–14% / 0
Hall and Vanderporten (1977)	1973	police	minimum, maximum average annual	(1,0) formal negotiations	<10%
Becker (1979)	1975	hospital employees	average wage	(1,0) occupation covered by a contract / (1,0) occupation is nonunion job in hospital with some contracts	7% / 8%
Ichniowski (1980)	1976	firefighters	min., max., average hourly and annual wages and contributions to fringes	(1,0) presence of contract	$0-3\frac{1}{2}$% (wages) / 18% (fringes)
Feldman and Scheffler (1982)	1977	hospital employees	average salary average fringe costs	(1,0) presence of written agreement	salary 8–12% fringes
Ehrenberg, Sherman and Schwarz (1983)	1977	libraries	minimum, maximum annual salaries	(1,0) any collective bargaining agreement	0
Moore and Raisian (1981)	1962–77	noneducational (individual data from CPS)	hourly wages	(1,0) union member	0–18% higher in later years

[a] Obtained from two-stage least squares framework.

using two years' data and a fixed effects model, to eliminate the biases caused by unobserved variables that may be correlated with collective bargaining coverage.

The unionization variable in these equations varies across studies. Some use a $(1,0)$ variable to indicate whether collective bargaining negotiations take place. Others use a $(1,0)$ variable to signify whether a formal contract governs wages and conditions of employment. Still others look at union membership, focusing on either the percentage of employees who are union members or whether any employees are union members. In each case, however, the estimates reported in the final column of the tables may be interpreted as *our* estimates (based upon their results) of what Jacob Mincer has called the "wage gap"; the relative wage differential associated with the union variable taking on the value of one rather than zero.[12]

What is most striking is how small most of these numbers are! The estimated relative wage differentials associated with union membership or collective bargaining coverage are typically smaller than 10 percent and rarely exceed 20 percent. These estimates are considerably lower than the estimates obtained from private sector studies (see Chapter 20 by Lewis in this Handbook) and they suggest that the relative wage effects of unions have been less in the public-sector than the private sector.[13] In addition, two studies that use data on individuals, rather than on bargaining units [Baugh and Stone (1982) and Moore and Raisian (1981)], tend to find that the union/nonunion relative wage differential increased between the early and late 1970s. Most students of public-sector labor relations find this latter result strange since their consensus was that while public-sector unions *may* have won large wage gains in the early years of bargaining when municipal employers were not fully prepared to bargain, over time these gains have eroded.

What accounts for these two findings? Does collective bargaining really have a smaller effect on union/nonunion wage differentials in the public than private sector and have the public-sector differentials grown over time? Or are there methodological problems with these studies which may account at least partially for the results?

Turning first to the question of the size of the union/nonunion wage differential in the public-sector, we should stress once again that the laws governing dispute resolution in the public-sector differ from those in the private sector. Most states prohibit strikes by public employees which may weaken their bargaining power and should lead to lower observed union/nonunion wage differentials. However, some states provide for alternative forms of dispute resolution and, as discussed below, some provide for binding arbitration, either

---

[12] In the case of the percentage unionization variable, the estimate should be interpreted as the relative wage differential between cities with some union members and those with none. See Ashenfelter (1971, footnote 16), for a proof of this statement.

[13] Edwards and Edwards (1982a), however, come to the opposite conclusion for solid waste collection employees.

of a conventional or a final offer form, as the terminal stage of their impasse procedures. The literature we review below suggests that the nature of the impasse procedures available may well affect the bargaining power of unions. Somewhat surprisingly, however, there are no studies that have empirically looked at how the nature of impasse procedures affects the union/nonunion wage differential; this represents a fertile area for future research. In any case, the smaller estimated differentials in the public-sector *may* reflect smaller actual differentials caused by the different nature of the laws governing bargaining in the sector.[14]

Several methodological problems may also cause these studies to understate public-sector unions' impact on their members' relative wages. First, most of these studies ignore the interdependence of wage settlements across different public-sector bargaining units in the same city (e.g. police, fire, sanitation) and the interdependence of wage settlements across geographic areas (e.g. cities in an SMSA) for a given category of employees (e.g. police). Such occupational and geographic wage interrelationships lead union wage gains to "spillover" across bargaining units in a given city and across contiguous cities.

Studies that take account of these spillovers often find much larger union relative wage effects. For example, Ehrenberg and Goldstein (1975) found union/nonunion wage differentials in the range of 6–16 percent for various categories of municipal noneducational employees when they considered only the unionization of employees in the category. In contrast, when occupational spillovers of union wage gains were permitted, the estimated union/nonunion wage differentials in cities where *all* categories of municipal employees were organized rose to the range of 20–32 percent. The same study also illustrated the importance of geographic spillovers finding that when a matched set of central city and suburban observations were used that, on average, the presence of a public-sector union in a category in one city in the pair caused wages of employees in the category in the other city in the pair to be significantly higher.

More recent studies have confirmed the importance of the occupational and geographic spillover of union wage gains [see, for example, Victor (1979), Feldman and Scheffler (1982), Cain et al. (1981), Becker (1981), and Chambers (1977)]. Ignoring them may well have caused most researchers to underestimate the magnitude of public-sector union/nonunion wage differentials.

Second, most public-sector wage studies have treated collective bargaining coverage as exogenous. However, one might expect employee pressure for organization to come first in cities where public-sector wages are below average for cities with comparable sociodemographic and economic characteristics. If this is

---

[14]Some people have also argued that the smaller estimated public-sector union differentials may reflect the fragmented nature of bargaining in the public-sector – with bargaining done often at the local level by "occupation". Since a similar bargaining structure exists in construction where union/nonunion differentials considerably exceed the private-sector average differential, we are suspicious of this explanation.

the case, subsequently contrasting wages in those cities where unions are present to those in which unions are not present will understate the true public-sector union/nonunion wage differential.

Attempts to allow for the endogeneity of collective bargaining coverage have not all yielded similar results. Cain et al. (1981) and Ehrenberg et al. (1983) estimated union/nonunion wage differentials in the context of models that corrected for selectivity bias; neither found systematically larger differentials using such models. Ichniowski (1980) used a fixed-effects model and panel data to eliminate the effects of any unobservable variables that might be correlated with both collective bargaining coverage and wages and again found that such a method did not significantly affect his estimated differential. However, Bartel and Lewin (1981) did find much larger estimated differentials when unionization was made endogenous.

Third, most of the studies summarized in Tables 22.1 and 22.2 have tended to focus on hourly or annual earnings, rather than fringe benefits or total compensation. Might such a focus understate the relative union/nonunion compensation differentials in the public sector? Studies of union effects in the private sector have often found that union/nonunion relative total compensation or fringe benefit differentials exceed union/nonunion wage differentials [e.g. Freeman (1981)]; an explanation for this result is that unions serve a collective voice function and can help to aggregate the preferences of individual workers for fringes and communicate these preferences to management. Since in the public-sector the ultimate financers of settlements (taxpayers) are not explicitly represented at the bargaining table and since it may be easier to hide the true costs of generous fringe benefit settlements than wage settlements from taxpayers (via underfunding of pensions or withhold information on the "true" costs of fringes), one might expect union compensation gains to be skewed even more towards fringes in the public-sector.

There is some evidence that this may have occurred. For example, Ichniowski (1980) found the relative union/nonunion fringe benefit differentials for firefighters to be roughly four times as large as the comparable wage differential; a relationship which is much larger than that found by Freeman (1981) in his private-sector studies. Edwards and Edwards (1982b) similarly found much larger fringe differentials than wage differentials for sanitation workers. Other investigators, however [e.g. Bartel and Lewin (1981), Becker (1979), Feldman and Scheffler (182), Cain et al. (1981)], found union/nonunion fringe differentials for public employees that appear to exceed the union/nonunion wage differential by only a small amount.[15] So while union/nonunion relative wage differential estimates in

---

[15] Rogers (1979) actually found that union/nonunion fringe benefit differentials were sometimes *negative* for certain categories of fringes, suggesting a willingness of unions to trade off some benefits for others.

the public sector probably do understate the comparable total compensation differentials, it is not obvious that the understatement is greater here than in the private sector.[16]

Finally, while most recent studies of union relative wage effects in the private sector have used data on the wages paid to specific individuals, studies in the public-sector have tended to focus on minimum, maximum, or average salaries for a particular category of public employees. If public-sector unions are dominated by senior workers, one might expect to observe smaller union/nonunion differentials at the entrance than at the maximum salary levels. Moreover, if public employers respond to union-induced wage gains that are skewed to favor older workers by seeking to increase the proportion of their workforces that are younger workers, estimated union/nonunion average salary differentials will also be less than maximum salary differentials and may actually be less than minimum salary differentials.[17] If public-sector wage studies focused primarily on average salaries, this might partially explain the lower union/nonunion wage differentials observed in the public-sector.

Although many public-sector studies, especially those for noneducational employees, have focused on average earnings others have focused on minimum and maximum salaries. A quick reading of Tables 22.1 and 22.2 also suggests that the union/nonunion wage differentials estimated from the latter studies are not appreciably higher than those estimated from the former. Moreover, the evidence on whether these differentials are actually larger for older than for younger workers is mixed [see, for example, Ehrenberg et al. (1980), Ehrenberg (1973b), Bartel and Lewin (1981), Thornton (1971), Gustman and Segal (1977), Chambers (1977), and Gallagher (1978)].

---

[16] The realization that the total compensation of labor includes a host of pecuniary and non-pecuniary job characteristics, as well as money wages, naturally led students of public-sector labor markets to consider the issue of compensating wage differentials. The studies in this area break down neatly into two sets: the first deals with the trade-off between public school teachers' wages and nonpecuniary job characteristics [see Antos and Rosen (1975), Eberts and Stone (1983), Gustman and Clement (1977), Toder (1972) and Kenny and Denslow (1980)], while the second deals with the trade-off between wages and fringe benefits for public employees [see Ehrenberg (1980), Ehrenberg and Smith (1981), Inman (1981), R. Smith (1981) and Woodbury (1983)]. Space constraints preclude a discussion of these studies here, the interested reader may refer to Ehrenberg and Schwarz (1983b) or, since the methodological issues are identical to those raised in private sector studies, to Chapter 12 by Rosen in this Handbook.

[17] Suppose initially that there are two types of employees, junior workers who get paid W_j and senior workers who get paid $(1 + s)W_j$, and that half of a city's workforce is in each category. Suppose also that a union increases wages of the two groups by α and αm percent, respectively, $(m > 1)$ and the city responds by increasing the share of junior workers it hires to $\gamma (> 1/2)$. Then the union/nonunion average wage differential is $[W_j(1 + \alpha)\gamma + W_j(1 + s)(1 + \alpha m)(1 - \gamma)]/[W_j(1/2) + W_j(1 + s)(1/2)]$ or $[(1 + \alpha)\gamma + (1 + s)(1 + \alpha m)(1 - \gamma)]/[1 + (s/2)]$. This will be less than $(1 + \alpha)$ provided that $[(1 + s)(1 + \alpha m)(1 - \gamma)] < 1 + (s/2) - \gamma$. For example, if $s = 1$ (initially senior workers get paid twice as much), $\alpha = 0.1$ and $m = 1.5$, then any value of $\gamma > 0.542$ will yield the union/nonunion average wage differential to be less than the comparable minimum wage differential.

We turn next to the question of whether the public-sector union/nonunion wage differential has grown over time. The estimates that suggest it has come from studies [Baugh and Stone (1982), Moore and Raisian (1981)] that utilize data on individuals and that completely ignore information on the economic and sociodemographic characteristics of the cities in which public-sector employees are located. We know from the bargaining unit studies cited in the tables that, ceteris paribus, public-sector wages tend to be higher in large, densely populated cities. These cities also tend to be the cities in which collective bargaining arose first and in which it has grown most rapidly. Hence, even if the actual union/nonunion wage differential is constant across high and low wage cities at a point in time and does not vary over time for each type of city, it is straightforward to show that the observed average union/nonunion wage differential will increase over time. Put another way, omitted variable problems may well have biased the studies based on individual data and we do *not* find the evidence that public-sector union/nonunion wage differentials have increased over time compelling.

As noted above, in addition to providing estimates of union/nonunion wage differentials, many of the studies of public-sector wages have taken great care to emphasize the importance of various characteristics of the environment in which bargaining takes place. To take one example, numerous studies have sought to estimate whether public employers have monopsony power, focusing on measures like the number of school districts in a county [Baird and Landon (1972)], the percentage of a SMSA's population which resides in a jurisdiction [Ehrenberg and Goldstein (1975)], or concentration ratios such as the fraction of an area's hospital beds in the four largest hospitals in an area [Feldman and Scheffler (1982)]. To the extent that variables like these are good proxies for monopsony power, the first should be positively associated with wages and the latter two negatively associated; these and other studies suggest this is the case.

To take another example, a set of studies has focused on the effects of form of government on wages. Historically, at least partially because of the belief that professionally trained managers could "produce" a desired set of services at lower cost than could an elected nonprofessional, a substantial proportion of all U.S. cities have chosen to employ a city-manager as the principal operating officer rather than an elected mayor or set of commissioners. If professionally trained managers are better negotiators, are more aware of market conditions, and/or are more efficient than elected officials in "producing" public services from a given number of employees, one might expect that city-manager cities would have lower wage costs than other municipalities and that union/nonunion wage differentials would be lower in them, ceteris paribus.

To date, however, only one study [Edwards and Edwards (1982b)] found that the form of local government affects the size of union/nonunion wage differentials. In particular, it found that union/nonunion differentials for municipal sanitation workers are zero in city-manager run cities but positive in other cities. Moreover, the evidence on the effect of governmental form on salary *levels* is mixed [see Ehrenberg (1973b), Ehrenberg and Goldstein (1975), Edwards and Edwards (1982b), and Bartel and Lewin (1981)].

Finally, a number of studies have examined how the effects of parity provisions in collective bargaining contracts, that require that two groups of employees (e.g. police patrolmen and firefighters) receive the same wages, affect wage settlements [Ehrenberg (1973b), Hall and Vanderporten (1977)]. The evidence here, not surprisingly, suggests that these provisions positively (negatively) influence the wages of groups that are in excess supply (demand). Other studies have begun to look at how municipal laws, such as civil service laws, residency requirements that mandate that public employees live in the municipality where they work, or prevailing wage laws that at least partially determine wages via reference to compatibility studies, affect wages [Lewin (1983), Hirsch and Rufolo (1975, 1983a, 1983b)].

This latter group of studies are suggestive of a direction in which future research on public-sector wage determination might proceed – to more fully analyze the relationship between the legal environment, public–sector wages, and public-sector union/nonunion wage differentials. The legal environment includes state statutes governing public-sector dispute resolution; as noted above there have been no studies of the effects of dispute resolution statutes on union/non-union differentials and only a limited number (to be discussed below) of their effects on the level of wage settlements.

Dispute resolution statutes are only one part of the environment, however. Surprisingly no one has addressed the effects of a host of other laws. Some states require taxpayers to approve local school budgets at annual budget referenda, while others do not. In the wake of the passage of Proposition 13 in California in the early 1970s, some states now have limitations on state or local taxes and/or expenditure levels, while others do not. Some state constitutions require that state governments operate balanced budgets, while others do not. Finally, some states have agency shop provisions in their public-sector bargaining laws that require public employees to join the union representing them or pay the equivalent of dues, while other states explicitly prohibit such provisions [Hanslowe et al. (1978)]. Surely these laws should all be expected to influence public-sector union bargaining power and hence the level of wages.

The fact that these laws vary across states provides a form of natural experiment that should allow researchers to investigate their effects on wage levels and differentials. Of course, the possibility that the laws are endogenous should be considered and appropriate econometric methodologies used. To analyze the effects of such laws obviously requires a national sample of bargaining units; it is interesting that many of the studies cited in Table 22.1 were confined to a single state.

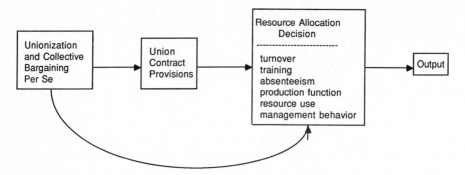

Figure 22.1. The routes via which unions affect productivity in the public-sector.

3. Unions and productivity

Recently, a number of economists have directed their attention to estimating the effects of unions and collective bargaining on nonwage outcomes in the public-sector. As is well known, the traditional neoclassical view of unions is that by creating noncompensating wage differentials and negotiating work rules that limit employers' flexibility to allocate resources, unions cause efficiency losses. In contrast, drawing on hypotheses put forth long ago by institutional economists, the "Harvard School" holds that unions may well increase productivity via a number of routes including reducing turnover, increasing morale and motivation, and expanding formal and informal on-the-job training. Indeed, several studies suggest that union/nonunion productivity differentials in the private sector are often positive.[18] It is natural to similarly ask, then, what the effects of unions have been on productivity in the public-sector.

Figure 22.1 presents a simple schematic diagram that illustrates the routes via which unions affect productivity. Unionization and the collective bargaining process per se lead to the establishment of union contract provisions (grievance, seniority, staffing, sick leave, wages, etc.). These provisions directly influence both employer and employee resource allocation decisions in areas such as turnover, training, absenteeism, and the nature of the production process and managerial behavior. Unionization per se may also influence these decisions independent of any specific contract provisions; for example, management behavior may be altered due to the mere presence of a union. Finally, the sum of these resource allocation decisions may affect output.

This figure highlights a number of important points. First, unions affect productivity both through the specific union contract provisions they negotiate

[18] See Freeman and Medoff (1984) for a summary of these studies.

and administer and via the unions' mere presence. A complete analysis would focus on both routes; however, as will be seen below, most public-sector studies have focused on estimating the effects of a specific set of provisions or the sum of the effects of unionization across the two routes. Second, because the unit of observation in the public sector is the bargaining unit and public-sector labor contracts are often readily available, one would expect many more analyses of the effects of contract provisions to have occurred in the public than in the private sector. To some extent this has occurred; while private-sector studies have focused on (1,0) collective bargaining coverage variables, a number of the public-sector studies have examined contract provisions. Third, the difficulties involved in trying to measure output and specify production functions in the public-sector are well known. As such, one might expect much of the public-sector research to focus on the effect of unions on resource allocation decisions, rather than on productivity, per se, and this has also occurred.

Turning first to studies that have attempted to estimate the effects of unions on productivity in the public-sector, these have all been single year cross-section studies that treat collective bargaining coverage or unionization only as a (1,0) variable and that use a production function or derived demand for public services approach. For example, Ehrenberg and Schwarz (1983a) and Ehrenberg, Sherman and Schwarz (1983) focused on municipal public libraries because of the availability of various measures of output and found no union/nonunion productivity differential. A similar result was found by Noam (1983) who studied municipal building departments.

Sherman (1983) and Eberts and Stone (forthcoming) studied elementary and secondary schools, using student test scores as measures of output. The former found that unions were associated with significantly *lower* mean test scores for students and a *higher* variance of test scores. The latter, who used data on individuals, found that unions were associated with higher test scores for "average" students but lower test scores for both below and above average students. Both papers caution, as Brown and Saks (1975) have emphasized, that school districts and teachers must make decisions about the allocation of resources across different categories of students. As a result, when one observes union coverage associated with the entire distribution of educational outcomes across school districts, it is difficult to disentangle unions' effects on the educational production function from their effects on how resources are allocated across students.

In principle, "production function" estimates could be extended to other public services, e.g. police, fire and sanitation, for which measures of "output" can be obtained. One must remember, however, that the association of union coverage with productivity does *not* imply a causal relationship; of the above studies, only Ehrenberg and Schwarz (1983a) and Ehrenberg, Sherman and Schwarz (1983) considered the endogeneity of unionization, modelling it in a sample selection framework. Future research in this tradition must continue to consider this problem, using either a similar approach and/or longitudinal data that would permit one to use a fixed-effects model to control for unobservables correlated with both union coverage and output.

Turning next to the studies of union effects on resource allocation, these have focused almost exclusively on public education and again have been primarily cross-sectional in nature. Eberts (forthcoming) found that teachers in unionized schools spent less time per school year in instructional activities and more time on preparation, administration and parent conferences. He also found that unionized districts had more teachers and administrators per student (but fewer secretaries and aids), a result that contrasts with Hall and Carroll's (1973) finding of lower teacher/student ratios in unionized school districts.

Most of the studies in this area, however, have focused on the effects of specific contract provisions. For example, Winkler (1980) found that various contract provisions relating to sick leave policy were associated with the number of short-term absences observed for a sample of teachers. Murnane (1981) studied the turnover of public school teachers in a system in which pay was determined strictly by seniority and found that the seniority provision did not cause the more productive teachers, as measured by principals' evaluations and/or the teachers' marginal effects on student performance, to quit their jobs more frequently.

Eberts (1982b) also focused on teacher turnover, studying whether contract provisions that specify maximum class sizes, and those that specify that reductions in force (RIF) due to declining enrollment be governed by seniority, affect the probability either that teachers voluntarily leave their school district or that they transfer from one school to another within a district. He found that class size provisions were associated with fewer quits but more within-district transfers and that RIF provisions were associated with a lower probability that experienced teachers would leave the school district (these teachers would have relatively more job security under RIF) but a higher probability that teachers with little seniority would leave. In related work, Eberts (1982a) found that districts with RIF provisions experienced, ceteris paribus, a smaller reduction in the level of resources available for education duing a period of declining enrollments and fiscal stress. Similarly, Eberts (1983) found that an index of the number of contract provisions contained in a contract and the presence of a set of specific provisions were all associated with a larger share of the school budget being devoted to instructional purposes, ceteris paribus.

While these latter studies are useful first efforts, they have at least three limitations. First, we have been careful to use the words "associated with" rather than "cause" when talking about the contract provision studies because, save for Eberts (1982a), none of them allow for the possibility that some omitted variables influence both the contract provisions and the resource allocation decisions. Again, what seems called for is an explicit simultaneous equations approach or the use of longitudinal data that would permit the estimation of a fixed effects model. If the latter approach is used, one would want to focus on how changes in contract provisions affect changes in outcomes, differencing out the fixed effects. If the former approach is used, one could explicitly address the issue of how state laws governing public-sector collective bargaining and dispute resolution affect contract provisions and hence, indirectly, resource allocation.

Second, while these studies are a substantial improvement over prior private- and public-sector studies that focus on $(1,0)$ union variables, they do not go quite as far as they might. Virtually all use $(1,0)$ variables to parameterize specific contract provisions when often more detailed data is available.[19] Is it the presence of a maximum class size provision or the level of the maximum student/teacher ratio that matters? Future studies should try to parameterize contract provisions in a more detailed fashion.

Finally, all of these contract provision studies deal with resource allocation decisions, but only Eberts and Stone (forthcoming) attempt to evaluate how these decisions subsequently affect output or productivity. What is needed are estimates of public-sector "production functions" that include variables such as absentee or turnover rates directly in the production function. Alternatively, one might ignore such variables and estimate "quasi-reduced-form" production functions in which the underlying contract provisions appeared explicitly. But again, here account must be taken of possible simultaneity between contract provisions and productivity.

4. Dispute resolution

As noted in Section 1, most states prohibit strikes by public employees, substituting instead a formal system of impasse procedures in which assistance is provided to local governments and unions to help them resolve collective bargaining disputes. For those categories of public services that are often thought to be essential (police and firefighters), about 20 states have adopted forms of binding arbitration as the terminal stage of the impasse procedures. This takes the form of either *conventional arbitration* where the parties present their final positions and supporting evidence to an arbitrator (or panel of arbitrators) who fashions a binding final settlement based upon the evidence and any other factors deemed to be relevant, or of *final offer arbitration* where the arbitrator is required to issue a settlement that corresponds to the final position of one of the parties, either on a package (one party "wins") or issue-by-issue (each party may "win" on a number of issues) basis.[20]

---

[19] Winkler (1980) is an exception.
[20] In Iowa, the arbitrator may also choose a neutral fact-finder's recommended settlement.

These unique forms of public-sector dispute resolution lead to a number of empirical research questions that economists and industrial relations specialists have devoted considerable resources to answering. For example, in spite of prohibitions against strikes in the public sector, strikes do occur and it is natural to study their determinants.

To take another example, conventional arbitration statutes were introduced in the hope that they would reduce strike activity. But concern is often expressed that these statutes will have a *chilling effect* on bargaining; if the parties believe that arbitrators' decisions tend to "split the difference" between their final positions, the parties will have reduced incentives to make concessions during bargaining since any concession would come back to haunt them if the dispute went to arbitration. As a result, conventional arbitration statutes may lead to a reduced level of bargaining and heavy use of the arbitration procedures. Final offer arbitration, where the "reasonableness" of a party's position influences the likelihood that the arbitrator chooses it, was developed to avoid this problem.[21]

These alternative forms of arbitration and the issues they raise lead naturally to the study of whether arbitrators tend to split the difference under conventional arbitration, whether a conventional arbitration statute increases the probability of a dispute going to arbitration vis-à-vis a final offer statute, and whether arbitration statutes tend to have a *narcotic* or *addictive* effect, in the sense that once the parties go to arbitration, this increases the probability that they will go to arbitration again in future rounds?

The empirical research addresses the outcomes of bargaining as well as the process itself. It is again natural to study whether the existence of an impasse procedure per se affects either the mean level or dispersion of contract settlements in a state, whether settlements systematically differ between bargaining units that use the procedures and those that settle on their own, and whether arbitrators exhibit bias in the sense that most of the cases that go to arbitration are won by one party (e.g. unions)?

These questions are all important because industrial relations specialists tend to evaluate public-sector impasse procedures by their effectiveness in inducing the parties to settle on their own (i.e. to not use the procedures) and by their effectiveness in *not* influencing the nature of the settlements. Before turning to the empirical evidence on these points, however, it is useful to remember that these are all somewhat ad hoc criteria. Indeed, recently a number of economists have provided analytical models of the arbitration process that suggest that some of these criteria may not be useful ones to focus on and we turn first to a discussion of these models.

In a series of papers [Farber and Katz (1979), Farber (1980a, 1980b, 1981)] simple two-party zero-sum models of parties' bargaining over a single outcome

---

[21] See Stevens (1966).

are presented. The first, Farber and Katz (1979), considers the case where the parties form expectations of a conventional arbitrator's award; each party's expectation is assumed to be normally distributed and to have a specified mean and variance. Each party seeks to maximize its expected utility from the negotiations and risk aversion of the parties leads to a contract zone; a range of settlements that is preferred by *both* parties to facing the uncertainty of the arbitrator's decision. In this framework, uncertainty is the cost of the arbitration process that leads to the contract zone and a key assumption of the model is that the larger the contract zone is, the more likely the parties will settle on their own.

The Farber–Katz model leads immediately to two important implications. First, if over time the parties' uncertainty about arbitrators' decisions diminishes, the size of the contract zone and thus the probability the parties will settle on their own will decrease. To avoid ever-increasing use of the arbitration process, one must increase the cost to the parties of using the process.[22] Second, if one assumes that the bargaining power of each party (the "share" of the contract zone the party will win in bargaining) is fixed, then necessarily the settlements that go to arbitration will differ from those where the parties settle on their own. This occurs because the more risk-averse party will willingly settle on its own for a smaller share of the pie to avoid the risks of going to arbitration. Thus, any difference observed between arbitrated and negotiated settlements does not indicate that the process is unfair. Rather, it suggests only that the arbitration process per se necessarily affects the nature of negotiated settlements.

The Farber–Katz model takes the arbitrator's notion of a fair settlement as given. Suppose instead that the arbitrator considers both the "intrinsic" fairness and the parties' positions in framing his award, with deviations of the parties' positions from his notion of intrinsic fairness reducing the weight he assigns to their offers in determining his award.[23] Farber (1981) shows that such a model will lead the parties to endogenously select their offers in an attempt to influence the arbitrator's decision and that, in equilibrium, the offers will be structured so that it appears that the arbitrator is "splitting the difference". Evidence that arbitrators are splitting the difference thus may imply only that expectations of arbitrators' decisions influence the parties' positions.[24]

Finally, Farber (1980a, 1980b) models final offer arbitration (FOA) as well as conventional arbitration. Under FOA a party has incentives to make concessions because, although such concessions reduce a party's expected utility if its position is chosen, they increase the probability that the party's position will be chosen. Thus, as under conventional arbitration, the parties' offers are endogenous under FOA [Farber (1981)]. As such, Farber shows that it is not necessarily the case

---

[22] See Kochan et al. (1979) and Hirsch and Donn (1982).

[23] Bazerman and Farber (1983) present evidence that supports this hypothesis.

[24] Farber (1981) also shows that the more weight the arbitrator puts on the parties' positions, the smaller the contract zone will be and thus the higher the probability of arbitrated settlements.

that FOA will lead to more uncertainty about the arbitrator's decision, and thus one cannot conclude that FOA provides the parties with more of an incentive to settle on their own than does conventional arbitration. Moreover, he also shows (1980b) that if the arbitrator awards the final offer closest to his notion of a fair settlement and the parties choose their final offers to maximize their expected utility, then the contract zone will be skewed against the more risk-averse party. Put another way, the more risk-averse party will win a greater share of the arbitrated awards but the awards it wins will be closer to the arbitrator's notion of intrinsic fairness than will the awards that the other party wins. Hence, evidence that one party (e.g. unions) wins most of the cases that go to arbitration may imply only greater risk aversion on that party's part, not that arbitrators are systematically biased in favor of that party.

This series of papers illustrates how simple economic models can be used to contrast alternative institutional arrangements and to call into question the criteria by which industrial relations specialists evaluate the effectiveness of public-sector impasse procedures. However, lest we appear too sanguine about the papers' importance, we should note that they have been subject to a number of criticisms. Crawford (1981) stresses that there is no theoretical justification for the key assumption that the size of the contract zone is positively related to the probability of reaching a negotiated settlement. To see this, suppose that there is only one point on the contract zone – only one bargaining outcome that both parties consider preferable to an arbitrated solution. Surely it should be easier for the parties to agree on that point than it would be for them to agree on one point out of five hundred on a contract zone, which all differed in their distribution of the pie between the parties. Without the assumption of the positive correlation between the size of the contract zone and the probability of reaching a negotiated settlement, many of the model's results concerning dependence on impasse procedures vanish.

Similarly, an important assumption in a number of the models is that the "bargaining power" of each party is fixed, in the sense that a negotiated settlement would give each bargainer a fixed proportion of the difference between the two end-points of the contract zone. This assumption leads to the result that settlements will be skewed against the more risk-averse party under both conventional and final offer arbitration. However, Crawford (1981) challenges the idea that it is meaningful to talk about bargaining power independently of the parties' risk aversion; more risk-averse parties surely have less bargaining power.[25]

One should not, however, go too far in dismissing the usefulness of the Farber–Katz line of research. In recent work, Ashenfelter and Bloom (1984) have

---

[25] Crawford (1981) also questions whether the results from these models will hold when more than one outcome is being negotiated. For his own work, which considers bargaining over a number of outcomes when arbitrators' decisions are assumed to be known with certainty [see Crawford (1979)]. Generalizations of the Farber–Katz model are found in Bloom (1981a) and Hirsch and Donn (1982).

looked at data on police wage settlements under the first three years of a binding arbitration procedure in New Jersey. This procedure allows for conventional arbitration if the parties agree to it and otherwise mandates final offer arbitration. The raw data suggest that unions win over two-thirds of the final offer arbitration cases, that there is about a two to three percentage point spread between the typical union and employer final offers, and that the means of the conventional arbitration awards in each year are very close to the means of the union offers under final offer arbitration. These data are very suggestive (assuming that conventional arbitration awards are good measures of arbitrators' intrinsic notions of fair awards) of a Farber (1980a) view of the world in which the more risk-averse party (the union) is positioning its offers closest to arbitrators' intrinsic views of fairness and thus winning the majority of the cases.

Ashenfelter and Bloom formally test whether this is occurring. They assume that an arbitrator has a normally distributed set of preferred settlements and chooses the party's offer which is closest to a random draw from this distribution. This leads directly to a simple probit model of which party's offer is chosen that can be estimated from data on the parties' final offers, the arbitrator's decision, and the variables that determine the expected value of the arbitrator's preferred decision (such as private wage settlements). From such a model one can infer the mean and variance of the distribution of arbitrators' preferences.

They show that it is straightforward to extend the model to allow for the arbitrator's preferred award to be influenced by the parties' final offers, as suggested in Farber's models, and to test if arbitrators are unbiased in the sense that they weigh both parties' offers equally in arriving at their preferred award. Finally, from conventional arbitration awards they show that one can again estimate the determinants of arbitrators' preferred settlements and see if these are the same under conventional and final offer arbitration. Without going into the details of their work, suffice it to say that strong support is found for the underlying framework.

Turning to the literature on strike activity in the public-sector, it suffers, as does its private sector counterpart (see Chapter 20 by Kennan in this Handbook), from the lack of any single analytical model that is universally accepted as providing an explanation of strike activity. Although many public-sector studies draw on existing theories of bargaining and strike activity, such as those found in Hicks (1966) and Ashenfelter and Johnson (1969), for our purposes it is best to think of them as quasi-experimental designs in which some measures of strike activity is regressed on a set of variables designed to capture the effects of public policy in an area, and a set of variables included to "control" for other factors. That is to say, the studies in the main seek to estimate the effects of public policies on the level of public-sector strike activity.

One early study [Thornton and Weintraub (1974)] examined the level of strike activity in the twelve-month periods before and after the adoption of "permissive" public-sector bargaining legislation – legislation which permitted collective bargaining – for teachers in 27 states, concluding that the level of strike activity tended to increase after the adoption of a statute. No conclusions can be drawn as to the causal nature of the relationship, since they failed to control for any other factors that may have influenced both the propensity of public employees to strike and the passage of a state law. A second paper of theirs [Weintraub and Thornton (1976)] tried to improve upon the methodology, using aggregate time-series data on various dimensions of teachers' strike activity, which were specified to be a function of the percentage of school districts in states with permissive bargaining legislation and a vector of control variables. While the bargaining legislation variable tended to be positively associated with the strike measures, it also tended to move like a time trend, making it difficult to separate out its effects from those of changes in any other variables (e.g. teacher militancy).[26]

A second set of studies uses cross-section or pooled cross-section time-series data at the state level and focuses on more aspects of state bargaining laws. Burton and Krider (1975) used data on four dimensions of local government nonteacher strikes (strikes per employee, striking employees per employee, mandays idle per employee, and duration of strikes) for the 1968–71 period and regressed these outcomes on a vector of control variables, as well as a vector of public-sector bargaining law characteristics. The latter included dichotomous variables for the existence of a permissive bargaining law, the requirement that the parties meet and confer, the requirement that the parties bargain in good faith, the existence of third-party impasse procedures, and the existence of laws penalizing strikers. The authors found no consistent pattern of significant effects for any aspects of the laws, either in individual year cross-sections or in the pooled data, and noted the low explanatory power of their models. The latter result is a characteristic of virtually all studies of public employee strikes.

Subsequent studies using state-level data have followed in the Burton and Krider (1975) tradition and occasionally have found specific bargaining law provisions significant; however, no consistent pattern of results has appeared across studies [see Perry (1977), Rogers (1980), and Partridge (1983)]. Their usefulness is limited by their treatment of state statutes governing bargaining as exogenously determined, by the collinearity of various provisions of the laws which makes it difficult to disentangle their independent effects, and by the fact that the unit of observation does not correspond to the bargaining unit which makes it difficult to control for other forces that might influence the level of strike activity. Several recent studies use data on individual bargaining units and go at least part of the way towards resolving these difficulties.

---

[26] Nelson, Stone and Swint (1981) is another aggregate time-series study, but the only public policy variable they included was a dummy variable for the passage of the Landrum–Griffin Act (which applies only to private sector unions).

Olson et al. (1981) used data on teachers, nonuniformed municipal employees, and police and firefighter negotiations in a number of states. Logit probability of a strike occurring equations were estimated separately for each employee group, with an arbitration dummy variable included in the police and firefighter equations and a state dummy variable in the other equations to control for state public policies. Their results suggest that in states where strike penalties were harsh *and* frequently enforced the frequency of strikes was lower, as it was for police and firefighters in states with an arbitration statute. While this study treated state laws as exogenous, Ichniowski (1982b) used data for a number of years on police work stoppages and estimated a fixed effects model to control for the endogeneity of statutes. His results suggest that a change from no law a "duty to bargain" law increased strike activity, while a shift from the latter to a compulsory arbitration statute decreased strike frequency.

A final study that utilized bargaining unit data has moved the analyses away from estimating the effects of state statutes back towards understanding the economic determinants of strikes. Olson (1984) argues that most theories of strike activity imply that higher costs to the parties of strikes will lead to a lower level of strike activity. In the case of teachers, these costs will be inversely related to the probability that a school district will opt to reschedule school days lost during a strike. He models this probability as a function of the community's demand for education and the penalties imposed by the state if the length of the school year falls below a mandated state minimum.

Using data on all school districts in Pennsylvania over a four-year period, a two-equation bivariate probit model was estimated that simultaneously determined the probabilities that lost school days will be rescheduled and that a strike will occur. The latter was specified to be a function of whether strike days were rescheduled in the past (if a strike occurred) and their probability of being rescheduled in the current round. His findings suggested that both of these variables positively influenced the probability of observing a strike.

Turning next to the studies of the usage of third-party impasse procedures, these have been of three types.[27] The first addresses the issue of the "chilling" effects of arbitration statutes, asking how the statutes influence various measures of the amount of bargaining that occurs (willingness to compromise, number of issues taken to impasse, etc.). A number of these studies analyzed a modified final offer arbitration statute introduced in Iowa in the mid-1970s [Gallagher and Pegnetter (1979), Gallagher and Chaubey (1982) and Gallagher, Feuille and Chaubey (1979)], while other studies used data from several states [Feuille (1975) and Wheeler (1978)]. Each used a very simple quasi-experimental design – a before–after comparison or a comparison of differences across bargaining

---

[27]Due to space limitations our discussion here is necessarily brief. For a survey of the empirical arbitration literature [see Anderson (1981)].

units – without any attempt to control for factors other than differences in the laws that might cause the outcomes to differ over time or across units.

The same criticism can be directed at the second type of study: those which address the issue of the chilling effect by looking at variations in the frequency of impasse over time and across areas. Somers (1977) and Lipsky and Barocci (1978) for Massachusetts, Kochan et al. (1978) for New York State, and Olson (1978) for Wisconsin, all found that the percentage of police and firefighter negotiations going to impasse increased after the passage of arbitration statutes. Similarly, Lipsky and Drotning (1977) found the shift from legislative determination to fact-finding as the final stage of the impasse procedure for teachers in New York State was associated with an increased percentage of negotiations going to impasse. Finally, Wheeler (1975b) conducted an interstate analysis of the percentage of firefighter negotiations going to impasse and found it to be higher in states with arbitration statutes than in states where the procedures terminated with fact-finding.

The third type of study addresses whether the procedures create a narcotic effect – a tendency once the parties use a procedure for them to become increasingly reliant upon it in future negotiations. The methodological approach used in these studies is somewhat more satisfactory than those used in the studies cited above. Equations of the form

$$Y_{it} = X_{it}B + \theta Y_{it-1} + \varepsilon_{it} \tag{2}$$

were estimated, where Y_{it} (Y_{it-1}) takes on the value of one if bargaining unit i goes to impasse in period t ($t-1$), X_{it} is a set of economic, political, structural and organizational variables expected to influence the probability that unit i goes to impasse in period t, B is a vector of regression coefficients, and ε_{it} is a random error term.[28] A positive estimate for the coefficient θ would suggest that prior impasse experience positively influences the probability of going to impasse in the current round.[29]

Estimates of variants of eq. (2) are found in Kochan and Baderschneider (1978) for police and firefighters in New York, Olson (1978) for the same groups in Wisconsin, and Lipsky and Drotning (1977) for teachers in New York. All found evidence that θ is positive, which they interpret as implying that prior impasse experience has a narcotic effect. But does it really mean this?

[28] See Kochan and Baderschneider (1978) for a behavioral model that yields implications about the variables that might enter into the vector X.

[29] The model is easily extended to allow impasses in rounds prior to $t-1$ to have an effect. Some of the researchers cited below have also looked at aggregate statistics on whether the conditional probability of going to impasse depends on prior impasse experience. It should be evident that this is equivalent to estimating eq. (2) without any X variables, so criticisms of that approach given below are equally applicable to these efforts.

The problem here is one of distinguishing between a true narcotic effect and unobservable heterogeneity across bargaining units. If any unobservable variables that influence the probability of going to impasse exist and remain roughly constant over time, estimates of θ will be biased in a positive direction. Butler and Ehrenberg (1981) show how one can correct for this bias using either a fixed or random effects model, along with an instrumental variable approach. Indeed, when they reanalyzed the Kochan–Baderschneider data using these methods, the estimates of θ they obtained proved to be negative – suggesting that a negative narcotic effect was present. That is to say, once unobservable heterogeneity was controlled for, the experience of going to impasse in the past appeared to *reduce* the probability of going to impasse in the current round.[30]

Studies of the *effects* of impasse procedures have focused on whether unions or management tends to win under arbitration, what the effects of the *use* of the procedures are on economic outcomes, and what the effects of the *availability* of the procedures per se are on economic outcomes. In the first group are studies by Ashenfelter and Bloom (1984) for New Jersey and Somers (1977) for Massachusetts that indicated that unions won over 60 percent of police and firefighter cases under final offer arbitration in the early years of the statutes. As we have previously discussed, Ashenfelter and Bloom have emphasized [following Farber (1980b)] that such a finding does *not* imply that arbitrators are biased in favor of unions.

Some of the studies of the effects of the use of impasse procedures have simply contrasted the mean wage levels or wage changes in a state of units that settle at different stages of the process.[31] Others have estimated wage level or wage change equations across bargaining units in a state, including a set of explanatory variables to control for other forces that might be expected to influence wages.[32] The consensus of these studies seems to be that the usage of arbitration per se, or the stage of the impasse procedure one settles at if an impasse is reached (mediation, fact-finding, or arbitration), has no effect on wage levels or wage changes; the former result is not consistent with the Farber–Katz (1979) model. In contrast, in areas where strikes are at least de facto legal, there is some evidence that settlements arrived at in negotiations that do wind up in a strike are higher than those arrived at when the parties settle without reaching an impasse.[33]

Many studies of the effects of the availability of different forms of impasse procedures have used national samples (either at the individual or bargaining unit level) and estimated wage equations that included dummy variables for the form

[30] Explanations for why a negative narcotic effect might occur are found in Butler and Ehrenberg (1981). See also Kochan and Baderschneider (1981).
[31] See, for example, Gallagher, Feuille and Chaubey (1979), Subbarao (1970), Lipsky and Barocci (1978), and Thompson and Cairnie (1973).
[32] See, for example, Bloom (1981b), Delaney (1983), Anderson (1979), and Auld, Christofides and Wilton (1981).
[33] See Delaney (1983) and Subbarao (1979).

of impasse procedure present.[34] Others have estimated wage level or wage change equations across bargaining units within a single state, including a number of years' data and dummy variables for years after a (new) impasse procedure was put in place.[35] While the latter suggest that the presence of an arbitration statute does not affect wages, the former strongly suggest that the availability of a statute increases wage levels by some 6 to 10 percent. Similarly, the availability of a strike option also seems to be associated with higher wages.[36]

One must interpret these results with caution, however. The studies of the availability of the various procedures have not included data on actual use; it is therefore difficult to disentangle the effect of availability from that of use. More importantly, virtually all of the studies treat both the use of impasse procedures and their availability as exogenous. The former treatment seems strange in light of the work of Kochan and Baderschneider (1978) who model the usage of impasse procedures. The latter seems equally strange since the types of impasse procedures that exist are not randomly distributed across states. For example, arbitration statutes seem to have been enacted first in states where public-sector unions are strong and where one might expect to observe above average wages even in the absence of the statutes. It is not surprising then, that the national cross-section "availability" studies show arbitration and/or the right to strike statutes having a positive effect on wages. Before these results can be taken at face value, the endogeneity of the availability and use of impasse procedures must be addressed.[37]

Finally, to reiterate a point made first in Section 2, the availability studies focus on only one aspect of the legal environment governing public-sector bargaining in a state. The effects of the "availability" of impasse procedures more appropriately should be estimated in the context of a model that permits consideration of other aspects such as budget referenda requirements, expenditure and tax limitation legislation, agency shop provisions, and constitutional requirements for balanced budgets.

5.   Public/private pay comparisons

The pay of most federal workers in the United States is determined through a comparability process that ties their wages to the results of government surveys of "comparable private employees", subject to possible Presidential and Congres-

---

[34] See, for example, Olson (1980), Kochan and Wheeler (1975), Delaney and Feuille (1983) and Delaney (1983).

[35] See, for example, Kochan et al. (1978), Lipsky and Drotning (1977) and Stern et al. (1975).

[36] Delaney (1983).

[37] Only two studies have addressed these issues. Olson (1980) used a random effects model to try to handle the endogeneity of availability. Delaney (1983) reports some estimates of the effects of use in the context of a model in which use is endogenous.

sional modification. Other federal workers, for example postal workers, have their wages determined via collective bargaining, as do many state and local government employees. However, as noted above, the dispute resolution procedures which govern collective bargaining in the public and private sectors differs substantially.

Given these differences, many researchers have sought to ascertain whether comparably qualified workers performing comparable work in the public and private sectors receive equal total compensation. That is to say, do the variety of institutional arrangements for determining wages result in a compensation structure in which public employees are doing no better (or worse) than they would if they were employed in the private sector? Even in the case of federal workers covered by the comparability surveys this question is difficult to answer because the surveys historically focused only on wages and ignored nonwage benefits and nonpecuniary forms of compensation.[38] Moreover, the jobs performed in the public and private sectors are not always comparable and subjective decisions must be made as to how a job should be classified.

As a result, instead of focusing on the earnings of workers with comparable job characteristics, researchers have focused on the earnings of workers with comparable measured personal characteristics. The basic methodological approach [discussed most fully in S. Smith (1977a)] is identical to that used in studies of sex, race, or union wage differentials. Equations of the form

$$Y_i = \sum_{j=1}^{n} \alpha_j X_{ji} + \alpha_{n+1} d_i + \varepsilon_i \tag{3}$$

are estimated over a sample of public- and private-sector workers, where Y_i is some measure of the natural logarithm of earnings, the X's are a vector of personal characteristics expected to influence earnings, d_i is a dichotomous variable that takes on the value of one if the individual is a public employee and zero otherwise, and ε_i is a random error.

Estimates of the parameter α_{n+1} provide information on the public/private earnings differential. In practice, a vector of dummy variables is often used to indicate the level of government at which the individual is employed (federal, state, or local), separate estimates are obtained by race or sex, and/or separate earnings equations estimated for public and private employees. In the latter case, one can estimate the public/private differentials by the wage differentials that would exist if government employees with a given set of characteristics were paid according to the private wage equation, or by the differentials that would exist if private employees with such characteristics were paid according to the government wage equation.[39]

---

[38] Hartman (1983) discusses recent attempts to include fringe benefits in the surveys.

[39] Whenever authors used the latter approach, the estimates in Table 22.3 reflect their (or our) estimate of the average differential obtained from the two methods.

The major work in this area has been done by Sharon Smith in a series of articles and books; our summary of the estimates obtained by her and several other researchers for selected years between 1960 and 1981 appears in Table 22.3. The studies are not directly comparable for a number of reasons. Some use annual earnings, while others use hourly earnings. The variables included in the vector X vary across studies; for example, only about a half include a measure of unionization. The definition of who is a public employee, especially at the state and local level, also varies. Finally, the private-sector comparison group varies across studies; in most it is all private nonagricultural workers, but in the Wachter and Perloff (1981) study it is private-sector service industry employees.

Despite these differences, these studies paint a fairly uniform picture.[40] The federal/private-sector differential is positive but appeared to diminish during the 1970s. Postal workers, whose salaries are determined via collective bargaining, receive earnings differentials relative to private-sector workers, that are about equal to the differentials received by other federal workers whose salaries are determined by the comparability process.[41] The federal/private differentials appear to be larger for females than for males and for nonwhite males than for white males; this may reflect a lesser level of race and gender discrimination in the federal than in the private sector (see the next section).

A similar result occurs in both the state and local sectors, where again, public/private earnings differentials are larger for females than for males. Moreover, as we move from the federal, to the state, to the local government level, the size of the government/private earnings differential gets smaller. Indeed, after controlling for personal characteristics, on average males employed by local governments, and possibly also males employed by state governments earn *less* than their private-sector counterparts.

What factors cause the public/private earnings differentials to decline as we move from the federal to the state to the local level? One possibility is that taxpayer information about the effect of public employee wage increases on tax burdens is much easier to obtain and understand at the local level. It may also be easier to hold local politicians accountable for such financial decisions; each federal legislator is just one out of hundreds of representatives who vote on scores of issues besides government employee pay. As such, pressure to hold down public employee wage scales may be greatest at the local level of government.

A serious deficiency with most of these studies (often acknowledged by the authors) is their focus on measures of earnings, rather than total compensation.

---

[40] We exclude the Wachter–Perloff study from our discussion, since by including only low-wage private-sector service workers as the reference group, their estimated public/private differentials are inflated relative to those of other studies.

[41] S. Smith (1977a), however, presents evidence that as of 1975 female postal workers received higher compensation than comparable females employed in other federal positions. See her Table 6.7.

Table 22.3

Estimates of public/private percentage earnings differentials: by level of government, race, sex, and year.

Year/study	Federal									State				Local			
	A	M	F	WM	WF	NM	NF	P	WP	A	M	F	WM	A	M	F	WM
1960 S. Smith (1976a, 1976b, 1976c, 1977a, 1977b)	21			8	19	15	27										−3
1970 Quinn[a] (1979a, 1979b)				22					20				12				
S. Smith (1976a, 1976b, 1976c, 1977a, 1977b, 1983)				4	8	15	15										
1973 S. Smith (1977a, 1982)		20	38								−3	14			−7	6	
1975 S. Smith (1977a, 1982, 1983)		15	21								−7	6			−7	1	
Bellante and Long (1981)	20	18	24							2	−3	8		−5	−4	−2	
1978 S. Smith (1981, 1983)		11	21								2	11			−4	−2	
Wachter and Perloff (1981)[b]	34							33		16				7			
1981 B. Dunson (1983)[c]				14													

Notes:

A – all employees in group
M – male   WM – white male
F – female   WF – white female
NM – nonwhite male
NF – nonwhite female
P – postal workers
WP – white male postal workers

[a] Quinn studies focus on white males 45 +.

[b] Wachter and Perloff study uses private-sector service workers as reference group. As a result, their public/private earnings differential estimates are artifically high.

[c] Dunson focuses on white-collar workers.

The latter should include all present and expected future forms of pecuniary (e.g. fringe benefits) and nonpecuniary (e.g. working conditions and stability of employment) conditions of employment. Presumably, if labor markets were competitive, one would observe equality of total compensation, as defined above, across sectors, not equality of current earnings.

Some limited research has been conducted on outcomes other than earnings levels. For example, several authors have examined various components of fringe benefits. Bellante and Long (1981) and Quinn (1979b, 1982) find that fringe benefits in the public-sector tend to exceed those in the private sector, with the difference being greatest for federal workers. Similarly, Quinn (1977) uses survey data on disamenities of the workplace (pace of work, degree of supervision, danger, etc.) and finds that private-sector workers tend to be employed in situations with more disamenities. These results suggest that positive public/private wage differentials are not compensating differentials for either lower fringe benefits or unfavorable working conditions.

Other authors have examined the question of stability of employment. In a number of her studies Sharon Smith uses both hourly and annual earnings as dependent variables to control for annual variations in hours of work. Bloch and Smith (1979) also directly examine the probability that an individual will be employed at a point in time, and find that it is higher for white male federal employees and for all race/sex groups of state and local government employees than it is for comparable private-sector workers. Public/private wage differentials are apparently not compensating differentials for relative instability of employment in the public-sector.

Somewhat surprisingly, there have been relatively few attempts to explain why public/private earnings differentials vary over time and across regions and states; the geographic variation has been noted by Smith and by Borjas (1982b). A notable exception is Borjas (1982a) who presents and tests a theory of why federal/private wage differentials vary over the electoral cycle and Borjas (1982b) who presents and tests a political model of a vote-maximizing bureaucrat to explain why state government/private differentials vary across states.[42]

Neither of these studies, however, explicitly considers the role of institutional variables. To return to a previous theme, no insights are offered about the effects of state laws such as those governing public-sector impasse procedures, those establishing tax or expenditure limitations, or those governing public-sector union security arrangements, on public/private pay differentials. Save for studies of postal workers, there have also been no studies of federal/private net wage

---

[42] In an earlier work, Borjas (1980a, 1980b) uses a similar model to explain why wages should vary across government agencies for individuals with comparable personal characteristics.

differentials for federal workers whose wages are determined via collective bargaining; we have little evidence then about whether the comparability process leads to larger, or smaller, relative wage differentials than one would observe under collective bargaining.

All of the studies of public/private wage differentials have treated individuals' sectors of employment as exogenous. However, if individuals nonrandomly sort themselves into public or private jobs because of differences in tastes for public service or preferences for nonrisky employment, then the possibility of sample selection bias arises. Evidence presented by Bellante and Link (1981) suggests that public-sector workers are more risk averse and that, holding risk aversion constant, many of the same factors that influence wages in the public and private sectors also influence an individual's sector of employment [see also Blank (1983)].

In view of the conceptual and measurement problems involved in trying to estimate public/private pay comparability, some investigators have suggested focusing on quit rates instead [e.g. Adie (1977)]. Since holding constant characteristics of individuals, better pecuniary and nonpecuniary conditions of employment should lead to lower quit rates, the argument is that public/private quit rate differentials would be prima facie evidence of public/private total compensation differentials. The evidence on quit rates seems compelling; both gross quit rates [e.g. Adie (1977), Wachter and Perloff (1981)] and net quit rates after controlling for personal characteristics [e.g. Long (1982)] are lower in the public than in the private sector.

A problem with these studies, however, is that they contain no controls for job characteristics. One key characteristic is the size of the employer; ceteris paribus, the larger an employer, the more likely an unhappy employee can improve his lot by an intrafirm change. Hence, quits should be negatively related to firm size [Utgoff (1983)]. Since federal and state governments and some local governments are obviously large employers, their lower quit rates may be at least partially be due to this fact.

A second key characteristic is the amount of specific training required. In situations where specific training is involved, an employer's goal is to minimize the sum of hiring, training, and compensation costs, not simply compensation costs; as such, a high-wage, low-quit policy may prove optimal. Thus, one cannot simply focus on relative compensation *or* quit levels in judging comparability; one needs to know the savings in hiring and training costs from pursuing a high-wage policy. Although many researchers have looked at public/private quit and wage differentials, only Adie (1977) has examined (for postal workers) if the differentials could be possibly "justified" by lower hiring and training costs.[43]

---

[43] See Ehrenberg (1979a) for a more detailed discussion of this point.

6.   Discrimination in public-sector labor markets

Studies of public/private wage comparisons suggest that public/private wage ratios are higher for females than for males and for nonwhites than for whites (see Table 22.3). This *may* reflect a lesser extent of gender and race discrimination in public-sector labor markets; a result that might be expected for two reasons. First, the highly structured nature of government employment with civil service and/or collectively bargained work rules, often requires equal pay for all individuals with the same seniority and qualifications who are employed in a given job. Thus, discrimination can primarily take the forms of slower promotion rates or unequal access to initial jobs, not of unequal pay for equal work.[44] Second, the oldest U.S. programs to combat race discrimination in employment are equal employment opportunity programs for government employees. The federal programs started during the New Deal and, by 1945, thirteen states had similar provisions for their employees – predating the Civil Rights Act by some twenty years. If these programs had any "teeth", one would expect to observe less race discrimination in the public-sector.

A number of researchers have focused on estimating the extent of race or gender discrimination in the public-sector and their methodologies are fairly standard. Returning to eq. (3) of the previous section, let the sample now refer to white federal employees, let d_i now take on the value of one if the individual is a male and zero if the individual is a female, and let all other variables be defined as before. Estimates of the parameter α_{n+1} now provide information on the male/female earnings differential that exists for whites employed in the federal sector, after one controls for the other variables in the analysis. One can similarly do analyses of gender differentials for nonwhites employed in the federal sector, and for employees of state and local governments. By restricting the sample to employees of one gender and letting d_i stratify employees by race, one can obtain estimates of race differentials for public employees. Finally, rather than inserting a dichotomous variable in (3), one can again estimate separate equations by gender (or race). In this case, the male/female (white/nonwhite) government employee earnings differential is estimated by the differential that would exist if female (nonwhite) government employees with a given set of characteristics were paid according to the male (white) wage equation.

Studies that have utilized such approaches with various micro-data files suggest that, after controlling for personal characteristics of workers, the earnings of minorities and females employed in the government sector are often substantially lower than those of white males. However, the magnitude of the differences tend

---

[44] One should, however, not discount the possibility of different job titles for males and females who perform essentially the same work; for example, male prison guards and female prison matrons. More generally this leads one to the issue of "comparable worth" – an important policy area in which public-sector research is just beginning.

Table 22.4

(A) Estimates of the percentage by which male employees'
earnings exceed those of female employees
with equivalent personal characteristics.

Sector/year	1973	1975
Federal	23	34
State	22	19
Local	19	16
Private	36	28

(B) Estimates of the percentage by which black employees'
wages are less than those of white employees
with equivalent personal characteristics in 1975.

Sector/gender	Male	Female
Federal	13	5
State	5	2
Local	8	−2
Private	11	4

Source: Authors' interpretation of results presented in
S. Smith (1977a, Ch. 6). In cases where separate earnings
equations were estimated by gender (or race) the male
(white) equation was used by us to calculate the earnings
differentials.

to be slightly less than comparable gender and race differences in earnings found in the private sector [see Corazzini (1972), Long (1976), Borjas (1978), and Borjas (1983)].

As in the case of public/private pay comparisons, perhaps the most comprehensive study is S. Smith (1977a). Some of her results, obtained using 1973 and 1975 Current Population Survey data, are summarized in Table 22.4. They confirm that, ceteris paribus, males appeared to get paid more than females and whites more than blacks at all levels of government.[45] However, the race and gender differentials she found were smaller at the state and local than at the federal level. Indeed, Antos and Rosen (1975), who confined their analyses to local government public school teachers, found virtually no evidence of gender differentials and only little evidence of race differentials.

To the extent that race and gender earnings differentials observed in the federal sector can be interpreted as estimates of labor market discrimination, one must conclude that federal government EEO programs directed at its own employees have not been completely effective. However, this does not imply that

[45] Black females were actually estimated to earn more than their white female colleagues in local government in 1975 (see Table 22.4), however, this differential was not statistically significant.

federal government employment per se has not reduced the extent of labor market discrimination in the economy. These studies suggest that gender and race differentials are smaller in the public-sector and the studies summarized in the last section imply, ceteris paribus, that federal government employees earn more than private employees with comparable characteristics. As such, if the probabilities that females or nonwhites obtain employment in the federal sector exceed the comparable probabilities for males or whites, the presence of government employment will cause the average female (nonwhite) wage in the economy to rise relative to the average male (white) wage. D. Alton Smith (1980) demonstrates that this condition appears to have been met.

In a recent article, Borjas (1982c) moves the discussion away from measuring gender and race earnings differentials to a discussion of discrimination in different federal agencies. It is well known that both the fraction of an agency's employees who are minorities (females) and the fraction of these minority (female) employees who are in upper-level jobs varies widely across agencies. After providing evidence that the magnitudes of gender and race earnings differentials also vary across agencies [Borjas (1982c, 1983)], Borjas provides an explanation for why this might occur.

Based on previous work [Borjas (1980a, (1980b)], he presents a model of a government trying to maximize its political support. The constituency of each government agency is assumed to have a "taste" for discrimination and he shows that the vote-maximization hypothesis predicts that the economic status of minorities (females) in an agency will depend upon how important minorities (females) are in generating political support for the agency. Operationally, the race (gender) composition of an agency's constituents is measured by the race (gender) composition of employment in the industry the agency "relates to" and/or the race (gender) composition of the population in states where the agency expends funds. The expenditures made by an agency on civil rights activities is also used as a measure of its affirmative action orientation. His empirical work does indeed lead to the conclusion that a portion of the interagency variation in race and gender earnings differentials can be explained by interagency variations in the above variables.

Finally, two recent studies have sought to ascertain whether specific federal programs relating to public-sector labor markets have significantly reduced gender discrimination. Simeral (1978) estimated wage equations for a sample of participants who held Public Service Employment (PSE) program jobs and finds that male/female wage differentials actually rose after program participation. Hence, she concludes that the PSE program did not lead to less gender discrimination.

Eberts and Stone (1982) focused on gender differences in promotions of public school teachers to administrative positions in New York and Oregon. They sought to analyze the effects of Title IX legislation, which prohibited gender discrimination against students and employees in public schools. Using longitudinal data they estimated logit probability of promotion equations for periods prior to and after the passage of the legislation, and found that gender differentials in promotion rates to administrative positions tended to decline in the latter period. One must caution, however, that their approach did not permit them to disentangle the effects of the law from the effects of any other "macro-level" variables that changed at the same time. In particular, since the decade of the 1970s saw an ever-increasing movement of women out of traditional female occupations, such as teaching, one might question whether higher female promotion rates to administrative positions would have occurred even in the absence of the law.

7. The demand for labor in the public sector

The motivation for studies of the demand for labor in the SLG sector is two-fold. First, to provide estimates of wage elasticities of demand to shed light on whether the same market forces that constrain union power in the private sector would exist in the public sector, if the same institutional rules governed collective bargaining in both sectors. Second, to provide estimates of whether federal funds provided to SLGs under public service employment programs were actually used to increase employment. That is, to what extent were these funds used to hire people who would have been hired anyway?

Turning first to the estimates of wage elasticities of demand, the earliest studies are faithful to economic theory, in the sense that they provide estimates of *complete* systems of demand equations that permit one to test, or impose, the restrictions suggested by classical demand theory. For example, Ehrenberg (1972, 1973a) provided estimates of the demand for eleven categories of SLG employees based upon a utility-maximizing model of a representative decision-maker.[46] These estimates were based on a variant of the Stone–Geary utility function that allowed for minimum required employment levels in each category; these were specified to be function of lagged employment levels and this specification allowed him to test for the presence of incremental budgeting.[47] Similarly,

---

[46] See Downs (1957) and Tullock (1967) for discussions of the "median-voter" or "representative decision-maker" model. An alternative approach, for example Reder (1975) and Brennan and Buchanan (1980), is based upon the premise that bureaucrats seek to maximize their own welfare.

[47] The Stone–Geary utility function is described in Stone (1954). Its modification to allow for minimum required consumption levels to be functions of prior consumption occurs in Pollack and Wales (1969). The system of employment demand equations actually estimated was

$$\log\left(\frac{M_j^t}{P} - \frac{\alpha_j M_j^{t-1}}{P}\right) = b_{0j} + b_{1j}\log w_j + b_{2j}\log\left[\left(B - \sum_{k=1}^{n} w_k \alpha_k M_k^{t-1}\right)\Big/P\right]$$

$$+ \sum_{k=1}^{m} C_{Rj}\log SD_r, \quad j = 1,2,\ldots,n,$$

Ashenfelter and Ehrenberg (1975) used a variant of the *Rotterdam*, or differential demand, system to test if the restrictions implied by classical demand theory (homogeneity, symmetry, and Engel aggregation) were met.[48]

Each of these studies used pooled cross-section time-series data at the state level. Aggregate time-series evidence on the demand for all SLG employees was provided by Ashenfelter (1979) in a later paper. Finally, two recent papers have focused on specific groups of educational employees; Thornton (1979) used cross-section state data to study the demand for public school teachers, while Change and Hsing (1982) used pooled cross-section time-series data to study the demand for college faculty in public universities. All of these studies, save for Ashenfelter (1975), treated public employees' wages as predetermined and ignored supply side considerations.

The estimated wage elasticities from these studies are summarized in Table 22.5. In the main they suggest that demand curves for labor in the SLG sector are inelastic. However, the estimated elasticities do not appear to be substantially lower in absolute value than the private-sector wage elasticities, summarized in

---

where M_j/P is per capita SLG employment in category j, α_j is the minimum fraction of last period's employment in the category that must be employed this period, w_j is a measure of the category's wage rate, B/P is the per capita SLG employment budget, the SD_j are those sociodemographic variables expected to influence the demand for category j, there are n employment categories, and the b's and C's are parameters to be estimated. With this system, decisions are made about increments of employment above "committed" levels and only the total employment budget *less* "committed" expenditures is free to be allocated. To be consistent with the Stone–Geary utility function b_{1j} should equal minus one and b_{2j} equal one for all j; a very severe restriction which was *not* imposed in the estimation.

[48] See Barten (1968) or Theil (1971). Ashenfelter and Ehrenberg estimated the system of demand equations

$$f_j d \ln(M_j/P) = \sum_{k=1}^{n} \Pi_{jk} d \ln w_k + u_j \left[\sum_{k=1}^{n} f_k d \ln(M_k/P) \right], \quad j=1,\dots,n \quad k=1,\dots,n,$$

where f_j is the average share of category j in the total SLG employment budget. The equation is expressed in terms of the change, over time, in the natural logs of the variables and the expression in brackets on the right-hand side can be shown to be approximately equal to the change in the real per capita employment budget. The u_j and Π_{jk} are parameters to be estimated; the former is interpreted as the marginal budget share allocated to category j. It is straightforward to show that to satisfy the budget constraint the u_j must sum to unity and that utility maximization implies that $\Pi_{jk} = \Pi_{kj}$ (symmetry) and $\sum_k \Pi_{jk} = 0$ (homogeneity). Thus, the restrictions imposed by the utility-maximization hypothesis can be tested directly.

Since this system is expressed in first difference form, any variables that might affect only the intercept term of the demand equations drop out. However, to allow for the possibility that population density might affect other parameters in the model, separate estimates were provided for high- and low-density states.

Table 22.5
Estimates of wage elasticities of demand for labor in the state and local sector.

Category	(1)	(2)	(3)	(4)	(5)
Education	-1.06	-0.08 to -0.57	-0.57 to -0.82	-0.89	
Noneducation	-0.38				
Streets and highways	-0.09	-0.44 to -0.64			
Public welfare	-0.32	-0.33 to -1.13			
Hospitals	-0.30	-0.30 to -0.51			
Public health	-0.12	-0.26 to -0.32			
Police	-0.29	-0.01 to -0.35			
Fire	-0.53	-0.23 to -0.31			
Sanitation and sewage	-0.23	-0.40 to -0.56			
Natural resources	-0.39	-0.39 to -0.60			
General control and financial administration	-0.28	-0.09 to -0.34			
All categories					-0.53

Sources:

(1) Orley Ashenfelter and Ronald Ehrenberg (1975) "The demand for labor in the public sector", in: Daniel Hamermesh, ed., *Labor in the public and nonprofit sectors*. Princeton, NJ: Princeton University Press, Table 6.

(2) Ronald G. Ehrenberg (1973) "The demand for state and local government employees", *American Economic Review*, 63:366–379.

(3) Robert J. Thornton (1979) "The elasticity of demand for public school teachers", *Industrial Relations*, 18:86–91.

(4) Hui S. Chang and Yu Hsing (1982) "A note on the demand for faculty on public higher education", *Industrial Relations*, 21:256–260.

(5) Orley Ashenfelter (1979) "Demand and supply functions for state and local government employment", in: Ashenfelter and Wallace Oates, eds., *Essays in labor market analysis*. New York: Halstead Press.

Chapter 8 by Hamermesh in this Handbook.[49] Before one draws conclusions about the market forces that constrain union wage demands in the public sector, one should remember that unions strive to make demand curves less elastic to improve the wage/employment trade-offs they face. To the extent that current public sector bargaining legislation limits unions' ability to do this, it is plausible that less restrictive legislation would lead to less elastic demand curves.

This suggests an obvious omission in the public-sector labor demand literature. Public-sector unions seek, through the collective bargaining process, to reduce the substitutability of capital for labor, for example by establishing maximum student/teacher ratios in education or minimum patrolmen per patrol car

[49]A bit of care is required here. Many of the public-sector studies hold the real employment budget constant and it it most natural to compare their estimated elasticities to output-constant industry level elasticities of demand in the private sector. Many of the output-constant private sector studies surveyed in Hamermesh, Table 1 are for the aggregate economy or aggregate manufacturing. However, the statement in the text appears to be true even for studies which use data at the two-digit manufacturing level.

ratios.[50] Public employees are also voters and, through the political process, seek to increase the demand for their own services.[51] Finally, public employee unions, via the lobbying route and their support of favorable legislation further seek to increase the demand for public employees. Yet in spite of these observations, there have been no studies that deal with the effects of unions on the levels, or wage elasticities, of public-sector labor demand curves, or that examine whether the form of local government influences the public-sector demand for labor (the process by which city managers might affect the demand for public employees was discussed in Section 2).

Several other omissions are also obvious. Most studies have used data from the 1960s and early 1970s. Somewhat surprisingly, there have been no studies that examine whether the presence of tax and expenditure limitation legislation per se influences the demand for labor in the public sector.[52] The updated studies required would also enable one to test if public-sector wage elasticities are more elastic in times of fiscal stringency than in expansionary periods. Finally, as in the case of the public-sector wage determination studies cited in Section 2, none of the demand studies has examined the role of other state legal or constitutional statutes (e.g. annual municipal budget referendum or balanced budget rules) on labor demand in the public sector.

Turning next to the studies of the *net job creation* effects of public-sector employment programs, the approaches here have been varied. One of the early studies [Johnson and Tomola (1977)] used quarterly aggregate data and found that while initially PSE funds stimulated increased public-sector employment, the net job creation effects seemed to be close to zero after five quarters. That is, eventually the federal funds simply displaced, or were substituted for, local resources. Borus and Hamermesh (1978) performed some reanalyses of the same data that illustrated how sensitive the aggregate time-series results were to choice of lag structure, functional form, and sample period, concluding that little can be concluded from the aggregate time-series data.

Other studies use different methodologies. Bassi and Fechter (1979) used cross-section data for cities, counties, and states for fiscal years 1976 and 1977, and a structural econometric model and found net job creation effects in the range of 40–50 percent.[53] Nathan et al. (1981) was a noneconometric study based

---

[50] For evidence on the former, see Hall and Carroll (1973).

[51] On these points, see Courant, Gramlich and Rubinfeld (1979, 1980). The latter show that SLG employees appear to want more SLG spending than either private or federal employees.

[52] The "median voter" approach suggests that such legislation should only reflect changes in other forces influencing the demand for public services and should have no independent effect. In contrast, the "bureaucratic-maximization" approach suggests that passage of restrictions based on voters' preferences might affect public sector outcomes. Shapiro and Sonstelie (1982) present evidence in favor of the bureaucratic model, however, they do not focus on labor demand.

[53] A similar estimate is found in Perles (1983). Bassi (1981) updated the cross-section analyses to FY 78 and 79 and found results similar to those in Adams et al. (1983) that are cited immediately below.

on the perceptions of field observers in 40 local governments and concluded that net job creation effects were in the rate of 80 percent in fiscal years 1977 and 1978. Finally, a third study, Adams et al. (1983), used pooled time-series cross-section data for 30 cities from FY 1970 to FY 1979 and concluded that of every dollar of PSE program funds, 30 percent actually went to increase local government wage bills in FY 1977, with the estimate rising to 70 percent in FY 1978 and FY 1979.

Although the methodologies differ, the consensus of these studies appears to be that the net job creation effects of the program increased over time. This is not surprising for, as Congress increasingly became aware of the possibility that federal funds could be used to substitute for, or displace, local funds, it continued to redesign the program in a way that limited such substitutions. For example, in the latter years of the program it became more difficult to switch employees from regular municipal payrolls to the PSE ones and to employ people on PSE projects for extended periods of time.

Several cautions are in order here, however. First, the Adams et al. (1983) study focused on the total wage bill not the employment level. Thus, we have no way of knowing whether this study's results imply that PSE funds went for increased employment or for increased wages for existing employees. Indeed, one relatively unresearched area is the effect of federal grants on SLG employees' wage levels, and the role that unions play in this process. Second, since the Nathan et al. (1981) study did not use formal statistical methods, no statements about statistical significance or confidence intervals can be associated with it. Finally, as Borus and Hamermesh (1978) note in the time-series context and Bassi and Fechter (1979) hint at in the cross-section context, many of these results are very sensitive to model specification, sample period, and choice of variables. Prudent researchers probably should not draw strong conclusions from this literature.[54]

8. Concluding remarks

A long summary of the literature requires no summary. However, several themes and substantive propositions have emerged from our review that are worth repeating.

First, one unique aspect of public-sector labor markets is that the laws governing impasse resolution vary across states. This provides an opportunity for researchers to estimate their effects on union/nonunion wage (and nonwage)

---

[54] The net job creation effect of a PSE program is not the sole criteria one should use in evaluating it. Other criteria include its success in targetting jobs on specified groups and its effects on participants' earnings. For some evidence on the latter points, see Bassi (1983).

differentials, on wage levels, on the demand for labor, and on public/private pay differentials. However, other aspects of the legal environment that influence bargaining also differ across states; these include budget referenda requirements, expenditure and/or tax limitation legislation, balanced budget requirements, and agency shop provisions. Studies are required that consider all of these forces simultaneously and that allow for the possibility that many of them are endogenously determined.

A second unique aspect is that the unit of observation in public-sector studies often tend to be a bargaining unit (e.g. a city or school district), and the underlying union contracts in areas where bargaining takes place are typically available to researchers. As such, in contrast to private-sector studies that have focused on estimating union/nonunion productivity differentials, there is much more room in the public sector for studies of how specific contract provisions influence resource allocation decisions and productivity. One must stress here, though, both the need to model the determinants of contract provisions and the fact that unionization per se may influence productivity independently of specific contract provisions.

Third, in spite of the rapid growth of collective bargaining in the public sector and the variety of institutional arrangements for determining wages in the sector (collective bargaining, comparability, etc.), many studies of public-sector labor markets make no mention of the role of unions and/or the effects of the institutional arrangements. For example, while there are private-sector studies that examine whether unions affect the demand for labor [e.g. Freeman and Medoff (1982)], no public-sector counterparts exist. Similarly, there are no studies that address how the institutional arrangements for determining wages influence public/private wage differentials and the extent of race and gender discrimination in the public sector. Clearly, there is room for research here.

Finally, many of the empirical studies of arbitration statutes use somewhat ad hoc criteria such as whether arbitrated settlements are the same as negotiated ones, or whether unions and management each win roughly half of the cases that go to impasse, to evaluate how the statute is performing. However, simple economic models of the arbitration process suggest that a priori neither of those outcomes is likely to occur. This suggests that the empirical studies may have focused on inappropriate criteria and it emphasizes the general proposition that the criteria used in evaluations of social policies should be based on explicit conceptual models.

References

Adams, Charles F., Robert F. Cook, and Arthur J. Maurice (1983) "A pooled time series analysis of the job creation impact of public service employment grants to large cities", *Journal of Human Resources*, 18:283–294.

Adie, Douglas K. (1977) *An evaluation of postal service wage rates.* Washington, D.C.: American Enterprise Institute.

Anderson, John C. (1979) "Determinants of bargaining outcomes in the Federal Government of Canada", *Industrial and Labor Relations Review*, 32:224–241.

Anderson, John C. (1981) "The impact of arbitration: a methodological assessment", *Industrial Relations* 20:129–148.

Anderson, John C. and Thomas A. Kochan (1977) "Impasse procedures in the Canadian federal service: effects on the bargaining process", *Industrial and Labor Relations Review*, 39:283–301.

Antos, Joseph R. and Sherwin Rosen (1975) "Discrimination in the market for public school teachers", *Journal of Econometrics*, 3:123–150.

Ashenfelter, Orley (1971) "The effects of unionization on wages on the public sector: the case of firefighters", *Industrial and Labor Relations Review*, 24:191–202.

Ashenfelter, Orley (1979) "Demand and supply functions for state and local government employment", in: Orley Ashenfelter and Wallace E. Oates, eds., *Essays in labor market analysis.* New York: Halstead Press.

Ashenfelter, Orley and David E. Bloom (1984) "Models of arbitrator behavior, theory and evidence", *American Economic Review*, 74:111–124.

Ashenfelter, Orley and Ronald G. Ehrenberg (1975) "The demand for labor in the public sector", in: Daniel S. Hamermesh, ed., *Labor in the public and nonprofit sectors.* Princeton, New Jersey: Princeton University Press.

Ashenfelter, Orley and George Johnson (1969) "Bargaining theory, trade unions, and industrial strike activity", *American Economic Review*, 59:35–49.

Auld, D. A. L., L. N. Christofides, R. Swidinsky, and D. A. Wilton (1981) "The effect of settlement stage on negotiated wage settlements in Canada", *Industrial and Labor Relations Review*, 34:234–244.

Baird, Robert N. and John H. Landon (1972) "The effect of collective bargaining on public school teachers' salaries: comment", *Industrial and Labor Relations Review*, 25:410–416.

Balfour, Alan G. (1934) "More evidence that unions do not achieve higher salaries for teachers", *Journal of Collective Negotiations in the Public Sector*, 3:289–303.

Bartel, Ann and David Lewin (1981) "Wages and unionism in the public sector: the case of police", *Review of Economics and Statistics*, 63:53–59.

Barten, A. P. (1968) "Estimating demand functions", *Econometrica*, 36:213–251.

Bassi, Lauri (1981) "Evaluating alternative job creation programs", Project Report. Washington, D.C.: The Urban Institute.

Bassi, Lauri (1983) "The effect of CETA on the postprogram earnings of participants", *Journal of Human Resources*, 18:539–552.

Bassi, Lauri and Alan Fechter (1979) "The implications for fiscal substitution and occupational displacement under an expanded CETA title VI", Final Report submitted to U.S. Department of Labor. Springfield, VA: National Technical Information Service.

Bazerman, Max H. and Henry A. Farber (1983) "Arbitrator decision making: when are final offers important?", National Bureau of Economic Research Working Paper No. 1183. Cambridge, MA: National Bureau of Economic Research.

Becker, Brian (1979) "Union impacts on wages and fringe benefits of hospital nonprofessionals", *Quarterly Review of Economics and Business*, 19:27–44.

Bellante, Don and Albert Link (1981) "Are public sector workers more risk averse than private sector workers?", *Industrial and Labor Relations Review*, 34:408–412.

Ballante, Don and James Long (1981) "The political economy of the rent-seeking society: the case of public employees and their unions", *Journal of Labor Research*, 2:1–14.

Binkin, Martin and Irene Kyriakopoulos (1981) *Paying the modern military.* Washington, D.C.: Brookings Institution.

Blank, Rebecca (1983) "An analysis of worker sectoral choice: public vs. private employment", Industrial Relations Section, Worker Paper No. 171. Princeton, NJ: Princeton University.

Bloch, Farrell E. and Sharon P. Smith (1979) "Human capital and labor market employment: errata and extension", *Journal of Human Resources*, 14:267–269.

Bloom, David E. (1981a) "Is arbitration really compatible with bargaining?", *Industrial Relations*, 20:233–244.

Bloom, David E. (1981b) "Collective bargaining compulsory arbitration, and salary settlements in the public sector: the case of New Jersey's municipal police officers", *Journal of Labor Research* 2:369–384.

Borjas, George (1978) "Discrimination in HEW: is the doctor sick or are the patients healthy?", *Journal of Law and Economics*, 21:97–110.

Borjas, George J. (1980a) *Wage policy in the federal bureaucracy*. Washington, D.C.: American Enterprise Institute for Public Policy Research.

Borjas, George J. (1980b) "Wage determination in the federal government: the role of constituents and bureaucrats", *Journal of Political Economy*, 88:1110–1147.

Borjas, George J. (1982a) "Electoral cycles and earnings of federal bureaucrats", Mimeo, University of California, Santa Barbara.

Borjas, George J. (1982b) "The earnings of state government employees in the U.S.", Mimeo, University of California, Santa Barbara.

Borjas, George J. (1982c) "The politics of employment discrimination in the federal bureaucracy", *Journal of Law and Economics*, 25:272–294.

Borjas, George J. (1982d) "Labor turnover in the U.S. federal bureaucracy", *Journal of Public Economics* 19:187–202.

Borjas, George J. (1983) "The measurement of racial and sexual wage differentials: evidence from the federal bureaucracy", *Industrial and Labor Relations Review*, 37:L79–91.

Borus, Michael and Daniel S. Hamermesh (1978) "Estimating fiscal substitution by public service employment programs", *Journal of Human Resources*, 13:561–565.

Bough, William H. and Joe A. Stone (1982) "Teachers unions and wages in the 1970s: unionism now pays", *Industrial and Labor Relations Review*, 35:368–376.

Brennan, Geoffrey and James Buchanan (1980) *The power to tax: analytical foundations of a fiscal constitution*. Cambridge, MA: Cambridge University Press.

Brown, Byron W. and Daniel H. Saks (1975) "The production and distribution of cognitive skills within schools", *Journal of Political Economy*, 83:571–594.

Burton, John F., Jr. and Charles E. Krider (1975) "The incidence of strikes in public employment", in: Daniel S. Hamermesh, ed., *Labor in the public and nonprofit sectors*. Princeton, NJ: Princeton University Press.

Butler, Richard J. and Ronald G. Ehrenberg (1981) "Estimating the narcotic effect of public sector impasse procedures", *Industrial and Labor Relations Review*, 35:3–20.

Cain, Glen C., Brian Becker, Catherine G. McLaughlin and Albert E. Schwenk (1981) "The effect of unions on wages in hospitals", in: Ronald G. Ehrenberg, ed., *Research in labor economics*. Greenwich, CT: JAI Press, Vol. 4.

Chambers, Jay G. (1977) "The impact of collective bargaining for teachers on resource allocation in public school districts", *Journal of Urban Economics*, 3:324–339.

Chang, Hui S. and Yu Hsing (1982) "A note on the demand for faculty in public higher education", *Industrial Relations*, 21:256–260.

Corazzini, Arthur (1972) "Equality of opportunity in the federal white-collar civil service", *Journal of Human Resources*, 7:424–445.

Courant, Paul, Edward Gramlich and Daniel Rubinfeld (1979) "Public employee market power and the level of government spending", *American Economic Review*, 69:806–817.

Courant, Paul, Edward Gramlich and Daniel Rubinfeld (1980) "Why voters support tax limitation amendments: the Michigan case", *National Tax Journal*, 33:1–20.

Crawford, Vincent P. (1979) "On compulsory arbitration schemes", *Journal of Political Economy* 87:131–159.

Crawford, Vincent P. (1981) "Arbitration and conflict resolution in labor–management bargaining", *American Economic Review*, 71:205–210.

DeNisi, Angelo S. and James B. Dworkin (1981) "Final-offer arbitration and the naive negotiator", *Industrial and Labor Relations Review*, 35:78–87.

Delaney, John (1983) "Strikes, arbitration, and teacher salaries: a behavioral analysis," *Industrial and Labor Relations Review*, 36:431–447.

Delaney, John and Peter Feuille (1983) "Bargaining arbitration and police wages," in: Industrial Relations Research Association, *Proceedings of the Thirty-Fifth Annual Meeting*, December 28–30, 1982, New York City. Madison, Wisc.: IRRA.

Donn, Clifford B. (1977) "Games final-offer arbitrators might play", *Industrial Relations*, 16:306–314.

Downs, Anthony (1957) *An economic theory of democracy*. New York: Harper & Row.

Dunson, Bruce (1983) "Are DOD white-collar workers overpaid?", Mimeo, Washington, D.C.: Federal Trade Commission.

Eberts, Randall W. (1982a) "Unionism and nonwage effects: a simultaneous equations model of public school teacher collective bargaining," Mimeo, Department of Economics, University of Oregon, Eugene.

Eberts, Randall W. (1982b) "Determinants of teacher turnover during the 1970s: the case of New York State school teachers", Mimeo, Department of Economics, University of Oregon, Eugene.

Eberts, Randall W. (1983) "How do unions affect management decisions? Evidence from public schools", *Journal of Labor Research*, 4:239–248.

Eberts, Randall W. (1985) "Collective bargaining and teacher productivity: the effect on the allocation of teacher time", *Industrial and Labor Relations Review*.

Eberts, Randall W. and Joe A. Stone (1982) "Sex differences in promotions: EEO at work in public education", Mimeo, Department of Economics, University of Oregon, Eugene.

Eberts, Randall W. and Joe A. Stone (1983) "On the contract curve: a test of alternative models of collective bargaining", Mimeo, Department of Economics, University of Oregon, Eugene.

Eberts, Randall W. and Joe A. Stone (1985) *Unions and public schools: the non-wage effect of collective bargaining in American education*. Lexington Books.

Edwards, Linda N. and Franklin R. Edwards (1982) "Wellington-winter revisited: the case of municipal sanitation collection", *Industrial and Labor Relations Review*, 35:307–318.

Ehrenberg, Ronald G. (1973a) "The demand for state and local government employees", *American Economic Review*, 63:366–379.

Ehrenberg, Ronald G. (1973b) "Municipal government structure, unionization and the wages of firefighters", *Industrial and Labor Relations Review*, 27:36–49.

Ehrenberg, Ronald G. (1979a) *The regulatory process and labor earnings*. New York: Academic Press.

Ehrenberg, Ronald G. (1979b) "The effect of tax limitation legislation on public sector labor markets: a comment", *National Tax Journal*, 32: 261–267.

Ehrenberg, Ronald G. (1980) "Retirement system characteristics and compensating wage differentials in the public sector", *Industrial and Labor Relations Review*, 23:470–483.

Ehrenberg, Ronald G. and Gerald S. Goldstein (1975) "A model of public sector wage determination", *Journal of Urban Economics*, 2:223–245.

Ehrenberg, Ronald G. and Paul Schumann (1982) *Longer hours and more jobs?*, Cornell Studies in Industrial and Labor Relations No. 22. Ithaca, NY: ILR Press.

Ehrenberg, Ronald G. and Joshua L. Schwarz (1983a) "The effect of unions on productivity in the public sector: the case of municipal libraries", in: Werner Z. Hirsch and Anthony M. Rufolo, eds., *The economics of municipal labor markets*.

Ehrenberg, Ronald G. and Joshua L. Schwarz (1983b) "Public sector labor markets", National Bureau of Economic Research Working Paper No. 1179. Cambridge, Mass.: National Bureau of Economic Research.

Ehrenberg, Ronald G., Daniel R. Sherman and Joshua L. Schwarz (1983) "Unions and productivity in the public sector: a study of municipal libraries", *Industrial and Labor Relations Review*, 36:199–213.

Ehrenberg, Ronald G. and Robert S. Smith (1981) "A framework for evaluating state and local government pension reform", in: Peter Mieszkowski and George Peterson, eds., *Public sector labor markets. Washington, D.C.: Urban Institute*.

Farber, Henry S. (1980a) "Does final-offer arbitration encourage bargaining?" in: Industrial Relations Research Association, *Proceedings of the Thirty-Second Annual Meeting, December 28–30, 1979, Atlanta*. Madison, Wisc.: IRRA.

Farber, Henry S. (1980b) "An analysis of final-offer arbitration", *Journal of Conflict Resolution*, 24:683–705.

Farber, Henry S. (1981) "Splitting-the-difference in interest arbitration", *Industrial and Labor Relations Review*, 35:70–77.

Farber, Henry S. and Harry C. Katz (1979) "Interest arbitration, outcomes, and incentives to bargain", *Industrial and Labor Relations Review*, 33:55–63.

Feldman, Roger and Scheffler, Richard (1982) "The union impact on hospital wages and fringe benefits," *Industrial and Labor Relations Review*, 35:190–206.

Feuille, Peter (1975) "Final offer arbitration and the chilling effect", *Industrial Relations*, 14:303–310.

Feuille, Peter and James B. Dworkin (1979) "Final-offer arbitration and intertemporal compromise or it's my turn to win," in: Industrial Relations Research Association, *Proceedings of the Thirty-First Annual Meeting August 29– 31, 1978, Chicago*. Madison, Wisc.: IRRA.

Fottler, Myron D. (1977) "The union impact on hospital wages," *Industrial and Labor Relations Review*, 30:342–355.

Freeman, Richard B. (1981) "The effect of unionism on fringe benefits", *Industrial and Labor Relations Review*, 34:489–510.

Freeman, Richard B. and James L. Medoff (1984) *What do unions do?*. New York, NY: Basic Books.

Freeman, Richard B. and James L. Medoff (1982) "Substitution between production labor and other inputs in unionized and nonunionized manufacturing", *Review of Economics and Statistics*, 64:220–233.

Freund, James L. (1974) "Market and union influences on municipal employee wages," *Industrial and Labor Relations Review*, 27:391–404.

Frey, Donald E. (1975) "Wage determination in public schools and the effects of unionization", in: Daniel S. Hamermesh, ed., *Labor in the public and nonprofit sectors*. Princeton, NJ: Princeton University Press.

Gallagher, Daniel G. (1978) "De facto bargaining and teacher salary levels: the Illinois experience", *Journal of Collective Negotiations in the Public Sector*, 7:243–254.

Gallagher, Daniel G. and Monmohan D. Chaubey (1982) "Impasse behavior and tri-offer arbitration in Iowa", *Industrial Relations*, 21:129–148.

Gallagher, Daniel G., Peter Feuille and Monmohan D. Chaubey (1980) "Who wins at factfinding: union, management or factfinder?", in: Industrial Relations Research Association, *Proceedings of the Thirty-Second Annual Meeting, December 28– 30, 1979, Atlanta*. Madison, Wisc.: IRRA.

Gallagher, Daniel G. and Richard Pegnetter (1979) "Impasse resolution under the Iowa multistep procedure", *Industrial and Labor Relations Review*, 32:329–338.

Goldstein, Gerald S. and Ronald G. Ehrenberg (1976) "Execution compensation in municipalities", *Southern Economic Journal*, 47:937–947.

Gunderson, Morley (1980) "Public sector compensation in Canada and the U.S.", *Industrial Relations*, 19:257–271.

Gustman, Alan L. and M. O. Clement (1977) "Teachers' salary differentials and equality of educational opportunity", *Industrial and Labor Relations Review*, 31:61–70.

Gustman, Alan and Martin Segal (1977) "Interstate variations on teachers' pensions", *Industrial Relations*, 16:335–344.

Gustman, Alan L. and Martin Segal (1978) "Teachers' salary structures—some analytical and empirical aspects of the impact of collective bargaining", in: Industrial Relations Research Association, *Proceedings of the Thirtieth Annual Meeting, December 28– 30, 1977*, New York City. Madison, Wisc.: IRRA.

Hall, Clayton W. and Norman E. Carroll (1973) "The effect of teachers' organizations on salaries and class size", *Industrial and Labor Relations Review*, 26:834–841.

Hall, Clayton W. and Bruce Vanderporten (1977) "Unionization, monopsony power and police salaries", *Industrial Relations*, 16:94–100.

Hamermesh, Daniel S. (1975) "The effect of government ownership on union wages", in: Daniel S. Hamermesh, ed., *Labor in the public and nonprofit sectors*. Princeton, NJ: Princeton University Press.

Hanslowe, Kurt, David Dunn and Jay Erstling (1978) *Union security in public employment: of free-riding and free association*. Ithaca, NY: New York State School of Industrial and Labor Relations.

Hartman, Robert W. (1983) *Pay and pensions for federal employees*. Washington, D.C.: Brookings Institution.

Hartman, Robert W. and Arnold Weber, eds. (1980) *The rewards of public service: compensating top federal officials*. Washington, D.C.: Brookings Institution.

Hicks, J. R. (1966) *The theory of wages*. New York: St. Martins Press, 2nd ed.

Hirsch, Barry T. and Clifford B. Donn (1982) "Arbitration and the incentive to bargain: the role of expectations and costs", *Journal of Labor Research*, 3:55–68.
Hirsch, Werner Z. and Anthony M. Rufolo (1975) "A model of municipal labor markets", *Journal of Urban Economics*, 2:333–348.
Hirsch, Werner Z. and Anthony M. Rufolo (1983a) "Effects of prevailing wage laws on municipal government wages," *Journal of Urban Economics* 13:112–126.
Hirsch, Werner Z. and Anthony M. Rufolo (1983b) "Economic effects of residency laws on municipal police", Mimeo, University of California, Los Angeles.
Holmes, Alexander B. (1976) "Effects of union activity on teachers' earnings," *Industrial Relations*, 15:328–332.
Ichniowski, Casey (1980) "Economic effects of the firefighters' union", *Industrial and Labor Relations Review*, 33:198–211.
Ichniowski, Casey (1982a) "Public sector union growth and bargaining legislation: the case of police," Mimeo, National Bureau of Economic Research, Cambridge, Mass.
Ichniowski, Casey (1982b) "Arbitration and police bargaining: prescription for the blue flu", *Industrial Relations*, 21:149–166.
Inman, Robert (1981) "Wages, pensions and employment in the local public sector", in: Peter Mieszkowski and George Peterson, eds., *Public sector labor markets*. Washington, D.C.: Urban Institute.
Johnson, George and James Tomola (1977) "The fiscal substitution effects of alternative approaches to public employment", *Journal of Human Resources*, 12:3–26.
Kasper, Hirschel (1970) "The effects of collective bargaining on public school teachers' salaries", *Industrial and Labor Relations Review*, 24:57–72.
Kenny, Lawrence W. and David A. Demslow, Jr. (1980) "Compensating differentials in teachers' salaries", *Journal of Urban Economics*, 7:198–207.
Kleiner, Morris M. and Charles E. Krider (1979) "Determinants of negotiated agreements for public school teachers", *Education Administration Quarterly*, 15:66–82.
Kochan, Thomas A. (1979) "Dynamics of dispute resolution in the public sector", in: Benjamin Aaron, Joseph R. Grodin and James L. Stern, eds., *Public sector bargaining*. Madison, Wisc.: Industrial Relations Research Association.
Kochan, Thomas A. and Jean Baderschneider (1978) "Dependence on impasse procedures: police and firefighters in New York State", *Industrial and Labor Relations Review*, 31:431–449.
Kochan, Thomas A. and Jean Baderschneider (1981) "Estimating the narcotic effect: choosing techniques that fit the problem", *Industrial and Labor Relations Review*, 35:21–28.
Kochan, Thomas A., Mordechai Mironi, Ronald G. Ehrenberg, Jean Baderschneider and Todd Jick (1978) *Dispute resolution under factfinding and arbitration: an empirical analysis*. New York: American Arbitration Association.
Kochan, Thomas A. and Hoyt N. Wheeler (1975) "Municipal collective bargaining: a model and analysis of bargaining outcomes", *Industrial and Labor Relations Review*, 29:46–66.
Layard, R., A. Marin, and A. Zabalza (1982) "Trends in civil service pay relative to the private sector", Center for Labour Economics Discussion Paper No. 121, London School of Economics.
Lewin, David (1983) "Pay determination in municipal building departments under unionism and civil service", in: Werner Z. Hirsch and Anthony M. Rufolo, eds., *The economics of municipal labor markets*. Los Angeles: UCLA Press.
Long, James E. (1975) "Public-private sectoral differences in employment discrimination", *Southern Economic Journal*, 42:89–96.
Lipsky, David B. and Thomas A. Barocci (1978) "Final offer arbitration and public safety employees: the Massachusetts experience", in: Industrial Relations Research Association, *Proceedings of the Thirtieth Annual Meeting, December 28–30, 1977, New York City*. Madison, Wisc.: IRRA.
Lipsky, David B. and John E. Drotning (1973) "The influence of collective bargaining on teacher's salaries in New York State", *Industrial and Labor Relations Review*, 27:18–35.
Lipsky, David B. and John E. Drotning (1977) "The relation between teacher salaries and the use of impasse procedures under New York's Taylor law: 1968–1972", *Journal of Collective Negotiations in the Public Sector*, 6(93):229–244.
Long, James E. (1976) "Employment Discrimination in the federal sector", *Journal of Human Resources*, 11:86–97.

Long, James E. (1982) "Are government workers overpaid? alternative evidence", *Journal of Human Resources*, 17:123–131.

Moore, Gary A. (1976) "The effect of collective bargaining on internal salary structures in the public schools", *Industrial and Labor Relations Review*, 29:352–362.

Moore, William J. (1978) "An analysis of teacher union growth", *Industrial Relations*, 17:204–215.

Moore, William J. and John Raisian (1982) "A time series analysis of union/nonunion relative wage effects in the public sector", in: Industrial Relations Research Association, *Proceedings of the Thirty-Fourth Annual Meeting, December 28–30, 1981, Washington*. Madison, Wisc.: IRRA.

Murnane, Richard J. (1981) "Selection and survival in the teacher labor market", Mimeo, Yale University.

Nathan, Richard P., Robert E. Cook, V. Lane Rawlings, and associates (1981) *Public service employment*. Washington, D.C.: Brookings Institution.

Nelson, William B., Gerald W. Stone, Jr., and Michael J. Swint (1981) "An economic analysis of public sector collective bargaining and strike activity", *Journal of Labor Research*, 2:77–98.

Noam, Eli M. (1983) "The effect of unionization and civil service on the salaries and productivity of regulators", in: Ronald G. Ehrenberg, ed., *Research in labor economics*, Greenwich, Conn.: JAI Press, Supplement 2.

Olson, Craig A. (1979) "Final-offer arbitration in Wisconsin after five years," in: Industrial Relations Research Association, *Proceedings of the Thirty-First Annual Meeting, August 28–31, 1978, Chicago*. Madison, Wisc.: IRRA.

Olson, Craig A. (1980) "The impact of arbitration on the wages of firefighters", Industrial Relations, 19:325–339.

Olson, Craig A. (1984) "The strike impact of anticipated employer bargaining tactics", *Industrial and Labor Relations Review*, 37:515–528.

Olson, Craig, James L. Stern, Joyce M. Najita and June M. Weisberger (1981) *Strikes and strike penalties in the public sector*, Final Report submitted to the U.S. Department of Labor, Labor-Management Services Administration. Springfield, VA.: National Technical Information Service.

Partridge, Dane M. (1984) "The determinants of strike incidence on the public sector", Master's Thesis, Cornell University.

Perles, Susan P. (1983) "Impact of CETA-PSE on local public sector employment expenditures", in: Werner Z. Hirsch and Anthony M. Rufolo, eds., *The economics of municipal labor markets*. Los Angeles: UCLA Press.

Perry, James L. (1977) "Public policy and public employee strikes", *Industrial Relations* 16:273–283.

Pollack, Robert A. and Terence J. Wales (1969) "Estimation of the linear expenditure system", *Econometrica*, 37:611–628.

Ponak, Allen and Hoyt N. Wheeler (1980) "Choice of procedures in Canada and the United States," *Industrial Relations*, 19:292–308.

Quinn, Joseph F. (1979a) "Postal sector wages", *Industrial Relations*, 18:92–96.

Quinn, Joseph F. (1979b) "Wage differentials among older workers in the public sectors", *Journal of Human Resources*, 14:41–62.

Quinn, Joseph F. (1982) "Pension wealth of government and private sector workers", *American Economic Review Papers and Proceedings*, 72:283–287.

Reder, Melvin (1975) "Theory of employment and wages in the public sector", in: Daniel S. Hamermesh, ed., *Labor in the public and nonprofit sectors*. Princeton, NJ: Princeton University Press.

Rodgers, Robert C. (1981) "A replication of the Burton–Krider model of public employee strike activity", in: Industrial Relations Research Association, *Proceedings of the Thirty-Third Annual Meeting, September 5–7, 1980, Denver*. Madison, Wisc.: IRRA.

Rogers, David. (1979) "Municipal government structure, unions and wage and nonwage compensation in the public sector", Master's Thesis, Cornell University.

Schmenner, Roger W. (1973) "The determination of municipal employee wages", *Review of Economics and Statistics*, 55:83–90.

Schneider, B. V. H. (1979) "Public sector labor legislation: an evolutionary analysis," in: Benjamin Aaron, Joseph R. Grodin and James L. Stern, eds., *Public sector bargaining*. Washington, D.C.: Industrial Relations Research Association.

Shapiro, David. (1978) "Relative wage effects of unionism in the public and private sectors", *Industrial and Labor Relations Review*, 31:103–205.

Shapiro, Perry and Jon Sonstelie (1982) "Did Proposition 13 slay Leviathan?", *American Economic Review*, 72:184–190.

Sherman, Daniel (1983) "Teachers' unions and the production and distribution of educational outcomes: the case of California", Master's Thesis, Cornell University.

Simeral, Margaret H. (1978) "The impact of the public employment program on sex-related wage differentials", *Industrial and Labor Relations Review*, 31:509–519.

Smith, D. Alton (1980) "Government employment and black/white relative wages," *Journal of Human Resources*, 15:77–86.

Smith, Robert S. (1981) "Compensating differentials for pensions and underfunding in the public sector," *Review of Economics and Statistics*, 63:463–468.

Smith, Robert S. (1983) "Salaries and pension funding: are public safety officers given preference over taxpayers?" in: Werner Z. Hirsch and Anthony M. Rufolo, eds., *The economics of municipal labor markets*. Los Angeles: UCLA Press.

Smith, Sharon P. (1976a) "Are postal workers over- or underpaid?", *Industrial Relations*, 15:168–176.

Smith, Sharon P. (1976b) "Pay differentials between federal government and private sector workers", *Industrial and Labor Relations Review*, 29:179–197.

Smith, Sharon P. (1976c) "Government wage differentials by sex", *Journal of Human Resources*, 11:185–199.

Smith, Sharon P. (1977a) *Equal pay in the public sector: fact or fantasy?*. Princeton, NJ: Princeton University Press.

Smith, Sharon P. (1977b) "Government wage differentials", *Journal of Urban Economics* 4:248–271.

Smith, Sharon P. (1981) "Public/private wage differentials in metropolitan areas", in: Peter Mieszkowski and George E. Peterson, eds., *Public sector labor markets*. Washington, D.C.: Urban Institute.

Smith, Sharon P. (1982) "Prospects for reforming federal pay", *American Economic Review Papers and Proceedings*, 71:273–277.

Smith, Sharon P. (1983) "Are state and local government workers overpaid?", in: Werner Z. Hirsch and Anthony M. Rufolo, eds., *The economics of municipal labor markets*. Los Angeles: UCLA Press.

Somers, Paul (1977) "An evolution of final-offer arbitration in Massachusetts", *Journal of Collective Negotiations in the Public Sector*, 6(3):193–228.

Stern, James L., Charles M. Rehmus, Joseph Loewenberg, Hirschel Kasper and Barbara D. Dennis (1975) *Final-office arbitration*. Lexington, Mass.: Lexington Books.

Stevens, Carl (1966) "Is compulsory arbitration compatible with bargaining?", *Industrial Relations*, 5:38–52.

Stone, R. (1954) "Linear expenditure systems and demand analysis: an application to the pattern of British demand", *Economic Journal*, 64:511–527.

Subbarao, A. V. (1979) "Impasse choice and wages in the Canadian federal service", *Industrial Relations*, 8:233–236.

Theil, Henri (1971) *Principles of Econometrics*. New York: John Wiley.

Thompson, Mark and James Cairnie (1973) "Compulsory arbitration: the case of British Columbia teachers", *Industrial and Labor Relations Review*, 27:3–17.

Thornton, Robert J. (1971) "The effects of collective negotiations on teachers' salaries," *Quarterly Review of Economics and Business*, 11:37–46.

Thornton, Robert J. (1979) "The elasticity of demand for public school teachers," *Industrial Relations*, 18:86–91.

Thornton, Robert J. and Andrew R. Weintraub (1974) "Public employee bargaining laws and the propensity to strike: the case of public school teachers", *Journal of Collective Negotiations in the Public Sector*, 3:33–40.

Tullock, Gordon (1967) *Towards a mathematics of politics*. Ann Arbor, Mich.: University of Michigan Press.

Utgoff, Kathleen C. (1983) "Compensation levels and quit rates in the public sector", *Journal of Human Resources*, 18:394–406.

Victor, Richard B. (1980) "Municipal unions and wage patterns," in: Industrial Relations Research Association, *Proceedings of the Thirty-Second Annual Meeting, December 28–30, 1979, Atlanta.* Madison, Wisc.: IRRA.

Wachter, Michael L. and Jeffrey M. Perloff (1981) *An evaluation of U.S. Postal Service wages*, Mimeo. Washington, D.C.: U.S. Postal Service.

Weintraub, Andrew R. and Robert J. Thornton (1976) "Why teachers strike: the economic and legal determinants," *Journal of Collective Negotiations in the Public Sector*, 5(3):193–206.

Wellington, Harry H. and Ralph K. Winter (1969) "The limits of collective bargaining in public employment", *Yale Law Journal*, 68:1107–1127.

Wheeler, Hoyt N. (1975a) "An analysis of firefighter strikes", *Labor Law Journal*, 26:17–20.

Wheeler, Hoyt N. (1975) "Compulsory arbitration: a narcotic effect?", *Industrial Relations*, 14:117–120.

Wheeler, Hoyt N. (1978) "How compulsory arbitration affects compromise activity", *Industrial Relations*, 17:80–84.

Winkler, Donald R. (1980) "The effect of sick-leave policy on teacher absenteeism", *Industrial and Labor Relations Review*, 33:232–240.

Woodbury, Stephen (1983) "Substitution between wage and nonwage benefits", *American Economic Review*, :166–182.

Zuelke, Dennis C. and Lloyd E. Frahreich (1977) "The impact of comprehensive collective negotiations on teachers' salaries: some evidence from Wisconsin", *Journal of Collective Negotiations in the Public Sector*, 6:81–88.

INDEX